Praise for *The Journals of Woodro...*

'The most explosive political memoirs of modern times'
Express

'A wicked satire on British society'
Craig Brown, *Evening Standard*

'Wyatt has done the country a service in giving us the unalloyed truth about how this country's governing and social elite still operates'
Andrew Neil, *New Statesman*

'Lord Wyatt joins Pepys and Clark in punishing the hubris of the mighty'
Frank Johnson, *Independent on Sunday*

'The more we see of him the more compelling is his portrait of the world in which he moved and shook. Roll on volume two'
Alan Taylor, *Scotsman*

'The most entertaining and talked-about read . . . Full of juicy anecdotes about the famous, they are funny, gossipy, malicious and spiteful'
Evening Standard

'The great and the good are mercilessly mocked'
Spectator

'A rich pudding of gossip, indiscretion, impish humour, malice and politics'
Sunday Times

'A fascinating insight into the old claret-stained establishment'
Sunday Express

'This is an authentic account of his times, and useful and readable because of it'
Andrew Marr, *Observer*

Woodrow Wyatt was born in 1918 and served throughout the Second World War. He was Labour MP for Aston 1945–55 and for Bosworth 1959–70 and parliamentary Under-Secretary in the War Office in 1951. In 1955, he began *Panorama* with Richard Dimbleby. He was a columnist on *Reynolds News* 1949–61, the *Daily Mirror* 1965–73 and the *Sunday Mirror* 1973–83. From 1983, he was the *News of the World*'s Voice of Reason and a columnist for *The Times*. He was Chairman of the Horserace Totalisator Board from 1976–97. Knighted in 1983 and created a life peer in 1987, he sat on the cross-benches in the House of Lords. His books include an autobiography, *Confessions of an Optimist*. Woodrow Wyatt was married four times and died in December 1997, aged 79.

After reading classics at Oxford, **Sarah Curtis** was a journalist on the *Times Educational Supplement* and *The Times*. She edited the RSA Journal from 1989 to 1995 and began work on Woodrow Wyatt's journals in October 1997.

The Journals of

WOODROW WYATT

Volume Three

Edited by Sarah Curtis

PAN BOOKS

First published 2000 by Macmillan

This edition published 2001 by Pan Books
an imprint of Pan Macmillan Ltd
Pan Macmillan, 20 New Wharf Road, London N1 9RR
Basingstoke and Oxford
Associated companies throughout the world
www.panmacmillan.com

ISBN 0 330 48574 1

1 3 5 7 9 8 6 4 2

A CIP catalogue record for this book is available from
the British Library.

Phototypeset by Intype London Ltd
Printed and bound in Great Britain by
Mackays of Chatham plc, Chatham, Kent

Contents

Contents

List of Illustrations

Introduction

In April 1992, when this final volume of Woodrow Wyatt's memoirs begins, John Major had just won the general election for the Conservative Party by a slim majority of twenty-one. Woodrow Wyatt's career was also delicately poised. He was writing a fortnightly column in the *Times* and occasional book reviews; he was 'The Voice of Reason' each week in the *News of the World*; he was still Chairman of the Tote, having finessed his reappointment with successive home secretaries since 1976; and he held a couple of substantial consultancies – but he was seventy-three years old.

At that age how could Wyatt maintain his influence as well as the standard of living he required for himself and his family? There were precedents he loved to cite of octogenarians running countries as well as writing columns but it took all his inimitable energy and formidable network of contacts to maintain his position. His memoirs finish in September 1997. By then New Labour were the party in power and Tony Blair was Prime Minister. Wyatt lost his *Times* platform in May 1997, after the election; he was eventually replaced at the Tote on 1 August 1997, but he was still writing fortnightly for the *News of the World*. His last article appeared on 30 November and he died on 7 December 1997.

Woodrow Wyatt's memoirs are of historical significance for the light they throw on contemporary political processes. On 3 May 1994 he wrote, 'It has been the most exciting two days of my life in a way, getting these people together and trying to influence the course of events in the way I want them to go, which is to keep Major there.' The people concerned were the Prime Minister, John Major, and the media mogul, Rupert Murdoch. They had never met before. Wyatt invited them to a secret dinner. His account is entertaining for his Pooterish fussing over the household preparations but the occasion was important for the contact established between Major and Murdoch. Wyatt remained a go-between, fixing further meetings and relaying messages. He eventually lost his battle to keep the

Murdoch press on-side for Major but his fight demonstrates the uneasy relationship between politicians and the press.

Like his predecessor Margaret Thatcher, John Major emerges in these pages as honest, not compromising solely for media favour, despite being painfully conscious of the power of the press. Wyatt frequently appears to lean on him (over personal matters, too, canvassing for honours for worthy friends or his own reappointment at the Tote) but Major follows due process and never interferes in 'quasi-judicial' matters. What cannot be known, however, is the subliminal effect lobbying has on politicians. Wyatt claimed one of the debts Rupert Murdoch owed him was that through Mrs Thatcher he stopped Murdoch's media holdings being referred to the Monopolies Commission. In this volume Wyatt repeatedly presses the right of Murdoch to own television companies as well as newspapers; and his rights to 'the little black box' for digital television are held to be a factor influencing whether the Murdoch press would support Major or Blair in the 1997 general election. These memoirs raise the question of how much lobbying is an inevitable concomitant of political life, with the only safeguard against corruption being the capacity of the ministers concerned to make balanced decisions.

Wyatt discusses other factors influencing proprietors and editors of national newspapers. Even if proprietors are precluded from directing editorial policy, as was ruled in the terms of the Murdoch acquisition of the *Times* and *Sunday Times*, editors may think their jobs depend on readership figures. If increased circulation is their primary aim, will they have the confidence to try to lead public opinion or will they merely follow the polls? Wyatt constantly attacks the BBC for bias but he raises the question, both deliberately and unconsciously, of whether Britain's much-praised free press gives the facts on which readers can make up their own minds.

By the end of Major's term of office the telephone calls between Downing Street and Wyatt's house in Cavendish Avenue were almost as frequent as they had been in Margaret Thatcher's day. Through shortage of space I have not been able to include in these volumes the full text of all his conversations with Major and Thatcher. Many of their talks mainly ran through current events, in Major's case from the latest Tory escapades to the cricket scores. As with any conversation recounted by one person, even if immediately after it has taken place, the words recalled may not be exact but I think Wyatt always tried to give the gist of what was said accurately.

As ever, Wyatt took the optimistic view, cheering his friends onwards and upwards, often contrary to common sense. 'My intention was to spread good cheer all around,' he says of one of his compliments to a lady of a certain age. Such social parries, often involving white lies, are harmless, but was his encouragement damaging to Major? Wyatt constantly argued, like a latter-day Candide, that it would all turn out fine for Major in this glorious, if sleazy, non-socialist world. Major's memoirs show that he was well aware of the way the tide was flowing. Wyatt was only one of a number of intimates and it is perhaps good for anyone's morale to have a friend on whose shoulder to groan, if not cry. And it was also useful to have Wyatt's columns supporting him, if no one else's.

For whatever reason, John Major only mentions Wyatt once in his autobiography, as writing an encouraging column when Major resigned and won re-election as Leader of the Conservatives in June 1995. Similarly, Wyatt receives only one mention in Margaret Thatcher's *The Downing Street Years*. There is no dispute, however, about the frequency of his contact by telephone with these prime ministers. They both took the time to talk to him and usually rang him back quickly after he had called. One can only deduce that they enjoyed talking to him as well as valuing his columns.

As far as Wyatt himself is concerned, why did he transfer his loyalties from Margaret Thatcher to John Major, the successor she constantly criticized? Does this show that his main concern was his *amour propre* – did he want to retain the ear of the Prime Minister whoever held the office? The answer is that in his own terms Wyatt never did transfer his loyalties but stuck to his principles, even when such obstinacy threatened his relationships and his livelihood. He saw Major as the inheritor of Thatcher's policies but tempering their presentation, especially with regard to Europe. In his opinion Thatcher was reneging on her previous stance towards Europe and Major was consistent. He dreaded the scolding he might receive when he telephoned Lady Thatcher but continued to adore her personally and tried to effect a rapprochement between her and Major with another lovingly described secret dinner.

For Norman Lamont he had a special loyalty because their friendship was based on personal as well as political confidences. Wyatt risked the closeness he had begun to enjoy with Major when the Prime Minister effectively removed Lamont from the government in May 1993. (There are several accounts in this volume of aspects of the events of Black Wednesday – the day in September 1992 when Britain withdrew from the ERM – which should be added to other records of it.) He wholeheartedly attacked Major in the press but when he considered Lamont's indignation about his treatment went too far, he told Lamont so. In neither case was there a fundamental rift. By May 1994 he was able to say, 'I am on entirely the old footing I was on with Margaret now with John.' Towards the end of his life, he relates his satisfaction that he is back on the old friendship terms with Lamont.

The most convincing evidence that Wyatt remained true to his principles can be seen in his refusal to change horses and back Blair at the end of the electoral race. He had said in December 1992, when a conflict arose between his desire to promote a bill on privacy and the activities of his proprietor's tabloids, 'I am sorry but I cannot sell my soul. I have never written anything I don't believe.' He had survived a bitter row with Murdoch in October 1994 over what he saw as the harassment of Lady Thatcher about her son Mark's business interests. 'I sat by the telephone on the floor of my library but the brute never rang,' he says of his attempts to contact again his great friend and employer. On 17 March 1997 came the announcement that the *Sun* was backing Blair. 'Rupert has behaved like a swine and a pig,' raged Wyatt, who by now was using his memoirs as a means to vent without inhibition his deepest feelings.

There followed 'a great commotion' at the *News of the World* when they received his column attacking the *Sun*'s decision but it was eventually published, including its hint that Blair had given 'some secret promise to help Rupert's business in exchange for the *Sun* (and probably the *Times*) backing Blair'. Courage was a quality Wyatt never lacked.

It would be misleading to say that Woodrow Wyatt's final years show only decline, although his newspaper articles were cut in length and frequency. (To his chagrin 'The Voice of Reason' was at one time confined to the gardening page.) In contrast to his struggles in journalism, his tenure of the Tote chairmanship is remarkable not just for the fact that he managed to hold it for twenty-one years, outwitting all the manoeuvres to unseat him of home secretaries, civil servants, magnates of the racing world and even some Tote Board members. The main reason for his success was that at every stage he had a game plan for the Tote and they did not. This volume shows him as almost frenetically active in his attempts to increase the Tote's profits and to maximize its contribution to racing. When a journalist said the chairmanship of the Tote was a sinecure, he was justifiably angry.

I have been able to include only a proportion of the thousands of words he dictated about the bid to run the National Lottery made by the Enterprise consortium. Its members were GEC (the Weinstock connection), Hambros (the Keswick connection) and the Tote, with the American firm Autotote as the potential operators, but the bid was initiated and fuelled by Wyatt who made himself believe that they would win, just as he tried to make others believe in equally doubtful outcomes. 'This is the great dream I had, that I could leave something solid and achieve something really important before I finally disappear from the scene,' he says of the Lottery bid.

The final attempts to choose Wyatt's successor at the Tote were farcical. With a general election imminent in 1997, his term was extended for a few months and then extended again, as Jack Straw found it as difficult as Michael Howard had to get a candidate agreed. Wyatt's account of his role would be high comedy were it not for his distress.

What did he enjoy most about racing? He conscientiously did the rounds of the racecourses and revelled in the social side but one feels he took most pleasure in belonging to, as much as running, an organization of disparate, jolly people, from the Tote ladies in their uniforms designed by his wife, Verushka, to his long-suffering executives.

It was racing that brought him into regular contact with Queen Elizabeth the Queen Mother. The last letter he wrote to her, on 30 July 1997, accompanying five books he had selected for her birthday, sums up his devotion. After describing the books he says: 'Ma'am, I thank you for your many kindnesses to me – including the presentation of the glorious gold cup. [She had presented him with a special cup at his final Cheltenham appearance in the previous March.] I thank you for that wonderful sense of duty which is an example to us all – and for your humour, and lightness of touch, for your elegance and beauty, your interest in all you meet, young and old. Your entrance into a room lifts the atmosphere and stimulates the brain. Ma'am, I hope you have a lovely birthday and holiday in Scotland. I am, Ma'am, your most admiring and devoted servant, Woodrow (Wyatt).'

The Queen Mother's handwritten reply on 14 August comments with delight on the little library of books, sends her very warmest thanks and hopes they may meet racing that winter, a hope not to be fulfilled. Wyatt's letter is of more than courtly interest. It encapsulates his views about all he likes best in women. He loved women for their shape, their elegance and their charm but he also wanted brains. He liked pretty heads but hated empty heads. His ideal dinner party neighbour was witty and spirited as well as beautiful. He believed that women, from Tote ladies to merchant bankers, should be encouraged in their careers – in his view it was odd for a clever woman to be reluctant to consign her children to the care of a nanny.

Yet his constant refrain when he met a woman who argued with him about politics resembles that of Henry Higgins in *My Fair Lady*, 'Why can't a woman be more like a man?' Only Margaret Thatcher was allowed to remain with the men when the ladies withdrew after dinner. His adherence to the tradition of withdrawing was not one of convenience, to allow everyone to tidy up and gentlemen and ladies alike to talk to their own sex after sitting next to someone of the opposite sex. He enforced it because he did not think women *au fond* were interested in affairs of state, a rule he even applied, somewhat oddly, if a female cabinet minister or MP came to dinner, other than Thatcher.

By April 1994 both Verushka and his daughter Petronella knew he was keeping some kind of diary – and that was why he kept his library door locked. In a family row on 26 June 1995 he asks Petronella for secrecy: 'I don't think either of you realize the dangers and risks you are playing with. What I am doing could be accurately described as collecting material for memoirs, which won't be published until after I am dead, as a sequel to *Confessions of an Optimist*. I am trying to make a small fortune for your mother after I am dead and the pair of you are trying to destroy it.' His family could hardly help themselves from overhearing him from time to time dictating – he spoke his thoughts at convenient moments into his 'talking machine'; his loyal secretary, Mrs Wendy Tamborero, then typed them up and he corrected 'the manuscript' – and they may have seen some pages of the manuscript if he left them out when correcting them. But he does not seem to have told them about the contract he eventually signed with Macmillan. Petronella records in her memoir, *Father, Dear Father*, published in 1999, that 'During the reading of his will, Mother and I discovered the existence of Project X. This sounded like something from Agatha Christie or Conan Doyle, but it turned out to be a secret diary, which Father had been keeping for years . . . When we did finally read his Diary, it was in the newspapers.'

Wyatt, as he said above, began his memoirs to provide for his widow but by March 1993 he was conscious of making a contribution to history. He explains: 'The manuscript is not merely intended as a source of income for my estate when I am dead. It is becoming more and more in my mind to be the only memorial I can ever leave. Perhaps it really does have a view and a sweep which nobody else contemporaneous can match.'

I would also suggest that dictating events as they happened eventually became a lifeline to him, a form of therapy, a means to confide his true reactions beyond the *badinage* of ordinary social exchanges. He reveals this aspect, and the essential honesty of his intentions, in 1996 after marking a passage which he says should not be published for many years (there are only four such prohibitions of short passages in the whole manuscript). He says, 'If I don't put in things which have hurt me, and when I behave badly, it won't be a true record and won't have the meaning I wish it may have for future generations when we are no longer here.' The dilemma, however, for his editor has been where to draw the line between revealing his naked thoughts and protecting others.

In the five years covered by this volume Wyatt wrote much more than previously about his family, especially Petronella, now launched on a high-profile journalistic career which delighted him. He adored her, as everyone must know, and was deeply fond of his son, Pericles, too, of whom he saw little because he lived in California. He recounts all his family's triumphs but also his paternal worries, writing with total frankness, as he did about everyone. He gave no guidance as to what he thought should be published or omitted. I think he would have enormously enjoyed the book Petronella wrote about him, having told her in October 1993 that he and her mother would make good comic characters, but I have tried to respect her privacy, that of her half-brother and step-brother and of other younger people who crossed his path, making a distinction between what is in the public domain and what is not.

Throughout the three years I have spent on these memoirs I have been conscious of what Lord Wyatt wrote about me on the first of the three times he met me: 'I wondered whether her prejudices wouldn't guide her editing selections. The manuscript is mine, not hers, and I don't want it to be altered in its flavour and approach by someone antipathetic to my political views or maybe to other aspects of my life.' He seems quickly to have withdrawn his reservations when I politely wrote him a thank-you letter for lunch, I not realizing how he always warmed to thanks. He was, however, acute in his analysis of me. I immediately saw the historical importance of his journals but I hesitated long before I was sure that I could take on the responsibility of selecting the material to present what he, rather than I or anyone else, thought was interesting, important and fun.

I have tried to the best of my ability to give the balance I believe he would have wanted. The cutting has been even more extensive for this last volume than for the preceding two: this book represents less than a fifth of the 1,380,000 words he dictated from April 1992 until the last entry on 7 September 1997, three months before he died. A major difficulty when cutting has been to avoid doctoring his style, which had by now become diffuse. I remember well his many imprecations on sub-editors who dared to change a word. I have made cuts but I have not changed words. He did, however, appreciate those who saved him from errors. Just as he liked someone to pick up his clothes from the floor, he relied upon a solicitous sub-editor to spot his mistakes. Towards the end he made many small corrections of words on the manuscript but he did not have an eye, for example, for the way people spell their names. I apologize if there are errors I have failed to see.

Three years is a long time to spend immured in someone else's life and thoughts. I have found the contradictions in Woodrow Wyatt fascinating. He could appear a bully and a braggart but underneath the veneer of confidence he is painfully and curiously lacking in self-esteem. To have been an MP for twenty-one years, chairman of a body like the Tote for another twenty-one years, a columnist in leading newspapers for about forty years, friend and host to many of the mighty, a knight and peer of the realm, would seem achievement enough. But he is haunted by his failures. The sale of his Banbury newspaper and the collapse of his Banbury printing business rankled for the rest of his days. He recalls that he did not reach the top in politics, his play did not reach the West End, he did not continue to write short stories. He despises his schoolmaster father for concealing the fact that he got a pass degree at Oxford but this perhaps masks his own dissatisfaction with himself for only getting a second. He repetitiously records praise he receives for every article he writes, every speech he makes, needing such reassurance to convince himself that he is making the grade. And he is convinced he is lazy when even to read his day's schedule would make many people feel tired.

On the personal side he is both cynical and sentimental but the tears he weeps for the death of friends, or in the case of Simon Weinstock, for a friend's loss of his son, are real. Behind his schoolboy, scatological self, there is a literary man *manqué* who loves the company of intellectuals. He often tried to make peace with his foes, from youthful journalists to eminent civil servants, by inviting them to lunch, and he usually ended liking them. ('But I like him,' is often a postscript when he has just indicated someone is a rogue.) He counted the cost of all he gave and was given, but it is his deeds that matter. He was a most generous host. Most of us would suppress in our minds the thoughts he voiced about his aged mother-in-law, Nadje, but how many of us would have looked after an incontinent, troublesome old lady in our homes for twenty-nine years?

At his farewell lunch with staff of the Tote at Wigan, Wyatt relates, 'I said I thought the purpose of life was basically to enjoy it. Most people of any worth really enjoy it, if they are doing something useful.' The thought is not original but who could resist someone who contributed so much to life and was so much fun? As a diarist Wyatt shows energy, curiosity, diversity, humour, and shrewdness. He offers a unique perspective of our time close to the centre of political power. He lays bare the pretensions of others and his own soul. Historians in future will look to his journals and readers will enjoy them just as they have other great diaries, from Channon, Crossman and Clark in our day, back to Greville, Pepys and Saint-Simon.

*

Biographical details of some of the principal figures in the journals are given at the end of this volume on pp. 781–91. An asterisk at the end of a footnote refers the reader to the biographical notes the first time such a person is mentioned. I have also included a short appendix on racing and a chronology.

At the end of three years my thanks go again to Lady Wyatt for her understanding of my role as editor; to Diana Rawstron, of Goodman Derrick, WW's lawyers, for introducing me to this project and for her constant support; to Geoffrey Webster, public relations director at the Tote when WW was chairman, for answering my questions about racing; to Catherine Whitaker who has remained my excellent editor at Macmillan though based in New York; to Kendall Duesbury, Becky Lindsay, Nicky Hursell and others at Macmillan in London who have all been helpful; and to my patient family, especially my son Quentin for his continuing encouragement from the US and my husband who must often have wondered whether there was not a third person in our marriage.

SARAH CURTIS

May 2000

Woodrow Wyatt

Baron Wyatt of Weeford in the County of Staffordshire (knight 1983, life peer 1987) was born Woodrow Lyle Wyatt on 4 July 1918, son of Robert Harvey Lyle Wyatt (d 1932), founder and headmaster of Milbourne Lodge School, Esher, and Ethel, née Morgan (d 1974). He was descended from Humphrey Wyatt (d 1610), ancestor of the Wyatt architects, painters and sculptors.

Woodrow Wyatt was educated at Eastbourne College and Worcester College, Oxford, where he took a second in Law.

He married 1 (1939–44) *Susan* Cox, an Oxford contemporary; 2 (1948–56) Nora (*Alix*) Robbins, later Coleman; 3 (1957–66) *Lady Moorea Hastings*, now *Black* (daughter of the 15th Earl of Huntingdon (*Jack*, d 1990) and his first wife (Cristina, d 1953, daughter of the Marchese Casati, Rome) by whom he had a son, *Pericles*, b 1963, m (1989–91) *Maria*; 4 (in 1966) *Verushka*, née Racz, widow of Baron (Hungary) Dr Laszlo Banszky von Ambroz, by whom he had a daughter *Petronella* (b 1968), and a stepson, *Nicholas Banszky von Ambroz* (b 1952), merchant banker, m (1984–95) *Caroline*, née While (two daughters – *Genevra*, b 1985, *Antonella*, b 1987). Verushka's mother Ilona (*Nadje*, d 1996) lived with the Wyatts. Her sister, *Livia*, a translator, lives in Budapest.

Major Robert David Lyle, WW's older brother (d 1989), married Irene Joyce Francis (*Joy*, d 1984). He owned the family estate Bonython in Cornwall; his son and heir was WW's nephew *Robert Lyle* (b 1952, m (1991) Hon. *Tessa* Mayhew, solicitor).

R. E. S. Wyatt (*Bob*, 1901–95, m *Molly*, d 1996, son *Jonathan*), the famous England cricketer, was WW's first cousin; another first cousin was Mrs *Honor* Ellidge (previously married to C. Gordon Glover, mother of the actor *Julian* Glover and *Prue*).

After serving throughout the 1939–45 war (he was mentioned in dispatches in Normandy in 1944), during which time he founded and edited the series of books called *English Story*, WW entered Parliament in 1945 as Labour MP for Aston, Birmingham. He was personal assistant to *Sir Stafford Cripps* on the Cabinet Mission to India to prepare for independence in 1946. He lost the Aston seat in 1955 through redistribution, but was returned as MP for Bosworth 1959–70 and was Parliamentary Under-Secretary of State and Financial Secretary, War Office, from May 1951 until October 1951, when Labour lost power.

While still an MP he opposed his party on some issues, voting with Desmond Donnelly to hold up the nationalization of steel when Labour had a tiny majority, and once out of Parliament he moved further to the right. However, he never joined another party and when Mrs Thatcher made him a life peer in 1987 he sat on the crossbenches.

Throughout his career WW was an active journalist: on the *New Statesman*, 1947–8; as a weekly columnist on *Reynolds News*, 1949–61; at the *Daily Mirror* 1965–73; and the *Sunday Mirror*, 1973–83. He was under contract to BBC Television 1955–9 and a regular presenter of *Panorama* in the days of its early fame. It was through television as well as when an MP that he fought Communist domination of the unions, particularly the engineering union (AEU) and electricians' union (ETU). In the 1960s he owned a chain of Midlands newspapers and the Banbury Press, introducing non-heat-set web-offset colour printing to England in 1962. He was a member of the Council of the Zoological Society of London 1968–71, 1973–7.

In 1983 WW joined Rupert Murdoch's newspapers with a fortnightly column in the *Times*, book reviews and a weekly column called 'The Voice of Reason' (not his title) in the *News of the World*. He was chairman of the Horserace Totalisator Board (first appointed by Roy Jenkins when Home Secretary) from 1976 until 1997, the year of his death. He wrote for the *Times* until the close of May 1997, when his contract was ended; his last column for the *News of the World* was on 30 November 1997. By then he was ill with cancer of the throat. He died of a burst artery on 7 December 1997.

His books include the ten volumes of *English Story* he edited (1940–50); an edition of the short stories of O. Henry (1967); *What's Left of the Labour Party?* (1977); *To the Point* (1981), a collection of short *causerie* pieces; two children's books about *Mr Saucy Squirrel* (1976 and 1977); his autobiographies *Into the Dangerous World* (1952) and *Confessions of an Optimist* (1985); a selection from *English Story* (*The Way We Lived Then*, 1989); and a play, *High Profiles* (1992).

Names in italics are of people WW mentions in this volume.

1992

Friday 10 April

Rupert[1] rang in a great state. What an appalling campaign it had been and how they were lucky to have got in and how they had been helped by the *Sun*.[2]

I said, 'I don't know why people don't just read my predictions. For ages I got it absolutely right.'

He said, 'You were only guessing.' I said, 'I was not. I worked it out extremely clearly and put a number of bets on, based on my predictions.'

There is something wrong in the atmosphere between Rupert and myself. Perhaps Andrew Neil[3] and Simon Jenkins,[4] two enemies of mine, have been getting at him.

He then said, 'Lamont[5] must go. Major should make Alan Walters[6] Chancellor of the Exchequer or at least Governor of the Bank of England.' I said, 'Rupert you really are talking rubbish. Norman Lamont should not go. He did it exactly right. It was his Budget and

1. Rupert Murdoch, chairman and chief executive, The News Corporation, news-paper and media proprietor.*
2. The Conservatives won the April 1992 general election with an overall majority of 21; the Murdoch press had supported them.
3. UK editor, *Economist*, 1982–3; editor, *Sunday Times*, 1983–94; executive chairman Sky TV, 1988–90; publisher, European Press Holdings, including the *Scotsman*, *Scotsman on Sunday*, *Sunday Business* and *Edinburgh Evening News* since 1996 (and the *European*, 1997–8). See Vol. 1, pp. 75, 195–6, 451, 535, and Vol. 2, pp. 142, 238–9, 247, 389–90, 472–3 for examples of animosity between WW and Neil; there are also examples of their mutual tolerance, if not good relations.
4. Editor, the *Times*, 1990–2, and *Times* columnist since then.
5. Norman Lamont, who had been Chancellor of the Exchequer since 1990.*
6. Former economic adviser to Margaret Thatcher; his opposition to the views of Nigel Lawson when Chancellor of the Exchequer precipitated Lawson's resignation in 1989.

tax cuts and the demolition of Smith's[7] phoney budget which cinched the election.'

He said. 'They shouldn't have gone into the ERM.' I said, 'But Margaret [Thatcher] took them in there. Anyway, it's not quite as bad in it as you think it is.'

He said, 'Interest rates are still too high. Look what that's been doing to small businesses.'

This was getting rather taut for a conversation between Rupert and myself.

We then talked a bit about the *Financial Times* coming out on Thursday for voting Labour.

He is now seriously considering starting a rival *Financial Times* which just sticks to the business and commercial world.

Rupert then brusquely asked, 'Are you close to Major and can you get through to him easily?' I replied, 'Not like I could with Margaret but I do have some ways of contact.' 'I thought not,' Rupert said in a nasty voice with the implication that I was no longer any use to him in influencing Number 10 as I could before. I don't care for his new, putting-down attitude.

I couldn't really contemplate not writing for the *News of the World* where I have this wonderful audience but I do wonder whether I should go on with the *Times* now they have cut me down to six hundred words.

Saturday 11 April

The day of the Cabinet changes. I was nervous about dear Norman but he told me early on that he saw Major at nine o'clock this morning and that it is OK, there is no intention of moving him and there never had been. He said if he had been moved, he would have left politics altogether.

Later I spoke to Ken Baker[8] who said he had been offered Wales with a peerage to make way for Chris Patten[9] because of course he has got a huge majority in his seat.

---

7. John Smith (1938–94) succeeded Neil Kinnock as Leader of the Labour Party later in 1992 but at the time of the 1992 election was principal Opposition spokesman on Treasury and Economic Affairs.
8. Conservative MP, 1968–97; Home Secretary, 1990–2; life peer 1997.
9. Conservative MP, 1979–92, he lost his seat in the 1992 election, having been Chairman of the Conservative Party and Chancellor of the Duchy of Lancaster since 1990.

Ken said, 'I told him what he could do with that. I am certainly not going to leave the Commons for Chris Patten.' He dislikes him as much as I do. He told me the new Home Secretary was going to be Kenneth Clarke.[10]

Ken said, 'When he said Wales to me I thought of Peter Walker.[11] That's where they put out-of-favour people out to grass in a non-job.' He said that last part to the press, which was a little foolish of him.

During the day I spoke a lot to Pat Chapman, editor of the *News of the World*, to keep her in touch with what was going on.

I said it was safe to say that Clarke is Home Secretary and that David Mellor[12] has got this fancy new job, overall in charge of sport and the Lottery, the arts and English Heritage.

Wakeham[13] is going to the Lords as Leader of it. Rather strange because he said he was too shell-shocked still from his injury at the Brighton bombing to go on being Leader of the House of Commons or in the government as Secretary of State for Energy.

She had a head start over everybody else for her front page (or her first page on the election because the front page was taken up by the new IRA bombing which destroyed the Commercial Union building, among others, in the City).

Yesterday I had a ridiculous article from the *Wall Street Journal*, sent me specially by Rupert after we spoke. It was idiotic drivel saying the Tories had lost their way, they didn't believe in what they used to believe in, which is definitely not true. He has gone very peculiar, Rupert.

I kept altering my article to make it as perfect as I could. I put some jokes in it as well and a sop to Chris Patten whom I don't want to have as a permanent enemy.

In the morning I was rung up from the *Morning Post* of Hong Kong which happens to be owned by Rupert. They wanted to know who

10. Secretary of State for Health, 1988–90, for Education and Science, 1990–2.
11. Conservative MP, 1961–92; Secretary of State for Energy, 1983–7, Secretary for Wales, 1987–90; life peer 1992.
12. He had been Chief Secretary to the Treasury, 1990–2, Secretary of State for National Heritage, April–September 1992.
13. John Wakeham, Conservative MP, 1974–92; seriously injured (and his first wife killed) by the IRA bomb at the Grand Hotel, Brighton, during the 1984 Conservative Party conference; Chief Whip 1983–7, Leader of the House of Commons, 1987–9, Secretary of State for Energy, 1989–92; life peer 1992.

the next Governor of Hong Kong would be. I said it could be a Labour man of solid worth. Would that be acceptable? They asked who and I said, 'I am not going to tell you because it would absolutely wreck his chances.'

They said, 'Would it be Denis Healey?'[14] I said, 'I am not discussing this.' Actually I had in mind not Denis Healey, who might be good, but Ivor Richard.[15]

Now there's a ludicrous proposal that wet Chris Patten should be Governor – a disaster.[16]

Sunday 12 April

Norman poured his heart out to me. He said he had the devil's own trouble over his [March 1992] Budget, before delivering it, with the Cabinet and with Major, too, in large part. They didn't want him to do the tax cut for all down to the new 20p device.[17]

At one point Shaun Woodward[18] and the people who were supposed to be running the campaign wouldn't even return his calls.

I said, 'You have got some good people now in your department and in the spending department. You have got Michael Portillo[19] who is a great Thatcherite and who will be determined to cut spending

14. Labour Party elder statesman; former Chancellor of the Exchequer, Deputy Leader of the Labour Party and shadow Foreign Secretary; life peer 1992.

15. Labour MP, 1964–74; UK Permanent Representative to UN, 1974–79; EEC Commissioner, 1981–4; leader of the Opposition, House of Lords, 1992–7; Leader of the House of Lords, 1997–8; life peer 1990.

16. WW wrote to Chris Patten on 21 April, commiserating with him on losing his seat in the general election and telling him Mrs Thatcher's reaction when the result came through: 'Characteristically she thought it very unfair of the people of Bath after all you had done.' (See Vol. 2, p. 690.) He added: 'May I suggest that you should not go to Hong Kong if you are offered the post?' WW argued that the hauling down of the British flag would be a more painful occasion than losing Bath and Patten would then be out of the mainstream of British politics instead of winning a by-election and returning to the Cabinet.

17. A new tax band so that the taxpayer paid only 20 per cent on the first £2,000 of income.

18. Former BBC TV journalist; Director of Communications, Conservative Party, 1990–2; elected Conservative MP, 1997; crossed to Labour, 1999.

19. Minister of State for Local Government, Department of Environment, 1990–2, at this time promoted to Chief Secretary at the Treasury.

down to prevent everything going overboard. Peter Lilley,[20] who thinks exactly the same way, is now at Social Security.'

Then he said he very much wanted to see Margaret: 'I am trying to keep up her ideas and I am the strongest person in the Cabinet trying to do it but I don't want to be lectured by her as though I were a small boy in shorts – which she usually does.'

Norman said he also wished they hadn't gone into the ERM because it was constraining him on interest rates. I said, 'But it is a good discipline as far as inflation is concerned.' He said that was true but they went in at the wrong time and at the wrong rate.

I talked to Tessa Keswick[21] who is going to be the political adviser to Ken Clarke again. I said, 'I am sorry about Ken Baker. He was very good but it is a really hot seat you've got at the Home Office,' and I told her what I thought about the whole set-up and all the semi-lefties and the delaying people and the inefficiency.

I said, 'You will be in charge of the Tote. It's not going to David Mellor?' She said 'no' and I said, 'Then you had better get me my appointment [as Chairman of the Tote] extended. I was told it was going to be by Ken Baker and Waddington,[22] if necessary, at the end of my two years. I want another two years at least.'[23]

Monday 13 April
Had a long talk with David Mellor, particularly about lotteries. I told him the Tote is going to bid [to run] the Lottery.

Talked to Ted Pickering.[24]

Pick can't understand what Jenkins means about my being too right-wing because I am no more right-wing than he is.

---

20. Secretary of State for Trade and Industry, 1990–2, now made Secretary of State for Social Security.
21. The Hon. Tessa Keswick, former journalist and Conservative Councillor, Kensington & Chelsea, had been special adviser to Kenneth Clarke since 1989; m 2 (1985) Henry Keswick, Chairman, Matheson & Co. and Jardine, Matheson Holdings, Hong Kong.*
22. David Waddington, Home Secretary, 1989–90, Lord Privy Seal and Leader of the House of Lords, 1990–2; life peer 1990.
23. WW had been appointed as Chairman of the Horserace Totalisator Board by Roy Jenkins when Home Secretary in 1976; subsequent Home Secretaries had all renewed him in the post.
24. Journalist and newspaper manager; formerly *Daily Express*, IPC, Mirror Group; executive vice-chairman, Times Newspapers, since 1982; knight 1977.

Dinner with Irwin Stelzer[25] at the new Oriental Restaurant at the Dorchester.

We had Calon-Ségur 1966 which was excellent and surprisingly good against the Chinese-type food. It was decanted well and I complimented the Chinese wine waiter because I didn't expect he would be able to do it properly.

Irwin still attacks Norman.

I said, 'You have got Norman entirely wrong and I had better arrange for a meeting with you.'

Afterwards Verushka[26] said I had been very aggressive to him but I thought the evening had passed off pleasantly enough. I like Irwin very much. He doesn't mind, I think, these strong arguments.

Tuesday 14 April
David Waddington, who was not a very good Home Secretary, and not a very good Leader of the Lords, is now going to be Governor of Bermuda. So I wrote to him, too. I like him very much. I congratulated him on a 'sunshine and sea change for the better'.

Wednesday 15 April
Off to Newmarket in time to see the last three races.

It was a jolly dinner [at the Howard de Waldens[27]].

People are very strange. He is immensely rich and very nice but careful about small things. For example, there weren't any cigars. Fortunately, I always take my own so as not to be in the horrible position of having had a good dinner and no cigar to follow it. I am smoking four or five a day.

I am very fond of Gillie, his wife. She still looks very trim and attractive.

John was very pleased because he had a winner today called Pursuit of Love. I said, 'That's a very appropriate name for you.' (He's healthily keen on girls still, at eighty in November.)

---

25. American economist and journalist; Director of Regulatory Studies, The Hudson Institute; *Sunday Times* columnist.*

26. WW's Hungarian-born fourth wife, née Racz, widow of Baron Dr Laszlo Banszky von Ambroz.*

27. John Howard de Walden, 9th Baron (1912–99); senior steward, Jockey Club, 1957, 1964, 1976; racehorse breeder and owner, including the 1985 Derby winner Slip Anchor; m 2 (1978) Gillian (Viscountess Mountgarret, née Buckley).*

It is an awful nuisance staying away. It is difficult to use the telephone in somebody else's house, particularly as they only seemed to have one. I like my breakfast at a quarter to eight but there wasn't any breakfast till nearly nine o'clock. When Robbie [WW's chauffeur] arrived with a whole stack of newspapers, Gillie said, 'It's marvellous having you to stay. We get a whole lot of extra newspapers.'

John Howard asked me how long I had left with the Tote. I said, 'Officially I am supposed to retire at the end of next April but I would like to stay on because I have so much left to do with the Lottery and developing our device which Coral are using in their shops.'[28]

Saturday 18 April

I have been writing the odd letter to various new Cabinet Ministers.[29]

I think it important to keep friendly with these people so I can keep in the swing of political circles which matter. This could influence them [towards] the way I want them to go and it also helps me get my articles accurate in their interpretation of what is going on.

Monday 20 April

For the second time running Mrs Tamborero[30] gave up her Bank Holiday to come and do the article for the *Times*. She is a noble girl.

It was in defence of Norman Lamont. I had talked to him and got his political adviser to get me a lot of cuttings. It began with a terrific attack on the *Sunday Times* and even on the *Times* itself.

Everything got very nervous at the *Times* because Simon Jenkins was away. They said it looked as though I was making an attack on Andrew Neil. I said, 'I am making one. I don't know why anyone should fuss about that. I was attacked for nine months by the racing correspondent of the *Times*, Richard Evans, and I'm a columnist in the same ruddy paper. Simon Jenkins wouldn't call him off so I don't see

---

28. A computer terminal enabling clients in betting shops to place their bets directly into the Tote pools on racecourses.
29. They included Virginia Bottomley (Health), Kenneth Clarke, Patrick Mayhew (Northern Ireland), John Patten (Education), and Malcolm Rifkind (Defence), all of whom replied warmly, most in their own handwriting.
30. Wendy Tamborero, WW's secretary since 1989.

why I shouldn't make comments about the *Sunday Times* or its editor who has behaved disgracefully to Norman Lamont.'

After a lot of to-ing and fro-ing we agreed a formula.

But when it appeared, they had cut out the bit where I had said the *Times* and the *Sunday Times* get it wrong because they lack understanding of politics and economics.

When I reported this to Norman, he said, 'It's extraordinary how sensitive they are. When I said on the television that the *Sunday Times* is a bloody awful newspaper, Andrew Neil rang up Number 10 to complain and said I ought to be made to withdraw the remark.'

Tuesday 21 April
Rosemary [Lamont][31] came round to go with Verushka to a dressmaker who makes for about £350 exact copies of all the latest fashions from the great houses (but you have to bring your own material). Rosemary is sprouting out quite a lot and enjoying herself enormously.

When Norman told me he had been given Dorneywood, he was over the moon.[32]

It is not only the fact of the house he has got (which Willie Whitelaw[33] had for nine years and often goes to the Home Secretary, as it did to Ken Baker) but that it shows the confidence the Prime Minister has in him. You don't give a chap a residence like that and then move him out in a year or even two.

We went to the Boltons to have dinner with Aly Aziz[34] and his charming Spanish wife from Costa Rica.

She has a pleasant round face and lively laughter. Her figure is not bad but her legs are a bit thick. She must be forty plus. Verushka is going to introduce her to her circle of friends, like Netta [Weinstock],[35]

---

31. Rosemary, née White, m (1971–99) Norman Lamont.*
32. Country house near Slough, offered in recent years to Chancellors of the Exchequer for entertaining, conferences and weekend relaxation; from the 1950s to the 1970s it was used by Foreign Secretaries who were subsequently given Chevening.
33. (1918–99; cr. viscount 1983); Home Secretary, 1979–83; resigned post of Leader, House of Lords, in 1988, after suffering a stroke; m (1943) Cecilia, née Sprot.
34. Chairman, Dashwood Group; investor in Cornish Spring Water, WW's family's company.
35. Née Sobell, m (1949) Arnold Weinstock, Managing Director GEC (1963–96), WW's close friend.*

Eva Pejacsevich[36] and Diana Wilton[37] – the touring team which goes from one grand hotel restaurant to another.

Only Harry's Bar is an expensive venue and Netta or Marcelle Quinton[38] always pays for that.

I said, 'You're a magic man with money. That's why I am certain we are going to make a success of Cornish Spring Water, if we can get Tessa and Robbie to behave in a sensible manner.'[39]

He said that when he was giving a dinner to Princess Margaret – I don't know where it was – there was Cornish Spring Water on the table and she said, 'Whose coat of arms is that?' He said, 'Woodrow Wyatt's.' Princess Margaret said it looked very grand.

I used to get on with her very well but I find her so difficult now that I never even ask her to the house for dinner. You never know what mood she is going to be in. I used to talk to her about books and send them to her, as I do to her mother.

The house was the same side of the road as Tony Crosland[40] had a flat when I was in Tregunter Road.

That was where he had the famous row with Kingsley Amis[41] over gramophone records. When Kingsley wanted to put one on, Tony said, 'It's my bloody gramophone.' Kingsley said, 'They're my bloody records.' It was a very funny squabble between two high-powered intellects quarrelling like children over a toy.

------

36. Countess Pejacsevich, wife of Count Mark Pejacsevich, merchant banker; Hungarian-born friends who frequently played bridge and dined with WW and Verushka.

37. Née Galway, m 1 David Naylor-Leyland, m 2 (1962) 7th Earl of Wilton (John, d 1999).

38. American-born sculptor; née Wegier, m (1952) Anthony Quinton, philosopher (life peer, 1982).*

39. Robert Lyle (Robbie), WW's nephew, son of his brother Major Robert Lyle; m (1991) the Hon. Tessa Mayhew, solicitor; Robbie inherited the family estate, Bonython, in Cornwall, on his father's death in 1989. See Vol. 2 for the history of Cornish Spring Water and the development of the wind farm, Cornish Light and Power.*

40. Anthony Crosland (1918–77); Labour writer and politician; his *The Future of Socialism* (1956) was a major influence on contemporary politics.

41. (1922–95); novelist, poet, critic and *bon viveur*, knight 1990. WW first told this anecdote in his 1985 autobiography *Confessions of an Optimist*, p. 178, and used it again in the article he wrote for the *Times* on Amis' death.*

Wednesday 22 April
Spoke to Margaret.

We talked at some length about what she wrote in *Newsweek*. This has caused a furore. It has been taken as a pretty severe attack on John Major personally.[42]

When I asked her if she wrote it before the election she said, 'No, afterwards.'

She said, 'It was an interview but they sent me the text of it and I made some alterations. I am not saying I don't take responsibility for it, though they did leave some bits out which would have clarified it more.'

I said, 'My worry is that you will lose some of the influence you should have. They will try to marginalize you and say you are of no account. They will compare you with Ted Heath and I don't want that to happen. Your pronouncements should be ones that can't be misinterpreted.' She said, 'I am going to make a lot of those. I only said I would keep quiet during the election time, not saying what I really thought, for example, about the £28 billion deficit.'

A confidential, secret letter arrived from the Home Office which I told Brian [McDonnell][43] to open though I was nervous in case it was something about me, bad. It was merely to know whether I wanted John Sanderson[44] and Peter Winfield[45] to continue [on the Tote Board]. I said, 'Of course I want John Sanderson but Peter Winfield is older than God.' Brian started laughing because of course he is younger than me. He is sixty-five. But he can hardly walk. Anyway I find him very tiresome. He may be useful in some ways but I shall never forgive him for trying behind my back to get me out.[46]

Brian said, 'I think you would be right in saying that some rotation is needed from time to time and that Peter Winfield could go.' So

42. See Vol. 2 for her criticisms of the Major government following her defeat in the 1990 leadership contest.
43. Chief Executive of the Tote, 1981–96.
44. Member, Tote Board, since 1983; chief executive of International Racing Management, responsible for Doncaster, Catterick and Redcar racecourses, chairman of Wetherby and a director of the British Horseracing Board (BHB) on its establishment.
45. (1927–99); Senior partner, Healey & Baker, surveyors, auctioneers and estate agents, 1975–88; trustee, Guy's Hospital, 1974–96; member, Tote Board, 1981–92; racehorse owner.
46. See Vol. 2, pp. 409–10, for Winfield's opposition to WW continuing as chairman.

that is something I will have to organize and sack him very discreetly if I can.

During the day I rang Richard Ryder[47] and said I thought that making Peter Brooke[48] the Speaker would be a great mistake.

Betty Boothroyd[49] would make a very good Speaker. She is Labour and it is about time Labour had its turn. It also should be a woman.

Saturday 2 April
At Oare [the Keswicks' house in Wiltshire].

I gave Tessa a long run down on how the Tote works and how it fits into racing.

To dinner came Amabel Lindsay[50] and her son. There was much talk about the young and Tessa talked a lot of rubbish about how we have to follow what the young think – green stuff, ozone layers, environmentals.

Tessa feels her boss, Kenneth Clarke is a very good egg, tough and resolute.

We had a very good Château Latour 1967, not necessarily the best year. The trouble is that Henry doesn't decant these things properly and there were dregs in it.

Sunday 26 April
Off to see Pyrrhic Dance.[51]

Pyrrhic Dance had been coughing but looked really beautiful, with a lovely easy action and powerful. John Hills [trainer] said he wouldn't force him into racing until he was absolutely ready for it.

When I looked at him in the box, there was a lot of torn up newspaper on the floor. I said, 'What on earth is all that rubbish?' John said, 'It's mostly the *Financial Times*.' I said, 'That's excellent.

---

47. Government Chief Whip 1990–5; life peer 1997.
48. Conservative MP, 1977–97; Paymaster General and Chairman of the Conservative Party, 1987–9; Secretary of State for Northern Ireland, 1989–92; for National Heritage, 1992–94.
49. Elected Labour MP 1973, having being a candidate in general and by-elections since 1957.
50. Widow of the Hon. Patrick Lindsay (d 1986), daughter of the 9th Earl of Hardwicke.
51. WW leased a share in this horse in 1991.

They're the people who told everybody to vote Labour.' The paper on the floor was to stop his throat being irritated.

I had to get back fast because James Joll and his wife were to be there [at Oare] for drinks before lunch.

I told James Joll this with great glee. He is the financial director of Pearsons, owner of the *FT*. He was once a journalist, a very good one.

Next weekend the Keswicks have Conrad Black[52] and his paramour. They couldn't decide whether to put them in the same room or not. Verushka said, 'Why don't you put them into the rooms we had? He can sleep in the dressing room if he wants to or go across into her room.' This is a bedroom attached through the bathroom.

George Weidenfeld[53] is also going to be there with the girl he is going to marry. This will be amusing because Barbara Amiel was his girlfriend for ages. I said to them, 'Do you realize that?' Tessa said when she mentioned who their fellow guests were, Barbara Amiel said fine, no trouble at all.

Before I went down to Oare I had written in the *News of the World* that Chris Patten should do very well as Governor of Hong Kong, though I am somewhat dubious about it in practice. In the *Financial Times*, on the way to Oare, I read that Henry also welcomed the appointment.

We had come to the same conclusion that he has to be backed whatever the doubts.

John Major, it seems, did not want Patten to go to Hong Kong.

It was Douglas Hurd,[54] who is a long associate of Chris Patten, who backed him.

Henry is an extraordinarily able businessman but he pretends it is all luck. It isn't. He says it is very easy to make money in Singapore and Asia. Perhaps it is but a lot of people can lose and do lose it.

I am worried about Henry. He eats in gargantuan quantities as well as drinking heavily. He is getting redder in the face and larger round the girth. He cannot walk easily now.

---

52. Canadian proprietor of the Telegraph newspapers, now a British citizen; m 1 (1978–92) Joanna (formerly Shirley) née Hishon, m 2 (1992) Barbara Amiel, newspaper columnist.*

53. Publisher; m 4 (1992) Annabelle, née Whitestone; life peer 1976.*

54. Conservative politician; Home Secretary, 1985–9, Foreign Secretary, 1989–95; life peer 1997.*

At breakfast this morning he had eggs, bacon, sausages and mush-rooms, then followed that by a kipper.

When I said in front of Tessa, 'I wish you would eat and drink less,' she agreed, but why does she give him all this food covered in cream sauces? He dotes on her and follows her every whim. The reverse is not over evident.

When I got home I found I had put on over two pounds in weight and am now 12 stone 3 or 4 pounds, which is far too much.

Monday 27 April

Betty Boothroyd's great day. I took the Oath of Allegiance early in the Lords so that I could nip round and watch the proceedings in the Commons.

I have known her for a very long time but have not seen anything of her for years. She was secretary to Sir Geoffrey de Freitas, the highly respectable Labour MP who married an American heiress.[55]

He had a nice smile. He was generally on the side of the angels.

He had been at Haileybury. Attlee made him his PPS when he became Prime Minister in 1945. Attlee was at Haileybury. Just as old Etonian Prime Ministers did their best for old Etonians and old Harrovian Prime Ministers like Baldwin did their best for old Harrovians, so Attlee did his best for old Haileyburians. That's how Christopher Mayhew[56] got early promotion – he was at Hailey-bury.

In 1946 Geoffrey became Under Secretary for Air but he never got further than Under Secretary at the Home Office. He was partly of West Indian ancestry, or at least his family had been there. He had a slight look of the tar brush about him, but not very noticeably.

Miss Betty Boothroyd has been pretty secretive about her past life, or at any rate selective. She was a Tiller girl when she was seventeen or eighteen after the war.

Her working-class father was shocked by her appearing on the stage as a chorus girl. It was all highly respectable. The Tiller girls were well

---

55. (1913–82); Labour MP, 1945–79; m (1938) Helen Graham, daughter of Laird Bell Hon. KBE, of Illinois, USA.

56. (1915–97); Labour MP, 1945–50 and 1951–74, Minister of Defence, 1964–6 (resigned); joined the Liberal Party, 1974, Liberal MP, July–September 1974; life peer 1981. His daughter, Tessa, m (1991) Robert Lyle, WW's nephew.

clad, mainly showing their pretty legs, which Betty Boothroyd had certainly got.

I am sure she will make a very good Speaker and I rooted for her in the *News of the World*. She has a lot of charm but strong authority in her nature.

Wednesday 29 April
Book of The Year party at Hatchards.

Philip Zeigler[57] is very excited over his book about Harold Wilson. I said, 'Can you make it interesting and exciting and romantic?' He said, 'It's a very hard task. I certainly can't make it romantic.'

I said, 'I suppose you could say Harold had been romantic with Marcia[58] at one time.' He said, 'I doubt if there was much romance in it.'

David Owen[59] and Debbie were there. She greeted me with great enthusiasm. She said, 'Wasn't it wonderful the way David won the election for Major?' I said, 'What?' She said, 'Yes, by coming out to support him.' I said, 'Every little helps but I don't think he can really claim to have changed the election result.'

He told me that Major had offered him the job at Hong Kong but then he had to give it to Patten and he understood why.

Then he told me he was coming to the Lords with the first batch of dissolution honours which I gather will be in June.

I was told that Salman Rushdie[60] was there and would I like to meet him. I said, 'No. Now I know he's here, I'm leaving before the bombs go off,' which remark was duly reported in the *Evening Standard*.

---

57. Historian, biographer and publisher, he wrote the life (1985) and edited the diaries of Earl Mountbatten of Burma; his life of the Labour Prime Minister Harold Wilson was published in 1993; as editor-in-chief at William Collins, he was WW's editor for *Confessions of an Optimist*.
58. Marcia Williams was Wilson's private and political secretary, 1956–83; life peer (Lady Falkender) 1974.
59. Labour MP, 1966–81, Foreign Secretary, 1977–9; joint founder of SDP, 1981; SDP MP, 1981–92; leader SDP, 1982–87; m (1968) Deborah née Schabert, literary agent; life peer 1992.
60. Novelist against whom Ayatollah Khomeini issued a fatwa death-threat in 1989 for writing *The Satanic Verses*.

Sonia was there and her husband, Andrew Sinclair.[61] He said, 'I see you're still going on writing in the *Times* despite the new regime. They've dropped me.'

I have an uneasy feeling that marriage won't last. She is somewhat older than Andrew who I don't feel is a very nice person.

I am very fond of Sonia, scatty and absurd though her politics have been.

Jilly Cooper [novelist] was there smiling away at me. I have no inclination to follow her suggestion that I should take her out to lunch.

She was looking very toothy as usual. At one point she was standing with her back to me and it was extremely scrawny and unattractive.

I haven't read her sex books on polo etc. but I should imagine they owe more to her imagination than to her experiences.

I have been eating nothing but bananas plus low fat yoghurt for lunch.

Thursday 30 April

Went to Sonia's party at 16 Tite Street. It was very crowded. Tarquin Olivier was there and thought I didn't remember him. He said, 'I'm Laurence Olivier's son. You may have heard of him.'

Tarquin has a vague look of his father, without the distinction. I said, 'Have you killed your father yet in your book?'[62] He said, 'What do you mean? I got on quite well with him.' I said, 'In the sense of getting him out of your system and coming to terms with it.' He said, 'Yes I have done that now. I think he was a much nicer person than I thought he was originally when I was going through his papers.'

Conrad Black was there with Barbara Amiel. I had a long talk with Barbara, basically about the poor quality of journalism, the lack of research and energy, and how journalists utterly failed to realize how wrong the opinion polls were [during the election].

---

61. Sonia Lady Melchett, novelist and board member, Royal Court Theatre from 1974, Royal National Theatre, 1984–94, m 1 (1947) the Hon. Julian Mond (later 3rd Baron Melchett, d 1973), m 2 (1984) Andrew Sinclair, writer and former academic, his third marriage; they are still married. WW constantly revised his views about friends and grew to like Sinclair.*
62. 'Have you killed your father yet?' was the question Sir Osbert Sitwell once asked WW – see *Confessions of an Optimist*, p. 36.

David Stevens was there with his wife.[63] I quite like his new wife. David was still convinced he had won the election single-handed which is a lot of bilge.

───────
63. Chairman, United Newspapers, since 1981, Express Newspapers, since 1985; m 2 (1977) Melissa Milicevich (d 1989), m 3 (1990) Meriza Giori; life peer 1987.

Saturday 2 May

To dinner at No 4 Grove End Road where Colonel J. Stephenson[1] lives in a tiny house once used by Gubby (Sir G. O.) Allen.[2] He had put in a door which let him straight into Lord's cricket ground.

It was for Bob's birthday.[3] It was a strange little party. His wife cooked the dinner tolerably well, with a wonderful birthday cake with ten candles on it to represent Bob's ninety-first birthday.

When people put on what they think is a very grand dinner, which is very ordinary, I often wonder what they eat when they are alone.

Paul Getty[4] was very jolly and wanted me to go to his house to watch some great match captained by Imran Khan[5] which is taking place at his new cricket ground in the country. It is apparently very beautiful and has a lake by it. Bob said it is the only cricket ground he has ever seen with ducks floating on it so that those who get out for nothing can join the ducks.

We had a tough argument about Gatting whose case goes to the International Test Cricket Control Board in July with the opinions of the MCC. Stephenson was all in favour of saying the ban against him should be continued because he knew the rules when he went to South Africa and he made a lot of money there.[6]

---

1. Secretary, Marylebone Cricket Club (MCC), 1987–93; m (1962) Karen Margrethe Koppang.
2. (1902–89); played in 25 Test matches and captained England in 1936, 1936–7 and 1948; President, MCC, 1963–4, Treasurer, MCC, 1964–76.
3. WW's famous cricketer cousin, R. E. S. Wyatt (1901–95), who first captained England against Australia in 1930; his wife, Molly, d 1996.
4. John Paul Getty Junior, millionaire philanthropist; m 1 (1956–66) Gail, née Harris, m 2 (1966) Talitha, née Pol (d 1971), m 3 (1994) Victoria, née Holdsworth; honorary KBE 1986; took British citizenship, 1997.
5. Former Pakistani cricket captain.
6. Mike Gatting, England cricket captain 1986–8, captained the unofficial England team touring South Africa, 1988–9, against the ITCC ruling; the ban was lifted later in 1992.

I said, 'Don't you realize it was a wholly immoral rule made by the anti-apartheid screaming mob, Peter Hain[7] and all those ghastly communists at the United Nations? It put off the ending of apartheid because cricket has been a marvellous unifier in South Africa.'

Paul Getty agreed and so did Bob in the end.

Bob and Molly made all kinds of embarrassing remarks about the people they know, the Lords and Ladies.

Sunday 3 May
Had a long talk with Norman who rang from Dorneywood where he is very happy.

Had I read 'my friend' Irwin Stelzer's article in the *Sunday Times* this morning? I hadn't. He said, 'It's another attack on me. He says I mismanage the economy and have done it all wrong.'

Why should poor Norman be bullied by an American economist who is led by the nose by Andrew Neil and talks a lot of rubbish on this particular subject, though not on other things?

Norman is getting on well with Major. I said, 'Does he recognize that you won the election, or at any rate clinched it, by your Budget and by insisting on the exposure of the Smith tax proposals?' Norman said, 'Not quite. He thinks he did it.'

I asked Norman whether they are going to take seriously and immediately the [task of] getting the boundaries redistributed, as I wrote in the *News of the World* this morning. He said yes, they were. 'And what about Scotland and Wales?' He said, 'I think they may not take in Scotland and Wales, for fear of stirring up more nationalism. There is certainly no intention of letting them have regional assemblies so they may still want to give them an undue number of seats.'[8]

7. Brought up in South Africa; Labour MP since 1991; Parliamentary Under Secretary of State, Welsh Office, 1997–9, Minister of State, FCO, since 1999.

8. The impartial Boundaries Commission reviews Parliamentary seats in England, Scotland and Wales according to shifts in the population; political parties try to manoeuvre the changes in their favour; under the Redistribution of Seats Act 1993 the changes, completed in 1995, gave negligible overall advantage to the Conservatives but the constituencies of certain MPs, including Norman Lamont's, disappeared. WW argued in his *News of the World* article of 3 May that 'shrunken Labour voting inner cities still return as many MPs as when their electorates were double the size'.

Monday 4 May

Bank Holiday. At a quarter past eight in the morning I rang William Purves, Chairman of Hong Kong and Shanghai Bank in Hong Kong.

NERA[9] are very anxious to see if they will give us the job of preparing their case against referral to any monopoly and mergers commission or Brussels or elsewhere in their bid to get the Midland Bank.[10]

I did get through to him instantly, which shows I still have some influence around the world.

I told him we were complete experts on Brussels, the Office of Fair Trading and the Department of Trade and Industry, the Monopolies and Mergers Commission and all the rest of it, because half NERA staff come from one or other of these sources. So maybe that will put a feather in my cap with NERA and get us a nice rich job.

Tuesday 5 May

I had a disturbing conversation with Bernard [Levin].[11] I had been puzzled where he had got to and had left a message on his answering machine, having not spoken to him for weeks: 'Where are you? Are you living in a cave?'

He told me he has been having an awful condition for the last three years. He has seen eleven doctors including the very best neurologist in America which cost him £3,500. He gets into panics unexpectedly when his mind is seized with fear and inability to think or do anything. He cannot now give a public lecture or speech (which he used to do often); he can't do television work because he can't make the commentary properly.

He still writes pretty well OK but I didn't like to tell him it's not as good as it used to be; now I know why.

I said, 'You're not going to the right neurologist. I know the best one in the world. Also, I am very close to the Royal Free Hospital at Hampstead and they've got a very good neurologist.'[12] He said, 'I don't want to see any more doctors. There's no point in it.' I said, 'Of course there is, if they're not treating you right.'

---

9. National Economic Research Associates for whom WW was a consultant.
10. Purves became chairman, Midland Bank, in 1994; knight 1993.
11. Journalist (*Times* columnist at this time), critic and author.
12. WW was referring to Professor Giovanni Ricci (father of Aliai Forte) and Dr, later Professor, R. E. Pounder at the Royal Free Hospital.

He sounded very gloomy and disturbed. Of course he always has had this melancholia, like Dr Johnson, ups and downs. But this is the worst that has ever happened to him. It's rotting him away. Oh dear.

Wednesday 6 May
I had rung Margaret about all this commotion in the press that she was going to be a Life Countess.

She said, 'They won't do it at Number 10, I don't think.'

I said, 'Why can't you be a real Countess?' She said, 'I thought it was enough to be a life peer. There is a hereditary baronetcy for Mark.'

Earlier she had said, 'I do have a few friends like you, Woodrow,' and I was very touched. I always feel the tears starting in my eyes when we talk about her deposition and the consequences of it because she should be there still, urging them on. Of course if she had been, Saddam Hussein would have been knocked out, the Kurds wouldn't be being murdered, she would have taken a grip of the Serb-Croatia affair and wouldn't have allowed Croatia to have been overrun or Bosnia Herzegovina. It was an appalling thing which was done to her. Major is good in his way but he is not a patch on her and never can be.

At tea in the Lords, after the Queen's speech, George Thomas[13] said to me, 'You have a very "twist in the knife" way of writing your wonderful articles. I agree with them all, just about.' I said, 'You shouldn't, George. On the whole they're anti-Labour.' He said, 'In a way that's why I agree with them. But don't tell anyone.'

Went to see Allan Davis's[14] play at Wyndhams. *The Straight and Narrow*, all about queers.

I told Allan I thought it was well constructed and how well he had directed it, how good the acting was and all the rest of it. He promptly asked me if I would give it a favourable mention in the *News of the World*. I have done so. I was not truthful in what I said in the *News of the World*.

---

13. (1909–1997); Labour MP, 1945–83; Speaker of the House of Commons, 1976–83; cr. Viscount Tonypandy, 1983.
14. (1913–2001); Director of WW's play *The Division Belle* (subsequently published as *High Profiles*) which was staged at the Theatre Royal, Margate, in October 1989; his productions included *No Sex Please, We're British*.

Thursday 7 May
Went down to the Lords.

Sitting on the front bench were three brand new Ministers and peers: Lynda Chalker (Overseas Development), John Wakeham (Leader of the House) and Robert Cranborne.[15] I went and sat behind him briefly and asked him if he'd like a PPS. He said yes, and if I was looking for the job, the duties were very onerous – he would like to be given lunch twice a month at Wiltons.[16]

In the Elysian Fields of the Lords I think life is lovely – and outside it. Though I work hard and long, I am lucky in enjoying it all.

To The Other Club.[17] A remarkable turnout. Ted Heath,[18] Peter Carrington,[19] even Andrew Devonshire[20] whom I haven't seen there for a long time, Norman Tebbit,[21] Paddy Ashdown,[22] William Waldegrave,[23] etc.

Before dinner Robin Day[24] kindly told everybody that I was the only person who got it right, meaning the election, to which Peter Walker said, 'He always does.' I hadn't seen Peter Walker for some time – the great trimmer who survived in Margaret's Cabinet, with considerable success, as the statutory dissenter.

Paddy Ashdown was extremely friendly considering what I had said about him during the election.

Ted Heath was beaming away. I sat nearly opposite him and threw

---

15. Viscount Cranborne, heir to the Marquess of Salisbury, Conservative MP, 1979–87, at this time Parliamentary Under Secretary, Defence.
16. Restaurant in Jermyn Street.
17. Winston Churchill and F. E. Smith (later Lord Birkenhead) founded The Other Club in 1913 because they were not wanted by a club called 'The Club'. Its membership consists mainly of politicians from all parties.
18. Sir Edward Heath, Conservative Prime Minister, 1970–4.
19. 6th Baron Carrington; Conservative politician; Foreign Secretary, 1979–82; Secretary General, NATO, 1984–8; chairman, Christie's International, 1988–93; chairman, EC Peace Conference, Yugoslavia, 1991–2.
20. 11th Duke of Devonshire.*
21. Conservative politician; MP, 1970–92; Secretary of State for Employment (1981–3), for Trade and Industry, (1983–5); Chancellor of the Duchy of Lancaster and Conservative Party chairman (1985–7); life peer 1992.
22. Leader, Liberal Democratic Party, 1988–99.
23. Conservative politician; Secretary of State for Health, 1990–2, Chancellor of the Duchy of Lancaster at this time; 2nd son of 12th Earl Waldegrave.
24. (1923–2000); television and radio journalist; knight 1981.

a piece of bread in his face to alert him. I told him he conducted the affairs as Father of the House in tremendous fashion during the election of the Speaker.

I said, 'I've always remained very fond of you, as you know, despite your contrariness from time to time.' He said, 'Yes, you've often been rude about that.' I said, 'But I've more often said what a good egg you are.' He beamed away very happily as the spiffing new Knight of the Garter he now is.

There was a tremendous memento signed photograph for the chap who has looked after the Club for forty-five years.[25] Jim Callaghan[26] had said he would like to sign it. Michael Hartwell[27] said, 'You can't because you've resigned.' He confirmed to me that his reason for resigning was because I had said he was the worst Prime Minister since the war, with the exception of Wilson who was slightly worse. Callaghan thought that was very insulting. Despite the rules of the Club, which allow for asperity in Party matters, he went. My comment was in a review in the *Times* of his autobiography which was appallingly bad.

I sat next to Arnold Weinstock. I started discussing with him the possibility of his joining in the tender for the National Lottery with us. He said, 'We could help.'

I said, 'I will have a look at it, if you are talking seriously, but I don't think you would be easy to handle.' He said, 'We are in it for the same thing. I want to make money and you want to make money.' I said, 'Yes, but not for myself, for the Tote.' 'No difference,' he said.

There was a superb 1967 Château Latour, given by Anthony Montague Browne, the boring last private secretary to Winston Churchill. I was amazed at his generosity.

On my other side sat Arnold Goodman.[28]

He is losing his memory, the dear fellow, as well as the sharpness of his brain.

---

25. Frank Mondelli, maître d'hôtel des salons privés.

26. Labour Prime Minister, 1976–9; his memoirs *Time and Chance* were published in 1987; life peer 1987.

27. Life peer 1968 (formerly the Hon. Michael Berry); chairman and editor-in-chief, *Daily Telegraph* and *Sunday Telegraph*, 1954–87; Conrad Black acquired control of the *Telegraph* titles in 1985 after sixty years of ownership by the Berry family.

28. (1913–95); solicitor; Master of University College, Oxford, 1976–86; chairman, Observer Editorial Trust, 1967–76; life peer 1965.

Friday 8 May

Budapest. Warm and pleasant. Mark Pejacsevich meets me at the airport with Witold's car.

Poor Witold.[29] He was a pleasant, feckless Pole. Just before he died he sold the little house they had given him in Poland in compensation for the loss of his pre-Communist property. He had about twenty-five thousand dollars left and was able to buy a new car. He left it all to Livia who is desolate.

On the drive in we picked up a young soldier, twenty years old.

He is looking for a job when he comes out, in the architectural field. I said, 'Will you get one?' He said, 'I think I will because I have got connections.' When I mentioned this to the Prime Minister later he said, 'I suppose it happens in every country that it's easier to get a job if you've got connections.'

I stayed with the Prime Minister for two hours.

I saw him in the same office where I once saw Pozsgay and the others just before the Communists decided to have an election, free and fair.[30]

József Antall, the Prime Minister, is short and dark and with a scholastic appearance. He was at one time a schoolteacher. Then he was thrown out of his job and arrested but not seriously imprisoned. He got a job running a medical museum where he did a great deal of writing. He is ill, but not seriously, merely saying he has cancer.[31] He doesn't smile much. He has an intelligent face. He has some charm and was very agreeable.

When I asked him what his achievements had been in the two years since he became Prime Minister, he emphasized very much the international aspects of what he had done, getting out of the Warsaw Pact and joining NATO and so forth. But they want more British and American investment in Hungary to outweigh the German and Japanese and that of other countries. He thinks it is a safeguard for keeping America in Europe and to deal with the threats which he believes will arise to Central Europe and even the rest of Europe from the break-up of the Soviet Union. He sees these old Soviet generals almost behaving like warlords under certain circumstances.

I was asking him about the old communists and whether there was

---

29. Former husband of Verushka's sister, Livia, a translator, who lives in Budapest.
30. See Vol. 2, pp. 32–3, for WW's interview with Pozsgay in February 1989.
31. He died on 12 December, 1993, still in office.

difficulty in getting them to run private enterprise which needs a vastly different approach.

He replied that true belief in communism was held by about one per cent of the communists running the administration and the economy.

Monday 11 May

To Stationers' Hall for the party for the eighty-year-old executive vice chairman of the *Times*, Sir Edward Pickering. Rupert was very friendly. I told him how his business is getting on in Hungary and what I was trying to do to get the articles of association or the conditions altered so that he could run it more effectively.

Tuesday 12 May

I went to lunch at the Savoy, the great annual David Stevens United Newspapers lunch.

I saw the appalling Andrew Neil, patted him on the back and said, 'You've been proved utterly wrong.' 'What do Conservative Central Office pay you to write all that stuff supporting Norman Lamont?' I said, 'I do it because I think it's right.'

It was a fairly acid conversation but not totally unfriendly.

Then it was off to the Tote, then back to NERA, and then dashing down to the Lords to make sure of my attendance money.

I was accosted by Alexander Hesketh.[32]

He said he was in trouble because people were saying he had been rubbishing Chris Patten and Shaun Woodward. He was going to deny it. I said, 'You mustn't be so rough with people and aggressive with them. I want you to go into the Cabinet.'

Arnold wanted an early dinner. We originally said we were going to Pratt's but they were having a special Duke of Devonshire cocktail party, including women, to which this year we had not been invited.[33] So we went to Wiltons, and blow me down, just as we were reaching Wiltons the [car] telephone rang. Verushka wanting to know where I was and what I was doing.

I said to Arnold, 'Verushka and Netta ought to run a private detective agency. We are under surveillance all the time.'

---

32. 3rd Baron Hesketh, at this time Government Chief Whip, House of Lords.*
33. The Duke of Devonshire is the owner of Pratt's.

Friday 15 May
Mrs Thatcher startled everyone by making a vigorous morning speech at The Hague about the European Community. The *Evening Standard* misinterpreted it immediately, saying it was a great blast which would damage Major.

At half past six the full text of it arrived from her to me. It read extremely well, brilliant, setting out in the most thoughtful way the problems facing the European Community and Britain. I rang her to say so.

She was helped by Norman Stone,[34] John O'Sullivan,[35] [Robin] Harris[36] and one or two others. 'Though the thoughts are all mine. I worked it all out,' she hastened to add. She said she couldn't see why John Major would object to anything in it. She made some very friendly remarks about him.

Saturday 16 May
Last night William Shawcross[37] delivered to me a huge typed manuscript of his book about Rupert. Would I read it and tell him what I think of it? It is not too late to make some alterations.

As far as I could judge from a quick flip through the book, it seemed racily and well written and thoughtful.

Basically, he disapproves of Rupert because he is rather left-wing, certainly left of centre. The other night Olga [Polizzi] said to me that William is very wet and she could never marry him, though he would like to marry her. I was surprised to hear he is wet because he certainly stirred up Henry Kissinger with his violent attack on him in his book about Vietnam.

---

34. Professor of Modern History, University of Oxford, and Fellow of Worcester College, Oxford, 1984–97; since then Professor of International Relations, Bilkent University, Ankara.

35. Journalist who helped Margaret Thatcher with her memoirs; Editor at Large, *National Review*, 1999.

36. WW recorded Robert Harris here but he must have meant Robin Harris, Director, Conservative Research Department, 1985–8; Prime Minister's Policy Unit, 1989–90; assistant to Margaret Thatcher since 1990.

37. The Hon. William Shawcross, writer; his *Sideshow: Kissinger, Nixon and the Destruction of Cambodia* was published in 1979; m 3 (1993) Olga Polizzi, née Forte.*

Sunday 17 May
Margaret and Denis Thatcher and Norman and Rosemary Lamont to dinner.

I decided to provide a 1979 Louis Roederer champagne plus a bottle of the first-class pink champagne, with gin and Martini ready for Denis. Plus some of the miraculous Château Margaux Pavilion Blanc 1933, to be followed by Château Margaux 1967.

Margaret drank a lot of the excellent Louis Roederer and she got very chatty with Verushka about running houses and so forth.

The first course was very good: artichoke hearts stuffed with quails' eggs on top with bits of caviar (imitation). Then came the lamb. Denis said his wasn't cooked enough.

So some was sent down to be cooked again. (I had told Rebecca to overcook at least one chunk of the three large racks but she doesn't take any notice and just does what she likes.) On the second helping Margaret asked if there was any more of the brown one and she had some brown ones, too. It seems that in Grantham and Dulwich and wherever Denis came from, we don't have the French taste for pink, nearly red, delicious young lamb cutlets.

The conversation got cracking when the dinner began. I congratulated her on her speech and said it was absolutely brilliant and put the choices clearly between the edifice which Delors[38] wants to construct which would collapse on itself and the open free market based on the Single Market but including more countries.

Then she started saying that John Major and the government had let the whole thing slide and it was inevitable that we were going to have a federal state, a single currency and a Central European Bank.

At one point Denis called out from the other end of the table (there were only six of us), 'Margaret, listen to what the Chancellor is saying,' because she was brushing aside his remarks and talking across him. So she did calm down a little.

Then she made an astonishing statement. Her peerage was being delayed so they could get the vote out of the way in the House of Lords against Maastricht before she could be in the Lords to lead the opposition to it and stop them passing it. I said, 'That's utterly absurd. You know perfectly well the Government can't be defeated on an issue like that. You mustn't go around telling Tories to vote against it, even privately.'

---

38. Jacques Delors, President, EC Commission, 1985–95.

She said, 'Of course the Government must win.' I said, 'They won't win, if you go on like this.'

She said, 'They want to stop me having free speech.' She is always going on about that. I said, 'I don't think that's true either. In fact John Major's comment on your speech was that it was very interesting, and so it was.'

Then we began on government spending and she said she hoped Norman is going to take a very hard line because it will take some years to get the thing straight again. He said yes, he is going to but it was inevitable, when you didn't have the revenue coming in during periods of recession, that there was over-spending.

She said, 'What about Michael Heseltine, *President* (sarcastically) of the Board of Trade? He's going to try to spend a lot.' Norman said, 'I've already had clashes with him and I'm not going to let him.'

She was sniffing a little as she had a bit of a cold. I said, 'Have you stopped taking ascorbic acid, the Vitamin C?' She said, 'I'm afraid I have.' I said, 'Please go back to it.'

Norman ventured to say that he didn't think the single currency was a serious matter.

I said, 'We had a single currency with India before the war. We had one with Ireland where it was really our currency but they just called it something different.' She said, 'Yes, but we're calling this the ecu.' I said, 'Margaret, you yourself put large sums of money into the very first stage of the ERM to support and fortify the ecu.'

She doesn't like to be reminded of things she let us in for.

When we discussed David Mellor, she said, 'He's no good.' I said, 'You mean he's too keen on favourable publicity and shirks from doing anything unpopular.'

She was clearly thinking about the difficulty we had with him about getting the Broadcasting Bill amendments about impartiality through.[39]

Margaret said, 'You have got to do what is right and not bother about the public relations. They take care of themselves in the end, if you've done the right thing.'

At about a quarter past eleven she said, 'I think it's time to go,' and she got up, after this tremendous battle of words which she had clearly enjoyed. As she got up, she said, 'Ministers should slip out first.' Norman said, 'Former Prime Ministers should slip out first.' She

---

39. See Vol. 2, pp. 349, 351 and 356–7, for WW's struggle to get Mellor to accept the amendments.

obviously wanted to stay behind a bit and talk to me about what had
been said. But so did Norman. Slightly grudgingly she went out and I
saw her into her car. She waved and was very friendly and jolly.

When I came back Norman went on a great deal about the single
currency.

I said, 'What about all you have always been saying, that it interfered with your ability to raise taxes?' He said, 'It doesn't at all. It
doesn't make any difference.'

Norman wants an independent Bank of England.[40]

Thursday 21 May

I rang Tessa Keswick from the car in response to a message. She asked
me all kinds of questions about Jeremy Deedes[41] – age, background
and what he did. I said, 'But it's all in the c.v. I sent to Johnson at the
Home Office.'

Henry Keswick, her husband, is on the Board of the *Telegraph* and
he would know about him, too.

I said, 'I have wanted him [on the Tote Board] for years. He will
be thrilled to bits.'

She said, 'The government is not going to do anything about trying
to curb the influx of immigrants from outside and inside Europe, and
it is not even going to do much about political asylum.'

I said, 'Won't Kenneth Clarke be tough about it?' She said, 'No.
The trouble with these "Europeans" (as he is) is that they think it's
fine.'

I said, 'He has to be absolutely cracked. There are going to be
violent explosions. The coloured people who are here already are going
to suffer the backlash.'

We then had a jolly chat about horses.

I think she is not a bad girl, Tessa.

But she is the sort of girl who understands a little and then misinter-

---

40. The Bank of England was made independent by the new Labour government in
    1997; in February 2000 Michael Portillo, appointed shadow Chancellor of the
    Exchequer, announced that the Conservatives would not reverse the change.
41. The Hon. Jeremy Deedes, b 1943; son of Lord Deedes (Bill Deedes, former
    Conservative MP and editor, *Daily Telegraph*); executive editor, *Daily* and *Sunday
    Telegraph*, 1986–92, editorial director, 1992–6, managing director, Telegraph
    Group, since 1996; member, Tote Board, 1992–8.

prets the total. Unfortunately, many women are like that. They can also be obstinate with it.

Nick Lloyd and his wife Eve Pollard,[42] Frank Johnson,[43] Petronella,[44] myself and Verushka at dinner at 19 Cavendish Avenue.

Anthony Howard[45] has been appointed as consultant to Simon Jenkins, advising him on the structure and content of the paper. They must be surely mad. He is a former editor of the *New Statesman*, very left-wing, assistant editor for a long time on the *Observer*.

The new daily supplement, 'Life and Times', is a poor joke, attempted trendiness for the young to whom it certainly doesn't appeal.

Some of the great editors of the *Times* must be turning in their graves. The last one who was any good was Charlie Douglas-Home,[46] although even Charlie Wilson[47] was a good, workmanlike constructor of a newspaper and knew how to run the news side.

The *Independent* is also losing its way so the *Times* ought to be making hay as a decent paper. But its reporting is now poor and I am beginning to think I can't keep it as my paper of record for information.

Its foreign coverage is lamentable. The only thing it has over the others is the Letters. Peter Stothard[48] and leftie Mary Ann Sieghart[49] are dreary and useless, though Janet Daley [columnist] writes quite well sometimes.

Nick Lloyd spoke of John Major's extraordinary touchiness and vanity and concern about what is written about him. The *Daily Express* had written a jokey comment about him wearing a suit which came from some downmarket, ready-made establishment. The next time Lloyd, who had forgotten about this, saw him, he opened his coat, held it open wide and said, 'See, that's Austin Reed. It's not the place you wrote about in your paper.'

---

42. Nicholas Lloyd, editor, *Daily Express*, 1986–96; knight 1990; m 2 (1979) Eve Pollard, editor, *Sunday Mirror* and *Sunday Mirror Magazine*, 1988–91, *Sunday Express* and *Sunday Express Magazine*, 1991–4.

43. Associate editor, *Sunday Telegraph*, 1988–93, deputy editor, 1994–5; editor, *Spectator*, 1995–9.

44. Journalist daughter of WW and Verushka.*

45. Editor, *New Statesman*, 1972–8, the *Listener*, 1979–81; deputy editor, *Observer*, 1981–8; reporter, BBC TV, 1989–92; obituaries editor, the *Times*, 1993–9.

46. (1937–85); editor, the *Times*, 1982–5.

47. Editor, the *Times*, 1985–90.

48. At this time deputy editor of the *Times*.

49. Assistant editor, the *Times*, since 1990.

As it was getting late and I thought I must get up early to do my article and perhaps I had drunk a bit too much – and I thought that Petronella ought to be allowed to talk to her journalistic peers – I left the dining-room.

I tried to get Verushka out, saying, 'Your mother[50] wants you,' and that kind of thing, but she would go back in.

All they were doing after I left was continuing to talk about sex, particularly about George Weidenfeld. They were fascinated about how he gets so many women. Eve Pollard said he was immensely charming and he had tried it on her but she didn't feel in the least bit attracted to him.

But it is strange, many women do like fat men like that. After all, Barbara Skelton who was the mistress of King Farouk then married Cyril Connolly[51] (fat) and George Weidenfeld (even fatter).

The girl he is going to marry now is thin.

Friday 22 May

I tried to wake myself up and alert myself by ringing Margaret whom I had not spoken to since she came to dinner last Sunday. She went on a lot about how awful it was that the government twisted the arms of the Tory backbenchers, particularly the new ones, saying they would never get a job if they voted against the government and didn't support it on the Maastricht debate. I said, 'Margaret, all governments do that.' She said, 'Mine didn't.' I said, 'Of course it did. The Whips didn't tell you what they were up to.'

She said, 'Look how Major is dishing out the jobs. What is Jonathan Aitken[52] doing there? They're just trying to stop him making trouble about the Community.' I thought to myself, you didn't have him in the government because he behaved so badly to Carol [her daughter] after having had an affair with her, thinking that might get him a job in the government.

---

50. Verushka's mother, known as 'Nadje' (the Hungarian for grandmother), now over ninety and bedridden, had lived with the Wyatts since before their marriage.

51. (1903–74); author, editor and literary critic; m 2 (1950–6) Barbara, née Skelton, who then m (1956–61) Weidenfeld as his second wife.

52. Conservative politician, journalist and businessman; MP, 1974–97; convicted of perjury for his evidence in his libel action against the *Guardian*, 1999; Major had appointed him Minister of State for Defence Procurement; see Vol. 1, p. 340, for his courtship of Carol Thatcher.

She then said, 'John Major is too vain. He always wants to be popular. He is too weak. He won't really carry all these things through.' I said, 'I think he will.' She said, 'No he won't. You'll see.'

When I had spoken to her I rang Norman.

Norman said he likes Chips Keswick[53] more and more and what sound judgement he has, very wise and sensible. I said, 'Then why don't you let him be a Director of the Bank of England?' He laughed and said, 'I knew you'd say that when I praised Chips Keswick.' I said, 'Do something about it then.' He said he was going to try.

We were then due for dinner, wearing a black tie, at the Connaught Hotel for Irwin Stelzer's birthday. I took him in a special box six of the wonderful forty-year-old pre-Castro Romeo y Julieta special selection cigars which had been kept in bundles. I have only got thirty-eight left now.

Joe Flom was there and his wife.[54] I like both of them. He said how much he had liked the Chancellor and how intelligent he thought he was. He thought he had a very good grip on the situation.

I made a little speech when the birthday cake came in and said that though Irwin can be very cantankerous (which everybody laughed at), I find him my best friend, extremely loyal and I am very fond of him.

I shouldn't have said he was my best friend because I don't quite know who is. But I do like him very much and he has certainly been an enormous help to me. He introduced me to Skadden Arps and all the rest of it.

Saturday 23 May
Dear Livia is going on Monday.

We had a barbecue. Originally we were going to eat in the garden but it got a bit windy. The barbecue was on the steps outside the kitchen. The South African Minister from next door rang up and said, 'I don't think you know it but there is an enormous amount of smoke pouring out of your house.' He thought the whole place was on fire.

Petronella was going to the South of France, Nice, the next morning

---

53. Chairman and chief executive, Hambros Bank, 1986–95, non-executive chairman, 1995–8; younger brother of Henry Keswick.*
54. From Skadden Arps, the US lawyers for whose firm WW held a consultancy; WW had introduced them to Lamont in November 1989; see Vol. 2, pp. 194–5.

early, having to leave the house at a quarter past six. She is writing
about some great Grand Prix at Monaco.

Could she borrow my alarm clock? I said yes. She forgot to take it
upstairs and I was just on the verge of sleep at ten past twelve when
she came and demanded it and how to set it.

Sunday 24 May

At about five in the morning I woke up worrying about whether
Petronella had left in time to catch this damned aeroplane because she
is so disconnected in her ways and had been watching television until
well after midnight. Eventually I went up at just gone six and said,
'Did the alarm clock go off?' She said yes and I said, 'Then why aren't
you getting out of bed?'

She got very annoyed. I said, 'I am only trying to help you.' Then
I had to go downstairs – I was wearing absolutely nothing – to answer
the doorbell because her cab came for her and she wasn't ready. She
had decided to wash her hair. When she left, typically, she left all the
lights on in the bathroom and in her bedroom and a general mess all
round.

Monday 25 May

Bank Holiday. I saw in the *Daily Telegraph* that John Major as well
as Queen Elizabeth the Queen Mother was at the first match on Paul
Getty's cricket ground

I wished that I had gone because I want to get to know John Major
a bit better and be on more friendly terms with him.

On the other hand, I felt it was darling Livia's last day and it would
have been unduly selfish of me to have gone.

Tuesday 26 May

Dinner at the Metcalfes.[55]

Barbara Amiel was there.

She has had several facelifts, that's obvious, but she doesn't look
bad and her figure is good.

She protested greatly when the ladies were taken upstairs, as is the

---

55. David Metcalfe, son of Major Edward 'Fruity' Metcalfe who was best man at
    the Duke of Windsor's wedding; director, Sedgwick James Management Services
    (insurance brokers); m 3 (1979) American-born Sally Cullen Howe, interior
    designer.

English custom. Conrad Black, who had some other engagement first, had by this time joined us at the dinner table. He also said it was a barbaric custom but stoutly, David Metcalfe took no notice.

Wednesday 27 May
Graham Turner[56] came again.

He asked a whole lot of questions, including 'Had I written a diary?'

He said, 'You should have recorded it all. It would be an important historical document. It is the most fascinating thing you have ever done, this close association with Mrs Thatcher.'

I didn't tell him that I have actually been keeping a manuscript but only since 1985. I once told Margaret I didn't keep a diary. I thought it would put her off telling me as much as she did, if she knew I was keeping one. People are well aware of what Dick Crossman[57] did, writing all the confidential secrets of the Cabinet when he was in it, as did Barbara Castle[58] and Tony Benn.[59] It is not a good idea to have a diary known. I am terrified this will get out.

Graham Turner wants a great lunch held here: Kingsley Amis, Bernard Levin and Paul Johnson.[60]

The *Sunday Telegraph* would fund it and so forth and it would be a great and jolly occasion. It might be.

Just as I was leaving at 12.25 to go to Corney & Barrow [wine merchants], Rupert rang. A little bird had told him that I had read the Shawcross book. I said, 'Not exactly. I spent three or four hours on it. It has about a thousand pages and I just glanced through it but my impression was favourable.' He said Anna[61] didn't like it. I said, 'I can understand that because it describes you, warts and all. It includes criticisms of you by other people.'

I said, 'You should serialize it in the *Sunday Times.*' He said,

---

56. *Sunday Telegraph* journalist.
57. (1907–74); Oxford don, Labour MP and cabinet minister, prolific writer and journalist whose diaries gave insight into the relationship between cabinet ministers and civil servants.
58. *The Castle Diaries* were published in 1980 and 1984.
59. His three volumes of diaries were published in 1988, 1989 and 1990.
60. Writer and political journalist (editor, *New Statesman*, 1965–70), he had moved from the left to support Mrs Thatcher.
61. Novelist wife (1966–99) of Rupert Murdoch.*

'That would look as though I were giving it the stamp of authority.' I said, 'Not at all because it would have passages which were critical of you in it. It would show what a big person you are and you don't give a damn. It puts you more on the side of the angels than of the devils. It is very moving, particularly about your relations with your father and also how you had to deal with the wayward bank in New York which nearly brought your empire down completely.'

He said, 'He did ask me if I would read it but I told him I wouldn't. I think that was the right decision.' I said I agreed.

I said, 'He hadn't finished the last chapter which was a final assessment of you. But from the first two paragraphs it looked as though it was going to be extremely favourable. I will get on to him and ask when I can see it.'

I asked when he was coming to England again. He said he wasn't quite certain but it would probably be in July. I said, 'I had better set up a lunch or dinner with you and Norman and perhaps John Major as well.'

We then talked about Ross Perot,[62] the man I say has a name like a mineral water, and his chances of winning. Rupert said, 'Don't underestimate him. I know him quite well. He is a very tough businessman. He has got bags of money. He can fund his own campaign. If there were an election tomorrow, he'd win it.' I said, 'I think he'll vanish like Paddy Ashdown.'

Then to the Corney & Barrow lunch. It was heavenly.

I ventured to the BBC party for sixty years of the World Service. I was greeted warmly by John Tusa[63] and thanked for having praised the BBC World Service in the *News of the World*.

I had an argument with Mark Bonham-Carter[64] about Rupert Murdoch whom he regards as an enemy of the people, silly fellow.

Then it was to Palace Gate House where Forster, the biographer of Dickens, once lived. He built the house in 1862.

---

62. Contender at that time for the Republican nomination for US President.
63. Managing Director of the BBC World Service, 1986–92.
64. (1922–94); Liberal politician and publisher (Collins); MP for Torrington, 1958–9; first chairman, Race Relations Board, 1966–70; vice-chairman, BBC, 1976–81; life peer 1986.

It is now Maxim's Casino which Nigel Kent-Lemon[65] and his partners own and run, as well as Lingfield.

It was a dinner given, supposedly, by the French trotting people (Jacques Chartier).[66]

I wondered what Forster would think about his house now becoming a gaming den.

Saturday 30 May
To Lingfield Park. The Prix du Tote was the 3.35 race. I had arranged for it to be included in the Jackpot and the Placepot, to the fury of many horseracing aficionados. I was greatly attacked by Monty Court, ex-editor of the *Sporting Life* still writing a column in *Sporting Life*.

He is a nice man and always very friendly but he likes to have real goes at me. He said he was counting the days – three hundred and thirty-five – to when my shelf life would be over and I would cease to be Chairman of the Tote. (He may get a surprise about that.) This would be a good thing because I had clearly gone quite barmy, advocating trotting and wasting Tote money on sponsorship for it which could have gone to some better cause.

He seems unaware that in Australia and New Zealand, America, Italy, France, Germany, trotting attracts as much if not greater support as other forms of horseracing.

I have been urging the Jockey Club for years to take control of it so it does not fall into other hands and damage orthodox horseracing.

Peter O'Sullevan [racing commentator] said how much he liked trotting and hoped it would succeed.

Julian Wilson, the BBC commentator, on the other hand, when I asked him what he thought of it, said, 'I plead the Fifth Amendment.' He is a stuffy young old man.

---

65. (1946–98); chartered accountant; consultant to the casino industry; visiting lecturer, Institute for the Study of Gambling and Commercial Gaming at the University of Nevada, Reno; chairman, City Clubs; chairman, Lingfield racecourse, 1991–8; joined Tote Board 1998.
66. WW saw possibilities for increased revenues for the Tote if trotting races gained favour in the UK – see next entry.

Sunday 31 May
I rang Martin Gilliat[67] at nine o'clock. I asked him to show my [*News of the World*] article about Bomber Harris to Queen Elizabeth the Queen Mother before she went to the unveiling ceremony.[68]

I am considering whether I should write another article about the Bomber Harris affair but from a different angle for Tuesday in the *Times*: what makes us dislike our heroes and how short a memory we have for history?[69]

------

67. (1913–93); private secretary to the Queen Mother from 1956 until his death; knight 1962.
68. The controversial statue to Sir Arthur 'Bomber' Harris, commander-in-chief Bomber Command, 1942–5, was at St Clement Danes, the RAF church in the Strand.
69. WW's *News of the World* article praised Harris and justified the bombing raids on Germany in the Second World War.

Monday 1 June
Saw Douglas Hurd at the Foreign Office for a chat which lasted an hour. It was a *tour d'horizon*.

[I was] pressing him about identity cards helping to deal with the immigration problem, forced upon us to greater heights by Brussels.

He was very sympathetic on the matter, more so than I expected. Sometimes he reflects a somewhat 'liberal' side.

I told Douglas, 'I have ticked you off in the *Times* for tomorrow morning for no ministers going to Bomber Harris's statue unveiling yesterday.'

Douglas said, 'But a minister did go. Didn't Archie Hamilton go?' he asked his Private Secretary. Archie Hamilton is a junior minister at the Department of Defence. The Secretary said, 'I think so. I think somebody called Aitken went, too.' They rushed out to find out and it was Jonathan Aitken. I said, 'Oh my goodness, I said no other minister went and ticked off Rifkind for not going. I must get the *Times* straight away.'

So the Private Secretary in the Foreign Secretary's office rang the sub-editors at the *Times* and said, 'Lord Wyatt for you.' I said, 'I don't want any inaccuracies to go into the *Times*. There have been thousands in the past and there will be many in the future but I don't want to be responsible for one. Can you quickly change it to "no other Cabinet Minister went".' I thanked Douglas who said, 'I am very glad to have helped you save your reputation.'[1]

I asked Douglas what he would do if the Danes voted against the Maastricht Treaty. He said he didn't think they would. I said, 'That was Margaret's view as well when she came to dinner. But I am not so sure.'

He asked after the family and I asked after his. Of Petronella he

---

1. The corrected article began by protesting that neither Rifkind, Minister of Defence, nor any other Cabinet Minister, was present at the unveiling of the statue.

said, 'Is she thinking of getting married?' I said, 'I don't think so. She seems to vary her choice almost weekly of people she goes out with.'

I said, 'She likes older men like you, Douglas.' He blushed and the Secretary laughed and then so did Douglas.

Tuesday 2 June
Quite an entertaining lunch with Stoker Hartington[2] at the Berkeley Hotel which he likes.

I told him about our bid to get the National Lottery and that one argument we were using is that our profits go to racing.

He was also delighted that I am on the panel to choose merchant bankers to be used over the sale of United Racecourses. He said did I think RHT [Racecourse Holdings Trust][3] would get it. I said, 'If I have anything to do with it, they will.'

Wednesday 3 June
Blow me down. The Danes did vote no.

Funny little Denmark. Well done them. They have led the way. They have also justified Margaret's demand for a referendum here.

Leon Brittan[4] had been warning everybody, including me, that we had to stop Delors being reappointed and we have done nothing about it. We have gone along with it. I said to Norman [Lamont], 'I hope it's not too late. We've got to put up a candidate. It needn't be British though, on the other hand, Leon Brittan might be quite good at it himself.'

I had a dream last night which was part of a sequence of similar dreams. I dreamed that I was feverishly trying to mug up the facts and material for an Oxford examination for which I ought to have prepared myself beforehand. I knew I was going to fail completely because I had not left enough time to get ready. It must be something to do with my recurring feelings that I haven't enough time to do all the things I want to do before I die.

As a member of the Levy Board, I, and Verushka, acted as hosts at

---

2. The Marquess of Hartington, eldest son of the Duke of Devonshire, senior steward of the Jockey Club, 1989–94.*
3. A subsidiary of the Jockey Club.
4. Vice-President, European Commission, 1989–92 and 1995–9; knight 1989, life peer 2000.*

one of the tables in what is normally the Board Room of the great new stand at Epsom, the Queen's Stand.

The architects seem unaware that betting has anything to do with racing. They were annoyed at the Tote demanding a proper place for its credit facilities and for its cash counter operations. They had wanted to put us in a dingy little corner where no one could see us. And we had paid for part of the stand.

Twice Sir Martin Gilliat came in from the Royal Box, which was next door, saying the Queen Mother would like to see me.

So I duly reported.

When she saw me, Queen Elizabeth came tripping up in her beautiful way: 'Come and sit beside me.' She thanked me profusely for my messages during the Sunday and for what I had written about her and Bomber Harris. She thought that the interrupters were Communists, revolutionaries.[5] I said I didn't know that and she said, 'That was what I was told.' She was startled but she soon recovered herself and had a very nice time talking to all the veterans afterwards: 'Wasn't it good that Mrs Thatcher came?'

When I was about to go, saying that I had to be looking around and taking care of Tote affairs, Piers Bengough,[6] the great courtier, came up. He said, 'Woodrow, your tie isn't quite straight.' Queen Elizabeth promptly said, 'I've been longing to straighten it. It's a beautiful tie but I thought it would be impolite.' So there was jolly laughter.

On my way out, at the huge table at the end was the Queen, dressed rather agreeably in yellow. She said, 'I am just doing our household Derby sweepstake and I am arranging the tickets they have to draw.' I said, 'It's a very unpredictable race so no one will know whether their ticket is worth anything or not.' She said, 'Yes, but I am told the last four furlongs are quite soft underfoot.' She always plunges into these technical horseracing matters. But she was quite charming to me.

I am rather popular in the Royal Family these days because I keep on defending them against charges that the Queen ought to be paying tax and the Royal Family are letting the country down and so forth.

---

5. There had been scuffles and arrests at the unveiling of the statue.
6. Colonel Sir Piers Bengough, Her Majesty's Representative, Ascot, 1982–97; Jockey Club steward, 1974–7 and 1990–2; former amateur jockey, riding in four Grand Nationals; knight 1986.

We went to watch the actual Derby in John Derby's[7] box.

He is the only person, incidentally, who gets a box free because he is John Derby and it is the Derby.

On getting back from Epsom I went down to the Lords to earn £60 attendance money.

I thought it would make up a little for my losses in the Derby where only one of the ten horses I had backed in one form or another got a place.

Thursday 4 June

Dinner with the Wolfsons[8] at Mark's Club. Also present, Tony Quinton and his wife, Marcelle. Plus a man called Bellinger who used to be Lord Mayor of London and is now retired, aged eighty-two and looking extremely fit, which I found very encouraging.

I found the dinner tedious. Estelle, the new wife, is nice but not hot on interesting conversation – not as good as Ruth was at it.

Tony Quinton at one stage insisted that Naomi Mitchison[9] had been married to George Strauss,[10] the Labour peer, so I bet him £10 she hadn't. Marcelle said, 'You shouldn't do that. He always wins his bets.' When I came home I looked up in the relevant reference books and, of course, Naomi Mitchison had never been married to anybody other than Dick Mitchison.

George Strauss, as I had told him, had originally one wife and a mistress and when his wife died he married the mistress. He is still alive though very old. He was a strong socialist, backing *Tribune* at one time. Appropriately, he lived, and still does, in Millionaires' Row and remains very rich from a family firm in the City.

---

7. (1918–94); 18th Earl of Derby.*
8. Leonard Wolfson, chairman, Great Universal Stores, 1981–96, m 1 (1949–91) Ruth, née Sterling, m 2 (1991) Estelle Jackson; life peer 1985.*
9. (1897–1999); writer; m (1916) Dick Mitchison (d 1970, Labour politician, life peer 1964).
10. (1901–93); Labour MP, 1929–31 and 1934–79, m 1 (1932) Patricia O'Flynn (d 1987), m 2 (1987) Benita Armstrong; Palace Green, London W8, with its mansions and embassies adjacent to Kensington Palace, is known as Millionaires' Row.

Friday 5 June

The night before last I had read through the final draft of William Shawcross' final chapter of the book on Rupert. Yesterday I had dictated a long letter to him to be sent by fax.

He soon rang up and said, 'It was a very tough letter.'[11] I said, 'It was meant to be. I wanted you to re-think what you were doing and not let yourself down by finishing a fine piece of writing with low-level, sub-intellectual rubbish. It made me wonder whether I had really read enough of the whole book you had let me see before I said how good I thought it was and a fair picture.'

He said he would take very seriously what I had said and jig it about considerably. But he said, 'I am already being attacked by a number of my friends who think I have been too kind to Rupert in the earlier parts.'

I sent a fax to Rupert of the letter. He was in Los Angeles but when he got out of bed and read it (being on a different time-scale), he rang to say what a marvellous letter. He thanked me very much for it and said, 'You are a dear friend.'

I haven't told William I sent him a copy of it. When I told Rupert that William had said he was being attacked by his friends who had seen it for being so pro-Rupert, Rupert said, 'The chattering classes have got at him.' I said, 'I am afraid, scratch him and in the end he is still a clichéd intellectual left-winger. But maybe we can improve him. Perhaps writing this book will have opened his mind to the importance of making money and that doing great things in the commercial world is not necessarily evil but actually *pro bono publico*.'

Sunday 7 June

My usual little chat with Norman. I urged him not to shove a lot of money to the Maxwell pensioners[12] but to make the institutions do it and have a fund like they do with holiday travel agencies.

---

11. WW criticized the draft chapter for suggesting that the problems of underdeveloped countries had anything to do with Murdoch; for quoting the belief of Harold Evans, former editor of the *Sunday Times*, that if he had continued to work for Murdoch he would have been corrupted; for attacking Murdoch's support of private enterprise and the concentration of his newspapers on sex and sleaze. WW conceded 'a vague republicanism' but did not find Murdoch anti-English and thought his TV news services the fairest.
12. Those from the *Daily Mirror* whose pensions had been stolen by Robert Maxwell (1923–91), Mirror Group chairman and former Labour MP.

We discussed, too, the latest attack on him in the *Sun* about interest rates. I said, 'I suppose it is partly because Rupert's businesses would do a great deal better if he didn't have to pay such high interest.'

We also talked briefly about the Princess Diana and Prince Charles business in the *Sunday Times* and the *Daily Mail* yesterday.[13]

The *Sunday Times* was the paper which brought us the authentic Hitler diaries, ha ha. I want to put that in my article in the *News of the World*, too.[14]

Monday 8 June

Spoke to Robin Janvrin,[15] the Assistant Private Secretary to the Queen. I said, 'I will do anything I can to help. I don't believe it was all true.' He said certainly it wasn't. I said, 'Have they considered a libel action?' He said they are considering it but it is very risky because some of the things may be true and they might not be able to stand it all up.

The unfortunate Camilla Parker Bowles has been made a focus of attention in this extraordinary newspaper campaign about Princess Diana and Prince Charles.

Actually, she is not at all a *femme fatale*, far from it. It is ridiculous they should imply she is his mistress.

A very large dinner party given by Charles Allsopp[16] and his wife in Cottesmore Gardens [Kensington].

Andrew Parker Bowles was there but not his wife, Camilla.

---

13. The *Sunday Times* was serializing Andrew Morton's book *Diana: Her True Story*; the press took up allegations that Princess Diana had made several suicide attempts and was jealous of the relationship between Prince Charles and Camilla Parker Bowles.

14. WW gleefully recounted in the issue of 14 June how the *Sunday Times*, just before Neil became editor in 1983, had to cancel its serialization of the Hitler diaries when it was shown they were forged. He forecast that 'the decent, caring Prince and Princess will one day be on the Throne together. If they can't always grin they know their duty is to bear it.'

15. Press secretary to the Queen, 1987–90; assistant private secretary, 1990–5; deputy private secretary, 1996–9; succeeded Sir Robert Fellowes as private secretary, 1999; knight 1998.

16. Chairman, Christie, Manson & Wood, 1986–96; m (1968) Fiona, née McGowan; succeeded father as 6th Baron Hindlip, 1993.

Jacob [Rothschild][17] was also there. He said about Serena's race-horses that at one time he had the least expensive wife in the country because she never bought dresses and didn't mind what she wore. Now he has got the most expensive wife because she is besotted with the stud and the racing.

He is a curious fellow, tall Jacob. He always looks shifty as he leans down towards me with a sort of half smile on his face. I like him. There's a split marriage for you, Jacob and Serena. She doesn't bother him and he doesn't bother her but they meet at weekends. He said, 'She is not here tonight because she says she doesn't go out in June in London,' which Jacob thought rather peculiar and I thought very funny.

On my left was Caroline Benson, Charlie Benson's ex-wife.[18]

I asked her why she married him in the first place and she said, 'He makes me laugh.' I said, 'That's a very sexy thing. Do you like fat men?' which Charlie Benson certainly is. She said, 'I don't mind them,' and that must be so. I said, 'You're a very good-looking girl.' She's got a daughter of eleven. 'You should find a steadier, more solid person and I'm sure you can easily. But he won't be quite as exciting or amusing as Charlie Benson. You must meet lots. There are a lot of rich bankers here, some of them quite young.'

There were several Barings. I thought it a strange mixture, immensely rich people and intelligent paupers like myself.

She said, 'So few Englishmen know how to talk to women.'

I said, 'Working-class male attitudes to their wives and women are precisely the same as the upper-class and aristocratic males. They are rather frightened of women – but I love them.'

My neighbour on my right was Jane Fellowes, sister of Princess Diana. She is married to Sir Robert Fellowes, Private Secretary to the Queen.

Jane, has a similar height and bone structure but her figure isn't so good and her legs are slightly too thick. Her face is not so pretty either, not just because she doesn't spend as much time on make-up – it is that Diana is a pretty, almost beautiful girl, and allows art to assist nature and vice versa.

---

17. Banker; Chairman, National Heritage Memorial Fund at this time; m (1961) Serena, née Dunn; succeeded father, Victor Rothschild, as 4th Baron Rothschild, 1990.*

18. Charles Benson, racing journalist, formerly 'Scout' in the *Daily Express*.

Wednesday 10 June

Great commotion. Norman rings in a panic at about half past four. He has just been given lunch by a reporter of the *Sun* who said he had been instructed by the editor himself to do a vicious attack on him, saying, 'As they said at Nuremberg, I'm only obeying orders.'

The reporter claims it is because circulation is going down and Rupert's business is so heavily in debt, he needs to have the interest rates cut and so forth. There is to be a dreadful huge front page with a dart board and Norman's face being spattered with darts. HATE is written at the top and so forth. I get on to Rupert in Los Angeles.

He said he would ring [the *Sun*] at once. He said it was totally untrue that he knew anything whatever about it.

Meanwhile, I decided to write to Stoker about having the Derby on Saturdays. Attendance has been declining like mad.

The Diana and Charles story gets more and more peculiar.

I think she is going slightly barmy, that girl, Diana.

Thursday 11 June

It was evident that Rupert had intervened because the Norman story was not on the front page.

When Norman spoke to me, he said that in the country editions it was on the front page and they had a different editorial.

Later Rupert rang and said he had managed to get it off the front page but it was all true.

I said, 'Please don't talk such nonsense. He is stoutly against creeping federalism. Margaret thinks very highly of him and understands his position.'

Today is the great [*Sunday Telegraph*] lunch. Fortunately, we were able to have it in the garden.

We had wines all connected with Margaret in some form or another. First was the 1979 Pol Roger Churchill cuvée magnum of champagne. That was the year she won her first election. It was also Churchill's favourite champagne. Then came a 1983 Pavillon Blanc, the white wine of Château Margaux, because that was the second time she won an election. Then came a 1961 Rauzan-Gassies (second growth), the year in which she first became a junior minister in a government. Then came a 1925 La Tour-Carnet, first growth. That was the year she was born. Finally, there was a 1975 Tokay, which was the year she became Leader of the Conservative Party.

Graham Turner arrived first, wearing no tie.

Kingsley Amis was delighted with the enormous amount of wonderful drink. He helped himself to a reasonable amount of the magnum of champagne, but very little else was drunk because Paul Johnson said he wasn't going to drink anything and Graham Turner said he didn't drink at all. (I thought to myself, you might have told me and then I wouldn't have put so much out.) I made Paul Johnson and Bernard Levin have a regulated amount of each wine. Otherwise they would not have performed their function of celebrating Margaret properly.

We discussed her at considerable length and how she had a transformation from being an ordinary, conventional Conservative into having her mission to save the country.

Paul Johnson said he thought we could claim we had a lot of influence on moving the mood of the country in the various things we wrote and the fact that we had come out for her, after being in the Labour Party.

He said he was sorry she had gone to the Lords. I said, 'Not a bit of it. It's perfectly all right. She has got a very good platform there. If anything extraordinary happens, she can always surrender her peerage and go back to the Commons as Leader again.'

Kingsley said he thought it was pure snobbery which did her down. They thought she was so common.

Bernard disagreed with me about Bomber Harris. When he had gone, Kingsley Amis said, 'You know Bernard is the one who retains the left-wing drag on him longer than any of us.'

I forbore to tell Kingsley that it was I who got him his knighthood after pressing for it several times.[19] He will never know that unless he is alive when my manuscript is published.

When they had all left, including Kingsley who was the last to leave at four o'clock, I rang Margaret.

I detailed all the wines to her and the dates of them in her life and she trilled away.

We then talked a little bit about Maastricht and I said, 'John knows he can't get a majority for it in the Commons and cannot possibly bring it forward. One of the things you say about his vanity is, I fear, true. He is so proud of what he thought he had achieved at Maastricht that he doesn't want to let go of it all.'

At The Other Club Chris Patten was in the Chair.

He invited us all to go and stay with him in Government House [in

―――――
19. See Vol. 2, p. 309.

Hong Kong]. Presumably one or two at a time and not the whole lot together.

Hugh Trevor-Roper[20] said he had once, as a member of the board of the *Times* and the *Sunday Times*, tried to stop the appointment of Harry Evans as editor of the *Times* because he said it would be a disaster. It all got overruled by Rupert who took no notice.[21]

Roy [Jenkins][22] and I briefly discussed the Diana situation. He said he thought it would be very serious indeed if they have a divorce, constitutionally, and it could raise the question on the whole issue of the monarchy.

I am considering introducing a Bill on privacy.

It is difficult to define but I have some material from the Lords library about it.

Friday 12 June
In the evening there was a great party at Forbes House, West Halkin Street.

There were about three hundred people. It was all given by Simon and Laura Weinstock.[23]

Charles Allsopp said that when Peter Carrington, who is the head of Christie's, was rung up by the Dutch to ask him if he would be the arbitrator for the European Community in trying to get peace between Serbia and Croatia and what remain of the warring parts of Yugoslavia, Charles was in the office. Peter turned to Charles and said, 'Do you think I should accept?' He said, 'No. You have quite enough to do here and you won't get any glory out of it.' But he said, 'I think I shall.'

Charlie could see his eyes light up at the thought of all the television cameras and the interviews and the new fame he would get politically

---

20. Regius Professor of Modern History, Oxford University, 1957–80; Master, Peterhouse, Cambridge, 1980–7; director, Times Newspapers, 1974–88; life peer 1979 (Lord Dacre).*
21. Evans was editor of the *Times*, 1981–2.
22. Former Labour Home Secretary, Chancellor of the Exchequer and President of the EC; joint founder of the SDP; at this time Leader of the Social and Liberal Democratic peers in the House of Lords; OM 1993.*
23. Son of Arnold Weinstock, m (1976) Laura, née Legh.*

and in the world, which he had lost since he ceased to be Foreign
Secretary at the time of the Falklands War. He is very vain, Peter, and
Charles's advice was right. He has made a total mess of it.

Before I went out, Pat Chapman, editor of the *News of the World*,
was very startled by my article and the attack on Andrew Neil [con-
cerning his stance on the monarchy]. She said, 'Did you realize we had
reprinted the stuff from the *Sunday Times* in our later edition?' I said
no. She said, 'I think you should make some reference to it.' So I
popped in a sentence saying, 'Sadly, for me, they [the arguments] were
reprinted in the *News of the World*.'

When we got back it seemed that Andrew Knight[24] had been trying
to get hold of me, obviously something to do with the piece I had
written in the *News of the World*.

He rang from the airport in Scotland where he has gone to see his
daughter at her school, Gordonstoun. He said he thought my piece
was unfair to Neil and he was not a republican. I said, 'You could
have fooled me.' He said it would be bad for Rupert. I said, 'On the
contrary. What I have written is very good for Rupert because it shows
that it isn't him who is pushing this appalling serialization.' However,
I took out a few words to please him.

As I was sunbathing in the garden, there was a call from Irwin. I
thought, 'Oh my God. Trouble about that damned article.'

But it wasn't anything of the kind. It was Irwin saying that Rupert
was coming to dinner that evening at Aspen, Colorado. He wanted to
give him a bottle of 1978 Pétrus. I said, 'My God, that's very expensive.
How much have you got of it?' He said, 'A dozen bottles.' I said, 'They
must have cost about £2,000.'

I told him to open it two hours and twenty minutes before they
came and decant it. I gave him close instructions as to how to do that
and put it back in the bottle it came out of, after it was washed
out.

How strange to ring up from Aspen, Colorado, to ask what he
should do about the bottle of wine he was giving to Rupert and Anna
for dinner.

---

24. Editor, the *Economist*, 1974–86; chief executive and editor-in-chief, Daily Telegraph plc, 1986–9; executive chairman, News International, 1990–3, non-
executive chairman, 1993–5, director, News Corporation, since 1991.

Monday 15 June
Dinner at Sydney Lipworth's.[25]

The swimming pool was amazing, almost a full size pool. We had
our coffee by it. On request that the floor for dancing should be
lowered, a signal was given to the machinery. Ten minutes later the
floor began to sink and the water poured in, [making a pool] 6ft 3 at
one end and 3 ft at the other.

It was a pity the guests were not as entertaining. Sir Sydney himself
is now retiring from the Monopolies and Mergers Commission. He is
pleasant enough and not dull. He made a great deal of money in South
Africa and will go on making more.

Before that I went to Nick Lloyd's fiftieth birthday party. I talked
to Esther Rantzen[26]: I had mentioned her favourably in the *Times* this
morning about her interviewing passers-by over the Diana book. She
seemed extremely pleased. She said of course I had also written in the
News of the World previously that she ought to be given the sack.

David Stevens was complaining about the admission of Jeffrey
Archer to the Lords and so was Lord King.[27] I said, 'I don't mind
about that. There are all kinds of people there, including jailbirds.
Jeffrey Archer hasn't been a jailbird.' There were various views that he
should have been.

When I was reaching the exit, suddenly David Stevens reappeared
and said, 'Are you going? Aren't you going to talk to John Major?' I
said, 'Maybe he doesn't want to talk to me.' I heard a voice say, 'Yes,
I would like to talk to you, Woodrow.' Then he said, 'Many thanks
for all the support you are giving to Norman. Would you like to come
and talk to me a bit now?' I said yes but he strode so fast I couldn't
keep up with him, so I couldn't be bothered and turned round and
went the other way home. It's no good talking to people at cocktail
parties about serious matters.

Tuesday 16 June
First day of Royal Ascot. My article in the *Times* today on the book,
Diana: Her True Story, attacks the *Sunday Times* from a different angle

---

25. Chairman, Monopolies and Mergers Commission, 1988–93; chairman, Zeneca,
    1995–9; deputy chairman, National Westminster Bank since 1993; m (1957)
    Rosalie, née Liwarek; knight 1991.
26. Television journalist and presenter of investigative programmes.
27. Chairman, British Airways, 1981–93; life peer 1983.

and stresses the importance of French-style criminal privacy laws which would have prevented the book appearing here or being printed.

Bernard Donoughue[28] said how completely he agreed with me and we must get an all-party group together to push such a law through, as the Press Complaints Commission has manifestly failed.

Lunch with Piers Bengough.

Piers said we were to have tea with the Queen after the fourth race which was better than having it on a Wednesday or a Thursday, which it usually is, because we have our own party in our entertainment room [then] and we are on our own today.

On arrival outside the entrance to the Royal Box, there was Princess Anne talking to Andrew Parker Bowles to whom she gave an affectionate kiss. She turned to me and said, 'Very good. Thank you. (Meaning what I had written.) No wonder you have been asked to tea,' and she laughed and rushed upstairs.

I thought she looked very pretty. Obviously things are going well with her lover. Her skin was glowing.[29]

Once upstairs, when we were assembled in the receiving line, Princess Margaret was extraordinarily friendly and charming, unusually so, and with a sweet smile said, 'Thank you for what you have done. Well said.'

Prince Philip said, 'Very good, very good. I would like to talk to you.' That was before tea and I never saw him again after tea.

Then, of course, dear, sweet Queen Elizabeth the Queen Mother, whom I was told to sit next to.

I told Queen Elizabeth how Rupert is frightened of his mother and she is a terrific monarchist, not only for Britain but for Australia.

I said, 'He would never launch direct attacks on the monarchy himself, though he does have this thing about some of the younger members of the Royal Family.'

I told Queen Elizabeth how I had missed the cricket match which she went to with Paul Getty at his ground because I had stayed behind to be with Livia, my Hungarian sister-in-law whose husband had died.

Queen Elizabeth looked at me and said, 'I think you would be a

---

28. Former academic, banker and journalist; senior policy adviser to Prime Ministers Wilson and Callaghan, 1974–9; Labour spokesman in House of Lords on Treasury matters, 1991–2, on National Heritage, 1993–7; Parliamentary Secretary, MAFF, 1997–9; life peer 1985.
29. The Princess Royal married Commander Timothy Laurence in December 1992.

very good comforter. In fact, I am sure you are.' I said, 'Yes, but I have
many defects. One of them is an extremely bad temper.' She said, 'For
what sort of thing?' I said, 'If I lose my glasses, for instance, I shout
around the house and complain like mad. Little things which are really
quite unimportant annoy me and I get very cross but I have forgotten
all about it in two minutes and can't understand why anybody else
minds.' She laughed.

Meanwhile there was a message from Daniel Johnson,[30] passed on
from Simon Jenkins. He had left a note just before he left for Aspen
(where obviously he is going to see Andrew Neil and co.). It said,
'Tell Woodrow we won't review the [Morton] book at all now.' So
immediately I rang Andrew Wilson[31] at the *Evening Standard* and said
would he like the review?

Wednesday 17 June
On my left [at lunch at Ascot] was the darling Annabel[32] whose glorious
mother was Pandora. Everyone who knew Pandora was in love with
her.

Annabel said, 'I have been going through all her letters and love
letters. There are hundreds of them. She kept every one of them.

'For over a year David Harlech[33] was madly in love with her and
wrote passionate letters to her.'

I said, 'Your mother could be quite naughty.' She said, 'That is
true.' 'But not with me,' I said, which is true also.

Kenneth Baker was there and talked away on Maastricht.

He said, 'You have got three ex Home Secretaries here.'[34] I said,
'That shows I never abandon my friends.'

Peter Lloyd, the Minister of State at the Home Office who is supposed to be in charge of racing matters, was there. He was extremely

---

30. At this time literary editor, the *Times*; assistant editor, 1996–8; son of Paul and
    Marigold Johnson.
31. A. N. Wilson, novelist, critic and journalist, at this time literary editor of the
    Evening Standard.
32. Annabel Sheffield, née Jones, m (1976) 4th Viscount Astor (William); Pandora,
    née Clifford (d 1988), m 1 Timothy Jones, son of Sir Roderick Jones and the
    writer Enid Bagnold; she m 2 the Hon. Michael Astor (1916–80), son of 2nd
    Viscount Astor.*
33. 5th Baron Harlech (1918–85); Conservative politician; British Ambassador in
    Washington, 1961–5, and friend of President Kennedy.
34. Whitelaw, Baker and Waddington.

untidily dressed. His waistcoat looked as though it didn't fit him, hanging loose. I think somebody told him to keep his top hat on as he walked about at Ascot, which he was doing. He is very friendly. He is one of the people who is trying to see that I can carry on at the Tote.

Sonny [Marlborough][35] says that Camilla Parker Bowles is still the Prince of Wales's mistress and there is no doubt about it. Whether he is right or not I don't know. When Verushka told me that I said, 'Has he seen them in bed together?'

Then water started coming down. It splashed like heavy rain just outside the Tote Information Office so nobody could get at it, and just outside the side door into Tote Credit. Some got into our entertainment room which is directly below the Royal Box.

A plumber arrived and said it came from the lavatories. They had either been pouring too much champagne down them or ejecting champagne into them after pouring it through their bodies with enthusiasm.

Someone said, 'It's the Royal wee.' I told Petronella, 'You could use that.' She said, 'No, I don't think the *Sunday Telegraph* would like it.'

We had a superb lunch, beginning with all sorts of goodies. Not only red caviar but enormous helpings of ordinary best Russian caviar came around. I had to say it all fell off the back of a lorry but actually it was sold through Eva Zarach[36] who came in with a ghastly Hungarian friend afterwards. I think she is very vulgar, that girl, but what can one do?

When I got back I found in my engagement book that I could not go to the dinner which Willie Whitelaw is giving for Margaret and a party of twelve in the Carlton Towers on July 12th because I had promised to go to the stag party for George Weidenfeld.

An idiotic fax arrived from Irwin Stelzer saying I had been very rancorous, deeply unfair and all the rest of it to Andrew [Neil], which was such a pity because he was so friendly with both of us.[37]

The new final chapter by William Shawcross for his book about Rupert is fair and reasonable.

So I sent a fax to him, William, saying it was a very great improvement and is now in keeping with the rest of the book. I will tell Rupert so.

35. 11th Duke of Marlborough; m 3 (1972) Rosita, née Douglas, painter.*
36. Born in Hungary; m Neil Zarach, designer and entrepreneur; see Vol. 2, p. 533, for Chinese caviar for which Eva Zarach had a concession.
37. Stelzer first thanked WW for his excellent tips on decanting.

Thursday 18 June

Another, and our last, party at Ascot.

Cecil Parkinson[38] arrived twenty minutes late. His feeble plea was that he had to go and see Robin Butler, the Cabinet Secretary, because his memoirs had been vetted by the Cabinet Office. (They always do that when somebody has been a Cabinet Minister.)

I had on my right the delicious Brazilian Ambassadress, very lively and jokey.[39]

She said she would back in the first race a horse called Source of Light. I asked why and she said, 'Because my name is Lucia,' and blow me down, the damn thing won.

She proceeded to win again and again. As she put large sums of money on each time she was winning £150 a shot.

She is a very intelligent girl.

I was amazed she should know all about John Brown and Queen Victoria[40] and the relations between Disraeli and Queen Victoria.

I said to the Ambassadress before Cecil Parkinson arrived, 'I don't know why he is so late. There are enough attractive women in the room for him to want to come and look for,' which made her laugh.

I also pulled off a baby coup of my own. I had a Yankee, which is betting four horses, doubles and trebles and so forth, for £1 each way with quite good odds on each horse, with Coral. All four of them got a place and one of them actually won. I won over £800.

Norman was in rather a state because the *Evening Standard* had done another vicious attack on him.

His secretary rang him up in the middle of lunch and wanted to talk to him about it so I told him where to go in the Credit Office where there was a public telephone. When he came back I said, 'How did you get on?' He said, 'I was shouting down the phone in the Credit Office that I am not going to cut interest rates whatever they say.'

After the excitement of the last three days, and the exhaustion of talking to all kinds of different people politely – and showing great

---

38. Conservative politician who resigned from the government in 1983 on the revelation that his secretary, Sara Keays, was pregnant with his child; life peer 1992.*
39. Wife of HE Paulo-Tarso Flecha de Lima.
40. WW told her that Queen Victoria and John Brown had married in Craigie Church but 'the records were suppressed by the Royal Family afterwards.'

interest in whatever banality they might come up with – I didn't want to go out to dinner at the Channons.[41] I thought I would be bored. I was wrong.

The Channons' house at 96 Cheyne Walk, on the corner, is fabulous. It is really an old country house. The site was where Thomas More lived by the river and received Henry VIII.

The food was pretty good but I was already full. The Pichon-Lalande, neighbouring Latour, was 1970, a great year and it should have been magnificent. Alas, the super rich are too often, as in this case, utterly incapable of treating a splendid wine properly. It had not been decanted. It had been shaken up. There were dregs discolouring the wine all the way through, diminishing what would have been a most beautiful flavour and nose. What a waste.

Before the evening ended I went to sit near where an astonishing woman was sitting talking to some people. She immediately turned to me.

She is an amazing girl, full of sexual vitality which pours out at you. At one point she grasped my wrist and arm and got her sexuality on me. She was looking at me hard with her eyes. She must be like an octopus to go to bed with, wrapping her legs all around you. She has tremendously long legs. She looked very pretty. She wore an extremely short skirt. I noticed though that her breasts were not as firm or as youthful as no doubt they had been once. She has a lovely face.

She remembered well meeting me [before] and said, 'I met you in the House of Lords.'

I was going up the stairs and she was coming down. At one point I was standing over her, when we were introduced, so our faces were level. Ordinarily I think one would need library steps to get anywhere near her unless she were lying down.

You wouldn't have thought from the gaiety of his Channon relations that the Earl of Iveagh died today.

He was a real chump who claimed not to have known anything about what was going on [at Guinness], though he was chairman of the company. He might well have been expected to inquire.

---

41. Paul Channon, Conservative MP, 1959–97; son of Sir Henry (Chips) Channon and his wife, Honor, née Guinness; m (1963) Ingrid Guinness, née Wyndham.

Somebody mentioned the miraculous recovery which Ernest Saunders[42] had made from his senile dementia or Alzheimer's disease.

And wasn't it extraordinary that he had been given a pension larger than the Prime Minister's salary? I said, 'Not at all. He multiplied the fortune of the Guinnesses at least fifteen times by his activities; they profited from him and disowned him. Guinness was the only company in which people were accused and brought to trial over share pushing which did not pay for the defence of their employee.'

Saturday 20 June
Went to Paul Getty's box at Lord's.

Dickie Attenborough [actor and director] and Sheila Simms, his wife [actress], were there.

He said I had always been one of his heroes. I said, 'If you read my articles, you would have known your side, Labour, couldn't possibly win.' He said, 'I felt a lot of the time you were probably right but I hoped you weren't.'

Jeffrey Archer was extraordinarily friendly.

He knew about the dinner which Norman Lamont had come to with Denis and Margaret.

Paul Getty was very chatty when he came in later. When Archer had gone, he asked me, 'Was she (meaning Mary) really 'fragrant', as the judge had said?'[43] I said, 'Yes. She is a beautiful girl and marvellously clever. She was a don at two colleges at once at Cambridge and she is a fine scientist.'[44] He was quite surprised.

Paul Getty said he didn't think a lot of him. He felt on the whole he was a scoundrel. I wondered why he had him in his box.

Roger Gibbs,[45] the brother of Christopher Gibbs whom I met on Thursday, was also in the box.

---

42. Convicted of various offences connected with the take-over of the Distillers' Company. He was imprisoned but released early because of his health. In December 1996 the European Court of Human Rights ruled that Saunders' trial had been unfair because of the use of evidence given before the inspectors without the right of silence.
43. In the summing-up of the libel case Archer won against the *Star* in 1987.
44. Fellow of Newnham College, Cambridge, and Lecturer in Chemistry, Trinity College, Cambridge, 1976–86; Visiting Professor, Dept of Biochemistry, Imperial College, London, since 1991.
45. Roger Gibbs, Chairman, Wellcome Trust since 1989, (knight 1994); Christopher Gibbs, art dealer and trustee, J. Paul Getty Jr. Charitable Trust.

Roger said, 'We are doing something to help the Royal Free – a couple of million or so.' I said, 'I know you are, but we want you to give some more and would you look into it?'

Sunday 21 June
Yesterday, in an interview I had with McCririck[46] on Channel Four, he said I was a great survivor.

I stuck up for the Tote rather well and gave it some solid advertising boosts.

Eva Zarach said I was much better looking on television than I am in real life. I wasn't quite sure how to take that.

We left at just after 11.15 to go to dismal polo at Windsor Great Park, Smith's Lawn Polo. I would have much preferred the cricket.

David Swaythling,[47] the Chairman of Rothmans, sponsoring the event, wished he had been there at Lord's as well. We go to support him because he is on my Board. I am very fond of him and he has been quite decent.

Prince Philip was in charge. When I came back from one of my visits to find out the cricket score from the car, which was conveniently close, he came up the steps. He spotted me and came straight up to me, to the annoyance of Meriza Stevens.

He said, 'I had a marvellous polo pony once which was given me by Lord Rosebery. It was a granddaughter of Hyperion.' Nobody knew what he was talking about except for me. Hyperion was the smallest Derby winner in history and belonged to the Derbys. Naturally it would breed small horses good for polo.

Polo is the most boring game out, as I told almost everybody in sight. It is very complicated and they all cheered every time anybody hit the ball. They don't cheer in a football match every time someone kicks the ball and they do it all the time without missing it.

In the *Mail on Sunday* there was an attack on me in a long-winded article by one of these professional Royal biographers, Anthony Holden.[48] He said I had described Princess Diana as whinging and slightly barmy, etc. He omitted to put the whole passage in which I

---

46. John McCririck, racing journalist, famous for his fast talk on television and bookie-style hand signals.
47. 4th Baron Swaythling (1928–98); banker; Tote Board member for 12 years; m (1951) Ninette, née Dreyfus.*
48. Journalist and author; his *Charles: A Biography* was published in 1989.

had said, 'Princess Diana is described as,' etc. Maybe I should write a letter to the *Mail on Sunday* but it gets so boring following all these things up.

Grey Gowrie[49] was there with his very pretty Prussian wife. They seemed affectionate enough but God knows what she makes of him being exposed going to massage parlours. That is another matter which would be covered by a criminal law of privacy.

I got back to London in time for the last hour and a half of the amazingly exciting test match which was just lost by England.

Paul Getty, again very jolly and friendly, got terribly excited. He turned to me and said, 'Have you got another cigar, Woodrow?' I was smoking one as usual and I pulled out my case. There was one in it, a very large hefty No. 2, torpedo-like Montecristo. He said, 'You've only got one.' I said, 'Never mind, you have it.' He said, 'I haven't smoked for two years but I feel so tense and excited I must.'

I was amused at helping out one of the two or three richest men in the world by giving him a cigar.

At the end, as I was leaving, I noticed John Major who was standing at the bottom of the stairs leading to the President's box where he had been. I didn't take any notice of him and walked by. He turned round, saw me and caught me up: 'Woodrow, I didn't know you were here. I would like to talk to you but I can't stop now.'

I then bumped into Jeffrey Archer.

I asked Jeffrey if he had talked to Major about my subsidiarity point.

He said, 'I think you should write to him about subsidiarity and how it needs a definition.'[50]

I had a very nice letter from Daniel Johnson about my review in the *Evening Standard*.[51]

---

49. 2nd Earl of Gowrie, Conservative politician; Minister for the Arts, 1983–5; chairman, Sotheby's International, 1985–6, Arts Council of England, 1994–8; m 2 (1974) Countess Adelheid, née von der Schulenburg; see Vol. 2, p. 482, for the press publicity when he was seen going into a massage parlour.

50. WW sent a letter by hand to Downing Street next day.

51. Johnson described the review, which was headed 'A princess much maligned', as 'trenchant'; he also explained that the powers that be at the *Times* had changed tack yet again and the book was to be reviewed after all, by Elizabeth Longford.

Tuesday 23 June
A Levy Board meeting. Kenneth Clarke was to be the guest so I stayed
on for lunch, unusually.

At the end of lunch there were no cigars offered.

I said, 'Would you like a cigar, Kenneth?' He said he would love
one. I pulled out my case and he said, 'You've only got one,' (like Paul
Getty).

He never bothered a hoot, when he was Secretary for Health,
about anybody at the Department of Health where they keep telling
everybody not to smoke.

I then went on to the Lords where I was in time to ask a question.[52]

Alexander Hesketh spotted me on the way out.

He said, 'Charles has been bonking away like mad with Camilla
Parker Bowles.' I said, 'Is there any evidence?' He said, 'Yes, plenty.'

I said, 'What about her [Diana's] relations with [James] Gilbey and
others?' He said, 'Yes, but there is no evidence.'

He said, 'Morton, the author, has tapes of her talking to him,
dishing out all the dirt on the Prince of Wales and Camilla Parker
Bowles, and putting her side of the story, why she is fed up and hates
them all, etc.' He knows that for a fact from his connections and there
is no doubt whatever about it. She not only approved of her friends
helping to write the book but took a leading part in it herself.

He said, 'No doubt her bulimia caused her to be unbalanced but
her behaviour has been outrageous.' I said, 'Are you afraid the monarchy won't survive?' He said, 'I'm not saying that quite but it has
been greatly damaged.' I said, 'I feel sorry for Prince Charles.' He said,
'I do a bit but he's a bit peculiar as well.'

He said, 'The main trouble is that the courtiers are useless.'

Wednesday 24 June
Anthony Howard wrote an article on the main feature page of the
Times today saying that Labour still needs its trade union cart-horse.
He then quoted me as follows: 'Woodrow Wyatt's description of the
late Frank Cousins in 1959 as "the bully with the block vote" was not
just a damaging phrase: in the electorate's perception of Labour it lit
a candle that has never really gone out.'

---

52. WW asked for assurance that there would be no attempt to get the Maastricht
    Treaty through Parliament unless there was a clear definition of what subsidiarity
    meant.

Quite a compliment. I remember Hugh Gaitskell[53] getting very upset about my using that phrase. Hugh had asked me to say something about the trade unions' overweening role at Labour Party Conferences and I thought of this phrase 'the bully with the block vote' which caused a great amount of perturbation because it was thought, as everybody knew I was a great friend of Hugh Gaitskell, that it came from him.

Andrew Roberts[54] came to see me to talk about Mountbatten in India and why I thought he had got it wrong over the partition and so forth. He is a very lively fellow, short and with a keen face.

He asked me did I seek consciously to be present at the right moment in history. I said, 'I don't think I did that at all.'

I said, 'I think I sense the mood of what is going on around me. I don't think I consciously think "I'm now going to choose a historic moment and be in the thick of it".'

Last night, when Petronella came back, she was practising her singing, 'Lili Marlene' and all that, because she has got to sing for Norman's dance tomorrow night.

She skipped around singing and dancing with Verushka in the dining-room and then, when she stopped, loud clapping came from Rebecca down below where she could hear it from the kitchen because the lift was up.

Thursday 25 June
Dinner at Cavendish Avenue before the ball at Number 11.

George Weidenfeld and his new fourth wife are going on honeymoon to many places but at some point they come to Italy where George will go to stay with the Pope – no women allowed – at Castel Gandolfo. I said, 'Good Heavens. How can the Pope do that? Here is a man who has been married four times; he can't possibly approve of that.' But George claimed to be in enormous favour with the Pope who thinks he is absolutely marvellous. They talk about music and literature and goodness knows what else.

George sat on the other side of Ingrid Channon and once again said that he had known me longer than anybody else in England.

He described how we shared a house.

---

53. (1906–63); Leader of the Labour Party from 1955.
54. Historian; his biography of Halifax, *The Holy Fox*, was published in 1991, that of Salisbury in 1999.

I said, 'You always were egging me on to take a wider interest in girls so as to have a real variety of girlfriends. But I was very innocent and didn't follow your line.' So he laughed and said, 'I don't think you're accurate about that.'

Number 11 was immensely crowded so you could hardly move from one room to another. I spoke briefly to the Brazilian Ambassadress who I decided on second viewing is not as attractive as I had thought her.

William Waldegrave dashed up to me across the dance floor and said, 'I must congratulate you. You have done marvellously well over the Prince of Wales. Thank you very much.' That of course comes pretty well via the Palace because his sister is a lady-in-waiting to the Queen and her favourite one.[55]

David Mellor was there and said we must meet very soon but he never seems to say when. He says he can't now come to dinner on July 21st, which he had said he could originally, and he never makes an appointment to talk about the National Lottery. He is a very rum fellow. He always has been since I first came across him when he made all the promises to Gino Corsini about getting Kew to look at Gino's arboretum. I had to do it myself because he never did anything and Gino never heard from him again.[56]

Petronella had great guts to get up in front of this crowd of sophisticated people – or semi-sophisticated, some of them – and sing to them with the orchestra. In her surprisingly deep and marvellous singing voice she sang 'Lili Marlene', all the words, wonderfully, exactly as used by Marlene Dietrich, and some other songs.

Norman rushed up and kissed her and said, 'Please sing "Lili Marlene" again,' and by popular acclaim she sang it again.

In the *Evening Standard*, when Peter Oborne wrote about Norman, he referred to her singing as being part of the great entertainment which he was suggesting the Chancellor should not have been holding at Number 11, using it as a private house. Peter Oborne I had thought was moderately intelligent but he seems to be barmy like almost every other journalist.

First when I saw Norman dancing very affectionately with a blonde

---

55. Lady Susan Hussey, wife of Marmaduke (Duke) Hussey, at this time Chairman of the BBC.
56. See Vol. 1, p. 617, for this incident in 1988, and Vol. 2, p. 144, for Marchese Corsini's delight at WW's help over Kew.

I thought he must be dancing with his own wife. It wasn't. It was the blonde bombshell, Lady Walters, the PR lady for the Jockey Club at one time. Her husband[57] was the tiresome, twin sneering opposer of Mrs Thatcher with Ian Gilmour.[58] I always thought she was extremely attractive. She had her hand on Norman's back and they were dancing cheek to cheek. It was rather rash, I thought, in front of that large number of people there.

She is a bit younger than Rosemary but very much more beautiful, though built in the same style and design.

I didn't dance at all, naturally, but Verushka did quite a lot.

A Tory MP whose name I can't remember came up to me where I was sitting and said, 'Still the same old Woodrow, observing the scene cynically and laughing at it.'

He was quite right. These elderly, middle-aged people for the main, prancing up and down like fifteen-year-olds, trying to recapture their youth, fat and ill shaped for the main part, looked utterly ridiculous.

Friday 26 June
Went to stay with Henry and Tessa Keswick in the country at Oare.

Tessa knew Victoria,[59] who is the current girlfriend or mistress, or perhaps combination of girlfriend, mistress and nanny, of Paul Getty, when they were much younger in Rome.

I had thought Talitha Pol had committed suicide. She said, 'Not at all.'

Talitha took more drugs than she should have done and went unconscious. This was in Rome.

Henry said, 'I am so glad to hear the news of your appointment.' That was when we were alone. I said I didn't know anything about it. He said, 'Goodness, don't say anything for heaven's sake. It might not go through perhaps but I thought you knew.'

Maybe at the last moment Major will take a dislike to what I have

---

57. Sir Dennis Walters, Conservative MP, 1964–92; m 3 (1981) Bridgett, née Shearer; knight 1988.
58. Conservative MP, 1962–92, and former *Spectator* editor; 3rd baronet, life peer 1992.
59. Victoria Holdsworth and Paul Getty married in 1994.

been writing in the *News of the World* this week as I haven't been one hundred per cent for him.[60]

Saturday 27 June
I ate an enormous breakfast. Henry ate an enormous amount, too. I said to him 'Please don't eat so much. You'll die much younger than you need to.'

When Tessa was talking about Sarah Keswick, she said the Keswicks make wonderful husbands; they spoil their wives and do everything for them, 'like Henry does for me,' which was nice of her. I got on pretty well with her this weekend.

Sunday 28 June
My letter to the *Mail on Sunday* was printed, edited somewhat but not so badly that it was worth taking it [the matter] to the Press Complaints Commission.

Actually, of course, the truth is she [Princess Diana] is slightly barmy and whinging, making a bloody nuisance of herself and behaving incredibly badly, enthusing people to attack her husband through the Morton book. But I don't want to be represented as saying that.

Another swim and another enormous breakfast, then off betimes to get to the Paul Getty cricket match.

The ground is amazing. I said to Paul, 'It's as though some *deus ex machina* had swooped out of the sky and scooped up great mounds of earth from the valley and put this cricket ground down among the hills.' He said, 'That is roughly what did happen.'

Today in the *Sunday Telegraph* appears the great piece by Graham Turner with a photograph of us having lunch in the garden at Cavendish Avenue. He left out the 1961 date and he also didn't mention the Pavillon Blanc, but I suppose it wasn't too bad.

In the same *Sunday Telegraph* was a long interview of Petronella's with Mrs Thatcher about the record she had been making of the Gettysburg speech, hoping to make money from it for her foundation. I didn't think it was a very kind article. It talked about her voice being high pitched and I thought it was snide in some respects, in the way

---

60. WW urged Major 'to get the answer right on that mouthful of a word, subsidiarity'.

that Barbara Amiel says she mustn't be – she will damage her own career because people won't be willing to talk to her.

When we got back I talked to Margaret.

She said she probably would make a maiden speech about Maastricht on Thursday when there is a debate in the Lords.

She is over-doing it a bit and I can't restrain her. I said, 'Your maiden speech is supposed to be non-controversial.' She said, 'But I shall only be following precedent. Macmillan in his maiden speech attacked me.'

Monday 29 June

Petronella had two tickets for the first night of *Spread a Little Happiness: a Celebration* by Vivian Ellis.

It was an enormously happy affair, without rape or violence or any grizzly message or people traumatically disordered, disabled mentally or physically. In short it was romantic. I clapped so hard I nearly broke my thumb.

Tuesday 30 June

Margaret was introduced into the Lords today. The house was absolutely packed. I have never seen it so full. I managed to find a seat on the Opposition side, high up, because it all has to be rearranged when the introduction ceremony is on. Then pretty Baroness Hollis (Labour) came in to squeeze in beside me. She said, 'Do you mind?' I said, 'I never mind sitting next to a pretty girl.'

When Margaret came in, it was like a lioness entering into what she must realize is something of a cage. She was very dignified, fairly pretty but not quite as pretty as usual. When the ceremony finally finished and she shook hands with the Lord Chancellor on the way out, a very substantial 'Hear, hear,' went up twice all round the chamber from all sides. They are looking forward to the fireworks.

She then came back without her robes, wearing a very attractive black dress and a beautiful diamond brooch, large, and sat where all the Tory Prime Ministers sit on the bench nearest the lobby, just apart from the normal Ministers' front bench. She listened with great interest, particularly to Lord Stoddart[61] asking why we couldn't have a referendum on Maastricht. At one moment I looked across at her from

---

61. Labour MP, 1970–83; chairman, Campaign for an Independent Britain, since 1985; life peer 1983.

where I was sitting on the crossbenches and she saw me and I blew
her a kiss and she smiled very sweetly.

In the lobby outside was Denis Thatcher and his family, all very
enthusiastic, saying what a great honour it was, which was piffle
because it isn't an honour at all for her to go into the Lords like any
other life baroness. It was very mean of Number 10 not to arrange for
her to become a life countess.

Wednesday 1 July
My speech [in a House of Lords debate on the press] went down very well.

Everybody referred to it and argued either for or against my law of privacy.

I rebuked Mark Bonham-Carter for making a stale repetition of his dislike of Rupert Murdoch.

David Stevens had told me he was going to support a law of privacy. When he spoke he did the opposite.

Young William Astor had to reply for the government. He told me what he was going to say yesterday, a sort of on the one hand and on the other hand kind of speech. He didn't rule out having some kind of statutory situation rather than the voluntary Press Complaints Commission and he didn't even rule out some kind of law of privacy. But as Bill Deedes pointed out in his speech, which was pretty good, 'Let's be blunt about it: the government did pretty well out of the press in the last election so they are not going to do anything which is likely to annoy it.'

Thursday 2 July
To the Lords to meet the two prize-winners and the consolation prize-winner, schoolboys from Eastbourne College, of my special prize in honour of H. J. Belk for the best essay on the conditions which would make the writer a happy life.[1] This year the increasingly tiresome master in charge brought two other masters with him.

This was maddening because it meant I had to get a table for six in the dining-room for tea, as well as making it much more difficult for me to get admission tickets for them to the Lords and later to the Commons. Not only that, it inhibited the boys from the jolly, friendly conversation.

---

1. Belk was WW's housemaster at Eastbourne College, 'the only civilized master in the school,' (*Confessions of an Optimist*, p. 47).

The party at the *Spectator* was as usual impossibly crammed.

Poor Peter Jay,[2] once the glamour boy billed as our future Prime Minister, was there looking haggard and drained, much older than his age. Conrad Black was there looking surly – the sale of his *Telegraph* shares is flopping.

Elizabeth Longford[3] was there who wrote a review, in the Life and Times section of the *Times* last Thursday, of the book by Morton which they said they weren't going to review. She said, 'For once I agree with you.' I said, 'Nonsense. You agree with me a lot but you don't like to tell Frank that.'

Andrew Neil is now about to serialize Goebbels' diaries, allegedly discovered in the archives of the Russian secret service and handed over to a dreadful man called David Irving who claims the certain knowledge that the holocaust never happened and that Hitler was really a decent guy.[4]

Spoke to Margaret when I got home and congratulated her on her speech.

We discussed the press immediately trying to make it a great rift between her and John Major. She said, 'I asked particularly in my speech not to drag personalities into it but they never take any notice.' I have written an article for the *News of the World* which I hope will satisfy both Major and Margaret because really they are on the same side and the quarrel between them is now becoming utterly pointless.

Margaret said she was very nervous making her speech in the Lords. I said, 'Yes, it's like wondering whether you can swim as well in a new pond as you did in the last one.'

Saturday 4 July

A number of people kindly sent me birthday cards, more than usual, which touched me. Perhaps they think the number of my birthdays is now extremely limited.

Pericles[5] rang shortly before we left.

---

2. Born 1937; writer and broadcaster; Ambassador to the US, 1977–9; chief of staff to Robert Maxwell, 1986–9; economics editor, BBC, since 1990.
3. Biographer; m (1931) The Hon. Francis (Frank) Pakenham, now 7th Earl of Longford, Labour politician and prison reformer.
4. David Irving in April 2000 lost a libel case in which he claimed he had been defamed over his views concerning the holocaust.
5. WW's son by his third marriage, living in California.*

It was nice of him to remember.

The party at Nether Lypiatt Manor was for Prince Michael of Kent's birthday which he shares with me. We bought him a handsome silver, velvet-lined box for carrying his cufflinks, dress studs and so forth when he has to travel.

We had arrived, as instructed, at 12.30 and were given lots of Pimms of which I drank copiously and many agreeable little bits to eat, a lot of them hot. It was two o'clock before lunch was announced. In the meanwhile I had gone into the house and found a television set for the news of the cricket and the tennis final between Steffi Graf and Monica Seles. In the end the little girl was beaten by the bigger one and I was sorry because Graf has won quite enough.

Many of the guests were business-type people.

Richard Branson was there, presumably because he flies them backwards and forwards across the Atlantic free and performs other such services.

Edward Montagu (Lord Montagu of Beaulieu) told me that Margaret Huntingdon[6] is in a very bad way with advanced Alzheimer's disease.

After his tribulations in prison with Michael Pitt-Rivers, on the buggery convictions for which there would be no grounds today,[7] he has matured into a reasonable fellow with a lot of sense. He seems happily married with children.

Marie-Christine [Princess Michael] is a clever girl with good taste.

Those two have found a way of living together.

They clearly go on liking each other and make a good public show, much better than the Prince and Princess of Wales and the Duke and Duchess of York.

A friendly and, I am sure, genuine letter came from John Major today. I am certain it is true that I focused his mind, as he says in his letter, on the need to clarify and get a good, acceptable definition of subsidiarity to get him out of the difficulties facing him on ratification of the Maastricht Treaty.

---

6. (1907–94); novelist, biographer, and journalist, writing as Margaret Lane, her maiden name; m 2 (1944) 15th Earl of Huntingdon (1901–90), artist; she was WW's step mother-in-law when he was married to his third wife, Moorea, daughter of the Earl of Huntingdon by his first marriage.

7. Before the decriminalization in 1967 of homosexual acts between consenting male adults.

At last my *High Profiles* will be published by Samuel French. It will be available in public libraries as well as to amateur dramatic societies who want to act it. So I can now write in *Who's Who* that I'm a playwright as well, with a printed and performed play to prove it.

Tuesday 7 July
Lunch at the Lords with Pat Chapman in the Barry Room.

She looked charming in her yellow outfit. She has a chubby face, not exactly attractive but not far short. I said, 'Would you like some champagne?' She said, 'Yes, perhaps a glass.' So I said, 'We'll have half a bottle.'

As we went on, she got more and more talkative and cheerful, so I ordered the other half.

She asked me if I thought it was reasonable to point out that an eye surgeon has got AIDS. This is big news at the moment. I said, 'Of course it is. Also, it is fearful rubbish to talk about this being as much a heterosexual situation as a homosexual one. We should be bold and say it's the "buggers' blight".' She said, 'What a marvellous phrase. Why don't you use it?'

Dinner at Lord and Lady Stevens'.

He wanted to know where we were going for our holiday. I said, 'We always take the same house in Porto Ercole in August.'

Then he said, 'Why haven't we been asked?' I said, 'Applications for invitations take a good many years to process and there is a long queue. It's like waiting to get into White's and you might never get in at all.'

Saturday 11 July
The Benson & Hedges final, Hampshire against Kent. I really only wanted to see Gower bat because he does it so beautifully.

A consulting physician and an orthopaedic surgeon were in the box. There is a great man called Muirhead[8] who could now do the [hip] operation on Bob with an eighty per cent chance of success of him not being killed. He is in great pain.

Paul Getty said to me, 'We must get him to have this operation,' so I had a long talk with the medical people and then talked to Paul and Molly and then to Bob.

---

8. W. F. G. Muirhead Allwood, orthopaedic surgeon.

Bob is only ninety-one. He could well live to be a hundred if he has this operation.

After dinner Petronella wanted to talk to me. It was a great secret. She is proposing to leave the house towards the end of August and live in a flat which has been more or less given to her by Hugo Vickers[9] who has two flats in Kensington.

Meanwhile, the law of privacy or something like it is hotting up. Calcutt[10] has been made to reconvene himself and consider what should be done. He will be spurred on by the extraordinary action of the *Independent* in publishing that Virginia Bottomley was a mother of three months when she married her husband. It was a wholly unnecessary intrusion into privacy with nothing to do whatever with her job. The *Sun* ran a leader saying it is a disgraceful intrusion of privacy (very funny coming from them).

Sunday 12 July
Just before dinner last night Arnold rang and spoke to me for twenty minutes. Poor old chap, he has been so ill.

He had water in his chest and his lungs and goodness knows what else. He is very gloomy about the economy, as usual. However, I congratulated him on increasing his profits which he has done.

In spite of all his arrogance and outward show, inside him he is very vulnerable.

To Norman Lamont's at Dorneywood for lunch. Twenty people present.

The butler greeted us like long-lost friends. He was there with Willie Whitelaw and Kenneth Baker and earlier Home Secretaries who used Dorneywood. Surprisingly, Rosemary and even Norman is uncomfortable with him.

Patricia Rawlings,[11] the very attractive, dark, MEP, said, 'I heard on the BBC this morning that you have been attacking Norman for not cutting interest rates.' I said, 'I thought I had done exactly the opposite.' She said, 'I was teasing you.' I didn't think it was much of

9. Author; his books include the authorized biography of Cecil Beaton (1985).
10. Sir David Calcutt QC, Master of Magdalene College, Cambridge, 1986–94; chairman, Committee on Privacy and Related Matters, 1989–90, Review of Press Self-Regulation, 1992–3.
11. Conservative politician; MEP, 1989–94; life peer 1994.

a tease. I had brought the *News of the World* for Norman. He was delighted.

I sat on Rosemary's right and Lord Alexander, Chairman of the National Westminster Bank, sat on her left. I asked him whether it was practicable to construct in an effective way a law on privacy. He used to be leader of the Bar Association and acted for Jeffrey Archer in the famous libel case.

I said, 'Do you think I should get in touch with Calcutt?' He said, 'Yes, of course.'

Ronnie Grierson[12] was there with his pleasant, faded wife. He gets himself in everywhere, hoping no doubt to make some mileage with his contacts by impressing them with his friendship with Norman. Cabinet Ministers allotted Dorneywood tend to have a few high-flying commercial and businessmen there, with an eye, no doubt, to what they can get out of them when they leave their jobs.

Monday 13 July
To the stag party of George Weidenfeld at the Garrick. It was exceedingly boring. I wished greatly that I had made some excuse and gone to the Carlton Towers where Willie Whitelaw was entertaining Margaret.

My presence was quite unnecessary and though I had known him since 1943 and longest (apart from somebody who knew him in Austria), he didn't ask me to make any speech. I felt slightly hipped because I would have made quite a funny one.

Tony Quinton was there. So was the Cardinal Archbishop of Vienna who didn't even say grace. Teddy Kollick, a very old acquaintance, said I hadn't recognized him. I said, 'That is true. Your hair is no longer blond.' He was of German origin and was Mayor of Jerusalem. I said, 'I remember well the jolly days we had in a kibbutz when you showed me round and explained everything to me in Israel in 1949.'

I sat between David Metcalfe on my left and Peregrine Worsthorne[13] on my right. He asked me why I had changed my views about Europe. I said, 'I have done nothing of the kind. It is Margaret who has changed hers.'

He said, 'Have you deserted her?' I said, 'Of course not. I speak to

---

12. Vice-chairman, GEC, 1969–91; chairman, GEC International, since 1992; knight 1990; m (1966) Heather, Viscountess Bearsted, née Firmston-Williams, (d 1993).
13. Editor, *Sunday Telegraph*, 1986–91; knight 1991.

her every week. I argue with her and I am arguing with her at the
moment, trying to stop her going overboard in the wrong direction.'

Thereafter I got very bored with David on my left and Perry on my
right and fell asleep.

Tuesday 14 July
The Weidenfeld saga has become the oldest established floating crap
game, à la *Guys and Dolls*,[14] swinging into the National Portrait
Gallery this evening. Most of the usual people were there.

Wednesday 15 July
To Drue Heinz's[15] party in the amazing, huge, rambling house with
courtyards off a mews in Mayfair. Once again the oldest established
floating crap game was in evidence. Stephen Spender[16] was there again,
the Channons, Carla Powell and Charles Powell,[17] etc.

Margaret Thatcher plus Denis made a slight change from the usual.
She thought that Petronella had written a good article about her
recording of the Abraham Lincoln Gettysburg speech.

I was slightly nervous talking to her because of what I have been
writing recently which doesn't precisely square with her views on
Maastricht and referendums and all the rest of it. But she was very
friendly and gave me her usual kiss and squeezed my hand.

Then I went to speak to Denis because Robert Rice of the Royal
Free had asked me to try to enlist him to badger rich friends to give
money to the Royal Free.

The party was ostensibly in honour of David Hockney, the painter.

William Shawcross was there and he said did I know who was
going to be the new editor of the *Times*? I said I had no idea.

---

14. WW's point is that a number of similar parties were given to celebrate the Weiden-
    feld marriage, with more or less the same guests; this reminded him of the famous
    floating crap game in the musical *Guys and Dolls* which the players continued in
    different locations.
15. Philanthropist widow of Henry John (Jack) Heinz II (1908–87).
16. (1909–95); poet and critic; Professor of English, University College London,
    1970–7; knight 1983; m 2 (1941) Natasha Litvin, pianist.
17. Charles Powell, diplomat, Private Secretary to Margaret Thatcher as Prime Min-
    ister, 1984–91; director, Jardine Matheson Holdings, since 1991, National
    Westminster Bank, since 1991; knight 1990, life peer 2000; m (1964) Carla née
    Bonardi, from Domodosolla, Italy.

Some would like Charles Moore[18] to be editor but I am not sure he would make a good one. Many were horrified to learn Paul Dacre[19] of the *Evening Standard* had been asked to be editor – because he is really a tabloid journalist, though quite pleasant according to Marigold Johnson.[20] She said, 'Unlike most journalists he is actually a gent.'

Yet another part of the seemingly never-ending oldest established floating crap game. This time at David Metcalfe's.

James Hanson[21] greeted me with cheerful affection. I told him I thought he had made a good choice in having Ken Baker, the former Home Secretary, on his Board because his judgement is good, his intelligence shrewd and he has imagination as well as being highly reliable.

Evelyn de Rothschild[22] was there with his pretty wife, Victoria. He is in a wild state with the Levy Board over Epsom.

He is a very insecure man, deeply so, never quite conscious of the impression he is making and worried about it, with all his bragging and bullying behaviour.

I quite like him. He has a charm and is not without intelligence.

After dinner Kenneth Clarke, the Home Secretary, turned up with Henry Keswick attached.

I only spoke to him briefly, more or less to say goodbye when I left at getting on for twelve. I said it was my bedtime, which I hope didn't make him think that I was already gaga.

Henry told me that at dinner there had been heavy emphasis by him and Tessa on the need to reappoint me, otherwise The Voice of Reason might turn belligerently against the Government. Henry told me Kenneth is pretty pro me, so that sounds fairly safe.

George has been exaggerating about the cosy one-to-one state he has with the Pope. It is really a seminar George is going on, at Castel

18. Editor, *Spectator*, 1984–90; deputy editor, *Daily Telegraph*, 1990–2; editor, *Sunday Telegraph* 1992–5, *Daily Telegraph* since 1995.
19. Editor, *Evening Standard*, 1991–2, *Daily Mail*, 1992–8, editor-in-chief, Associated Newspapers, since 1998.
20. Former Labour parliamentary candidate; née Hunt, m (1957) Paul Johnson.
21. Chairman, Hanson plc, 1965–97; life peer 1983.
22. Chairman, N. M. Rothschild, 1972–89; chairman, United Racecourses (including Epsom), 1977–94 (the future of United Racecourses, a subsidiary of the Levy Board, was being decided at this time); director, *Daily Telegraph*; m (1973, separated 1999) Victoria, née Schott; knight 1989.

Gandolfo with a lot of scholarly people, which happens once every two years.

The girl he is marrying seems a very nice woman, having been secretary or general factotum or mistress to Rubinstein,[23] the pianist, for some years. She must be thirty-five years younger than George and I can't imagine what kind of sex they have with his vast bulk, almost unable to waddle, although I can imagine it really. She is attractive and can presumably get many men. I hope George's money lasts the course because I don't think she has got any.

Thursday 16 July

In the report and accounts published by the Tote and submitted to Parliament is a glaring error. It says that my salary for the year had been £93,000 up to 31 March 1992. It was actually £89,000. The *Racing Post* and the *Daily Express*, among others, said that although the Tote had not had a very profitable year, it had been a very profitable one for me because my salary had gone up 13.4 per cent. This was horrifying because it had been agreed with the Home Office, Ken Baker, last summer that Board Members wouldn't have more than 7 per cent and my own staff would be pretty annoyed to see I had got an enormous rise when they had been held back to 8.5 per cent.

I knew mischief had been afoot, and it had been.

My expenses for going to the Arc de Triomphe and Prix d'Amérique, neither of which were jolly jaunts but involved long talks with PMU and with trotting officials and all the rest of it, [had been included].

There was a hell of a row and I had to get the auditors to issue a certificate altering the salary figure which was wrong and blow up Tom Phillips, the Financial Director, for letting it go through.

It really was only 7.1 per cent which I got extra, as agreed with the Home Office.

I went to The Other Club dinner, a dullish one.

Jack Cunningham, the Labour Shadow Leader of the House, agreed with me when I said, 'You're making a frightful mistake in going for John Smith and Margaret Beckett. You should have had either Tony Blair or Gordon Brown and one could be the Leader and the other the Deputy Leader.'[24]

---

23. Arthur Rubinstein, 1887–1982.
24. Beckett had become Smith's Deputy Leader, Blair was Chief Opposition Spokesman on Home Affairs and Brown on Treasury and Economic Affairs.

Sunday 19 July

The Jeffrey Archer annual party.

We were greeted effusively by Jeffrey who said, 'Would you like Bucks Fizz or Pimms or Krug?' I said, 'I'll have some champagne.' He said, 'You mean Krug,' and gave me a glass of it. He always wants everybody to know he is giving Krug.

He then said, 'You are sitting at a special table, the only one which will be waited on, with Margaret and Denis and Cecil Parkinson and his wife.'

Cecil Parkinson and I worked on Margaret, sitting on either side of her, not to gas about referendums and argue about Maastricht but to wait to see what happens.

We talked about her accepting the consultancy ('I never would become a director because of the legal liabilities,' she said) to Philip Morris, the great tobacco firm owning Marlboro cigarettes. She said, 'Of course they have enormous amounts of food chains and stores in America and in Europe. It isn't necessarily anything to do with smoking.'

She is going to get about a million pounds out of being a consultant, possibly to help them in relation to what goes on in the European Community.

Naturally there was a discussion about the unfortunate David Mellor.[25]

Previously I had been talking to Ken Baker who said he doesn't have to resign but he's finished because every time he gets up in the House the Opposition will jibe at him and say, 'Were you too knackered to prepare your speech today?'

The woman sold the story to the *People* for £40,000 with lots of explanations and details.

Margaret believes he shouldn't resign but should just carry on. I said, 'You were always very good about that sort of thing,' looking hard at Cecil Parkinson who had the grace to smile a bit. She never threw him out for all the things he got up to with the dreadful woman,

---

25. The *People* had splashed his affair with Antonia de Sancha, an actress. Stories followed about Mellor making love dressed in Chelsea football club strip and having a penchant for toe-sucking. Matthew Parris in his book *Great Parliamentary Scandals* says that de Sancha 'was not accused of having tipped off the press, or assisted in any way in the first "scoop" '.

Sara Keays, but he did have to go in the end because of what was published in the *Times*, interviews with her and so forth.

When Margaret came up to me before lunch I was talking to Clive James[26] and I introduced him to her. He was very complimentary to her. But when she drifted away before the lunch began he said, 'I got the best of both worlds at the general election. To satisfy my conscience I voted Labour but I got a Tory government which was what I really wanted.' I told her that and she said, 'Gosh, he has no principles at all.'

Margaret hopes Bush[27] will win but was inclined to agree when I said what I had written in the *News of the World* this morning, that Bush is an indecisive wimp and Clinton, his opponent, is an ass. Nevertheless, she thought he would be better than Clinton. Maybe he will be and I think he will get in all right, now that Ross Perot has suddenly withdrawn.

After she had gone I thought it safe to go and talk to Leon Brittan who had been carefully tucked out of the way so as not to annoy Margaret, right on the other side of the lawn. I said, 'Why the hell don't you get on with making the British conform with EC betting laws so we can have Sunday racing?' I went over the argument of the competition angle again.

I then rang Rupert Murdoch to ask what he was doing about the editorship of the *Times*. I said, 'What about John O'Sullivan?' He said, 'He would be very good on policies but I am not sure about the rest.' He is thinking about the Deputy Editor [Peter Stothard]. I said, 'He is very good. But I'm not sure if he has got the flair.'

He doesn't think Charles Moore could do it.

He was very jolly. He had his mother staying there.[28]

To cap the day, I had a long conversation with Norman Lamont.

I told him that just before I went Jeffrey Archer had said he was having dinner with the Prime Minister tonight. He said, 'That's very odd. I am talking to him at 6.45 this evening so it must be a very late dinner or he isn't really having that dinner with him at all.'

Norman hadn't realized it was Tote Credit at Wigan who were

26. Writer and television presenter.
27. George Bush, US President, 1989–93.
28. Dame Elisabeth Murdoch, widow of Sir Keith Murdoch, the Australian newspaper owner.

taking all the telephone calls[29] for the National Savings Bond. He said, 'I may have to cut the interest on that a little.'

I said I thought it would be a good idea, by enough to stop the building societies putting up their mortgage interest which would then have an adverse effect on inflation.

Monday 20 July
Spoke to Norman Lamont.

I told him, 'We have had thousands of calls again today at Wigan, the biggest number we've had so far (for the National Savings Bond) after your announcement that there will be a different rate of interest after twelve noon tomorrow. We've had to take on another fifteen people.'

He thanked me for convincing him it was the right thing to do.

I seem to be advising everybody on everything at the moment.

Tuesday 21 July
I had a long chat with my friend Patsy Chapman, a rumbustious girl. 'High jinks,' I said when she picked up the telephone. I asked her whether she had refrained from using the Mellor story because she was afraid of my law of privacy. She said, 'Not exactly but we were unhappy about the sources who were providing us with the story.'

I said, 'I can see you had no option but to follow suit when the *People* did it.'

She told me that though she is a member of the Press Complaints Commission, she had refused to attend on Wednesday, saying it was nothing to do with them and she doesn't agree with them if they do condemn the press for talking about Mellor. She thinks the press have a right to do it because he is concerned with the law of privacy and he got himself photographed all over the bloody place with this girl, coming out of the bedroom in which they had made love and so on, having during the election traded on the show of what a happy family he has.

I said, 'I don't really approve of it all but I must admit it's quite hilarious.'

---

29. This was the Tote's telesales company, Intrac.

Wednesday 22 July
I replied to David Calcutt's nice letter.[30]

Dinner at St James's Palace with David Airlie.[31] Very formal with grand invitations sent, with Buckingham Palace printed on them, from the Lord Chamberlain, which he is. The entrance is squitty, a little door which might be the door to a kitchen.

Once inside it unfolds into a country house type residence behind thick brick Tudor walls.

Verushka sat on the left of David Airlie. On his right was the Japanese Ambassadress, a funny looking little creature. Her husband sat next to Ginnie Airlie who has been Lady of the Bedchamber to the Queen since 1973. The tiny Japanese Ambassador looked altogether too squeaky and polished in his immaculate dinner jacket over a spotless shirt.

The most amusing person there was the new Baroness James, better known as P. D. James, the writer of remarkable thriller and detective stories. We talked about thriller writers, particularly women ones.

She is a dumpy creature with a broad, plain face, but beaming with intelligence and kindness. She was a civil servant. She worked in the police department and the criminal policy department so she knows what she is talking about when she writes about detectives and murders. I have praised her in my *Times* review of Len Deighton's latest book.[32]

The Chief Scout was there.[33]

'Do Scouts still have to do one good deed a day?' I enquired. 'Yes,' he replied. 'What was yours today?' He was startled and had to think very hard.

---

30. Calcutt thanked WW for sending him various items and said he had asked for WW's name to be included on the list of those from whom his Committee was seeking evidence. WW's efforts 'on the French front' would be extremely welcome, although the Committee had reservations about how well the laws of one country travelled to another.

31. 13th Earl of Airlie, Lord Chamberlain of the Queen's Household, 1984–97; m (1952) Virginia, née Ryan.

32. WW began his review of *City of Gold*: 'As a thriller writer, Len Deighton is not in the same elegant class as practitioners such as P. D. James, who bring a literary distinction to their work that is superior to all but a few Booker prize-winners,' but he recommended Deighton's book as excellent holiday reading.

33. Garth Morrison, Chief Scout, 1988–96.

Sunday 26 July
Sunday racing at Doncaster, a great success particularly as far as the
Tote was concerned.[34]

Monday 27 July
Went to David Mellor's office at National Heritage in Whitehall. There
were the regulation cameraman and crew waiting outside.

He said, 'I thought I'd like to talk to you without any officials
present.'

He thanked me for the support I had given him in the *News of the
World* and my messages.

I said, 'I supported you as a matter of principle. I have been in
pickles just as bad as yours. I have been four times married and
understand how these things happen. It would have been very unfortunate for me if one or two of the things I had done in the sex line had
been revealed. I think it is unwise to have friends like Paul Halloran
of *Private Eye*.'

He was obviously heartened by Major's loyal support to him. Mellor
usually rings him on a Sunday but yesterday he didn't. The moment
Major left the cricket match at Headingley, Major rang him to see how
he was getting on and tell him not to worry.

I said, 'I think there must be some action on the use of tapes and
recordings and photography inside private places, bugging and that
kind of intrusion.' He agreed with that but said, 'I'm against a law on
privacy.'

On the question of the National Lottery, which I had ostensibly
been called to see him about, he was highly supportive of the Tote's
wish to be an agent and of the drafting of the necessary passage in the
law to make sure nobody could accuse the Tote of acting *ultra vires*.

I spoke to Chris Hudson at the Home Office and he told me that
Peter Winfield had written an umpteen page letter to the Home Secretary saying how he is an owner, a breeder, goes to foreign countries
to watch racing and all kind of rambling, inconsequential stuff, and
how fit he is and all the rest of it. I said we couldn't possibly have him
back anyway, after his behaviour in writing to the Home Office. He

---

34. WW argued in the *Times* on 28 July that punters should now be able to bet at
    racecourses on a Sunday. Tote Credit customers could already do so; they had put
    £118,363 into Tote pools on the 26th.

said there is no intention of allowing any such thing at the Home Office and he is drafting a reply in general terms. So it is settled.

Wednesday 29 July
Off [to Italy] at last, forgetting things, no doubt, all the way.

Arrived at Perignano. Gingo[35] has not been at all well. I think he won't live much longer. He has emphysema. He is not his old lively self but seemed querulous because I smoked cigars in his little library.

Anna Lu is more lively than Gingo. She came down the steps outside the house. I followed her. I said, 'You have very pretty legs, Anna Lu, and the skirt is exactly the right height for them just to be seen and suggest excitement if one saw more.'

When we were ready to go the day after, she came up to me in the garden and we embraced. She said to me, 'I shall remember what you said. I shall say to myself, "Woodrow says I have got lovely legs." '

Ginevra (Gingo and Anna Lu's daughter), with the husband descended from Brutus, was there.

She has a lovely, round face, a little like a Madonna's, round and kind and sweet, but plump and sexy.

He is a nice fellow, her husband, but he really should have been born with a great deal of money rather than into a family which has run down over the last two thousand years, not accumulating enough and losing bits of what it had.

---

35. Count Sanminiatelli (known as Gingio which WW always spelt 'Gingo') married to Princess Anna Lucrezia Corsini (1933–2000, known as Annalù which WW always spelt 'Anna Lu'); the Wyatts regularly began their Italian holiday by staying with the Sanminiatellis at Perignano.

Saturday 1 August

The garden at Villa Safir in Porto Ercole looked brown and terrible.

However, the swimming pool is in good condition and the views are still wonderful looking out over the sea and the fort. I found various tiny rearrangements in the library which slightly discomposed me until I put them all straight again. I'm afraid I removed Mrs Reinhardt's pictures of her husband and put them face down somewhere else away from the desk I write on.[1]

Sunday 2 August

The Wiltons arrived. It was a great pleasure to see them. But Diana is a bit scratchy. She asked me rum questions about who vetted my expenses at the Tote.

Saturday 8 August

The Keswicks arrive.

Tessa is very friendly. I talked to her a lot about the Lottery and the Tote's need to get it.

She said Kenneth Clarke is very supportive. He is unlikely to go racing but he would, no doubt, go to the annual Tote lunch and make a speech. Tessa said that it is undoubted that I am to be reappointed against the wishes of the civil servants.

She told me that Kenneth Baker was extremely unpopular at the Home Office. When he arrived, he just took off his coat and threw it at one of the civil servants, sat down and started bullying everybody and being very rude to them.

I was surprised. I had nothing but courtesy and kindness and intelligence from him.

---

1. The Wyatts had rented this villa each year since 1988, except for 1990; Mrs Reinhardt's late husband had been US Ambassador to Rome. See Vol. 1, p. 612.

Sunday 9 August

Invited by Filippo[2] and his wife, Georgiana, to go and see the wild
boar they keep in an enclosure and watch them being fed. We went
miles to their enormous castle which seems to have been built only in
1900 – one of the many properties the Corsinis have.

We tramped through the grounds, like being on safari, and through
the forest. There were many midges about.

We saw no wild boar. The keeper commented it was too hot for
them to come out.

The boar hadn't even bothered to eat the vast consignments of
water melons which were lying in a clearing untouched. These are
ones Filippo gets for nothing because there is overproduction and, by
European Economic Commission rules, the farmers are paid for them
although they can't sell them, except on the side.

We then went on a long drive along roads which were not roads
but tracks, through brush and trees. It was ages before we got to the
top of a hill where there was a spectacular view and a picnic on tables
brought up there specially.

Verushka hated it because curiously it grew cold up there. She
snuggled up to Henry because she said he was a good hot water bottle,
which with his enormous size he is.

Tuesday 11 August

Charles Powell and Carla arrive. She is extraordinarily bossy. She goes
into the kitchen and cuts up tomatoes without asking anybody. Henry
employs Charles, who is doing very well with numerous directorships.
He sits on the National Westminster Board, for one. He says in their
three thousand branches they can see no sign of recovery at all.

Charles is interesting on Margaret. Of her famed insulting behaviour
towards her Ministers he said, 'They are grown men and they should
have been able to stand up to it. But what they couldn't cope with was
her directness, particularly coming from a woman.'

On Maastricht he was certain that she would have done much the
same as John Major. He said that again and again he watched her at
3.00 a.m. in the morning, at meetings of the European summits, when
she would finally make concessions to prevent the thing running off
the road. She has been badly advised and egged on and stirred on by

---

2. Prince Corsini, brother of Anna Lu, wife of Gingo Sanminiatelli.

Nicholas Ridley[3] who has gone partly mad and is very ill. She also seems to have formed a new alliance with Tebbit who stirs her up and talks a lot of nonsense.

He said she would not have gone on to Baghdad, as I keep saying she would have done, and eliminated Saddam Hussein. She was very much piping down on that because we had to keep within United Nations resolutions and it was absolutely clear that intervention by force into Kuwait was limited to getting Saddam Hussein out of Kuwait.

He may well be right about that.

We lamented Margaret's departure and wished she was still there.

Wednesday 12 August

I had a call from Paul Connew, deputy editor of the *News of the World*. He said they had a story, and knew it was true, that the *Mirror* (he didn't want to reveal their sources) were sending out reporters and photographers to follow Norman [Lamont] everywhere when he gets here and show pictures of him luxuriating in the sun by the swimming pool and going to restaurants, drinking and smoking large cigars, while Britain is an economic plight with unemployment going up, more houses being re-possessed, businesses collapsing and so forth. That was rather alarming.

He apologized for disturbing my holiday. I said, 'I am extremely grateful. You have rung me just after we heard that our house in London has been burgled.'

It seems that somebody had rung up asking if our windows should be cleaned.

Rebecca [the cook] had told the bogus window cleaners we were away. Someone broke through the French windows into Verushka's bedroom and broke open the door of my library. They turned everything upside down in her room, going through her jewellery, and had stolen a lot of costume jewellery and some rather valuable rings which she hadn't put into the safe, unfortunately.

I spoke to the police at some length.

---

3. (1929–93); Conservative MP, 1959–92; Secretary of State for the Environment, 1986–9, for Trade and Industry, 1989–90; life peer 1992.

Thursday 13 August
The Keswicks departed after lunch, she particularly reluctantly. She is very supportive of me for which I am grateful. She is still quite pretty, with very nice legs. She was not at all abashed by my swimming naked in the pool. She has a very strong will but in the end Henry triumphs on big matters.

Carla is endlessly on the telephone to England talking to her son or anybody she wants to. She is extremely restless and tiresome. She never asks if we mind her telephoning but just does it. I can't get a line to speak to the Tote.

Friday 14 August
Brigadier Moggi was brought by Gino Corsini to see me at nine o'clock. He was taken round the garden to see where the paparazzi could photograph from. He suggested moving the white umbrella at the swimming pool to the other side which would block them a bit.

He thought it would be fairly difficult to prevent them photographing but would Norman Lamont like two guards with him all the time. I said, 'No. that wouldn't do at all. Anything rather than that.' He gave me a special telephone number to ring. In Italy you can clear anyone off your property at once if they are trespassing and they can be arrested. It is better than it is in England for the protection of privacy.

After they had gone there was some more news. There were two young men, looking rather scruffy, skinheads, English, who went to the Pellicano Hotel and asked where Lord Wyatt's villa was. Evidently they think the villa belongs to me but they don't seem to know the name of it. They said they were friends of mine and they had an appointment with me.

Later I heard they had been down in the marina. Fortunately, we had primed everybody down there not to say where we were staying.

Norman's secretary rang from London yesterday and said she had heard the *Sun* were doing it. I said, 'I don't know about that but certainly the *News of the World* aren't,' and I told her how I had been tipped off about the *Mirror* people.

Maybe they will find out in the end where we are but one doesn't know how long they are prepared to stay, wasting their newspaper's money. They can't speak Italian.

In the marina this morning they asked to be shown Lord Wyatt's boat. No such object. At about half past four this afternoon Eduardo, the gardener husband of the cook, went down to Verushka at the swimming pool and told her to follow him. They went up the road going up the hill. He had spotted two young men, one wearing glasses, just disappearing. They left behind a film case. Obviously they had been taking pictures of the swimming pool into which the umbrella had fallen. The Brigadier's advice to move it to the other side had been pointless as a shield against photographers.

Norman, somewhat disturbed when he arrived, started to ring the Ambassador. I said, 'That won't do any good. I am in direct contact with the police here.' But he insisted on doing it. He overreacted. Then more photographers turned up, two from the *Today* paper and two from the *Sun*. I rang Rupert in Los Angeles. I had a brisk argument with him. He said, 'Anyway, it's true, isn't it? He is having a luxurious holiday with the famous Woodrow Wyatt in a wonderful villa.' I said, 'Possibly, but what has that got to do with the economy?'

I said, 'Rupert, the Calcutt Committee recommended two years ago that photography into people's private property, and intrusion into their privacy where they live for the purpose of disseminating the stuff in newspapers, should be a criminal offence. Calcutt is now reviewing the situation to see whether that should become law. He is recommending it again. It is the worst possible time for your newspapers to be intruding on privacy here, trespassing and taking photographs of swimming pools with people swimming in them and all the rest of it.' He saw the point and said, 'I'll see what I can do. But tell him he ought to get out of the ERM.' He was as good as his word and the *Sun* and *Today* have been called off and have now left.

But the *Mirror* is still lurking around, their two youths having at last discovered where the Villa Safir is.

Saturday 15 August
The police were again sent for because the photographers were waiting outside.

The carabinieri are taking more sensible action here by our local persuasion than the silly Ambassador in Rome who keeps saying, 'I can't just go to the Minister of the Interior and ask him to do something.'

They chased them away from their view on a road in the hills overlooking our swimming pool and they hamper them at every turn.

It does feel somewhat like being besieged and it is uncomfortable to feel you are being spied on and watched wherever you go. I occasionally risk naked bathing but I am terrified it is going to appear in some juxtaposed photograph of me standing naked in the swimming pool and some naked lady by my side.

The Powells left today. Charles is extremely nice but she, I am afraid, is awful, immensely pleased with herself.

It is a great joy to see Mark and Eve Pejacsevich. But I miss Charles who was extremely interesting about Mrs Thatcher and her methods.

Sunday 16 August
It was Hilaire's birthday today.[4] A cake was arranged and candles put upon it. He was delighted.

In the evening Mrs Johnson came to dinner. She is fiftyish, perhaps a trifle more, blonde, plump, plain and Polish. She seems to have left Poland at a very young age in 1939. Her father, she said, was an army officer. Eventually she married, as his third or fourth wife, Mr Johnson of Johnson baby powders and Johnson wax polish. She was well educated and had some job working in his household. She told me that she had been married to him for fourteen years before he died which was some four years ago. She has about £750 million.

She is a tough cookie. She gave entertaining accounts of how she had dealt with Walesa, the President of Poland. He thought she was just going to give vast sums of money for them to run the shipyards at Gdansk at a loss. She said, 'No, certainly not. I want to know what your plans are for making it efficient with a proper basis for conditions of work.'

She did appear to have kindness below. She was anxious to help her country and she donated to all kinds of charities to help Polish people.

Monday 17 August
Somehow the *Mirror* people found out that Norman and Rosemary and family, and Verushka etc., were going out on Carmelo's[5] boat this morning. They were waiting just outside it when he arrived. Photo-

---

4. The Lamonts' son, b 1977; their daughter Sophie was also there, b 1980.
5. Carmelo Calabro, a Porto Ercole friend of the Wyatts.

graphs were being taken.[6] They asked Carmelo how much he charged
to charter it, thinking the Lamonts must have hired it or I must have
hired it for them. What very great simpletons they are if they think I
have got that kind of money, also to say that I am the owner of the
villa they describe as worth £1.5m.

Carmelo is very annoyed. He'd never charter his boat but if he did,
it would be £1,500 a day – not the measly £500 the *Mirror* reported.

Norman is worried about the continuing presence of the photographers. Also, by some belief in his office that the Prime Minister
wants him to return tomorrow to discuss the financial crisis with him.
I said, 'That would be crazy. Everybody would think the pound was
going for six.'

Tuesday 18 August
The Prime Minister rang Norman in the morning so I left my library.
They had a long talk. It was all a misunderstanding about Norman
coming back. The Prime Minister had completely forgotten he was on
holiday with us. He agreed it would be calamitous for Norman suddenly to dash back to London.

Norman told him what I had done to stop the *Sun* and *Today* and
he was very pleased that Rupert Murdoch had responded so well.

It seems that the *Mirror* have now called everything off, tired of the
story.

I think they were stymied by our carabinieri whose surveillance
prevented them taking pictures of Norman in the swimming pool and
all that kind of lark. Norman is very sensitive and did not want himself
photographed in a swimming costume because he thinks he looks too
fat and not elegant enough.

Wednesday 19 August
The *Mirror* now has much more to gossip about. They have done nine
pages on the Duchess of York topless and lolling about with her semi-
naked lover who tried to get an injunction to stop the pictures. But
the judge said, 'There is no law of privacy in this country though there
is one in France. There is nothing I can do about it. Complain to the

---

6. They appeared in the *Daily Mirror* next day, 18 August, under the heading 'Glad
   I'm not there'. A short item had appeared in the *Sunday Mirror* of 16 August,
   'Lamont's bad times bolt-hole'.

Press Council.' Maybe I should complain to the Press Council, too, about what the *Mirror* did to us but I won't.

Norman says that the Queen is very exercised about the income tax question. When he went to see her before his last Budget, she only wanted to talk about whether she ought to pay income tax. She is beginning to think maybe she should. I said, 'The true answer is for those estates which she surrendered, the Crown Estates, to be given back to her and then to pay tax on those. She would make many times the amount of the Civil List which is for necessary duties.'

Norman said the Queen Mother is the one who is most extravagant. She far exceeds her Civil List and the Treasury gets very het up about it. I said, 'No one is going to object to her. She is very good value. No one ever attacks her.' Norman said they do to him in the Treasury.

Went to La Torre de Carla in the mountains. Wonderful wild boar to eat and a marvellous tagliatelli with white truffles.

Petronella sang a bit, there was dancing in the restaurant and it was all extremely friendly.

It is a very ancient town with a beautiful church, outside which the most blatant pornography was being sold.

Shenanigans with the Treasury. What to do about the sinking dollar and the pound sinking with it. There is too much pressure on it and the reserves are being used up to defend it.

Thursday 20 August
Fresh disturbances about the ruddy pound. Norman had to give all kinds of instructions and held a three-way conversation with Brady, Secretary of the US Treasury, who was at Bush's convention where he was about to make his acceptance speech and outline his policy – which turned out basically to be that he was going to cut taxes across the board. He said that last time and didn't do it.

To Norman's surprise, Brady was worried about the dollar going so far down that he was anxious to help. He had various plans. One last resort is to put up interest rates briefly to steady the pound because on no account will we have a realignment.

He had a long conversation with John Major also, taking place in my library. Norman said, 'Don't go.' I said, 'No. I'm going to leave you to it. I don't want to hear all this and anyway it's distracting to you for me to be sitting there while you talk to John.' But it meant I couldn't get on with my play because there was such a commotion going on all day.

Poor Verushka was badly affected by something she ate at the hill-top restaurant which was not her sort of place at all, fairly rough.

She is distressed because her holiday is being ruined, to say nothing of messages from Cavendish Avenue that Nadje, my mother-in-law, has been leaning out of her window shouting for help because she was being kept a prisoner there. The neighbours got the police in. Then the ambulance came but she refused to go to hospital. Fortunately, Caroline [Banszky], who for once behaved rather well, went to see her and calmed her down and told her not to behave in such a crazy way. The next thing will be all that in the newspapers, too.

So I am not getting the peaceful holiday I had hoped here.

Friday 21 August

Rosemary is frightfully pleased with herself, now she is well ensconced in Number 11. Norman very sensibly said, 'You know we wouldn't get all these invitations if I weren't Chancellor of the Exchequer. You will find you have got very few friends when I leave that job.' He is very practical. I said, 'I will always be your friend.' He said, 'I know that.'

I got through to Pericles and wished him a happy birthday for the 22nd. He has now abandoned his Trusthouse Forte job. It doesn't pay him enough, too long hours. He's working for the Raspberry Review Bar Restaurant where he earns double the money for much fewer hours.

Saturday 22 August

The saga with sterling continues. Washington, the Prime Minister, the Governor of the Bank of England and goodness knows who else are trying to do something about averting putting up interest rates.

This little library is now used as a centre for Norman to conduct all the arrangements to defend the pound. He is chucking money at it. They are probably losing a lot because all the banks which are supposed to come to the rescue haven't done much about it, for either the dollar or the pound.

Sunday 23 August

Norman's conversations with the Prime Minister go on. Norman is going to go back tomorrow but not motoring through France.

Today was their last evening, I had promised Sophie that we would have the great game where you act out plays and songs and films and books. To dinner came Mr and Mrs Burrell, Margot and Mark (the mother and father) and Anthony and William the sons.[7] There was a daughter of sixteen or seventeen who I thought rather pretty. Also came Daisy Corsini.[8]

I appointed Sophie to be captain of one of the two teams, which thrilled her.

I proposed that Norman should be made to act the Iron Chancellor, which he did extraordinarily well but they guessed it immediately. They did not guess my Madame Butterfly.

Monday 24 August
Before Norman went I told him, 'If you have to put interest rates up, then put them up by a full point. That would annoy a lot of business people but it won't matter. You won't have to do it for long but it will be a token that you are absolutely determined not to go the devaluation route.'

I enjoy it when the Lamonts stay. I like Sophie very much and am deeply fond of Norman. He and his daughter very much resemble each other in gentleness, though Norman is extremely tough when it comes to politics and dealing with the pound.

Livia arrived looking rather thin, poor dear, and pale. I think she is very sad and lonely and acutely missing Witold.

Norman rang. There are photographs of him in the *Star* and in the *Mirror* as well, at the Pellicano when we went there to lunch on Saturday. He was sitting next to Eva [Pejacesvich] in one picture and in the other he was playing table tennis.

I don't think it matters very much but he felt it was so harassing that he couldn't even have a game of table tennis, having gone to lunch as a guest of the proprietor and then being pictured in a luxury hotel as though he had paid a fortune for it.

I said, 'How are you getting on with the more serious subject?' He said, 'Not very well. It is very difficult indeed. Yesterday the pound was just on two dollars. It strengthened mildly towards the Deutschmark but the dollar is so linked to the pound that we go down with it in the end, if we can't do something about it.'

---

7. Mark Burrell, development director, Pearson, since 1986 (executive director, 1986–97); director BSB Holdings from 1987, BSkyB Group 1991–4; m (1966) Margot, née Pearce.
8. Daughter of Gino and Amy Corsini.

Norman was amazed when Rupert made Peter Stothard editor of the *Times*. I said so was I. We both think he will be useless. He doesn't write very well. He is as wet as anything and rather too left in many respects.

Friday 28 August

William Shawcross arrived. Olga is thrilled and delighted. They are like a honeymoon couple. He teases her about Charlie Allsopp.

She smirked away like a girl of eighteen instead of over forty. I am very fond of Olga. She is sweet and kind and she does have a beautiful figure, though her face is not exactly beautiful but handsome.

William said he had been derided for not attacking Rupert in his book. It came out too late for him to talk about his extraordinary behaviour to Richard Searby. This is a lifelong friend of Rupert's who was chairman of the whole shooting match.

He gave up his law practice and all the rest of it to be with Rupert. Then suddenly Rupert got rid of him with no explanation. Searby is a very nice man. I met him often with Rupert. He is too nice to make attacks on Rupert and he is completely stunned.

William said, 'The trouble with Rupert is he has got no one at his court who ever dares to disagree with him.' I said, 'I do,' and I explained what had happened with Norman.

I thought, 'Maybe I will get the chop suddenly.'

Olga is going on to Portugal in the Forte company jet. Rocco[9] wants her to persuade her father to stand down as chairman and become a distant president, leaving Rocco to run the business entirely by himself.

My own view is that old Charles Forte knows far more about running it than Rocco ever will and has much better judgement.

I asked Olga what she would do. She said, 'I will try to work out some little compromise. When my father plays golf, which he loves doing, he likes me to go round caddying for him. I will talk to him and raise the subject with him and see if we can get something arranged which Rocco will feel is all right and my father will feel is all right.' Olga is his favourite child, as well she might be because she has such guts and liveliness of brain. If she had been a boy, he would have handed the whole business over to her.

William said that when Richard Searby was dismissed by Rupert, his oldest friend who was at school with him and had stuck by him

---

9. Only son of Lord Forte, brother of Olga.*

through thick and thin, Rupert couldn't face telling him himself but got the head man in Australia to hand him a letter to say his appointment as Chairman had terminated. Rupert is very curious and shy and embarrassed when this sort of thing happens but I think he should have had the guts to speak to Richard himself.

William said, 'Of course it may well be it is no good having him as Chairman of News Corporation now as it is such an American-oriented company based in Hollywood and Los Angeles.'[10]

Saturday 29 August
Had another long conversation with Gino Corsini who is almost in despair as to what was to be done about Italy.

Corruption operates at every single level. It's a way of life. That's why the Italians want the EC in Brussels to be a complete political union in the hope somebody else will run the country for them.

Monday 31 August
I have booked the house for next year but I don't know if I shall have any money by then. Most of what I bought on the stock exchange is half or less the price I paid, sometimes a tenth.

---

10. Twentieth Century Fox is one of News Corporation's companies.

Tuesday 1 September
Norman is not at Number 11 because repairs and alterations have to be done. Dorneywood is closed and he has a secret address.

I rang him there and asked him to look and see if they had got one of my shirts. Rosemary first said no, then looked while I was talking to Norman and said yes, she had it. Norman is still having a rough time trying to avoid putting up interest rates.

I was very bad at sending out postcards this year.

I remembered to send one to Peter Stothard, the new editor-to-be of the *Times*. I am not convinced he will be all that good but he may be.

I got back a very nice letter from him which I found comforting. I hope he may give me more space than Simon Jenkins.

I can't quite remember what he looks like but he has certainly been here to this house for lunch, among others with Kingsley Amis.[1]

Friday 4 September
Spoke to Duke Hussey having failed to get John Birt[2] who is on holiday. Ian Orr-Ewing[3] and Julian Lewis[4] are in a state of uproar. It was reported in the *Times* that Liz Forgan[5] is about to be appointed Deputy Director-General of the BBC. As I couldn't get hold of John Birt, I asked Duke Hussey if that was true.

He said he thought it must be nonsense.

1. On 28 January 1986 and, with Amis, on 18 September 1986: see Vol. 1, pp. 76–7 and 192.
2. Deputy Director General, BBC, 1987–92, Director General, 1992–2000; knight 1998, life peer 2000.
3. (1912–99); Outside Broadcasts Manager, BBC, 1946–8; Conservative MP, 1950–70, Civil Lord of the Admiralty, 1959–63; baronet 1963, life peer 1971.
4. Research director and director, Coalition for Peace Through Security, 1981–5; director, Policy Research Associates from 1985; Deputy Director, Conservative Research Department, 1990–6; MP since 1997.
5. Director of Programmes, Channel 4 Television, at this time.

He told me he thought the reforms were going to cause a great deal of trouble and one of the difficulties is that Checkland[6] still hangs on as Director-General, though he knows he is going.

He said, 'That was the only way I could get the governors to agree to John Birt's appointment, which most of them didn't want and most people in the BBC don't want either, by allowing Checkland to serve out his time.'

Sunday 6 September

Norman is against the Queen paying income tax but there is some suggestion that she might. He said the handing back the Crown Estates lark wouldn't work. That's because the Crown Estates previously used to pay the army and part of the civil service and so forth.

Tuesday 8 September

At twenty to eight Rupert rang from his car on the way to work in Wapping but he didn't stop talking until five past eight when he actually arrived. He was going on about the interest rates and so forth, admitting this time that the world is in a hell of a mess – but we are making it worse for ourselves.

However, he did agree that Norman had done quite well in arranging the surprise loan to prop up the pound.[7]

Yesterday I had spoken to Peter Stehrenberger of the *Times*. I said, 'This is the time of year when we discuss my increase. Last year I got nothing. There has been 10 per cent inflation in the intervening period so I should at least go up by 10 per cent but I think I should go up by 15 per cent because of all the extra things I do for Rupert.' He said he understands that and they were particularly pleased with what I did in Hungary to help them so they could run the paper properly and get rid of the old dead-beat Communists who were stifling it.

The great drinks party at Rupert's apartment in St James's. Anna was very friendly telling me about their marvellous yacht. They hope to sail down to see us at Porto Ercole next year.

Young Peter Stothard there.

I said, 'Perhaps you will give me more than my six hundred

---

6. Michael Checkland, Director General, BBC, 1987–92; knight 1992.
7. The Government had taken a £7 billion foreign currency loan to support sterling.

words I have been cut down to, though they gave me a bit more this morning.' He remarked on what a good article it was.[8]

Norman Lamont came.

He talked for quite a long time to Rupert and Rupert was very friendly with him. I went up to them and said, 'Now you say to Norman what you say to me and let him give you his answer,' which Norman did with apparent effectiveness to some degree.

Rupert had asked John Major to come. He said he couldn't but what about dinner, so he was going over to the Stafford Hotel after the party to give John Major dinner, taking young Peter Stothard with him.

Eventually we left with Mrs Stothard to go to dinner with Irwin Stelzer at Harry's Bar. Gerry Malone,[9] one of the two deputy chairmen of the Tory Party, came too, plus his aggressive, boisterous not entirely unattractive doctor wife who works in a Glasgow hospital.

Mrs Stothard sat on my right. She is a novelist and writes under the name of Sally Emerson. She was also the editor of *Books and Bookmen*. She said I used to write for it sometimes.

She said she makes about £20,000 a year [from her novels]. She said the one she liked best was *Separation* so I am going to read that. She is a pleasant woman. She had enjoyed being in Washington.[10] She looks a bit older than Peter Stothard.

Someone asked me did I keep a diary. I said no rather stoutly. I was told I ought to.

I talked to Mrs Stothard about Barbara Pym[11] and told her what I knew about her, my relationship with her through Julian Amery[12] and how she had this great affair with my cousin's husband, C. Gordon Glover.

Gerry Malone was talking about the general election and the

---

8. WW had written about corruption in Italy.
9. Conservative MP, 1983–7 (Aberdeen South) and 1992–7 (Winchester); deputy chairman, Conservative Party, 1992–4, Minister of State, Department of Health, 1994–7; editor, *The Sunday Times Scotland*, 1989–90; m (1981) Anne née Blyth.
10. Peter Stothard had been US editor, the *Times*, 1989–92.
11. Novelist (1913–80). WW says in Vol. 1, p. 15, that 'Jay', an early Pym lover, was Julian Amery; C. Gordon Glover was married to WW's cousin Honor.
12. (1919–96); Conservative politician and minister; life peer 1992.*

Conservative, the dreadful Browne,[13] who had been thrown out of the party for his disgraceful conduct in not disclosing his interests to the House of Commons, to say nothing of his appalling treatment of his wife whom he managed to make just about bankrupt by claiming all kinds of rights from her because of her previous husband's money.

Browne said to Gerry Malone, 'We don't really want two Conservative candidates here. We're just splitting the vote. Let's toss a coin. If I win, I'll be the Conservative candidate and you will support me, and if I lose, it will be the other way round.' Gerry Malone was absolutely furious. He said, 'Of course I wouldn't do anything so damn silly. You're finished anyway.' The outcome was that Gerry Malone's vote increased the majority for the Conservatives.

Mrs Malone was really too rumbustious.

She said at one point that the people in her hospital, the staff, were amazed when they discovered she was a Conservative MP's wife. 'You are so caring,' they said.

At Rupert's party I was astonished to see Caroline Banszky, for some reason with her brother-in-law. She kissed me very affectionately which I thought was a change.

Her brother-in-law is now a partner in Arthur Anderson who are the accountants to Rupert's News International.

Not for the first time I had kissed the wrong woman. It was not Caroline Banzsky but her twin sister who looks exactly like her and now does her hair in precisely the same way.

Thursday 10 September
Brian [McDonnell] came for a sandwich lunch with Roy Hilsley[14] as a preliminary to our meeting [about the Lottery bid] with the Chairman of the Post Office and the Managing Director of Post Office Counters. The meeting went extremely well. Like them, we may join

---

13. John Browne, Conservative MP for Winchester, 1979–92, was censured in 1990 by the Commons Select Committee on Members' Interests for non-disclosure of foreign payments. He was awarded £175,000 in the divorce settlement with his first wife Elizabeth, née Garthwaite, to whom he had been married for 18 years (1965–83); he returned to court in 1986 for the enforcement of the final £65,000, leaving her apparently almost destitute. After deselection he contested the seat in 1992 as an Independent Conservative but was defeated by Malone.
14. Tote Technical Director.

several consortiums. They agreed we had a very good product in our device.[15]

They are talking of some thirty thousand outlets plus the possibility of pubs, which I don't think will happen.

Friday 11 September
I rang Rupert to ask him how the dinner had gone with the new editor of the *Times* and John Major.

'Did John make some impression on Peter?' He said, 'Yes, quite a lot.'

I said to Norman that I thought Peter Stothard might probably make quite a good editor. He promptly said, 'That's not what you said in Italy. You said you thought he wouldn't be any good, too weak and not strong enough on the right.' I said, 'At the party on Tuesday he told me what a fan he is of mine.'

Norman laughed. He said, 'Remember what you said in *To the Point*.[16] You said that Beaverbrook charmed you with his flattery and you would always defend him thereafter, which you have done.' I said, 'Yes, flattery makes a lot of difference.'

Sunday 13 September
I had been dodging Margaret because I was nervous of her reactions to my support for Major and Norman over interest rates and not devaluing and so forth. I hadn't spoken to her since before the end of July when I went on holiday. I thought I must not be a coward and ring her. She was very friendly.

On Douglas Hurd she thinks he is now hopeless, quite ineffective over Yugoslavia. She said, 'Owen was a fool to accept the job of mediator. He won't do any good at it and Douglas was wrong to give it to him.'

She is off to Washington in the morning. She is going to raise more money. I said, 'You're doing well for the Foundation?' She said, 'Yes, but also with the lectures.'

Then I said I thought Bush would win. She said, 'I hope very much

---

15. The plan was to adapt for the Lottery the Tote machines which linked betting shops to the Tote pools on course.
16. *To the Point* (1981) was a collection of short *causerie* pieces by WW; 'Flattery' is on p. 97.

he does. It will be a disaster otherwise.' I said, 'I am not so sure about that. Nothing much would change.'

She then said, 'It's appalling that they are contemplating giving Neil Kinnock[17] the EC Commissioner job with a large salary at Brussels. He is the enemy we have fought for years and he will only combine with our other enemies in Brussels and do Britain down because he is a deep-dyed socialist.'

In the end she said to me, 'Cheer up.' I said, 'I think I am not so gloomy as you are. I think Britain has still got a lot of life in it. Your achievements were so solid that you've made it possible for Britain to advance and I think somehow or other it will.'

Monday 14 September
Rang Norman before going to bed. He is quite pleased at the result of his efforts so far. I said, 'It was entirely due to you that the Germans reduced their interest rates at all [this morning].' He said yes, that was so. 'The point everybody is missing is that the reduction, even though it is only by 0.25 per cent, is an indication to everybody that they are not going to put them up which is vital at the moment.'

Wednesday 16 September
Horrifying stories on the wireless and in the newspapers. The German Bundesbank and Germany are saying they expect a realignment of currencies and the pound will be devalued. Senior officials from the Treasury were anonymously quoted as saying there probably would have to be a devaluation, or realignment as it is politely called but it is the same thing, because a two per cent or three per cent interest rate increase wouldn't hold the pound.

As soon as the markets opened the pound was under great pressure again. I rang Norman and said, 'Look here, are you starting to give in?' He hadn't seen the report on the right-hand side of the *Times* so he read it and was very cross about it. He said, 'I don't know where all that comes from. It's a lot of rubbish.'

I said, 'Have you spent all that £7.2 billion you borrowed?' 'Oh no,' he said. I said, 'You're not going to do anything about devaluation, are you?' He said, 'Good heavens, of course not.'

Later there were amazing convolutions.

Norman put interest rates up by two per cent. No good. He put

---

17. Leader, Labour Party, 1983–92; EC Transport Commissioner, 1995–9.

them up another three per cent. Still no good. The pound didn't hold to its permitted low level in the ERM. Then came Norman's announcement that he had suspended our membership of the Exchange Rate Mechanism and the pound would therefore be allowed to find its own level. I rang the private office and said, 'Whatever happens you must say this is NOT a devaluation. A devaluation is when you are tied to a fixed rate and you decide on a figure by which you devalue. This did not happen.' They said they would make that point.

Naturally all the ignorant commentators say it is devaluation, but it isn't.

Thursday 17 September

Norman rings at twenty-five past seven. He has amazing energy and resilience. I was much impressed that he was still so lively and so early in the morning. I said, 'Were you up all night?' He said, 'No, not quite.' There was a meeting of finance ministers in Brussels and hoo-ha going on with the Germans and Norman was quite roughly attacked. I said, 'You have done exactly the right thing and there may be a lot of advantages.' He said, 'Don't say this but my intention is that we don't go back into the ERM for a very long time.' I said, 'I hope we never do, certainly not until we're in a much stronger position.'

He had hoped to keep us OK with the two per cent increase in interest rates and then with the three per cent one. When he saw the two per cent had absolutely no effect whatever he was dumbstruck. That is why he went on with the three per cent. I said, 'Have we lost a great deal?' He said, 'It is quite severe.' Gradually I got the impression we had actually lost only about twenty per cent of the money we had borrowed and put into it so it may not be as bad as he thinks.

He said it was terrible that we got so near to pulling it off and then it slipped away. He said did I agree it was OK not to give any time for when we would go back into the ERM. I said, 'Oh yes. You must vague it out and say the situation will be watched to see what conditions are.'

After lunch Christopher Haines came from the Jockey Club. He is very friendly these days. He asked how could he help us get the Lottery to be run by the Tote. I explained what we had done about it, saying that racing will benefit from us if we run the Lottery, which is some compensation for the loss racing is bound to sustain from the Lottery in the betting shops and therefore the levy.

Friday 18 September

Last night, before going to bed and in bed, I read the novel *Separation* by Peter Stothard's wife. To my surprise it is extraordinarily good.

It should have been entered for the Booker prize and it ought to have won it.

The newspapers are plastered with demands that Norman should resign. They don't like to say the Prime Minister should go, though it is his policy as much as Norman's. Norman quite rightly says there is no question of it.

The stock exchange has soared. Business seems very pleased about something they are trying to condemn him for.

I spoke to Tessa Keswick. She said she thought maybe he ought to resign because, after all, it looks a bit untidy at the top of the Treasury, bumbling about.

At lunch time Norman rang. I told him what I was going to say in my article in the *News of the World*. He said, 'Don't go too hard on not reducing interest rates because I propose to have some [reduction].'

I therefore adjusted my article a bit.

Kohl had just called for Norman's removal saying he wasn't fit to be a minister. His actual remark was his conduct was 'inappropriate for a minister.' I said to Norman 'That's fine. I'll put it in my article that Kohl wants you sacked, so sucks to him, or words to that effect,' which was duly done.

Norman is going off to the IMF, Washington, tonight. He said Mrs Thatcher was ringing all her friends saying, 'Isn't it marvellous, I told you so, etc.'

I think the calls for Norman's resignation are very likely to die down. Why not Major's? He was in it just as much as Norman.

This whole affair ought to unite the fanatical anti-EC people and the moderately pro-EC people in the Tory Party. There seems to be nothing left to quarrel about.

On one of the occasions when I was trying to get Norman and I got Rosemary, she was very appreciative of my backing of Norman. She said she heard at one point that Major had prevented him doing something he wanted to do. I asked Norman about that later and he said he didn't know anything about that. He might have not been willing to tell me.

Saturday 19 September
Rupert rang in the afternoon from America.

He said Norman ought to resign.

I said, 'Nonsense. They pulled off a great coup. You seem to have misunderstood it. The Germans wanted to force us to formally devalue but we didn't.'

He said, 'I don't go along with blaming the Germans.' I said, 'You should. It's their policy. They lost two wars because of us and now they're trying to conquer us by other means. Read my article in the *News of the World* tomorrow.'

He said, 'Lamont and Major have been discredited.'

I said, 'I don't think they have at all. You wanted us to be out of the ERM and now we're out of it.'

I asked him whether he had spoken to Peter Stehrenberger about my pay. He said, 'Andrew Knight is dealing with that. He'll be in touch with you about it.' That sounded a bad sign but Rupert is never able to talk directly to his friends about anything he finds awkward.

Monday 21 September
Andrew Knight rings up pursuant to what Rupert told me.

After he complained that we hadn't asked him to dinner and he hadn't seen us lately, he said, 'Don't you think there should be no pay rises at all in the present situation?' I said, 'Not in my case. I have been without a pay rise for two years, not even catching up with inflation. Also, I do things other than mere journalism,' and I pointed out what I did in Hungary as well as making William Shawcross's book a good deal less hard on Rupert.

He said, 'What about £110,000?'

I said, 'I'll suggest a compromise so make it £112,500.' He said, 'All right then. I'll tell Rupert I was defeated in a difficult negotiation.'

We then talked about his role in News International.

He said, 'People think I am expecting to take over when Rupert dies but that has never been the case. I'm only here running it for Rupert until his children are able to take over. The three of them are very able, Elisabeth particularly.'

Tuesday 22 September
Left for Brussels at a quarter to seven from Cavendish Avenue and returned at a quarter past four. Interesting meeting with EC officials. Concluded it is now impossible to get them to do anything about

persuading or overriding the British gambling laws which would enable Sunday racing to take place properly. Also impossible to get them to insist that the French let us bet into their pools and them to bet into ours because this is only one European partner with another and it is not a major cross-border problem. However, the meeting was worthwhile. Then it was off to Olga Polizzi's house where the publishers were giving a party for William Shawcross's book.

Paul Johnson said Mellor should resign at once because it was disgraceful taking money for his air fare.[18] I said, 'I don't think that necessarily stands up. Churchill, for example, was not only bailed out often by his friends but he accepted lavish hospitality from them including air fares, and so have many other politicians.'

Paul Johnson kept saying that all the working classes want her [Margaret] back now.

How he would know such a thing I cannot imagine because he doesn't know any working-class people.

I felt rather sad when I saw Petronella's flat on Monday evening. It's nice and she likes to be on her own. But it is somehow cheerless, not warm enough. I felt she looked a fragile little figure sitting in it. It's all glass in the front, too clinical, not yet a friendly place.

Wednesday 23 September
Spoke to Norman for the first time since he got back from Washington. I asked if he had seen the *Sun* this morning.

The *Sun*'s new policy is that Lamont must stay. That's because he has cut the interest rates and they have suddenly decided they like him. I said, 'I think it must have been at Rupert's instigation. But I am a bit worried about your interest rates. I think one whole point down might be a bit too much but I suppose you know what you're doing.' He laughed and said, 'I hope so.'

Went to Levy Board meeting.

I am getting a bit nervous. Some days I am not as alert and on the ball as I should be. But I think I can overcome that by will power.

---

18. From Mona Bauwens, at whose villa in Marbella the Mellors had a holiday; her father was a prominent funder of the Palestine Liberation Organization.

I then saw Jane [McKerron].[19] She maintains that the manuscript is wonderful and my descriptions of people are good, although I should have more of them.

I said, 'Sometimes I think I go on a bit too long.' She said she thought that was true on some subjects but they could be weeded out eventually.

I said, 'Yes but I want this to be published in its entirety one day after I'm dead, the whole damn lot, even if it has to wait fifty years or more before everybody concerned is dead.' She had thought of trying to get prepared for a first edition, as it were, the first one to come out as soon as I am dead. I said, 'It is very difficult to judge exactly what you should put in that until you see the thing in the round. In just the same way I have several times thought about writing an introduction, but it would be a different introduction according to when I wrote it. In the end I think I shall just say why I decided to keep the diary, having not kept one before, and leave the thing to speak for itself.'[20]

Thursday 24 September

The lead item in the news is, 'Is Mellor going to resign? Shouldn't he resign?' and all that kind of lark. Hardly the most important matter facing the nation. He said that he would resign if it embarrassed the Prime Minister and the party for him to stay. I don't know how much further he thinks he can go in embarrassment, but he has a very good point: why should the tabloid newspapers decide who should be in the government and not the Prime Minister?

A dinner party in advance of Verushka's birthday, at Cavendish Avenue. As Micky Suffolk[21] was coming, I gave them some of the new Tursan white wine produced by Monsieur Guérard, owner of Les Prés d'Eugénie and Le Couvent des Herbes at Eugénie-les-Bains. It is a

---

19. Journalist and author; former wife of Brian Walden (television presenter and newspaper columnist; Labour MP, 1964–77); WW had designated her as editor of his journals and sent her copies of the manuscript as it was typed up.

20. WW never did write an introduction but from time to time he gives his reasons for keeping a diary. The three volumes now published contain 750,000 words. The full manuscript totals over three million words, a huge amount to be published in its entirety, though some of the material omitted might be of interest after the passage of years. The introduction to this volume explains how the selection was made by the present editor, it is hoped in the manner WW would have wanted.

21. 21st Earl of Suffolk and Berkshire; wine connoisseur.

three-star restaurant and he serves this wine at it. It is difficult to get and very expensive.

William Shawcross sat at the head of the table at the opposite end to me with Verushka on his right. Olga was also there, so were the Wiltons. Tessa Keswick was there by herself because Henry was in Hong Kong. Sandra Howard came by herself with Michael to join later, after the great debate on the pound and Maastricht finished in the Commons. Tessa had to go early to hold Kenneth Clarke's hand while he was making a broadcast on the situation. William had to go early because he was doing a programme about his Rupert Murdoch book. His place was taken by Robin Day who came in after doing something else.

I told Frank Johnson that on no account was he to attack Norman.

Robin Day was bellowing away about Mellor, whose resignation was announced in the late afternoon.

Robin said, 'He shouldn't stay with people like that. It was all right for Churchill and Bonar Law in those days [to accept hospitality].'

I said, 'What you mean is Mellor is very common and the others were gentlemen. That is your snobbish explanation of why you don't mind what gentlemen do but you do mind what people like Mellor do because they don't do it in the right style.'

Michael Howard turned up. Anxiously I asked him how Norman had got on. He said, 'Extremely well. He spoke with great authority, completely floored his critics, tied up Gordon Brown and John Smith, and there is not the slightest suggestion left that he should resign.'

Michael Howard said that Gordon Brown, in winding up for the Opposition, had referred to the great party which Norman Lamont had given at Number 11 on June 25th. He was recounting how Norman had been wasting time instead of attending to affairs of state and the star of the dance and the dinner had been the Hon. Petronella Wyatt who sang 'Lili Marlene'. When Petronella was told this she was justifiably delighted.

Saturday 26 September
To Ascot and lunch with Piers Bengough in his room.

After doing my rounds I went up to the Royal Box and had a long conversation with the Duchess of Gloucester whom I had never spoken to properly before. I complimented her on her very pretty outfit and the brooch which adorned it. It turned out that she was dressed by

Franka.[22] She is Danish. We talked about the Danes and their referendum. She was very intelligent about it, saying that many Danes
regretted what they had done.

If only the Princess of Wales and the Duchess of York had been
something like her there would have been no trouble at all.

Dinner with Rupert Murdoch.

Rupert said he thought Major was turning out to be not much
good, nothing like Mrs Thatcher and would probably be going soon.
I said, 'I think that's extremely unlikely.'

However, Rupert is still full of praise for Norman, telling me to
give him advice that he should not only cut interest rates but take
away mortgage relief and capital gains tax because it was costing the
country so many billions.

He said he thought Mellor's resignation had been engineered to
come just on the day when Major had to make a big speech in the
Commons to distract attention. I said, 'I think that's making John out
a great deal cleverer than he is.'

For some reason the conversation got on to Barbara Amiel and
Conrad Black. I said, 'She's a very attractive girl and very amusing
and intelligent and she writes very well. But I think she's extremely
neurotic and would be hell to live with.'

Suddenly we saw them at a table behind us.

We all wondered whether they had heard us talking about them. We
assumed not because there was a good deal of shouting and it wasn't
necessarily very distinct.

Sunday 27 September
Spoke to Norman and said, 'What is all this rot in the newspapers
about you and Major being divided and leading separate wings of the
party?' He said, 'Of course it is rot and I am very annoyed about it.'

So when I had finished talking to Norman I rang Downing Street.
I was put through to John straight away. I said, 'I am so annoyed
about the unfair way you're being treated by the press, rubbishing all
you've been doing. I'm ringing you up to say take no notice.'

He said, 'I knew that once David [Mellor] went, I would then be
the target and they would move the attack on to me.'

After a good deal of friendly conversation I said, 'Be of good cheer.'

---

22. Couture dressmaker, born in Croatia, m Baron Jan Staël von Holstein; Verushka
    was among her other fashionable clients.

He said, 'I always feel better when I talk to you, Woodrow.' So that was nice.

It was like when I used to ring Margaret when she was under fire and I tried to cheer her up.

Rupert rang before leaving on his world-wide tour to collect longer-term money at lower interest rates which would strengthen News International and News Corporation considerably. He said he thought the profits would double this year and they have already been very good.

Tuesday 29 September
To my horror, in the *Daily Telegraph* I saw that dear, darling William Douglas-Home[23] was dead. True, he was eighty but I fear all the lights are going out around me. I felt very sad and remembered all the jolly, happy times we had together and the jokes he made. He was a terrible gambler and I dare say he was left with no money at all except for the continuing royalties from his plays.

---

23. Playwright, younger brother of the Conservative Prime Minister, Sir Alec Douglas-Home.

Thursday 1 October

Norman rang at twenty past eight. What did I think of the latest state of the row? The German Ambassador leaked to the press a confidential document from the Bundesbank railing against Britain and vice versa – what the Bundesbank should have done to help the pound and how they helped the French more, and so forth, denials and counter denials, Norman should resign and all the rest of it.

I asked him what John Major thought. He said, 'He is so fed up with all these rows with the German Bundesbank and everyone else that he now wants to rush the Maastricht Treaty through Parliament immediately.' I said, 'That's very unwise. He's got to collect the codicil about subsidiarity first and if he doesn't, he might come a cropper.' Norman said he doesn't seem to care.

It was a beautiful day at Newmarket.

I had come to see Pyrrhic Dance for the first time on a racetrack.

It was a very smart Maiden with extremely grand horses, trainers and owners.[1] Serena Rothschild had a horse in the same race. She rushed across and greeted me with great enthusiasm, flinging her arms around me. She was looking rather pretty in a blue outfit with a white thing in the front by her neck. I am very fond of that girl. She said what a lark it was that we both had a horse in the same race.

Little Miss Olga Gold, another of the partnership, was there by herself. A neat girl, nicely dressed in a black and yellow outfit. She works in medical research at Oxford. I am surprised she had the money.

Mrs Hills said didn't I think Pyrrhic Dance looked a very nice horse going round. I said, 'Yes, but unfortunately so do most of the others.'

The jockey, brother of John Hills, was wearing my old colours, the Hastings[2] original ones. He came in eighth. He said he almost dropped out halfway through but he said to Pyrrhic Dance, 'Oh no, you're not

---

1. A Maiden is a race for horses which have not previously won prizes.
2. Hastings is the family name of Moorea, WW's third wife, daughter of the 15th Earl of Huntingdon.

going to do that,' and gave him one or two slaps and then he finished quite brightly with nine rather grand horses behind him. One of them was Serena's which came in ninth.

So it could have been worse.

Friday 2 October
Spoke to Norman early in the morning.

He said he was pretty cheerful but they weren't so cheerful at Number 10.

The Tory press has gone mad attacking Major for having no policy which is quite untrue. Our press and media think they perform the function of informing and therefore must be free. The real function they perform is that of misinforming.

Now the *Sun* is running a great campaign, a telephone poll, 'Would you like Mrs Thatcher back?' She is cock-a-hoop; so is Tebbit and some of her friends.

Saturday 3 October
Norman said they are still in a great state at Number 10 but at least John Major has calmed down about suddenly rushing through the Maastricht Treaty.

Reading the Beaverbrook book[3] reminded me of how I had failed, in that at one time I had hoped to be a kind of newspaper magnate like Rupert Murdoch or Beaverbrook. Beaverbrook urged me to go into newspapers or business, to have a business of my own to protect me against outrageous fortune if I got flung out of Parliament, as one does from time to time. I tried and I failed from over-enthusiasm and conceit, thinking I could advance more rapidly than was possible.

At one time I had the lovely little *Banbury Guardian* and if I had been more cautious and taken time over it, I could have built it up into a network and done something with it nationally. It was sheer vanity that I didn't, thinking myself cleverer than I am. It was also bust up by the divorce with Moorea because she had provided the money for the enterprise. I had to raise £300,000, one way or another, and that included selling the *Banbury Guardian*. So I just had the printing works, which was really not my cup of tea, and that finally went bust.

---

3. *Beaverbrook: a Life* by Anne Chisholm and Michael Davie which WW reviewed in the *Times* of 1 October.

Sunday 4 October
A conversation with Norman about his speech for the Tory Party
Conference. It is mundane, more or less OK but not enough kick in it.
I drafted this morning for him a passage in which he should attack the
press, enlarging on what they think is their duty to inform into their
right to misinform, etc. He thought it was very interesting but he didn't
think he dare do it because he didn't want bad relations with the press.
I said, 'You have them already.'

A little later on he rang me and said would I find out something
about Margaret. He had heard that she intends to speak just before
him, saying he had got it all wrong and denouncing him. I said, 'That
doesn't sound very like her.'

I said, 'I am mildly terrified of ringing her. I know she is going to
tick me off because I have been supporting John. But I suppose I shall
have to screw up my courage and do it.' So at a quarter past six I
rang her.

Mark answered the telephone.

He said, 'Mother's on the telephone to somebody in America. I'll
tell her you've rung and I'm sure she'll call you back.'

Nothing happened until a quarter to eight. Then she rang. For ten
minutes I got a terrific dressing-down.

I said, 'John's in a difficult position. He promised the others to
ratify the Maastricht Treaty.' She said, 'It's only his vanity which is
making him stick to it.' I said, 'But I thought you believed he was the
best Prime Minister to follow you.' She said, 'Really it wasn't that at
all. It was just that he was the best of three bad candidates.' As she is
very disappointed with him, she now says she never thought him any
good at all.

Then she said, 'We shouldn't have any Commissioners in Brussels
at all. We should only have civil servants. The Commissioners should
be abolished and the civil servants should just do what governments
tell them and nothing else.'

Actually I think she has got something there.

She said, 'Woodrow, they've clouded your vision,' by which she
meant I was wobbling like mad and departing from the true faith,
which I suppose is partly true.

'Do you speak to Norman at all?' She said, 'No, I haven't seen him
since I had dinner at your house when he said he thought a single
currency wasn't a bad idea. Terrible, I don't know what's come over
him.'

She said, 'Norman should say tomorrow that we're not going back into the ERM.' Curiously, that was what Rupert had said when he rang from an aeroplane this afternoon on his way to Boston.

I said, 'Why don't you say some of these things to them yourself? Have you had any contact with Major?' She said, 'No. He doesn't speak to me at all. You've got to tell them, Woodrow. They won't listen to me.' (I thought, poor little me if I've got to carry all this. It's a very difficult trick for me to perform.)

Then she said, 'There are four people in the Cabinet who should stop the whole thing: Norman, Lilley, Portillo and Howard. They should say they will resign if they go ahead with Maastricht. But they haven't got the guts or the courage to stand by their principles.'

So I got a real earful.

She went on, 'I hope Major will speak for Britain at the party conference.' I said, 'We don't want him to go, do we?'

She said, 'We don't want to get rid of him because the alternative, if Labour got in, is too awful to contemplate.' (This seems slightly inconsistent with her view that Labour is exactly the same as the Tories now.)

I said, 'Maybe, I sometimes think, there might be a possibility of your returning.' She said, 'No, I don't think that is ever going to happen. I've given up all thought of that. What I can do is to try to stop them letting down the country and breaking all their promises. The whole affair, getting out of the ERM, the manner in which it was done, was too incompetent for words, absolutely ghastly.'

I rang Norman and gave him the gist of it.

Norman giggled a bit at some of the things. I said, 'But you can't disregard her, you know. She's not a lone voice.' He said, 'I wouldn't disregard her anyway, even if she was a lone voice.'

When I put down the telephone, I remembered that Norman had a row with Gordon Brown about his speech in the emergency debate when he had referred to Petronella.

Actually, she didn't mind a bit.

Norman adores Petronella. I don't always adore her.

She overspends like a lunatic. She gets it all from her mother. She has never heard of public transport. She takes taxis from Kensington to the Isle of Dogs or wherever the *Sunday Telegraph* is. But I suppose I am proud of her because she is incredibly intelligent and clever and writes like a dream.

Wednesday 7 October
I went to see Hayden Phillips, Permanent Secretary at the National Heritage ministry.[4] I knew him of old when he was Roy Jenkins' *chef de cabinet* when he was President of the Commission.

We [the Tote] are definitely going to get the alteration to the legislation put into the new Bill.

Friday 9 October
Got my article off to the *News of the World* and set sail for Venice. We were met at the airport by Alistair McAlpine's[5] motor boat and his boatman. It was cold and wet. Alistair and Romilly were on the plane with us.

We said we would take them out to dinner because they hadn't had time to organize anything in their house which is by the Arsenal. It was the first naval dockyard in the world and that is why every similar naval centre is called Arsenal. There is an absolutely beautiful entrance to it with lions from Athens and other places, looted from time to time by the Venetians.

I had not known Alistair very well before though I had always liked him. He is very funny. Thoroughly anti-Major but pro-Norman. He said Norman ought to resign and then become Prime Minister in two years' time. Alistair is writing a column every week now in the *Sunday Express*. He said he had to take up journalism to earn some money because there are no dividends coming in from the great McAlpine building and construction company: times are so bad.

He likes doing it very much, actually, because it gave him another angle on power and influence.

He is still passionately pro-Margaret though he thinks she has been rather foolish lately. He has written a book called *The Servant* which is based on his serving Margaret which he did for a long time, particularly when he was Treasurer of the Tory Party and raised all the money they needed.

He is a great collector. He has boxes full of 1920s ties at the

4. Deputy *chef de cabinet* to EC President, 1977–9; permanent secretary, Department for Culture, Media & Sport (formerly National Heritage), 1992–8, Lord Chancellor's Department since 1998; knight 1998.
5. Alistair McAlpine, businessman and writer; Hon. Treasurer, Conservative Party, 1975–90; life peer 1984; m 2 (1980) separated (2000) Romilly Thompson, née Hobbs, businesswoman.

moment. At one time he had collected modern sculptures and art. When Ted Heath won the election in 1970, he was so pleased he gave the whole lot to the Tate Gallery.

They used to see a great deal of Margaret and stay with her at Chequers. They even went on Christmas Day. Once, when the guests were getting towards the end of their lunch, Margaret made them march off to the television to watch the Queen's speech and then asked everybody what they thought of it. They had to stand to attention when 'God Save the Queen' was played and stand up while they watched the Queen speaking. I said, 'How odd.' Alistair said, 'It wasn't all that odd because it was a way of getting them all to go. Denis by that time was always fed up with the guests.'

One Christmas they had been given an enormous quantity of caviar by Lord Hanson. Margaret asked Romilly, who used to own a food shop called Hobbs in South Audley Street, how much it was worth. She said, 'About £1,500.' 'Good Heavens!' said Margaret. 'We can't leave that lying about for people to eat. [Let's] keep it for Denis when he is alone by himself. Can we put it in the fridge?'

They found in the kitchen that no tinfoil had been put over anything in the fridges and the place was very dirty. Margaret started cleaning it up, putting tinfoil over things and carefully prepared the foil for the caviar. They thought it very funny that Margaret was washing up and doing all the sort of things the servants should have done in this dirty kitchen.

Saturday 10 October
The time for the great dinner arrived for Henry Anglesey's[6] seventieth birthday.

John Julius [Norwich][7] made a very poor speech giving us a history lesson, not entirely accurate, on Venice. He talked a lot of rot about eighteenth-century aristocrats like Henry who came to Venice and bought cheaply Canalettos and took them back to England.

Henry was saying, 'I wish to God we had.'

---

6. 7th Marquess of Anglesey, historian.
7. Viscount Norwich, son of 1st Viscount Norwich (Duff Cooper) and Lady Diana Cooper; he and Henry Anglesey are first cousins through their mothers, daughters of the 8th Duke of Rutland; writer and art historian, former diplomat; chairman of Venice in Peril Fund since 1970; author of *A History of Venice* Vol. 1 (1977), Vol. 2 (1981).

I was unable to sit next to Arabella[8] which I would have preferred. She is Liz Paget's daughter (and Henry's niece). But I was able to talk to her for a bit.

Arabella is married to a very rich fellow, Michael Heathcoat-Amory. When we went I whispered in her ear, 'I have to look out for my wife, you know, but we will meet again.' She laughed.

Sunday 11 October

I woke up feeling strange. It was pouring with rain, a very bad day. I decided I would go with them down the Grand Canal and have a look around.

We set off, Alistair, Verushka and myself, in the motor boat to get off by St Mark's Square. The water had risen very high and parts of St Mark's Square had been flooded again. There was an enormous swell in the sea which was pretty rough. I was smoking a cigar. When we came to get out, the boat yawed away from the side of the jetty and as my foot was going over on a slippery part to get on to the jetty, I fell right into the lagoon, still smoking my cigar. I went into the water above my waist.

Verushka thought I was going to be drowned, so did the boatman, so did Alistair. But they got me out. I badly bruised my leg and I was soaked. I had not been submerged above my waist and I came up still smoking my cigar. The boatman was delighted about that, but they were all very concerned about me.

We were immediately taken back to Henry's house by the boatman. I took off my clothes and went to bed and fell asleep for two hours which seemed to me the best way to shake off any ill effects.

Alistair was saying how badly the campaign to keep Margaret as leader went. He talked of one extraordinary thing. Before she went to Paris, Alistair was there when Peter Morrison,[9] her wet campaign manager, read out to her the numbers and said, 'You're quite safe. You can go to Paris without anybody going over your head in votes.' She

8. Arabella, daughter of Raimund von Hofmannstahl (son of the Austrian poet, playwright and librettist, Hugo von Hofmannstahl) and Lady Elizabeth Paget (one of the five daughters of the 6th Marquess of Anglesey); m 1 (1964–9) Baron Piers von Westenholz, antique dealer and former Olympic skier, m 2 (1975) Michael Heathcoat-Amory, banker.

9. (1944–95); Conservative MP, 1974–92, Deputy Chairman, Conservative Party, 1986–9; knight 1990.

turned to Alistair and said, 'That's exactly what they said to Ted Heath, giving him the numbers showing how he couldn't be defeated, when I won the leadership and defeated him.' She felt by instinct that something awful was going to happen.

Alistair has had six by-pass operations. He had them all at once. He now walks a tremendous lot. He still overeats but he doesn't smoke cigars any more and he doesn't drink wine any more, having sold his wine cellar because of it. But he has a large glass of whisky every night.

Thursday 15 October

I see in the *Financial Times* this morning that Olga Polizzi's mediation when she left us to go to her parents from Porto Ercole seems to have had effect. Charles Forte is no longer Chairman. At the same time Rocco sensibly brought in two high-class players, Anthony Tennant,[10] as Deputy Chairman, and Paul Girolami,[11] Chairman of Glaxo. They are both very hot stuff. Charles Forte will be President and continue to serve on the Board but I don't think he will be able to have a directing role in the same way as before with those two heavyweights on the Board with Rocco.

It is very sad really. Charles is eighty-four. Whether Rocco is right or wrong, Charles has certainly allowed him to do one or two very foolish things lately.

To dinner at George Weidenfeld's for the publication of Cecil Parkinson's book. I found myself sitting with Carla Powell on my left and Rosemary Lamont on my right.

Rosemary said it was a great relief for Norman to have a diversion about the miners.[12] I said, 'Yes. And now that Major is doing something strong and decisive, everybody says he shouldn't have done it.'

Sunday 18 October

Norman rang me back after he had read my article in the *News of the World*.[13]

---

10. Deputy Chairman, Forte, 1992–6; Chairman, Guinness, 1990–2, Christie's International, 1993–6; knight 1992.
11. Director, Forte, 1992–6; Chairman, Glaxo, 1985–94; knight 1988.
12. The sudden announcement of thirty-one pit closures had met fierce opposition from the miners and in Parliament.
13. Headed 'Why we can't turn back the clock to save the pitmen,' one of only a few attempts in the press to support the government.

He said there wasn't really a Cabinet discussion about the pit closures. I said, 'There was no need for one, was there?' He said, 'No, but perhaps it should have been minuted – there was some reference to it in a Cabinet committee meeting.'

To my surprise Norman agreed with what I had written about Major's success at the Birmingham EC summit. When I said, 'There are quite a lot of good things in Maastricht really,' he said, 'I know, that's quite true.' That is a complete change of mood from two days ago when he said, 'I hate the bloody Community and I wish I had never heard of it.' However, I dare say people's moods change.

Monday 19 October

Sent some roses to Margaret, twenty, with a little note saying I would have sent them before but she had been out of the country, giving all my love, etc. I must always try to remember that birthday because I always did send them to her when she was Prime Minister. She rang, very delighted, and chatted away, full of charm.

She said, 'When Haslam was Chairman of the Coal Board, he came to me and said he had to close fourteen pits all at once and very quickly.' She said to him, 'No, you can't do that. You must phase them out. It would be too much of a shock, fourteen at once.' She said, 'That is what they should have done.'

I was expecting her to have some triumphalism over her deadly enemy, Heseltine,[14] but she made no particular comment about him. For the moment I think she has switched off a bit, is getting on with her memoirs and waiting for the great Maastricht affair to arrive in Parliament.

The farewell dinner to Peter Winfield on his retirement from the Tote Board.

I made a little speech, gave some compliments to Peter and made a few jokes. He replied in an amiable manner, no longer bitter about being removed, wishing us all well.

---

14. As Secretary of State for Trade and Industry responsible for the decision, he bore the brunt of the attacks.

Tuesday 20 October
Large reception given by Mark Lennox-Boyd[15] and his wife in the Foreign Office where are the handsome interiors done by Sir Matthew Digby Wyatt.

I asked Peter Stothard, new editor of the *Times*, 'Did you read what I said about you in the *News of the World*?' He said, 'I don't read the *News of the World*.' I said, 'That's exactly why you're so out of touch.'

At the moment, of course, he has got the public behind him, but he won't have in a few months' time. He has done it by talking vicious rot, particularly in the now-running *Times* campaign to say Major is ill and had a nervous breakdown during the monetary crisis on so-called Black Wednesday, which is total piffle.

Wednesday 21 October
We went to dinner with Leonard and Estelle Wolfson. It was the first dinner party they had given since they were married, the first Portland Place dinner party not presided over by Ruth Wolfson.[16] There was Château Beychevelle. It hadn't been decanted.

The food wasn't very good. But the people were more interesting than usual. Jocelyn Stevens[17] and Vivien Duffield[18] were there. Jocelyn and I agreed how terrible David Stevens had been. He is now launching attacks on Major and Norman Lamont, saying they are hopeless and writing pompous and idiotic articles in his newspaper.

Another very agreeable fellow there was Alex Alexander.[19] He used to be head of Lyons and Allied Breweries, a big businessman. He has done a tremendous lot for Covent Garden as Chairman of the Royal Opera House Trust.

He told me the difficulty with Covent Garden was that it wasn't

---

15. The Hon. Mark Lennox-Boyd, Conservative MP, 1979–97; knight 1994; m (1974) Arabella Lacloche, Italian-born garden designer; gold medallist at Chelsea Flower show, 1998.
16. See Vol. 2, pp. 437, 447, for Wolfson's divorce.
17. Grandson of Sir Edward Hulton; former journalist and deputy chairman, Express Newspapers; rector and vice provost, Royal College of Art, 1984–92; deputy chairman, ITC, 1991–6; knight 1996.
18. Philanthropist daughter of Sir Charles Clore; chairman of the Clore Foundation since his death in 1978.
19. (1916–94); Chairman, J. Lyons and Company, 1979–89; Chairman, Royal Opera House Trust, 1987–91; knight 1974.

big enough. The reason why some of the big opera houses, like Milan, got on so well was they could seat four thousand without an increase in their overheads for staff.

Leonard said I had given him some 1841 sherry from the cellars of Sir William Gladstone so I must now try some brandy he had which was dated from 1860.

I took some of this stuff and it was filthy.

'What did you think of it?' I said, 'Interesting,' in a non-committal manner.

How pleasant to be among the ultra-rich and laugh at and berate them.

Thursday 22 October

I asked Norman had they worked out the cost yet of the disastrous giving-in over the coal mines and was he concerned with it. He said no, he wasn't concerned with it at all. They just did it and he has got to pay the bill.

Norman is very worked up about the absurd attacks not only on him now but on Major by the *Times* and the *Telegraph* and so forth. I said, 'Well, don't read the newspapers, and Major mustn't either. Is he depressed?' He said, 'He does get rather depressed at times from all the vicious attacks from people who should be on his side.' I said, 'But surely there is no truth in that story that he had a nervous breakdown on the famous Black Wednesday?' He said, 'No, that was rubbish. But he does go up and down somewhat.'

I said, 'I feel maternally protective towards him. Also I hate injustice and I think he has been very unjustly treated.'

It was then off to The Other Club. I fear it was somewhat dull. The bright Labour fellows, Gordon Brown and John Smith and Tony Blair don't come, or they haven't been coming lately. I said to Nicko Henderson, who is the secretary, 'Why don't they come?' he said, 'They will when things are settled down.' I said, 'I thought perhaps it was because the dinner has gone up to £19.'

Nicko had been looking at the very first members in 1911 and said the Portuguese Ambassador had been a member. I said, 'Why don't we have some ambassadors now? For goodness' sake, why don't we have von Richthofen, the German Ambassador?[20] He is a very good egg, very pro British.'

---

20. Baron Dr Hermann von Richthofen, German Ambassador to the UK, 1988–93.

At that point Montague Browne, who used to be Churchill's secretary, said, 'It is absurd. At one time the Queen's Private Secretary was always a member but when Sir Robert Fellowes was proposed the other day he was turned down. He didn't get enough votes. It ought to be automatic.'

If the Queen's Private Secretary were there, he would have some very good feelings from a slightly wider section of knowledgeable people, experienced in politics and in the world, about how the Crown is getting on in relation to the people and what should be done.

When talking to Norman I said, 'Why don't you put Chips Keswick on the Board of Directors [of the Bank of England]? You would then at least have one friend there. He is a great supporter of yours.'

Friday 23 October
I spoke to Chips to ask him how he felt things were going.

I told him what I said to Norman about putting him on the Board of Directors. He said, 'You are a marvellous fellow.' 'I told him you wouldn't want to be Governor.' He said, 'I would love to be Governor,' but I can't start on that one now.

Wednesday 28 October
Talked to Norman. I said, 'Are we still going on with this mad scheme to bring Maastricht back to the House on November 4th and have a head-on collision?' He said, 'I suppose so,' but he wasn't taking much part in those proceedings.

He said, 'All the uncertainty is definitely having an adverse affect on the pound. I am writing my Mansion House speech and all the business people seem so despondent.'

I told him he is doing fine, which he is, and to keep right on in his course.

Ken Baker called.

I said to him, 'Do you think Major is going to have a head-on collision?' He said, 'He might do but there is talk now of a procedural motion, saying we ought just to get on with the debate.'

I watched Pyrrhic Dance run an extremely moderate race at Yarmouth.

I really think I would be mad to carry on with that horse next year.

The only bright part of the day was meeting Ken Clarke. He said how well I looked. Fortunately, it was a day when my feet were moving properly with no hesitation, despite the fact that I kept waking up in the night trying to remember all kinds of things I had to do and get sorted out, particularly with regard to my income tax.

The good news was his saying that I would have another two years [as Chairman of the Tote] but he could not guarantee a further two years at the end of that, suggesting it might even occur. I told Brian McDonnell, 'Look out. I might be around for a very long time.'

Thursday 29 October

I made an early start to Tommy Wallis's funeral at Sandhurst in the chapel.[21] As the great building came into view, I began to think of James Wyatt. The RMA Sandhurst was his last great work, done between 1807 and 1812.

Johnnie Henderson[22] made an excellent speech about his curious betting behaviour and all the other eccentric things he did, including once forcing his way into where a bride was just getting ready to go to the church to be married and saying, 'You've got time: if you want a really good honeymoon, you must back this horse. It's in the three o'clock. I'll let you know if it's won or not as you come down the aisle.' He put some money on for her and as she came down the aisle he had to say it had lost.

I had to hurry like hell because I was due to have lunch with Chips Keswick and people from Skadden Arps.

I had introduced Skadden Arps to Hambros and they are now collaborating over deals in Central Europe and in the former Soviet Union.

Then it was on to the Levy Board.

After that I popped into the Lords to find out the latest news on all the high jinks on the Maastricht debate next Wednesday. Curiously, I didn't feel tired.

Arnold came to dinner. He conceded that GEC wasn't doing all that badly, through its own efforts with no help from the government. I said, 'Why do you want help from the government?' He said, 'Other countries give their industry help.'

He said Major is no good. I said, 'That's what you used to say about Margaret. Do you want a Labour government?' He said he wasn't quite sure about that. I said, 'I know you might like it because

---

21. Managing director, Racecourse Holdings Trust, a subsidiary of the Jockey Club, 1975–89.
22. Chairman, Henderson Administration, 1983–90; member of the Jockey Club.

you think you would get contracts more easily and you wouldn't have to go through such rigorous tests for your defence equipment. But there isn't much defence stuff going now.'

He was in a very jolly mood and told a lot of jokes. I was glad to see him.

Friday 30 October
Richard Ryder gave me the motion they are putting down before it was published, which was useful. It was quite clever. It referred to the promise made to have a debate before the House began its committee stage on the Treaty. The Bill, of course, is called the European Communities (Amendment) Bill and doesn't mention Maastricht.[23]

I now think they will get by all right.

We arrived at Oare in time for dinner. Then began the great drinking and eating.

David [Swaythling] was there with Ninette. Also Jessica Douglas-Home.[24] She was married to Charles who was the editor of the *Times* until he unfortunately died so early. She was getting way over-heated about Maastricht. She was seeing all kinds of goblins and dangers and the end of Britain and so forth. I kept trying to tell her and Tessa it was not so and it became quite acrimonious once or twice.

I said, 'The whole purpose of getting Maastricht through is that those dangers will be curbed. It would be dotty to try and unseat the government.'

Jessica said, 'You wouldn't have to do that. You could have another Prime Minister.' I said, 'Who?' None of them could agree on one.

---

23. The vote, on 4 November, was on a paving motion to proceed with the Bill.
24. She m 1 (1966) Charles Douglas-Home (1937–85), m 2 (1993) Rodney Leach, director, Jardine Matheson Holdings since 1984.

Sunday 1 November

I suddenly realized they hadn't got Sky Television at Oare. I said, 'Why don't you have it?' Henry said, 'I don't know. I suppose we'd spend all the time watching television.' I said, 'You don't have to watch it. But you love all the sports and you can have it easily.'

I thought how strange; they have masses and masses of money, they must be some of the richest people in the country, and they can't even arrange something he likes so much.

We both agreed that Chris Patten had done remarkably well [in Hong Kong].

He is standing up to the Chinese government and putting some steps towards democracy forward which Douglas Hurd wouldn't agree to when I tried to make him do it. He has got the right approach: more elections, more direct universal suffrage, elected seats in the legislative assembly.

Wednesday 4 November

Bill Clinton got his great victory. I lost my £5 bet with Arnold.

After our Tote Board meeting I went down to Parliament.

As the evening wore on, it got more and more exciting. Right up to the actual voting there seemed no certainty that the government were going to win – on the contrary. But when they did, by six votes on the first division and three on the second, it showed Major's gamble had come off. Now his authority must be a great deal stronger in his party.

There has been a lot of talk about arm-twisting and bullying and blackmail and goodness knows what by the government Whips against the Tory rebels.

Margaret's old private secretary (political) at Number 10, John Whittingdale,[1] was in floods of tears when he had seen her. She had

---

1. Political Secretary to Thatcher as Prime Minister, 1988–90, manager of her private office, 1990–2; Conservative MP since 1992.

accused him of all kinds of treachery for not voting against the government. In the end he abstained which really helped the government, in direct opposition to her.

I have no doubt that my position is delicate with her, too, after the article I wrote in the *Times* saying that the Tories in Parliament simply had to support John Major.

Monday 9 November
To the Lords and there was Willie Whitelaw. The moment he saw me get up he came out. He said, 'You know there is something terribly rotten in this government. They are making so many fearful mistakes.'

He was very gloomy. I said, 'I am not really because I am a great optimist. I think that the worst never happens and it never does.'

Willie said that Margaret did bully people and it was pretty awful.

I said, 'Yes, but you used to argue with her and Major needs somebody like you to restrain him and make him more sensible.' He quite liked that idea.

Tuesday 10 November
Spoke to Norman.

He said he met Margaret at the Cenotaph on Sunday and she was very friendly to him. He was greatly disturbed by reading in Nigel Lawson's book that she had tried to prevent him being in the Cabinet as Chief Secretary when Lawson was Chancellor and Lawson had a great fight to get him there.[2]

I said, 'I always told her what a good egg you were and she never gave me any indication she was reluctant to put you in the Cabinet.'

Norman gets very worried about what those in high places say or write or think about him, such as Margaret, or even Lawson. He has a very sweet and trusting nature. He plugs away at what he is doing and believes that when he is open with others, they will be equally open with him. Sometimes he can be disappointed in his sincerity being met with the enmity of others.

There is another new scandal, about the sale of arms to Iraq in 1989 or thereabouts. The trial collapsed of three men prosecuted for

2. See p. 728 of Lawson's memoirs, *The View From No 11*, published in 1992; Lawson was Chancellor of the Exchequer from 1983 until his resignation in October 1989 over differences with Mrs Thatcher about Europe and her adviser, Alan Walters.*

breaking regulations. It turned out they had been acting under instructions from the government.[3]

Margaret was the Prime Minister when all these things were going on. It was said that he, Major, had not been at the Cabinet discussions relating to the sale of arms to Iraq, which made me think of Macavity the cat who was 'never there'.[4] He was not there when Margaret was deposed because he had toothache, an abcess which stopped him talking and required him to go into hospital during the early part of the leadership contest following Margaret's deposition, so he was out of action and could not be accused of having betrayed her or having plotted against her. He has this amazing ability to dodge the blame. It may not be so easy over the sale of military equipment to Iraq.

Thursday 12 November
Norman's autumn statement was a terrific success. The Tories cheered him, Labour looked sullen and disappointed about the lack of broken election pledges. It was a very clever rearrangement that Norman did and it stopped all the talk of his resignation. When I was just about to go to bed Norman rang to ask me what I thought about it. I said, 'You made a splendid job of it and that is what I am writing in the *News of the World*.'[5]

Friday 13 November
In the evening it was dinner with Irwin Stelzer and Cita and the editor of the *Times*, Peter Stothard, and his wife. I like her. I asked her to sign her book, *Separation*, and told her how good it was, so she wrote an inscription: 'To the man I suspected was my perfect man but now I know he is. With love, Sally.'

We had an excellent Beychevelle 1961.

This was at the Connaught where the food is very good but heavy.

---

3. The Scott Inquiry into export licences and the sale of arms to Iraq was set up on 10 November after the collapse of the Matrix-Churchill case in the light of the admission by Alan Clark, former Minister of Trade, that the exports had received tacit official approval.
4. 'Macavity: the Mystery Cat' from T. S. Eliot's *Old Possum's Book of Practical Cats*; the refrain of the poem is 'Macavity's not there!'
5. WW praised Lamont for not raising income tax or VAT, while allowing growth in spending on the NHS, education and social security, and while asking MPs to limit their own pay rises to 1.5 per cent as an example to others.

Not surprisingly, I woke up in the night feeling weighed down.

Saturday 14 November
In the evening we went to Dorneywood for dinner. Apart from Norman and Rosemary and their son, the Powells were there. It was quite amusing. Charles seemed very certain that the [fact of] arms going to Iraq was well known to Margaret. He is coming round more to Major's side. He has written an article in the *Mail on Sunday* to that effect. That won't please Margaret any more than my article will. I daren't ring her up for the moment.

Charles, plus Carla, was screaming away, saying the monarchy was no good and we ought to get rid of it, why couldn't we have a President.

I said, 'You don't seem to understand the issues at all. It doesn't matter how badly they behave. Look what happened with the Prince Regent and Caroline of Brunswick. And they mirror what is going on in the country. Of everybody who gets married next week, half of them will be divorced in two years. They have got a very good cross-section in the Royal Family.'

I said, 'We have got to have a proper law of privacy, not just for the Royals but for everybody.'

Charles Powell said when he was Private Secretary to Margaret at Number 10, he was plagued by Princess Michael. She was always writing letters demanding to be put on the Civil List.

I said, 'But Prince Michael is really quite intelligent. He speaks very good Russian.' Charles said, 'He does not. He says he does. He told us that and when Gorbachev came to a great dinner, he was put to sit next to him. Gorbachev couldn't understand a single word he said nor could Prince Michael understand anything Gorbachev said.'

I was very surprised and told him about how he had been to the tent at Farnborough where there was a special Russian aeroplane. He made a report on it to the Ministry of Defence. He spoke to the guards in Russian. Charles said he didn't believe it, but that is what he told me. There is something wrong somewhere with these stories.[6]

Sunday 15 November
Off to the dismal prospect of the Sunday racing at Cheltenham.

God it was dreary. I had lunch in the National Hunt room where the Jockey Club were entertaining people. Verushka decided, rather

---

6. See Vol. 2, pp. 79–80 and 309, for Prince Michael and Gorbachev.

wisely as it was such a ghastly day, that she would say she was ill. She did feel a bit ill and the more she thought about going to Cheltenham the iller she felt.

At my table were Mark Zetland and his wife.[7]

He said it was a pity Verushka wasn't there and how fond he was of her and that, 'I expect she is in bed with her lover now.' I said, 'If she is, I hope she's having a jolly time.' I got the slight impression he wouldn't mind being in bed with her. He thinks she is very amusing with her Hungarian voice and oddish observations on the English racing scene. He himself is as mad as a hatter, though he did seem quite sincere when he congratulated me on having another two years and on some of the things we were trying to do.

Alan Meale,[8] Labour member on the Home Affairs Select Committee, has said that my reappointment shows that once again I have made rings round the Jockey Club. Meale hasn't quite got it right. By this time it seems that Stoker Hartington and Christopher Haines actually want me to go on. They can see what I can get done for racing which they can't possibly do.

Tuesday 17 November
Dashed off in the morning to the BBC to be interviewed by Anthony Howard on trade unions after the last world war.

I found what I wanted in *Confessions of an Optimist* and the book I had written about trade unions, *The Peril in our Midst*, which gave a history of what had gone on, the corrupt falsification of ballots in the ETU and also in the AEU when I saved them from having a Communist executive.

Anthony Howard was very friendly. He is a funny boy. He looks most extraordinary with a face that seems as though it has been bashed in on one side. He is quite small. I suppose there could be somebody uglier but not many. He has got a nice, friendly, inquisitive manner. He has cut me up once or twice in articles in the *Observer* and elsewhere but in a curious way I think he quite likes me.

---

7. 4th Marquess of Zetland; director, Redcar and Catterick Racecourses; director, British Horseracing Board, 1993–7; member of the Jockey Club, steward, 1992–4; m (1964) Susan, née Chamberlin.
8. Labour MP since 1987; Opposition Whip, 1992–4; Parliamentary Private Secretary to John Prescott, in opposition and as Deputy Prime Minister, 1994–8; Under Secretary of State for the Environment since 1998; m (1983) Diana, née Gillespy.

I pointed out that the unions owed a great deal to Mrs Thatcher and her reforms which have made them more respectable and the Labour Party more electable.

Our dinner party was really for George Weidenfeld and his bride, Annabelle.

I asked her about her life. She had been to a convent school and felt repressed. She then started some kind of concert agency business which she built up: rather clever of her.

They [she and Rubinstein] lived in Paris and she continued with her operations from there. I said, 'Are you continuing to do all that sort of thing now?' She said, 'I can't. I can't keep up with George.'

George has got amazing energy, devouring books and people and living a high society life. I am very happy for his now revelling in the fact that he is no longer dependent on women for his money, as he was on his previous wives – the unfortunate Jane Sieff and the Witney lady – or on Anne Getty (married to one of the Getty brothers) who provided him with a lot of money for a failed publishing business in New York which her husband put a stop to. His publishing, though with flair, has always been a rocky, unprofitable business.

Part of their honeymoon, which extended over some months, was spent on the Gettys' yacht.

George always wanted to leap ashore and go on long expeditions and see everything he could.

Before and after dinner there had been conversation about how one could ever make sense of Yugoslavia and some of the other countries of what was the Soviet [bloc]. Democracy is a very good idea for places like Britain where it really works but it is not such a good idea where they have no comprehension of it. The only way to control these mixed-up peoples, with their boundaries all over the place, is to sit on their heads, as Tito did.

Wednesday 18 November
Edward Pickering, 'Pick', came to lunch at the Lords. I told him that Andrew Knight saw his role as stand-in for Rupert until the boys are old enough to take over and if necessary standing-in for Anna until that happens. I said, 'How effective do you think he is?' he said, 'His trouble is that he is no communicator. He doesn't get on very well with people and they don't quite know what he means or what he is after.' I said, 'You mean he doesn't have jolly chats with Kelvin MacKenzie?'

Kelvin MacKenzie is the rough bloke who is the editor of the *Sun*.[9] Fastidious Andrew simply wouldn't know how to begin being on the same wavelength as him.

Pick said Rupert had been taking a lot of interest in the *Times* and his newspapers lately. There was a long discussion when he was last here with the editor of the *Times* and the others concerned. He laid out the paper and went through everything and made his sparkling comments.

'Is it true that Simon Jenkins went voluntarily or was he pushed?' He said, 'The situation was that he had agreed when he joined that he only wanted two, or at the most three, years as editor of the *Times*. He wanted to write on his own behalf.' I said, 'Yes but if Rupert thought he was a real success he would have asked him to stay longer.' He said, 'Yes that is true.'

We both agreed what a splendid girl Patsy Chapman is. He said when she joined the Press Complaints Commission everybody was horrified on it, having the *News of the World* editor there. Now they ring up and ask her advice.

I told him the sort of law of privacy I wanted.

Pick is quite amazing. He certainly doesn't look eighty. His lean face is still quick. He moves much better than I do, nippier.

He is kept very busy running News International where he is Deputy Chairman.

The *Times* itself makes no contribution to overheads but the publications associated with it, the various education supplements and so on, make £5 million a year profit, which means that the *Times*, when connected with its sister publications, is not losing money.

There was much amusement at the Levy Board this morning about the story in the *Evening Standard* describing my falling into the lagoon smoking my cigar and still smoking it when I came up. There were considerable inaccuracies in the story but I thought the whole thing had been very funny.

To the Hong Kong Trade Development Council dinner at which Christopher Patten was to speak.

Sir Hal Miller,[10] the Chief Executive of the Society of Motor Manu-

---

9. Editor, the *Sun*, 1981–94, managing director, British Sky Broadcasting from 1994.
10. Conservative MP, 1974–92; chief executive, Society of Motor Manufacturers and Traders, 1991–3; chairman, Cosmopolitan Holdings, director, The Car Group, since 1996; knight 1968.

facturers and Traders, said he was talking to the editor of the *Daily Mail* and said, 'Why don't you publish the great success story of the British motor industry?' The editor said, 'In Fleet Street we only want stories of doom and gloom.'

I said, 'I would like you to send me some details,' and I gave him my fax number.[11]

On the way out I saw young David Cameron [from Lamont's office] who had dinner with us last night. He thanked me profusely and said how much he had enjoyed it. He said when he told Norman about it, he had asked who was there and he had mentioned Eva Pejacsevich. Norman said, 'Oh yes, she has got the most wonderful legs.' David said, 'Typical of Norman, don't you think?'

Thursday 19 November
Had lunch with Joe Elmaleh.

He was born in Beirut. He is Jewish of course. He went to various countries, finally came to England and went to the London School of Economics, taught economics and political philosophy and all that kind of lark. Then he decided to start making money and by God he has.

He kept wanting me to go over to where Autotote are, near Las Vegas somewhere, and see their machines. I said, 'No, I would have to go with one of our technicians and they are too busy getting ready our new device, with Coral and [for] the National Lottery.'

He said, 'I think Autotote might well like to adopt it and sell it on a royalty basis.' I said, 'Then tell them to come over, perhaps in the second part of March when we have got it all out and working.'

The Other Club. Jacob Rothschild was there. He doesn't often come.

Jacob said Soros[12] is a financial genius, particularly on money markets. He had got bored with Quantum and its associated funds at one time but he couldn't bear the idea that they were not being managed as well as when he was directly the manager.

Therefore he had taken over the running of the funds again. I said, 'That's excellent news.'

---

11. WW made the main story in his *News of the World* column of 22 November, 'The car men drive home the good news about Britain'.
12. Hungarian-born financier and currency dealer; WW held some shares in his companies.

Jacob also said Soros is very upset about Hungary. They won't do what he wants financially and even worse than that, he feels there is a big anti-semitic drive beginning there. I said, 'I am going to Hungary over Christmas and I shall investigate this thoroughly. I don't believe it is very serious, merely some semi-fascist nutter who gets a little backing in the country but not much.'

Opposite me was Jack Cunningham. He is Labour Shadow Foreign Secretary. I said that Labour must more whole-heartedly embrace capitalism and reduce taxation, not increase it, and look after the middle levels.

Both sides [in the US] are completely wedded to the capitalist system. Therefore there is no fear, as there is here, of awful things being done if the Conservatives are replaced by Labour.

I said I think it is bad for the country indefinitely to have no change of government.

He said, 'Our people, one for one, are better than the Tories.' I said, 'I am not quite sure about that. Blair and Brown but not, I'm afraid, John Smith. I wish you had taken the quantum leap to go straight up to Brown.' He agreed but said it should be Blair and not Brown as the leader. He is cleverer than Brown and better.

I said, 'I think I had better appoint myself as adviser to the Labour Party.'

Roy [Jenkins] said that after Clinton has been President of the USA for eight years and can't stand again, it would be an interesting idea for Oxford University to ask him to be Chancellor. That is supposing that Roy is dead. He will continue to serve as Chancellor, as Macmillan did, until he drops off the perch.

Tuesday 24 November
John Martin Robinson[13] has rung me about the Wyatville rooms which were destroyed in Windsor Castle.

The poor Queen is in a terrible state and said today, at a celebratory

---

13. Librarian to Duke of Norfolk since 1978; Maltravers Herald of Arms Extraordinary since 1989; author of *The Wyatts: An Architectural Dynasty* (1980). Windsor Castle had been badly damaged by fire, including work by Sir Jeffry Wyatt (who was renamed Wyatville by George IV). WW wrote about the restoration of Windsor Castle and the 'vendetta' against the Royal Family in the *Times* of 1 December.

lunch for her fortieth year since accession, at the Guildhall, that it had been an '*annus horribilis*'.

This only started another burst in the press and on the wireless with Labour MPs saying she ought to pay for the restorations at Windsor, being the richest woman in the world and all that kind of rubbish.

Wednesday 25 November
The fortieth birthday party given by Peter Saunders for *The Mousetrap*.

We found a very good table with Jack Profumo[14] and his wife, Valerie, who was Valerie Hobson who played in *The King and I* and many other roles. Then we were joined by Susan Hampshire, the everlastingly pretty girl, and her husband, Eddie – with a beard but I can't remember his surname.[15]

She told me that her mother-in-law, aged eighty-eight, lives with them but in a slightly separate cottage. I said, 'Mine has been here for twenty-six years, living with me, and she is ninety-one.' I told her how difficult she is and how she behaves. She said hers does exactly the same sort of thing. I said, 'Central Europeans like my wife think it is a great disgrace to put your old people out into a home, though I often wish I could. Sometimes, when I think I might be about to do it, I have a recurrence of cowardly good nature and don't pursue it because I think she is far from her original home and they lost everything they had.'

Then John Major got up.

He made far too long a speech (which made me late because I couldn't go until he had finished) about Agatha Christie being a great literary figure and how he read all the books when he was in hospital for a year when he had a car accident when he was very young; and then about the Lottery and how it was going to help the theatre. I am not sure he is right about that because no extra will go to the Arts Council, as far as I know, and that is where theatres get their help from at the moment.

---

14. John Profumo, Conservative politician; Secretary of State for War, 1960–June 1963 when he resigned over his lie to the House of Commons about his affair with Christine Keeler; president, Toynbee Hall, since 1985; m (1954) Valerie Hobson, actress (d 1998).
15. Kulukundis, shipping magnate and theatrical impresario; m (1981) Susan Hampshire, actress; knight 1993.

I got down to the Lords and earned my £59.

William Astor wanted to know about my unstarred question for next Wednesday [on impartiality in broadcasting]. When I was talking to him, the very nice Ferrers,[16] said, 'Are you giving him a rough time?' I said, 'No. I love William dearly, almost as much as I love his wife.'

Thursday 26 November

Norman deep in trouble again, splashed all over the *Sun*. This is the story that Norman didn't pay off his credit card bills in time. He has had legal warnings before, according to the *Sun*, for exceeding his limit, and so forth.[17] Not only that, he bought a bottle of champagne at Threshers' off-licence for 'a mystery tryst' and a packet of peculiar Raffles cigarettes. Now he must go.

He spent £17.47 at an off-licence in Praed Street, the supposed red light district, on Monday night. That was what the shop-assistant swore to. Actually, he was at various meetings with people who can give complete evidence of that fact; he did not go into this place at all that night and could not have done at the time stated.

Later in the evening two reporters turned up on our front doorstep.

Verushka opened the door. One was black and one was white, showing at least they paid attention to the Commission for Racial Equality. They assumed it wasn't a tart he went out with but Petronella he had gone to see, and she lived near Paddington, which our house is in. The reporters wanted to know if she was at home and if she lived with us. They said, 'We want to know about the affair your daughter is having with Norman Lamont.' (This, incidentally, has been rumoured around Fleet Street for months.) Verushka laughed and said, 'I wish you would print that. She would be delighted. She would be able to sue for no end of money and she would have some real money for the first time in her life.' They began to laugh and withdrew.

There is a determined campaign against Norman, just as there has been against the Queen.

---

16. 13th Earl Ferrers, at this time deputy leader, House of Lords, and Minister of State, Home Office. See Vol. 1, p. 482, for his ancestor who in 1760 was the last member of the House of Lords to be tried by his peers and hanged for homicide.

17. In his 1999 book *In Office* Lamont explains that for some years he had simply paid his credit card bills every two or three months to save the bother of writing endless cheques: 'The cost was marginal and [it] seemed to me an entirely private matter.'

Robin Janvrin rang me from Buckingham Palace earlier in the afternoon. He said he wanted me to know that John Major was going to say that when talking to the Queen three months ago, she volunteered to pay income tax.

It is a terrible mistake. Now the tabloids and the *Sunday Times* have scented blood, they will be after the Queen about what tax she pays.

Friday 27 November
Norman, naturally, was in a very worried state. He was just coming back from Brussels and talking with the European finance ministers about their demand that we should cancel the rebate of £2 billion a year which Margaret Thatcher won for us. The press don't give a damn how much they put him off his stroke. The whole thing is so bloody dishonest. I shall have to write about that for the *News of the World*.[18]

What actually happened was that on Sunday Norman went to the Connaught Street off-licence, Threshers, and bought three bottles of red wine to take home with him on his way back from Dorneywood. His driver is witness to this. I advised him to sue the *Sun* and the *Star* and all these people.

Mark Pejacsevich insisted on coming to see me to discuss something with me personally.

It turned out that all he wanted, and this prevented me from finishing my article, was first, for me to intercede with Norman and say could Flemings have a slice of the job of selling some of the government shareholding in BT. I said, 'That's a little embarrassing but if you send me a note I will send it to him without any comment.' The second thing he wanted was that I should get Soros, the great international financier, to meet Robin Leigh-Pemberton, Governor of the Bank of England.

I said, 'Surely Leigh-Pemberton can just go straight to him.' Mark said, 'No, he doesn't want to do it that way round. He doesn't want it to look as though he is seeking a meeting.'

Presumably this was all to do with the way Soros bangs the pound about whenever he feels like it and makes fortunes from it.

---

18. WW on 29 November attacked the National Westminster Bank for giving the alleged details of Lamont's credit card transactions and the *Sun* for publishing them.

Saturday 28 November
I should have been at the opening of the new stand at Newbury by Queen Elizabeth the Queen Mother.

We ran into the most hideous traffic.

I had to send messages on the car phone to apologize.

I was deeply embarrassed. She said, 'No, no, not at all. I understand how these things happen,' and was her usual sweet self.

During the course of the afternoon we did talk. I said, 'This is the most fearful thing which is being done,' and she agreed. I was referring to the Queen paying income tax.

She said, 'She let Major persuade her. Of course Mrs Thatcher is such a patriot. She never would have suggested that or allowed it.' In this she was quite right. The suggestion was that Major isn't such a patriot.

Then Queen Elizabeth said, 'There is too much talk of money all the time. We're not rich at all, not in serious terms, as you know.'

I said Norman Lamont didn't want the Queen to pay income tax. He had said adamantly that she shouldn't but he was overruled by the Prime Minister.

Then she said, 'The Queen is absolutely dedicated. She thinks of nothing but her job and what she promised the country to do at the coronation.'

She said that nearly everything being said about Prince Charles is absolute lies but he can do nothing about it.

I said how well she was looking but I was sorry to hear about the sciatica, or whatever it was she had. She started rubbing her thigh and said, 'I had this terrible pain here. I have still got it a bit.' People must have wondered what she was doing, holding up her leg and rubbing it while she talked to me.

As soon as I got back I heard a new disaster or trip-up for Norman. It was announced that when he had trouble with the tart who took his house,[19] his legal bills were partly paid for by the Treasury. The press gloated over it as much as they could, the fact that the bill was £24,000 and the Treasury paid £4,000.

It was not a decision of Norman's at all. It was the Permanent Secretary, Sir Peter Middleton in the first instance, and then confirmed by the next Permanent Secretary, Sir James Burns. They said it [the

---

19. See Vol. 2, pp. 493–5, for the 'Miss Whiplash' story about the tenant of the Lamonts' house.

payment] was in connection with his necessary duties and functions as Chancellor of the Exchequer. They had to make all kinds of press statements arranged with his lawyers, have press conferences and find out what it was all about, to protect his name because he was attacked as Chancellor of the Exchequer.

Poor Norman was remarkably cheerful. I said, 'Did John Major know?' He said, 'Absolutely.' I said, 'I can't see how, if the Treasury decided it was their duty to pay a small part, there can be any complaint.' But of course Margaret Beckett, Labour Deputy Leader, and various others immediately said he must resign as a matter of honour.

Sunday 29 November
Blow me down! The *Sunday Times* had on its front page, carried on to the second page, how for £200 you can get immediately a full dossier on anybody you care to name, any public figure or even not a public figure.

I said to Michael Howard, 'It just shows we have got to have a law of privacy to stop all this. But how are you going to stop it, if it is so easy to get the information? That's the most serious aspect of the whole business.'

Monday 30 November
I had to see Peter Brooke, Secretary for National Heritage, about three things. One was to put the Tote's case for running the Lottery.

He said, 'Of course, when we get a bit closer to the time, although we'll make certain by law that you are able to tender, it will have to be very much at arm's length. You won't get any special preference.' I said, 'I understand that. It will be purely on our merit and I intend we shall win it on our merit.'

I talked to him about a possible privacy bill.

He agreed that something should be done. He said he can't prejudge the Calcutt Committee.

I then talked to him about the Windsor Castle fire. I congratulated him for doing exactly the right thing in immediately saying the government would pay.

Then I put to him the idea that John Martin Robinson should be on a Committee of Taste, as they had in George IV's time. He said it was a very helpful suggestion.

Back home at about a quarter to seven. Norman rang.

He said. 'The man at that particular Threshers in Paddington has now admitted he made the whole story up and that he did it for a joke. He has actually come forward and confessed he had never seen me in his life.' Now more and more of these things are shown to be lies, he is holding back about a statement to see how it evolves.

Allan Davis had told me that Frank Finlay, the famous actor, is now interested in reading my play. I said, 'But isn't he a bit old for the part? He was born in 1926 so he is sixty-seven.' Allan said, 'But he can make himself look much younger and he could get away with it. He would be marvellous to have in the part because he is so well known.' Now we will see what happens about that.

Tuesday 1 December

To a party at the Garrick, the *Times* op-ed Christmas party.[1]

Enoch Powell[2] was there. I didn't speak to him to begin with. I am shy of him. He is a frightening fellow in his way. Then he saw where I was talking and came across and said, 'Woodrow, I just want to congratulate you on your most extraordinary ability to fill the left-hand column of the *Times*.' I said, 'You could do it much better.'

Enoch said, 'They have never asked me to.' I said, 'Well, here is the editor.'

I don't know if I embarrassed Peter Stothard by suggesting Enoch should write for him, but I think he would like to.

Once again I said, 'Will you ever overcome your dislike of the non-hereditary peerage? You should come to the Lords.' He said, 'No, never. It's full of corrupt scoundrels.' I said, 'Jesus Christ went among the publicans and sinners.' He laughed and said, 'That was just a code word for gentiles.' He is a very religious fellow, Enoch Powell.

Frank Longford said was I still a Thatcherite. I said, 'Yes, always.' He said, 'But you are supporting Major.' I said, 'Not all the time.' He said, 'How can you support both of them?' I said, 'Perhaps I am more of a Thatcherite than she is – she is not so much of one as she used to be. I try to make a bridge between them.'

When she came into the Lords, he went up to her and said, 'I do hope you are going to liven things up here.' She looked at him and said, 'How is Lady Longford?' just as if she were the Queen, not wishing to answer a question she thought too personal.

When I was leaving the room, there was that nice girl, Miriam

---

1. The 'op-ed' page, opposite the editorials, carries political articles, news articles and articles by columnists.
2. (1912–98); Conservative, then Ulster Unionist, politician; classical scholar; dismissed from Edward Heath's shadow cabinet in 1968 for his 'rivers of blood' speech about what he saw as the consequences of immigration.

Gross.[3] She is a great fan of Petronella's and says how sweet she is. I said, 'Yes I love her, too. But I was pretty annoyed with her a few minutes ago because she made me late going down to Parliament. She said she had to be dropped in Harley Street. When she got out, she gave the door an enormous bloody slam, which does it a great deal of harm, and she also trapped the strap of her bag in the door so we couldn't open it for a while and she went off without it. She had to be chased up the street to hand it to her.'

Miriam looked at me quizzically and said, 'Could she by any chance take after you?'

I laughed, 'I'm afraid she does. I was exactly like her at her age. People used to put it down to the thoughtless arrogance of youth. Now, fortunately, they put it down to my senility.'

Miriam Gross was once a very beautiful woman with a lovely dark face and hair and a nice complexion. Beautiful eyes. She doesn't look at all bad even now. She has charm and sweetness.

Wednesday 2 December
I got together a reasonable speech for my unstarred question on bias in television.

I launched a pretty hefty attack on Liz Forgan, director of programmes Channel 4. McIntosh, now Deputy Leader of the Labour Opposition, got into a terrible state of excitement, saying I was being libellous and saying things I would not be able to say outside, abusing Lords privilege. Eventually he moved a motion that the noble Lord be not heard.[4] Afterwards I said I was willing to say anything I had said in the Lords about this woman outside as well.

Noël Annan[5] popped up to say about Liz Forgan that the dealings he had had with her were highly unsatisfactory, when she made a programme for Channel 4 saying that the civil war in Greece ought to

---

3. Arts editor, *Daily* and *Sunday Telegraph*, 1986–91; literary and associate editor, *Sunday Telegraph*, since 1991; m 1 (1965–88) John Gross, writer, editor and critic; m 2 (1993) Geoffrey Owen, former editor, *Financial Times* (knight 1989).

4. He withdrew the motion after Viscount Astor (William), a Government Whip, intervened.

5. (1916–2000); Provost of King's College, Cambridge, 1956–66; Provost of University College London, 1966–78; Vice-Chancellor, University of London, 1978–81; life peer, 1965.

have been won by the Communists and it would have been if the British Government had not been so reactionary.

Thursday 3 December
The *Evening Standard* tonight carries the ghastly Liz Forgan talking about my wild outburst and there being no evidence for what I said.

If I repeat these things outside the Lords, she will bring a libel action.

She would, of course, have the finance behind her of the Channel 4 Board and I would just be a private individual, unable to go to all the expense they could. I shall have to think very carefully what to do now.

Friday 4 December
Talked to Norman Lamont. He is in a very bad way now, thinking he may have to go. He can't stand it any more; his life is being made impossible; the *Daily Mail* have rung two hundred Thresher shops to find out more about his wine-buying habits; and he is being attacked everywhere.

He thinks the whole of the Miss Whiplash saga, and his letting the house when they moved to Number 11 Downing Street, was actually arranged by the press. They persecuted him about the bill for the hotel when he was at the party conference which he paid as soon as he got it. He was not late in paying it; they were just late in sending it.

I fear he is extremely careless and slack with his own financial arrangements, though of course they don't have any money. He says he is going to bring libel actions, or threaten to. He has issued writs against six newspapers.

It is very difficult to defend him sometimes from all the scrapes he gets into, but he must be defended.

Saturday 5 December
Norman is utterly miserable. I said, 'Don't give up now. Arnold [Weinstock] thinks recovery is on its way and you are going to be a hero again and they will forget about all these silly little events you have got caught up in.' He said he was going to ask to see Mrs Thatcher to talk to her and ask her advice.

During the day I spoke to Philip Freedman.[6] He has been a leader

---

6. Member of Jockey Club since 1995; racehorse owner and breeder (Cliveden Stud).

in trying to get VAT the same here as in Europe on bloodstock. He thought there may be some chance of having a situation in which owners could be registered for VAT and then the VAT could be recoverable so it would be a nil situation for them. But Customs and Excise say, according to Brussels and their own understanding, being an owner is not an economic exercise. I said, 'That's rather silly. It is for many though it isn't for others.'

Now I must speak to Norman tonight before we go to dinner with some ghastly people called Gourlay. They are very rich and they live near Princes Risborough.

He is an investment banker and knows Soros, which could be useful. She is a fairly overblown, largish, dark lady, once pretty, very florid in her face and behaviour.

I suppose they are very kind-hearted and maybe he is the anonymous benefactor who saw Norman through with the balance of the bill he had from Carter-Ruck [libel lawyers] over the Whiplash affair.

I rang Molly [Wyatt] who came up with Bob for his operation this morning.

It was very successful. That is what they feel at the moment.

Sunday 6 December
Andrew Neil's leading article included the following sentence: 'Mr Lamont needs to keep sight of the wider picture: if he paid more attention to what most sensible commentators were saying (instead of seeking solace from his discredited cheerleaders, such as Lord Wyatt and Sam Brittan[7] etc.) . . .'

One thing Norman did say last night was that Major is now so annoyed about all the press have been doing that he is determined to apply the same rule as they have in America, which is that nobody who is a foreigner can own both newspapers and a television station, so Rupert would have to choose. This would be totally ruinous for Rupert. I have told Irwin, not where it had come from but that it was a very definite proposition and of course Labour would support it.

John Major has now made it very clear that Norman will continue as Chancellor of the Exchequer, at least into the next Budget. Also there is a little poll of Tory MPs which says by a fairly substantial majority that he should go on. So I said to Norman, 'Cheer up. Your darkest hour is over.' He said, 'I have heard that before.'

---

7. Principal Economic Commentator, *Financial Times*; knight 1993.*

Meanwhile, poor Bob nearly died, it seems, on Friday night. His kidneys stopped functioning and all kinds of terrible things happened.

Later I rang Molly at the hospital and Bob insisted on speaking to me. I said, 'I'll come round then,' which I did. By this time they had got him out of bed. He is in considerable pain still in his hip but they got him walking about and he seemed altogether more cheerful.

During the day I have been arguing with Piers Bengough about Pyrrhic Dance.

I told him I am going to exercise my right not to go on with it. He was haggling away, saying we should keep the horse in training for the fun of it until the end of the year because maybe we would get the benefit of it in its third year, if it turns out to be better then. I said, 'But there's no fun whatever in watching a horse get nowhere.'

Monday 7 December

I wrote a letter to the *Sunday Times* saying what a ruddy lot of nonsense it was saying the Treasury didn't know where Norman Lamont was on his holiday, that he had 'borrowed' my villa, etc. I sent the letter to the Chancellor's Private Secretary to check before sending it.

Like an idiot I had allowed myself to say that I would be interviewed by Naim Attallah[8] at five o'clock.

He is a curious fellow. He has a kind of appealing, dog-like face, but he is a very high-powered chap, with a publishing firm and controlling Mappin & Webb and Asprey. He could see I was very restless so he went unhappily away with a promise from me that he could come back, which I immediately regretted.

There was a lot of preparation for the dinner party this evening.

Carmelo Calabro, whom the dinner was really for, the fellow who always entertains our guests on his boat at Porto Ercole, arrived looking terribly smart. I had never seen him before wearing other than dreadful beach clothes or swimsuits.

There were sixteen sitting down altogether. We had two round tables.

When we went into dinner I banged on the top table and said, 'Be quiet everyone. I have a dismal announcement to make. Twenty-six years ago today the poor, unfortunate Verushka married me and she

---

8. Proprietor, Quartet Books, since 1976, The Women's Press, since 1977, the *Literary Review*, since 1981, the *Oldie*, since 1991, The Academy Club, 1989–97; chief executive, Asprey, since 1992, managing director, Mappin & Webb, since 1990.

has been suffering ever since. So perhaps you can just drink a little toast to commiserate with her.' Everybody laughed and raised their glasses to her. I said, 'What is more, I forgot it was today,' which they thought very unfeeling of me.

Irwin said, with regard to my letter, that the *Sunday Times* had been told the Treasury didn't know my telephone number in Porto Ercole. I said no doubt they didn't give it because they didn't want to give it to the press.

Tuesday 8 December
A high-powered lot from GTech came to Cavendish Avenue in the afternoon. They run a large number of lotteries in the USA and in various countries throughout the world.

I wanted to see if we could get going with them in a sort of consortium. I said, 'Are you committed to anybody?' The said no, not yet. They got more and more interested in our device and how I have a certain entrée which would enable us to make sure we had a very good chance of being successful with our tender.

Then it was off to Mark's Club to have dinner with Sir John Laing of the construction company. The host was Prince Michael who is on the Laing Board.

He had on his right the Russian Ambassador.

I thought, 'Here comes the great test – is he going to speak to him in Russian at all?' Later on he did. He talked to him for about six minutes in Russian and the Ambassador was replying, obviously, in Russian. The Ambassador's English was pretty good but he seemed to like it more when Prince Michael was talking to him in Russian. So it is not true what Charles Powell said, that he can't speak Russian and that he hadn't and couldn't when he sat next to Gorbachev. But the explanation could be that sometimes people like Gorbachev like to have official translations by their own interpreters to make sure there is no mistake on either side.

We went over the difficulties facing Russia.

At the end of the dinner he said would I please write my thoughts which were full of such common sense and interest, as he wanted to pass them on to Yeltsin.[9] I thought to myself, 'My God, that's another thing I will have to do, and I can't really remember what I said anyway.'

---

9. President of Russia, 1991–9.

Wednesday 9 December
At last I plucked up my courage and spoke to Margaret.

Could she let me have her Frankfurt speech because I hadn't got a proper copy? I had been talking to Norman Stone about it who had told me he had helped her write it. She was a little bit stand-offish and miffed. 'He gave me the historical background.'

She doesn't like to admit that a lot of the ideas and so forth in her best speeches have really been provided by somebody else, although they are in line with her thinking.

I said, 'Has Norman [Lamont] spoken to you and has he asked to see you?' She said, 'Very privately and confidentially he is going to.'

She said, 'He's the best man they've got in the government. Absolutely the best.' I said, 'He's tried to follow your stance.' She said, 'I know that. But they have overspent like crazy.'

She was very friendly and went on talking for about a quarter of an hour, though I don't think she feels I am one hundred per cent for her the whole time, which in a way I am not because she is handling herself so badly.

There was a good debate in the Lords on Hong Kong. Hartley Shawcross at the age of ninety was brilliant.[10] He showed that what Chris Patten is proposing is clearly outside the agreements in the Joint Declaration and the Basic Law. He demolished Margaret's speech in defence of Chris Patten. My feeling now is that if the Legislative Council in Hong Kong want to support his proposals, it is up to them, but he, Patten, should try to get off the hook by saying they were only proposals and they could reach some compromise with Peking.

Thursday 10 December
The great dinner at Mosimanns, perhaps a hundred and fifty people. It was supposed to be a Christmas party given by Conrad Black.

The seating arrangements at this vast party were strange. Mrs Thatcher sat in a little separate room with Conrad Black on her right and the Lloyd Webbers at the same table. What on earth Mrs Thatcher and the Lloyd Webbers have in common, God only knows.

---

10. Chief Prosecutor for the UK before the International Military Tribunal trying Nazi leaders at Nuremberg after the Second World War; Labour MP, 1945–58; Attorney General, 1945–51; m 1 (1924), Rosita Shyvers, d 1943; m 2 (1944), Joan Mather, d 1974; father of William (b 1946); life peer 1959.

Astonishingly, Barbara Amiel (now Black) sat with George Weiden-feld on her right.

Friday 11 December
Heard an astonishing story about Diana.

One day at Highgrove the Queen was coming to visit them. Prince Charles's car was in the front of the house so the Queen couldn't have drawn up to the front door properly and he had to move it. He went to his car to see where the keys were which he had left in it and couldn't find them.

The whole house was turned upside down. Everybody was asked. Diana said she hadn't seen them, the servants said the same.

Then came the moment when the Queen's car was just arriving. Diana leant out of a top window and shouted, 'There are your lousy rotten keys,' and chucked them out on to the drive. She had them all the time. She was just trying to annoy him, and also to annoy the Queen. Apparently it is absolutely typical of the way she behaves all the while.

These things are humiliating in front of servants.

Sunday 13 December
Blow me down, the *Sunday Times* did publish a part of my letter, having chopped off the essential bits which criticized their incompetence.[11]

I had rung Charles Wintour[12] and said, 'Are you still the ombudsman?' He said yes and I told him what had happened. He said he thought I had a cause for complaint.

---

11. In his letter WW began by saying that the *Sunday Times* on 6 December had claimed to uncover 'a chain of incompetence' in the handling of the pound leading up to its suspension from the ERM; he then pointed out factual errors in the piece relating to Lamont's stay with the Wyatts in Italy; he ended by saying, 'Getting so much wrong in so short a space indicates a "chain of incompetence" on your part, suggesting that probably much of the rest you published in News Review was also tripe.'
12. (1917–99); former editor, *Evening Standard*, *Sunday Express Magazine*, *UK Press Gazette*; ombudsman, *Sunday Times*, 1990–5; when Wintour was at Cambridge and WW at Oxford, they together edited *Light and Dark*, an Oxford and Cambridge magazine.

Monday 14 December

I popped into the Lords. It is soothing and restful and I can begin to think as I listen to the quite intelligent speeches droning around my head.

Then it was on to a party given by GTech.

The party was very peculiar They had John Moore, now Lord Moore, the sacked Minister of Health in Mrs Thatcher's government. He looks a fairly miserable creature these days. He is now a consultant for GTech but God knows what he does except find the way around Whitehall for them.[13]

The chairman of this great company was there, an American.

He said, 'Would you come to meet a few friends?' I said all right and when I went across to see them, it turned out to be a live television broadcast, a two-way one, from their HQ in distant Texas.

Setting up a private two-way link across the Atlantic to Texas by satellite is no mean feat. I hope we may be able to do business with them.

Tuesday 15 December

There is a foul and vicious attack on me in the *Sun* this morning, all about my desire to have some curbs on the licence of the press and intrusion into private lives. They have put a horrible picture of me looking about a thousand years old. I decided to try to take it light-heartedly.[14]

Irwin Stelzer has been getting agitated that I am not serving Rupert's interests, as he calls it. Andrew Knight got on to me after his very unsatisfactory telephone call to me last night. (He had told me the *Sun* was going to attack me and I was letting the side down over the privacy law, by attacking Andrew Neil and so forth.)

He started saying how horrible it was of me to have mentioned Andrew Neil's association with a prostitute: 'This is a great personal enmity. You are attacking him all the time.' I said, 'He's attacking me

---

13. Conservative MP, 1974–92, Secretary of State for Health and Social Security, 1987–July 1989; a director of Camelot since 1993; life peer 1992.
14. The article, headed 'A ramble with Wyatt Twerp', was in the column 'The Sun Says'. WW faxed Kelvin MacKenzie saying he expected to be around for a few more years 'laughing with and at you'. MacKenzie faxed back saying WW had missed the point about the dangers of shackling the press.

all the time.' He said, 'Oh no, it's all you.' I said 'Don't be bloody ridiculous' and put the telephone down on him.[15]

I got to the All Party Lords Broadcasting Group at four o'clock. I raised my quandary over saying on December 2nd that I was quite prepared to publish outside Parliament what I said about Liz Forgan.

My solution may have to be that I will say I don't know how to say it outside because no one will publish while Liz Forgan threatens legal action.

There is terrible excitement at 19 Cavendish Avenue with Verushka very worried I'll be sacked by the *News of the World*. Irwin and Cita are saying I should drop my row with Andrew Neil and I should by no means take the subject of my doctored letter to the Press Complaints Commission.

Verushka was terribly upset at around 1.00 a.m. because she says we will lose £100,000 a year and how could we live without it.

I said, 'I am sorry but I cannot sell my soul. I have never written what I don't believe and I am not going to be censored by Andrew Neil. It is much better for Rupert in any case to have somebody independent writing in his papers and showing that they do put the other side of the case when it comes to the Royal Family and also to the question of dirty tricks, as used against Norman Lamont, David Mellor and so forth, with Peeping Tom photographers and tapping phone conversations.'

Wednesday 16 December
I popped into the House to hear the tail end of the debate but really to get my £59.

Jeffrey Archer made his maiden speech.

Lady Trumpington, when winding up, said he made an excellent maiden speech, 'beyond reasonable doubt' (the title of his play), but it was clear she didn't think much of it.

We are now off to his Christmas party so I shall have to tell him I heard it was very good, not wishing to fall out with him.

All this excitement buzzing around in my head, getting written

15. See Vol. 2, p. 229, for Neil's libel case in 1990 against the *Sunday Telegraph* and Peregrine Worsthorne over his relationship with Pamella Bordes and pp. 472–3 for WW's article in the *Times* of 27 February 1991 in which he upbraided Neil for attacking the morals of Lord Althorp, Princess Diana's brother, in view of his own 'exploits with Pamella Bordes'.

about in every damn newspaper, one after the other, makes me feel that anyway I am still alive and kicking; however they may try to mock me, they must be taking me seriously.

Later Major came in [to the Archer party].

I said, 'What are they [Tory rebels] going to do with the Maastricht Treaty in the Commons? They certainly can't vote with Labour against opting out of the social chapter.' 'No,' he said. 'We've got the bastards by the balls.'[16]

Thursday 17 December
To the Royal Free Hospital for lunch with the Dean of the Medical School, Vere Rothermere,[17] Professor Schapira[18] and Miss A. Brennan, the girl from the Students' Union.

I think it possible that Vere will produce something now for the Royal Free.

To Norman Lamont's party at Number 11. I talked at some length to Sir John Cope, the Paymaster General, about the VAT problems of racing.

He said, 'There are complications but one solution might be to get the owners registered for VAT by putting advertisements on their saddle cloths or something on the back of the jockeys' shirts, and charging, say, £500 a time.' But, he added, the Jockey Club were rather stuffy about all that and 'perhaps you can tell them not to be'.

Friday 18 December
During the morning Stoker rang.

I told him evening racing seems imminent but he must keep that under his hat. I told him I talked to Cope and he and the Chancellor are very keen on getting something done about the VAT.

'Thirdly,' I said, 'you've got to do something about these Stable

---

16. It was later, in July 1993, that Major made the much publicised remark, 'Do we want three more of the bastards out there?'; see *John Major: the Autobiography*, p. 343, and this volume, 27 July 1993 note.

17. (1925–98); 3rd Viscount Rothermere, chairman, Associated Newspapers (*Daily Mail*, *Mail on Sunday* etc.), from 1970; m 1 (1957) Patricia Brooks, née Matthews (Bubbles), d 1992, m 2 (1993) Maiko Joeong-shun Lee.

18. Professor Anthony Schapira, Royal Free and University College Medical School, chair of clinical neurosciences since 1990.

Lads. The trainers refuse to give a ha'penny more. It's all right with the decent trainers who pay well over the minimum but it is wicked with a lot of bad trainers.'

He said, 'Leave it to me but for goodness' sake don't say I know anything about it.'

In the evening we went to San Martino, a restaurant at the end of Walton Street.

I said to Irwin, 'I don't know what you and Andrew Knight are fussing about. In the first place there wouldn't have been a *Sunday Times* at all if I hadn't arranged with the electricians' union to move in when the printers' union refused to take part. Also the *Sunday Times* wouldn't have avoided the Monopolies Commission.'

At which point he said, 'That was overruled. They didn't have to go there.' I said, 'I know. I stopped that through Margaret. You mustn't say it to anybody. I also prevented this business, which they are now maybe going to reintroduce, that you can either have television stations or you can have newspapers but you can't have both. I helped Rupert get his Hungarian newspaper on its feet, and now I am trying to see that the privacy bill isn't as bad as it might be, but there is going to be one. I want to get it on a proper basis and I have a better chance of doing that than anybody else, from what I say in public and what I say in private.'

Saturday 19 December
During the morning Norman rang in a great state. He said, 'Do you think I can continue with these attacks all the time? There is a new one in the *Sun* this morning. Now my honesty is being impugned.'

I said, 'Don't worry. When the economy picks up, all that will be forgotten. And it is going to pick up, I think, in the second half of 1993.' He said, 'I hope it is going to do it before that.'

I said, 'Will you promise me you won't do anything which might get into the newspapers?' He said, 'I am living a monastic life.' I said, 'Are you sure? He said, 'Absolutely.' I said, 'Then you must be getting very restless.'

He said they would try as best they could to do something about the VAT on bloodstock because everybody understands the employment issues involved and the cost and the loss of valuable earnings from auction houses moving off to Ireland or France.

I sent a Christmas card to the Queen with a message.[19] I also wrote a longish letter to Queen Elizabeth the Queen Mother and sent her a couple of books including the one which Livia had given me, *Kingsmead* by Bettina von Hutten.[20]

Sunday 20 December
The *Sunday Times* printed 'The *Sunday Times* and Lord Wyatt' on page five. Charles Wintour had done a pretty poor job in acting as the ombudsman. He ended by saying that both the *Sunday Times* and myself were right about that fateful week because, as reported by William Keegan in the *Observer* on August 30th, on his way to me the Treasury didn't know where to find him. This may or may not be true but it has no relevance to the famous week, beginning on the 17th and ending on August 24th, when the *Sunday Times* said he wasn't in touch. However, Charles upheld my complaint over implications that I had not been telling the truth.

I am now contemplating whether to go to the Press Complaints Commission or whether to drop it.

I noticed that Mrs Thatcher had a party at her house to which I wasn't invited. I am clearly off the menu for sticking up for John Major.

Monday 21 December
I am feeling very tired. Sometimes I sleep OK and sometimes I don't.

Subconsciously I must be worrying a great deal about the row with Andrew Knight who has been mildly supported by Irwin.

Rupert last week had rung 19 Cavendish Avenue and said he would ring later that evening but he never did.

Norman is in a state of frenetic worry while simultaneously snoozing on a bed of optimism.

---

19. WW wrote, 'I pray that 1993 will be for Your Majesty an "Annus Felicitas (Roman goddess of Good Luck)" '. To have been grammatically correct, he should have written 'Annus Felicitatis'.
20. WW had told the Queen Mother about von Hutten in his letter of 23 October, when he invited her to present the 1993 Tote Cheltenham Gold Cup: 'I find her fascinating about goings-on in "high society" in pre-war (pre-1914) times.' In her letter of 27 December thanking WW for tracing a copy of *Kingsmead* for her and for other books, the Queen Mother said how deeply touched she was by what he wrote about the Queen.

Now he is being attacked again by a House of Commons committee saying he ought to have declared on the register of members' interests that he had received an anonymous donation from some Conservative benefactor or benefactors to pay off the part of the bill he didn't pay himself (apart from the bit paid by the Treasury) for employing Peter Carter-Ruck.

When you think of the corruption there always used to be, and how Churchill had his bills paid for him and never had to put it down on a register of members' interests, and how Lloyd George was corrupt, personally pocketing a lot of the money people sent in for buying peerages, how Beaverbrook and Lloyd George had mistresses all over the bloody place and nobody seemed to mind a bit, or they didn't know because newspapers didn't expose it all in those days, Norman's little escapades seem utterly irrelevant.

Tuesday 22 December
Lunch with Andrew Knight and Irwin Stelzer.

I said to the wretched Andrew Knight, who is such a creep, 'Why is it the bruisers Andrew Neil and Kelvin MacKenzie need protection against my little pop-gun?'

I said, 'What do you think it was like when Mrs Thatcher was always being foully attacked by Andrew Neil in the *Sunday Times*? She was always getting on to me and saying, "How can Rupert allow this?" and I had to defend him and say he is not all that much in charge of what his newspapers write and he has to give editorial freedom to the *Sunday Times* and so on.

'And what do you think she felt when Andrew Neil said she must go and Heseltine was the man to succeed her and backed him in the leadership election? That was after all she had done for Rupert and Rupert did nothing about it. It is possible that Neil persuaded two Tory MPs, by his leading articles and by going on TV, to vote the wrong way and that was enough to stop her going on being Prime Minister.'

They said, 'You still want this privacy law?' I said, 'Of course I do and there is going to be one.'

I laid into them good and proper. I may send my complaint now to the Press Complaints Commission. I left them rocking about that.

Wednesday 23 December

Norman rang up very anxious to know what had happened at my lunch and I gave him a full account of it. He said, 'Are they going to take your column away from you?' I said, 'I don't think so.'

He has obviously been talking to John Major about the possibility, as he would be somewhat concerned about losing his main supporter in the Murdoch press.

The altercation does not seem to have affected Patsy Chapman deeply, though I was disturbed that she, according to Andrew Knight, had wanted him to look at my articles.

Anyway, Patsy sent me a wonderful box of *News of the World* Christmas crackers and a lovely bottle of 1987 Château Margaux.

Off to Hungary, Budapest, at what seemed like the crack of dawn.

Livia's flat, where we are staying, is very pretty. She has got some lovely old furniture she bought with excellent taste and some which she got from her family. I have a fantastic Biedermeier writing desk to work at in the far side.

Friday 25 December

We entertained the Hungarian Ambassador and his wife and his school-mistress daughter, aged about thirty.[21]

We went to the Gundel restaurant, the famous one started in 1894.

My old friend, Gyorgy, the leader of the gypsy band, previously at the Hilton, was there. He serenaded Petronella and she sang to the accompaniment of it and the diners clapped. I got very drunk. I gave them about £100 as a tip, pretending myself to be the representative of the old Austro-Hungarian Hussars or whatever.

Saturday 26 December

Boxing Day. Pericles arrives. He rings from the airport, a bit late but he managed to get to Livia's under his own steam, unlike Petronella.

I talked to Count Paul Teleki on the telephone. (His grandfather committed suicide when the Germans forced them to declare war against England. He was Prime Minister at the time.) Paul Teleki is now a member of the government, though he is an American, and he is in charge of privatization, which is going slowly but tolerably well. I got a lot of information from him about anti-semitism and about the state of the country.

---

21. Sir John Birch was British Ambassador to Hungary, 1989–95.

Monday 28 December

Pericles and I went down with Petronella into the town by the Atrium Hotel where I wanted to change some money.

I had walked quite a long way when Petronella came running after me and said, 'Pericles has found a way of changing money here.' He was talking to some men who approached him to sell currency to them. He said, 'It's marvellous. They're giving a hundred and sixty forints to the pound.'

He had just changed £100 which I had given him, and then I handed over another £100. But it was all a clever conjuring trick. We were caught like naïve idiots. They did a sort of slapping about with their books, laying one thing on top of the other, etc. I got a few pounds worth of forints back on it in the end, likewise Pericles.

Wednesday 30 December

It was sad leaving Budapest.

I gave Pericles a hug.

I am worried about him starting a restaurant on his own.

Five minutes after I walked into the house, Cavendish Avenue, James Hanson rang: 'What kind of cigars do you smoke?' I said, 'Why?' He said, 'I have just been reading your article in the *Times*.[22] It's terrific. And on behalf of Imperial Tobacco, which we own, I want to send you a box of your favourite cigars.' So I said Montecristo No. 2, which was the first I could think of. I then wished I had said Churchill in tubes or Romeo y Julieta.

Thursday 31 December

Chips Keswick has got a knighthood in the New Year honours. I spoke to him and he is very thrilled. I said, 'You asked for a knighthood and you have got one. I am still working on getting you made a director of the Bank of England.'

He is the first of the three brothers to get a knighthood so I suppose I shall now have to work on getting Henry one.[23]

Chips Keswick was thrilled with my article on smoking.

----

22. The article was headed 'Light up for a long life'. WW cited as evidence *Smoking and Common Sense* by Tage Voss, a Danish doctor, and the work of Dr Hugh Sinclair on smoking and diet.
23. Simon Keswick is the third brother.

I said Hanson had rung and wanted to send me a box of cigars on behalf of Imperial Tobacco.

Blow me down, within about an hour arrived by hand fifty delicious cigars, bundled and boxed.

1993

Friday 1 January
The day was complicated by having to go out to a New Year's Day lunch with Diane and Harold Lever.[1]

Cita had been pleased with the piece of Herend china[2] I sent her. I sent exactly the same one to Diane Lever who was also delighted. Herend is all the rage now in England and in America. Irwin wanted to know whether they had been privatized yet and I said no, and I didn't think they would be, not in a formal sense, other than giving the workers a lot of shares.

They are terrified of it getting into foreign hands, which is not unreasonable.

Quite a large piece I wrote [in the *News of the World*] was about poor old A. L. Rowse[3] not getting any kind of an honour and he is now ninety.

Saturday 2 January
I spoke to Norman yesterday. He said, 'I am just playing ping-pong with the Secretary for the Environment (Michael Howard). We are fifteen all in the final game of three. Michael Howard is complaining that you're giving me a breather.' I said, 'Let's speak tomorrow then.'

Today we did speak. He is still worried deeply over all these things being written about him in the newspapers.

Today Verushka tells me that she and Petronella are both due to go to Florida next Friday. She will be away for a week. I said, 'But Virginia

---

1. (1914–95); Labour politician; Financial Secretary to the Treasury 1967–9, Paymaster General 1969–70, Chancellor of the Duchy of Lancaster 1974–9; chairman, SDS Bank, 1984–90; life peer 1979; m 3 (1962) Diane, née Bashi.
2. Made in Hungary.
3. (1903–97); Cornish-born historian and writer; Fellow of All Souls College, Oxford. He identified from the Forman papers the dark lady of Shakespeare's sonnets as Emelia Lanier, daughter of an Italian musician. With his many interests and decided opinions, he was a controversial figure among academics.

Bottomley is coming to dinner on the 12th.' She said it can't be helped and she will get Diana Lever to act as hostess.

Petronella is going on behalf of the *Spectator*.

Sunday 3 January

Along with the usual attacks on Norman in the *Sunday Times* and elsewhere, there is a new set of rumours, said to emanate from Downing Street, to the effect that John Major is very angry with Norman because he said publicly that he doesn't want any other job but Chancellor of the Exchequer and that is the one he wants to stick to. This seems to take away from the Prime Minister, according to so-called Downing Street sources, his right to move members of the Cabinet around as he pleases.

When Norman rang I asked him whether there was anything in this. He said wearily he hoped not.

The gloomy Naim Attallah came.

I am utterly sick of these interviews. They waste my time, as I told him, because I always hear 'Time's wingèd chariot' hurrying near and I have so much to do, including wanting to write my play. Some of his questions were plain daft and he could just have easily got the answers from my *Confessions of an Optimist* as asking me.

He did a lot of amateur psychology about my attitude to my father and so on. I said, 'I don't think much about him at all now. Maybe I was unfair to him. I don't know what I would do if I met him. I would probably be embarrassed.'

I don't see why I should have my blood sucked by him. He wants to put it not only in the *Oldie*, but in a book which no doubt would sell very well.[4] It would be money from a book with material I would like to make money out of myself.

However, I felt rather sorry for this man.

Norman rang in the evening and said not long after he had spoken to me John Major rang him up and said, 'Where do these extraordinary stories come from? I am not at all annoyed at your saying you want to stay on as Chancellor of the Exchequer. I understand that and am quite in favour of it, as you know. Do these stories come out of the Treasury?' Maybe they do. There is somebody behaving oddly there.

---

4. *More of a Certain Age*, Attallah's second collection of interviews, was published later in 1993.

Monday 4 January
A girl called Caroline Phillips from the *Evening Standard* wanted to come tomorrow to interview me. I said to her 'What is the point of doing it for the *Evening Standard*? I seem to be in the *Evening Standard* almost every day and they get it all wrong anyway.'

A very silly thing in the *Evening Standard* the last time said I was estranged from my son who lives in Canada. First, I am not estranged from my son and, second, he is not in Canada.

Tuesday 5 January
I was still agitating with myself whether to send to the Press Complaints Commission the manner of the treatment of my letter to the *Sunday Times*. I finally decided not to bother any more. The Press Complaints Commission are no damned good either.

Wednesday 6 January
Arnold rang.

I said, 'Don' t forget you owe me ten quid.' He said, 'Why?' I said, 'Because you said Norman wouldn't be Chancellor of the Exchequer by the end of the year and he is.'

Friday 8 January
David Stevens rings, interrupting my trying to get on with my article. Had I seen the attack on him in the *Sun*? I had. It accused him of living on immoral earnings from pornographic telephone calls.

The *Sun* used to do that and so did the *News of the World* but they have more or less stopped doing it now. So they unctuously wash their hands with virtuous soap and attack David Stevens.

David Stevens said, 'There was an understanding in the past that proprietors and chairmen of companies owning newspapers didn't attack each other.' I said, 'Yes, and I think that was a very good rule.' He said, 'I have consulted my lawyers and they think it is libellous. Can you do anything about it or talk to Rupert?' I said, 'I can't talk to Rupert because he is on the other side of the world at the moment. But why don't you ring Andrew Knight?'

Then he said, 'We have always been very lenient to Rupert. Why shouldn't we expose his private life?'

He said, 'What about his daughter getting married to this black man? It could be very interesting to have a series on the tribal customs of both families, the Murdoch family and the black man's family.'[5]

This reminded me I hadn't sent a message to Liz, which I proceeded to do during the day.

Liz is attractive and amusing and I do actually like her. She is extremely highly sexed.

I rang Andrew Knight and told him what had happened and that I had told David Stevens I don't suppose that Rupert knew anything about the article in the *Sun*. Andrew said this was not so. Originally the article was going to be headed 'Lord Porn' and he himself had asked Rupert what he thought about this appearing in the *Sun*. Rupert had said let it go ahead.

Rupert himself had in fact stopped the pornographic advertisements in the *Sun* at a time when it was very difficult for them because they owed so much money and hardly knew how to pay the salaries.

I said, 'Why don't you ring him?' He said, 'I would rather do anything than that. I think I shall just disappear for the weekend.'

I was very annoyed to find that David Swaythling had made a very silly remark when he spoke at some racing lunch yesterday.

The real damage was in answer to a question. David said he expected the BHB (this new body, the British Horseracing Board, which is quite bogus because it is really controlled by the Jockey Club in the end) to take over the Levy Board and the Tote and that would happen in two or three years' time. Once again, all the staff will wonder, my God, are they up for grabs again because should this happen, it would be a virtual privatization. The Office of Fair Trading, the Department of Trade and Industry, the Monopolies Commission, everyone would weigh in to say it was a privatization and therefore the whole Tote operation was up for grabs, including of course Tote Direct and our chances of getting the National Lottery.

Saturday 9 January
Mrs Tamborero and I went to see a very remarkable play, *Lost in Yonkers* by Neil Simon. He is Jewish himself and understands the whole set-up of a Jewish family and their reactions. He had a number of interesting devices, one or two of which I might incorporate into my play, so I could not consider myself to have been wasting my time.

---

5. Elisabeth Murdoch m (1993) Elkin Pianim, economist, from Ghana; they separated in 1997.

Sunday 10 January
David Swaythling rings up. He makes a feeble explanation of his absurd statement.

He is obviously sucking up to Stoker, wanting to become a member of the Jockey Club which he longs to be although he pretends not.

Damien Thompson[6] came to dinner. I want him to advise me on my play about the religious accuracy.

He is a Roman Catholic, mad keen on the rituals and all the rest of it.

He really is very nice. He looks like a lost dog seeking help. But I can't help the entire world, unfortunately.

Tuesday 12 January
Andrew Knight is not at all pleased with my article on privacy law in the *Times* today. On the other hand Sir John Sparrow[7] told me he thought it was a very courageous article and I was absolutely right to put it as I did.

All were asked for dinner [here] at 8.15. At 8.20 only James Gourlay had arrived. I began to wonder whether I had got it all mixed up. Diane [Lever] was supposed to be there much earlier, before eight, but couldn't because she was waiting for a doctor to see Harold.

Virginia Bottomley sat on my right and Sally Stothard on my left. As we sat down the place for Aliai Forte was still empty because Rocco had not found her at the party he went to pick her up at.

At about twenty past nine she came in, looking absolutely lovely in a wonderful gold and black trouser suit, gilt edged, with her hair beautifully done. She is far more poised than when she first came to England, with a more attractive, mature beauty than her early, slightly brash prettiness.

The time of the vote became ten o'clock so the three voters, Kenneth Baker, Peter Bottomley and Virginia Bottomley, didn't leave until just before a quarter to ten. There were two votes and they were back by twenty to eleven.

I said, 'Normally when a great lady politician comes, like Margaret

6. Journalist; religious affairs correspondent, *Daily Telegraph*, 1991–5.
7. Director, Morgan Grenfell Group, 1971–88; seconded as head of Central Policy Review Staff, Cabinet Office, 1982 until 1983 when Mrs Thatcher closed the unit; chairman, Morgan Grenfell Asset Management, 1985–8, Universities Superannuation Board, 1988–96, Horserace Betting Levy Board, 1991–8; knight 1984.

Thatcher, we always stay in the same room, but perhaps the ladies would like to get away from us for a bit,' and so Diane took them out.

Then Ken Baker went to great lengths to say he thought Major was doing extremely well and that he would be Prime Minister for a decade.

His latest idea is that interest rates must be cut immediately by another two points.

Naturally, Rocco agreed with that because they are all in debt to the banks in the hotel world.

Peter Stothard was fairly critical of the government in a sort of Timesian way. But privately he said to me before we went in to dinner, about my article in his newspaper that morning, that though he didn't want it said outside this house, he actually agrees with my views on the ending of all these electronic devices, bugging and dirty tricks.[8]

Virginia, with her fair hair and fair complexion, is an attractive girl though a tiny bit too tall and slightly ungainly as she walks. She has a good figure, she is very feminine and very pleasing to talk to.

I told her how appalling it was that her Department wasted millions of pounds trying to stop people smoking when it may well turn out to be one of the things which aid health. I said, 'You have got to read this book, *Smoking and Common Sense* by Tage Voss.' I gave her a copy before she left. She left early because she, poor girl, had all these papers to read and her boxes to read at home before she could go to bed.

There was some disagreement to the proposition that Major would remain Prime Minister for the rest of the century or thereabouts from Peter Stothard and James Gourlay.

They said, 'What about Blair? If he took over from Smith, it would make all the difference.' I said, 'It would not make any difference unless they [Labour] renounced socialism and made it quite clear that they had. Until they make that quantum leap I don't think they ever will get elected. I would rather like to be able to advocate voting for a Labour government, saying it would now be completely safe.'

James Gourlay is much nicer than I thought he was.

Rocco Forte was funny about Sir Hugh Wontner.[9] He died just in

---

8. The *News of the World* on 17 January flanked WW's column calling for a privacy law with a column by Paul Connew, deputy editor, putting the opposite view: 'We must fight for our right to the truth.'

9. (1908–92); chairman, Claridge's and the Berkeley Hotels, from 1948; President, The Savoy Hotel, from 1990.

time. They were about to push him out of his free lodgings at Claridge's. There he lived in great style in a huge suite. He could order anything he wanted to eat – caviar, wines, anything. He also had a free valet and servants. He started from nothing and worked nowhere else but in the Savoy Group which includes Claridge's. He died several times a millionaire, having made the money out of his perks, basically.

Out in the street, as Ken Baker was going, I asked him whether Norman would get by his latest troubles with the select committee.

Ken moved his hand backwards and forwards underneath the lamplight and said he thought he would probably just get away with it. He sees no reason why Norman should resign and he said several times how strongly he supported him.

Thursday 14 January
A funny little chap with spectacles called Jones from the racehorse owners' section of the BHB came to see me.[10] He had said what a disgrace it was that I was allowed to go on at my vast age and that I should be replaced. I think he came with a kind of olive branch, basically. But he seriously wanted my advice on the BHB and who should be appointed as the chief executive. I gave the pros and cons quite honestly and trustingly. I hope he won't let me down. It is between Christopher Haines and Tristram Ricketts.[11] I had given a slight edge to Tristram Ricketts.

I think I have made an ally of Jones now.

Sunday 17 January
Norman thought my article in the *Times* last Tuesday was splendid.

Continuing his saga, he said his private office had a telephone call; a girl secretary came to him, very embarrassed, and said, 'It's a woman who says she was approached by the *Sun* with a six-figure offer to help them in their enquiries about your mistress. They know her address and they are watching the house. The woman who rang said it was supposed to be her, though she had never even met Mr Lamont, and what should she do about it?' They told her to speak to her lawyers and

---

10. Peter Jones; chief executive, Omnicom UK, 1989–94; president, Racehorse Owners' Association, 1990–3; member, BHB, 1992–6, Levy Board, 1993–6 and from 1997; he eventually succeeded WW as chairman of the Tote Board in 1997.
11. Haines was chief executive of the Jockey Club, Ricketts of the Levy Board.

Norman spoke to lawyers, too. Of course, it could be a terrific libel action if they ever published anything about it.

Verushka and Petronella arrived back, deadbeat, in the morning. They had an entertaining time. Mary Rothermere, whom they were staying with, was tedious because she was so bossy.[12]

Tuesday 19 January
Went to Number 10 to see John Major.

Out came Sarah Hogg[13] who greeted me very affectionately.

She said, 'The Prime Minister is just putting his coat on to receive you.' I said, 'Tell him he needn't bother about that.' Then Jonathan Hill, his Political Secretary, came along and we went into the Cabinet room. I remembered how I had sat there from time to time when there were meetings of the Defence Committee in Attlee's day and I had to represent the War Office.

I went straight into efficiency and fairness in the government and how it must be maintained.

On the Matrix-Churchill affair I said, 'You know it really isn't fair that these people lost their jobs. If Alan Clark[14] had told the truth instead of perjuring himself, they would still have their jobs. I think something ought to be done about it.' He said he certainly thought it was Alan Clark's fault and he would think about it.

I then went on to the privacy situation.

After a pause he said, 'I am thinking that we should make a law that foreigners, non-British residents, should not be allowed to own newspapers. Look at all that stuff attacking me and the government the whole time in the *Daily Telegraph*, as well as in the *Sun* and the *News of the World*.'

I said, 'All these new electronic devices and long distance lens photography – it's like living in Stalin's Russia. You know, the *Sun* has

12. Daughter of Kenneth Murchison of Dallas, Texas, Mrs Mary Ohstrom m (1966) 2nd Viscount Rothermere (Esmond, 1898–1978), his third marriage; d 1993.

13. Journalist and economics editor; head of Policy Unit 10 Downing Street, 1990–5; life peer 1995; daughter of Lord Boyd-Carpenter, Conservative politician, m (1968) Douglas Hogg, Conservative politician, son of Lord Hailsham.

14. (1928–99); Conservative politician, historian and diarist; Minister for Trade, 1986–9, and Minister of State, Defence, 1989–92. At the trial of Matrix-Churchill directors in November 1992, Clark admitted he had been 'economical . . . with the *actualité*' in his evidence to the prosecution.

been spending thousands renting an apartment opposite a house where they think you have a girlfriend.'[15]

He blanched at this and looked very startled. I said, 'They spend thousands watching the house to see if you go in or out. Obviously you don't.'

WW moved on to caution Major against further defence cuts, intervention in the former Yugoslavia and putting up taxes.

Then he reverted to all these attacks on him. He said, 'Of course you know where they all come from,' (meaning Margaret and co.).

I said, 'In a way I understand her position. There she is, only sixty-six and full of energy. I have been trying to be a bridge between the two of you, as you know, but I think the bridge has now collapsed.'

'The civil servants here all say to me that she would have done exactly the same as I did about Maastricht. She would have signed it and carried it through Parliament.'

WW then enumerated, item by item, what he thought Major's 'defined plans for the future' should be – he should continue with privatization, continue to fight federalism in the EC, maintain links with the US, and improve education, thus creating genuine classnessness.

He thought my statement of what should be his aims a very good summary.

I said, 'You don't want to take any notice of all these attacks on you. Just ignore them. Your opponents haven't got anything to offer.'

I said, 'I am sorry to blather away like this but we had a very short time.'

Major doesn't look grey at all and is far more confident.[16] He has a good, upright walk and a neat, trim, slim body and he has this terrific smile which lights up his face with eagerness and enthusiasm.

I spent a lot of time trying to explain to him that Rupert Murdoch didn't necessarily agree with his editors and how difficult it was for him to get rid of them because of the basis on which the newspapers were handed over, with him not to interfere with editorial control. But he didn't seem very convinced.

I told John I thought Conrad Black was basically a pretty decent fellow who wrote letters to his own newspaper contradicting what they say. But he didn't think that much of an excuse, either, considering

---

15. WW had been told in December 1992 that the *Sun* had done this.
16. Major had been lampooned as 'grey'.

all the attacks he got in those papers from everyone else editing or writing in them.

Wednesday 20 January
Today that sweet creature, Audrey Hepburn, died. Sixty-three years old only. She died of cancer. She was marvellous in *My Fair Lady* and in many films and on the stage in *Gigi*. She was once the girlfriend of James Hanson when she was very young.

She did terrific work for deprived children all round the world.[17]

It seems extraordinary that my mother-in-law upstairs who had done nothing for anybody all her life of any value except for look after her grandson a bit when his parents were out, still lives and is thirty years older than Audrey Hepburn was.

Dinner at the Connaught.

I told Irwin in great secret and confidence, without giving him the name of the source, what John Major had said about having a law to stop residents abroad, who are not British subjects, owning newspapers here. He said, 'Does that apply to Black, too?' I said, 'Certainly.'[18] He said, 'It is logical.' I said, 'Yes, but what am I to do about it? Should I tell Rupert?'

After a while we decided that he, Irwin, would revolve the subject in his head but say absolutely nothing to Rupert about it.

Thursday 21 January
I rang Irwin and said, 'You know they had that poster in the war which I suppose you couldn't put up now without causing all the feminists to scream. It read, 'Be like Dad. Keep Mum.' He laughed and said, 'Yes, I've got the message. I will certainly do so.'

That extraordinary fellow, Clinton, has been kneeling in prayer at the grave of John Kennedy with a battery of cameramen to watch him. He was trying to get strength and inspiration from Kennedy, his hero. He hoped to be like him. He clearly is like him in one respect: he is a terrific womanizer.

To The Other Club. Before dinner I found myself sitting next to that dreary man who was Winston Churchill's last private secretary, seconded from the Foreign Office, Montague Browne.

---

17. She was Special Ambassador for UNICEF from 1988 until her death.
18. Conrad Black is now a British citizen and has been a resident in Britain since 1989; Rupert Murdoch is an American citizen.

The former private secretary looked around the room and said, 'Most of these people shouldn't be in the Club at all.'

He said, 'Look at that fellow Robin Day, and Bernard Levin. Neither of them should be allowed in here. They are journalists.' I said, 'So am I.' He said, 'Not exactly because you have been in politics, too.'

If this fellow had his way, there would be about three or four people left talking to each other, mostly bores.

I talked at some length to Duke Hussey about the BBC. I said, 'I got your letter. I haven't replied to it yet because I was stunned by your falling for that girl [Liz Forgan]. It's a typical case of an old man being charmed by a young woman.' He blushed and smiled a bit.

'She has a lively, original mind, the most original in broadcasting.' 'Anybody can be original if they do the opposite of what they are supposed to be doing. Grace Wyndham Goldie[19] was a splendid woman before she got drunk so often, but in fact she was able to produce objective programmes and make us all do so, whatever our political views.'

I told Ian Gilmour he had written a damn good article on the privacy laws required, meaning that he had put the same arguments as myself, but in a different way.

He was clearly glad to find us on the same side again, at least on one topic.

John Smith was very friendly considering what I continually say, that he is too drab and uninteresting to get the Labour Party elected.

I was glad to hear from Robin that he has now got a contract for a year with Central Television.

Robin is really impartial, and knows what objectivity means.

As he was leaving, Nicholas Soames[20] made a particular point of coming over to me and saying how good my articles had been on the Royal Family and that we would meet again at Cheltenham when he would be staying with Queen Elizabeth the Queen Mother. You would think he had never said all those horrible things about me, once to my face at the All Party Racing Committee[21] and a great deal behind

---

19. Producer of *Panorama*, retired from the BBC in 1965, d 1987.
20. Conservative MP since 1983; son of Mary Soames (writer, chairman, Royal National Theatre, 1989–95; daughter of Sir Winston Churchill and widow of Christopher Soames, Conservative politician and life peer 1978).*
21. In February 1991; see Vol. 2, pp. 459–60.

my back when he was trying to stop me being re-appointed as Chairman of the Tote.

Friday 22 January
Yesterday at the Levy Board it was announced, as I knew already, that Tristram Ricketts was going to be the Chief Executive of this famous new BHB at £100,000 a year. We [the Levy Board] immediately appointed Rodney Brack his deputy, an accountant who is much more efficient and sensible and worldly wise than Tristram Ricketts, even though he has not been there as long and is much younger.

Wednesday 27 January
This morning I thought I must no longer be a coward. I must ring Margaret and probably get a roasting. It was not quite half past eight when she answered the telephone at home. It was nearly nine when she put it down, saying 'Cheer up,' which was slightly odd as I had been telling her that despite everything I remained optimistic.

On the £50 million deficit projected for 1993–4: 'Norman doesn't seem to have any idea of the seriousness of it, nor does Major. They're just drifting along, overspending.'

She then turned to attacking the House of Lords. She said, 'I didn't realize how absolutely useless they are. There they are, they just go along to collect £15,000 a year.' I said, '£15,000? How do you work that out?' She said, 'Well, grossed up they collect seven to eight thousand and that brings in fifteen thousand because it's tax free.

'They've got no guts. They should be defending Britain against the transfer of power to Maastricht and our loss of sovereignty and our loss of identity.'

I said, 'Go easy, some of the Lords have a very keen sense that if they push things too far, they'll be wiped out and have the only little power they have left taken away.' She said, 'If they were bigger men, they would take the risk. Actually, I think they are quite useless and they ought to be abolished. They are no good at all,' which was somewhat contrary to her support earlier for our institutions and not having them undermined.

She said about Norman that the attacks on him were monstrous, got up by the press and a lot of them were lies. 'He is having a terrible time. I think it stops him thinking properly about what to do with the economy.'

She said, 'Nigel Lawson is a very clever man indeed and he was very good. He had much imagination until he went wrong, but we won't go into that again now. Norman hasn't got a first-class mind.'

I said, 'There is one comfort which is that it doesn't matter what they do nor how badly they behave, the government, because the other side will never get elected, so long as Labour refuses to behave like Clinton and embrace capitalism and all its faults with enthusiasm.'

'You may have a surprise. I have been amazed at John Smith, that he hasn't fought back harder and done better. I think they will try to get rid of him. If they do, some of those younger ones may easily win the next election.'

I asked how she was getting on with her memoirs and she said she expected the first volume to come out by October or thereabouts.

I think nobody will be spared in these memoirs. Probably I shall get a few swipes, unless for old times' sake she doesn't mention me at all.[22]

She obviously still likes me and likes to talk to me, though I don't think I have much influence on what she thinks at the moment, except when I write an article about privacy or India or whatever it may be which she agrees with, and give her new facts she hadn't thought of.

I didn't go to the Lords today. Partly because I felt hit by Margaret grumbling about people claiming their £59 for attendance.

It is not a good idea to go every day just in order to collect that cash. But usually when I do go something interesting occurs.

Thursday 28 January
Talked to Norman about the great deficit.

I told him Mrs Thatcher's reaction and her saying the government doesn't seem to care about it, wandering along doing nothing.

Norman is really more interested in the John Major affair which is splashed all over the papers this morning. This is the allegation printed in a little paper called *Scallywag* and now taken up by the *New Statesman* in today's edition. The suggestion is that John Major has been having an affair with a cook at Number 10. She also has a catering business, providing meals for lots of people. She doesn't look attractive but maybe it's just a bad photograph.

Of course she denies there has been any hanky-panky.

---

22. For whatever reason, Lady Thatcher only mentioned WW once in the first volume of her memoirs, on p. 370 when she says she met some of the working miners at a private buffet hosted by WW at the end of March 1986. See p. 290.

On hearing about this, John Major went into session in his last few hours in India with his colleagues there, his private secretary and others in his entourage. He then decided to get in touch with his solicitors to issue libel writs against the two papers.

I said, 'You know I had warned him that the *Sun* had taken an apartment opposite a house where they thought he might be visiting a woman. They have found nothing yet but you have all got to be jolly careful. Otherwise, if you visit somewhere you shouldn't, people will put two and two together and make five,' to which Norman replied immediately, 'Or make four?' and laughed.

It is certainly true that Norma Major spends very little time at 10 Downing Street and is always at home in Huntingdon if she can possibly manage it. But she told me that when I first met her some years ago in the French embassy, long before he was Prime Minister, that she didn't like the political life.[23] Maybe John is friendly with the woman who has never yet been married, but it doesn't mean to say he is having an affair with her.

Friday 29 January
How I long for that Channel Tunnel to open!

We arrived at the Ritz Hotel at a quarter to seven local time, being due to be out to dinner with Luc de la Barre de Nanteuil[24] at 8.30. Our journey from Cavendish Avenue had taken an exhausting over five hours.

Poor Hedwige had just had her latest therapy for her breast cancer.

We had bought her some flowers at the Ritz for £30, just a dozen tulips. They did look beautiful but it was ridiculous paying that amount.

Luc was in tremendous spirits. It is all clear about Hedwige, everything is going to be all right, there are going to be no problems at all and no lasting effect. So we rejoiced with him in that.

Luc had never liked Mrs Thatcher. But he said she was magnificent. He recalled an occasion when Rocard was Prime Minister.[25] He was invited by Mrs Thatcher to meet her at half past four one afternoon. When he got there, he was shown into her little study upstairs (the

---

23. The French embassy dinner was on 3 July 1990; see Vol. 2, p. 322.
24. French Ambassador to the UK, 1986–91; m 2 (1973) Hedwige Frerejean de Chavagneux.
25. Michel Rocard, French Prime Minister, 1988–91.

one I know well), and was plonked down in a chair. Then Mrs Thatcher began to harangue him on her latest fad of the moment which was the danger to the ozone layer. After a bit she said, 'What are your views?' So he said a few things and then she charged off into her next attack, on the European Community.

Rocard was absolutely fascinated and hardly dared say a word. At a quarter past five she got up and said, 'Thank you very much Monsieur Rocard. This has been a very interesting discussion.' Completely shaken, he left the room.

I said, 'Doesn't that show what a miraculous, extraordinary woman she is? Here we are still talking about her.'

He said about Maastricht, 'It is very unsensible of Mrs Thatcher to make such a fuss about it. It is a romantic thing in Europe and in France. We have set an impossible goal of political union. We know it is impossible. We will keep our national identity and you will keep yours. The Germans will keep theirs. We like to say these things but they don't really mean anything. It's just like a Utopian dream. But you in England take it all so literally.'

Luc was very funny mimicking Mrs Thatcher, her voice and her expression.

Sunday 31 January
We had arranged to get to Vincennes [for the trotting races] very early.

Alan Meale was there and his quite attractive wife (except for her teeth which are extremely bad and irregular: something ought to be done about them). She is an economist. He was very friendly, very keen on trotting. He is a supporter of mine, though he made some foolish, deprecatory remark which he said he was misquoted on when I was reappointed.

Monday 1 February

The Duff Cooper Memorial Prize at the Mayfair Hotel. Moët et Chandon had provided the champagne which wasn't too bad, nor were the little bits to eat. The hotel had provided the Crystal Room free. I don't know if Denis Healey, who was to make the speech on the presentation of the prizes, was free or not. Perhaps.

I talked to Edna Healey[1] a bit. She has still got a very pleasing, voluptuous face. In some ways she is cleverer than her husband, Denis. I congratulated her on the book she had been writing about the Coutts family.

Denis looks a strong fellow, aggressive always but with a good sense of humour. I think they must be very happily married. She is the soft side of his nature but she is also a strong woman.

I always remember him describing how they would stop on their walks in the hills and make love at the side of a field. They have both been fairly lusty.

They really are an engaging and admirable couple, even though Denis on the whole prostituted himself, particularly when backing a Labour Party believing in nuclear disarmament, which he didn't believe in at all.

I asked Sue Baring[2] what she was doing there and she said she had now written a book. I said, 'Have you?' and she said well, she was now writing one. She still attracts men like a candle attracts moths.

Then I talked to Marigold Johnson who was also there with her husband, Paul, and a couple of her children.[3]

He is a difficult fellow to live with. He goes up and down and has these terrible moods.

---

1. Edna, née Edmunds, writer; her *Coutts & Co. 1692–1992* was published in 1992; m (1945) Denis Healey.
2. JP; former Alliance and Liberal Democrat parliamentary candidate; née Renwick, m (1955–84) the Hon. John Baring, now 7th Baron Ashburton.
3. Daniel Johnson was literary editor of the *Times*.

Norman said to me that he had gone up to him at a party recently and said to him, 'I hear you have been in a loony bin recently and you are frequently there. I am not surprised.' Paul Johnson had walked away. Norman did this in return for all Paul's vile comments about Norman, saying if he was a man of honour he would resign.

Miss Artemis Cooper,[4] who is a bit of a silly girl, made a speech which wasn't too bad – she made one or two tiny jokes. When I wrote to John Julius, thanking him for the evening, I said what a brilliant speech she had made. That proves something, namely that I am a liar when I think no harm is done.

I am trying to send half a dozen bottles of champagne to Graham Paterson who is getting married at the end of the week. He is the Features Editor of the *Times* and looks after my copy. I am very friendly with him and he likes what I write, even when News International are very definitely against me, and he still gets me as much space as he can. As indeed does Peter Stothard, rather decently because almost everything I write now contradicts something he has just written in rather scatty leading articles.

Wednesday 3 February
The Prime Minister has made a speech which was quite good, setting his notion of a classless society just along the lines which I had suggested to him. It was to the Carlton Club members, all in their dinner jackets, shown on television.

I don't know what the viewers made of the dinner jackets on upper-class, prosperous men, thirsting for a classless society.

Thursday 4 February
A dinner to say goodbye [from SIS] to Bruce Matthews[5] at the Langham Hotel, owned by Ladbroke.

When he made his little parting speech, which was extremely dreary (he is a very dreary man, Bruce, though I quite liked him) he referred to how I had brought him into SIS.

It is true I introduced him to it when he was leaving Rupert's English

----

4. Writer, daughter of 2nd Viscount Norwich and his first wife, Anne, née Clifford.
5. (1926–96); former managing director, News International; see Vol. 1 for his becoming chairman of Satellite Information Services (which provides television pictures of races in betting shops).

operation, about which he was also bitter, but I see now why Rupert got rid of him.

I made lots of jolly jokes about Clive Hollick,[6] whom I like. He is the fellow running the *Mirror* now, more or less, with David Montgomery.[7] He was quizzing me about having left the Labour Party and going back on my ideals. I said, 'My God, there you are, a ruddy great socialist capitalist, you're going to be a multi-multi-millionaire because you are very young, and you accuse me of not keeping up my ideals. I have kept up with them completely. The Labour Party has just sailed away from me.'

Sunday 7 February
Dinner at the Lennox-Boyds was pretty noisy. Michael Howard was there and I asked him if he thought Major was wise to go on with the libel action. He was a bit cagey as it was in front of a journalist called Xan Smiley who is actually a very reliable fellow, at the moment political editor of the *Economist* and writing the column 'Bagehot'.

I was talking to Richard Ryder in the morning, too, and he was there.

We were discussing the serious danger that the government will be defeated over the pits closures and also that there might be enough madmen on the Tory side to combine with Labour to vote against Maastricht. They would have to be quite insane, but silly Tory MPs do get insane at times.

Arabella had been looking very cuddly. She squeezed my arm as we sat next to each other on the sofa after dinner. She said had I noticed she was getting thinner. I politely said yes, but she still has a longish way to go.

---

6. Chief executive, United News & Media (formerly MAI) since 1974; director, SIS, 1990–4; special adviser to President, Board of Trade, 1997–8; life peer 1991.
7. Chief executive, Mirror Group, 1992–9.

Tuesday 9 February
It was with some apprehension that I went to the Marje Proops[8]
luncheon given by Christina Foyle[9] in honour of the launch of her
book. Hugh Cudlipp[10] was Chairman.

My neighbour, Beryl Bainbridge, is a writer I have always thought
is very good and I have one or two of her first editions, *The Bottle
Factory Outing* and *Sweet William*. We talked away about writing and
how women were very good writers of novels. She said she was brought
up in Liverpool. She was married but divorced and she has got grandchildren now.

She is a jolly sort of lady.

I said, 'I have a paperback on order right now, your book about
Scott.'[11] She said, 'That is one of my best.' I said, 'Can I send you my
first editions of yours to sign?' She said, 'Yes, please. And I will send
you a hard copy of the Scott one.' I thought that was very generous
of her.

She said her publishers are Duckworth but she sells a lot in paperback with Penguin and also in paperback in America. I said, 'You
don't sell much with Duckworth?' She said, 'No. They are gentlemen
publishers and they don't bother about making money.' She said she
had always been with them ever since she started writing. I said, 'Why
don't you get a proper publisher who would promote your books?'
She said, 'I am not really interested in money. I have enough to live
on.' She lives in a little house in Camden which used to belong to one
of the managers of the railway. She said they are little houses, not
slummish but built for middle managers when the railway revolution
started in the 1830s and 40s.

She was once shortlisted for a Booker prize.[12] I said, 'Obviously
your book had a plot and real people instead of all that dreamy stuff
and that is why you didn't win.'

8. Born c. 1911, died 1996; *Daily Mirror* journalist and agony aunt; *Marje: the guilt
and the gingerbread* by Angela Patmore, published 1993, had revealed her long
affair with the *Daily Mirror* legal manager, Phillip Levy (d 1987).

9. Bookseller; began Foyle's Literary Lunches 1930; died 1999.

10. (1913–98); journalist and newspaper publisher; former chairman, Daily Mirror,
IPC; life peer 1974.

11. *The Birthday Boys*, 1991.

12. For *An Awfully Big Adventure*, 1989; two of her books since this date have also
been shortlisted for the Booker: *Every Man for Himself*, 1996, and *Master Georgie*,
1998.

Hugh Cudlipp made a very funny speech, saying Proops was very innocent in supposing that they would not concentrate in the reviews and comments in the press mainly on her secret sex life for twenty years or so: 'I didn't know that Phillip Levy was not only working all day for the *Mirror* but working at night as well for the *Mirror*.'

In the House I bumped into Alistair McAlpine. I said, 'Please stop rubbishing and attacking Norman. He has done everything you asked for, cutting interest rates and setting the stage for recovery. Margaret thinks he is the best man in the Cabinet.'

He promised not to do it any more. That is in his column in the *Sunday Express* which is not good but can be very spiteful and I daresay is read fairly widely.

Wednesday 10 February
The highlight of the day was the golden wedding celebration of Cecilia and Willie Whitelaw. There were about a hundred and twenty people in the National Portrait Gallery which is a very good setting for that kind of dinner.

I was very honoured to be invited to this great gathering – I am not even a Tory.

On my right was a tiny little charming lady, quick and interesting with a very pretty face, particularly when she got animated.[13] She talked a great deal. I enjoyed it.

Her husband is Sir Robin Butler who is Head of the Civil Service and Secretary to the Cabinet, a very clever fellow.

They were at university together.

While they were living together before marriage and away on holiday, Robin got a telegram from his father which read rather oddly considering she was staying with him. It said, 'Congratulations on your first love.' There was no comma between 'first' and 'love' and they could not make out whether he was talking about Robin's success in his examination or about being with her, who, in his father's mind, was his first love.

Beryl Bainbridge sent me a number of her books, first editions, which was sweet of her. She wrote on them various little messages.

I was very amused by her letter saying she would have put in her inscription in the book 'lots of love and XXXs' but 'you being a Lord

---

13. Gillian, née Galley, m (1962) Robin Butler (Secretary to the Cabinet and Head of the Home Civil Service, 1988–98; knight 1988, life peer 1998).

and all that, I didn't think I could.' This was a on a scrap of exercise book paper.

In the afternoon I gave tea in the Lords to Judith Heimann, a strange, Germanic lady by birth. She wanted to talk to me about Tom Harrisson[14] on whom she is deeply researching a book, goodness knows why.

She said how upset Tom Harrisson had been when Zita Crossman[15] had left him for another lover. She was quite amusing. She wanted to know a great deal about Biddy [Harrisson] who was three parts mad but had a hold on Tom, as I told her, because she had a very comfortable house. It was big and she had some money. Tom needed money.

She asked what did I think of Biddy. I said, 'She had sex with anybody, anywhere at any time, immediately she could get it.' I added hastily, and it's totally true, 'But never with me because I wouldn't have anything to do with her like that.' I quite liked her and when I went to Normandy I had a letter from her, asking questions about what war was like. I wrote an answer while I was awaiting court martial[16] which was published in *Horizon* in 1944.

I also sent around to Mrs Heimann on Thursday morning some extracts about Tom which I had written in my early book, *Into the Dangerous World.*[17]

Friday 12 February
I rang Irwin.

I said, 'I have an idea. I think the *Sun* should not go on resisting

---

14. (1911–76); ethnologist, joint founder and chairman of Mass Observation, m 1 (1941–54) Mrs Betha Clayton (d 1961); WW wrote the *Dictionary of National Biography* entry on him; see Vol. 1, p. 196. Judith Heimann's book, *The Most Offending Soul Alive: Tom Harrisson and his remarkable life*, was published in 2000.

15. Richard Crossman (1907–74), the Labour politician and writer, m 1 (1937) Inezita, née Baker (d 1952).

16. For writing an adverse report on a senior officer; the outcome was that Field Marshal Montgomery wrote on the papers, 'This officer is right. But it would be bad for discipline if he were to continue to serve in 21 Army Group. He may keep his rank and choose to serve in any other theatre of war . . . ' See *Confessions of an Optimist*, pp. 99 ff. *Horizon* was the literary journal Connolly founded and edited, 1939–50; WW's memorable 'Letter From France' was in Vol. X No. 58, October 1944.

17. WW's first autobiography, published in 1952.

this action for damages over publication of the Queen's Christmas broadcast two days before it occurred.' He said, 'Why don't you ring Rupert?' So I decided to do so as I hadn't spoken to him for some time.

I told him very firmly that it was impossible for me to defend him at the moment if he goes on insulting the Queen.

He said, 'I read what you said in the *Times* and I don't agree with it.'[18] I said, 'About our history and so on?' He said, 'Yes. It doesn't mean a thing,' with an overdone Australian accent put on to tease me.

I said, 'You can say that she has done what was asked of her, she turned up trumps over paying income tax and, as a gesture of goodwill, you would like to say you won't defend the action and that you will pay a settlement at once into the Save the Children Fund, which is Princess Anne's [charity] and very popular.' He said, 'What, all those Africans?' which is what Irwin had said to me. I said, 'Yes, it's a very popular charity and you should pay them £200,000.' He quickly broke in, '£100,000.' I said, 'No, that's not enough. It's got to be at least £200,000.'

A little while later he rang back and said, 'I'm drafting a letter for the front page of the *Sun*.' He started reading this. It began, 'Dear Ma'am, Sorry about upsetting your Christmas. We didn't mean to do it. It was only a bit of fun.' (I said to him, 'It wasn't, you know. It was spite.') 'You've agreed to listen to the people and of course we will go on having our disagreements and arguments but I hope we can do it in a friendly way. Meanwhile, that's what we would like to do . . . '

I said, 'You can't address the Queen in that way.'

He said, 'Why not?'

I said, 'First of all, it totally lacks respect. Who is signing this letter, you?' 'Oh no, Kelvin MacKenzie will sign it. I'm just working it out.' I said, 'But Kelvin MacKenzie is trying to behave as though he were the equal of the Queen.' 'He is,' says Rupert. 'We've got twelve million readers. She hasn't.' I said, 'But she's got most of the whole nation. In any case, all the readers by a long chalk don't agree with what you've been doing, insulting the Queen and trying to order her about.'

I said, 'There are all kinds of things they are thinking of here, you know. For example, about cross-ownership of television stations and newspapers. That's going to come back again. Also there may be VAT

---

18. WW's article of 9 February was a defence of the monarchy as a symbol of national identity.

on newspapers.' 'I don't mind about VAT on newspapers. The *Mirror* will suffer worse than us.'

I said, 'There are people in this country who actually have power to do things to you, Rupert. You must get that into your head.'

In the end he said, 'I appreciate your suggestion. It's very friendly of you and very helpful. We're working on it and we'll go on working on it.' I said, 'Will you send me a fax of the final thing?' 'Oh no, I can't do that.' I said, 'Why not?' He said, 'You'll try to influence us.' I said, 'Yes, certainly. What is more, when it's about to happen, I would like to ring David Airlie and say it is coming up and please take it in the spirit it's intended.'

He said, 'No, no, I don't want you to do that, no, no, no.' So I don't quite know where I am now. That was the last thing I heard before I went to bed.

Reflecting on Rupert I am beginning to wonder whether he hasn't gone absolutely Citizen Kane.[19] He was shouting away telling me how important he was and how he has a great media empire and when I said, 'It's not very helpful, you know, doing this film about Diana and the Prince of Wales on BSkyB,'[20] he said, 'Ah, well, they have got to put up with it. It's all their fault.' He admitted to me that he did want a republic. I forgot to say to him, 'Have you told your mother that yet?' because he was telling me he had more power than the government in England.[21]

Sunday 14 February

I began to wonder whether I might not do a play with that curious girl, Beryl Bainbridge, she having been an actress and her daughter on the stage as well. Two of her works would make very good plays.

Eventually at eleven o'clock at night I got hold of Norman.

Norman said Conrad Black had promised him when he met him at his party that he would stop the attacks in the *Telegraph* papers and the insistent demands that he should resign. Having done that, three days later the demands arose again. 'Doesn't he have any control over his newspaper or is he just a liar?'

---

19. The megalomaniac newspaper proprietor in the Orson Welles film, based on William Randolph Hearst.
20. Based on Andrew Morton's book *Diana: Her True Story*.
21. WW often cites Dame Elisabeth Murdoch as supporting the monarchy.

Monday 15 February

I tried to get Norman to say that whatever happened he mustn't give
any indication that I had anything to do with the front page of the
Sun this morning when the famous letter appeared. It was pretty well
OK, as re-written by me.

I then got hold of Sir Robert Fellowes, the Queen's Private Secretary,
at the Palace at about 8.30.

I said, 'Now you must get the response right.' He read to me what
he thought the Queen should say.

He said, 'There's another thing. Princess Anne has agreed that half
of the £200,000 will go to the Cheshire Homes which was the subject,
largely, of the Queen's Christmas broadcast.' I said, 'That's fine. I never
thought of that. I had forgotten. You're quicker witted than I am.' He
laughed, 'That's the first time I've been told I'm quick-witted.'

I also said to him, 'Will you please make sure that nobody says
anything about my connection with this because it would fatal to anything I can do to help at other times.'

I said, 'I am sure the Queen is a very confidential lady so I don't
mind your telling her.' He thought that was quite funny.

I spoke to Fellowes again at about half past four in the afternoon.

He told me the other side had agreed to pay costs which in a sense
was an admission that they were wrong. He then said, 'I would like
your advice. I am the Queen's Private Secretary but I have never met
Rupert Murdoch and I think I ought to.'

I said, 'We will have a quiet dinner here next time he comes
to England, by ourselves, just the three of us. We won't eat in a
restaurant which would be very dangerous.'

I spoke to Irwin and told him it is absolutely essential that my name
be kept out of this.

He said, 'This sounds very mediaeval.' I said, 'Of course it's mediaeval. We have a long history and these things have to be done secretly
at times. He who denies his history denies himself.' He said, 'Did you
think of that?' I said, 'Of course I did. All the things I say are original
to me.'

I said, 'It very much applies to your people, the Jews. That's how
you have kept surviving, keeping to your traditions and your past
because it gives you strength in the present and confidence for the
future.'

So that was one of the more interesting days of my life. Maybe it
is the most important thing I have ever pulled off. To weaken the

monarchy or destroy it would be absolutely ghastly, fatal for the country.

Tuesday 16 February
Dinner party at Cavendish Avenue.

Vere Rothermere had rung me earlier in the morning from France. He was ill and couldn't come. Chips who came instead was jolly decent about it.

When Princess Alexandra came in she of course knew Chips and knew Amabel Lindsay as well. I said to them, 'I fear Vere couldn't come. He is ill with diarrhoea.' The Princess looked rather shocked at my saying that, although the Royal Family are always making lavatory jokes. I said, 'Chips was the nearest in size I could think of to come.' Actually Chips isn't as tall and not nearly as fat, though he is pretty fat.

Angus Ogilvy said that Prince Andrew, poor fellow, is still in love with Ferguson. He also said that Prince Charles is much to blame for the way in which he resumed his affair with Camilla in such an indiscreet way that it was flaunted in Diana's face, and she is a very unstable girl anyway, so it was not altogether surprising that she jumped over the traces.

Princess Alexandra rather nervously asked me, when she was sitting next to me at dinner, did I think the monarchy would survive. They are obviously all very rattled.

Pierre Salinger has a very attractive, craggy face. He was Kennedy's spokesman and speech writer and generally his chief factotum while he was at the White House. He said that Reagan had made a terrible mistake in the bombing of Libya. It now turns out, and American intelligence are completely satisfied it is true, that the Libyans had nothing whatever to do with the Lockerbie bomb in the aircraft which was blown up. It was Iran and Syria who put the bomb on board at Frankfurt. But of course it can't be published, at least not at the moment though it will get out one day.

Nicole Salinger is very pretty and charming. She has only been married to Pierre for four years and is his fourth wife. She said, 'You are on to your fourth wife, too, aren't you?' I said, 'Yes but we have been married rather longer than four years.' She is French.

Verushka asked me not to keep the men in the dining-room for more than twenty minutes after the ladies left the room. I said all right and timed it.

The food was very good, wild duck. Everybody enjoyed the wine and of course the champagne beforehand which was either 1976 Krug or 1947 Mumm. Angus at this stage was only drinking water and so was the Princess. She is still a handsome-looking woman. She is over sixty,[22] not unintelligent and very charming.

When the pictures of Fergie semi-nude with her boyfriend, [John] Bryan, appeared in August, the Queen saw them first thing in the morning. She put them all round the breakfast table for when the Duchess came down for breakfast. She saw them there and immediately left Balmoral.

The Queen is very distressed with her behaviour and that of her children.

None of them had a proper marriage, they have all been divorced apart from Edward who has never got married at all and there is still a great question mark around him.[23]

This all came from Angus Ogilvy who talked quite freely about it.

The flowers, a huge, huge bunch of magnificent roses, sent by Vere, were very much admired. We needn't have got any flowers at all, had we known.

Wednesday 17 February
Beryl Bainbridge came to lunch with me. I couldn't book a table in the Lords Strangers' dining-room so I had to have one in the Commons next door.

Everywhere I went she was greeted by people who knew her. It was like going around with a film star.

One whom she knew, a Mrs Kenneth Carlisle, an MP's wife, had a baby with her. They carry their babies in there now. I didn't know they allowed that. They certainly didn't when I used to be in the Commons.

I got her a seat in the Lords to see the introduction of Shirley Williams.[24]

She was introduced by Bill Rodgers, who has only just become a peer, and Roy Jenkins. As usual, Shirley muffed it. First of all, she didn't always stop at the right place or turn when she was supposed

---

22. She was 56 (born 25 December 1936); m (1963) Angus Ogilvy, younger brother of Lord Airlie (David), knight 1989.

23. He married Sophie Rhys Jones in 1999.

24. Former Labour Minister of Education who founded the SDP in 1981 with Bill Rodgers (life peer 1992), Roy Jenkins and David Owen.

to have done. Then, instead of giving a little head bow which is the correct one, she gave a waiter's bow, quite low.

I saw Beryl sitting up there, absolutely enthralled by everything, her face darting around the chamber.

She is rather pro the monarchy. She is not at all left-wing except in tiny bits.

I brought her my *Confessions of an Optimist*. She said, 'Is that your autobiography?' I said, 'Yes it is.' She said, 'I have written mine, you know, in my novels. I have expressed my feelings and my life in many ways in them.' She has the most original mind and remarkably strange ways of thinking, but she writes in a fascinating manner.

I also introduced her to Eddie Shackleton.[25]

I said, 'This lady has written a book called *The Birthday Boys* about Scott's last expedition. She says that Scott was always very jealous of your father.' He said, 'Yes.' They had a little chat and he was very interested.

Thursday 18 February
In the Chair at The Other Club, so I could select those who would sit on either side of me. On the right I had Paddy Ashdown and on the left Ian Gilmour.

Ian Gilmour was in a jolly laughing mood as of old. He talked of the feeling in the Tory Party against Major being snobbery. I remembered the snobbishness about Mrs Thatcher (but never mind). He recounted his dance with her at a Tory Party Conference when the Chairman of the Young Conservatives said he couldn't dance so Ian had to take his place. It was then alleged that he had trodden on her toe, on purpose. But he hadn't because he was never close enough to her. 'Can you dance?' 'A bit but she dances well.'

I had an entertaining conversation with Paddy Ashdown. He said I had been miles ahead of my time in advocating the Lib-Lab pact in 1961.

Paddy said, 'That would have swept the country in a similar pattern as now, when it would do the same.' I said, 'Yes, but you would find it very difficult to get Labour to swallow their pride.' But maybe he could now. They seem to be getting a bit closer.

He said he greatly admired Mrs Thatcher. It is extraordinary how, when politicians gather together, they never stop talking about her. He

---

25. (1911–94); son of the Antarctic explorer; Labour politician; life peer 1958.

thought power had corrupted her in the way that absolute power corrupts everybody. She was needlessly rude to people in public like Geoffrey Howe[26] and she became, perhaps, too arrogant. But she was extremely vulnerable, just a little girl inside.

I said, 'You have the qualities of a leader in you. If you get the Lib-Lab pact going again, you will have a chance to do something practical and need no longer waste your time as you are doing now.'

I was pleased about making a friend of Paddy Ashdown who has quite a lot to him.

Friday 19 February
Tried to ring Chips who has now been made a director of the Bank of England, which he longed to be. I found he was ill in bed with 'flu and a temperature. I left him a message saying, 'It's Chips with everything,' meaning he had also just got his knighthood.

Saturday 20 February
On arrival at Oare Henry met us by the car. As we walked towards the house I said, 'Would you like a knighthood?' He said, 'Who wouldn't?'

I said, 'I will see what I can do. But please don't say anything to anybody because it might muck it up.'

I said, 'After all, you have been backing Chris Patten against the mood of the business community in Hong Kong and in defiance of Peking; you have been very brave about that and very helpful.'

There was a jolly dinner.

Nicholas Soames said he can't come to Cheltenham because he has something he has to do in the Commons. He is Minister of Food now.

He said he hadn't been asked to the Tote lunch. I said, 'All right, I will see that you are. I don't know why that was. They were revising the lists trying to keep the numbers down, but certainly you shall come.' Actually, I'd struck him off for disloyalty.

Sunday 21 February
Henry showed us his prize yearling which is called John Major and a Welsh cob which gambols in the field called Norma after Mrs Major. I said, 'Have you told them that?' He said he didn't dare.

---

26. Conservative Chancellor of the Exchequer, Foreign Secretary and Deputy Prime Minister whose resignation from the Thatcher government in 1990 precipitated her fall; life peer 1992.

Monday 22 February

Having done my article for the *Times*, I had to rush down to the Lords.

I had thought the Newall amendment [to stop the evening opening of betting shops in summer] would be coming on after four, but it actually came on at twenty past three. Fortunately, I was just in time.

During the debate Mark Zetland referred obliquely to me: 'The Noble Lord sitting on the crossbench was responsible for getting the levy increased and the tax reduced by the Chancellor of the Exchequer.'

That was very handsome of him. He made a pretty effective speech, for him.

We got a great victory, one hundred and ten votes to fifty-six in our favour, so all was well.

I then rushed back to Cavendish Avenue. I was told that Rupert was going to ring. Eventually he did. He is still a trifle quarrelsome, complaining I had said the press were inaccurate and full of dirty tricks and so on in the *News of the World* on Sunday which he had already seen on return from his trips all round the place.

I told him Robert Fellowes would like to meet him and he said he would be happy to do that. He is coming over in April.

I said, 'It is of the utmost importance that my name is kept out of having anything to do with all this, otherwise Kelvin MacKenzie (editor of the *Sun*) will have my guts for garters.' 'He will anyway,' said Rupert cheerfully.

Tuesday 23 February

Fearful news from darling Anne Tree.[27] Colefax & Fowler in which they had all their money has blown up. They had undertaken not to sell their shares for two years, though they could have got out before it all collapsed. Now they have got to sell the house at Donhead St Mary and use a little house belonging to her sister somewhere in Chelsea. They are selling the Eaton Square flat.

I said, 'How dreadful to lose that wonderful garden you have made.'

---

27. The Lady Anne Tree, née Cavendish, daughter of the 10th Duke of Devonshire, sister of the 11th Duke (Andrew); m (1949) Michael Tree (1921–99), painter, director of Christie's and Colefax & Fowler, interior designers; great-grandson of Marshall Field, the Chicago millionaire; he succeeded his mother, Nancy Lancaster, at the helm of Colefax & Fowler. The Trees owned Mereworth Castle in Kent before Shute House in Dorset where they made a water garden with Sir Geoffrey Jellicoe, the landscape architect.

She said, 'I mustn't feel sorry for myself because so many other people are worse off.'

Dear, sweet Anne. I felt absolutely wretched hearing her. But she is a noble soul, not merely 'noble' because she is the daughter of a duke.

To make it worse, poor Jeremy Tree cannot see and is getting more and more confused in his head. Not so long ago he was in full command of all his senses and was one of the most brilliant trainers ever.[28]

Tuesday 23 – Wednesday 24 February *In Cornwall*
After the [Cornwall Light and Power] board meeting which was conducted with observers from the NatWest Bank who have put in all the finance, off we went to the Goonhilly Downs to see the windmills, of which nine are up already.

I set off walking in front of them because I couldn't be bothered to wait for them all to get into the jeep. I was up the hill and just on to the grass where the windmills are situated before they overtook me. It was a good, fresh air walk, though I was smoking a cigar.

We expect to be putting electricity into Mullion by they end of next week. I climbed into the control set-up at the bottom of one of the hundred-and-fifty-foot towers with the blades on top. It is very elaborate, [with] marvellous controls recording every bit of wind and amount of electricity generated and passed on to the South West Electricity Board [SWEB] for Mullion.

If the wind speeds are somewhere between 6.8 and 7.1, a lot of money can be made [though] we won't be able to pay off the debt to NatWest or get rid of some of the other debts for a long time.

Tessa [Lyle] was unusually friendly, particularly when I said I thought she should be paid a proper salary by the board for virtually managing it all on site. She has done that extremely well. She bargains with everybody, all the suppliers, and beats them down till they go nearly mad. I don't have to be there when she does it, so good luck to her on that aspect.

I took away my grant of peerage, the illuminated one with my new supporters stuck on my coat of arms, which had been hanging in the hall at Bonython. I don't think they minded at all. I put it there in the first place because my brother liked it there. I think they realize that perhaps it was symbolic, because I don't intend to go there again,

---

28. Michael Tree's brother; he died from his brain tumour on 13 March 1993.

at least not very often, if I can avoid it, and I will not be buried in the Cury Church because it will now be a family vault in Mayhewland.

Thursday 25 February
Spoke to Norman and urged him to have a look at the situation after they had taken the quarter per cent off the betting tax: were they getting more in total revenue or not? I told him it had been a very bad year and suggested they consider knocking another quarter per cent off.

Saturday 27 February
I hoped, when I recommended National Service be brought back again in the *Times*, it would produce a lot of letters but so far they haven't put one in. I think they don't put letters in about my articles on purpose.

I decided in my *News of the World* article to attack the government for overturning property contracts and creating uncertainty. If they can do that with property, they can do it with anything. The new Bill [the Urban Development Act] about leaseholds is legalized theft.

Tuesday 2 March

The *Evening Standard* and the *Times* both rang Beryl Bainbridge. They had heard she had a great new friendship with me and they wanted to run a story about it, that I had given her a bottle of champagne, etc.

I told Verushka about the story. She knew I had met her at the lunch for Marje Proops given by Christina Foyle, but I had not told her I had given her lunch in Parliament. So I did this evening – and how everybody there knew her and I suppose put two and two together and made seven.

When I spoke to Beryl on the telephone in the car, she said, 'Of course it is true that I have been going around boasting about knowing you.' I thought that was terribly sweet because there is nothing to boast about. It should be the other way round.

John Junor[1] wrote in his *Mail on Sunday* column about Rupert Murdoch liking privacy only for himself.

Vere Rothermere got into a terrible state. He said, 'You are not ever to write anything like that again attacking Rupert Murdoch. I have an understanding with him that I am not going to attack him.' The reason is that News International have got a whole lot of letters from Bubbles, his wife who has just died, which are quite extraordinary. She was crazy. She wrote to Vere attacking his life with his Korean mistress with whom he had been living for years in Paris. If Murdoch is attacked, this is all going to be published, in the *Sun*, probably, or the *News of the World*.

Bloody marvellous. These great press owners will happily publish, in Vere Rothermere's case, all the dirt and stuff they can get about Princess Diana from the Morton book and the Prince of Wales, all the tapes and anything they can get hold of, the pictures of Fergie naked and so on. Rupert does the same.

They think it is the right of the press and they mustn't be censored

---

1. (1919–97); former editor, *Sunday Express*; knight 1980.

and everybody has the right to know. But apparently nobody has the right to know what the press barons get up to. Ha ha.

In the *Evening Standard* tonight, in a column called Mr Pepys, there is a reference to me. It says I depend for my valued cigars, fine wine and champagne on Rupert Murdoch and this is now in jeopardy because I have been writing so many things in my column in the *News of the World* slamming News International newspapers for attacking the Queen and the Royal Family. Ho ho.

Pericles sent me very proudly a photograph of the outside of the café he is taking over and leasing, and plans of the location and the area. The square is supposed to be like some kind of English village, three miles or so from Monterey. It looks attractive. I hope to goodness it works. Dear boy, I tried to ring him this evening but he wasn't there so I left messages to say how good it all looked. I do hope he succeeds. I am worrying about what happens to him, and also what happens to my feckless, clever Petronella.

I was touched by getting A. L. Rowse's new book *The Sayings of Shakespeare*, to be published on March 25th. He had written in it, 'Woodrow, Good luck, from A. L. R. Look at the dedication.' It was dedicated to 'Margaret, Historic Figure, English Patriot'. I must make one last effort, before the poor old boy dies, with John Major to get him a knighthood.

I have also written today to Douglas Hurd asking if he will recommend Henry Keswick for a knighthood. I could write to John Major myself but it wouldn't be one millionth as good as Douglas doing it.

Thursday 4 March
In the evening, dinner party at Rocco and Aliai Forte's. The first person I spoke to was Alistair McAlpine. I thanked him for not making any more attacks on Norman Lamont in his weekly column in the *Sunday Express*.

Rosita Marlborough saw us talking and came up.

She asked was I up to some mischief. I said, 'No, I am trying to stop Alistair making some.'

I had a very jolly talk with Aliai.

We discussed infidelity in marriage.

I said, 'It's absurd this notion that there is only one person in the entire world who can match just one person from the opposite sex and live happily ever after. Infidelity in marriage doesn't mean you stop loving people. It just means that most people from time to time are cheered up and made to feel romantic again by a diversion. It doesn't necessarily have to be so deep as to wreck the marriage.' I hope I didn't put any new ideas into her head.

On my other side sat a girl called Emma Sergeant, daughter of Sir Patrick Sergeant, a financial journalist who made a fabulous fortune out of a magazine called *Euromoney.*

She is a painter and charges £10,000 for a portrait. I said, 'Good heavens, that's far more than I could afford. When Olwyn Bowey painted Verushka and had a stab at painting me she didn't charge anything like as much. I couldn't have afforded it.' She had never heard of Olwyn Bowey, but she is a member of the Royal Academy and so is Carel Weight she is married to.[2] She didn't think much of the Royal Academy but she doesn't have to if she can charge all that much at her age, thirty.

Norman was enjoying himself. I was surprised they had asked him to the house because of the distress Papa Forte had felt over the scandal when he got the famous black eye which he has never been able to live down in the gossip columns and the press. The Fortes don't seen to mind about it now.[3]

The person who made the most impact on me at that party was Stephen Fry. He acts Jeeves perfectly in the film productions of the Jeeves stories.

He said that sometimes it was rather difficult to act in the way Wodehouse had laid down. 'How do you raise your eyebrow imperceptibly?' I said, 'How do you?' He said, 'I just try and think that it's going up so therefore it's imperceptible.' I said, 'You've just done it with great accuracy.'

Friday 5 March
As I had been writing about the wickedness of the Archbishop of York, I started reading the Bible and the New Testament.

I had originally written the Archbishop of York is evil but the lawyers got very frightened so we compromised by saying he was

---

2. Carol Weight (1908–97) and Olwyn Bowey never married but lived next door to each other.
3. The incident was in 1985; see Vol. 1, p. 18.

wicked and demonstrated it by saying he should surely know that his
sympathy for the criminals encourages crime.[4]

Tuesday 9 March
I rehearsed my speech [for the annual Tote lunch] several times to try
to get some life into it. Then it was off to the Hyde Park Hotel.

I had Kenneth Clarke on my right and Norman Lamont on my left.
On his left was Stoker Hartington and on his left was Douglas Hurd
and on his left was Robin Butler.

They roared with laughter at my joke about John Birt who has been
very much in the newspapers. He is the Director General of the BBC
now. Having made himself a private company while employed by the
BBC, he got all kinds of tax allowances which he wouldn't have got if
he were working for the BBC properly [as an employee].

On Verushka's expensive clothes I said, 'Unfortunately, unlike John
Birt, I haven't found a way of making them tax-deductible.'

Later I went down to the Lords to vote against the government on
this legalized theft [the Urban Development Act].

In the lobby Margaret was busy haranguing Tories who were about
to vote for the amendment which would at least stop some of the theft.

I thought this was slightly rum.

It is hardly consistent with her opposing Maastricht.

Oh dear, I do love that woman so much but, my God, she has
become very stupid.

The amendment was only defeated with the aid of Labour votes.

When I said to Robert [Cranborne], 'You're a traitor,' his father
[Lord Salisbury] came up to me and said, 'You're absolutely right. It's
abominable what he's doing.'

Robert said to him, 'I'll pair with you if you like.' He said, 'No, I
want to record my vote against you.' He was really quite cross with
his son. Robert had to do it because he is in the government, as were
a number of young men on those benches, hereditary peers who hated
the whole ruddy Bill but had to pretend they liked it.

---

4. WW in the *News of the World* of 7 March attacked Dr Habgood, Archbishop of
   York, for saying Major was wrong to state we should condemn offenders more
   and understand them less.

Wednesday 10 March
Panics from poor old Mark Zetland. They are very much on the danger list at Redcar where they have been losing money. He has lost the sponsorship of his famous two-year-old race and would we sponsor it? I was sympathetic to him because it is in the North.

This evening I went to see dear little Beryl Bainbridge and took her a bottle of red wine. She was rather sweet and she showed me all the way round the house, pictures of herself and, extraordinary, the hole underneath the stairs at the top of the house where her crazy mother-in-law, who hated her because she got divorced from her son, came in with a pistol and shot her. She was just planning to knock the gun away (she must have been extremely brave, the then young Beryl) when the bullet glanced off her and hit behind, underneath the stairs. You can still see where the hole was.

I said that she ought to be more optimistic. She said no, she couldn't be and she felt she was going to die alone. I said, 'Don't worry, you don't have to think about that.' She asked if I minded about dying. I said, 'No, not a bit. I know nothing will happen after it. I feel annoyed that I have to die because I enjoy life so much.' But she doesn't, or she does only in parts.

It was very dark in the house. She wanted to show me everything, where her books were, where her bed was, what she put behind the bed. There was wrapping paper from Carnaby Street used as a Union Jack on the wall. There was an animal standing on one landing with a cigarette dangling out of its mouth. She smokes a lot of cigarettes. In the hall was a big buffalo which she had told me about. It was rotting in parts. She said that was caused by central heating.

She was very sweet. She gave me some smoked salmon sandwiches. The champagne wasn't really cold but would I open it? I said yes and she said, 'Do be careful, you'll break the window. It will pop up into the ceiling and cause some damage.' I said, 'No it won't. My dissolute youth has given me more knowledge of opening champagne bottles than anybody you could meet.' I carefully took the cork out and then I said, 'All you have to do is push against the pressure and let the air go out.'

Thursday 11 March
Had an argie-bargie with Margaret.

Naturally we talked a bit about Nicholas Ridley (who had just died) and what a great human being he was. He always stuck to what he believed, even though he was wrong.

I said, 'How do you think the government are doing?' She said, 'They have got no sense of purpose.' I said, 'They have got to get Maastricht through.' She said, 'Why?' I said, 'Well, if they don't they'll fall.' She said, 'No, not at all. It is the general view of the people that nobody wants it.'

At the end of it all she said, 'God bless you', a little bit like old times but not quite.

The next jollification of the morning was the Archbishop of York. He wrote to the editor of the *News of the World* saying unless they retract and prominently apologize for the article I wrote about him on March 7th he is going to take it to the Press Complaints Commission. I spoke to Paul Connew [deputy editor] who said of course they are not going to retract or apologize. They thought what I said was perfectly justified.

Saturday 13 March
There was a sweet postcard from Beryl Bainbridge. She is a very good person as well as being a brilliant, amazing writer. I have added her to the list of people I think about before I go to sleep to give them some protective shielding.

Sunday 14 March
I had to get cracking on readers' letters. I must have done about a hundred of them by the time I had finished.

I was feeling pretty weary by the afternoon but we had to go out to drinks with the Levers where Margaret and Denis were going to be.

Margaret delivered a long spiel about helping Yeltsin with money. I said, 'That's not much good because it's not money he needs, it's know-how. You yourself made very good arrangements for the distribution of food by sending out people from supermarkets here to show them how to distribute it. They've got plenty of food. They just can't get it distributed.' She was half complimented but half annoyed.

When they finally got up to go, normally she kisses me on the cheek and I kiss her on two cheeks, but she turned away then slightly relented as I squeezed her arm. I am afraid things are not what they used to be.

In some ways I feel disloyal to her but what can I do? I can't say what I don't believe, particularly when what she is trying to do is dislodge the government, which is silly.

Fortunately, the Tories have decided not to have Alan Clark as the candidate at Newbury. He is as mad as a hatter. He would not have won Newbury for them.[5]

Continue to read the Bible quite a lot, partly to defeat the ludicrous Archbishop of York and partly to have a look at the truths, which are many, in the New Testament. But I think it odd of Jesus Christ to say that the reason to behave yourself properly is because you will be rewarded in heaven. The reward ought to be in behaving yourself properly.

Monday 15 March
Count Paul Teleki came to dinner.[6]

I gave him the most marvellous wine, 1970 Calon-Ségur with the heart on the bottle. The Marquis de Ségur centuries ago owned Lafite and Latour and said, 'I make wine at Lafite and Latour but my heart is in Ségur.' That is why there is a heart on the bottle.

He said that the great Tokay Imperial vineyards and the stocks of wine, a hundred and fifty years old and more, some of it, are up for grabs. There is debt of seven million dollars to a Hungarian bank and they are going to foreclose. Maybe some Americans would buy it but they might disperse these wonderful stocks of wine to make a killing, not continue with the vineyard and the great Imperial Tokay would be no more.

I said I would try to see what I could do.

Tuesday 16 March
By the time Mark Pejacsevich had rung I had already spoken to Chips Keswick who is going to try to organize via Hambros somebody to pick up the [Tokay vineyards] debt.

When Norman rang from his Budget party at Number 11, there was a lot of laughter and talking in the background, as well there might be.

He said, 'I saw you in the Gallery with your yellow tie and I was very grateful to you for coming to support me.'

---

5. Nor did the candidate they chose; the seat was won on 6 May by David Rendel for the Liberal Democrats.
6. WW had met him in Budapest at Christmas – see 26 December 1992.

I said, 'I had to queue up first to get in but that wasn't any great sacrifice because we had a jolly gossip outside waiting. There was Baroness Hollis[7] whom I mistook for Blackstone[8] which caused a great sensation because they're both very pretty.'

Norman said, 'Do you mean the one with the red hair sitting next to you?' So there he was, doing his Budget speech and looking up to eye the girl with red hair next to me.

Norman said, 'Of course those are the only things worth talking about, aren't they, sex and love? They're the only things that really matter.'

He maintain his jolly attitude though perfectly serious.

That's not a bad approach to keep him balanced. But it gets him persecuted ever since that blasted black eye with Olga Polizzi's boyfriend outside her house.

Thursday 18 March
Sat next to Queen Elizabeth the Queen Mother [at Cheltenham].

She thinks Major lacks experience and didn't seem to know what he was doing and where he was going, not at all like Mrs Thatcher who did have experience.

I remembered, though, that when Margaret was doing the poll tax, she was sending messages through me to Mrs Thatcher saying she had gone too far and the English didn't like all these changes which were all a great mistake.[9]

I said, 'I think Major has done much better than people realize and he will turn out to be an excellent Prime Minister.' She did not appear convinced but I think I made her feel a bit better about him.

I told her about my row with the Archbishop of York. She thought it amusing. She thinks the Church has been appalling in its lack of taking a lead on morality and for all the same reasons that I do. She also agrees with my desire to return to having National Service.

Queen Elizabeth said everyone is so keen on money these days.

---

7. Reader (previously lecturer) in modern history, University of East Anglia, since 1967; Parliamentary Secretary of State, DSS, since 1997; life peer 1990.
8. Master of Birkbeck College, University of London, 1987–97; Minister of State, Department of Education and Employment, since 1997; life peer 1987.
9. See Vol. 2, p. 256, for the Queen Mother saying, 'Can't you get her to be more flexible?'; WW continued, 'Referring to the community charge, Queen Elizabeth said the British don't like too many changes.'

Kenneth Clarke, when he arrived, said he didn't quite agree that people were so keen on money as all that. He got on with her well.

I told Queen Elizabeth that I had backed a horse at 100 to 1, £2 each way, called Royal Athlete. She looked at me and laughed and said, 'This is one of your wicked jokes.' I said, 'No. It's perfectly true. Look what it says in the official race-card.' There it said that it had been improving and could well be near at the finish. When it came in third she was delighted, as I was, and very amused.

Also at lunch was David Stevens. He said he had ordered the *Express* to say the Budget was very good and I congratulated him on his turnround.

Princess Anne has this dim-looking husband who didn't seem any more lively than the last one, Mark Phillips.[10]

When I was saying goodbye to Queen Elizabeth, she said how much she had enjoyed talking to me and very quietly, 'Were we indiscreet?' I said, 'Yes, but I don't think anybody heard us.'

Saturday 20 March

It was very jolly at the Uttoxeter racecourse but it was up very early to get there.

Stanley Clarke, who is Chairman of Uttoxeter and puts a lot of money into it, as he is very rich with his Modwen Properties, was full of jolly greetings and congratulations about my Tote lunch speech.

I am beginning to think it is the most brilliant speech since Cicero exposed the Catiline conspiracy.[11] At least I bet mine was funnier.

Then it was on to Weeford via Lichfield. I left in good time so I could look around the cathedral.

Eventually when I got to Weeford, the Vicar, John Martin, who is the vicar of St Giles, Whittington, on the edge of Lichfield, and of St Mary's, Weeford, met me.

We looked at the tomb of John Wyatt and Jane Jackson, his wife. John Wyatt died in 1742 and his wife in 1739. From his brother Benjamin stemmed all the twenty-eight architects, painters, sculptors, inventors. There never before was such a flowering of genius in one family in the history of England nor since.

Thirteen first cousins married each other and numerous second and third cousins, so I am descended from them all ways round. They

10. Princess Anne had married Commander Timothy Laurence on 12 December 1992.
11. As Roman Consul in 63 BC.

stopped this excellent practice and the genes ran out; they were left with nothing but me and my cousin, R. E. S. Wyatt (Bob), to make any kind of splash in the world.

First of all we examined the top of the tomb in which my great-great-great-great-great-great-grandfather (and maybe another great to be added) was buried. There is a lovely poem written on the top in the slate which probably came from Leicestershire.

The problem with the slate on the top of the tomb is that it keeps getting cracked in the frost. The local stonemason from Lichfield wanted to put an entirely new slate on but he could never equal the beautiful lettering which had been inscribed, though he said he could.

The Vicar, who is a sensible bloke, agreed with me that it should not be touched. I said, 'We have just got to find out how to get it somehow sealed and not made any worse.'

I resolved to ring John Martin Robinson (which I did the next day and he is investigating it).

I agreed with the Vicar that I should be buried close by the John Wyatt and Jane Jackson tomb.

James Wyatt built a new church on the site of the previous church which had been there for centuries and was in a state of terrible collapse, as one can see from old prints of it. James, however, was buried in Westminster Abbey in Poets' Corner. Though a number of them got knighthoods, none of them ever got a peerage, though extremely distinguished.

I have to arrange to give them some money both before I die and afterwards. They haven't done much in the way of upkeep of the grave although I have been giving them money for some time.

At least I shall be part of the ground where my ancestors were for four to five hundred years, farming all around. That would be better than being with rather dodgy Cousin Molly[12] and probably a whole lot of bloody Mayhews at Cury. I don't suppose my brother will mind the distance between him and me. March 20th was his birthday and I thought about him a lot with considerable affection as I wandered around Weeford.

---

12. See *Confessions of an Optimist*, pp. 14 ff., for Cousin Molly and Bonython, the Cornish house of the Lyle family.

Tuesday 23 March
I spoke to Andrew Knight about the monstrous attacks still going on Norman Lamont.

He said he can't do anything with those two editors, meaning Andrew Neil and Kelvin MacKenzie.

We then had quite a friendly chat. I said, 'Did you see on Sunday night, it shook me rigid, Dennis Potter, who writes those musical films like *Pennies from Heaven* for the BBC? I have never heard such libellous stuff as he was saying about Rupert.'[13]

Rupert, apparently, had already thought of bringing a libel action but decided not to because it would only spread the story around more. He was accused of everything under the sun, including dishonesty.

So was Andrew Knight, who was accused of being a tax dodger.

Andrew said he is not a tax dodger.

All he has got is a trust in the Channel Islands, mainly for the benefit of his children, or entirely perhaps. If he sells any of that, he will have to pay sixty per cent tax on it.

He has turned out to be about the third largest shareholder in News International and News Corporation. I was cursing myself for not being bolder a couple of years ago and only bunging £2,400 into News International.

[After the Levy Board] I went to the Lords.

I looked up and saw baleful, hostile, hating eyes glaring at me. They belonged to the Archbishop of York.

On my way out I met McGregor, Chairman of the Press Complaints Commission.[14] I said, 'Have you ever heard anything more from the Archbishop of York about his complaint?' He said, 'Yes. We just had it this morning. Actually, in confidence, I think it is nonsense. You were merely expressing a political opinion which you have every right to. He is in the rough and tumble of it and he must accept what he gets.' So it looks as though the complaint will be rejected, which is very amusing.

Wednesday 24 March
Last night I had a dream that I was in a hairdressing shop and there were a number of ladies lined up with white things around their

---

13. In an interview with Melvyn Bragg; Potter died of cancer in 1994.
14. (1921–97); Professor of Social Institutions, University of London, 1964–85; Chairman, Press Complaints Commission, 1991–4; life peer 1978.

shoulders. The hairdresser was pouring water down their necks in order to make their hair grow. This must have been related to the fact that I have been pouring water into the bottom of my little Christmas rose which I bought for myself, one of my few treats, in Lichfield.

Saturday 27 March
This manuscript is not merely intended as a source of income for my estate when I am dead. It is becoming more and more in my mind to be the only memorial I can ever leave. Perhaps it really does have a view and a sweep which nobody else contemporaneous can match. Perhaps if it were read years and years after my death, there will be messages which will achieve an echo in the minds of some readers with the same kind of thinking.

Monday 29 March
Nadje started yelling her head off at about half past ten.

She announced that she had said to the doctor, 'I would like to kill myself,' and he said, 'I don't blame you.' I thought, 'Unfortunately, there is no chance you will.' This was very unkind, no doubt.

She is a tremendous example of Shakespeare's crabbed age. I am trying to avoid it and be more agreeable but it is quite tough going.

Wednesday 31 March
Berjis Daver, the Chairman of Ladbroke Racing, came to lunch. He is a Parsee and, like his race, tenacious and highly intelligent. He came from Bombay originally. He didn't drink much but he had some champagne, some Sancerre and a chunk of my 1984 Cos Labory. He is clearly interested in joining in the party in Tote Direct.

I went to hear John McCririck, racing's comedian, at the All Party Racing Committee. He got a very good house. He talked much nonsense about how the BHB wouldn't work. He thought bookmakers should be on the BHB as it's the new controlling body of the sport. He thought there should be no Tote monopoly – no monopolies at all. He thought the Tote should be privatized: 'There is his Lordship who writes every week in his column about the virtues of privatization but when it comes to his Tote, no, it is special and different and can't be privatized.'

Rupert, having bought the *New York Post*, which he was able to do because it was going bankrupt, is not now coming to England till much later in April. I think he's an idiot. He is splashing out far too much again. He only just got round the last corner. His shares will fall because the *New York Post* cannot possibly make any money.

He wants influence in New York and through New York in politics in America.

No one man can possibly straddle Hollywood and such vast media concerns all over the world, his newspapers in England and so forth and really do it properly. Also, it will heighten the demand in England not to have this foreigner owning so much of our press and television. I shall have my work cut out to help him.

The day of the great dinner party for fourteen people.

The drawing-room never looked so lovely with beautiful flowers everywhere. Some were presents and some had been bought by Verushka. The dining-room table was splendid with all the silver candlesticks and the full regalia of my crested plates which I got twenty-six years ago when we were married, specially made.

Robin Day had been asked at the last minute as one man had fallen by the wayside. He was the first to arrive and immediately said, 'May I give your daughter a present?' to me in his gallant, old-world style. As the others began to come in, already Robin and Petronella were starting to sing which amused everybody.

I had the delicious Allsopp girl on my right.

I said, 'Why do you keep moving? Do you make money each time?' She said they have done so far. It seems they never stay in a place for more than a couple of years before they move on to the next one.

He makes a lot of money as Chairman of Christie's in London but I think it is all income rather than capital, though he will succeed to his father's peerage when he dies.

On my left was Tessa. Sometimes I think she doesn't like me at all. I may be right. She always quarrels about politics, about which she knows zero though she thinks she knows everything, having been on Kensington Council for some time and being political adviser to Kenneth Clarke. She says she keeps him posted on what goes on in the real world. She hasn't a clue what goes on in the real world, being a Lovat married to one of the richest men in the world, Henry Keswick.

She thinks Major is hopeless.

Verushka had a good idea to do something we have never done before. Just after the coffee arrived all men moved three places to their left. Thus there was variety.

Then the women left except for Olga Polizzi who insisted on staying behind for a while.

Somebody said how lovely she is. I said, 'We've all been in love with Olga, everybody here.'

She has that dark, Southern Italian beauty and immense vivacity and high intelligence and quickness and a terrific sense of humour.

However, she did go after about twelve minutes and the men were left alone.

Chips expressed himself worried because he thought the pound was sinking too far; it was going to be very dangerous and cause a great deal of inflation.

Chips is a great admirer of Norman, as well he might be, because that is how he got on to the Board of the Bank of England and got his knighthood.

When we got back into the drawing-room all the singing began again.

Eventually they began to go at about half past twelve. But Andrew Parker Bowles and Petronella were still dancing and singing. She had put on a lot of records from the little television room which adjoins the drawing-room.

When I came back I said, 'You don't need a chaperone, do you?' pointing at Verushka.

Eventually Verushka went up and they were left singing and dancing downstairs till about half past one or later. Then they went out somewhere, perhaps to a night club.

Andrew Parker Bowles was very worried about what is being done to the army. He is a Brigadier in the Household Cavalry. He said my article in the *Times*[15] attacking Rifkind for crippling the army had been reprinted and passed around everywhere among all the officers in the household troops.

15. On 23 March.

Thursday 1 April

Solly Zuckerman[1] has died aged eighty-eight. That brought up memories of happy days. I used to stay with him and so did Roy Jenkins when we were Labour MPs, in Birmingham in his house in Edgbaston.

Then I was on his Zoo Council for years when he was very effective in raising large sums for the zoo by persuasion and what Prince Philip used to call 'lion hunting'.

He had many affairs but he was really happy with Joan, his wife – granddaughter of the great Marquess of Reading who became Viceroy of India.

Another dinner tonight.

When Norman had agreed to come, a secretary from his office rang up and asked if she could be told who the other guests were. I said, 'Mr and Mrs William Cash (he's the frantic, mad leader of the Tory rebels on Maastricht), Norman Tebbit and his wife, Lady Thatcher and Denis Thatcher.' She began to say, 'Are you sure?' I said 'Yes. Isn't that what the thought police want to know about?' In the end I said, 'I'm just pulling your leg,' and told her who the real guests were.

I think it is quite a serious thing, actually. They have to say to Number 10 Downing Street when they go out to dinner who they are going to be with.

We asked questions of Hartley Shawcross whom Norman and Richard Ryder had never met before.

About Nuremberg he said Goering was easily the outstanding figure. He dominated the court at the war criminals' trial from start to finish and you could really see, wicked though he might be, what a powerful personality he had and what a tremendous leader he must have been.

There was a lot of talk about the Royal Family again. Hartley said in his view they were finished and Charles could never become king.

---

1. Lord Zuckerman OM, Chief Scientific Adviser to HM Government, 1964–71; president, Zoological Society of London, 1977–84; m (1939) Lady Joan Rufus Isaacs (d 2000), daughter of 2nd Marquess of Reading; life peer 1971.

Nobody ever knew what was going on in royal circles until this happened. I said, 'Absolute nonsense.'

'In the famous Lords trial of Princess Caroline of Brunswick, an Italian witness kept on saying, "Non mi ricordo, non mi ricordo," and this became a famous catchword throughout the whole of the country.'[2]

Arnold and I were arguing like hell, which he loves, when I suddenly turned to Caroline [Ryder] and said, 'You know this fellow (meaning Arnold) pretends to be frightfully tough and talks ruthlessly about sacking everybody, but he has got a wobbly, soft centre and he is not the tough guy he likes to pretend to be. He is the best friend in need that anybody could possibly have and he is really compassionate, although he loves to pretend what a beastly tycoon he is. I suppose he does business better that way.' Arnold was pleased and he was blushing away and not denying it.

Norman even got a little singing in with Petronella after dinner so he enjoyed that, but he can't sing for toffee.

Saturday 3 April
On my way to Wigan in the car, Verushka rang, terribly upset. Mary Rothermere died yesterday.

Monday 5 April
I went on the BBC Radio Four *Today* programme with John Humphrys about the Grand National affair.[3]

I finished up saying it was a complete P. G. Wodehouse farce. This caught on around the press and the television channels and I was deluged with requests to appear or speak. I said, 'No. I am not going to say any more about it. I have written my article for the *Times* and I don't want it leaked in advance.'

Michael Kovacs, who made a fortune here out of videos and records and made lots of money in various ways in Hungary before, by being pally with the Communists (although of course he was never a Communist), came to dinner.

Kovacs has become the Chairman of the Agricultural Bank in

---

2. The arraignment by George IV of his wife to answer the charge that while abroad she had carried on 'a licentious. disgraceful and adulterous intercourse' precipitated riots from the pro-Queen faction.
3. The race had been declared void after two false starts.

Hungary, a privately owned concern, and he wanted advice from Chips Keswick.

Chips is extremely forthright. Michael Kovacs was pretty shaken.

When he had gone, I was talking to Chips about the Tote and the Lottery.

I said I got £93,000 [as Tote Chairman] and he said he thought it was a very fair amount for a company which can't be worth more than £100 million.

He said, 'What are you worrying about? You're living very well now. You've got a chauffeur and a car and a secretary.' I said, 'Yes, but I won't be able to stay the same probably beyond the next two years, after the end of April 1995.' He didn't seem at all sympathetic. He seemed to think I was being overpaid, if anything.

Kovacs arrived early because he wanted to see my mother-in-law. Elizabeth went up to see if she was in good order which apparently she was and then up he went.

Wednesday 7 April

Before the Board meeting David Montagu [Swaythling] came to see me.

He said, 'I am involved with the BHB and there is a conflict of interest. I have so much to do with that I don't think I have time to go on with it [the Tote Board], though I love you and love being on your Board.'

In a way I am sorry to lose David because he was quite good in many ways, apart from betraying me behind my back.

I told Jeremy Deedes that he wasn't coming up to my hope that he would on the racecourses make himself known to the staff, go about the place and take an interest in their well-being, as Dame Elizabeth Ackroyd[4] and Priscilla Hastings[5] used to do.

But he is quite good on the whole and has a few not bad ideas.

I then met Diana Rawstron[6] at the RAC and gave her half a bottle of champagne. I thought I wouldn't have to pay for my legal consultation which it wasn't really.

She seems to read quite a lot of reasonable books. She is also

---

4. (1910–87); Director, Consumer Council, 1963–71; member, Tote Board, 1975–84.
5. A director of Newbury Racecourse; member of the Jockey Club; she had recently retired from the Tote Board.
6. WW's lawyer at Goodman Derrick.

extraordinarily good at legal matters. She is pretty in a curiously
schoolgirlish way but a trifle ungainly. (She is going to read this one
day after it's published. I send her my love. I think she is a very
worthwhile girl and will certainly be an excellent trustee when I've
gone and look after Verushka's interests and make sure people don't
muck about with my manuscript.)

Thursday 9 April
A disaster. During the night somebody removed the busts of William
Pitt and Spencer Perceval from the plinths on which they stood behind
the solid wooden garden gate [at 19 Cavendish Avenue].

They faced one coming down the steps to leave the house. On the
left was Spencer Perceval, on the right was William Pitt with a chipped
nose. Both were coated in green thickly from the ilex tree above, under
which they stood for many years.

Perceval was very friendly with Captain Charles Wyatt who, when
in the army in India, had built for Wellington's brother, [Richard]
Wellesley, the finest eighteenth-century building in India, which is still
there.[7] It was after the style of Kedleston where the Curzons lived.
That had been supervised to some considerable extent by one Wyatt
or another and Charles Wyatt was familiar with the plans.

The idea of this new palace to house the governor-general was to
impress all the Maharajahs which it certainly did.

Charles Wyatt made a lot of money in India, as people did in those
days.

He became MP for Sudbury in 1812 and was its member for another
six years.

I liked having William Pitt because of his great glory when 'England
has saved herself by her exertions and Europe by her example.'[8] Spencer
Perceval was there because of the uniqueness of his death[9] and his
connection with Charles Wyatt.

Later in the day Charlie Allsopp, who had seen them when he came
to dinner and thought they were rather nice, said he thought from the
one [of Pitt] in the Commons, by Nollekens, that mine could be worth
several thousands. I said I thought not because they ran them off on a

---

7. The governor-general's palace in Calcutta; it was completed in 1803.
8. Pitt's speech at the Guildhall in 1805 after the battle of Trafalgar.
9. He was the only Prime Minister to be assassinated in the House of Commons, in
   1812.

mass production basis during that period. Both were probably sculpted at the end of the eighteenth or beginning of nineteenth century.

I said I got them for a few pounds in a junk shop about thirty or forty years ago.

Later comes some good news for Petronella. She's to go to New York and Washington to report on the first hundred days of President and Mrs Clinton.

Saturday 10 April
We arrived at Badminton[10] a little late and they had started lunch. I sat next to Caroline who is getting a little deaf.

Anne, their daughter, who has got a baby called Eleanor after Eleanor of Aquitane about whom she is writing a book, sat on my right.[11]

Anne told me she is [also] writing about the Sir Thomas Overbury case. That was a famous early seventeenth-century murder, mixed up with various plots between Roman Catholics and Protestants.

We had the most wonderful 1975 Château Lafite at dinner which had been decanted properly.

Sunday 11 April
Petronella, after dinner last night, went up to the house where David and Caroline used to live and where Bunter (Harry) Worcester now lives with his wife Tracy.

She has put in an organic pond which means, she says, the frogs can live happily there, wrecking the wonderful garden that Caroline created for that house.

One agreeable thing about staying here is that not only do they unpack one's things and lay out one's clothes for dinner, they also take your shoes and clean them. My three pairs of brown shoes which I had brought look absolutely marvellous. They had never been cleaned

---

10. Seat of the Duke and Duchess of Beaufort (David and Caroline Somerset), parents of the Worcesters (Bunter and Tracy, environmentalist) and Anne, writer; see biographical notes under Beaufort for the rest of the family including Caroline's mother, the Hon. Daphne Fielding.*

11. The books of Lady Anne Somerset (m (1988) Matthew Carr) include *Ladies in Waiting* (1984) which mentions Eleanor of Aquitaine in the introduction; her *Unnatural Murder: Poison at the Court of James I*, about the Overbury murder, was published in 1997.

like that before, as Elizabeth and Maria simply don't know how to clean shoes.

David makes a lot of money in the art world.[12]

He talked to me quite a lot about Agnelli, his great friend who is the head of Fiat. He said he is being unfairly attacked now in Italy.

Everybody has to give bribes to get contracts in Italy.

He is now under attack, as well as half the Cabinet and Andreotti and the ex Prime Minister.

David read my article in the *News of the World*.[13] He said, 'Excellent, absolutely excellent. She is terrible that girl Diana.'

I said, 'I don't find Camilla Parker Bowles very attractive though she's a nice girl.' He completely agreed but he said Prince Charles is absolutely bowled over by her.

It seems to be not true that they have broken off their relationship.

I went to church at 11.15 with David; Caroline came a little later.

The children behaved absolutely abominably throughout. One of them next to me, I can't remember whose child he was now, was playing a Nintendo game.

At lunch was Daphne, who had been married to Henry Bath and is the mother of Alexander Bath who is as mad as a hatter. She is [also] Caroline's mother. She'd had a hip operation. She is eighty-five and she had just fallen down in the kitchen. Caroline is annoyed because she has to pay somebody to look after her the whole time. Caroline is quite firm with her.

We had a long talk about Rosa Lewis.[14]

She used to cook for Edward VII and do parties for him and stay with him. I asked, 'Do you think she was ever Edward VII's mistress?' 'She might have been but I think possibly not, although she was very beautiful. I think he just liked having her around and talking to her.' Strange arrangement. She made an awful lot of money. That was how she came to have the Cavendish Hotel.

---

12. Chairman of Marlborough Fine Art since 1977.
13. The article was headed 'Vain Princess Diana's addicted to the limelight'.
14. Daphne Fielding wrote a biography of Rosa Lewis, *The Duchess of Jermyn Street*, published in 1964 with a preface by Evelyn Waugh; Waugh used the raffish style of Rosa Lewis's Cavendish Hotel in Jermyn Street as a model for Shepheard's Hotel, Dover Street, in his 1930 novel *Vile Bodies*; Rosa Lewis was the model for its proprietor, Lottie Crump.

Caroline said old Lord Sandwich[15] stayed there.

He kept telling her he had some wonderful Roman coins and would she like to see them. She said she would. One evening she was in the bath when there was a knock, knock, knock on the door. Nothing was locked in those days. Lord Sandwich was there. He said, 'I've got some coins to show you. Can I come in?' She said, 'No, I'm in the bath.' 'Never mind,' and he came into the bathroom where she was lying in the bath.

'He didn't take any interest in my body.' She was rather aggrieved about it (in those days she was absolutely beautiful with a wonderful figure and a marvellous face, slim and really the most attractive thing you could imagine). 'He kept showing me these coins. They were quite interesting but the water was getting colder all the while.' It was stone cold by the time she could get him out of the room and stop lying naked in the bath.

At tea in the kitchen, which we made ourselves and helped ourselves to biscuits, that's the rule in that house, someone said it was really like a hotel staying there. I said, 'I like it. You don't have to see anybody you don't want. You can do your own thing: work, read or write in comfort, alone in your quarters. You must amuse yourself in your own way and you meet at dinner, just before dinner and after dinner, before lunch and after lunch.'

David made a lot of money last August when they made the film about the butler in a Japanese writer's book.[16] The butler here showed them how to open wine properly, serve and do everything properly. He instructed Anthony Hopkins who acted the butler. The book won the Booker prize. I did start to read it. I think I read most of it but found it pretty silly on the whole and very odd.

David has been immensely kind about Petronella's visit to New York and Washington. He is giving her a letter to give to Pamela Harriman[17] to ask her to put her in touch with the right people.

At dinner Caroline, whom I sat next to, said they had both lost an

---

15. 9th Earl of Sandwich (1874–1962), former Conservative MP.
16. *The Remains of the Day* by Kazuo Ishiguro, Booker Prize winner, 1989; Ishiguro's parents came from Japan but he was brought up in England.
17. Pamela, née Digby, b 1920, m 1 (1939–46) Randolph Churchill, son of Sir Winston Churchill, 2 (1960–71) the American producer Leland Hayward, 3 (1971) Averill Harriman, the American Democratic statesman (d 1986); she was US Ambassador to France from 1994 until her death in 1996.

awful lot of money at Lloyd's, she and David, and had I been a member of Lloyd's. I said, 'No. I was once or twice asked but I thought there wasn't such a thing as a free lunch and I daren't risk it.'

It was a help-yourself dinner. All the servants were out. David produced some very nice 1982 La Tour Haut Brion.

At the end of dinner David and Caroline went into the kitchen to start washing up, which they have to do when the servants have the night out, so they don't return to dirty plates.

I said, 'I am now going to organize this. Too many cooks spoil the broth but on this occasion many hands make light work.' So I went into the library and collected the others.

Then I sat back and said, 'I am the contractor. I have contracted to get this washing up done. You will all work away,' which they did.

Monday 12 April
For lunch came Jane Westmorland[18] whose husband is Master of the Horse, which the previous Duke of Beaufort had been till he died. He is sixty-nine and he had a stroke eight or nine months ago. She is afraid he will never be able to speak again. A consultant at the hospital said to her when he had the stroke, 'You'll probably be able to take him home but he'll be a cabbage, quite a pleasant cabbage, and you might enjoy looking after him.' She thought that was the most terrible thing to say.

I completely agreed because he may not be a cabbage at all. I told her about Guy Wint who had a stroke on a train at Paddington. He was going to Oxford. He was carted off to a hospital in an ambulance. For nine months he understood everything that everybody said to him and about him and they thought he couldn't understand anything because he couldn't speak or move. Then he wrote a book about it.[19]

Only one good thing happened today and that was Aston Villa winning one nil against Arsenal.[20]

---

18. Née Findlay, m (1950) 15th Earl of Westmorland (1924–93), former chairman of Sotheby Parke Bernet Group, Master of the Horse, 1978–91; the 10th Duke of Beaufort was Master of the Horse, 1936–78.
19. Fellow of St Antony's College, Oxford; his stroke was in 1961, he died in 1969; the book was *The Third Killer: Meditations on a Stroke* (1965).
20. WW had supported Aston Villa football club since he became MP for Aston in 1945.

Tuesday 13 April

This morning Petronella got up almost too late to catch her aeroplane to Washington.

I had got her talking to Arthur Schlesinger[21] on the telephone – she was very nervous to begin with. I said she is very pretty and very clever and he said if she is anything like her mother, she must be.

The election of Clinton must bring back many poignant memories to him of his days with Kennedy in the White House when he and Kenneth Galbraith[22] were his advisers, speech writers and policy formers.

Arthur keeps up the youthful idealism he had then and the belief that there will be and can be a better world in which all men are good but perhaps not quite so clever as he is. He was always very kind to me, as was Galbraith.

I don't think it's just because I am getting older that I think that Adlai Stevenson, though defeated twice by Eisenhower, would have been a far better President than his opponent. He was miles above that brash fellow. He was shining with proud idealism like the young Clinton with his appalling wife.

Saturday 17 April

I watched Pyhrric Dance in the 4.20 at Thirsk on the SIS programme.

It came in fourth. However, it did run rather better than usual in the sense that there were only one and a half lengths dividing the first four.

By the end of this season I will have spent £9,000–£10,000 on it which I would much rather have invested in one of Soros's funds or in News International or some such affair, where I could have doubled my money instead of just throwing it away.

Sunday 18 April

I woke up at half past six.

I went down to the RAC for my swim, thoroughly washed my hair, which I can't do in my own house because of Nadje occupying the top bathroom and making a hideous mess of it.

---

21. Former Professor of History, Harvard University; special assistant to President Kennedy, 1961–3.
22. Former Professor of Economics, Harvard University; US Ambassador to India under Kennedy; his best-known book is *The Affluent Society*.

I am now terrified of talking to Margaret. She went to Warsaw to open a newly restored hotel for Forte's, the new Bristol.

She made a long speech, I gather, about how the whole world should rush to its defence as Croatia is attacked by Serbia.

Earlier in the day Norman rang. He was just back from Japan where he found that they thought Britain was doing rather well, better than most countries, economically.

We discussed Margaret's absurd intervention over Yugoslavia. I said, 'The real criminal was Margaret for planning the cuts in our defence forces, and you and Major for going on with them. We can't intervene anywhere.'

Wednesday 21 April
As a result of David Swaythling leaving the Tote Board, I had to think of somebody else. So I asked Christopher Sporborg would he like it. He is Deputy Chairman of Hambros and a director of Huntingdon racecourse, a trainer and owner of horses. He was delighted, to my surprise. He comes off the Levy Board quite soon and he saw no conflict of interest in being just off the Levy Board and a member of the Jockey Club as well. I have written to the Home Secretary and hope he also agrees because I think he will be more interested and better at the financial side than David.

Dinner party at Cavendish Avenue. Alexander de Gelsey and his wife,[23] the Wolfsons, Sir Sydney Lipworth, just retired that day from being Chairman of the Monopolies Commission, the Quintons, Cita and Irwin Stelzer and Susan Crosland.[24]

Susan is a very jolly girl. I have been attracted to her since I first met her, long before she married Tony Crosland, when she was still married to Patrick Skene Catling. She came with some document which had to be witnessed.

She wanted me to do it specially because I had set her on the road to having some money when she was married to her first husband and I had guaranteed the mortgage for the house they bought. She has

---

23. Alexander de Gelsey, born Budapest, m (1969) Romy, née Cairns; chairman, Sericol International, 1955–98; Honorary Consul of the Republic of Hungary since 1990.
24. American-born author and journalist; widow of Anthony Crosland (d 1977), Labour politician and writer.

never forgotten it and I had never mentioned it again which she said she thought was very nice of me.

She was longing to see what I was going to put down as my occupation, expecting me to say Peer of the Realm. She hooted with laughter when I wrote Bookmaker. I said, 'It's true.'

I said, 'I have a licence to take bets. I have to because when we set up Tote Direct with Bass, a senior person from each organization was required by the licensing authorities to be the licence holder. It's quite legal for me to take any bet in this room now, though it isn't for anybody else.'

On my right sat Cita to whom I gave the paperbacks of *A Quiet Life* and *The Birthday Boys* by Beryl Bainbridge.

We wanted to plan to go to Oxford on Monday.

She said I would have to ask Irwin when I took him to the Saintsbury Club the next night because it was the anniversary of their marriage. She said, 'He might come, too, if you speak to him.'

When the women had gone, a tremendous argument, stimulated by me, broke out, with Irwin saying the Chancellor of the Exchequer was still no good, he had done it all wrong, we needn't have had the recession at all in England.

I am very fond of Irwin Stelzer, though he is very quarrelsome and argumentative.

I feel a little lift when I see him come into a room and we meet and start discussing things.

Thursday 22 April

There had been consternation because yesterday I said I had Beryl Bainbridge coming to lunch at one o'clock [today].

Verushka said the servants were going to give notice and all the rest of it. I said, 'I don't believe it.' She marched Elizabeth in and she said, 'We can't do it because there is so much washing up to do after the dinner party.' I said, 'Get somebody else in then.'

But I must say the lunch wasn't too bad. The first course consisted of a nicely presented haddock mousse from the night before. Then we had spring chicken with rather nice vegetables and then a beautiful apple tart which Beryl Bainbridge didn't want because she had eaten too much already. We also drank two-thirds of the bottle of Château Lascombes 1967 which hadn't been drunk the night before.

I took Irwin to the Saintsbury Club.

I introduced him to Alan Hare.[25]

When we had gone into dinner, Irwin asked why Alan disliked Andrew Neil so much. I said, 'His father was an Earl and his brother is the present Earl. They are not exactly a republican family. Many people in England hate Andrew Neil because of his consistent and persistent attacks, along with Kelvin MacKenzie and aided by Rupert, on the monarchy.'

I then told him that when the present Earl was at Eton, his mother used to send him hampers of food from Fortnum's because she didn't think the food was good enough and he wasn't getting enough to eat.

I said, 'But he became a socialist.' 'What?' said Irwin, amazed. I said, 'Yes, it's part of the eccentricity of the British class system which no one will ever understand, including you. He claimed that nobody needed more than x amount of money to live on and that was all they should be allowed to have. When his father died he said, "My eldest son says that x is the amount of money anybody needs to live on and that is precisely what I have left him." He [the son] has been penniless more or less ever since, although he was Governor of Burma and Secretary of State for India in Attlee's government. The rest of his property he left to the other brothers, most of it to the next one down who became Lord Blakenham.'[26]

I sat next to Merlin Holland, grandson of Oscar Wilde.

I knew his father very well. He was a friend of Jack Huntingdon's and they both put me up for the Saintsbury Club.

We talked about Rupert and to my surprise Irwin said he is over here secretly now, looking into the budget. He walked into the room where Irwin and Andrew Knight were sitting and said, 'I have come to look at my overheads,' meaning them.

I am hurt because Rupert has not got in touch with me.

---

25. The Hon. Alan Hare (1919–95), fourth son of 4th Earl of Listowel; chairman, *Financial Times*, 1978–84; director, Pearson Longman, 1975–83, president, Société Civile du Vignoble de Château Latour, 1983–90; his brother, the 5th Earl (1906–97) was Labour Secretary of State for India, April–August 1947, for Burma, 1947–8, and Minister of State for Colonial Affairs, 1948–50.*

26. 1st Viscount Blakenham (1911–82), Conservative politician; m (1934) the Hon. Beryl Pearson, (d 1994); cr. Viscount 1963; his son, 2nd Viscount Blakenham, chairman, *Financial Times*, 1983–93, Pearson, 1983–97, m (1965) his first cousin Marcia, daughter of Alan Hare.

I think he is nervous of me because I disagree with him so much and publish articles in his papers which clearly do disagree with him.

Rupert isn't a bit like other owners. He despises journalists.

Irwin said, 'You're quite right. He does. He thinks they are two a penny.' 'He is wrong. He must realize he couldn't hire easily another Kelvin MacKenzie or Andrew Neil.' Irwin said, 'He does realize that but he thinks writers are two a penny.'

When I asked Irwin about Monday and going to Oxford, he said tetchily, 'No, we're going off together alone.'

He is a very generous fellow, old Irwin, but I wouldn't really like to be on the wrong side of him.

Charles Wintour was there on crutches. I didn't speak to him. He was avoiding me.

I still remain fond of him. I think it was only because he was a friend of mine that he grudgingly conceded that some part of what the *Sunday Times* did wasn't fair. But he rejected my complaint as a whole.

I also said to Irwin that he must keep me in touch with developments on the business of trying to end the cross ownership of television and newspapers.

I said, 'I will do what I can behind the scenes as well as in front of the scenes in the Lords, but I must have the information soon. I will do whatever I can to protect Rupert's interests.'

Saturday 24 April
I have had a sweet letter from Beryl Bainbridge.

As she went [on the 22nd] she said, 'Of course, you know, we're still walking round each other a bit. We haven't really got to the nitty gritty yet.' She is very perceptive. I haven't really told her everything that's in my head nor has she told me.

I rang Norman. I told him I wanted to go to the reception for these weird European Bank people[27] on Sunday night because I could meet Paul Teleki there with Mark Pejacsevich.

Norman was very upset the press had picked up a remark he had made, particularly the *Sun*, when asked if he regretted anything. It was at the Newbury by-election where he had been speaking on Friday morning and he replied in French: 'Je ne regrette rien.' The silly press said he couldn't speak French very well so why did he put it in French, being utterly unaware of Edith Piaf's very famous song. I said, 'Don't

---

27. The European Bank for Reconstruction & Development (EBRD).

worry. The City is much more friendly to you. You've won through,' and I read him a chunk of what I have written for tomorrow's *News of the World* which pleased him a good deal.

John Major has stood very well by Norman so he will obviously be Chancellor still at the November Budget time.

James Hanson has written a pathetic letter saying they may not be allowed to go on presenting Melody, the wonderfully successful light music station. They have to re-apply and it is up for tender.

Would people like myself write letters of support, so I must certainly remember to do that. It is lovely and particularly useful to me when I am dictating this manuscript because I put it on and Verushka, even when in her bathroom with the thin wall against my bookcase, can't hear what I am doing.

Verushka rang Petronella [in Washington] early in the morning, before half past six, to make sure she got out of bed in time so as not to miss her aeroplane. She will be returning latish tonight.

Sunday 25 April
To the Natural History Museum where, among the dinosaurs, the guests of this strange European Bank for Reconstruction run by Attali, the extravagant Italian, were being given a party by Norman. He had warned me not to come because there would be no champagne because of all the shenanigans about the marble hall built by Attali.[28]

Paul Teleki outlined to me more about the Tokay operation.

Monday 26 April
There was the most extraordinary article in the *Times* about Tessa Lyle and Robbie.

Robbie had told them that the Lyle family had owned land in the area since 1691. Complete rubbish. They didn't own anything, at least they didn't buy Bonython and the part going on to the Lizard until 1839. There was a lot about being hereditary lords of the Lizard and a lot of waffle about how my brother had left the estate in a terrible mess, which was very unkind because he actually resurrected the whole damn place which was in a frightful condition when Molly died.

There was a great deal of explanation of how Tessa Lyle managed to get through the planning consent and how difficult it had been with

---

28. Jacques Attali's expenditure on the EBRD headquarters had been much criticized in the press.

regard to the wind farm. Not one mention of the fact that they wouldn't have got any permissions at all, or been on the list for having a wind farm from OFFER who dish out the contracts and put people on the list in Birmingham,[29] if I hadn't fought with the Ministry of the Environment and the local people and got enormous backing, things they couldn't conceivably have done.

During the afternoon while I was at the Tote, Rupert rang up from a car on his way to the airport. He said he had just come back from Italy where he was looking at this marvellous boat they had built.

I said, 'What about Fellowes, the Queen's Private Secretary?' He said, 'I forgot that.'

He grudgingly said that Norman was doing some of the right things now, but only because he was forced to by Soros.

People are very dangerous when they've made a lot of money and then they think they know all about politics and start laying down the law internationally.

It was an extraordinary evening at the Merchant Taylors Hall. It was [again] for the strange Attali European Reconstruction & Development Bank.

On my right was a nice, roundish-faced gentleman of about fifty with a foreign accent. He came from Luxembourg. I probed around a bit.

I said, 'But what do you yourself do?' 'Oh, I'm the Prime Minister.'

He thought Norman Lamont was a first-class Chancellor of the Exchequer and couldn't understand why people kept attacking him in England.

Tuesday 27 April
A dinner party at 19 Cavendish Avenue. It was supposed to be for Olga Polizzi and William Shawcross. Olga suddenly discovered that she as usual had double booked.

Desperately, we searched for a woman to take her place and found Miriam Gross.

Miriam Gross is the mother of the boy whose flat Petronella has [now] rented, doesn't like and wants to get out of.

Petronella was also coming to dinner, with Frank Johnson present.

---

29. See Vol. 2, p. 352, for WW's visit to the Office for Electricity Regulation at Birmingham on 20 September 1990.

I sat next to Sonia [Sinclair] and was pleased to chat away with her.

Her son, Peter,[30] refuses to marry, not believing in marriage, so he has a son who can't inherit the Melchett title. Couldn't I speak to him about it? His father would have been horrified. I said, 'It's all very well to make these decisions for oneself, but one's son is an entirely different matter. But I don't think he'll listen to me.'

Wednesday 28 April
Off to meet Bruce Buck, the Skadden Arps man in London, to give him lunch at the House of Lords.

He is interested in the Tokay project so we have sent him all the details in case he has got some clients who would be willing to do it.

He was interested in my ability to get Paul Teleki to see George Gluck, the Skadden Arps representative in Hungary, again to get more legal work, in particular in the privatization of oil in Hungary.

I do my best for him in all directions to ensure my £25,000 a year. I wondered if I dare suggest to him some more at some point.

Friday 30 April
Tomorrow we go to the Wiltons. We will have one room with two beds in it and a bathroom. That's because Petronella is going to be in the other room we usually have and the Hambledens are having superior accommodation to us. I suppose that is because he is a Viscount[31] descended from a tradesman, W. H. Smith, who started W. H. Smith's. I like him. I used to see a lot of him at one time but I think two days cooped up with him at the Wiltons will be a killer.

---

30. Executive director, Greenpeace UK, since 1988; Labour Whip, House of Lords, 1974–5; Minister of State, Northern Ireland Office, 1976–9.
31. 4th Viscount Hambleden, m 2 (1988) Mrs Lesley Watson.

Saturday 1 May

Newmarket where we were entertaining for the 2000 Guineas.

Petronella went to Liverpool Street to try to catch a train to Newbury. Of course there are none. She rang up her mother in desperate straits. I said, 'Why are you trying to go to Newbury?'[1]

Somehow the conversation [at the Wiltons] turned to smoking and I said what rot it was to say that people could die of cancer or of coronaries caused by smoking and passive smoking. Lady Hambleden began to get very indignant. We had quite a row.

Sunday 2 May

By the evening Lesley Hambleden had decided that a reconciliation must be put in hand and she greeted me in a friendly way saying, 'Hello, my adversary,' and we sat next to each other again at dinner.

When she smiled she had an attractive, moving, interested face.

Bank Holiday Monday 3 May

Harry Hambleden had breakfast with me in the kitchen. When he was in America for seven or eight years he was Prince Philip's representative on the wildlife conservation front.

Harry travelled a lot with Prince Philip. He said he was both impossible and charming.

They [once] went to a place called Niger.

They were sitting in their tent and Prince Philip came in and said, 'Hello, what are you all looking so gloomy about?' 'We've all forgotten to bring our towels.' 'Good heavens, what a lot of bloody fools you are. You shouldn't be allowed out by yourselves.'

Then Harry went over to his tent to ask him some question and he found Prince Philip cutting up an enormous Buckingham Palace bath towel into little squares to give to each of the four who hadn't got one.

---

1. The Wiltons' house, where they were all staying, was near Newmarket.

He brought them in and said, 'There you are. I didn't like to think of you all having no bath towels in this bloody awful place.'

Harry also told a funny story about Queen Elizabeth the Queen Mother whom he has known since he was a child. She was in some foreign part and he hadn't seen her for ages because he had been in America. He rushed into the room full of dignitaries and went up to her and embraced her. Without stopping him she said, 'Harry, remember who I am and where you are.'

Tuesday 4 May
I went along to hear the Dalai Lama in the Grand Committee Room in Westminster Hall. He is a genuinely holy man.

He is trying to reach some kind of compromise with the Chinese but he says every time he does he gets an aggressive answer. Their real response to Tibet asking for freedom is to pour vast new settlements of Chinese into the lower valleys.

Then they say the Chinese now outnumber the Tibetans.

Before I went to bed I rang Norman Lamont. 'For goodness' sake stop cutting our defences. And please remember you must never put our troops into Bosnia. I've been hearing rumours in the press that we're going to support the Americans in doing that.' He said, 'No, I don't think we are at all. We may go through the motions and allow a few bombing raids.' I said, 'They won't do any good either, just kill some more people.'

Wednesday 5 May
The three from the Tote, Brian, John Heaton and Tom Phillips, arrived at a quarter to nine. I managed to get ready in time and the Board meeting went pretty well. It was being conducted here so I could go to the memorial service for Solly Zuckerman.

Roy Jenkins made the main speech of tribute which he did extremely well though a little too flowery and a tiny bit stilted. He was followed by William Waldegrave who knew Solly well in government, and then the local Rabbi who didn't do at all badly.

I was rather taken with a girl dressed in rabbinical costume who did a number of readings from the Bible. They were all in English except for one or two. I thought she was an extremely pretty girl, very sexy, dark, full lips, tall. I couldn't see if she had very good legs but she was quite a luscious Jewish girl. I shouldn't think she was more than about twenty-five.

When we went out I bumped into Arnold.

I said, 'What did you think of the girl who read the readings?' 'Appalling. That's a cantor. It should have been a man. She had no business to be doing it at all. It's a ridiculously liberal synagogue.'[2] I said, 'Do I take it from that you would be opposed to women priests in the Church of England?' 'Yes completely.'

The Jewish religion is a very good one. It is basically the same as ours but with more common sense to it and it doesn't really claim that it knows who God is or what he is. I like very much its references, which obviously take place in a memorial service, to the brief time we live here and one should try for people to remember one as a good person who tried to do one's best.

So off went Solly, podgy, lively with that expressive face and quick urgent voice, with our memories to immortalize him.

I then went off to the Grand Committee room once more. This time it was Nelson Mandela.

He, too, is a good man with a touch of the quality of the really holy, laughing Dalai Lama but not so big a man.

He was tetchy when he was asked about persuading white business men not to leave the country. He is desperately keen that they shouldn't, understandably.

I was deeply touched by Robbie [chauffeur]. I said, 'Will you buy me a birthday card for Petronella who is twenty-five tomorrow.' He got me one which mirrored my sentiments completely, remembering the joy she gave me as a child and my pride in her now and her achievements as she has grown to be a woman and all that kind of thing.

Friday 7 May

I woke to the somewhat unexpected news that the Liberal Democrats had not only won Newbury but had swamped the Tories and Labour had lost their deposit. Horror all round. Immediately on the air went the silly asses in the Tory Party, including Sir Marcus Fox, the Chairman of the 1922 Committee, demanding the instant resignation of Norman Lamont though what it has to do with him I can't tell.

---

2. This was the Liberal Jewish Synagogue, St John's Wood Road.

Saturday 8 May
Off to Lingfield on a cold day.

One jolly surprise was that Jane's book was there, a copy for each guest.[3]

She had written and inscribed each one with her name and best wishes from her. I said to Nigel Kent-Lemon, 'Did you buy them?' He said, 'Yes. It's not a publisher's thing. She'll get some royalties from it. She said she knew you.' 'She certainly does.'

My review of the George Brown book by Peter Paterson[4] in the *Times* on Thursday has been an enormous success. It had been discussed on the wireless this morning and in the House of Lords people kept popping up and telling me how good it was. Even at the racecourse they had read it.

Curiously, they [the *Times*] seem to be much happier with my work on the review pages than on the feature page, from the way they keep cutting my articles down.

Then it was off to Dorneywood. I took a big cigar for Norman.

It was a fairly large gathering, about eighteen for dinner.

Norman was pretty concerned at all the attacks on him being remounted. He had spoken to Major who said don't worry about it and there is no question of his being asked to resign.

On my left at dinner was Mrs Portillo[5] who runs a head-hunting outfit. She was previously an accountant but got fed up with it. She does her own income tax returns but Michael Portillo won't let her do his. I said, 'Why not? It would save you money.' 'I know. Isn't it silly?' she said. I said, 'Perhaps he's making payments he doesn't want you to know about,' but she didn't seem unduly worried. She's not a bad-looking girl.

Also present was a very nice Tory MP called Sir Michael Grylls.[6] I congratulated him on the letter he had written in the *Times* setting out

---

3. *High Flier* by Jane McKerron, published 1993; Kent-Lemon was chairman of Lingfield racecourse.

4. Journalist, formerly on the *Sunday Telegraph*, *New Statesman*, *Spectator* and *Daily Mail*; the book was *Tired and Emotional – the Life of Lord George Brown*; Peter Paterson's son Graham is an assistant editor of the *Times*, chief assistant to the Editor and features editor, 1993–5, foreign editor since 1995.

5. Carolyn, née Eadie, m (1982) Michael Portillo.

6. Conservative MP, 1970–97; knight 1992.

what Norman had achieved. It was right after one of the usual *Times* articles saying he ought to go and was never any good.

The Brazilian Ambassadress said quite a lot about her very close friend, Princess Diana. There had been reports in the paper about her going to the Belgrave embassy secretly and I had wondered if she had a boyfriend there but this is not the case at all. She went with her last weekend to Paris where she spent a lot of money on buying clothes. She said she is a very difficult person, she doesn't know what she wants to do and she is very silly.

She said, too, she was very much taken aback when Major issued the statement saying there would be a separation but she could still be Queen. First of all, she didn't want an official separation. She wanted what she called a private separation, with no one to know about it. This would have been rather difficult. It was Charles who said if they were going to have a separation, it would have to be a proper one. Diana says she doesn't want to be Queen, she hates the idea and couldn't bear it. She just wants to gad about all over the world being an international television celebrity with her pictures everywhere.

I told them I had put £200 for the Tories to be the largest party in the next parliament on with Ladbroke this afternoon, tax free because it was on a racecourse. I got the bet at evens so it ought to be fairly easy to win.

The thing which really infuriated Major and co. was Margaret saying on the very morning of the [Newbury] by-election that the government was living in cloud-cuckoo-land and describing it as pretty hopeless. What an awful thing for her to do.

I haven't dared to ring Mrs Thatcher today. They are pretty annoyed with her, even Caroline [Ryder] who was her personal assistant and Ryder who was very close to her personally, too.

Sunday 9 May
I woke up quite early and the papers were full of denunciations of Norman and Major, apart from John Junor who surprisingly said, quite correctly, that the trouble with the voters in Newbury was that they were so damned unintelligent and they didn't seem to realize we were in a world recession and we were coming out of it rather well.

I rang Norman to thank him for the evening and said, 'I hope nobody's going to panic.' He said he thought John Major was still in the same frame of mind and there was no danger of him rushing around chopping people's heads off, particularly Norman's.

Monday 10 May
Norman was still in good heart. I hadn't taken him a birthday present
other than his large cigar. I sent him round six bottles of champagne
and the article in the *Sunday Times* by Edwin Bramall[7] showing quite
clearly that it's appalling how they are cutting our armed forces and
our defences.

Cecil Parkinson has written a silly article saying again that Norman
should go, which is surprising as he is supposed to be a great friend
of Norman's, and as for Cecil Parkinson, he was a bloody failure in
the Department of Energy and in everything else as a member of the
Cabinet.

Tuesday 11 May
Went to David Stevens' annual United Newspapers bash at the Savoy.

David Stevens stoutly defended Norman Lamont and the government and said, contrary to what all these people writing away in the
newspapers said, they were doing very well.

I then went to the House of Lords because it was the Report stage
of the Urban Development Bill which I describe as the Legalized Theft
Bill.

Micky Suffolk had come up for the day.[8]

When we had finished with Prime Minister's questions, we went to
the Lords. I said, 'I'll take you in. Are you going to speak?' He said
he wouldn't dare do that but he was here to vote and listen. I said, 'All
right. You go in and sit up on the left because that's where Tories sit.
I'm sitting on the crossbenches.'

Micky went into the chamber, and blow me down, an attendant
tried to eject him. 'I'm afraid you can't come in here, Sir.' I had to
explain that he was a lord, an Earl.

Wednesday 12 May
Mrs Tamborero got hold of me and said they were looking for me for
Newsnight.

They wanted somebody to come on to defend Norman Lamont.

So I raced down to the television studios in Shepherd's Bush and
got there at about ten to fifteen minutes past seven. I did a twelve-

---

7. Field Marshall Lord Bramall, Chief of the Defence Staff, 1982–5; life peer 1987.
8. He was affected by the Bill because his house, Charlton Park, Malmesbury, was
    divided into flats with leases; see Vol. 1, pp. 586–7.

minute interview. They began by asking me why did I think he was so unpopular and disliked by the press and had a bad image. I answered these questions and then a bit about human touches. I explained how well read he was, how balanced he was; he liked jolly parties and why not. And that he was a very good ornithologist with wide interests. I spoke about the Scops Owl in Italy when he stayed with us. I said, 'You're not going to cut me up? You are going to represent me seriously, aren't you? I hope I can trust you.' 'Oh yes', they said.

In the end they just used a snippet on the owl which made me sound a bloody fool and Norman a bit of an ass, too. It was done deliberately, of course, the way they cut it.

At dinner with the Swaythlings, I sat next to Claire Hesketh.[9] Alexander was there, too. He was not being exactly supportive of Norman, which annoyed me.

As we all watched *Newsnight* downstairs I was bitterly humiliated when the scrap of me came on and I could see everybody else thinking 'My God, that's not very good. I thought he was supposed to be a great television personality.'

Thursday 13 May
Sarah Keswick has known Prince Charles since she was fourteen. She said it is absolute lies, the story going around that he had gone up to a bedroom with Camilla Parker Bowles during the pre-wedding-day dance at Buckingham Palace.

They had broken off relations months before, when he first got engaged to Diana.

The truth of the matter was that after Diana became more and more tiresome and nasty, and she could see the whole marriage was in a terrible mess, five years later Camilla had an affair again with Prince Charles.

In the morning I first of all rang Richard Ryder and said, 'What the hell are you going to do now? Robert Adley has died.'[10]

He said, 'He was tiresome to the end.'

I said, 'At least he had a thirty-two thousand majority at Christchurch. I don't see how you are going to lose that.'[11]

---

9. The Hon. Claire Watson, daughter of 3rd Baron Manton, m (1977) 3rd Baron Hesketh.
10. Conservative MP for Christchurch.
11. The Conservatives did lose the seat, to the Liberal Democrats on 29 July 1993.

When I probed him about Norman's position he was rather cagey, saying, 'I'm sure he'll be all right. He has enough people supporting him.' I said, 'But what's the Prime Minister saying?' He said, 'I don't know. He hasn't said.'

I rang Norman.

When he asked if Richard was supporting him I said, 'I think he is very supportive of you but he was vague about what he thought Major's intention may be.'

Still fuming at the way I was cut up by the BBC *Newsnight* last night.

At The Other Club there was a very shrunken attendance. I had expected there would be more with all the excitement about the attacks on Major and Norman reaching a crescendo.

We fell to talking about new members. I said, 'What about John Mortimer?'[12] That was agreed heartily by Arnold Goodman. 'And Tom Stoppard?' I said. That was less enthusiastically agreed but it was agreed because he is a lively fellow. Arnold said he couldn't understand his last play.[13] I said, 'Maybe, but they [his plays] are very good.'

I also suggested Alexander of Weedon who was once head of the Bar Council, a brilliant lawyer and Chairman of Nat West. That was accepted. So we had three.

I wanted Peter Ustinov[14] and they protested vehemently, though Arnold Goodman and I thought it would be a good idea because he is so amusing. 'No', said Bernard [Levin]. 'He has only got thirty-six jokes and they are all repeated.' I said, 'That would take you through several years of this Club's meetings. We only meet ten times a year.'

Dear Michael Hartwell, who really runs the Club, protested that it was irregular because we hadn't got an election. I said, 'Why don't we have one?' He said, 'You should ask for one.' I said, 'Here's our list, signed by Bernard Levin and myself. Can you please arrange for them to be candidates.' So I don't know what will happen next.

I was saddened to find that Bernard had joined the hysterical nonsense about getting rid of Norman and Major. I said, 'You sound like a lynch mob like all the others. I am disappointed.' He said, 'It's what we need. The country needs a lynch mob.' I said, 'Lynch mobs often get the wrong victims.'

---

12. Barrister, playwright and author; knight 1998.
13. *Arcadia*, first performed in 1993.
14. Actor, dramatist, wit and film director; knight (1990).

At York [yesterday] I put £300 at evens for the Tories to get a larger number of seats in the next parliament, with Ladbroke's.

Friday 14 May
Norman had made a spirited defence of himself, and a very good one, at the Scottish Conservative Conference. He received a prolonged ovation. Norman told me it lasted three minutes but the newspapers said it was thirty seconds in their usual lying way, trying to denigrate him.

In the evening we went to the Garrick Club to have dinner with Norman Stone.

He arrived ten minutes after we did.

He is busy egging Margaret on. He is a very merry, friendly fellow and it is possible to take a completely opposite point of view to him in a most jolly and convivial way. That is not so with Noel Malcolm[15] who is small, serious looking, bespectacled, narrow-faced, a kind of puritan, fierce in his beliefs though they are not based on a wide appreciation of life. But he is only thirty-six.

While waiting for Norman Stone I wandered about looking at the pictures. In the upstairs Morning Room there is a marvellous portrait of Colley Cibber, the actor and prolific dramatist who lived from 1671 to 1757. He was as queer as a coot and the portrait shows that brilliantly.[16]

Saturday 15 May
To Oxford to the meeting of the International Nutrition Foundation Council.[17]

We agreed on one or two points about where we were to send Sinclair's money which will be in the order of £5 million now.

I toured some betting shops after lunch.

There had been a bomb placed yesterday two hundred yards away from the last one, in the Cornmarket in Oxford. I knew that but I hadn't told Robbie because I thought he would be terrified of parking there.

---

15. Academic, writer and political journalist.
16. The portrait by Giuseppe Grisoni shows Cibber in the role of Lord Foppington in Vanbrugh's *The Relapse*; perhaps WW did not realize this.
17. Founded by the nutritionist Dr Hugh Sinclair who died in 1990; see Vol. 2, pp. 320–1, for his work.

It is appalling that even darling Oxford is assaulted by these ghastly terrorists.

Then I went to see short, tubby, round-faced, cheerful-looking Dick Smethurst.[18]

We went for a walk across the fields. Until F. J. Lys's time, who was the Provost when I was there, the enormous acreage including the playing fields was a farm given to the Provost of the time to make money out of for himself.

I always feel happy there. It reminds me so much of the sunlit three years I had which for joy may have been the best of my life, uplifted by hopes of glory, revelling with friends and drink and good food, sunshine, in love with the lovely buildings of Oxford, the prettiness of Worcester's gardens. I floated on a tide of great expectations and had merry times with the *Oxford Camera*, the weekly newspaper which was banned by the Proctors and we changed it to the *Oxford Comment*. I had edited them both and started them. I had a very special love affair with Susan Cox, whom I married before the war began at the end of my time at Oxford.

Sunday 16 May

Lunch at Bowden [with the Weinstocks]. Alexandra Dacre[19] looks like a wizened old horse but is quite friendly. She tends to dominate Hugh Trevor-Roper, her husband, who was interested that Bowden was built by James Wyatt.

Charles Powell was there with his wife, Carla, to whom I sat next. She said how marvellous William Rees-Mogg is.[20] I said, 'He is very pleasant and amiable but he's an ass, has no touch with politics and writes elegant twaddle in the *Times*.'

Arnold said to me after lunch that he was alarmed by what William had written because he is on the GEC Board. It was extremely offensive

---

18. Economist; Provost of WW's college, Worcester, since 1991.
19. Lady Alexandra (d 1997), eldest daughter of Field-Marshall Earl Haig, m 2 (1954) Hugh Trevor-Roper, historian (Lord Dacre), Regius Professor of Modern History, Oxford University, 1957–80; Master, Peterhouse, Cambridge, 1980–7; director, Times Newspapers, 1974–88; life peer 1979.
20. Editor, the *Times* 1967–81; chairman, Sidgwick & Jackson (publishers), 1985–9; vice-chairman, BBC Board of Governors, 1981–6; chairman, Arts Council of Great Britain, 1982–9, Broadcasting Standards Council, 1988–93; director, GEC, 1981–97; chairman, Pickering & Chatto (publishers), since 1983; knight 1981, life peer 1988.

to John Major and could be very damaging in getting government contracts.

As we walked in the garden, he asked my advice about Charles Powell. When Jim Prior retires in a few years, would Charles be a good deputy chairman, to be groomed as Chairman for GEC? I said I thought he would be excellent because he knows everybody worth knowing in most capitals of the world, through having visited them when right-hand man for Margaret or met them when they came to Number 10 Downing Street. 'But wouldn't Henry Keswick object? Charles seems to be doing well with him.' Arnold replied, 'If the money's right, people always move.'

Monday 17 May
I said I would like nine hundred words for the *Times* in my defence of Norman. They said they didn't know if they could manage that but it would be seven-fifty. In the event, of course, they hacked it about as usual. Everybody is allowed to write reams, like William Rees-Mogg, saying how dreadful Norman is (and Major), but the defence is confined to a tiny space.

Tuesday 18 May
Dinner at Olga Polizzi's in her pretty house in Clarendon Close. It was for William Shawcross who is off again to Cambodia whence he has just returned.

Before dinner Mark Lennox-Boyd was quite emphatic that Norman had to go, and said lots of other people in the government thought so, too.

Olga said she believes in an after-life and going to heaven. I said, 'What, and the resurrection of the body? Which age do you want to be resurrected at?'

Thursday 20 May
To the meeting of the NERA Board. Sir Peter Middleton, who used to be Permanent Secretary at the Treasury, is on the Board. He is on several other Boards, too. He is quite competent, not all that brilliant but he beams a lot, as do all retired grandees like him.

Patrick Jenkin was there.[21]

---

21. Conservative MP, 1964–87, Secretary of State for the Environment, 1983–5; life peer 1987.

I gave him a lift back to the Lords and he started attacking Norman and Major.

He couldn't accept that Norman was any good because once he had been his junior in the Department of the Environment. That is typical of human nature. If somebody junior than yourself at school, suddenly becomes a great writer or is thought to be, you say, 'Of course he can't write at all. I knew him well as my junior.'

Friday 21 May

Visit from Maurice Berry and Carl Yates from Banbury. They are still in part of the old premises of WW Offset.

I told them I don't want any more commission from them in respect of *Coal News* and *GEC Topic*. When Banbury wound up, I managed to secure retention of both these [house magazines] for them and they have been paying me a percentage commission.

I said, 'Let's have a look to see if we can find some more things for you,' and I gave them a list of names which I had taken from the NERA meeting.

They said a lot of people in Banbury who were employed by me are deeply distressed. They now have jobs nowhere near so good and not so well paid.

I said, and they knew it, too, that Frank Chapple of the ETU told me the Communist Party would never forgive me for having got the Communists out of the ETU and for preventing them taking over the Amalgamated Engineering Union.

King Street, where the Communist Party Headquarters was, sent in 1978 a Communist to organize as much trouble as he could in the works.

He was aided by another Communist.

They, with the backing of the unions, told the employees they must not accept the shift working and the streamlining which would have saved us enough costs and got us the work to survive comfortably. If they did, they would be expelled from their union and never get employment again in the printing industry. That was the case in those days. You had to be a union member or you couldn't be employed. So they were frightened and did what they were told. The strikes began.

They were terrorized by the unions when in 1982 we had a bad debt of £300,000, from a free advertising sheet started in London.

And then we lost a huge telephone directory contract because a young ass in the collating department, working at nights with his

friends, thought it would be a great lark to stick some obscene pornographic literature into some of the directories. These caused outrage,
particularly in Scotland.

I said it was a one-off and wouldn't happen again; the man had
been dismissed. But the Post Office said they now couldn't rely on us
to do the collating properly.

Then came Arnold Weinstock's unfortunate intervention, induced
by Verushka who was frightened by my personal position.

He and my brother and Jacob [Rothschild] forked out £8,000 each
to satisfy the creditors. It was all quite unnecessary. I could have done
it all by myself and Jacob has despised me ever since.

We could have got by, just – although it had been made extremely
difficult by the unions and maybe the bank then took the view we
wouldn't actually get by because of the £300,000 bad debt.

I was glad to hear that the two Communists were not taken on by
any other printing firm because they knew what they had done to me
at Banbury.

Saturday 22 May
To Oare for the weekend.

There was a thirty-eight-year-old member of the European parliament, John Stevens, who sits for the Thames Valley.[22]

He is a very able young man. He has got a very good business of
his own, connected with, among other things, one of Jacob Rothschild's
activities. He drives around in a nice Rolls-Royce.

On Saturday evening Jacob and Serena Rothschild came to dinner.

Serena started talking about this great party which was held at the
National Gallery where Jacob had been Chairman and how lovely it
was to have only one's friends there. I thought to myself, 'Crikey, why
didn't they ask us?' I am among their oldest friends. But Jacob down-
rates me, because of Banbury, as a failed businessman.

Sunday 23 May
I swam before breakfast in the Olympic length, heated pool which is
very shallow at both ends so that the children won't drown. Before I
went to swim I discovered Henry having his pre-breakfast in the dining-

---

22. Banker; Conservative MEP, 1989–99; candidate for the Pro Euro Conservative
Party in the 1999 Kensington and Chelsea by-election.

room, eating large quantities of cereals. He blushed and said, 'I've just had a little snack before breakfast.'

I am very fond of Henry. He is an extremely astute businessman. He looks sleepy but my goodness he's far from it. With his Hong Kong Land Company he's taken over now Trafalgar House, Kwik Save, and all kinds of things.

He said, in front of John Stevens later, that the great future is not in Europe but in developing markets in Asia and the Pacific. That's where Jardine are going to fight away because they will be much bigger producers and consumers than we are. This made the young man blench.

A party went to Bowood where Charlie Shelburne (heir to the Marquess of Lansdowne) lives. I was asked did I want to go. I said, 'No, I've been there often for dinner and there's nothing new to see about it except for the famous bedroom.' 'What is the famous bedroom?' 'That's the one where Camilla and Charles slept. Charlie Shelburne could make a great deal of money by putting notices in it, saying "This is the bed where the Prince of Wales slept with Camilla Parker Bowles on various nights".'

Conrad Black is boring. He is limited. He has read some history books, which he understands somewhat, but I don't think he has really got a grip on the policy the paper ought to have, even if he were able to impose it.

He has done well in business and the *Telegraph* is becoming more profitable; even the *Sunday Telegraph* seems to be doing better.

He is very pleased with himself and thinks he is the most important person in the country because of the influence the *Telegraph* papers have. It is certainly true that they have an enormous effect on the Tory Party.

Henry wanted me to stay to watch the third one-day test against Australia. I said, 'No, I've got to go back. I'm under marital orders. We've got people coming to play bridge and I shall go to watch live the rest of the test match.'

Oh for the grace and glory which is Gower and away with the misery which is Gooch! The match was easily within England's grasp and everybody expected them to win except for me who knew their fatal flaw: bad leadership, no determination.

Monday 24 May
I was reading in the *Financial Times* that it is the intention to get rid
of Norman during the Whitsun recess so I rang Norman. He had heard
nothing about it and doesn't believe it for a moment.

Norman said he was very much looking forward to coming to
dinner tomorrow and would he be sitting next to Princess Michael. I
laughed and said, 'Yes, I think we can arrange that.' I don't know if
he now has his eye on rather larger girls. I said, 'Maybe she'll ask you
for a million from the Treasury.' 'Or a security guard. That's what
she's always wanting,' Norman replied.

I've been reading some of the Alan Clark memoirs. They're very
racy, lots of inaccuracies and lots of boasts in them. I don't think he
ever had any influence on her (Margaret's) policy though he pretends
he had. I note that they paid an advance of £350,000 for them, the
publishers, so that makes my advance extremely cheap, and they don't
cover anything like as wide a range as mine do.

Baroness Jay, who is having a tumultuous affair with a married
man and flaunts it all over the newspapers, asked a question this
afternoon from the front bench of the Labour Party.[23] I saw her sideways on. Though she has an attractive face she is thickening out
enormously.

Tuesday 25 May
Blow me down, the Blacks had not arrived by gone a quarter to nine.
The dinner was timed for no later than nine so we had to sit down
without them. Incredibly rude, which he is of course.

Black mumbled something about a telephone conference in his car
with Canada.

On my right was Princess Michael.

There's a film called *Indecent Proposal* in which Robert Redford
asks a married woman he's attracted by if she would sleep with him
for a million dollars. After a lot of struggling with her conscience she
says yes. I said to Princess Michael, 'I know what your answer would
be. You'd do it for a million.' She said, 'No, you've got it wrong. I'd

---

23. Margaret, née Callaghan, daughter of the former Labour Prime Minister, m 1
    (1961–86) Peter Jay, m 2 (1994) Professor Michael Adler, after his divorce in
    1994; former television reporter and producer; Minister of State, Department of
    Health, 1997–8; Leader of the House of Lords and Minister for Women since
    1998; life peer 1992.

do it for nothing. I think he's so glorious. He has a wonderful physique and body.'

Then she told me they're in frightful trouble, she and Prince Michael. They were and are names at Lloyd's and the whole of their syndicate has gone bust and they're being called on for everything they've got. I was horrified and said, 'What are you going to do?' She said the 'family,' meaning the Queen, has helped out enormously 'but most of the money comes out of the trust which was available for us and the children. The children are protected but we're not.'

The books she wrote, the last one about royal courtesans,[24] made a lot of money but it was all swallowed up by the debt to Lloyd's.

Norman was sitting on her right. He was absolutely fascinated as he had never met her before. He told me later her bosoms started almost popping out of her dress.

On my left was the very pretty girl, Grania Cavendish,[25] who had not long come back from her house in Italy which is an old convent she is converting, not far from where Tony [Lambton] lives.

Grania is a slight, small girl with a beautiful figure, wonderful dark green eyes, very well done hair, beautifully turned out, and extremely appealing.

A flourishing, noisy argument was getting up steam between myself and Conrad Black.

I said how disgracefully he had behaved towards the government and Norman.

Prince Michael was fascinated by the commotion.

Poor Robin [Day] looks very ill.

It's something to do with his heart all over again. I have a horrible feeling he's not long with us. He's very disconsolate about his life. He thinks it's been a fearful failure though I kept cheering him up and telling him it hadn't been, and it really hasn't been.

We [the men] were about to [return to the drawing-room] when Conrad came up to me and said, 'Would you mind staying behind and asking Norman to do so because I want to have a private and serious conversation with him.'

He said really he was very pro-Major and Lamont but it was all very difficult with the whole world against them.

---

24. *Cupid and the King: Five Royal Paramours* was published in 1991.
25. Grania Caulfeild m (1970) Hugh Cavendish, chairman, Holker Estate Group of companies; life peer 1990, a government Whip, 1990–2.

Max Hastings[26] had been offended by Norman's rudeness to him. Norman said, 'What do you mean by rudeness?' Conrad said, 'You saw him at a party the other night and you just turned away from him.' Norman said, 'I did nothing of the kind. I said, "Good evening, how are you?" and then he walked off so I thought he didn't want a serious conversation.'

Conrad said, 'Why doesn't Major ask him to lunch?' I said, 'Why should he? He's done nothing but insult him.'

Conrad then said, '[You] Norman may have done well, as Woodrow says, but you are thought to lack *gravitas*. Why did you talk about singing in the bath when we left the ERM?' Norman said, 'I never did say that. It was my wife who replied, when we were besieged by reporters asking how I was feeling, that I must be feeling all right because she had heard me singing in the bath.' Conrad then proceeded to the other remark which was supposed to have got Norman into trouble, 'Je ne regrette rien'.

At this point Conrad said would Norman like to write a complete defence of his actions and clear up the misunderstandings? It would get major billing in the *Telegraph* and in the *Spectator*.

Norman said, 'Would you leave in everything I said?' 'Oh yes,' said Conrad.

When I got into the drawing-room it was five to twelve. Prince and Princess Michael were ready to leave. I took them out and they walked up to their car hand in hand, which was touching. I think there's genuine affection between them.

I have told Princess Michael I really haven't got any money. She doesn't quite believe it but I said I haven't and do the best I can in the way I can while I am alive. What happens after me is another matter.

No multi-millionaire in the world could have given a better dinner party with better wine than that we had that night. They would not have been able to gather the right ingredients for conversation and interest nor deal with the wine in the way that I do, nor would the food have been done so well, nor would the rooms have seen such beautiful flowers, beautifully arranged, nor would the service have been smoother or better.

A most extraordinary thing happened in Palm Beach, where Conrad has long had a house, at a famous club there to which the best people belong and to which Conrad belongs. They realized he has now got a

---

26. Editor, *Daily Telegraph*, 1986–95, *Evening Standard* since 1995.

Jewish wife. He said he was going to bring her to lunch. They said if he did, no one would speak to Barbara and he would be thrown out of the club. Instead of standing up for himself and his wife and their rights, he tamely found an excuse not to go to the club.

It is very strange that this sort of thing goes on in Florida, America, which could never happen here. They might not always be willing to exceed their quota of Jews, or have too many Jews in a club, but once they are there no one would dream of treating anyone in the way Conrad was treated over Barbara. In fact, ours is a much more open and democratic and less class-conscious society than America's.

I can't exactly say to Black, 'If you support the government properly, I think you'll get a peerage,' but I may risk it later. I must think more about it and talk to Norman again. It would be a blatant bribe but a sensible one from the point of view of John Major who is assailed on all sides.

Wednesday 26 May
I spoke to Richard Ryder early in the morning and asked what was going on. I told him that as almost the government's only supporter in the press, I didn't want to be made a fool of.

He was somewhat guarded, which I felt was ominous. He asked where I was going to be over the weekend and for the next three days. I told him. He said he would have something to tell me, perhaps, a little later, on Friday or so.

I felt a prick of foreboding and once again said, 'Sacrificing Norman would look shameful and do John harm.' Would he pass that on? He said he would.

Had another conversation with Norman during the day. He was getting nervous. I said, 'Have you spoken to John?' He said no, he wasn't going to. It wasn't for him to do that at all. It would be beneath him.

I forbore to mention to Norman that I saw a picture of Major on the television sitting next to Kenneth Clarke at the one-day test at Lord's. That was worrying.

Thursday 27 May
Norman rang quite early in the morning and said he had just been asked to see Major. What should he do if he were offered another job in the Cabinet? I said it would depend on what it was. Leader of the

House or Foreign Secretary or Home Secretary might be a good thing and be OK.

He said Foreign Secretary wasn't available. That was what Selwyn Lloyd did when he was removed by Macmillan. Home Secretary I didn't dwell on too much because John might think that Norman, with the black eye incident and other curiosities, would cause the press to go for him and the *Sun* might shriek out what an extraordinary person to put in charge of law and order when he can't keep law and order over himself.

Norman said he had seen Richard Ryder go into Number 10 last night and stay there till twelve so they must have been plotting something. I was extremely worried for Norman.

About an hour later he rang back. He said, 'Yes. They are sacking me. I have refused to write a letter of resignation because I am not resigning. I was offered the Department of the Environment.' I said, 'It's quite an important department.' 'I loathe the very idea of it. Anyway it's obviously a demotion, an insult.'

He is pretty shattered, and so of course is Rosemary. I was just about in tears. It was a dirty trick. Major shows himself as hopelessly weak. He sacrificed David Mellor after saying he would stand by him and now he has done the same to Norman. As I said to Norman, 'It won't save his skin, you know, trying to do it without good reason. You were his protective shield, but I suppose now you have got the economy going on the right lines and improving, he thinks he doesn't need your protective shield any more. But he'll find out he does.'

Later on the *News of the World* rang and said could I ask Norman if he would write an article for them. I said, 'How much would you pay? Would you pay £10,000?' After consultation they said yes they would, provided it said something. I said, 'I'm sure it would.' I tried then to get hold of Norman but he had gone to Canterbury to take the children out from the King's School with Rosemary and tell them what had happened.

Eventually I left a message for Norman to ring. He rang later on that night. I told him about the *News of the World* offer. He said he wasn't very keen but he would think about it overnight.

I said, 'I was very amused that you only sent him a letter saying you were happy to have served your country, not him.' He said, 'I never sent him a letter at all. It was a press statement, a very funny press statement.' I said, 'Haven't you replied to his letter?' He said, 'No. It's here. I haven't even opened it. I'm going to throw it away unopened. I couldn't care less what he has written.' So the press were all speculating on his reply to Major's letter and he hadn't even looked at it.

It's terribly sad. Major gave way because of pressure by that little bastard, Norman Fowler, two-faced, slimy fellow, who chairs the Tory Party.[27]

Friday 28 May
There seems to be a wave of sympathy towards Norman [Lamont] this morning. He said he didn't want to do the *News of the World* article. I said he had to try to get a large advance for a book.

We went out for dinner after I'd finished the article for the *News of the World* and another special one they wanted me to write about Norman alone and what he was like on holidays and so forth. I charged them £1,000 for it which they were willing to pay. The dinner was at the Chinese restaurant with Irwin and Cita.

I had rung Margaret early in the morning.

I said, 'I've come to the same conclusion as you, that Major's weak and he's making a mess of it. But we've got him at the moment and I don't know who else we could have.'

Margaret said it was pathetic what Major had done.

She said, 'He's shuffling the same pack with the sole purpose of getting rid of one member of the Cabinet.'

She asked me whether I was going to speak at the Maastricht debate. I said I didn't think there was any point in it because we're in it now and if it doesn't work, it will collapse on itself.

She said, 'I'm just off to California on Monday. But God bless.' It was just like old times. I shall always go on adoring that woman but I wish she hadn't gone over the top with some of her extravaganza.

Apropos what I wrote about Norman being highly regarded in the capitals of the world by prime ministers and finance ministers, he said he was rung up by the Canadian finance minister who goes to the G7 meetings.[28] He said he couldn't understand what on earth had happened to us in England.

---

27. Conservative MP since 1970; former Secretary of State for Transport, Social Services, Employment; knight 1990.
28. Dan Mazankowski.

Saturday 29 May
I woke up early because I was going to Wigan. I set the alarm clock for seven o'clock but in fact I woke up at six, restless. So I rang up Norman.

Norman said that Margaret had rung him up and he had a very nice conversation with her. She said how sorry she was and how unfair it was.

As for Kenneth Clarke's appointment [as Chancellor], Norman doesn't dislike him at all. They were friends at Cambridge. He explained how he had been his best man. The four of them, Kenneth Clarke, Michael Howard, John Gummer and he had all been great friends there and they'd all officiated in one way or another at his wedding to Rosemary. Old university true friends in youth usually support each other through life. As with me and Julian Amery, and Hugh Fraser[29] and Alan Hare, Jerry Kerruish[30] and even to some extent Ted Heath.

It was also terribly sad that on Wednesday morning, after the dinner with Conrad Black, Norman had sent Conrad a letter reminding him of all he said: that he would now give Norman full space and publicity in the *Telegraph* and *Spectator* to put the whole side of his case and defence, justification for what he had done and how good it had been.

Sunday 30 May
Does he have a future in politics, Norman asked me. 'Yes,' I said. 'There's no reason at all why you shouldn't make a come-back. Two of your closest friends are now Chancellor of the Exchequer and Home Secretary.[31] One of them is quite likely to become Prime Minister because I think Major may be finished.'

Monday 31 May
Rosemary Lamont came to see Verushka to borrow a hat for the Derby.

They are going to sell their house where the tart used to be in the basement when they were in Number 11. They are going to buy a much bigger house because they think they need one now they are

---

29. (1918–84); Sir Hugh Fraser, Conservative MP from 1945; knight 1980; younger brother of 17th Baron Lovat; m (1956–77) Lady Antonia, née Pakenham, who m 2 (1980) Harold Pinter, playwright.

30. Canon, Salisbury Cathedral, and Fellow, Magdalen College, Oxford; d 1992.

31. Michael Howard had succeeded Clarke at the Home Office.

accustomed to living in bigger surroundings. It seems that Norman has an aunt who says she would leave him some money, a fair amount, if he behaved himself. She died quite recently (I knew nothing of this) and left him some money. This is why he is not so anxious to make money with his memoirs or writing an instant article for the *News of the World*.

Norman had lunch with Alistair McAlpine yesterday. I am very glad I persuaded Alistair months ago to stop attacking Norman in his column, which he had done. They are now pretty good friends, as I suppose they used to be.

One thing is fairly civilized about England. You may quarrel with people politically but there really isn't any need for enmity in the end. I have drifted away, obviously, from Mrs Thatcher. But we remain friends.

At lunch time Harold [Lever] was much brighter, argumentative, looking much more cheerful. The only other guest was (Sir) John Woolf.[32]

He said he owed me a great deal of gratitude and he had never acknowledged it before. When I was on *Panorama* he heard me talking about *Room at the Top* written by John Braine. I went to Bradford, where he was a librarian, and interviewed him.

I mentioned there was sex in the book and described what it was about, so it sounded very intriguing. He thought, 'God, I must buy the film rights for that,' which he did immediately. It was a fantastically successful film with Simone Signoret and Laurence Harvey.

He said, 'I made a lot of money out of it, thanks to you.' I said, 'Well, that is very kind of you. Perhaps if you die before me, you might leave me something in your will. All contributions gratefully received.' He is notorious as the meanest man alive.

It made me feel what a foolish fellow I am because I could have easily set a film up like that myself, if I'd had any gumption. I have never pursued money skilfully or relentlessly enough.

32. Film and television producer, d 1999; founder (1948) and chairman, Romulus Films, whose many productions included *The African Queen*, *The L-Shaped Room*, *The Day of the Jackal*, *The Odessa File*; knight 1975.

Tuesday 1 June

Michael Mates, Minister for Northern Ireland (which he got by grace of Heseltine because he managed his campaign for him during the leadership election), has done an incredible thing. Asil Nadir, the man who swindled millions out of everybody in his Polly Peck firm, and who has fled to Northern Cyprus from where he can't be extradited, was given a watch by Mates, inscribed, 'Don't let the buggers get you down'. This was sent to him by Mates when Nadir was arrested. He had his watch taken from him by the police. Mates has been bombarding the Attorney General and others in the government, attacking the Serious Fraud Squad and everyone else, saying Nadir is not being fairly treated. That's the sort of fellow we have got in the government now.

Dinner with Mrs More-O'Ferrall[1] in her flat in Eaton Square.

Mrs Cazelet,[2] the widow of the man who trained for Queen Elizabeth the Queen Mother at Fairlawn in Kent, sat next to me at dinner and I talked to her about P. G. Wodehouse, with whom she is connected via Edward Cazalet.

Mrs Cazelet said P. G. Wodehouse was an immensely dull man.

'I never thought he was funny at all. Women don't think he's funny, it's not their kind of humour.' I said, 'That isn't quite true. My daughter and Queen Elizabeth the Queen Mother both think he's very funny and I know other women who do as well.'

Wednesday 2 June

Arrived [at Epsom] at half past eight.

On the Downs side I saw a couple of Tote girls buying a bacon and

---

1. Widow of Roderick More-O'Ferrall, racehorse owner.
2. Zara, née Mainwaring, m 2 (1949) Peter Cazelet (1907–73), racehorse trainer; the High Court Judge, Edward Cazalet QC, (knight 1988), is Peter Cazelet's son by his first marriage to Leonora née Rowley (d 1944), the daughter of Ethel, Wodehouse's wife, by her first marriage to Leonard Rowley.

sausage roll. I said into the ear of one of them, 'That won't do you any good,' and she jumped nearly a mile high.

Verushka came with the Lamonts on the helicopter. They had been invited by Evelyn de Rothschild while Norman was still Chancellor. Typically the press reported the helicopter trip there and back as costing £1,000, as though he had paid it himself, but he was the guest of United Racecourses because he has done a hell of a lot for racing.

Willie Whitelaw talked to me about Mrs Thatcher and how badly she had behaved lately. He doesn't think anything of Major.

Margaret always put the policies first and the politics second. She stuck to her guns and tried to get through what she thought was right for the country. Major on the other hand, as he has said to Norman, puts the politics first and tries to make the party happy before going through with the policies.

Willie Whitelaw thought the Tories today were the most worthless party he ever could remember.

In the evening we went to Charles Forte's and Irene Forte's fiftieth wedding anniversary. It was upstairs in the Park Lane Forte restaurant establishment. It was very jolly with lots of nice music. The grand-children sang a little song written for them by Olga in praise of their grandparents. Willie was there again and so was Margaret.

Margaret was asked by Verushka if she would like to come to dinner again. She said, 'Yes, but not if Woodrow is going to be against everything I said, as he was the last time I came to dinner.' This was a somewhat misreading of what happened. I had merely pointed out that she would have signed up for Maastricht, as everybody knew.

Saturday 5 June

Norman had still not been able to get hold of Margaret. I think it is important that they don't both do their speeches on the same day, she on Maastricht and he on his dismissal from the government, because I want Norman to get the maximum publicity.

Talking to him, the more I realized how shameful the episode of his dismissal had been and how dithering and hopeless Major is. On the morning of 16th September 1992 [Black Wednesday], when Norman wanted to get out of the ERM straight away, he wasn't able to. There was a four-hour meeting of the inner circle at Downing Street – Major, Michael Heseltine (the mad pro-European), Kenneth Clarke (then Home Secretary and also very pro-Europe), Douglas Hurd and Norman. Heseltine and Clarke had no business to be there at all as it was a matter of financial affairs outside their scope. Hurd had some justification in the sense that he is Foreign Secretary and might be concerned with the implications.

They were all keen on jumping up the interest rates instead of backing Norman who wanted to go from the ERM immediately. Clarke still wanted to say, after Norman at the PM's request had jumped up the interest rates and we had to leave the ERM, that we would immediately go back in the ERM.

Norman had suggested even before September 16th that we should suspend our membership of the ERM but there was shock and horror from Major and the others. When all this charade happened on September 16th, Major passed him a note saying, 'I am not resigning, nor are you,' which was clear assurance, among many others he repeatedly gave, that he didn't want him to leave the Cabinet.[3]

Before all this happened Norman had said to Major after the election, 'You are under no obligation to me. I backed you and organized the campaign for you to be Prime Minister because I thought you were the best person, but don't feel you have to stand by me for that reason if you're not happy with me.' Major said, 'No, you're the best. I don't want anyone else to be Chancellor. You understand it and have done it very well. I like you very much. We've got to see this thing out without panic and you'll get through OK.'

What happened on September 16th in the four hours Major dithered about and consulted people who had nothing to do with financial matters, was that we lost £6 billion which was entirely Major's fault and not Norman's.

Norman told me he would actually have taken the Leader of the House position, though he would have preferred to be Home Secretary. He was not offered either of those positions. Why didn't Major talk to him the night before instead of plotting with Ryder and Fowler to get rid of him?

Now they are all scared stiff as to what he is going to say when the House meets again on Monday after the Whitsun recess.

At Longford [with the Radnors[4]] it is really very beautiful. Where I am dictating this now, I see a long way down the river out of the window above the formal gardens, beautifully arranged.

---

3. See Lamont's book *In Office*, published in 1999, p. 269, for this note, and pp. 246 ff., for Lamont's account of the events of this period, much as WW records here.

4. 8th Earl of Radnor (Jake) m 3 (1986) Jillean Pettit.

Sunday 6 June

Last night we had a jolly sing-song after a terrifically good dinner.

Barney [Miller[5]], the Argentine of US parentage, who is a very pleasant fellow, sang no end of ditties and very witty and skilful satires on modern life which his mother had written. She died two years ago. He is trying to find somebody else to help him write new ones. Would I help him? 'I don't think I'm good enough.' He takes his little party, himself, his wife and his twin daughters, from place to place for charity concerts.

He's sixty-four and he's going to umpire the cricket match on Sunday.

Jill was very funny about Conrad Black at our dinner. She asked him what he did. He said, 'I'm a proprietor.' She said, 'A proprietor of what? A shop? A business?' He said, 'No. A newspaper.' 'Oh, which one?' 'The *Telegraph*. Do you read it?' She said, 'No. We only take the *Times* and the *Independent*.' It was amazing to Black to meet somebody who had never heard of him; it healthily deflated his ego, though I like him a lot.

Norman is going to make his resignation speech on Wednesday. All with great secrecy, so it will give the utmost surprise to Major and the government.

Tuesday 8 June

Norman wants to come to have his speech typed by Mrs Tamborero. He said he would be coming at twelve. I said I had Lord Hartington visiting me at two to talk about the new British Horseracing Board so we would have to make sure they didn't clash.

In the event Norman was still with me in the garden when Stoker turned up. He probably noticed him but he didn't say anything. He was shown into the drawing-room while Norman left the house by another route. The press are chasing him like billy-o.

Wednesday 9 June

Board meeting at Cavendish Avenue at 9.15 a.m. That is because I have to go to the memorial service for Mary Rothermere.

---

5. Formerly Vice President, Johnson's Wax; he organized cricket in Argentina where he lived for many years; his team, the Troubadors, played the local Longford team most summers at this period; see Vol. 1, p. 574, for a similar weekend at the Radnors.

The service was pretty and light, just like Mary herself. Gayle Hunnicutt,[6] the actress and an old friend, gave a good address. We finished with Texan jazz: both Mary and Gayle originated from Texas.

I had to hurry back to Cavendish Avenue. Norman had been there since twelve dictating a different version to Mrs Tamborero and getting drafts of it out. We had some sandwiches and champagne as I looked through it and made some suggestions, most of which he accepted.

I had wanted Robbie to drive us through the other side of Parliament so we could have just gone by the House of Lords entrance and dropped him at the Commons entrance. Robbie was rather stubborn, or perhaps he misunderstood. He decided to come our normal way. We were halted by the traffic lights just beyond the entrance gate to the Commons and of course there was a thrusting of cameras into the window and they were popping off like billy-o. Norman didn't seem to mind but I was very annoyed and put my hand up to try to deflect them. A huge colour picture of Norman and myself (rather a good one of me smoking a cigar and Norman grinning) was splashed across the front page of the *Times* next morning.

The House was absolutely packed. Norman got up. He was nervous but that didn't matter a bit. He made a remarkable speech.

I had arranged afterwards to pick Norman up in the Central Lobby with Rosemary, who was sitting a little bit behind me, and smuggle them out via the back door through the Lords entrance where Robbie would pick us up to avoid photographers. I am not quite sure that Norman wanted to avoid photographers all that much.

Thursday 10 June

Just as I was beginning to read the newspapers and listen to the eight o'clock news they rang up from the *Today* programme. Would I be prepared to speak about Norman Lamont?

'When are you proposing?' They said, 'Now, in a few minutes after Michael Heseltine speaks.'

I explained Norman's speech was not intended to ruin John Major but to improve him and that if he behaved better, along the lines Norman indicated, his government would be more successful.

Chips rang last night to say how marvellous he thought Norman's speech was.

---

6. She m 2 (1978) Simon Jenkins, editor of the *Times*, 1990–2.

Chips said he agreed with every word, particularly the bits about shaping policy and the Bank of England.

Norman completely upstaged the whole economic debate and put the government in a tizzy. So our secret had been very well kept. No one ever spotted him here, at least if they did they didn't report it to the press. Surprise is always the best method of discomforting the enemy and at that moment the Prime Minister was the enemy, plus his hangers-on.

I had a very nice letter from Kenneth Clarke in answer to mine. I must keep intact normal relations with Michael Howard and Kenneth Clarke. When Major goes, as he well may do, there should be no bar to Norman going back into the government. On the other hand, we may not completely have burnt our boats with Major, mainly because it wasn't a malicious attack.

Friday 11 June

Spoke to Margaret. She said what Norman needs is a group of friends around him who will stand by him. He has been too much of a loner.

He should keep quiet and lie low and see how events develop. I passed this on to Norman and he didn't seem at all pleased. I have the horrible fear he is overdoing it and thoroughly enjoys all the press pictures.

Later My appearance on *Newsnight* was very successful.

The dreaded, sneering Jeremy Paxman was nowhere to be seen.[7] Anthony Howard was on the programme with me, being interviewed as well. He had done a pre-film of Anthony Eden's decline, comparing it with the situation Major is in. I said, 'But Major is not ill.' He said, 'You're not going to rubbish it, are you?' after the film had been shown. I said, 'No, I won't.'

Before they had us, Douglas Hurd was shown, trying to calm things down. He sounded very defeatist and even contemplated the possibility aloud of there being another leadership election, in which he said he would not stand.

Petronella says there is going to be a profile of me in the *Sunday Telegraph*.[8] I said, 'What a cheek. They haven't asked my permission.' She said they don't have to.

---

7. *Newsnight* presenter.
8. The peg for the profile on 13 June was WW's support for Lamont.

Sunday 13 June
On the BBC in *What the Papers Say* on Radio Four this morning, they
led off with my *News of the World* statement that I had not written
Norman's speech, as had been said in the newspapers, and they gave
a bit more of my defence of Norman. Verushka is terrified it will all
put me in wrong with Major, which in a sense doesn't matter because
I don't suppose he will renew my appointment with the Tote after May
1995 anyway.

Norman has spoken to Nigel Lawson who said, 'If you write
your memoirs, you won't be able to get back into politics if you
have written anything interesting, and if you haven't, they won't
find them worth publishing or at any rate not worth anything
much by way of an advance.' Norman is getting slightly depressed
now.

Monday 14 June
We have been having this morning arguments with Norman. I have
been trying to prevent him coming to lunch at Ascot on Wednesday
because Willie Whitelaw and Michael Howard, the new Home Secretary, as well as William Astor, who is a government minister, will all
be there and it could be extremely embarrassing to have them in the
same room, as the press would take pictures and pester everyone with
questions.

He had wanted to come down early with us. I think he has gone a
bit cuckoo at the moment.

Yesterday he had a parcel which he thought was suspicious. It
was addressed to Lamont, Notting Hill. He thought it might be
a bomb. So he walked all the way to the local police station
with it. They looked at it and closed the streets around before
they examined it. It turned out to be a CD, musical disk. The
police pretended to be annoyed and said it was very irresponsible
of him. If he thought it was a bomb, why was he carrying it through
the streets?

His reasonable explanation to me was he didn't want to ring up
Downing Street and he didn't want the police to know where he is
living to prevent being besieged by journalists and photographers, as
the police would tip them off.

Thursday 17 June

Appalling nonsense in the *Express* gossip column. It was said the reason why Norman didn't come to have lunch in the Tote room was because it would have embarrassed the guests present. This is a total lie.

I told him he should not come because journalists and photographers would follow him around.

Nick Lloyd [editor, *Daily Express*] came into our entertainment room after lunch today and I gave him a hell of a pasting.

I had to leave at a very early hour to go to the Lords for my amendment, which I had to move myself, for the Tote to operate or take part in any form in a National Lottery, to be made absolutely certain.

Saturday 19 June

William Golding, the Nobel Prize-winner, author of *Lord of the Flies*, died suddenly after the party on Thursday night to which he had invited me and Verushka. I regretted not having gone because I would have taken to him a first edition I have got of *Lord of the Flies* and asked him to sign it, which would have added £1,000 at least to the value of the book.

I was very sad for him because he was an extraordinarily good writer, independent of other writers. He carefully did not mix with the literati because he didn't wish to be confused by them or find himself influenced by some 'school' of writing.

Monday 21 June

I am getting nervous again that everything I do is looked at against my age and, if I slip up or it is not up to standard, they will think it is because I am too old.

I decided to map out a plan. I assume I will live five years with my brain more or less intact. Therefore, I have about one thousand, eight hundred and twenty-five days. Of these I intend to spend all but sixty-five days a year working.

I must keep up this manuscript and also find the time to write a decent play, while making money at the same time to maintain Verushka and my mother-in-law.

She is deeply selfish and ungrateful, yet I'm sorry for the poor old thing – totally useless all her life and looking like an overblown, decaying toadstool of gigantic size.

The plan is to start on July 4th 1993 when I shall be seventy-five. I will review it on July 4th 1998 when I shall be eighty.[9]

A party at the Gilmours where friendly relations have been resumed. Norman is getting very distressed.

He wants to have his memoirs put up for auction. I shall have to let him get on with it and make a mess of it in his own way. He is downcast that the City isn't rushing to employ him. But they won't, so long as they think he is totally out of favour at Number 10. They want ex Chancellors for the perceived influence they may still have in Whitehall.

I saw Andrew Parker Bowles talking to the Duke of Northumberland's sister just outside the house. He said, 'Is Petronella here?' 'Yes, she's right down over there talking to Robin Day and some of the Gilmour boys.' 'Oh, I must go off and see if she will have dinner with me.' I said, 'I don't think you'll get very far with Petronella.'

At lunch time I had gone to Lord's to see England's second innings dwindle away. Bob and Molly had been very kind and got around twenty-six signatures of famous cricketers on the two bats for Jill Radnor for her dyslexic society and for the Longford Park Cricket Club. Molly said there had been three hundred bats left in the pavilion for signing for one cause or another so it had not been as easy as expected.

Paul Getty was very friendly. Secretly he agrees that Major is not up to much but he thought it not a good idea for me to say so.

Molly complained, as did Tim Rice[10] who was there, that Major doesn't give honours to the right people. Why have they suddenly dug up Larwood[11] and given him a decoration and there is still nothing for Bob?

Tuesday 22 June
The great dinner party – Henry and Tessa Keswick, John Patten (Secretary for Education) and his pretty but not quite as pretty as she used to be wife, Louise.

She is now a director of Ladbroke, about which I teased her.

Alistair McAlpine and his wife, Romilly, were there. It was her

9. WW died on 7 December 1997 when he was seventy-nine.
10. Writer of lyrics for musicals; knight 1994.
11. (1904–95); England fast bowler, central figure in the 'body-line' controversy, 1932–3; awarded the MBE.

birthday. For some reason or other when Louise Patten arrived I confused her with Romilly, who she looks something like, and I said 'Happy Birthday' to her.

No wonder Alan Clark wrote in his diaries that I was gaga.[12]

Beryl Bainbridge was put next to John Gross who used to edit the *Times Literary Supplement* and knows all about writing.

Olga Polizzi was by herself because William is still going backwards and forwards to Cambodia or elsewhere.[13] His place had been taken by John Bowes Lyon.[14] He told Verushka the other day he was at a lunch party given by the favourite grandson of the Queen Mother, young Linley who is about to get married. Knowing she [the Queen Mother] knew Elton John (he sings or whatever and is very popular), Linley told her he'd be there. So Queen Elizabeth went heaped with diamonds and jewellery. When Elton complimented her, she said, 'Yes, I thought you would like it. That's why I dressed up in this way.' She adores being with queers because they butter her up so much. She feels they are sympathetic to women, as indeed they are, and gets on with them a treat.

Tessa Keswick says it is very cold and impersonal at the Treasury and even the Chancellor of the Exchequer's office is grim and uncosy. She doesn't have the same relationship with Kenneth Clarke there as she had at the Home Office.

She likes Sarah Hogg, she maintains, but I doubt it because of course Sarah is the boss lady above Tessa so far as giving advice politically on economic matters, which is all that now concerns Kenneth Clarke.

I think she will hang on in the hope he does become Prime Minister because then her advice of a more general sort will be needed. She is pretty good at warning him of the dangers of Brussels which he had been too lazy to understand until now.

The ladies eventually left the men behind. This astonished Beryl Bainbridge and even Louise Patten who has not been here before. Tessa meekly went away with her head boiling away at the indignity of women being removed.

---

12. Alan Clark actually wrote: 'With the exception of Macmillan (and *he* does it on purpose) Woodrow is the only person I know who seems to be more gaga than he is.'

13. His book *Cambodia's New Deal* was published in 1994.

14. Related to the Queen Mother; a director of Sotheby's, 1970–80.

Wednesday 23 June
I couldn't go to the Levy Board meeting and had to send Brian [McDon-
nell] instead. He is getting more and more like a bewildered flamingo
flapping his wings.

He now waits for me to take action and then says he agrees after
a bit of resistance behind the scenes and delaying things. But I am fond
of him.

Friday 25 June
Had a very funny letter from David Stevens. He was much hipped by
my saying he is considered a nonentity among press magnates (see
Paper Tigers book review).[15] He hadn't read what I said properly so I
sent him back a fax. He is very touchy. Soon after he rang up and said
'a nonentity' wanted to speak to me. Very funny. We have now made
our peace, as I explained to him I was only reporting what the others
say.

I asked Norman what he thought about Mates's resignation which
was announced yesterday. He said, 'It's just like what Major did to
me. I think he did his job pretty well and Major said he was going
to stand by him and then of course he didn't.'

Saturday 26 June
Rang Richard Ryder.

I said, 'I suppose I must resume normal relations with you now. I
wish Major would talk to me more often. I could prevent him making
some of the stupid mistakes he makes.'

He said, 'I think you should see him.' I said, 'Well he had better
ask me if he wants me to come to see him. I think he is pretty cross
with me at the moment for all the things I have written about him,
and I can understand that.'

---

15. In the *Times* of 24 June WW had reviewed Nicholas Coleridge's book about press
     moguls, *Paper Tigers*. The passage in the review read: 'Conrad Black's evolution
     from brashness to maturity is also fascinatingly described. For the other press
     magnates, Lord Stevens is a nonentity owning but a few shares in Express News-
     papers, of which he is chairman. He has created efficiency and saved money; but,
     without printers' ink in his veins, his rivals do not fear him as a damaging
     competitor.' Nicholas Coleridge, journalist, has been managing director, Condé
     Nast Publications since 1992.

Meanwhile, Heseltine has had a heart attack or a stroke or both. He was in Venice.

He is obviously not going to be able to do his job at the Board of Trade for some time if ever again. He is very young (sixty) and doesn't smoke and takes a lot of exercise. Another proof that smoking does not cause these diseases.

I went swimming early this morning. Then my blind eye, or practically blind eye, began to give me merry hell, like needles being stuck into it. It was agony.

It's because, Arnott[16] says, the eye is defective and the body wants to get rid of it; the eye resists and they fight over it. When it happens it is almost unbearable. It usually happens around once a week.

Sunday 27 June

Norman came to lunch. We had it in the garden. As he likes red wine, I gave him a bottle of 1963 Château Lafite, which he enjoyed hugely and drank two-thirds of. We also had champagne. He is terribly mixed up, confused between writing sensational memoirs and trying to get back at a senior level in politics.

I said, 'Let's get the objectives straight.'

'What you need to do is to acquire *gravitas*, as Margaret has said. You haven't got it now. You are perceived as a playboy.' 'But I'm not,' he said indignantly. 'I know that. I know you're deeply serious and have been perhaps the most brilliant Chancellor of the Exchequer almost of this century. So you have to write a book about your philosophy of finance. You might do essays on Keynes and what he would be likely to do in the present situation – Adam Smith, Keynes, Milton Friedman. Explain what you were trying to do, how you set about doing it, why it is a long-term approach and needs to be stuck to. It would be a lot of hard work but it would be worth it.'

He is in great difficulty about his constituency.[17] I said, 'Look for another one if you don't get adopted in one of the ones which emerge from the Kingston-upon-Thames present seat. Then you'll be in good stead for it, if you're being serious. As for money, why don't you pursue those libel actions?

16. Professor Eric Arnott, ophthalmologist specializing in cataract and lens implant operations.
17. Under the Boundary Commission changes, Lamont's seat, Kingston-upon-Thames, would cease to exist at the next election.

'They'll probably settle out of court. You should collect £200,000–£300,000 that way and it would be tax free. It's like winning the football pools, winning libel damages.' He began to warm to this idea.

'Should I see Margaret and ask for her advice?' 'Of course. But don't take it all too seriously. She's a bit out of touch. And don't go overboard with being anti-Europe. We're in the bloody thing now so what we have to do is make it work.'

He told me he would have abolished capital gains tax in the next Budget which is something I have often talked to him about.

Monday 28 June
Party at Sonia and Andrew Sinclair's.

David Stevens came in with his wife. He came up to me and said, 'I can't talk to you. I'm a nonentity.'

Then Nicholas Coleridge came up to Lady Stevens and they started a wonderful curious slanging match in which she said how appalling it was that he had said her husband was a nonentity and all the rest of it.

On the way out I was stopped by Andrew Neil. I told him I had written an article about him which was due to be published on Wednesday in the *Times*. 'I don't think you will altogether dislike it but I don't quite know who you are trying to break up, the Tory Party or Major or both.'

Then he said, 'I fight, you know, when you attack me.' 'Oh yes, I know that. So do I, when you attack me.' He suddenly became very amiable.

Funny fellow.

Tuesday 29 June
Pursuing Arnold's suggestion that we must get hold of a project manager if we are going to do this Lottery, I had another brain-wave. It was to speak to Joe Elmaleh who is connected with Autotote.

I tracked him down in Israel on Sunday. I said, 'I understand you are in touch with Autotote. I have had a look at it and it's clean, unlike [organizations] who have had executives in jail and cases brought against them continually for corrupting senators and other officials in the United States to get lotteries. Does Autotote really know about lotteries?' He said, 'Yes. It so happens that the Chairman and Chief

Executive of Autotote, Lorne Weil, is with me now in Israel.' 'Could he come over here on July 1st? I may be able to line up GEC.'

Then my problem was how to deliver Arnold. I spoke to him and said I wanted to bring the Autotote people to him on Thursday.

Wednesday 30 June
At eleven o'clock I went to see Louise Patten who has this head-hunting affair. I told her all I wanted in the way of a marketing director [for the Lottery project].

Thursday 1 July

I had Robbie pick up Lorne Weil and Jack de Vries [of Autotote] from the Berkeley Hotel. Joe Elmaleh was coming later from elsewhere.

We went to see Arnold and it was a terrific success.

Arnold has tremendous interest with his retail outlets in this country. He has got a foothold (for servicing and dealing with equipment) in about seventy-five per cent of all the service stations in Europe, Canada and large parts of the world, and these are one of the places where you could put [machines] for selling Lottery tickets.

Malcolm Bates was there who is one down from Arnold [at GEC].

I can see if we get this bid, the Tote will be getting about £15 million a year.

The world will be quite astonished when this consortium is announced but we must keep it dead secret at the moment. It will be a very powerful one, with all the GEC resources behind it, no question of falling down for lack of money; no question of the Lottery not being OK with Autotote who have got the biggest number of lotteries now in the world.

If I can pull this off, it will be terrific. Not only will racing get an enormous amount more from our Coral's venture, with the pools getting bigger and bigger,[1] but also it will get a fantastic amount from the Lottery.

Friday 2 July

A ridiculous letter arrived from Meriza Stevens.

She said she would see Jimmy Goldsmith[2] at a party in Paris.

---

1. Clients in Coral betting shops were now able to bet directly into Tote pools on course.
2. Sir James Goldsmith (1933–97); industrialist, environmentalist, member (for France) of the European Parliament; campaigner against political integration of Europe; Leader of the Referendum Party in the 1997 general election; knight 1976.

I said, 'If she takes this review [of the Coleridge book] with her, Jimmy Goldsmith will just roar with laughter. I have known him for many years, far longer than she has known him.'

Meanwhile, the government gets deeper and deeper into messes.

Major's poll rating sinks below the horizon, far lower than Margaret's ever was. The pro-Margaret faction, to which in a sense I partly belong still, wants Major to be given a year's grace before there is another leadership election.

In my own mind I am running both Kenneth Clarke and Michael Howard. Either would suit me – I get on well with both. But I think, if it comes to a contest between the two, it will be Kenneth Clarke because he has more skills in presentation and eloquence. Michael Howard is very nice and highly intelligent but sometimes appears a little bit oily or smooth, and that doesn't go down very well on television. But he is actually very tough.

Sunday 4 July
This was my birthday.

It was to the Theatre Royal, Drury Lane, for a concert, to be followed by dinner at the Waldorf.

The concert was amusing. Peter Ustinov conducted the presentation of it very cleverly. A fellow called Roger Moore (who used to do James Bond parts and I never realized how empty-headed he was until he started blathering hopelessly and pretentiously) was a kind of additional compère.

I was longing to go early [from the dinner] but Joe Elmaleh had prepared a birthday cake for me.

He'd had made a beautiful cake in my racing colours, the jockey's cap the right colour red and beautiful green and yellow striped sleeves and so forth.

Before the dinner I fell into a long conversation with Jeffrey Archer. I told him how good his book is. This was sheer hypocrisy.

I had turned down an invitation to be guest of honour at his Foyle's luncheon.

I didn't want to stand there with an array of Archer worshippers.

I have an affection for Jeffrey Archer. He fought back valiantly from his bankruptcy. He is a bit dodgy in many ways but he has got plenty of guts and he is a lively, worthwhile character. I told him I thought he ought to be Chairman of the Tory Party as Norman Fowler is absolutely useless.

Monday 5 July
To a party this time given by Conrad Black at Mark's Club.

Before the dinner proper began, during the drinks, I got involved with Charles Moore.

Then up came Rosita [Marlborough] in a very friendly manner. I said, 'Just a second. I am trying to explain something to Charles Moore.' Then I turned for a moment to put down my glass and she disappeared. I think she was rather huffy so I must send her a note. Standing up a duchess in favour of a common journalist must seem to her a terrible thing to do.

I spoke to David Stevens. I said, 'I don't know what all this fuss is about, this business about my not being a friend to you.'

'You said I'm a nonentity.' I said, 'I never said anything of the sort. If only you would read the bloody review properly, you would know I hadn't.' He got very angry and I wasn't best pleased.

Tuesday 6 July
To the opening by the Queen of the new gates in Hyde Park in honour of Queen Elizabeth the Queen Mother. These gates would never have been erected if it hadn't been for me. Prince Michael was getting nowhere with the Queen Mother, sending her the designs for them. He got on to me to ask her whether she would see him to talk about them. I thought this was odd because, after all, he is a cousin of the Queen's. But I did contact Martin Gilliat, the Queen Mother's Private Secretary, at the time. He said, 'Yes, by all means he can come to talk to her.'[3]

Prince Michael made an astonishingly well constructed speech and delivered it very well. He did it without notes, presumably having memorized it before, and without a falter. He looked regal with his military bearing and straight upright walk.

There was a reception afterwards.

Queen Elizabeth the Queen Mother came round and I said to her that I thought the gates were very beautiful, light and elegant and with her spirit in them. She smiled as though to say, 'I am not sure about that.'

Wednesday 7 July
To Newmarket to Prince Khalid Abdullah's house for lunch.

The Prince is dark and small with very finely made features and a

---

3. See Vol. 2, pp. 574–5, 577, 600.

neat small moustache. His hands are elegant and so are his movements. He has enormous charm and is clearly a very kind man. He is one of the most successful racehorse owners there has ever been in this country, winning Derbys, Arc de Triomphs, and goodness knows what else.

He is worried that in Saudi Arabia, where he is the King's brother-in-law, a Prince in his own right as well, they are not handling the situation properly. The fanatical religious people preach their version of the Koran, out-of-date, attaching conditions which appeared fifteen hundred years ago, and no one is allowed to oppose them or give a contrary view.

In some ways he is like a very civilized English country gentleman which presumably is why he has a house in Kent, a house in New-market and all those racehorses. In the box there were some Saudi ladies, quite plump and quite pretty.

Dinner at the Connaught with Arnold and Netta. Arnold said we can go ahead mentioning that GEC, Autotote and ourselves are concerned in a consortium to try to get the National Lottery. He suggested getting some kind of admiral to be chairman to make it all look respectable.

A dreadful worry has emerged in my life in the last few days. To be listed on the stock exchange, the debenture which the Tote is arranging with Hambros for £20 million needs information to be provided about the directors. (Tote Board members are equivalent thereof.) Two of the questions relate to this: 'Have you ever made a composition with your creditors or arrangements with them?' The answer to that I am afraid is yes, when Banbury collapsed and all the money I had borrowed from the banks to buy more equipment for Banbury and a very successful printing house.

Thursday 8 July
I had a shock. Arnold rang up and said did I realize that far from being a solidly based organization, Autotote had been making steady losses.

I had calls to Joe Elmaleh who said it is all right really. I said, 'Look at their record. They had better explain themselves pretty fast.'

Then it was on to the reception for Miriam Gross's wedding. She is marrying Sir Geoffrey Owen who is a previous editor of the *Financial Times*. He made an immensely tedious speech which I could hardly hear a word of. There was an extraordinary mix up of people, from

Grey Gowrie and Drue Heinz to the scruffiest out-of-work journalist.
Conrad Black was giving them dinner that evening and then they
were going on their honeymoon. Miriam was very pleased with the
champagne I had sent her.

Claire Tomalin,[4] who has just married a playwright, came up to
thank me for the champagne I had sent her for her wedding present.

Anthony Howard is firmly convinced I wrote Norman's speech
because of a particular phrase that I had used in a *News of the World*
article and which had turned up in Norman's speech, 'Having office
without power.' There were one or two phrases which I had suggested
or Norman had got in the back of his mind perhaps from reading
one or two of my articles.

There was some sensational news today which Rupert Murdoch
rung me up about. The ghastly paper called *Sport* today has published
pictures of the lady who joined in the libel action with John Major
against the *New Statesman* for saying they were having an affair. They
show her with an enormous dildo thrust at her at a Christmas office
party.

She actually is fully clothed but the party was obviously pretty
overboard. It happened nine years ago, so I don't see what connection
it can really have with whether or not she was having an affair with
Major.

Rupert thought that with the publication of these peculiar pictures
he might resign and go. I said, 'I think that's a bit premature.'

Friday 9 July

The ghost from my past – there was a composition of some sort made
with my creditors and also I was chairman of a company which went
into receivership – has been laid to rest. Chips is having all the details
required by the Stock Exchange filled in by each member of the Board
separately and sent to him to deal with. He says he may not even have
to show them to the Stock Exchange at all but if he does, he knows
they will just be put on the shelf and no one will think any more of it.

If I had to make a composition with my creditors today, I wouldn't
be allowed to be Chairman of the Tote Board, but it was OK at the
time because the law was different.

---

4. Writer and journalist; literary editor, *Sunday Times*, 1980–6; née Delavenay, m 1
   (1955) Nicholas Tomalin (d 1973), m 2 (1993) Michael Frayn, novelist and
   playwright.

Saturday 10 July
Faxes duly arrived from Autotote in New York.

Arnold then said he was quite happy.

John Heaton had a bright idea. Why not ask Richard Branson of Virgin fame (records, airlines, etc.) if he would like to be in on the consortium. He is young, bright, modern and clearly produces stuff the public like.

Norman Lamont rang.

He shouldn't be quite so bitter, having nothing to do with people who may well be useful to him in the future. Unwise.

Monday 12 July
Branson was already quoted in the *Sunday Times* saying he thought these things shouldn't be done for profit. However, I did ring him and gave him a reasonably long explanation as to why good works and charity would get a large slice and that he could do anything he liked with his profit.

He was very amiable and thanked me for the clarity with which I had explained it. This was rather remarkable as I had only just in time put my teeth in.

After dinner I wrote some letters to readers, one or two quite interesting about how much they'd smoked and how healthy they were.

I popped out with Verushka to see the flat she wants Petronella to buy with a mortgage. It could be very attractive when she'd finished with it and in not a bad position at all, on a bus route to Marble Arch, not that Petronella would ever use a bus.

Tuesday 13 July
Verushka is much exercised in finding out what goes on at the hotel next to the block of flats where Petronella is interested in getting a flat. It's a very rough area and the hotel lets out rooms to the Lambeth Council for the bed and breakfasting of homeless arrivals in England.

It could diminish the value of the flat. Verushka enjoys the spy work involved.

Wednesday 14 July
After lunch it was off to the Lords. First I had to go at four o'clock to hear John Birt at the Broadcasting Committee.

I asked Birt why they didn't implement the code about impartiality, the code being good.

John Birt was very friendly to me and explained some of his difficulties, which I believe. He is under heavy attack from inside the BBC. Their correspondent in Delhi, India, a well-respected BBC reporter for many years, had launched a tremendous attack on him.[5] John Birt ruefully remarked that if GEC had been making some alterations, or a company as big as that, and a branch manager in Delhi had made a complaint about the Managing Director, no one would have published the ruddy thing.

I then had to dash down to meet my four prize-winners from Eastbourne College of the essay on what conditions would give you a happy life.

The schoolboys, and the schoolgirl, aged seventeen to eighteen, all got in to hear Margaret Thatcher which was a great thrill. But her speech was very poor, illogical, contradictory, evasive about why she didn't have a referendum on the Single Act which caused all the trouble. She made an astonishing statement that she hadn't understood the Single Act and its preamble when she agreed to it, which is absolute piffle.[6]

It is very sad. She demeans herself by entering the arena in so carping a fashion. She also implied she had no faith in the strength of this country to overcome obstacles in the EC and win the day for what it wants. I don't like to hear her sounding such a defeatist.

Emily Blatch, a minister, asked me did I think the government would win. I said, 'By hundreds,' and that indeed was what happened, a huge vote for the government (four hundred and fifty-six) and the largest attendance in the Lords that anybody could remember this century.

As I was sitting on the Bishops' bench, Alexander Hesketh, who is of an enormous size and is the government's Chief Whip, came and sat next to me, trying to squash himself in. He then went and sat just behind the clerks in the middle of the chamber which he is entitled to do. Later he came back again and sat down next to me and told me to clear off – I had no business to be sitting on the front row of the Bishops' bench which was reserved for government ministers and the chairman of committees.

---

5. Mark Tully, Chief of BBC Bureau, New Delhi, 1972–93, South East Asia Correspondent, 1993–4, when he resigned from the BBC.
6. The Single European Act was passed in 1985.

Thursday 15 July

Debate [in the Lords]on Hong Kong passports.[7]

When it was coming to an end I sat down and spoke to Margaret.

She was delighted that in my speech I had explained that without her they would never have got any passports at all.

She was looking beautiful again today. She is an extraordinary woman. I think she is still fond of me and I am certainly fond of her. None of us know quite what on earth to do about Major now. He plunges from one folly to another.

Monday 19 July

Lunch with Beryl Bainbridge at Simpsons. She was very thrilled that they recognized her.

We discussed my idea that we might write a play together. She thought it was an excellent notion. She said, 'It wants to be a farce to make people laugh. There's so much to laugh at. We must make it hilarious.'

Lots more going on about the National Lottery – very exciting. Arnold now keen. He rang me up on Sunday and today several times. We have got Thorn-EMI in on it as well as Autotote and the GEC.

Now there is a possibility Petronella may go to St John's Wood High Street where there's a very substantial flat on two floors on top of a house there.

Tuesday 20 July

Lunch at Clarence House with Queen Elizabeth the Queen Mother. A little while after we arrived she said she wanted to talk to me and took me to two chairs in a corner of the drawing-room. Previously she'd asked what I would like to drink. Sherry was being offered. I said, 'I will have a little sherry.' 'I didn't think anybody drank that nowadays.' I wondered why it was being offered if she hadn't expected anybody to drink it.

I told Queen Elizabeth I couldn't understand why Major hadn't given A. L. Rowse a knighthood or something similar. It would fit in with his classless stance. 'I hate that classlessness. It is so unreal.' I said, 'But it applies particularly to A. L. Rowse, son of a farmworker who fought his way through the educational system when it was very

---

7. See Vol. 2 *passim* for WW's campaign for more passports to be issued to people from Hong Kong before it was handed back to China.

difficult and became a Fellow of All Souls, Oxford. Now all the Fellows there are trying to get him his due before he dies. Is there any chance? It is within the Queen's gift.' She said she would enquire again.

I said I thought it was a pity the press barons had not been dealt with more intelligently. 'If Vere Rothermere and his wife had been asked to stay the night at Windsor, Rothermere would have been so thrilled that there never would have been these attacks in his papers on the Queen.'

'I know it's a nuisance but you do have to have a lot of uninteresting people at Windsor, foreigners.' 'Oh no, they're not really uninteresting. Everybody has something interesting to say.' She took on board what I said.

Before lunch I was talking to Leslie Bonham-Carter.[8] Queen Elizabeth said, 'Don't talk to her any more. You'll have her at lunch.' I replied mischievously, 'I'd like to have her anywhere.' Leslie giggled.

Dinner at the [Henry] Keswicks in their new house in Smith Square. It is a Queen Anne house with some style inside, lots of panelling in the rooms and some handsome oak staircases and floorboards.

I found myself sitting next to Mrs Kenneth Clarke who sat between Henry and myself, Kenneth Clarke being the main purpose of the dinner. I got into a squabble with her, almost.

Mrs Clarke said, 'I can understand about being loyal to one's friends but sometimes one can carry loyalty too far,' meaning, I suppose, that I had been attacking Major because of Norman. But I have no need to be loyal to him – I am not part of the Tory Party. I did say I thought Kenneth was marvellous, which I do, and that one day he might become Prime Minister. She said, 'We mustn't have that sort of disloyal thought.' I couldn't see why that was disloyal.

I asked her about her children and she softened up a bit.

In fact we were quite cosy by the end of dinner.

After dinner people piled in through the doors – the neighbours. Virginia Bottomley lives next door with her husband, Peter Bottomley. She wasn't as friendly to me as she used to be. I have been ribbing her in the *News of the World* for continuing with the mad anti-smoking campaign. But she was friendly enough to give me a rather lukewarm kiss instead of the more emphatic one which I usually get.

Paul Johnson and Marigold came in and all the mad anti-Maastricht

8. Daughter of Condé Nast of New York, m 1 (1949–55) 2nd Baron St Just, m 2 (1955) Mark Bonham-Carter.

people – Rees-Mogg, who is frightfully pleased with himself, getting on the front pages with his idiotic action in the courts to try to rule Parliament as violating the law in passing Maastricht.

I quite like him. He is of course highly intelligent. But like many intelligent people the bloody fool is a buffoon.

Kenneth Clarke, as I said to his wife, is one of the people I categorize as a jolly joker, which it is absolutely vital to have among one's friends and acquaintances. They are people who are serious but not too serious and who don't think politics is the whole world – I am sure he wouldn't think it were the end of the world if he never became Prime Minister.

Thursday 22 July
Amabel Lindsay's party. I popped in, between Olga Polizzi's [party] and the House of Lords where I voted twice in the pro-Maastricht pro-government lobby.

When I first arrived young Lord Hardwicke[9] was there. I started helping myself to mushrooms with my fingers and one or two other little things. He said, 'Don't do that. It's the dinner.'

When I came back it was true, it was the dinner. Everyone was horrified at the scarcity of the food and the poor drink. Amabel is extremely rich, by her husband Patrick Lindsay who made a lot of money at Christie's.

Among those present were Andrew Parker Bowles and his wife Camilla. She was cheery in her greeting to me. I thought again, how could that immensely plain girl (she may once have been pretty) have excited such amorous enthusiasm of a really potty kind from the Prince of Wales.

Alexander Hesketh was rushing backwards and forwards, looking very important and saying what the motion the Prime Minister had put down for tomorrow meant. He didn't really know at all.

He also apologized to me for having been so rude to me when I was sitting on the overflow Bishops' bench. He said, 'You were quite right and I'm afraid I was wrong. You are allowed to sit there provided you don't speak.'

Everybody was supposed to be dressed as an Indian. Verushka had a marvellous pair of trousers on which were supposed to be Indian. I

---

9. Nephew of Lady Amabel Lindsay.

said they made her look like a zebra which didn't please her because
they had been very expensive.

Some people actually were Indians so they didn't need to dress up.

Saturday 24 July
It was a pretty ghastly day, raining all the time. England were making
their usual hash of the cricket.

I had spoken to Bob and asked him what he thought of the way
they played under Gooch's captaincy. The result was in my *News of
the World* article on Sunday 25th July. Ron Pell [sub-editor] wanted
me to say that it had come from Bob. I said, 'Good heavens, I could
never do that. He would have a fit and never forgive me.'

Bob remains remarkably well and intelligent. He thinks Atherton
ought to be the captain but they probably won't have him because he
is too well educated.[10]

Sunday 25 July
I had a long call from Rupert. He doesn't altogether agree with what I
say but he lets me say it.

Tuesday 27 July
I rang Richard Ryder. He was over the moon with my article in the
Times this morning.[11] I said, 'Make sure he reads it.' 'He will read it.'
I was referring to Major. But I still haven't forgiven him for the shabby
way he treated Norman.

Wednesday 28 July
NERA have been announced officially as advisers to the Lottery.

Thursday 29 July *Italy*
There were no visitors for dinner at Perignano, just jolly chats. The
Italians, particularly the women, are obsessed with talking about our

---

10. Michael Atherton read history at Cambridge; he was that week appointed captain
    of England in succession to Gooch who had resigned.
11. WW wrote that Major, reported as calling three cabinet colleagues 'bastards' in
    an unguarded moment and attacked for being indecisive, had won a notable
    victory by defying the Tory rebels not to vote for him on a confidence motion
    with which support for Maastricht was inextricably linked.

Royal Family, Charles and Diana and who did what and why and what does the country think and what the world thinks.

Gingo is not looking as well as last year.

Sunday 1 August

Verushka drove very well the long way down to Porto Ercole from Perignano. It became pretty hot though the car was air-conditioned. It had no power steering so if she had to turn when she missed the way, it was like turning a bus.

Everything is almost the same at the house. A few things had been shifted around a bit but I put them back to the way I had been accustomed to them and moved the family photographs so (a) they don't get damaged and (b) I don't have to look at them.

Monday 2 August

Livia came in the afternoon, arriving by train from Rome. Then late at night came the Wiltons.

Thursday 5 August

Carmelo Calabro to dinner because Verushka wanted to go on his boat and take the others. He's an interesting rascal.

He is highly indignant about the present state of affairs [in Italy]. He said there are a hundred and fifty-four MPs waiting investigation and claiming immunity.

'But where will it all stop?' he asked.

Carmelo looks like frog, squat and swarthy. He makes noises like a frog.

Friday 6 August

Four went on the boat and I stayed behind and managed to get cracking at last on my play, rewriting it. I suddenly realized I should confine it to the Bishop and his wife, his camp Father Herbert, the Archbishop when he turns up, and the lover.[1]

---

1. WW had been writing a play on ecclesiastical themes for some time. There is no copy of it with the manuscript so the details of the plot can only be surmised from what he tells us.

Sunday 8 August
Message from Rupert. He's coming down the coast on Tuesday or Wednesday, August 10th or 11th, to take us out on the boat.

Monday 9 August
George Weidenfeld arrived and was thrilled to be going out on Rupert's boat. So were Henry and Tessa Keswick who had also arrived.

Rupert had to stop the faxes for a bit because he was told by a doctor he must have at least thirteen weeks holiday a year, in bits, weeks at a time or taking long weekends off, two or three days.

Tuesday 10 August
It was remarkable, the ship.

The engines were as quiet as a Rolls-Royce, with the famous claim that you can only hear the clock ticking. The mast was a hundred and fifty feet high and the hull was a hundred and fifty-five feet long. It has a beautiful master cabin with lovely bathroom. There were changing rooms and enough beds to sleep eight, but of course not our twelve people. There was a crew of six. You had to take your shoes off and walk with bare feet so as not to leave marks on the wood from tar or oil you might have picked up.

It sailed triumphantly through the water and at times it was on its side to pick up the wind as it tacked towards the island of Giglio. It had a James Bond atmosphere. Electricity caused a whole row of steps on one side towards the stern to go up, you walked down and there you were, ready to walk straight into the sea.

I got in and swam right round the boat to great applause from Rupert and Anna, who had been particularly sweet. She has changed enormously. She didn't want to write any more books. I said, 'Why don't you want to do that?' 'Because my duty is to be at home and I am fed up with all this feminism.'

She is very much against women having their own careers now because she says they should be looking after their families.

I said, 'Of course you only did those books (her novels were quite successful) in order to show you could and you weren't entirely dependent on Rupert.' She said I was quite right and I said, 'Also you know you can say to him, if there was a terrible split, "I don't care, I can go off and I have enough to live on from writing by myself." ' She said that, too, was true.

But I had never seen them so happy together for a very long time.

I thought she was looking almost as beautiful as when I first met her some twenty years or more ago, which I told her to her considerable pleasure. She said she had read my interview in the *Oldie* magazine and, 'I know what you think about women. You are wrong to think they should all be given equal opportunities. Why should they? They should remember that their husbands and families should come first. They are not really happy either, those women.'

You are only allowed to smoke out in the open, otherwise Anna maintains anti-smoking.

Before dinner we went up to the top deck which is quite high. There were vast quantities of caviar and champagne. I haven't seen Rupert drink like that for ages, nor Anna who is usually very abstemious. I ate a great deal of caviar.

I said to Rupert he must be careful not to make mistakes about Britain. He had been quite wrong in attacking Norman's policies because they had turned out to be right and we are in a very strong position. He should be optimistic now.

I must remember to send him another message saying optimistic newspapers sell more copies. The reason he is losing circulation is because he is making everybody feel very defeatist.

At one point earlier Rupert had been accusing me of sucking up to Major. I said, 'You haven't been reading all my articles. I've attacked him a good deal, particularly over his disgraceful sacking of Norman Lamont.' Rupert agreed that had been disgraceful.

I said, 'Margaret doesn't want to rock the boat now against Major because she's afraid that Kenneth Clarke will get it who is much more pro European.'

Rupert talked to Tessa a bit. I had told him she was Clarke's political adviser, which he knew, of course, from the newspapers.

He had a long talk with Henry Keswick. They are going to develop joint activities in Hong Kong. Rupert has just bought out the satellite television there and is ready to move the uplink, if the Chinese get difficult, to somewhere else. They can't knock his satellite out without knocking things out for themselves.

The dinner was quite amazing. There were wonderful tournedos steaks with a delicious little sauce, followed by a fantastic cake cooked by the chef.

The wine was very much better than we've been serving. The dinner was far better than the lunch we gave them, which was a pity because ours could have been just as good in a different way.

Woodrow Wyatt at Cheltenham racecourse in 1995.

Rupert Murdoch with his second wife, Anna.

Petronella Wyatt.

Top: Lady Wyatt
(Verushka) in a Chanel
hat presenting the Tote
Gold Trophy to Kay
Bliss of the Elite Racing
Club, at Newbury on
11 February 1995.

Left: Lady d'Avigdor-
Goldsmid (Rosie)
with the Tote Autumn
Cup at Newbury on
18 September 1993.

Norman Lamont in Woodrow Wyatt's car on the
day of his resignation speech, 9 June 1993.

From left to right: Kenneth Clarke, Michael Howard (Home Secretary), Kenneth Baker, Wyatt, Denis Howell (former Labour Minister for Sport), Lord Wakeham, Lord Hartington (Jockey Club Senior Steward) and William Whitelaw at the 1994 Tote lunch. Baker, Clarke and Whitelaw were former Home Secretaries.

Lord and Lady Weidenfeld
(George and Annabelle).

Mr and Mrs Conrad Black
(Barbara Amiel).

Sir John Paul and Lady Getty
(Victoria Holdsworth).

Lord and Lady Stevens
(David and Meriza).

Woodrow Wyatt with Tote ladies in their new uniforms, March 1995.

It was very pretty on the ship at our candle-light dinner – a classical music background the whole time. We ate under the awning. The stars and the moon were clear and beautiful. It was just the night for sailing away on a honeymoon, which was what Rupert and Anna had been doing, which I found touching.

Wednesday 11 August
Verushka is worried that Rupert might sack me as I disagree with him so often. I said, 'Balls, he would never sack me, that is quite clear, even though he has sacked some other old friends like Searsby for not doing their job properly.'

Relations between Rupert and myself have very much strengthened again.

George and Annabelle are being extremely entertaining. At one lunch George, with her conducting, sang vigorously student songs from Germany. George now looks extremely impressive. He has matured tremendously. He has the head almost of a noble Jewish patriarch with stature and authority. He is busy writing his memoirs but he has to be careful on how far he goes. He read me one piece about Ted Heath. It was pretty sharp.

Thursday 12 August
I now have a bet with Tessa that Britain will not be opening its frontiers to illegal immigrants within eight months, as she says they will because they will be obliged to by the EC.

I keep telling her that if something from the EC doesn't fit in with national desires, it simply won't happen.

Nevertheless, I do like her. She has a pretty face and once had a pretty figure.

John Wilton remarked that he'd never known a Fraser 'who didn't know everything'. That wasn't true of Hugh Fraser, Tessa's uncle and my great friend from about the age of eighteen.

George makes sweeping attacks on many people. He said Goodman's a liar and dishonest. He had written his memoirs in which he attacked George – perhaps he said the same about him.

He [Goodman] has always been absolutely straight with me and insisted on honesty – at least I did always in any cases he has dealt with for me, believing that honesty is the best policy because the truth will out in any case and it makes a better impression.

On one occasion George started attacking Roy [Jenkins], saying he was no good as Chancellor at Oxford, he didn't raise any money for Oxford and they all thought he was useless.

The next morning I said to Annabelle, not in front of the others, 'You know, I was very angry with George last night. I spoke sharply to him. But I do that when any friend of mine is attacked, including George. People often criticize George and I round on them in the same way I rounded on George.'

George told everybody how I had been looking after his publishing concern when he went off to be secretary or assistant to Weizmann[2] in Israel after the war. I would send him reports saying it was doing badly and he had better make up his mind whether he wanted to have a career in Israel or look after his own interests here. He decided to come back, which I am sure was the wiser decision.

Suddenly Mrs Reinhardt rang from America when Verushka wasn't in. She said would I mind dreadfully if some Princess, daughter of the ex Queen of Holland, came to see the house if they rang up to fix a time.

It now turns out that this very minor royal princess is a friend of her daughter's and she is very anxious that she should take the house with her children for the whole of August, so we can't have it next year.

The Americans are worse than the British about royalty; they'd do anything to be known by them, even Fergie.

Sunday 15 August
Tessa went off with the Weidenfelds to catch an aeroplane.

I fear that Tessa's stay here has not improved my long-term relations with her though I tried to cover up the cracks by saying how pretty she is and how intelligent and how useful she must be to Kenneth Clarke and all that kind of lark.

Mark and Eva went. I was very sorry to see them go.

The Lamonts arrive.

Norman is thoroughly worked up about his future about which we had discussions immediately. He is not going to write a sensational book which I had warned him against. He has now collected bits and pieces for a consultancy and such-like which will bring him something like £165,000 a year including his parliamentary salary, some three times what he was getting as Chancellor of the Exchequer. He has a

---

2. (1874–1952); first President of Israel.

little team working with him. One of them is Sir George Gardiner[3] who is second rate but a dummy to try out ideas in speeches concocted by Norman.

Norman's policy now is the same as mine. We have to back Major for the time being.

Petronella arrives. It is a great delight to see her. As usual, she made a dreadful mess of her travel arrangements.

Monday 16 August

Robin Day arrives. I had not known he was coming until after I arrived on this holiday. He is staying for an immensely long time, namely until Wednesday August 25th. He is noisy, talks about nothing but himself or politics.

He is obsessed by Marcheses and titled Italians who he thinks belong to ancient aristocracies and believes their titles. Many are sons and daughters in any order of birth who assume the tenuous titles of their parents.

Robin went to some state school first and then to Bembridge School in the Isle of Wight, a very second-rate, unheard-of, minor public school, where Desmond Donnelly[4] was, too. Robin does not speak of his antecedents. But he speaks much of the grand people he has met.

Wednesday 18 August

Norman and I talked again about the extraordinary occurrences on Black Wednesday last September 16th. I said, 'Didn't you complain to the Prime Minister when he wanted to see you in Downing Street that morning and you found that he had invited Hurd (the Foreign Secretary), Clarke (Home Secretary), Heseltine (Environment Secretary) to be there to consult as to what was to be done?'

Major said to Norman before the meeting, 'I want to have them there to make sure we have the Cabinet behind us and that they agree with us. Then it will be OK.' Norman had to agree. By all the dithering which had been going on they had already lost, prior to September 15th during the previous few weeks, £24 billion from our reserves. This was when Norman was advocating suspending ourselves from the

---

3. Conservative MP, 1974–97; joined Referendum Party, 1997; knight 1990.
4. (1920–74); Labour (1950–68), then Independent (1968–70) MP; joined Conservative Party in 1971; with WW fought Labour (1964–6) to stop the nationalization of steel.

ERM but Major didn't want to do it. By that morning of September 15th there was only £8 billion left in the reserves. The delays which took place before the decision was taken as to what to do, two hours after they first met early in the morning, lost us another £8 billion of reserves, meaning that the whole of our reserves were wiped out.

Norman put the interest rates up because they wanted him to. He said it wouldn't work but they said, 'Do do it.' Clarke was very keen on it, so was Heseltine. So Norman did it more as a demonstration that the pound would collapse. He said it was, as I put it, like King Canute sitting on the beach surrounded by courtiers urging him to tell the tide not to come in.

We also discussed Number 10's reaction to Norman's publishing the fact that on that day in September he offered to resign and Major wrote him the note which said no: 'You are not resigning and nor am I.' The meaning was that they were both in it together.

After Norman mentioned in his resignation speech about the note, Number 10 were about to rubbish him. They rang up and said could he let them have a copy of the note. Norman sent back a message saying, 'I have the note' (which he hadn't as a matter of fact because he had thrown it away but he had a complete record of it). 'If there is going to be warfare of this kind, it would be better if the PM conducted it with me direct.' So Number 10 shut up. Norman, naturally, remains very bitter.

Wednesday 25 August
It was a delight to see Olga [Polizzi] and Romilly [McAlpine] and the Sinclairs. The last had brought Verushka and Petronella each a huge bottle of Chanel scent which Verushka said must have cost £40–£50 each, even in the duty-free shop. They brought me, which was extremely generous, all the way from England, six bottles of Château Talbot 1987 which is a very good year and they withstood the journey pretty well.

Thursday 26 August
The two new ladies, as well as Sonia, not only look very charming but they are very sweet and jolly. Olga had brought me a box of Romeo y Julieta cigars and Romilly had brought for Verushka and Petronella some wonderful hand-made glass beads from Venice which had been decorated and embellished by Alistair himself who is a very good craftsman.

We talked about Alistair's new way of getting thin, which is also being practised by Romilly. He sits in a cold bath filled with ice for two hours every day. Unimaginable.

He has already taken off half a stone which greatly improves his health.

Friday 27 August
Dorothy, Rupert's secretary, rang and wanted to know whether we were going to go to Elisabeth's wedding or not, which is on September 10th. I said no, that we couldn't because it was so far to go, I would get jet lag and I was very busy with the National Lottery and other things.

Whilst we were speaking Petronella butted in and said, 'I want to go, I want to go. I'll represent the family.' So I reported this to Dorothy, thinking nothing much of it.

A few minutes later Rupert rang. We passed the time of day.

What he had really rung up about, it emerged, was about Petronella going to the wedding. He said, 'You know I am very worried about it because she is a very bright girl, a very smart journalist and she knows a good story when she sees one. It would be terrible if she wrote anything about the wedding.'

- I said, 'Good heavens. She wouldn't dream of doing that. It's absolutely not possible. What she is really going for, which coincides with the wedding, is a story they want her to do for the *Sunday Telegraph* about the film industry in Hollywood, just nearby. Perhaps one of your people could give her some advice or talk to her about it at 20th Century Fox (which of course he owns).' He said, 'Oh yes. That would be fine. That I understand.'

Hardly a second or two had passed after putting the telephone down when Anna came on.

We passed the time of day very briefly and then she said very sharply, 'Can I speak to Verushka?' Verushka was just beside me. She then proceeded to say in a most nasty manner, 'If Petronella comes to Los Angeles and goes to the wedding and one word about it appears in any of the newspapers, the *Sunday Telegraph* or anywhere else, it's the end of our friendship. I'm telling you it's the end of our friendship. We wouldn't want to have anything to do with you at all, you or Woodrow. I am much tougher than Rupert and I'm telling you that now.'

I could hear her while Verushka talked to her. She sounded

extremely vicious and showed her really nasty side, just when I had begun to think she had softened up and become a more kindly, rounded person.

I was absolutely shocked and stunned and so was Verushka.

Petronella had doubtless told people at the *Sunday Telegraph* she had been invited to it, which she shouldn't have done in the first place because it was all meant to have been so hush-hush.

Nevertheless, it was rather strange, coming from Rupert and Anna, that nothing should be written about the wedding, considering the intrusions into privacy which all his newspapers have gloried in for years, crucifying Norman and all that kind of thing. When it comes to themselves, they think they should be inviolate and nobody should intrude on their privacy. Petronella had made one good point which was that the policy of Conrad Black, who controls the *Sunday Telegraph* and the *Daily Telegraph*, is never to attack another proprietor or send him up. But I suppose Anna thought she might be selling the story to somebody else.

Anyway, we have forbidden her to go.

Although Anna said her name had been taken off the invitation list, it wasn't quite clear whether she would be admitted if she did go. But it would be absolutely fatal now. It would ruin my whole relationship with Rupert and he might even ask me to stop writing for his newspapers, which I dearly love doing even though I don't think he pays me enough for it by any means. I like to preach my sermons to the largest possible audience, namely the biggest selling newspaper in the world, the *News of the World* – which are reinforced by the articles I write in the *Times*. And Rupert doesn't mind my taking the opposite view to his newspapers in either the *News of the World* or the *Times*.

I have been getting very friendly with Andrew Sinclair. We didn't argue in the same way about politics any more. He has stopped being so absurdly left-wing now.

Wednesday 1 September
To the Banqueting Hall, Whitehall, for the News Corporation special celebration relating to Sky Television. On arrival Rupert was very friendly (Anna didn't come over).

We exchanged a certain amount of gossip and he told me he was going to startle everybody with his price reduction for the *Times*, which will go down next Monday from 45p to 30p.

His son, Lachlan, was there. He has been working at the *Sun* under Kelvin MacKenzie.

He is dead keen on the newspaper business and he will be the one who takes over, presumably, from Rupert in due course.

Irwin said Rupert is finding an excuse to push Knight out now without a lot of fuss. He no longer relies on him.

To my surprise, Stoker Hartington was also there. I said, 'What are you doing here?' 'I was invited.' I think Rupert invited the heads of all kinds of sports because he was announcing in his speech that there would be another sports channel through Sky as well.

Rupert delivered it [his speech] from a teleprompter which made it look as though he was doing it not from a script. But he delivered it well and there were some fascinating things in it, particularly about the extension of his communications empire into Asia, Hong Kong and the means by which he was doing it.

I told Rupert how well he had spoken.

I said, 'You can't say it, but I am going to say it in a book or some appropriate place, that if you hadn't been a good democrat, which you are, all this power of the media around the world would have been very worrying. A dictator could have used it to suppress programmes. As it is, all the unelected governments are terrified of the democracy you are blowing into the area. Some of your actions can be attacked, and I have done so myself, but your standards are basically decent ones. They are spreading the message that free enterprise makes democracy and free choice and gives people what they want.'

Evelyn de Rothschild was there. I told him what a good idea it had been to give Norman a part-time job back at Rothschild's where he used to work for eleven years before he became a Minister.

Thursday 2 September
Had a talk with Irwin early in the morning. I said, 'Who do I now ask about my increase in salary?' He said, 'Leave it to me and I will find out.' He is very much on my side.

Irwin now seems to be the chief adviser to Rupert on just about every matter.

Monday 6 September
Irwin Stelzer is in a great state because he thinks they are going to be after News International from the Office of Fair Trading and the Monopolies Commission and that Rupert will be pilloried. Some Labour MPs have already sent a representation to the Monopolies Commission and the Office of Fair Trading people. I don't think the Minister should allow it to be considered.

I learn that the appalling horse, Pyrrhic Dance, was sold privately for some £7,000. I am amazed they could have got so much for such a rubbishy horse. Bengough was a pig not to agree to my proposition that whatever the lessor got should be shared equally with the lessees, of which I was one of the four, pro rata.

Wednesday 8 September
This is chauffeur Robbie's last day before going into hospital to have his hip operation. I began to feel sad. I am very fond of the old boy, though he groans and moans. Verushka said to me that she and Robbie have an association like a bad marriage. They quarrel when she is doing the shopping but nevertheless she finds him indispensable.

To the Redfern Gallery, Andrew Sinclair's reception for his book about Francis Bacon.[1]

Most of his book is quoting other people, which he probably does with some degree of perception.

I said to Stephen Spender, 'I see you in every gossip column.' He said 'Yes, isn't it awful.' I know he adores it.

On the way out I saw Anthony Howard and I congratulated him on the special obituary in the *Times* of the Sitwells' housekeeper. He said he had actually borrowed the idea when he saw it in the *Indepen-*

---

1. *Francis Bacon: his life and violent times*, a biography of the painter.

dent and thought it was too good a chance to miss, which was very honest of him. 'Now you are in charge of obituaries I hope you are not going to muck about with my obituary, or I will haunt you,' to which he replied he wouldn't dare, 'You are too great a man.'

Saturday 11 September
I am heartily sick of all this stuff in people's memoirs. Most of what Ken Baker says is untrue. He claims all the credit for everything that happened, like the betting tax and so on, to himself.[2]

Tuesday 14 September
Dinner party at George Weidenfeld's. The usual thing – about forty people and a bit of a muddle. The drinks are still lousy but the food is much better since Annabelle took over.

On the left of the German Ambassadress was David Stevens. I said, 'Hello, how are you?' He said, 'You can't see me. I'm invisible. I'm a nonentity.' I said, 'Do stop being silly about that, David. You know it's ridiculous. You're making a fool of yourself.' He began to thaw out a bit and we had a general conversation.

On the way out I saw the absurd Lady Stevens. I grabbed her by the hand and said, 'Now come on, give me a kiss and stop all this damn nonsense.' Instead of accepting this as a peace offering, she ran off screaming, 'No, no, I'll never speak to you again.' Stupid woman. I shan't be bothered with her any more.

Wednesday 15 September
David Swaythling's last board meeting.

I thanked David very warmly for his support (thinking not always, not when he and Peter Winfield went behind my back to the Home Office and said I ought to be sacked some years ago).

I also told them it was Christopher Sporborg, the Deputy Chairman of Hambros, who would succeed him because we wanted somebody with the same sort of stature as David and associated with finance.

---

2. Baker's book, *The Turbulent Years: my life in politics*, had just been published; see Vol. 2, p. 574, for WW telling Baker, then Home Secretary, that he had talked to Lamont, Chancellor of the Exchequer, about the possibility of lowering the level of betting tax.

Instead of opposing this, which I had supposed he might, he said, 'What a good appointment.'

Friday 17 September
I went to Harold Pinter's *Moonlight* at the Almeida Theatre, a tiny little theatre in Islington.

Before the play began – we were there early to collect our tickets which Diane [Lever] has as a patron of the place – we waited outside for a while. Along came Harold Pinter who had been talking to Andrew Sinclair who was also there. He was introduced to me and we shook hands quite warmly. He looked at me somewhat quizzically. I thought of all the fearful things I have said about him, and he about me, and all his idiotic pro-Communist activities in Communist countries and his damning of Margaret Thatcher at any attempt to help liberals and democrats in Nicaragua. I thought there'd be a *frisson* but there wasn't.

I nearly fell asleep during the first part of the play, either because I was tired or because it was a trifle tedious. But it improved. I suddenly woke up to Harold Pinter being Jewish. The play is really about the Jewish view of death which has no promise of an after-life. You only live on so long as you live in the memory of those who loved you or knew you or in the works you did.

Anna Massey was terrific in it.

Saturday 18 September
I must be careful how far I go about Major. Basically I don't think he is all that bad although he has got a vicious, very, part to his nature. I don't want him out of spite somehow to interfere with our getting the National Lottery.

To Newbury for the Tote Autumn Cup which I had to give away

At lunch, for which I arrived extremely late in the Royal Box, so-called, at Newbury, was General Inge.

He is Chief of the General Staff. It used to be called the Imperial General Staff, which sounded better.

In private, so others couldn't listen, we were soon engaged in a deep conversation about the appalling things the government is doing to the armed forces

He told me that Rifkind is very good, which surprised me. He said he does his best but he can't win against the Treasury and the Prime Minister who have no conception of the dangers.

Arnold came because he had a horse running.

It was in our race, won by Rosie d'Avigdor-Goldsmid's horse.[3]

I played the fool when I presented her with the great dish which is worth £2,000 (that is apart from the winnings) and put it on my head. I then put it on her head and her hat fell off. I tried to put it on for her. Then she hung on to the cigar [I had given her] which she had not yet lit. What the photographers made of it I don't yet know but they kept taking picture after picture as usual.[4]

Sunday 19 September
I rang Arnold and said I wanted John Heaton to go over the draft [Lottery] bid with him because there was a lot of valuable material in it but it was very long-winded and had to be turned into English.

In further discussion we [Heaton and I] thought, 'Why don't we ask for thirty per cent [as the Tote's share]? It looks very unequal with the two giants, GEC and Thorn-EMI, squashing the poor little Tote.'

I rang Arnold at Bowden at ten past one, after John and I had been further through the documents. I was nervous at his reaction. But he agreed.

Monday 20 September
Wrote for the *Times* article about the status of the Tory Party.

The gist of what I said was don't go on with this boring squabbling. It is all over now. Likewise to Lamont, keep quiet. If you want to be taken seriously, stop being an exhibitionist and make serious, thoughtful speeches. Also, consider your relationship with Rothschild's who have just given you a decent job.

By chance, Evelyn de Rothschild rang on Monday evening. He wanted to plead with me not to use my influence to have United Racecourses, of which he is Chairman, including Epsom with its Derby, sold immediately. I said I would not agree to that because I am in favour of getting rid of it.

We then talked about Norman.

He had spoken to him this morning and asked him to calm down but he said he still had to make his fringe speech at the Conservative Party Conference. I said, 'I will tell him to keep it low key.'

───────

3. Widow of Major Sir Henry d'Avigdor-Goldsmid (1909–76, Conservative politician, member of Tote Board, 1973–6); she had also been one of the shareholders in Pyrrhic Dance.
4. See illustration.

Then it was to dinner with the Lamonts. I told Norman what I had written, more or less. He was upset. I said, 'It's true. You are becoming an exhibitionist. You've got to pipe down.'

Peter Lilley was also at the dinner, very friendly. So was Kenneth Baker. He is frightfully pleased with his book.

I said to him, rather sharply at one moment, 'You were waiting to see which way the wind blew. When it blew you out of office, you'd nothing to lose. You thought your book would sell better if you attacked Major, though you would have happily stayed his Home Secretary.'

Notwithstanding my put-down, two days later a postcard arrived at Cavendish Avenue saying, 'You must watch my broadcast, the final one in the series for television, on my book on Saturday.' He's an ass if he thinks I am going to waste time watching that nonsense.

Tuesday 21 September
At the Levy Board in the afternoon John Sparrow and Anna McCurley, the silly ex Tory MP from Scotland,[5] were all for delaying the sale of United Racecourses. I led the attack on them and said, 'It must be done now. We have gone on subsidizing racecourses which have never paid us a single penny. Their management is appalling. We should ask for tenders of £20 million or more and see how it goes.'

That won general agreement. I want to arrange that Racecourse Holdings Trust, a subsidiary of the Jockey Club, buys it, even if it's on instalments. That is the sure way, apart from legal documents, of ensuring that racing always continues at Epsom and the Derby is never lost to it.

At the River Room in the Savoy, Prince Khalid held a fabulous party for some two hundred people, nearly all connected with racing.

I talked to William Astor. He is furious he has been moved to the Ministry of Social Security instead of doing the nice civilized things he was doing before, and that he won't be able to talk to me about the Lottery any more, as he could when he was at National Heritage. He thought Alexander Hesketh had given up the job of Chief Whip because he felt he would never get into the Cabinet.

I am sorry about that. Of course he is deeply against Major and remains rampantly pro-Margaret.

At the end of the dinner, suddenly there was a demand for silence

---

5. MP for Renfrew W and Inverclyde, 1983–7, Levy Board member from 1988.

and a great curtain which had been arranged at the back of the room opened. Charles Churchill[6] leaped on to the stage. He disclosed a huge orchestra and Liza Minelli. They had been flown all the way from New York to entertain Prince Khalid's guests. I thought it strange for Charles Churchill to be the introducer of bands and singers but he didn't do it badly.

She is a good entertainer, that girl, though she was once a drug addict. Perhaps she still is. But she seems to have partly cured herself, unlike her unfortunate mother [Judy Garland]. When asked to sing 'Somewhere over the rainbow', she said very simply, 'I'd rather not. I always promised my mother I never would. It was her song and I'd like to keep it that way.'

Wednesday 22 September
Had to see two advertising agencies hankering for the business of helping us with the National Lottery bid. Neither were particularly good.

John Heaton has done tremendous work and I have promised him a bonus specially.

He is to be seconded from the Tote to run the company we are setting up for the bid.

I have great hopes for John Heaton, if he sticks at it, but I don't want to lose him from the Tote, at least not while I am there.

When I got into the car, after leaving Arnold at GEC, I had a message to call Rupert Murdoch. He was bouncing with liveliness, commenting on my article in the *Times* yesterday. 'You are still defending the indefensible, I see.' He meant Major.

The circulation of the *Times*, he tells me, has gone up a hundred thousand.

Saturday 25 September
It was the Ascot Festival of Racing day, at which the Tote sponsor a big handicap.

We had lunch in Piers Bengough's rooms.

Princess Michael told me again about their near destitution.

She has organized a consultancy through Joe Elmaleh for Autotote.

I said, 'I am sure you will be very good at it. You are worth quite a lot to them.' Actually I didn't really believe that. I can't see what she

---

6. Lord Charles Spencer-Churchill, younger brother of the Duke of Marlborough.

can do of any real value but Americans, even tough Lorne Weil, are suckers for royalty.

She said, 'What I want is a very rich lover.' 'There must be many about.' 'Most of them are so bad-looking.' 'Why do you bother about that?' 'Because there must be romance. I must be in love with them before I go to bed with them.' She looks very handsome, still, though her legs are covered below the knees so you don't see how thick they are. She said she is getting too fat. I prodded her stomach and said, 'I don't think you are. You're not a bad shape at all. You've also been behaving very well. You're keeping a low profile. It looks as though you are the most discreet member of the Royal Family at the moment. But I notice that the others have calmed down somewhat.'

I find her very amusing, quite outrageous. She enjoys shocking me, which she can do.

Monday 27 September

The main feature [of the day] was the cocktail party given at Christian Dior. Verushka had been helping them. She suggested that Ungaro should merge with Dior in London, as Dior has never had a place in England before.

After it we went to dinner at the French Embassy which is housed temporarily in Regent's Park, Hanover Lodge, because the other one [in Kensington] got burnt down and is not ready yet.

On my left sat Alexandra Shulman. I told her that at a distance I thought she was her mother, Drusilla Beyfus. 'But she had a better figure than you,' I said, which was unkind of me. 'Everybody was in love with your mother with her beautiful elfin face, her lovely figure and her brilliance.'

Her father still continues to write for the *Evening Standard* and she, the daughter, is the editor of *Vogue*.

Tuesday 28 September

A ludicrous meeting with the Post Office at the top echelon. Counter Productions they call themselves. They are anxious to get into the Lottery business with us, as they have been with other consortia, but they do not know what time it is. At one point they were saying we could not select the post offices and sub post offices that we wanted but they would choose them for us and we would have to take the lot or none at all.

The more I talked to them, the more I thought, good heavens, it should have been privatized years ago. In addition, they wouldn't let me smoke in the building.

This morning I plucked up my courage and rang Margaret.

As usual, she hadn't said most of the things she was supposed to have said. But she remains vehemently anti-Maastricht.

Though not supporting Major much except in one or two items, she said she did make the statement attributed to her that there should be no election for the Leader of the Party while a Tory government is in office. This is what happened to her and it was a disgrace. She didn't want it to happen to him.

She said I had stood by him through thick and thin but, 'You see now he is really not worth it at all. He is really very low level. He has no sense of history, either.' I said, 'Absolutely right. I said in the book review I have just done [of Penny Junor's biography of Major] that he should read the newspapers less and read more good books on political history.' She said, 'He won't. He hasn't got the mind for it. He doesn't do any work. He doesn't do any reading up on anything. That's why all his actions or decisions are either vacillating or based very shallowly.'

At the end she was very, very friendly and warm, as she always used to be with me.

Later that day I met her at the great Conrad Black, *Daily Telegraph*, party at Spencer House.

The Spencer House occasion was strange. Princess Diana was there. I kept turning away in case I should even have to meet her or see her because I think she has utterly let the side down and had just said so to Margaret.

Barbara Black is extremely gauche. She didn't even go downstairs at the end to see Margaret off, as Conrad did. Her seating arrangements were ridiculous. Men were sitting next to each other. Yet with a little adjustment she could have had a man, woman, man, woman arrangement around the circular tables.

Spencer House looks lovely and no doubt Diana felt good in it, as it is still in the freehold ownership of the Spencer family though leased to a company of Jacob's.

Serena [Rothschild] was sweet. She made me sit down because I can't bear the standing up the whole bloody time.

I told her how I hoped to succeed in the bid for the National Lottery which would help racing a good deal. She said, 'Have you asked J. R. about it?' (meaning Jacob). 'No.' I told her confidentially who the consortium was and she said, 'Then you don't need any help from him on that. That's a very strong combination.' Curiously she looks prettier now than she used to, with her nice, round, crinkly face.

The guest of honour was Henry Kissinger.[7]

When people asked me what I thought of him, I said, 'Bloody boring. Nothing new at all. He is a fearful show-off, Kissinger, and very pleased with himself.'

I sat next to Peregrine Worsthorne.

He said, 'You ought to have resigned when Murdoch was making all those attacks on the monarchy and nearly brought it to an end.' 'Whatever for? I don't censor other parts of the paper and he doesn't censor me. There'd be no voice left at all in the Murdoch press backing the monarchy or saying how many of the government policies were right.'

Peregrine then said about his own memoirs, had I read them?[8] I said, 'I don't like to read them in the *Telegraph* serialization because I don't think serializations select the right bits. They concentrate on particular sensational issues out of context. However, I shall get the book.'

On my right was Drue Heinz. I am always having to sit next to her. I like her very much but very little goes a long way.

Verushka's spectacular Dior dress was greatly admired. It must encourage trade for them.

Norman at the moment is both a little peeved with me and apprehensive. He said he would confine his speech [at the Conservative Conference] to policy matters. He would talk about not having a capital gains tax and his economic philosophy.

Wednesday 29 September

GTech and their consortium [for the Lottery] with de la Rue and one or two others are bursting out all over. They have produced a very glossy in style presentation and a boastful press release. They've seduced a lot of press, hoping that nobody else makes a commotion as front runners. They call themselves Camelot. We are still playing it quietly. I do not want to arrive at the starting gate as the favourite, but as an outsider.

---

7. US Secretary of State, 1973–7.
8. *Tricks of Memory*.

Thursday 30 September
Verushka and her sister set off on their journey to Budapest.

It was very sad to see Livia go though she had become a little tetchy, unusual for her. This was from having to sit with her mother a lot, naturally, and listen to her complaining about the food and talking a vast amount of rubbish and nonsense.

They arrived all right and Verushka seemed pleased to be there, also with the Pejacsevichs. She said Budapest is full of aristocrats, the most famous names in Hungary, coming back to collect their vouchers. These are a tiny bit of compensation for the lands and property stolen from them by the Communists nearly fifty years ago. Verushka and her sister have some. Livia was able to use hers, because she was living in the flat, to buy it with.

Friday 1 October
The great *News of the World* hundred and fiftieth anniversary party at Butlers Wharf.

Ron Pell, my lovely sub-editor, and his wife came specially, though he is on holiday, in order to see me. He is a short, shy man. He had once a bad accident on his motorbike, as did his son who nearly died. Ron's head is flattened. He has an appealing, hesitant smile. His wife, Joan, is charming.

He always tells me how many lines need to be cut or added but he doesn't touch anything himself except very occasionally.

He often picks up a mistake of mine.

The speeches eventually began. For a start there was the ghastly Andrew Knight. He made Rupert sound ridiculous. He spoke of him as though he were God: 'He is thinking of you. He sent you a message. He wishes he could be here but he is in Hong Kong, or China, or Hollywood, I am not quite sure where – he hovers over the world and us.'

Then Patsy Chapman came on. As hers is a newspaper with sex in it, she felt obliged to make a number of sexy jokes. Perhaps she does enjoy them – I am not sure about that, but she puts on the appearance.

Patsy made way for Bob Monkhouse who gets £25,000 for a twenty-minute performance. All his jokes were obscene. He referred to imaginary and actual sexual adventures of some present saying, 'Get 'em up,' making crude sexual gestures.

From the ballroom there was a walkway covered with old and new editions of the *News of the World*, with front-page headlines prominently displayed. Poor Norman Lamont wasn't let off. The whip-lash vice girl in his flat and all that stuff.

What was very interesting were the street cries and the noises of Victorian times as one walked through.

There was a music hall, Victorian, in which fairly pretty girls danced the can-can and sang many old music-hall songs, which you could sing with them. At the end of the set piece can-can men were summoned from the audience to dress up in the can-can costumes and dance the can-can. This was received with cries of great delight. The English adore seeing men dressed up as women. It is a strange taste, not wholly understood on the Continent.

Then there was the great fireworks display on the Thames from a large boat opposite us in the rain.

There were fortune-tellers and jugglers wandering around. I have never seen so remarkable a scene in my life.

Petronella and I adored it all.

Sunday 3 October

Petronella is being extraordinarily sweet and friendly and companionable. She cooked the lunch which we had upstairs with Andrew Roberts.

He wanted to know why I didn't keep a diary. He keeps one himself and has done all his life. He said, 'So is Petronella.' 'I didn't know that, Petronella.' 'Oh yes, I do keep one.' 'When do you write it?' 'I scribble away upstairs.' 'Good Heavens. You should make a fortune. I don't in the least bit mind your writing about what happens in this house and about me. You can turn me into a great comic figure, like Clarence Day[1] did with his father in *Life With Father*.' (Oddly, Andrew Roberts had never heard of Clarence Day and *Life With Father*.) I said, 'I don't mind your making a fortune out of me as a comic figure, or out of your mother.'[2]

In the morning Elizabeth had rung for the ambulance without telling me. She said Mrs Racz [Nadje] looked grey and said she had a heart attack. I got into the ambulance with her and they did different tests. She seemed not well but improved in the ambulance. She was then driven off to the hospital, St Mary's, Paddington.

I decided not to tell Verushka. Then I did because Elizabeth said I must. There was a terrible commotion, tears and shrieks, even from Livia.

I had a very jolly dinner with the Stelzers at a Chinese restaurant just off Curzon Street.

---

1. (1874–1935); American essayist best known for his autobiographical collections, *God and My Father*, *Life with Father*, *Life with Mother* (published 1937) and *Father and I* (published 1940), in which he portrays upper-class *mores* in nineteenth century New York.
2. Petronella's memoir of WW, *Father, Dear Father*, was published in 1999.

Irwin has a wonderfully agile and enquiring mind. We spent some time arguing about the constitution of Britain and why it should have a republic, according to Irwin.

Monday 4 October
Eventually Verushka returns.

Her luggage, one suitcase of it, has been stolen with all the most valuable dresses imaginable in it, worth about £15,000 which could never be claimed on insurance or replaced because there are no copies of them. She was in a state of absolute desperation and despair, also about her mother.

At twelve o'clock the doorbell rang violently and there was Verushka's luggage.

Tuesday 5 October
The reports coming from the hospital about poor Nadje are dreadful. She doesn't know where she is. Sometimes she says, 'I'm in Liverpool,' sometimes she says she's at Conock, sometimes in Budapest.

There are all kinds of apparatus on her, tremendously expensive, costing thousands of pounds and all done mechanically and the nurses don't have time to be kind or nice to the patients.

Verushka, who finds her mother very tiresome when she is here, is now full of filial love for her and tenderness. Poor old soul, she ought not to be alive at all.

In the afternoon I went to NERA. They have done a terrific report on the expense of keeping people alive very long, exactly the same as my mother-in-law, as I described to them.

They had some ingenious suggestions in the NERA report. Everybody should be forced to pay compulsory health insurance so that all these new advances in medical science could eventually be paid for.

Thursday 7 October
Nadje is in a very bad way. She has been fighting the nurses, kicking them, throwing things at them, attacking one with a knife, swearing at them. She challenges the doctors saying, 'I don't think you've got medical qualifications. Show them to me.' She screams at them saying, 'If Lord Wyatt gets to know how badly you are treating me, he'll be very angry,' as though they would give a damn about that.

I was summoned to go to see her which I did for two hours. She promised me she would behave well.

Then came the great weakening. I had said to her would she like to come home and she had said she would. I have alternating thoughts about her: first that I wish she would die and stop occupying the top of this house, which prevents me from having a decent bathroom and from using the top sitting-room properly, demanding such enormous attention by the hour (and sometimes by the minute) from the servants who cost me a lot more than they need. The stair carpets are getting worn out with the bang, bang, bang on them the whole time. Her room up there smells like an old people's home with pee on the floor.

But then, I looked into her room which Elizabeth and Maria had so beautifully tidied up, putting all her things back again, hanging her night-gown up on her armchair ready for her to come back. Elizabeth's husband had painted the room to make it look nice and bright and clean again. I thought, 'Oh dear, how can I be so awful as to wish she was dead, thinking there is no point whatever in her being alive.' I was filled with shame and great concern for her. How awful to die in the ward where she now is.

The only roots she has got are here now. At least she has her room with her things and photographs, which she likes, of her grandchildren, Nicholas particularly.

So whatever it costs, I think she must come back.

Meanwhile, the Tory Conference is having a merry time with peace breaking out all over it, as I predicted it would in last Sunday's *News of the World*.

When Margaret did go to the conference, the cheers for her as she came on to the platform with Major were much muted. Quite a large section of the hall was silent and wouldn't applaud her at all. Others roared louder than they did for Major.

Norman himself did not disturb the atmosphere by his fringe meeting though the press tried to pretend he had been attacking the government.

Monday 11 October
I rang Margaret.

She went straight on to what I thought of Major's speech. I said, 'I thought it was an excellent speech, about going back to the old traditional values, using simple words everybody understands.'

Promptly she said, 'They are my values. They're mine. He was saying what I always said.' She ignored them being values of all time which were thought of before she came along, but I didn't say that.

She was very friendly and we went on for about twenty minutes. Then she said, 'God bless you.'

Nadje is coming back tomorrow. She is much better.

We are hiring, we hope, a cheap New Zealand nurse who will only charge about £80 a day or so. I think she will live another year at least. She is getting strong again and will probably be just as much trouble as before. But what can one do, poor old soul?

Tuesday 12 October
The nurse, hired from a New Zealand agency, is an extraordinarily pretty girl. If Alan Clark saw her he'd leap out of his trousers.

Lunch in the Lords in the Barry Room with dear Beryl Bainbridge.

She liked the Barry Room with its neo-Gothic columns and arches. There is a central table where spokesmen of all parties sit together. I pointed out Philip Noel-Baker's[3] mistress who is a peeress now, Patricia Llewelyn-Davies.[4] I had a horrible feeling she may have overheard me which would be terrible but Beryl said she could hardly hear what I was saying herself.

We then embarked on her idea for a play, a great farce which she and I are to do together. She outlined a good first scene. It was about a man who lost his memory, became very confused and was taken to hospital and all the extraordinary things that happened to him there, the things he thought he saw, and those he didn't see, the things which were real and the things which weren't. She said, 'You could carry it on. You've got your Hungarian mother-in-law. You told me how she was treated in hospital and drugged and thought they were poisoning her.'

It could be done. These things based on real life, as Beryl's are, are much more effective. I could put in quite a lot of the rows that go on in this house and that could be amusing.

The taxi she got was one from which Alun Chalfont[5] descended.

---

3. (1889–1982); m (1915) Irene, née Noel, d 1956; Labour politician and campaigner for world disarmament; Nobel Peace Prize, 1959; life peer 1977.
4. (1915–99); née Parry, m (1943) Richard Llewelyn-Davies (architect, life peer 1963, d 1981), Opposition Chief Whip, House of Lords, 1973–74 and 1979–82, life peer 1967.
5. Journalist and expert on defence; Minister of State, Foreign and Commonwealth Office, 1964–70; deputy chairman, IBA, 1989–90; chairman, Radio Authority, 1991–4; life peer 1964.

She said to me, 'I like the cut of his jib. He's very attractive, isn't he?'

Then began the extraordinary meeting with Baroness Cumberlege (Julia)[6] and her officials.

We let fly, or at least I did. I said they will look extremely silly and the public will be very angry with them when it is known that people over sixty or around sixty should be encouraged to smoke, not discouraged. Smoking delays the onset of Alzheimer's disease and senile dementia by at least five years.

The officials, when asked by Julia if they had anything to say, wouldn't speak.

But Julia appeared to listen with a more or less open mind.

I like that pretty girl, Baroness Cumberlege.

Wednesday 13 October

Margaret Thatcher's birthday. I sent her twenty roses. When Malcolm [WW's new chauffeur] took them down, not many other flowers were going in to Chester Square. Lost power quickly loses false friends.

A strange, fuzzy-haired and bearded figure, wearing scruffy clothes and floppy shoes, turned up [at the Lords] to swear in to his inherited peerage. Pat Llewelyn-Davies asked who he was. 'He's Alexander Bath. He's mad as a hatter. He wanted me to help him become King of Wessex. A pity he hasn't brought his wifelets with him. It would have enlivened the proceedings.' When he had taken the oath, he went to sit with the Lib Dems. I said to Pat, 'You're lucky. He's gone Lib Democrat.' They greeted this crazy man with great warmth. Dear Henry, his father, would have been horrified.

A long journey to Mark Zetland's house somewhere near Scots Corner, two hundred and fifty miles in the rain.

It is a splendid building. The Victorian part has been pulled down because Mark's parents couldn't afford to use it. The remainder is mainly Georgian.

Mark was very friendly. He produced three bottles of Château Ducru-Beaucaillou 1961. It was superb.

---

6. Parliamentary Under Secretary of State for Health in the House of Lords, 1992–7; life peer 1990.

Thursday 14 October
I walked all the way round the house during a brief spell without rain.
There is a beautiful lake in the front, designed by Capability Brown.

To Redcar, the course owned by Mark Zetland, for the occasion of
his two-year-old special trophy sponsored by the Tote.

Cape Merino led the whole way and held on to beat the favourite.

I handed the trainer[7] a glass of champagne. 'Oh no. I would like a
cup of tea. I'm a teetotaller.' That was the first time I ever met a trainer
who didn't drink.

Saturday 16 October
I think Margaret's memoirs have busted her as an effective player, at
least until the memory of the memoirs dies away. I have not been asked
to a single function connected with them. I am only mentioned once
as having 'hosted' a party for the working miners at 19 Cavendish
Avenue to which she came. I don't know if she left me out because she
had been so annoyed about my disagreements with her over Maastricht
and other matters or whether it's because I always said she had to keep
dead secret my association with her. Though she hardly did this in the
corridors of Whitehall.

It was announced that Vere Rothermere is to marry his Korean
mistress with whom he has lived for around twenty years. She is a
friend of Daisy Corsini. From his fiancée Vere got the Bhuddist bug.

Sunday 17 October
A message came for me to ring Gus O'Donnell at Number 10 to
arrange a meeting with the Prime Minister.

Monday 18 October
General Inge, Chief of the General Staff, came.

I said I was seeing the Prime Minister on Wednesday and it was
important to get their case over [against the proposed defence cuts]
without telling him where I had got it from.

He came very secretly. I didn't escort him to the gate, so even his
driver couldn't tell who he had been visiting.

---

7. Alfred Smith was the trainer of Cape Merino.

Tuesday 19 October
Spoke to Jonathan Aitken to get some details about how much we
would be losing in exports and how many jobs we would lose if all
these fearful cuts took place. He gave me all the figures and a big
build-up for John Major about what he had done on January 28th this
year, selling millions of pounds' worth of armaments.

Thank goodness it's now decided that Nadje doesn't need a trained
nurse.

Wednesday 20 October
I arrived at 11.55 at 10 Downing Street.

We sat, as usual, at the Cabinet table. Oddly, he seems to do all his
work there. Perhaps he likes the ambience of where great Prime Ministers of the past have sat.

He was very friendly, as ever. I said I had been angry with him
when he first got rid of Norman Lamont. I thought it very unfair; he
had given in to pressure which he shouldn't have done; Norman had
done a brilliant job and now was unable to complete it and get the
credit for it.

Major replied that he had been under unsustainable pressure for
months upon months and that Norman had not expected to go on
being Chancellor of the Exchequer after the election.

The unsustainable pressure, coming not only from the constituency
parties but also from his own party in the House, arose not really from
the actual policies which they didn't like but from the various troubles
and blunders which got Norman devoured by the press. Not all of it
was serious but some he could have avoided.

Major said, when it came to the meeting he had with him in
Downing Street, he had hoped very much that he would stay in the
government.

'For reasons you will well understand, I couldn't possibly have
made Norman Home Secretary.

'Nor could I make him Leader of the House. The other side would
have given him no mercy and he would not have been very good
dealing with the business managers on either side of the House.

'As for one of the other big ones, like Foreign Secretary, there was
no vacancy. He wouldn't take the job he was offered, though I did
offer him another house to live in on leaving Downing Street and
another in the country.'

I said, 'Of course he's burned his boats with you,' to which he replied, 'Not necessarily. I don't see why that should be so in a few years.'

He said he was upset by reports which got back to him that Norman keeps hinting at dreadful things he could and will reveal about Black Wednesday. 'There was nothing to be ashamed of or that I would mind being revealed at all.'

He said a great deal of the trouble in the Party was because Margaret kept stirring it up.

Major said, 'She's not doing Michael Portillo any good raising him as the next Prime Minister. Maybe he will be Prime Minister one day, but not if she goes on talking in that way.'

Then we went on to the billion pound arms cut business.

He said, 'Don't worry. It will be all right. They're not going to have cuts which will cripple them so they can't have all the latest developments.' He agreed with me that it was a mistake to believe there's a peace dividend.

I talked to him about the Post Office and our experiences with the Lottery.

After I told him about the extraordinary meeting I had, he said, 'Would you send me a blind letter.' He sent for his political secretary and told him. (Otherwise we were always alone, which was a great compliment, except when he sent for someone to copy material which he wanted me to have but not to say I'd got it from him.)

He said, 'This way perhaps I can make the Post Office see sense. It is very important in the constituencies. The sub postmasters are losing customers.'

The blind letter I sent later that evening. It gave the facts of the matter. It had no signature from me.

We got more and more friendly all the time. He has a charming smile and he sounds very sincere.

I suggested he shouldn't read the newspapers so much but read books about politics. He said, 'I don't really read them as much as people think I do.' However, I didn't believe him on that. He said [about Murdoch], 'I can't think what he expects. Does he want a Labour government which could ruin him? It would stop at once any cross-ownership between newspapers and television and it would also attack him for being a monopoly.'

I said, 'I think I have now resumed normal service of the kind I gave you when you first became Prime Minister with Margaret's blessing. I think you will be a very good Prime Minister.'

I left him at ten to one. We had at least fifty minutes' conversation of a warm and friendly kind which I think was useful on both sides.

There was a reception given by Mark Lennox-Boyd at the Foreign Office, quite posh.

I saw Verushka talking to a pretty woman I vaguely remembered. It was Simon Fraser's wife[8] whom I had sat next to at one of the Black dinners. Afterwards I had sent her a postcard about some poetry books to read. She said she had taken a day to decipher my handwriting. I said, 'My father used to collect pencil stubs. He wrote inside envelopes of letters which had been sent to him and returned them to the sender inside out. So I write in a very tiny manner. It's small but beautifully formed, my writing.'

Thursday 21 October
A letter from Film Rights saying that my play [*High Profiles*] is to be performed between November 17th and 21st at the Kenneth More Theatre in Ilford.

At The Other Club a goodish turnout.

Our new members were announced but not quite confirmed because the voting isn't completely finished. I think Tom Stoppard and John Mortimer may have got in, also Robin Cook whom I like – he is unpopular with most of the Labour leaders but John Smith, talking to me, said he is very good indeed, the best debater in the Commons.

John said, 'He's very keen on racing.' 'Yes, that's where I meet him.'

It also seems that John Major has been elected. I wonder how much he will come. He might enjoy it.

Sunday 24 October
In the evening we went to the seventieth birthday party of Robin Day in the Garrick Club.

At the door Robin Day introduced me to Sue Lawley. 'Of course you've had Woodrow on *Desert Island Discs*, haven't you?' She said, 'Oh, well. Perhaps he'll be coming along soon.' I laughed on the side because she once said the person she most detested in the world was me. I would seem to be a very unlikely candidate for the programme.

One item remaining in my mind from seeing John Major was his

8. Virginia, née Grose, m 1 (1972) the Hon. Simon Fraser, Master of Lovat (d 1994); m 2 (1998) Frank Johnson.

remark, 'I always put myself in the position of the person on the other side.'

For general purposes it is a very good maxim. I don't do it often enough.

Monday 25 October
Dear Jo Grimond[9] died overnight in the Orkneys, unexpectedly, at the age of eighty. It was thought he was worrying about Laura whose mind is wandering.

I went to see Douglas Hurd at the Foreign Office.

He confirmed that he was thoroughly Eurosceptic, like John Major: 'But we have got to work with these people and sell them our ideas.'

I telephoned Richard Ryder in the evening. I told him the Major meeting had gone well and normal services were being restored.

Tuesday 26 October
An All Party Media Group meeting.

They[10] were arguing that the Act preventing a newspaper having more than twenty per cent in a television station or a broadcasting station is nonsense and ought to be removed.

David English held forth at great length about the dangers of the monopoly being created by Rupert Murdoch.

He had got all the satellite channels and nobody else could get properly into that.

I pointed out that Rupert was not that big in America in either television or satellites so it couldn't be him doing the damage [to newspapers] there, yet he is supposed to be doing damage here. It could be because they are not so good at newspapers here as Rupert is.

Peter Mandelson, Herbert Morrison's grandson (a queer), who is high in the public relations counsels of the Labour Party, asked why the law had been passed about broadcasting in the manner it had been. My answer was that, though designed to clip the wings of Rupert Murdoch, like many well-meaning Acts of Parliament it had the reverse

---

9. (1913–93); Liberal MP for Orkney and Shetland, 1950–83; Liberal Party Leader, 1956–67 and May–July 1976; life peer 1983; m (1938) the Hon. Laura, née Bonham Carter, granddaughter of Asquith, herself a Liberal politician, d 1994.

10. Sir David English from the *Mail* and representatives of the *Telegraph* and *Guardian*.

effect to that intended. The eagle genius flew into the skies and nobody could catch him.

Petronella, Verushka and I went to a party at the Forte 86 Park Lane establishment in celebration of a restaurant called Chez Nico with which they are associated. There another coincidence, a fruitful one, occurred. Peter Jones, the young chap on the BHB who owns numerous horses and sits on the Levy Board, was there.

Peter Jones asked me how the Lottery was going. I told him we were looking for a new advertising and PR agency.

He said, 'I think I can help you.' He has twenty-eight per cent of the shares in the fifth largest advertising agency, which includes a PR wing, and I should talk to the man concerned the next day. He'd do it on a no foal, no fee basis.[11]

Before going to the Lords I spoke to Rupert. I gave him a very broad résumé, trying to make it as secret as possible, of my conversation with John Major last week. I told him that Major was unhappy with the attacks on him by the Murdoch press and [asked], 'What does he want, a Labour government?'

He said, 'I get the message. We have been toning down the attacks lately.' He agreed Major was doing better than before.

I told Rupert that David English had said that Rupert had wanted to buy the *Independent* and, 'You were probably going to do that to wreck the *Telegraph* and then you would have even more papers in your hands.' Rupert was very cross. 'I told him that in strict confidence. I was only just thinking aloud that I might have a bid for it and see what happens, as a way of knocking the *Telegraph*, and he put that in the *Spectator*. He is an absolute bastard.' 'There's a strong force against you in Parliament and you need me behind the scenes more than ever. Also with John Major. You can repair the bridges with John Major and I can get a lot of input there now.'

Then I mentioned my salary.

He said, 'It's all been sorted out. You'll get what you want.' So now I shall have to act on that, taking it that he means I will get my £150,000 instead of the present £112,500, which is what I have been demanding.

I said, 'I know it is like teaching your grandmother to suck eggs, but what are you doing about China? Shouldn't you be there more

---

11. A form of agreement when racehorses are put to stud; the agency was Abbott Mead.

often? I see they are saying that they will make it illegal for anybody to watch or listen to your broadcasts.' Rupert said, 'That's because the BBC has been putting out very anti-Beijing stuff, a lot of it inaccurate, and they think we are going to do the same. I shall tell them we will be absolutely impartial and they won't have any worries at all about us creating subversion in China.'

Then it was to the House of Lords to the Barry Room to entertain Richard Rapp and others connected with NERA.

I took them all on a guided tour which they liked very much. We went down into the crypt and I showed them the anti-semitic Judas Iscariot with a huge prominent Jewish nose and face surrounded by thirty pieces of silver. I explained it is well known that Jesus Christ was a nice English public schoolboy who had been done to death by those dirty Jews.

We drank several bottles of the house champagne plus some excellent white wine and a very good 1983 claret. The bill was £257 after I had given £50 for the tip which I always do there, to keep them happy.

Having been thanked by Richard Rapp, who is the head of NERA, and Dermot Glynn, who is the head of NERA in England, for my hospitality, I could hardly send them the bill for it. Instead I shall say, 'I do far more work for you, introduce customers to you and suggest more ideas than anyone else on your advisory board, so I would like a £2,500 increase in my pay.'

Wednesday 27 October
The great event of the day was the party for twenty (which became twenty-one when Olga Polizzi arrived after dinner was nearly over). It was in honour of Cita's fiftieth birthday.

I made a speech 'about this learned lady who seeks after learning for the sake of it, rather as monks did in monasteries, exuding a calm and benign atmosphere as she does.'

I had found a bottle of rare Tokay dated 1943, the year of her birth, so everyone drank her health in a little of that.

Thursday 28 October
Went to see Michael Baulk who runs Abbot Mead, the advertising and PR agency Peter Jones recommended. He agreed to just about everything with regard to the terms and I think they can do us very well.

Friday 29 October

Once again the article for the *News of the World* was interfered with by people ringing. One was Norman Lamont. He said, 'Are you busy? I have something very serious to ask you about.'

He wanted to know what I thought of his writing his memoirs.

The more I said he should get on with his book, the more he said he didn't think he would after all. He is doing very well at Rothschild and thinks he can make a lot of money there.

Once again I told him that all the bridges weren't burnt with Major. He doesn't believe me and I can't tell him what Major told me.

This rather inconclusive discussion went on for about twenty-five minutes. It drives everything out of my head when I am thinking about my article, sets me back a long time before I can get back into the mood of it again.

But I can't complain. I am working harder than I ever have before in my life, keeping my brain tolerably active and preventing the onset of Alzheimer's, which is what my mother got and I have the same gene. And I actually enjoy it when I consider what I have done in the day and feel progress is being made.

Tuesday 2 November
Called in at the Arnold Goodman reception in Wimpole Street for his book, *I'm on My Way*. I told him he was looking very well, which cheered him up.

In fact he's not but it is much better for him to think he is.

Wednesday 3 November
I showed the Tote Board the letter I had from Liz Scarbrough.[1] I said I had never had a letter from a girl before which began like that: 'Dear Woodrow, Can I please have £4,000?' When I told her after the Board meeting that she had got it, she said, 'If it had been that kind of trouble, it would have been much more than £4,000, wouldn't it?' She is a jolly girl.

Sunday 7 November
[At Oare] Tessa is very argumentative about the Lottery. She said, 'There is a lot of opposition to you.' I said, 'Yes, no doubt. But Henry says ours sounds like a blue chip consortium.' Tessa kept saying they didn't really want a betting organization in it. I said, 'That is simply untrue. Why on earth would parliamentary counsel have drafted my amendment in the Lords making it clear the Tote could run the Lottery? It had all-party support in both chambers.'

But I didn't dare tell them about my conversation with Major who, it seemed to me, would like us to have it very much.

---

1. Elizabeth, née Ramsay, daughter of 16th Earl of Dalhousie (and sister of Sarah Keswick), m (1970) 12th Earl of Scarbrough. Doncaster racecourse had offered a Charity Race Day for the Royal Naval Lifeboat Institution; as President of the Doncaster Guild she was asking for a subscription from the Tote. In a postscript she added, 'If you pay up you can come & stay & we'll have devilled kidneys for breakfast again.'

Monday 8 to Wednesday 10 November
A jolly but exhausting trip to the USA.

In the Concorde lounge there was a surly look cast at anyone smoking cigars or a cigarette. I had to go right to the back, behind a screen, to smoke my cigar. I also tried to go to the loo to excrete waste matter. I failed. And no one can say I shat on the Americans. I didn't get rid of waste matter until the Thursday morning after my return from America on the Concorde.

Immediately on arrival in New York I was dashed off to the Westbury Hotel where I had a magnificent suite for $225 a night. It had been arranged by Olga Polizzi's office. (She is away in Italy trying to find out which [hotels] of the Aga Khan's bankrupt hotel chain are worth taking over.) I got a fifty per cent discount.

I was whisked off to the Autotote headquarters. Lorne Weil seemed immensely busy. At one time I thought he was hardly taking any notice of me, but I think that was wrong.

Autotote have some wonderful new gadgets for betting. There are self-service, easy-to-use screens. They talk back to you if you make a mistake. This is stuff we have got to use.

Interesting to talk to the racecourse management and owners.

They reckon they are saving fifty per cent of their running costs with the new gadgets, despite having to bribe the unions by giving them some kind of bonus or share of the profits.

Thursday 11 November
In the evening I went to the most extraordinary dinner at Claridge's.

I was a guest of Christopher Sporborg. Hambros own the cigar firm Hunters & Frankau. The proceedings were conducted by a remarkable fellow, Marvin R. Shanken, who is the editor of an American journal which comes out every two months called *Cigar Aficionado*.

At the same table was Win Bischoff.[2] He repeated his willingness, in fact enthusiasm now, to talk to Bruce Buck. That is about Bruce Buck's worry that Bischoff had been rubbishing Skadden Arps.

I had never been at a dinner before where cigars were not only served before it began but during the courses. Naturally I couldn't smoke them entirely each time so I popped them in my pocket.

---

2. Winfried Bischoff, banker; group chief executive, Schroders, 1984–95, chairman since 1995; knight 2000.

Saturday 13 November
Reading *The Bridges of Madison County*,[3] I thought back into the
past. Of Doris Kaplan who, I suppose, was the greatest love I had. She
looked like a cross between Ingrid Bergman and Queen Soraya. She was
an American Jewess. I can see her sitting at one end of the drawing-
room at Tregunter Road, with her deliciously seductive half smile,
looking over a glass at me.[4]

I can see her with total clarity at this very moment and often think
of her.

Sunday 14 November
We went to Bowden.

In the afternoon Arnold talked to me about the problems of business
in the Middle East.

The story of how bribery in these parts occurs and is unavoidable
is fascinating. It has to be done in such a way that it is not detectable.
If it hadn't been done, thousands would have been out of work in
Britain.

Arnold has never got anything personally of that kind for anything.

He suggested Lord Craig, who was once Chief of the General Staff,
as the Chairman for our Lottery [bid].[5] He said, 'I am not doing that
because I owe him anything. On the contrary, he stopped me having
Nimrod – you'll remember the case – because he wanted AWACS from
America, and we lost a lot of money.[6] But he is very honest and it
would be a splendid figurehead.' So I agreed to get hold of him to
sound him out.

I am immensely fond of Arnold. He is vastly rich but he is not as
happy as I am. Always pessimistic.

---

3. Best-selling first novel by Robert James Waller, a professor at the University of
   Northern Iowa; WW was reviewing his second novel, *Slow Waltz in Cedar Bend*,
   for the *Times* book page of 2 December.
4. WW described this affair, without giving the name of his great love, in *Confessions
   of an Optimist*, pp. 186 ff.
5. David Brownrigg Craig; Marshal of the RAF, 1988; Chief of Defence Staff,
   1988–91; m (1955) Elisabeth, née Derenburg; knight 1981, life peer 1991.
6. See Vol. 1, pp. 225 ff., for the defence alternatives of Nimrod and AWACS (Air
   Warning and Control System).

Wednesday 17 November
The first night of my *High Profiles* at the Kenneth More Theatre in
Ilford.

It went very well. The man they had (Leonard Charles) doing the
main character, Philip, acted better than the professional we had at
Margate. Some of the others were not quite so good. There was a
smallish audience, the theatre only about half full. This was because it
was a very cold night so they didn't get the passing by trade that they
would normally have.

Beryl said it would make a very good television play.

Afterwards I felt determined again to go on writing plays. I really
do like that curious theatre atmosphere.

Thursday 18 November
The Other Club was entertaining.

I spoke to Richard Ryder, the Chief Whip. I said, 'I hope you and
John Major have noticed the atmosphere coming out of all the
Murdoch papers has greatly changed and is far more favourable to
Major since I talked to him.'

Arnold is furious with Chris Patten. He said he lost him a £5 billion
order in China because of his insulting behaviour. Henry Keswick is
losing orders for the same reason.

At the great meeting in Seattle with the Pacific countries, Clinton
was quite rough on the human rights issue.[7]

Arnold said, 'It's none of our business anyway.' 'It is to some extent.
Maltreatment of anybody in anybody's country involves the entire
world.' To which he dissented on the grounds that we have to look
after our own people first.

Saturday 20 November
Another early start.

I had to see betting shops in Salisbury before going to the William
Golding Memorial Service in Salisbury Cathedral.

The singing of the choir from the school, the Bishop Wordsworth's,
where Golding once taught, was lovely.

But Ted Hughes, the poet laureate, looking wild, couldn't stop his

---

7. Clinton met leaders of the Asia-Pacific Economic Cooperation group, amomg them
Jiang Zemin, President of China.

verbal exuberance. After a long preface with much about himself, he read a passage from *The Inheritors* by Golding.

The son, David Golding, read the 13th chapter of St Paul's First Epistle to the Corinthians. It contained the bits about when we are children we do childish things and shed them when we grow up. However, like many great men, Golding did not shed his childish myths. That is why he wrote so well about children.

Monday 22 November
Met Lord Craig, the retired RAF Air Marshal who was Chief of the whole General Staff when it used to be called the CIGS. At sixty-four he looks far younger, with a tight, neat and military bearing, a quick mind, black hair, good figure, good jaw, a thrusting energetic fellow with plenty of brain.

I told Arnold how good he was and Arnold was delighted.

Tuesday 23 November
Up at six o'clock in order to catch an aeroplane to Dublin.

John Heaton and I were on our way to talk to Ray Bates, in charge of the Irish National Lottery.

Bates was full of praise for GTech who run the operation on the ground for them. He warned us not to bid against them because we wouldn't win, GTech being so good.

He gave us a great deal of information which we need, particularly when commissioning MORI, as we have to, for a research into public attitudes. We know them all already but it is a requirement of the Director General of OFLOT so we are stuck with the task.

Thursday 25 November
A man came from Courteney Coatings, a firm in Birmingham, to estimate how much it would cost to put the whole of this house in good order externally and to some extent internally.

I got gloomier and gloomier as he said everything is falling apart, which it probably is. I think they will want to charge about £30,000 to put it all straight.

I am in a panic about the Christmas cards. So many have to be sent abroad and the over-printed House of Lords cards which were ordered well over a month ago have not yet arrived. I rang up the director of production of J. Arthur Dixon, the Isle of Wight printing firm, and gave them all total rockets yesterday.

Friday 26 November

On BBC *Question Time* this evening Sara Morrison[8] was on the panel.
She was dressed as a very upper class Englishwoman, with a blue jacket
with red facings as though she were part of some hunt.

She talked total drivel about the case of James Bulger who was
murdered by two boys. It was all wet and lefty about social deprivation
and so forth. Yet I like her for her wit and astuteness in private.

For most of the rest of the evening I was thinking about the Bulger
case. I was very much struck, having listened to extracts from *Lord of
the Flies* and read them again since I got back from Salisbury, by how
original sin was in the boys.

On the question of losing jobs, I got Bruce Buck of Skadden Arps
to see Win Bischoff of Schroders.

When he said that had gone very well, I said, 'I was just wondering
whether, in view of that and the other things I am able to do for you,
you'd now put my emoluments up to £30,000 from £25,000.'

He said, 'I daren't mention any increase. I couldn't. I'm not going
to put it forward because if I do, they'll discontinue it altogether.' In a
panic I said, 'My God, consider I've said nothing.' To lose that £25,000
a year would crucify me.

My mother-in-law is getting worse now that she is getting better.

Everything is mixed up so no conversation of any coherence is
possible. The other day she was saying that Petronella got married
twenty years ago.

She watches the television and sometimes reads the newspaper.
Then she secretes matches to smoke cigarettes in bed which she is not
supposed to do. There should always be someone with her when she
smokes in bed or she will burn the whole house down.

When I do go in to see her, she welcomes me with open arms and
I give her a kiss and talk to her for a bit.

Often it is extremely tiring in this house.

I try to explain to Verushka that Montaigne[9] had a tower in his
very large house, miles away from anywhere, and nobody, not his wife
nor anybody else, was allowed to come anywhere close to his tower

---

8. Director, GEC, 1980–98; vice-chairman, Conservative Party Organization, 1971–5;
   chairman, National Council for Voluntary Organisations, 1977–81; née the Hon.
   Sara Long, m (1954–84) the Hon. Charles Morrison (Conservative MP, 1964–92,
   knight 1988).

9. French essayist, 1533–92.

when he was in working and writing, with his library around him. He had total quiet and that is how he was able to write well.

Saturday 27 November
Norman rang me up just as I was going to bed.

He said he was going on the Frost breakfast programme on the BBC tomorrow morning and what should he say.

I said, 'Stick to what you're supposed to be talking about, which is what you think should be in the Budget. So far all the articles you have written on the subject have been very good.'

I persuaded Norman to say something nice in the *Times* in his advice to Ken Clarke on the Budget. I also sent a note to Ken Clarke asking him to say something agreeable about Norman in his Budget speech.

Tuesday 30 November
Ken Clarke was pretty good on the whole.

He referred to Norman twice in a friendly manner.

Norman called it a very good Budget. He had few criticisms, if any. So a little has been done to improve relations all round.

Wednesday 1 December

There was a great dinner given by Mr Lod Cook, President of Arco, the oil company, in Claridge's. Ex President Bush was the speaker.

Bush was funny when he referred to his terror of Margaret. During the Gulf War the Americans decided not to turn back an Iraqi ship carrying provisions of sorts, including arms, through the Gulf. He rang Margaret to tell her his reasons, to which she listened patiently. At the end she said, 'Don't be a wobbler, George. This is no time to be a wobbler.' Thereafter he said he never wobbled.

Sir Colin Cowdrey was there. I couldn't remember who he was when he came up to me and said he'd heard Bob had another stroke. I said, 'Yes he has but he's coming through it perfectly now.'

This reminded me that I hadn't thanked Harold Pinter for sending me his little booklet about Arthur Wellard, the well-known professional cricketer before the last war.[1]

You can't be all wicked if you're so fond of cricket.

Thursday 2 December

On the way to dinner with Alan Hare at Rutland Gate we met Julian Amery on the doorstep. He insisted on believing that the young couple who came in at the same time were going to dinner with the Hares, but they were not. I rather wish they had been. They were a handsome pair. Julian Amery is getting very deaf.

Sam (Nicholas) Baring[2] was there with his very agreeable wife to whom he has been married twenty-five years. She is not at all bad-looking, fairish with a good figure, and lively. She is marred in her brain by being a fluffy left-winger, feeling guilt at being rich. I said,

---

1. In his thank-you note dated 2nd December, WW told Pinter that Bob said Wellard hit the ball as hard as anyone he had ever seen 'but he was a risky player, a bit unpredictable'.

2. Deputy chairman, Barings, 1986–9; chairman, Commercial Union, 1990–8, National Gallery, 1992–6; m (1972) Diana, née Crawfurd.

'You're just like Beatrice Webb[3] and all those upper-class ladies who invent for the working classes what is good for them.' She said she was a friend of Shirley Anglesey.[4] I said, 'That makes sense as far as you are concerned. She is very left-wing and Henry [Anglesey] and I have had stiff arguments with her.'

Alan has had a repeat of his heart attack and stroke. For a moment they thought he was a goner. He now looks much better and quite steady on his pins. We drank some marvellous Latour Carruades. The 1970 real Château Latour was superb and well decanted.

Nicholas Baring to my surprise, said he is chairman of Commercial Union. That is after retiring from the Barings. 'Why did you retire?' 'It gets boring after a while. Anyway, banking is a young man's profession.' He looked gaunt because he had cancer. I like him. He is slight and fair-haired. He still has a boyish smile.

Monday 6 December
Ron Muddle's new Wolverhampton racecourse is beginning to look pretty good.

The floodlighting is fantastic. He will have a lot of trotting races at night and ordinary night racing as well. It is going to be a fully utilized course.

As usual the Tote had been niggardly in the terms they offered for trying to get the betting shops. I had to settle all this.

I [then] had to dash back to London to the advertising agency and PR firm, Abbott Mead, which is handling the [Lottery] pre-bid preparations, so far as they are affected by them, for the Tote consortium. I was amazed. I had to listen to a long, rambling statement from quite a pretty girl with red hair and a fair complexion with becoming freckles.

They kept banging on that we have got to do a lot of pre-bid

---

3. (1858–1943); Socialist intellectual and leading Fabian Society member; assisted Charles Booth's research for *Life and Labour of the People in London*; member of the Royal Commission on Poor Law and Unemployment, 1905–9; joint author with her husband, Sidney, of works on trade unionism, local government and welfare.

4. Née Morgan, m (1948) 7th Marquess of Anglesey (Henry); chairman, Broadcasting Complaints Commission, 1987–91; chairman, British Council Drama and Dance Advisory Committee, 1981–91; DBE 1983.

publicity and take advertising on television as well as in the newspapers.

I said, 'No. Absolutely no. I have said this again and again. We are lying low and we are having no publicity. We are not trying to influence the Director General from outside at all. You are trying to make us go the American way which other consortiums are going. They are getting no mileage from it at all – in fact the opposite.'

Tuesday 7 December

Our wedding anniversary. Verushka was very sweet. She said, 'I want to be adored.' I said, 'That's fine. I think we all do.' I sent her twenty-seven roses in colours which make up the Hungarian flag. The twenty-seven was for our twenty-seven years of marriage. I wrote her a little poem and sent her a telemessage which was delivered by hand at the door and also a wedding anniversary card. That created sweetness and light.

I then had a meeting at Thorn EMI with Simon Duffy, the financial director who is leading their team, Chris Goodall (consultant to Thorn EMI), John Heaton and myself.

Yesterday I calculated that there are only twenty effective working days between now and getting the bid ready and putting it in. Time is going by fast and Arnold hasn't even agreed to the memorandum of agreement between the consortium partners which is essential in order to make sure everybody pays their whack.

There is a hell of a lot of hard work to be done and midnight oil to be burned, particularly by the lawyers, curiously enough, but not really so curious as they come into every damn thing.

In the evening we went to the annual party given by Alastair Goodlad, Minister of State at the Foreign Office, and his wife.

Half the Cabinet was present, if not three-quarters. Douglas Hurd, as usual, chatted up Petronella, and so did many others.

The handsome Virginia Bottomley, tall and blonde like Juno, bore down on me. She had been flattered by my referring to her as Virginia the Goddess Bottomley in my last *News of the World* article. I had added, 'Strong men tremble before her. It must be her looks.'

I meant of course that it couldn't be her brains but was too polite to say so. Again she wanted me to realize how marvellous she had been in refusing to ban cigarette advertisements in Britain.

We had decided to go, Verushka and I, to a new Chinese restaurant opposite Harry's Bar run by a Malaysian. It was to celebrate our wedding anniversary. Petronella graciously consented to come too.

The bill for three was £150. It would have been double across the road at Harry's Bar and nowhere near so good.

I had a little bit of nostalgia with Verushka. We were remembering Mary Rothermere and her then new husband, Esmond Rothermere. The day we got married secretly at the Guildhall to avoid the press, we went to a great party and dance at Warwick House where Rothermere lived in tremendous grandeur. Only Mary knew we were married. She was singularly sweet and remained so with us for the rest of her life, although she could be very tiresome and difficult.

It is sad that she has gone, Esmond has gone and so many friends have gone. Eric Bessborough[5] has now suddenly died. I was talking to him only a few days ago. He supported me tremendously whenever I needed him, on Sunday racing or any other topic, for a vote.

He was large and shaggy like a dog, with a nice, round, kindly face. He had had mild political ambitions but he wasn't up to them.

Then Desmond Hirshfield,[6] whom I had also been talking to only a few days ago when he looked in reasonable health, died suddenly at eighty, the same age as Eric Bessborough. I knew him in days of old when we had the property company of which Hirshfield was a member. I was married to Moorea and Jack Huntingdon put money in it too. But when the divorce came, it all got split up.

It went on to make millions. So many things have slipped away from me.

Wednesday 8 December
In the morning John Heaton, Simon Duffy, Chris Goodall and I went to see Peter Davis, the Director General of OFLOT. We wanted clarification on some items in his draft invitation to tender. I had not met him before.

He said he would have to publish anything which might be of interest to other consortiums. (That was why I had crossed out a number of the questions Autotote, Thorn EMI and even John Heaton

---

5. (1913–93); 10th Earl of Bessborough; diplomat; Conservative politician (junior minister or Conservative spokesman, science and technology, 1963–70, member, European Parliament, 1972–9), film producer and playwright.
6. (1913–93); chartered accountant, chairman, Horwath & Horwath, 1967–86; treasurer, UK Committee for UNICEF, 1969–83, 1986–8; life peer 1967.

had wanted to ask because the answers would give information to our rivals and prevent them falling into elephant traps which I hope they will fall into and which we will avoid.)

I particularly hammered home the need, which he had neglected, to make sure any equipment proposed to be used was examined before any bid were accepted; to make sure the system worked, was modern, the cheapest available, with the least number of breakdowns and the quickest in response time for the public and for the central computer.

Autotote's newest, operational and fully tested system is the world's best.

In the evening a dinner party at Cavendish Avenue.

Peter Lilley improves steadily on acquaintance. He has an excellent brain and is very tough. He has got exactly the right ideas on maintaining the welfare state, making it affordable and only delivering benefits to those who need them. That was the original Beveridge idea.

He went to vote on the shops opening hours in the Commons and returned. Major, and Lilley himself, hadn't got what they desired, which was complete deregulation on Sundays. They only got the half solution which is that shops should be allowed to open for six hours on Sundays, if they were major shops, and little stores could open all day.

I said, 'Do you think this means we can now go ahead to try to get Sunday racing with betting on and off the courses?' He said, 'No. I don't see how you can. We only carried the compromise by eighteen votes against the Keep Sunday Special people.'

There was quite a lot of conversation about Margaret at the Scott inquiry. At first I thought from what I heard on the news that she had done badly. But Peter Stothard said she had done extremely well, really stood her ground and made them all look rather silly. That didn't turn out to be the general impression of all the newspapers, but I think Peter was right. Anyway, it is quite intolerable that one of the greatest Prime Ministers of all time should be pilloried and cross-questioned by some girl QC [Presiley Baxendale] and the idiot man, Justice Scott, who thinks there should be no secrets in government dealings with other countries.

Thursday 9 December
Obviously Margaret did know much more about the sale of arms to Iraq than she was letting on. But she was quite justified actually because

we needed the exports. We also got valuable information and we were trying to balance off Iraq and Iran.

Julian Muscat, the new racing writer on the *Times*, came to lunch at the Tote. He had written an absurd attack on me and the Tote without even checking his facts. He turned out to be quite nice.

I think he could now be a convert. We are sending him up to Wigan to see all our computers, etc.

Meanwhile, Stoker Hartington is an idiot and his BHB people are idiots, too. There was a great to-do yesterday at their absurd conference in which they proclaimed they were going to take over the Tote.

I spoke severely to Stoker. 'I am trying to get this Lottery for the benefit of racing. You are shooting yourself in the foot and me in the back. All our rivals will say how could you possibly give it [the Lottery] to the Tote, if racing is going to take over the Tote? How could racing possibly be responsible for a National Lottery?'

He said, 'It's only an aspiration and we've said it before.'

'What are you trying to do? Are you trying to get rid of me again now? I got you betting shops open for evening racing. I got you an increase in the levy. I got you reduction in betting tax and I've done no end of other things for racing. I made this great agreement with Bass which is going to vastly increase the pools. What on earth do you want now?'

Stoker said, 'It's fine as long as you're there. We're worrying about your successor.' 'I haven't gone yet, have I? I may be here for ever as far as you know.' He said he thought it unlikely that I wouldn't die. I said, 'You're right about that but when the time comes I shall make what arrangements I can to see that the next person shares my views.'

I wasn't having a real row with him but I was firm and friendly. He was then very contrite.

In the afternoon we at last saw the brand marketing manager at Post Office Counters. This was after I had talked to the Chairman of the Post Office, Michael Heron.

He clearly had a message from on high which had been instigated by Number 10 through my blind letters. He was much more amenable and he agreed straight away that we would be allowed to select the sub post offices we wanted.

I then spoke to Jonathan Hill, the Prime Minister's political adviser. I said, 'Will you please tell the Prime Minister what has happened. The blind letters seem to have worked.'

My dud eye continues to hurt like hell.

What compounds the agony is that my big toe on my left foot spends most of its day hurting extremely painfully so I am in pain at the top of my body and at the bottom of it, too, and trying to think clearly in the middle.

Monday 13 December
To the Archer party. They had three. This was the third. Margaret Thatcher was the main star for this one, John Major having been at the previous one, ensuring the two should not meet.

Leon Brittan's wife was there. I told her I thought he was a great hero, which I believe, and I have written him a note asking would it be helpful or harmful to him if I were to say that he ought to be the next President of the Commission.[7]

Denis was very tipsy. He was looking for somewhere to smoke. 'You can't smoke in here. Jeffrey says it discolours the pictures. I tried once and was nearly thrown out.' He then got hold of Susan Hussey and they did go and smoke in the corner and utterly refused not to.

He gets very fed up traipsing around with Margaret to parties he doesn't like. I suspect he reckons drains to Jeffrey Archer whereas she always liked him, despite his extremely dubious provenance.

Wednesday 15 December
Quite a good meeting at Abbott Mead, conducted by Peter Mead himself. He paid me a great compliment by saying, 'We think you were right about wanting to use the Cole Porter theme song "Who Wants To Be A Millionaire?" from *High Society*. We have now got an option on it.'

We have got to get the animations going with the type of advertising we are going to use so that the Director General sees them with the bid.

It is vital to show it is the 'tasteful' approach that he demands, while persuading everybody to put the maximum money into the Lottery. It's typical British hypocrisy that you pretend you don't really approve of the Lottery but you want to raise the maximum from it.

There was a very grand dinner in Broadcasting House in the third floor suite.

---

7. Leon Brittan had been a UK member of the European Commission since 1989; m (1980) Diana Peterson (deputy chairman, Equal Opportunities Commission, 1994–6).*

It was in honour of Margaret after the great television series they did with her.

The person I was most keen to see was Joanna Trollope, the novelist and relation of the great Trollope. She is married to Ian Curteis.[8] He was there because he had written the Falklands play which the BBC had rejected because it was too pro-Margaret. They are now considering doing it after all.

I had sent him my play asking could he give me some advice on it and how could I get it broadcast. I gather they pay a lot of money for those plays. When I saw him he said he had read half of it and it was very good, very witty and amusing and subtle.

I thought well, he might have finished it. It wouldn't have taken very long. He said he was writing to me about it.

We discussed mutual friends like Kingsley Amis and his last wife, Elizabeth.[9] I told her how awful it was when she was staying with us in Italy and she was madly in love with him still. He didn't write and she wrote every day. I said, 'He's probably in the pub,' and he certainly was. He always was. He hated abroad.

Margaret made a charming speech.

She said she had decided she was going to start a 'Rent-A-Spine Agency' but now she didn't think John Birt required it.

I had quite an absurd conversation with Peter Jay. He was saying that all single mothers should be dealt with severely. I said, 'Do you really think that, Peter? I don't think women really do have babies in order to get advanced on the housing list and social security benefit. I think it's a biological urge and they get trapped and that's it.' He fiercely disagreed and said I was getting very left-wing.

What I was really doing was somewhat teasing him, though he didn't seem to understand it. He has got an illegitimate child and he is at it all the time.

He should ask himself if the girl had his baby to get a flat and social security. Of course she didn't.

Thursday 16 December
Norman Lamont's party at Kensington Park Road. On the way I heard on the wireless his voice asking Major about Ireland. He was

---

8. They separated in 1998.
9. Elizabeth Jane Howard, novelist, m 3 (1965–83) Kingsley Amis (d 1995).*

rubbishing the whole policy, saying it didn't square with what Major had said before.

He can't resist trying to stick pins into Major. Therefore he is further and further away from ever getting back into the government or getting on in politics because even people like Kenneth Clarke won't have him now.

When I got to his house I pointed this out to him. I was about the first there because I had to go on to The Other Club where I was in the chair.

They have a huge picture in their drawing-room. It was painted when they were at Number 11 and the four of them are in it.

Robin Day was asked what he thought and he said he thought the frame was very good.

I got to The Other Club in good time. I asked Roy to sit opposite me and I had Noël Annan on my right and Duke Hussey on my left.

Noël Annan dotes on Petronella. He said, 'Does she have any boyfriends?' I said, 'Dozens of them. I don't enquire.'

William Waldegrave is upset. He has been severely attacked by Alan Clark who told the lies which got the Matrix people prosecuted. Clark is now trying to blame the lies he told on William Waldegrave. William said would I help him if the attacks get worse and he is in difficulties. I said I should be delighted to do so.

Major's unpopularity among the Tories is no doubt the reason why he was not one of the new members elected, though he was not far short.

Alexander of Weedon, Chairman of the National Westminster Bank, the great lawyer, was elected.

Kenneth Clarke, the new Chancellor of the Exchequer, was elected. So was Robin Cook whom I rather like.

Then there was John Grigg, who should have been Lord Altrincham. His father was a Permanent Secretary at the War Office and received a hereditary peerage but John thought it was improper for him to take it up because he hadn't earned it and it was meaningless. That was in his slightly revolutionary days when he was attacking the Queen. I suspect he wishes now he hadn't rejected it.

Max Hastings is another new member elected. So is John Mortimer whom I am very fond of, and also Tom Stoppard whom I like very much as well.

Friday 17 December

Had a very nice letter from Kenneth Clarke replying to mine congratulating him on his Budget. It was hand written from the House of Commons. He probably doesn't like his officials to know he's in communication with me.

I also had a very friendly letter from Leon Brittan in his own hand marked personal and private. He was flattered that I wanted to promote him as the next President after Delors, but would I carefully do it, not as a knocking of Delors but because of the good he, Leon, might be able to do for the Community. I duly obliged in the article I am writing today for the *News of the World* to be published on Sunday.

Monday 20 December

Max Hastings had a party at Brooks's, his club. He is very proud of being a member of Brooks's and thinks it's very grand.

I found Max Hastings and said, 'I am very glad you are now a member of The Other Club.' He purred. I hope that helps Petronella a bit.

Then it was on to the great dinner at Christie's being held by Charlie Allsopp and his wife for Olga and William.

I said to Charlie, 'Am I allowed to smoke? I am longing to smoke a cigar.' 'I'll have ashtrays brought at once,' which he did. He said, 'I have now told them to turn off the fire alarm which otherwise might be set off by the smoke.' So much for that Jeffrey Archer who won't let you smoke in his flat for fear of damaging the pictures.

I think the dinner had been mainly arranged by Vivien Duffield and will be paid for by her.

Vivien Duffield made a speech that was affectionately abusive of both William and Olga, saying how could she have got married to him? She had always said she wouldn't and now she has married this wretched man and broken up her set of girlfriends and all the gossip they usually have about Willie and other people. It was delivered in a firm, loud voice – a startling celebration of a wedding.

She has a lot of go and guts that Vivien woman.

One away was a man I didn't know. He hadn't got a cigar and none was being offered. He said he didn't know we were going to be able to smoke. I said to him, 'Here you are. I always keep one in reserve for a fellow cigar smoker who may be stranded.' I pulled out of my case a Montecristo No. 2.

Afterwards I asked who he was. It was Maurice Saatchi, the rich one of the Saatchi brothers.

Charlie Allsopp's father had died the night before so he is now, therefore, a peer, Lord Hindlip.

Tuesday 21 December

There arrived today a great object for me. I opened it and it was two cigars with a note from Maurice Saatchi saying these were two Churchill cigars which were better than my Montecristo (though very politely and jokingly). I immediately sent him back a card saying it reminded me of Gandhi who used to say, 'He who gives quickly gives twice.'

I am getting extremely annoyed with the slowness at which Autotote are reacting to our requests for information and a really thorough working-out of the bid procedures.

I was also angry that they were not getting on with making the device which we invented at the Tote and designed for Tote Direct, and which we had converted, into a machine would take Lottery tickets in low volume locations.

I rang up Jack de Vries at Owings Mill, Maryland.

De Vries said it would take nine months to get it ready and anyway, why couldn't they just use their own terminals?

I said, 'This is ridiculous. Can you not remember that when I got the law altered so that the Tote could go in for the bid, I led into it by saying we had this great device which was entirely a British conception?'

Wednesday 22 December

In the morning Lorne Weil rang up and I told him exactly what had happened.

He quite agreed with me and is going to put a bomb under them.

Vere Rothermere had a great party at Claridge's for his new bride, the girl from North Korea who is a Buddhist.

I had quite a long conversation with her about Buddhism. She is not all that beautiful but she has got something very appealing and agreeable about her. She has a charming face. By this time she must be about forty-five – those girls from the East retain their looks a very long time.

Friday 24 December
We arrived at Budapest airport ten minutes before time. This seemed a cheerful start until we discovered there were no cabs of any kind, everything having ceased at twelve noon on Christmas Eve in Budapest, which is the custom in Hungary.

In an hour and a half a cab arrived to take us to the centre of Budapest.

Sunday 26 December
I was afflicted by a sudden illness with a high temperature, something in the food or a bug. Various people got it including Verushka and Petronella.

We were all confined to bed and feeling very sorry for ourselves, ill and sick. Not a merry Christmas.

Monday 27 December
I am worried about the *News of the World*. The new acting editor [Stuart Higgins] has pushed my article down so I have less space because he likes to write all over the bloody place himself. This time his ire was directed at a wretched fellow called Tim Yeo, a junior Minister at the Department of the Environment.[10] The *News of the World* had got one of their jolly scoops. He had previously been having an affair with a thirty-four-year-old Tory councillor in Hackney and last July they had a baby born to them.

He's a bit of an oaf. One knows that morals have nothing to do with people's capabilities, but it seems rather careless not to use a condom or make sure his girlfriend does [use contraception].

---

10. Conservative MP since 1983; he resigned his ministerial post on 4 January 1994.

1994

Sunday 2 January
I read many of the stories in the new definitive edition of the collected short stories of Robert Louis Stevenson;[1] and a charming book given me by Livia who is so clever at finding these out-of-the-way novels by long-forgotten, pre-1914 but rather good writers. This one is *Through the Postern Gate* by Florence L. Barclay published by Putnam, New York, 1912, a first edition.

Extraordinary how many similarly dated books turn up in Budapest shops.

Tuesday 4 January
Genevra and Antonella[2] arrived at half past twelve to be taken out for their annual treat. This began at a Chinese restaurant run by a Malaysian which we went to before. I was somewhat against going there because I knew it would be expensive, and my God, it was – £84 for two little children and ourselves for what was really not a very big lunch. The tickets to *Starlight Express* cost £27 each, i.e. £108, and I had to buy each of them a £10 T-shirt with *Starlight Express* written all over it. The cost of the outing was over £200.

The performers rattled by on roller skates and the noise was abominable.

But the children adored it.

In a weird way I enjoyed it, too.

Wednesday 5 January
The Quintons gave a dinner at the Garrick.

There was a fair amount to drink but most of it was not very good.

---

1. WW sent the Stevenson stories to the Queen Mother; she was thrilled to have the two volumes as she had always loved the stories and thought it was a charming edition with lovely printing.
2. Verushka's grandchildren, daughters of Nicholas and Caroline Banszky, b 1985 and 1987.*

Henry Keswick said he longs for us to get the Lottery but he hears we are very far from being the favourite, more like an 'also ran'.

Henry is very susceptible to rumours.

Friday 7 January
A disconcerting letter from Stuart Higgins, the acting editor of the *News of the World*.[3]

I have never been told before that I have to consult with the editor about what I am going to write.

However, I rang him up.

'Which would you like most, the solid basis for Britain's riches (à la the books I had sent to Tessa Keswick[4]) or to start with Yeo and all his ridiculous problems?' He wanted me to do Yeo – he's that kind of an editor.

Norman Lamont came to dinner plus Rosemary. He is now getting better off and busier as he dashes round the world. Off to Canada tomorrow for Rothschild.

He still remains bitter. I said, 'You mustn't show it.'

Norman said, 'Major was often a very difficult man to size. I couldn't get him to make decisions when I needed them.'

He then said, 'I've told you what I told nobody else about what happened on Black Wednesday morning. Now I'll tell you something else nobody else knows. A few days before Black Wednesday there was to have been a meeting to which a number of Ministers were coming, including Treasury Ministers. We were to have a private discussion without officials with Major about the need rapidly to leave the ERM. When we got there to this great meeting, he said he was very sorry he didn't have time to discuss it with us because he had to go to a Conservative women's conference which was far more important. So for the sake of that they plunged on with the ERM when they could have got out of it before the crash

3. Higgins thought most *News of the World* readers would not have been interested in WW's lead item from Hungary the previous week; he suggested they should talk regularly, on a Thursday morning, about the content of the column.
4. At the Quintons' Garrick dinner on 5 January WW had recommended books on the history of British manufacturing by P. J. Cain and A. G. Hopkins.

and in much better order without losing billions of pounds in reserves.'[5]

It does seem an extraordinary attitude on Major's part. He never wants to get on with talking about the tough, serious things, but always with the more frivolous aspects.

Hence this absurd business about Back to Basics. It means absolutely nothing. He has now had to say it doesn't include personal morality, as so many of his Ministers are personally very immoral in their private lives.

Saturday 8 January
One scandal after another, allegedly, is emerging among the Tories, all to do with sex. The wretched fellow David Ashby, MP for Leicestershire, has been sharing beds with men in hotels alleging that no homosexuality takes place. They just do it to save money. I was amused by that because he was the ghastly man who attacked me violently at the Select Committee when the Tote was being examined.[6]

Friday 14 January
For the *News of the World* I wrote about the views of Verushka and why she had never left me alone when I was in the House of Commons when I married her twenty-seven years ago: she relied on the Hungarian proverb, 'Opportunity makes the thief.'[7]

Sunday 16 January
Had a very long talk with Richard Ryder.

The ghastly bearded Trevor Kavanagh from the *Sun* declares he knows what happened at a dinner at Number 10 for Gus O'Donnell, press secretary now retiring: Major said he was going 'to crucify these fuckers' who were making a mock of his Back to Basics campaign and

---

5. In his 1999 memoirs *In Office*, p. 226, Lamont records a secret meeting, set up to discuss withdrawal from the ERM shortly after Lamont's return from Italy on 24 August; but Major refused to talk about the ERM, saying, 'I don't want to discuss that at all, I want to discuss my speech for next week.'
6. See Vol. 2, pp. 528–9.
7. WW was discussing the problems of parliamentary marriages after the death of the Countess of Caithness which was followed by her husband's resignation on 9 January 1994.

trying to get him out and so forth. There wasn't a word of truth in it. Richard Ryder was present at the dinner.

Richard said, 'Does Rupert know what they are all doing?' I said, 'I haven't spoken to Rupert lately but I am not sure. He has a huge empire. He may be too busy looking after his interests in China, sucking up to them there to make sure he gets his enormous deal through with them on communications and TV and all the rest of it.'

The foul Andrew Neil is demanding that Major goes, so is the *Sun* and so is the *News of the World* idiot, Stuart Higgins, and the *Daily Mail*.

I said, 'I think perhaps I should see John Major. I have a number of notions.' He said he would arrange it.

I am now looking at non-executive directors [for the Lottery consortium]. I want women because we haven't got any women in anything to do with our Lottery. Arnold said, 'I don't want women. They're too bossy.' I said, 'That's what OFLOT will want. It's the flavour of the period we're in.' He then made some rather good suggestions.

Monday 17 January

We went to the Beefsteak Club in the evening to a party given by Andrew Roberts.

I had never been in the Beefsteak Club before. Andrew Devonshire says he won't go there any more because it is full of awful journalists who leak stories into the newspapers. It is quite a handsome room, just by Leicester Square.

Alan Clark was there. He started chatting in a very friendly manner. He was with his long-suffering wife. He said he was delighted with the Public Lending Rights money he's getting. I said to him, 'Your book was hilarious but you were dealing with the flip side of people, not with the honourable and decent side.' He said this was quite right.

He said he had not heard of one threat of a libel action and that had surprised him, though it had been read very carefully for libel.

Jane [McKerron] has now written to me, which was rather a shock, saying she didn't want to edit this manuscript because it was too long and too difficult. She was afraid of libel and goodness knows what else. So she wanted me to stop paying her monthly money.[8]

---

8. When he began his journal, WW designated Jane McKerron as its editor. She was sent the typescript in regular instalments. She gave him advice and represented him at some of the negotiations with publishers but had not started work on the editing.

I am considering, if I can choose the right moment and think he is really discreet enough, asking Andrew [Roberts] whether he might like to do it.

Tuesday 18 January
Went to Vintners Park Crematorium near Maidstone for the funeral of Joan Chapple.[9] She died of Parkinson's. Frank has got it also but nowhere near so badly.

There were many people there from the old days when I was instrumental in getting the Communists out of the ETU and getting into court the case which disqualified them all and showed how corrupt they had been.

They were very happy together.

I was glad I had gone.

During the day messages came, would I go to see John Major at six o'clock tomorrow. Immediately I rang Rupert.

We had a bit of a barney. He said he could do nothing about Andrew Neil because he is a law unto himself, but he could, he thought, 'have some influence on the *Sun* which is the only paper that matters. That was the paper which got the Tories elected last time.' I didn't demur over the *Sun*'s winning of the election though it is absolute rubbish.

During the day there were the usual commotions about the National Lottery.

Simon Duffy was to be nominated as Chief Executive of our Enterprise Lottery Company which will be owned by our consortium.

At one moment he had been saying he wouldn't go forward because it was all such a ghastly trauma, the Saunders and Guinness affair.[10] At the next moment he was saying, 'I don't think it matters.' I had to tell him, 'I'm afraid it does matter. You have to put yourself in the

---

9. Joan, née Nicholls, m (1944) Frank Chapple (General Secretary, Electrical, Electronic, Telecommunication and Plumbing Union (EETPU), 1966–84; member, Tote Board, 1976–90; life peer 1985).

10. Duffy was director of corporate finance at Guinness, 1986–9, and operations director of the Guinness subsidiary, United Distillers, 1989–92, before joining EMI Group (formerly Thorn EMI) as group finance director in 1992. He was thus working for Guinness when Ernest Saunders and others were charged in 1987 and found guilty in 1990 of offences connected with the takeover of the Distillers' Company.

position of the Director General of OFLOT who is trying to make certain everything is Simon Pure. He gives us the job of doing the Lottery and the first thing that happens is that nasty journalists dig up your past and say good heavens, we thought this was all going to be Simon Pure and here's this chap Duffy as Chief Executive who was mixed up in the Saunders affair.

'I am sorry but I have to tell you this: it's not worth risking the application by putting you forward.'

Wednesday 19 January
I had a fax from Rupert Murdoch. It looks very much as though he is going back on his word to me.[11]

I rang Margaret to ask her what she thought of the state of affairs. I was delighted to find she was immensely supportive on Major. She spoke of him warmly as she did in the days when he was her heir apparent.

When I said about Rupert not knowing what his papers were doing necessarily, she said, 'You know, Woodrow, he was always saying that. Every time it's his excuse. I think he knows perfectly well what they are doing.' And by the way, so do I.

My meeting with John was set for six o'clock. I was told he only had half an hour.

I told him what Margaret had said about him and he was delighted.

'What about Portillo?' 'Do you think they are really going to have a Spaniard?' He laughed. 'Somebody has got to take Portillo on one side – and perhaps you could do it.' I said, 'I know him tolerably well. I rather like him.' He said, 'So do I. Take him on one side and tell him they are making use of him but it is not doing his career any good at all. The boy keeps blowing off about Back to Basics and moral qualities and all that kind of thing, but it has nothing to do with what he is as Financial Secretary. So it's damn silly.'

I said, 'I thought I had got Rupert more under control and that he would be more reasonable. But I had a fax letter from him which I suppose I ought not to show you.' 'That makes me very much want to see it.' 'I will show it to you but it mustn't get out that I have.' We

---

11. Murdoch said he had been thinking about their talk and still agreed with Rees-Mogg rather than WW about Major who seemed to confuse leadership with manipulation and compromise.

repeated to each other there was total confidence on both sides so I gave it to him and he read it very carefully, three times.

He said, 'But these things aren't true. It isn't true that it [current prosperity] is entirely due to what happened in the Thatcher years. All my problems were based on the difficulties caused by the Lawson over-spending. That made things much worse than they would have been otherwise and it was Margaret's fault.'

I said, 'Why don't you ask Vere Rothermere to dinner at Chequers or Number 10 and butter him up?' He said, 'I did. He came to Chequers. We had a little lunch party and I had a charming letter from him and his wife saying how grateful they were, how much they admired me and so forth. And away they go, just the same in his papers. It's all that fellow who edits the *Daily Mail* (Paul Dacre).'

We then got on to the National Lottery.

I told him that I thought all the estimates being made of how much the Lottery would take in the first year were grossly low.

He was frightfully pleased with that. The reason of course is that the more they get in for good causes, the less the government have got to spend – and he has a great success.

It is obvious to me that the decision about who is to run the Lottery won't be made without consultation with Downing Street. This is right. *Quis custodiet ipsos custodes?* (Who will be the custodian of the custodians?) No government would let Peter Davis make such a decision by himself.

I think his nudge will be towards us at the moment. I am certainly doing all I can to get him on side but I am not saying anything about him which I don't believe.

I went on to the Waldorf Hotel where William Shawcross and Olga were giving a great party.

I wanted to go home.

But Verushka didn't want to go and she kept running around and hiding from me. I said to Drue Heinz, 'The next time I marry I am going to marry a really tall girl so she can't dodge me when I want to go home.'

Friday 21 January
There's been a ghastly young social services worker lurking around the house. He wants to have my mother-in-law psychoanalysed to find out why she always wants to get out of bed and says she is being impris-oned. Danger, danger, danger, flashed into my mind. This fellow will

put something into the newspapers about our ill-treating my ninety-three-year-old mother-in-law.

He said the social services provide all this free. I could see another great thing in the newspapers about the stinking rich Lord Wyatt having social services of this kind provided free for him. So he has been forbidden the house. I can see him saying, if she did die, which she is obviously likely to do, that we had murdered the pour soul – death by neglect and God knows what else.

Saturday 22 January
The *Sun* editor, Kelvin MacKenzie, has moved to run Sky Television and the acting editor of the *News of the World*, Higgins, is going to be editor of the *Sun*. A twenty-eight-year-old boy, Piers Morgan, who writes a funny column in the *Sun*, has come to be acting editor at the *News of the World*.

Tuesday 25 January
Some of the characters from the consortium meeting at GEC appeared at the great dinner party at 19 Cavendish Avenue.[12]

Lord and Lady Craig – I hope we have warriors of better brain and stature than nice Craig if we are involved in another conflict.

Arnold with Netta – it was just as well we had this dinner by chance at that moment. He had to soften down.

Kenneth Clarke agreed it is rubbish, this business of Major having to go, starting scares again.

He is certainly not to blame, so far as far as I can make out, for the rumours and destabilization directed at dislodging Major.

I was amazed that Mrs Clarke had read Florence Barclay. She had not read *The Mistress of Shenstone* so I thought I had better lend it to her, although it is from The London Library, and ask her to let me have it back when she had finished it.

Andrew Roberts was goggle-eyed for most of the dinner.

He has got plenty of brain and his family have the franchise of Kentucky Fried Chicken so they are rich.

I am thinking earnestly that he could be the editor of this manu-

---

12. There had been an acrimonious meeting on 20 January when it emerged that Avery, a subsidiary of GEC, had offered maintenance services to other Lottery consortiums.

script, if he wanted to be. I don't know how to deal with it because I am terrified of widening the circle which knows about it.

Wednesday 26 January
A jolly dinner at the Connaught Hotel with Irwin Stelzer. There was a beautiful bottle of 1966 Brane-Cantenac.

Poor Irwin is dealing with the Monopolies Commission tomorrow, at which he will have a pretty rough time, I reckon. I said, 'Please let me know if there is anything I can do.'

Monday 31 January
I rang John Major's sidekick, Jonathan Hill, his political adviser, and said to him, 'Please say to the PM about *that* letter [Rupert's fax], I do note some kind of softening. Of course Norman Lamont has made a total bloody idiot of himself again. He hasn't dared to ring me up because I would tell him the trouble was that the girl he was having lunch with was a pretty girl and he fell for her completely. Later he said it was not supposed to be on the record, but she just made hay of him.'[13]

At dinner [at Cavendish Avenue], after the men had left the dining-room, I told Bernard Donoughue where we stood [on the Lottery bid] and that we had a good chance.

The German Ambassador and his wife were there.[14] She is charming and easy to talk to. Robert Kee[15] sat on her right. He had been a German prisoner of war and speaks a bit of German. They got on famously.

On my left was Lady Inge who is pleasant enough and thrilled we

---

13. Lamont gave an interview on 6 January to the *Times*, published on Saturday, 29 January. He explains in his memoirs *In Office*, p. 408, that the journalist had said she wanted to write a sympathetic piece as she felt he had been badly treated by the press. When the profile appeared 'it was a hatchet job', claiming he had described the Prime Minister as 'weak and hopeless'. He was certain he had not said any such thing in the interview, 'though it was just possible I had said something to her later at the Ritz, after the article had "gone to print".' Lamont had agreed to have a drink with the interviewer and a friend of hers a few days after the interview.

14. Dr Peter Hartmann, Ambassador to the UK, 1993–5, m Baroness Lonny von Blomberg-Hartmann.

15. Writer and broadcaster; his books include *Munich; the Eleventh Hour* (1988) and many translations from German.

were asking them to Ascot in June. Her husband was Commander of the British Army of the Rhine for a few years and speaks perfect German.

Bernard Donoughue was a great success with the ladies.

Wednesday 2 February
Eventually I said to Simon Duffy, 'I'm sorry. It's all off. We can't have this backwards and forwards any more.'[1]

I said, 'I hope it won't affect your input into the bid application.' He said pompously, 'I have a duty to Thorn-EMI and I will do it responsibly.'

Simon told me when he left Guinness for Thorn-EMI, the latter just wrote out a cheque to him for £250,000 for the share options he had lost by leaving Guinness. It is amazing what fairly ordinary people running public companies give each other out of shareholders' money.

Thursday 3 February
Evelyn de Rothschild rang in a great bother. Could I do a favour for him?

He said, 'It's Norman and this latest stuff about John Major being weak and hopeless. Talking to this woman journalist he has started it all up again now. It is horrifying everybody at Rothschild and we are really going to have to get rid of him if he doesn't stop it.'

I rang Norman. 'You haven't rung me lately.' He said, 'No. I thought you'd be annoyed.' 'I am extremely annoyed.' I gave him a hell of a dressing down.

I said, 'You have lost your seat at Kingston and now no constituency in the country is going to give you one.' He said, 'There may be one anti-Major, like me.'

After a while he said, 'Have I now had six of the best?' I said, 'Yes. Is Evelyn there?' 'I don't know.' 'Well go and see him and say you are not going to do this any more.'

I think he has taken it to heart now.

---

1. A compromise had previously been reached whereby the Director General of OFLOT would be told that Duffy would stand down from the post of chief executive if it was thought his past position with Guinness would be an embarrassment.

Friday 4 February
The lawyers are arriving from Autotote in America and they are all going to sit in consultation with Rowe & Maw, the GEC contract lawyers, and John Heaton to get it [the Lottery bid] all sorted out.

My head is whirling around. Arnold says we will never get the application completed in time. I said, 'We will. I am seeing to it.'

Saturday 5 February
I told John Heaton that whether he liked it or not he had to be the Chief Executive of Enterprise Lottery. I said, 'I guarantee you that you can get back to the Tote if you want to. Perhaps you need only stay two years. We'll fix the salary and all the rest of it and you've got to do it.'

So he said he would, and he will do it very well.

In the afternoon I watched England v. Scotland at rugger, while poor John Heaton who adores rugger, having played for Richmond and nearly played for England, and was longing to watch it, had to be at Rowe & Maw.

Monday 7 February
The idiot, Jack de Vries, has arrived at last. They [Autotote] still haven't got all the specifications of the systems and equipment and how they work which are required by the Director General of OFLOT. Nor have they got the prices in. Their paperwork is indescribably inefficient. They haven't even put their declarations of honesty and integrity in yet. They simply can't be bothered. They say it's not like that in America. I get angrier and angrier.

As the day wore on, de Vries said, 'Of course we can't produce the terminals in time.' So total breakdown.

Arnold Weinstock was all for getting rid of them straight away, saying they are utterly impossible and abandoning the bid.

Tuesday 8 February
Emergency Tote Board meeting at Cavendish Avenue at 7.30 a.m. about the investment in the Lottery.

At the end of the Board meeting David Sieff[2] was very sensible. He

---

2. The Hon. David Sieff, director, Marks & Spencer, 1972–97; president, Racehorse Owners Association, 1975–8; member, Jockey Club, from 1977; board of Newbury Racecourse from 1988; Tote Board, 1991–8; knight 1999.

gave us all the authority we needed to show the consortium and the Director General.

Then off I went again down to the lawyers (Rowe & Maw) in Blackfriars, a very pretty building with lovely views. It is a little like Venice on one side. A narrow old street leads to the Thames. You get a marvellous backdrop of St Paul's.

We have sandwiches each day which are not too bad, and plenty of fruit which is OK. I decline drink because I know I would not keep awake sufficiently.

There were endless conversations backwards and forwards between Jack de Vries (who is only a messenger boy) and Lorne Weil who was having a holiday with his wife in the sun. He ought to have been over here. I cannot understand these people.

Eventually they came back to say they could get the terminals on the move.

I [had to] say the Tote would be willing to give them 2.5 per cent of our equity [in the consortium], which I am bloody annoyed about.

So it was on again. But they wouldn't agree to pay OFLOT penalty clauses if the machines didn't work.

It is a kind of nightmare. It is almost impossible to explain how the same point is argued by the lawyers over and over again.

Unfortunately, the Air Marshal will keep poking his nose in where he is not wanted and where he has no expertise or understanding, and saying, 'I smell a rat, I smell a rat.'

Wednesday 9 February
The marketing programme, produced by Abbott Mead, was repetitive and [full of] self-advertising for the agency.

I am very disappointed in Abbott Mead. They've also got a rotten printer so you can't make any corrections without rephotographing a page, which is light years behind modern practices.

Now they say they want to have a great publicity event, about what the consortium is all about, when we hand in our bid, if we ever do, on Monday February 14th. The Director General has said there will be a photo opportunity.

I said, 'First of all, we don't want any publicity. If we do have any, it'll be simple and something we can issue to the Press Association for nothing.'

I popped into the Lords for a bit. There I was congratulated, which is always agreeable to my vanity, by various people on what I had said [in the *Times*] on how the Tories will pull themselves together and how Labour really are doing badly. I think it is an article which will please John Major and maybe produce a favourable atmosphere for our bid.

Friday 11 February
Autotote were still not offering solid guarantees of the efficacy of their operation nor were they willing to take the liability for the thing going wrong.

There was supposed to be a [consortium] shareholders' meeting yesterday at six o'clock but it couldn't take place. Instead, the riot act was read again by Malcolm Bates [GEC] and I had to give in this time. So the bid was all off.

I went home to bed, as John Heaton did, very sad and miserable.

I was really shattered, thinking how can I go to Newbury on Saturday and face the announcement that we had all withdrawn from the bid.

I had warned Autotote and Lorne Weil, 'You know what a blow this is going to be to you. You'll never get another lottery anywhere, not a major one.'

In one sense we had them over a barrel because the damage would be far greater to them than to us. There would be no damage whatever to GEC who just regard the whole thing as a side issue, and so does Thorn EMI. The damage to my reputation would be immense because I organized it all, got the bid going, got Autotote in.

Verushka, who hadn't realized what was going on properly, was extraordinarily sweet about it and said, 'I do understand what it means to you.' I said, 'This is the great dream I had, that I could leave racing something solid and achieve something really important before I finally disappeared from the scene, a legacy which would go on working.'

At half past two in the morning I heard the telephone ringing again and again and again. I drowsily woke up – I had ear plugs in because I didn't want to be woken. I clambered upstairs. John Heaton and the very nice chap, Berd Ratzke, partner at Rowe & Maw and son-in-law to Malcolm Bates, were determined to have one more go.

They said, 'How would it be if we made a conditional bid, saying the details still had to be worked out on the prices for the systems supplied by Autotote which would follow later, but here is a rough idea of it, etc.' I said, 'It doesn't look too good, but it's better than nothing.'

Then I got hold of Autotote. By the morning they had agreed.

What we have arranged is to send Roy Hilsley, who has been a bit better than usual, and three chaps from GEC, immediately on Monday to the States to see what the hell they are doing.

If we win this bid, I am bloody well going to see that it is fulfilled, even if I die in the attempt.

Saturday 12 February
I went to Newbury.

Then it was back to London and long talks again with John Heaton as to where we had got to now.

Sunday 13 February
At Rowe & Maw they were sweating away.

They were all sticking things into the right boxes, hardly the labour one would have expected to be performed by such elevated, highly paid persons. But they were in good spirits.

Monday 14 February
Woke up at half past four.

Our statement went out to the Press Association as finally altered by me. John Heaton appeared on the television several times, and so did the Rowe & Maw man.

We were the first to arrive [to present the bid]. John shook hands with the Director General. He asked John how we were getting on. 'Fine. We are doing very well. We have set out everything as best we can.' He made no comment and started talking about the weather. But he was very friendly.

In the morning the idiot Branson, who has a wonderful popularity vote from the nation because he says he is going to give everything to charity, turned up at Trafalgar Square with Desert Orchid [racehorse] and led it down to the place where you hand in the bid boxes.

In fact Branson said they would only provide a billion a year for the charities. We are going to provide at least 1.5 billion a year quite soon and it will probably go up to two billion.

I have lectured Hilsley with instructions to ring me at least twice a day reporting on what is happening [with Autotote in the US].

I rang Richard Ryder and had a long talk with him.

I said, 'Can't you get a better type of person in the Tory Party now? They're all on the make, low, slimy and sleazy. As for that nonsense about Stephen Milligan having a great career ahead, he didn't have one at all.'[3]

I told him we had just put in our bid for the Lottery and I was hoping we would get it started in October if we heard by the middle of May that we'd got it.

I read in the *Times* that Caroline [Duchess of Beaufort] swooped over Badminton in a stunt aeroplane nose-diving onto Badminton house. She said she was terrified.

I rang her up to tell her not to behave like this any more. 'It said in the paper you are sixty-four. You can't do this sort of thing when you are sixty-four.' She said, 'I'm sixty-five.'

Tuesday 15 February
Appalling reporting by the *Financial Times* and the *Guardian* on the bids for the Lottery. The *Financial Times* leaves out altogether the link with Autotote and makes it sound as though we haven't got a proper bid at all. So does the *Guardian* which says we have given no information about who would run the organization or which company provides the marketing expertise.

I sent a fax to the editor of the *Guardian* enclosing the press release we had on Monday at 12 noon. My fax said, 'Why is your reporting so ridiculously wrong?'

Thursday 17 February
The works of Florence Barclay are having a strange effect on me.

What she makes me feel – and I can't believe in eternity – is that I do believe in goodness and people trying to do good.

I feel protective to my mother-in-law.

She is immensely selfish and yet she still has a woman's trick to seduce you with a smile, making you think how much she loves you or admires you or whatever. She still does this to me.

I am immensely selfish but I care about other people and feel sorry for them and like to help them. I patiently take up cases for *News of the World* readers when I think they are deserving. Perhaps I don't do that energetically enough. When I was younger and an MP I took enormous trouble over it.

---

3. The Tory sex scandals had continued with Stephen Milligan, MP for Eastleigh since 1992, found dead after some unusual solo sex play (suspected auto-erotic asphyxiation).

The Other Club.

Jacob was full of his visit to Jimmy Goldsmith and his Mexican palace.

He said, 'You'll never guess who else was there.' I said, 'Perhaps Soros was.' He said, 'You've got that right. Also there was Packer from Australia.'[4]

I said, 'What were you arranging? Another raid on gold?' Someone said, 'You shouldn't ask for information like that because it is insider trading.' I said, 'I can ask Jacob anything I like but he need not answer if he doesn't want to.'

Tuesday 22 February
To the Levy Board to see Rodney Brack.

He wanted me to take up with the Home Office, in my behind-the-scenes manner, the levy to be paid by the bookmakers which we think should remain the same as before, although they are all asking for a reduction.

I duly rang Peter Lloyd, the Minister of State in charge of racing. I told him why the levy should stay the same and also, as the Home Office has to approve the sale of United Racecourses, to take on board our duty as custodians of the future and not give it to people whose descendants might be against racing and would take advantage of any new 'legalized theft' Act.

Went to see *An Inspector Calls*, with Julian Glover, my cousin once removed (being Honor Wyatt's son), in the part of the hard-hearted industrialist expecting a knighthood. He acted extremely well.

To my surprise he is fifty-eight.

The production was very strange, quite different from the way it was done when Priestley's play was performed straight in three acts.[5]

Thursday 24 February
My lunch with Beryl Bainbridge at the Ivy.

She was dressed very nicely. She said, 'I have got on my daughter's coat.'

I said, 'It's usually the other way round with my daughter and her mother. My daughter is always pinching her mother's clothes.'

We discussed just about everything. I am very fond of that girl.

---

4. Kerry Packer, media magnate.
5. This was the prize-winning production directed by Stephen Daldry.

Saturday 26 February

To Oare in dismal weather. It was nice to see Henry Keswick as soon
as we got there. He has got a little thinner. I keep urging him to get
much thinner.

We talked at length about the idiotic campaign of Andrew Neil,
the BBC and the media against trade with Malaysia.[6] Henry agrees
completely with what I have written for tomorrow's *News of the
World*. He knows, obviously, masses more than Andrew Neil will ever
know about trade with the East.

Went to Beach's, the lovely old bookshop. To my horror I heard it
was about to close down as Mr Beach is clearly on his last legs, rents
have gone up and so forth. It is just outside the entrance to the
cathedral. I was immensely sad.[7]

Sunday 27 February

I couldn't get to sleep. I was rattled by the number of things I have to
do.

I don't think Tessa likes me at all, though she certainly, with Kenneth
Clarke, then Home Secretary, made sure I got reappointed at the Tote.
Maybe that was because there was a general feeling that I should be.

Mrs Hayden Phillips popped in briefly. She is the step-daughter of
Mark Bonham-Carter. I said, 'Don't give my regards or good wishes
to your husband. He'll think I am trying to influence the Heritage
Department to give us the Lottery. Just make sure you say I particularly
didn't send him any good wishes.'

Hayden Phillips withdrew his acceptance invitation to the Tote
lunch because, as he is a Permanent Under Secretary at the Department
of National Heritage, he felt he could be compromised over the Lottery
bids.

I find that the *News of the World*, without telling me, have changed
my reference to a sanctimonious investigation 'by the *Sunday Times*
and the media' by leaving out 'the *Sunday Times*' which is a sister
paper.

---

6. The controversy was about a possible link between UK aid for building the Pergau
   dam and the Malaysian government ordering arms from the UK; WW argued that
   contracts were frequently won by such means and thousands of jobs here would
   be lost by alienating the Malaysian government.
7. WW wrote to the owner asking whether anything could be done to make sure it
   kept open.

I wondered, vaguely, why they had not sent me a final proof by fax but now I know the reason. They are more frightened of Andrew Neil than they are of me.

However, vis-à-vis Rupert, my position is still strong. It will be helped by what I am trying to do with regard to the reduction of [the number of] American films being shown on TV and in cinemas in this country by fifty per cent as a result of a decree from Brussels.

To lunch among others came Simon Weinstock and his wife, Laura, Sonny and Rosita Marlborough.

On my left Rosita was bubbling away in good spirits. She is having an exhibition of her pictures now, I forget where, and she is actually selling them. I said, 'That's a great achievement. You're really doing something worthwhile in your life.' 'Oh yes', she said, 'You always think I have nothing in my head.' I said, 'That's as far as literature is concerned or reading. You are simply unable to read very much. I know you are a good painter but you have always been very shy of showing me your pictures.' She said, 'You can go to see them now.' But as I have forgotten where the hell they are, that will be difficult.

Like all of us, Rosita is looking a bit older but she is still very handsome. It always gives me quite a lift to see her and talk to her.

Henry and I both got into disgrace again because we kept rushing off to see the start of Aston Villa v. Tranmere Rovers on the second leg of their semi-final contest.[8]

Monday 28 February
When I got back home I found a message from John Heaton saying the presentation required by the Director General of OFLOT would now possibly be on April 14th. I told him I was supposed to be going to France the Easter weekend before.

I would never forgive myself if something went wrong because I had gone to France to stay with [David Swaythling] the man who had gone behind my back to try to get rid of me.

After a bit of a dust-up Verushka said, 'You have to ring them to tell them.' So I rang and explained the situation. Ninette was absolutely understanding, delightful, saying, 'Thank you for ringing so early.'

---

8. Aston Villa went through into the final of the Football League Cup.

Tuesday 1 March

Harold Acton has died.[1] I have happy memories of him.

He was once greatly annoyed with Tom Driberg[2] who stayed with him. First, he made a pass at one of his footmen. Then he asked Harold, who was very fastidious, which public lavatory he should frequent to pick up male prostitutes. Harold said it was one of the few times he was really angry. He was, of course, himself homosexual and used to have live-in lovers staying from time to time in the house.

He wrote beautifully about the Medicis and others and he wrote a very good novel. His manners were courtly and exquisite.

He had a double nature. Sweet, kind and malicious.

He was a great friend of Tony Lambton's.[3]

For the last year or so it seems he was nearly always drunk on vodka and losing his brains, which was very sad.

I am fighting like mad to make sure that the Racecourse Holdings Trust, owned by the Jockey Club, is the one which is able to buy Sandown, Kempton and Epsom.

A serious contester against the Racecourse Holdings Trust is Stan Clarke.

My point basically is that Stanley Clarke is sixty. He has done a good job at Uttoxeter, which is nowhere near the same thing as doing a good job with United Racecourses, but his grandchildren might well have the opportunity through another 'legalized theft' Act, introduced

---

1. (1904–94); writer and aesthete; lectured in English in Peking where he lived for seven years before the Second World War, after which he lived at his family villa, La Pietra in Florence; his novel *Humdrum* was published in 1928 but he is best known for his books on the Medicis, the Bourbons of Naples and memoirs; knight 1974.

2. (1905–76); Labour politician and journalist; life peer 1975.

3. Viscount Lambton; politician and writer; Conservative MP, 1951–73; Parliamentary Under-Secretary of State, Ministry of Defence, 1970–3; he resigned from the Commons in 1973 after photographs of him with a prostitute were offered to the press; since then he has mainly lived at his villa near Siena.*

either by a Tory government or a Labour one, to stop racing and use their courses for development.

Wednesday 2 March
On Tuesday I was in a tremendous panic because I couldn't see all day, everything was blurred.

I went off to see Eric Arnott.

At the end, Eric Arnott said to me, 'I think you're suffering from stress.'

He gave me a prescription for 75mg of aspirin I am to take every day.

Thursday 3 March
I have been having a lot of trouble with Piers Morgan, the twenty-eight-year-old acting editor of the *News of the World*. He will now be there permanently. Poor little Patsy Chapman is so ill or off-beam because of her illness that she will not be returning. Young Piers had the cheek in my article last Sunday to remove my reference to the *Sunday Times*.

Saturday 5 March
To Blenheim to the usual yearly evening in honour of Sir Winston Churchill, with an oration to be given by Martin Charteris (Lord)[4] and a concert.

Martin gave a pleasant but not really profound talk about Churchill. He had only met him as Private Secretary to the Queen and he was overawed by him.

Harvey McGregor, the Warden of New College [Oxford] was there with the New College choir and an older group of singers. Having done the usual classical stuff, he then proceeded to have them singing Cole Porter songs which were very jolly.

His own special item is to do the story of Barbar in French, reading it in a mincing voice to the accompaniment of the young man at the piano. I wondered what the previous Wardens would have thought, the great men who occupied this position.

---

4. (1913–99); Private Secretary to the Queen as Princess Elizabeth, 1950–2, Assistant Private Secretary to her as Queen, 1952–72, Private Secretary, 1972–7; Provost of Eton, 1978–91; life peer 1978.

Sunday 6 March
After breakfast Rosita came to me and said would I like to see her dirty den.

It's up a lot of stairways, narrow as you get towards the end, almost under the eaves of the house. It is long and narrow and there are all her paints and her drawings which she does very well. She gets the anatomy right.

To lunch came Conrad Black and Barbara Amiel. She was looking pretty but nervous. She had never been there before, to Blenheim.

I could see from the way Conrad Black's mind works that we went up enormously in his estimation, having stayed there the night and being on such intimate terms with Sonny Marlborough and Rosita.

We left after lunch while the Blacks were being given a tour of the house.

Black wanted to pee. He was shown where to go and did so. The others went on, either round the grounds or the gardens or other parts of the house. He found himself unable to open the door of the lavatory. He bashed on it and shouted and banged and banged but nobody heard him. Eventually, by using his very considerable weight and strength he broke the door down.

Monday 7 March
I am busy negotiating with Ladbroke to get them to take fifty of our Tote Direct machines in their shops as a trial. If we succeed in that, all the other bookmakers will come flooding in.

Tuesday 8 March
When Sonny Marlborough arrived [at the Tote annual lunch] he said gleefully, 'I got my cheque from Conrad Black. It was in compensation for having smashed my lavatory door.' He got a cheque paying for the repair of it and a handsome cheque for charity as well.

Michael Howard, the guest speaker, was on my right. At my table sat Willie Whitelaw, Ken Baker, the previous Home Secretary, Stoker Hartington, Denis Howell[5] to represent Labour and Robin Cook for the same reason. Also Richard Ryder, the Chief Whip.

---

5. (1923–98); minister with responsibility for sport, 1964–70; former football referee; life peer 1992.

In the afternoon I rang Irwin to ask his advice about what to do with young Piers Morgan trying to censor me.

Irwin said, 'Yesterday there was a big meeting at News International. There had been a row between the *Sunday Times* and Sky Television. Sky objected to being criticized by the *Sunday Times*, saying they were all part of the News International Group and it was said absolutely all over again that anybody may criticize anybody else within the organization. Otherwise it would add strength to the proposition that News International is too much of a monopoly and not even free expression is allowed, if it's contrary to what the proprietor or other editors may think. There is to be complete no-censorship of columnists.'

Wednesday 9 March
My lunch with Piers Morgan. He is tall and slight, a pleasant looking fellow with a strange accent which I don't know if he deliberately puts on – a non-upper-class accent nor a middle-class accent which is his background – or if it is natural to him.

Piers agreed he needed a drink and we had half a bottle of champagne.

I said, 'I have to tell you that I cannot put up with any censorship. I am very sorry about that and I cannot put up with you ringing up and getting me to alter my articles when I am halfway through them. My contract is not with *News of the World*. It is with Rupert Murdoch.'

'How did you get to know him?' and I told him all about that and made it quite clear the association was very strong.

I told him all that Irwin had said.

Piers said he now understands the position. I said, 'But I will let you know in the morning early what I am going to write about (he said he gets to the office at about half past eight). Of course I am always happy to make a mild adjustment to fit in with what you are doing but it is ridiculous to think we shouldn't have arguments in the paper.'

Then it turned out he was a great fan of cricket and I told him about Bob.

It all passed off on a very friendly basis and all, I hope, is now well.

Thursday 10 March

At twelve o'clock came Jerry Lewis[6] who wanted to talk to me about Cyril Connolly. I had tried to stop him but he would insist. He is writing a book about him. I said, 'I can't think of anything to add to what I wrote in my autobiography, *Confessions of an Optimist*.'

However, we did talk at some length, particularly about Lys Lubbock.[7] I said, 'Cyril treated her absolutely abominably and used to beat her with a hair brush, with the sharp hairs, on her bottom.'

I thought she was a very attractive, small, dark girl, very pretty indeed. Eventually she left him and married somebody in America. She is now dead. I said, 'I don't mind you putting that in, in that case, about her. Otherwise I wouldn't like to have hurt her feelings.'

Then he said to me, 'You might be flattered to know that a great many letters which Cyril Connolly wrote to Lys said, "I suppose you're attracted by that Woodrow and keep seeing him." ' She may have been, mildly. Perhaps she was, but she never displayed it very adamantly otherwise I think I would have responded in the appropriate manner.

I said, 'Cyril was a terrible snob and being Irish he felt inferior to the English, rather like Oscar Wilde, always having to prove himself by living among the high and mighty. He was a good soul, far more good than evil. It was a great pity he was so vain. He didn't dare write anything after middle life in case it wasn't good enough and he would be torn apart by the critics.'

I have been at war with that fool Michael Howard.

He didn't consult me before he made his speech at the Tote lunch. He talked a lot of tripe about the BHB one day taking over the Tote and the Levy Board or whatever. He then wandered around making it worse by talking to racing journalists, saying he expected it to happen in 1995–6, or words to that effect.

He had already agreed with me, after his speech, that he would write to the Director General of OFLOT saying there was no change in the status of the Tote contemplated, that it would be all quite a different ball game in any case if we got the Lottery, and also that

---

6. Jeremy Lewis, author and editor, former publisher and literary agent; his *Cyril Connolly: a Life* was published in 1997.

7. Lys, née Dunlap, m (1938) Ian Lubbock, actor; she lived with Connolly 1941–50 and changed her name to Connolly by deed poll in 1945 but they never married; she m 2 (1954) Sigmund Koch, an American academic.

a great deal of primary legislation could be needed which might not even get through.

Friday 11 March
I duly rang Piers Morgan at a quarter past eight but he wasn't there. I didn't get him until ten o'clock. He said, 'Oh, you've put me to the test. It was the first time I wasn't there.'

I said, 'I'll tell you what I'm going to write.' He thought it was splendid.

I spent a lot of time reading an excellent book by Mervyn Jones about Michael Foot,[8] of which I am writing a review.

Every single political issue he took up he was wrong on. Amazing. But he was charming.

I am getting extremely worried about the presentation to the Director General of OFLOT. Lorne Weil thinks it very important that Jack de Vries goes. I said, 'He made a very bad impression on everybody here.' 'But he knows all about running and setting up lotteries.'

I shall have to go myself. John Heaton is not very keen on that because obviously he wants to be seen as running the show.

Thursday 17 March
To Cheltenham for the Tote Gold Cup

I think Princess Anne was a little miffed that she hadn't been asked to present the prize. But it has always been my rule that if Queen Elizabeth [the Queen Mother] can't do it, then it has to be Verushka.

Verushka did look extremely pretty. She is remarkable. She brought two outfits down to see what the weather and the wind would be like and kept changing her mind about them until she got the ideal one in my view, a charming hat and a Dior coat (which will do her standing good at Dior because everyone saw her wearing it).

Friday 18 March
Once again, Piers Morgan was not in his office as early as he said he would be.

I think he is a nice boy. He likes the little bits about cricket and all the other funny things I do.

---

8. Labour politician and writer; Leader of the Opposition, 1980–3.

Sunday 20 March
Olga Polizzi came late to dinner. Carmelo Calabro was here from Italy
to get a renewal of his British passport.

The discussion at one stage was about the seven deadly sins.
Adultery is not considered to be one by me, but a natural event which
occurs throughout the ages and throughout the sexes and will never
be stopped.

This arose naturally from when we were talking about Bienvenida
Buck and Sir Peter Harding, the ex Chief of [Defence] Staff.[9]

Tuesday 22 March
After lunch I popped into the Lords and scored another 'L'.[10]

I then went to the Levy Board meeting. The main item was the
decision about to whom to sell United Racecourses. I had spoken to
Rodney Brack in the morning and discovered that all was OK for
Racecourse Holdings Trust belonging to the Jockey Club.

It was agreed *nem. con.*, except for Anna McCurley on my left, the
silly girl, making some idiotic point irrelevant to the subject. Poor
creature, she drives me nuts.

If it hadn't been for me, it would have gone the other way because
the St Modwen bid had enough money and energy behind it.

To Blakes Hotel for a suddenly arranged dinner. I had never been
to this place though have heard of it often. It is in a dingy street off
the Fulham Road.

We were greeted on the doorstep by the manager of Blakes and
taken to a recess [to wait] for the owner, Anouska Weinberg.[11]

After some twenty minutes Anouska turned up with Mark
Weinberg.

Then arrived Prince and Princess Michael of Kent.

Marie-Christine kept putting her arm round me at dinner and

---

9. Marshal of the Royal Air Force Sir Peter Harding, Chief of Defence Staff since
   1992, resigned when his affair with Bienvenida Buck was exposed in the press.
   She m (1990–3) Sir Antony Buck, (Conservative MP, 1961–92, knight 1983.) See
   Vol. 2, pp. 279–80, for the Bucks' marriage.
10. WW called collecting the tax-free attendance allowance at the House of Lords
   'scoring an "L" '.
11. Anouska, née Hempel, fashion designer and hotelier, m (1980) Mark Weinberg,
   chairman, Allied Dunbar Assurance, 1984–90, St James's Place Capital since 1991,
   J. Rothschild Assurance since 1991, knight 1987.

holding my hand, behaving in an extravagant manner planting kisses on me. It was a strange performance. They are desperately hard up. She says they have been prevented from going to Russia where Michael has a sales pitch and she wanted to do some more research for another book she is writing. They had arranged to go and they were told not to go till after the Queen had been there.

Marie-Christine said whenever he's in Russia people rush to kiss the hem of his trousers, hold his hand and bless him because he looks so like the last Tsar that they think it is him back to life again. They are a very superstitious lot, the simple people of Russia.

We discussed the affairs of the Royal Family and about Diana and so on. The two children will not be going to these crazy schools like Gordonstoun, but I gather they will be going to Eton. I said, 'I'm not so sure about that. It might be better to go to a more sensible school.' Their son is a great friend of William's, a few years older.

He has won a scholarship to Eton. I said, 'He must be damn bright.' She said, 'He is.' I thought it can't come from Michael's side of the family, but that is not quite fair because he is brighter than he seems.

All her claims to be royally connected and from the high aristocracy are absolutely true. During the evening she kept waving and shouting to Verushka 'We Hungarians', and so on. She is very proud of her Hungarian connections.

Wednesday 23 March
Went to meet Moorea[12] in the Barry Room at the Lords.

We talked of the many jolly things we had done in the past and how we had travelled to Russia and to Eastern Germany. When we raised electrically the roof of the Bentley and put it down again, I said to the workmen in East Germany, 'In England every working man has a car like this.'

I said, 'You know I always loved you.' She said, 'I know,' and she almost had tears in her eyes, as I did.

She has been very helpful with the entry in the *Dictionary of National Biography* about her father [the 15th Earl of Huntingdon]. She said what I wrote in my obituary in the *Independent* was 'very accurate and depicts the charming person he was'.

---

12. WW's third wife, now Lady Moorea Black.*

Thursday 24 March

I had lunch with Patric Dickinson.[13]

We had a fascinating discussion which will emerge when I write out my entry [on Huntingdon] for the *Dictionary of National Biography*.

Went to Pratt's, thinking it would be a dull evening. But Richard Needham was there. He is really the Earl of Kilmorey.[14]

We talked a lot about the eccentric Earl, his predecessor.

I said, 'He never went into the Lords, as the last Irish representative peer, unless it was to use the car park.' Richard said, 'Yes. He would be off to see his mistress who lived not far away.'

Sunday 27 March

Took John Heaton as my allowed guest to Wembley to watch the first Cup Final I have ever seen there, between Aston Villa and Manchester United. Aston Villa were the total underdogs and Manchester United were supposed to walk all over them. As often, it went the other way and to my enormous excitement, and I was sitting at the Villa end, the great Manchester United team was defeated by 3–1.

Wednesday 30 March

I published my great denunciation of Douglas Hurd, saying he'd let the side down and then blackmailed Major and the Cabinet into accepting a weak compromise.[15]

A lot of people totally agreed with me. Ralph Harris of High Cross,[16] who I had been sitting next to the night before, when I showed him the proof of my article, kissed it ecstatically.

Spoke to Margaret. She completely agreed.

'What do you think of the hysterical state the Tory MPs are in?' She said, 'It'll calm down over the weekend. I'm having nothing whatever to do with this vaunted leadership crisis. It won't happen, the challenge. They've got nobody to put in his place.'

---

13. Rouge Dragon Pursuivant of Arms, 1978–89, Richmond Herald since 1989, Treasurer, College of Arms, since 1995; an Oxford friend of Nicholas Banszky.
14. Conservative MP, 1979–97; Minister at the Northern Ireland office, 1985–92, Minister of State, DTI, 1992–5.
15. The argument was about altering the percentages needed for blocking EU proposals before the review of EU institutions due in 1996.
16. Economist; Founder President, Institute of Economic Affairs; life peer 1979.

Norman Lamont has been ringing me. First he began ringing from Canada, saying, 'He's got to go.'

I said, 'It would split the party from top to bottom. You can't have Howard because the country is deeply anti-semitic. You can't have Portillo because he's a Spaniard. And I don't think you could have Clarke because he's all above himself and not bright enough, apart from yelling the place down he wants to be Prime Minister.'

The second time he rang, when he had just got back from Canada, he said, 'There isn't anybody else, really. Perhaps we'll have to settle for Major.'

Thursday 31 March
I explained to Colin Southgate [Thorn-EMI] what we were trying to do at the [Lottery] presentation.

I said, 'The Director-General would say to himself, if I'm not there, "We've got the monkey but where's the organ grinder?" '

Friday 1 April
We would have been going to Oare today but for the most extra-ordinary deaths in Tessa's family. Her youngest brother chasing buffalo was killed by one he failed to kill with his original shots. Now Simon, the Master of Lovat and the heir, has fallen off his horse in a heart attack and died. He was overweight.

He quarrelled with his father who had handed everything over to him to save death duties. He has just about wrecked the entire estate. All is mortgaged. It will take very careful management for some time to restore the affairs of the estate. I expect it can be done. Doubtless that is why Tessa wanted Henry to go to Scotland to stay over the weekend.

Sunday 3 April
Went to Bowden. Peter Carrington and his wife were there.

Peter Carrington got very angry with me because I said Harold Macmillan had been the worst of three bad Prime Ministers – Wilson, Callaghan and him.

I said, 'He didn't fight for Britain at all, just for himself. He only cared about being Prime Minister. He accepted all the nationalization and said it couldn't be rolled back. It was only Mrs Thatcher who did it all.'

He then said I had been very unkind to Douglas Hurd. I said, 'Not at all. He is a Foreign Office apparatchik. You were to some extent but not entirely. The Foreign Office has been wrong on every damn thing.'

Carrington talked at some length about Rupert and his parents whom he knew well, the reason being that at a very young age Peter had been Governor General of Australia[1] and used to see Rupert's mother a lot. They always see her whenever she comes to England. 'Why does Rupert say all these dreadful things?' I said, 'Because he

---

1. Lord Carrington, b 1919, was UK High Commissioner in Australia, 1956–9.

wants to make money. He doesn't much mind what his editors do provided he makes some money.'

When I got home I found a message to ring the BBC. Would I appear at seven o'clock the next morning to defend Major as I was the only person who seemed to do so.

When I told Verushka about it she said, 'You mustn't do that.' 'Why not?' 'It's too risky. Why should you go through all that and get yourself into difficulties?' I didn't say any more to her about it but secretly arranged it.

Monday 4 April

The BBC car fitted out with its radio and so on came and sat outside the house. I came on after Rees-Mogg who made his usual attacks on Major.

Afterwards I got back again into my usual night-shirt and dressing gown.

However, one of the people putting in the new bathroom, a carpenter, came rushing in and told Verushka, 'Oh, he was wonderful, your husband. When I was coming here, I heard him talking on the radio, attacking all these people who are disloyal to Major, telling them all to shut up.'

My cover was blown but she didn't make any comment.

I can't see how it could have done me any harm. It isn't just that I want to make sure we get this bloody Lottery but far more that I think Major is being treated incredibly unjustly.

Tuesday 5 April

The tiresome little pip-squeak of an Air Marshal is giving an awful lot of trouble.

He has the impertinence to say that he proposes that he opens the ceremony of presentation to the Director General and that I speak last.

I sent him back a fax saying too late, we've already sent the agenda in.

He then gets furious and sends another memo round to everybody, which should never have been circulated, attacking me.

I explained to the Air Marshal that I have got to represent the shareholders. I have got to lead it all.

Wednesday 6 April

Verushka says she knows I am writing this diary and she knows I lock my library door to stop her coming in, not to stop Petronella pinching my first editions.

I said, 'I know very well that you have keys to everything in my library and you read everything I have written. What I hate is that I haven't any privacy anywhere. I explained to you about Montaigne and you don't understand.'

Thursday 7 April

My mother-in-law has been screaming and yelling the bloody place down. She decided it was Christmas and where was her money? Somebody had stolen her money and she wanted to buy everyone a Christmas present.

She gets into a state of alarm because she fears being burnt in hell and put in purgatory. What a ridiculous religion that is. I can't persuade her that when she dies she is just going to sleep for ever. Poor old soul. She is looking really cadaverous these days, but she has a strong will to live, despite her protestations to the contrary.

Sunday 17 April

Norman is just back from Korea, Formosa and distant parts of the East. He was persistent to know what I thought of the dreadful situation in Bosnia. 'I am frightfully busy. Would you mind reading the *News of the World* this morning. Don't you get it?' He said no, he was ashamed to be seen buying it. I said, 'Well ask my darling friend Sophie whether she would be kind enough to do me a favour, and you, by going out and buying one.'

Norman swears he is not engaged in any plotting. I said, 'You can't come to Italy if you do.' He thinks there is a mood arising in which people are saying it's better to stick to Major than have Heseltine or any alternative. Clarke, he feels and not just because he is jealous of him, is not up to the job of Chancellor.

On the off chance I rang Rupert's flat and he answered the telephone. I talked to him earnestly about fairness to Major in his papers and elsewhere.

I said, 'I am seeing him tonight. Have you got any different messages from the one I gave him last time?'

In an hour's time Rupert rang back.

A reshuffle he thinks would be a very good idea in the summer, to get rid of Hurd and to substitute the nice Hambro man as Tory Treasurer for somebody more able to get money out of one.

I said, 'What about Jeffrey Archer?' He thought that could be a good idea and the public would probably wear him as Chairman of the Tory Party.

Earlier Rupert had said that Major is such a miserable creature.

'He hasn't got a home life. His wife's never with him. She loathes 10 Downing Street and won't come up to London if she can avoid it.' I said, 'You mean he has got nobody to keep him warm?'

Rupert said, 'Maybe he's got somebody keeping him warm now. I hope so. I wouldn't blame him.'

A most extraordinary thing happened. My watch had somehow got slow and I arrived at Downing Street seven minutes late.

John said, 'I have got a call coming from Clinton at ten past seven.'

I thought, my God, how awful. Maybe he thinks I can't be bothered to come at the right time any more because he is so much on the skids.

We discussed at length the possibility of a challenge. I said, 'I can't believe it would happen.' He said, 'I think it very well may. We will do badly in the local elections and the European elections and I think there will be a challenge.' I said, 'That's crazy. Even Norman thinks you should stay now. He thinks there could be a reconciliation,' and I laughed. He said, 'I see.'

We discussed Clarke's failings and Heseltine's growing support, as he thinks, among the Tory MPs.

I said, 'He'd split the whole party. Margaret doesn't want him and she wants you to stay. She keeps telling me you've been abominably treated by the press.' 'I wish you could get her to say that publicly but I can't ask her to say it myself.'

We talked at some length about Rupert.

I said, 'Have you thought of inviting him to come to see you?' He said, 'I can't do that after all the attacks he's made on me.' I said, 'Supposing I suggest to him that he and you come to Cavendish Avenue and nobody need know that either of you have been there. It wouldn't look as though you had been having talks with Rupert and advising him and asking him to support you.' He said, 'It would be wonderful if you could arrange that.

'Thank God for you, Woodrow. You're the only person who supports me in the press, however black things look.' Then he thought there were one or two others who did – the *Express* newspapers do but they're not so important.

I told him all the things he had going for him, including the Lottery. I gave him quite a spiel on that, as far as I dared.

I also told him what a mess Howard had made after his speech at the Tote lunch.

At about a quarter past seven the Clinton call came through, but not before Major had shown me his brief for talking to Clinton (which he shouldn't have done) and how Clinton wanted to send more troops [to Bosnia] and all the rest of it.

Dear, oh dear. He really was down in the dumps, poor fellow.

I rang Rupert again.

'Can you be overheard?' He said no. I told him a lot of what I had said.

'I'll give you good notice and a number of dates and I'll fly back specially to have the dinner.'

Bob came into the conversation with John Major.

'What a marvellous cricketer he is, and a splendid fellow. He knows more about cricket than anyone alive.' (I thought to myself, I can't ask you any more, but for heaven's sake, can't you give him a knighthood? You've given one to lesser people in sport and he'll be dead soon. I should think the birthday honours in June will be about the last chance.)

Monday 18 to Sunday 24 April
This period is a jumble.

I had much difficulty persuading [the Enterprise representatives] that what I had to do was to induce a cosy atmosphere at the presentation with the Director General of OFLOT on Tuesday 19th April.

It worked brilliantly. I had made our team rehearse repeatedly like acting in a play so they would feel a team and it would show through.

The others had brought silly, slick slides and boring presentations of a stilted formal kind.

On Saturday I went to Sandown.

Queen Elizabeth the Queen Mother was talking to Evelyn de Rothschild who was furious that it was his last day as Chairman of United Racecourses.

She beckoned to me to come. So we sat side by side.

When we had finished, along comes Evelyn, 'Is Woodrow under control, Ma'am?' I said, 'She is the only person in the country I am frightened of.'

Monday 25 April
In the evening it was to Claridge's, wearing a black tie, for a dinner given by Prince Alexander, who calls himself Crown Prince of Yugoslavia. I quite like him but he is on a hopeless wicket, though he says he will not try to go back there again until there is an auspicious moment.

I had a row with the Danish Ambassador.[2] Very embarrassing. I said that England was more important to the Common Market than the other way round. He said, 'Nonsense, nonsense. You'd be broke without it.'

I also said our Foreign Office was no bloody good.

He said, 'Your Foreign Office is absolutely magnificent, the best in the world.'

I then had to say the names of all the Danes I could remember I admired, and how wonderful they were, their writers, and their beautiful, brilliant actresses like Ingrid Bergman.[3] I think he was slightly mollified but it had almost come to fisticuffs.

Wednesday 27 April
In the afternoon I went down to the Lords and actually spoke against the government on the privatization of coal bill. They are going to abandon the consumers' council, the silly asses.

In the Division Lobby a number of Labour peers said, 'Goodness, how awful to be in the same Lobby as you.' I said, 'No. It means you are beginning to learn at last.' The last bit I said particularly to quite a nice fellow called McIntosh, who is Deputy Leader of the Opposition and was put out of his job as Leader of the old GLC by a coup organized by Ken Livingstone.[4]

Friday 29 April
Arnold rang up in a very excitable state while I was writing my article. 'We have got to abandon the whole of this bid for the Lottery. I see that Archer is to be put in charge of it.'

---

2. HE Rudolph Thorning-Petersen was Danish Ambassador at this time.
3. Unfortunately, Bergman (1915–82) was Swedish, which could not have helped WW's attempt to conciliate the Ambassador.
4. Andrew McIntosh, member of the Greater London Council (GLC), 1973–83, Leader of the Labour Opposition on the GLC, 1980–1, life peer 1982; Livingstone was Labour Leader, GLC, 1981–6 (from when Labour won control of the GLC until it was abolished); Labour MP since 1987, elected Mayor of London, 2000.

I said, 'He's not going to be in charge of it. In any case it wouldn't matter. He can't put his hands in the till. The money goes direct from us to the Director General of OFLOT and then is handed over to a commission which has already been appointed and he has no say in how the money is to be spent. Don't be so fanciful, Arnold.'

I told Arnold, 'He is only going to be in charge of sport if he's in charge of anything, according to that story. I am not even sure that Major would risk that.'

Sunday 1 May

We had a jolly evening yesterday, playing bridge at Countess Karolyi's.[1]

We saw the literature about condoms from the National Health Service. It is idiotic: an imitation penis was sent and also various types of condom, the very thick ones being for buggers, with instructions how to put them on. Boritshka said she has a very uptight nurse of about seventy who works for her and when she saw this she said, 'Good heavens. They'd be lucky if they saw a penis like that (meaning standing so firm and erect).'

Monday 2 May

In the morning John Major rings from Huntingdon.[2] 'How are we to play the meeting with Rupert? Is it an informal social occasion?' I said, 'It's completely informal. I propose to try to keep it on a friendly basis but you are to say exactly what you like to him and address all the things you feel strongly about, the behaviour of News International and so forth.'

The Prime Minister wishes to arrive after Rupert, on my advice, it being the proper thing for a Prime Minister to do. Obviously Major is very nervous. He is in a ruffled state, poor fellow. He says the returns from the canvassing for the local elections are appalling: he is going to do extremely badly. I said, 'Don't worry. All will be well.' I have to say that repeatedly to him now.

I decided to give them a very good Veuve Clicquot 1983 followed by the Pavillon Blanc of Margaux 1989, followed by the Margaux itself, Château Margaux 1976 which was a pretty good year.

Rupert rings from his flat as soon as he gets there during the afternoon. 'What should I wear? Is it a formal occasion?' I said, 'No. Wear anything you like. We're in the country here. Do say what you want to. Don't just grumble to me. Grumble to him quite frankly.'

---

1. Countess Boritshka Karolyi is an NHS GP.
2. Huntingdon was his constituency.

Meanwhile, the telephoning round the garden gets quite frantic. The gate has to be left open so the two cars which take the Prime Minister and his security people behind him can get through into the garden without him being observed.

Rupert, I don't know if deliberately or not, decides to arrive a little bit later, so actually the Prime Minister arrives first, walks through the garden to the front door, passing Maria picking various herbs from the herb garden. She instantly recognizes him, having been told she is not to know who is going to be present.

Major was greatly interested in the drawing-room with the view of the Lord's Nursery Ground.

At last Rupert arrived, about five minutes after the Prime Minister. We start drinking champagne. I wanted to get them on a friendly basis before we actually begin dinner. We talked about things like the snooker match just going on, on the television in the little room behind the drawing-room, in which the unfortunate White who repeatedly had nearly won the world title looked like losing it again, against Stephen Hendry.

Then dinner was announced. I said, 'Now let's get down to the nitty-gritty. It is absolutely appalling, Rupert, the way your newspapers invent "facts", or misrepresent them. For example the instance at the time of the Sheffield Chamber of Commerce dinner when the Prime Minister was depicted as hanging his head in dejection and despair when he was really roaring with laughter at a joke being made by one of the speakers.'

John said only half joking, 'I am having such a wretched time I feel like getting drunk,' and helped himself liberally.

He made it clear to Rupert that he is down in the dumps – he went a little too far on that, perhaps, I am not sure; it probably makes Rupert pleased. He said he was very angry with Portillo, who should have been conducting the campaign in London, instead of which he starts talking about things which have nothing to do with it like the single currency. That starts an idiotic row with Rupert saying Portillo is right.

John said, 'My position is this. I have got only a majority of fifteen.' I said, 'I thought you had the Irish Unionists, giving you twenty-five.' He said, 'Yes, but I can only call on them in a confidence vote, not on anything else. I have got some forty to fifty ultra-Europeans who want to have a federal government. I have got twenty to thirty passionately anti-European fanatics. The rest are in the middle. They don't know which way they're going except they vaguely think Europe will be all right if we can resist all the restraints Delors and Brussels try to put on us.' He said he thought there would be a leadership election, a challenge in the autumn.

He told us how well he had got on last week with Kohl.[3]

Kohl is in favour of a European parliament and a sort of political union because he is terrified his own people will go overboard, particularly now that they have got neo-Nazis. But he doesn't want to give any further powers to Europe at all.

At about this point Elizabeth came in saying there was an urgent call from Number 10 for the Prime Minister.

He came back and said, 'That was Nelson Mandela. He was ringing up, now that his victory is assured, to thank me and Britain for all the support we have given in getting rid of apartheid and getting to this particular situation.'[4] He was talking to him for about fifteen minutes.

Meanwhile, we were having lots of laughter and jolly jokes. Rupert was drinking very much more than I have seen him do for a very long time.

I was getting them friendlier and friendlier. We talked about Andrew Neil. I said, 'He's the fellow who went utterly against you, Rupert, in backing Heseltine against Margaret. His last editorial may have been the tip-over factor.' John said, 'She would have won that if she had somebody properly organizing her campaign instead of her Chief Whip, Renton, and hadn't gone to Paris at that moment.'

Rupert was fairly silent on the subject of Andrew Neil. I said, 'I know you've got these rules about not being able to order the editors of the *Times* and the *Sunday Times* about. But you can easily tell the *Sun* what to do. For goodness' sake tell them to come out before the local elections (which are on May 5th) and say, "Even if you don't like Major, you have got to vote Tory. Otherwise you will get a calamity in which the Lib Dems and the Socialists may be able to form a coalition after the next general election." '

Rupert was starting to complain about Brussels. I said, 'You know what John is doing, do you? He is resisting completely all the attempts from Brussels – particularly instigated by the National Union of Journalists here, and there is a great green paper about it from Brussels

---

3. Helmut Kohl, German Chancellor, 1982–98.
4. Mandela and the African National Congress had won South Africa's first fully democratic general election.

– to say there should be no cross media ownership so anybody who owned a television channel as well as newspapers would have to give up one or the other. Also, he is resisting the attempt to make your television stations, and all television stations in England, have this ridiculous quota which they must maintain of films made in Europe.'

I think it had some effect on Rupert, showing him which side his bread ought to be buttered.

Rupert said there should be a reshuffle. John said, 'That is so. But if I do it now, people will say I am only doing it because it's just before the [local] elections and if I do it immediately afterwards, they will say I am only doing it because I have done badly in them. So I have to choose the time carefully.'

John started asking us who we thought should be the new Chairman of the Tory Party.

He has got a candidate called Jeremy Hanley, son of the comedian of wartime fame.[5] I said, 'Has he got a round face? You need one with a round face.' He said, 'Yes he has, and he's very tall and he's very amusing.'

We talked about Jeffrey Archer. Rupert said, 'Don't have him.' Major said, 'I'm afraid I can't. There's too much risk.' We went very frankly through the rest of the Cabinet and he gave his views on each of them, no good, or quite good, or fairly good. He thinks very highly of Stephen Dorrell [Financial Secretary to the Treasury]. He doesn't trust Hunt, the Employment Secretary, really, because he is a friend of Heseltine's.

John then said, 'What would you do?' to Rupert. 'Be much tougher about Europe.' 'Yes, but I have got my difficulties in doing that. I can't say we're going to come out of Europe or Brussels. It's not the time for it. I'd split my party doing it and my small majority would be done for.'

Rupert admitted he cut the price [of the *Times*] down as low as it is in order to ruin the *Daily Telegraph* (though that hardly matters now politically, in the sense that they are both against Major).

Rupert said he didn't agree always with Neil. I said, 'No. He just makes money for you. That's why you keep him there.' He enjoyed

---

5. Conservative MP, 1983–97; Parliamentary Under Secretary of State, Northern Ireland, 1990–3; Minister of State for the Armed Forces, 1993–4; knight 1997; his father was Jimmy Hanley and his mother, Dinah Sheridan, actress.

my saying that, laughing at his own cynicism to which I have no objection.

Then he made some complaints about Sarah Hogg and the secretariat of the Cabinet saying it wasn't strong enough, to which John agreed in part, but not about Sarah Hogg.

We discussed who our candidates should be, if at all, for the next EC presidency. John said at one time he thought it could be Leon Brittan, but he is now far more *communitaire* than anybody. Then he mentioned the Dutchman [Ruud Lubbers], saying he wasn't too bad at all.

I said to John Major, 'You know we have got a couple of fascinating things coming along to cheer people up. We've got the Eurotunnel and then the Lottery.' Rupert said, 'Good heavens. Yes, of course, that dreadful Lottery. It offends my Presbyterian instincts.'

I said, 'It doesn't seem to offend Rupert's Presbyterian instincts to parade all the sex lives of anybody who may be prominent.' However, we all agreed that it didn't matter about the silly things Major's MPs and Ministers had been doing.

I said, 'What about that fellow Norris,[6] though?' to Major. 'He's got three mistresses at once. Probably the country admire him for it.'

Major was complaining about Richard Ryder. He wasn't even sure of his loyalty. He said, 'It's the job of the Chief Whip and I was very nearly a Chief Whip myself – I was in the Whips' office – to dispose of these people for the Prime Minister of the day, telling them they must resign at once or he would just have them booted out.' But Ryder was urging that Yeo should be given more rope and Mellor should be given more rope, which was all wrong. Major said he was hamstrung by not having a hatchet man as the Chief Whip.

Having arrived at ten to eight, it wasn't until half past eleven that the Prime Minister said, 'I must go now because I have got some work to do,' but he didn't really want to go. He almost pleaded with Rupert to give him a fair wind.

When John had gone Rupert said, 'He's a nice guy, but is he strong enough?'

Before he left he said, 'Something will happen tomorrow which will please you.'

---

6. Steven Norris, Conservative MP, 1983–97; Under Secretary of State, Transport, 1992–6; unsuccessful Conservative candidate for Mayor of London, 2000; the alleged number of his mistresses later increased to five.

Tuesday 3 May

Soon the PM was on to me. I was trying to get to the Tote for our Board meeting. 'How did it go?' he asked.

He thought he had made one mistake when he asked Rupert, 'What would you advise me to do on such and such?' He should have said, 'This is what I'm going to do.' He's so nervous, poor chap. He really is in the dumps.

Rupert rang later in the day to say Andrew Neil was going to America but it was not really anything to do with our conversation. But I knew very well it was to do with what I had been saying to him before. He said the *Sun* would come out to say vote Tory and he wasn't backing Heseltine any more. He said to me, 'I am doing this, Woodrow, because you are convinced Major will win through and you are usually right about these things.'

I duly rang the Prime Minister who had some important meeting at Downing Street. He came out to talk to me. I told him, 'We are getting some movement.' He said, 'God bless you, Woodrow. Thank you very much. It is absolutely marvellous what you are doing.'

Rupert rang me twice from the car on his way to Heathrow. I do get the impression that I have got him on board, at least nearly on board, at last, and that he is going to start coming out in favour of Major.

It has been the most exciting two days of my life in a way, getting these people together and trying to influence the course of events in the way I want them to go, which is to keep Major there.

Wednesday 4 May

The *Sun* did come up with a decent leader after all, but not with something all over the front page as I had hoped.

I am on entirely the old footing I was on with Margaret now with John. When I said, 'Do you mind if I ring you up from time to time?', he said, 'No, please do any time you like. I value it a great deal.' He now rings me up without my prompting him. He knows I shall be absolutely loyal to him, which is perfectly true because I think it is monstrous what they are doing to him and he happens to be the ablest Prime Minister in sight.

I told him yesterday that Rupert had said on the telephone that about eight Cabinet ministers had been ringing editors saying that they were no longer backing him, John, but were backing Heseltine or somebody else, and that even Jeffrey Archer had rung newspaper editors saying that of course he was completely loyal to the Prime Minister but he wasn't sure now that he could be saved. I said I'd be very surprised if Jeffrey did say that and I hope he didn't, to which poor old Major said, 'It's par for the course,' indicating that he thinks even Jeffrey Archer may be a fair weather friend.

He really is in a very crumpled state. I have got to stiffen him all the time.

I sent to Downing Street a selection of very pro-Major letters I had after my *Times* article, saying how disgusted they were with the disloyalty of the Cabinet, Tory MPs, the *Times* and the Tory press.

Meanwhile, preparations continue at No. 19 for the great party which Petronella is having for her birthday tomorrow, the day before her birthday.

We are going to have Lascombes 1967, which is in the Margaux Commune, next door to Margaux. It is a marvellous wine, and a very good year 1967 – the year Petronella was conceived marking the true date of her entry into the world. (1968, the year she was born, was not a good year.) There will be dancing and a marquee which is being put up this afternoon. It looks pretty and jolly. Everything is getting very amusing and I am feeling quite light-hearted as well as being rather tired. I love that girl Petronella – she has a touch of genius and its waywardness.

The Garrick, that curious place, to have lunch with Robin Day. He was very down in the melancholy dumps. He didn't feel well. He wasn't drinking anything. He has got no job and he has two sons to educate and a divorced wife to pay maintenance to.

He thought he had been wrong to have abandoned *Question Time* but he had got bored with it. Now he is out and it is very difficult for him to get back into TV.

I left Robin feeling sad. Poor old boy.

He wants Michael Heseltine to be leader of the Tory Party. Mad.

Thursday 5 May
I popped along to the Lords after lunch for Questions. I asked a supplementary about cross-media ownership, television stations and newspapers.

I had to order more champagne and pink champagne and special Heidsieck Monopole which Verushka says is better than the ordinary one I get from the Majestic wine store. (It isn't really though she thinks it is.)

All was cooked in the house, the salmon to start with and also the pudding, except the middle course which they brought from a restaurant which Netta and Verushka go to and which is very fashionable.

The band was marvellous, the Spring Beans. They wore shovel hats, dark. They looked real desperadoes, like relations of Al Capone.

I had Rosita Marlborough on my right and darling little Annabel Astor on my left. She told me her mother had kept masses of diaries. I said, 'She wrote well. Are you going to publish them?' She said, 'No, certainly not while anybody is alive. She wrote a great deal about you. She adored you.'

She (Pandora) was the most beautiful girl of her time.

Annabel's daughter was also there so we had two generations of Pandora.

Rosita was looking very pretty, extraordinarily so. She'd sent some pictures for the Royal Academy Summer Exhibition and was anxious to see if they would hang them. I said, 'You ought to do it under quite a different name.' She said, 'Why?' 'Because if you send them in as the Duchess of Marlborough it will go against you.'

She had already put Rosita Marlborough on them. 'It's been my name for the last twenty-five years and I am not going to start putting myself anonymously.'

Sonny himself enjoyed it all enormously, dancing with Petronella, dancing with all the pretty girls and there were a lot of them.

Norman Lamont came and Peter Lilley was there. Much attention was paid to the little TV room through the drawing-room arch, as local election results began to come.

Norman keeps protesting he has no dealings at all with the ghastly Heseltine but I am not at all sure he is telling me the truth now.

The Allsopps were there, the divinely beautiful Fiona Allsopp.

Their daughter came, too, a dream of plump lusciousness.

Petronella sang beautifully, which I was very pleased about. She sang all my favourite songs, including 'Lili Marlene', to great applause.

Micky Suffolk was beside himself with joy and excitement.

Frank Johnson was drunk by the end. Peter Mackay was there who writes various things in the newspapers. He said how much he admires what I write and I returned the compliment, naturally, though I don't really at all. Then he said, 'I suppose you will be loyal to this Prime Minister until there is a new one and then you will be loyal to him.'

That is simply untrue.

All greatly admired the wine and thought the food was very good, including the middle course. It had some special sauce on it and it did taste a great deal better than it looked on arrival. But as it was £11.50 a head and £700 altogether in cost including VAT, it jolly well ought to have been.

The police came at about half past twelve and said we were making too much noise. The band did then reduce the noise a little bit but not too much.

Friday 6 May
I slept until gone nine o'clock.

Verushka had done it all beautifully. No one can take away from her the great gift she has for organizing a party: the food and the flowers and the seating arrangements, all most magnificently done.

The Weinstocks met Simon and Laura on the way out. Arnold said, 'What are you doing here so late? You've got a job to do tomorrow,' rather severely to his son.

Simon is getting more at ease than he used to be and Laura improves all the time.

Earlier in the evening Pericles had rung Petronella.

He is a sweet boy, Pericles. He never forgets things like that.

Sunday 8 May
I spoke to John Major when he came back from Huntingdon. I said I thought the local election results had improved his position. He said he thought it was still pretty dreadful.

We discussed a new Leader for the Lords because we both feel that Wakeham is useless. He doesn't want to make any new peers from the Commons for the purpose. I said, 'I have been thinking about Hesketh.'

I told him I had spoken to Margaret. 'She felt it would be unwise to have a private meeting with you at the moment in case it got out – it might do you harm. I am sure we can count on her at the right moment. I will try it again later, a private talk.'

To my surprise he said Rupert had not kept secret our dinner and conversation on the previous Monday. He had leaked it. He said, 'Alistair Burnet (who is a member of the *Times* Board) told me he talked about it at the *Times* Board meeting.'

I said, 'It may not be too bad actually because it will help get across to them that the line is changing. But it would be fatal if it gets out widely.'

John Heaton believes we must be the last two in the race for the

Lottery. BT have been pressing him so hard, and our Autotote experts from America, to make sure all the interfacing of the different systems worked.

Monday 9 May

I had my usual argument with the *Times*. Peter Stothard rang up and wanted me to take out various unfriendly references to the *Times*.

He also objected to my saying that William Rees-Mogg was part of the *Times*'s campaign against Major. He said there wasn't such a campaign.

After a lot of haggling and mucking about, in which I think at one moment the article almost never got printed at all, it was printed, slightly mutilated, but most came over including the attack on Sir John Nott, the incompetent Defence Minister at the time of the Falklands War who Margaret was delighted to see the back of. He had written in the *Sunday Telegraph* that it would be a good thing if the Tories lost the next election so then they would refresh themselves.

The man is a real idiot. Once Labour got in with the support of the Lib Dems to keep them in office, they would benefit from the prosperity that Major's policies have created which would last until the next election (although the underlying damage would be great to the Thatcherite revolution) and they would win a second election. No government since the war has ever failed to have at least two bites of the cherry, except for Ted Heath's government in 1970.

When I told John that I was attacking Nott he was very amused. He said, 'He's the only one of that Cabinet who hasn't been given a peerage. That's why he is so cross.' I said, 'I should keep it that way if I were you.' He laughed and said, 'I will.'

He was still depressed. I said, 'You have nothing to worry about. The situation's getting better. You must fight on. I remember Hugh Gaitskell, my dear friend whom I loved. He said at the time of that nuclear disarmament stuff in the Labour Party, "I shall fight and fight again to save the party I love," and he did. And you have got to do that. It is your duty to the country. It's coming our way.'

Tuesday 10 May

I arrived late for the great Lord Stevens of United Newspapers annual lunch at the Savoy. Blow me down, I was sitting on the same table as John Nott.

Eventually he said, 'I hear you wrote something rude about me this

morning in the *Times*.' I said, 'Yes, indeed I did. Didn't you read it?'
'No, I only just heard about it,' but he obviously had read it.

Nott said I was sucking up to Major because he was the Prime
Minister. I said, 'In which case you don't read my articles, because you
didn't see the serious attacks I made on Major when he sacked Norman
Lamont and compared him with Macavity the Cat, which wasn't
sucking up to a Prime Minister, was it?'

Wednesday 11 May
Had lunch with Ian Chapman and Diana Rawstron, sandwiches and
a bottle of champagne at the Waldorf Astoria.

Ian wants me to go to Macmillan [to publish my memoirs] where
his son, thirty-nine years old and now Managing Director is working.[7] There is a great deal in favour: it is a long-established firm
and would take what I have done for my diary seriously and not
just skim the froth off and then forget it. There is a mass of
material here. I told them how I had thought of Andrew Roberts as
the editor but discarded him as so rich that he wouldn't bother to get
it out quickly.

'Of course, you know this conversation will be going into the
manuscript.' Ian said, 'That's something we have to live with. We
mustn't stop your saying what you want to.' Diana also laughed. She
was looking rather pretty.

There was great excitement today in the racing world. By a very
cunning device James Paice,[8] whom I do not much care for and who
is Chairman of the All Party Racing Group, won the vote for an
amendment in the deregulation Bill about betting on Sundays on and
off the course.

Thursday 12 May
In the morning was announced the death of John Smith from a heart
attack. I wasn't surprised. He was terribly overweight, as I told
him.

My first thoughts were that this absolutely settles the Tory leader-

---

7. Ian Chapman junior was Managing Director at Macmillan until December 1999
   when he moved to Simon & Schuster. WW made the decision to go to Macmillan
   later that month.
8. Conservative MP since 1987.

ship question. No one could vote for sixty-one-year-old Heseltine now with his dodgy heart. He might immediately blow up. Also, why have the Tory Party divided when the Labour Party is entering what usually is a somewhat fractious leadership contest?

John Smith would never have won the general election, though it was being claimed by all that he was the next Prime Minister and was just about to step into Number 10, etc. etc.

Parliament decided only to meet for tributes in both houses.

John Major made an excellent little valedictory speech. He got the mood absolutely right.

He said he hoped we could give up party bickering because it had gone too far. We were using all these dreadful, personal insults to each other. Everybody said, 'Hear, hear,' in the Commons. The whole nation did, maybe.

Went to The Other Club where there was a good deal of talk about John Smith but not so solemn or religious.

Talking about Smith's successors, it was the first time I heard that Gordon Brown has got a bad eye which he can't see out of properly – not that that would make any difference. His eyesight was damaged playing rugger.

Arnold would not agree that Heseltine was now finished because of his heart attack if not for any other reason. Anyway, Blair, who seems the most likely candidate, is only forty-one so Heseltine would be no good against him.

John Mortimer had been asked to make a tribute to John Smith, a member of the Club. He did, with considerable grace and charm. He feels Labour has lost a lot by losing John Smith but not as much as when Kinnock went.

John Mortimer said at seventy-one he didn't have an opportunity with attractive girls any more, or only very few. People forget that men go on liking sex. I said, 'Women do, too, to a very advanced age, in fact so long as they are alive, so far as I can see.'

Friday 13 May

Already little gangs of rivals are emerging in the Labour Party. Tony Blair, and Gordon Brown who says he doesn't think he is going to stand down, and Robin Cook would like to have a go, and so would the man of the people, John Prescott.

I wrote my *News of the World* article with a bit extra about my D-

Day letters.[9] We have had about six hundred. Many of them are very touching.

I am so used to getting about twenty to twenty-five per cent of letters saying how awful I am, how they hate me and why don't they have my column stopped. This volume from a much wider section made it very clear that I am actually esteemed by a lot who love my column.

They also made me feel very proud to be British because they were from people who, even if they hadn't been in Normandy or in the services, felt enormous pride in their country and what we did to save the world.

Sunday 15 May

I have been beginning to lose confidence in myself, even in my [repeating] 'Every day I am getting better and better and so are my finances,' followed by 'The Tote will get the Lottery,' which is uppermost in my mind. Often there are messages that such and such a person I care about should be looked after and I repeat the name so he or she will be all right.[10]

In the Sunday papers there was reference to the Lottery in the *Times* Business Section. We weren't even mentioned.

Monday 16 May

Tea at the Lords for Tish Newland.[11] I hadn't seen her for two or three years. She looks a trifle fatter. 'I am sure you would like to see, as a good Communist, the warrant for the execution of Charles I.' So off we pottered to the Royal Gallery.

We are now going to get two-thirds of the money [for the Library] but I must send her £100 to be one of the contributors.

---

9. In response to his article on the forthcoming fiftieth anniversary of D-Day.

10. WW was following the Coué system, believing that repeating his hopes helped to determine events. Emile Coué (1857–1921), a French psychologist, developed a system of psychotherapy by autosuggestion, usually of an optimistic nature. Among his followers was the writer Arthur Koestler who scratched on the wall of his prison in the Spanish civil war, 'Every day in every way, things are getting better and better.'

11. WW had struck up a friendship with Tish Newland, librarian of the Marx Memorial Library in Clerkenwell, through his efforts to obtain funds for the restoration of the building which contains a mural painted by Jack Huntingdon; see Vol. 2, pp. 488–9, 615.

Then I went to Sonia Sinclair's party.

There was one good egg there, Simon Jenkins. I said, 'You and I write the only sensible columns in the *Times*.'

The *Times* ought to be more serious but it's doing well. Of course it is a livelier paper and the price is so cheap. In some respects Peter Stothard isn't a bad editor for that kind of downmarket stuff.

I was told by someone that Kelvin MacKenzie has now got or is getting the ghastly Richard Littlejohn from the *Sun* to do a special programme on Sky attacking politicians and anybody that Kelvin and he don't like, really biased programmes, a prejudice show run by Littlejohn. He also puts pressure on the Sky TV News to be more anti-Major.

Tuesday 17 May
A party at Pratt's.

Along came a lady with a bright dress, red and blue checks. A nice outfit. She had blonde hair. Andrew [Devonshire] introduced me to her.

She was Valerie Eliot, second wife of T. S. Eliot. She worked for him as his secretary for eight years before he dared to propose to her, thinking she was so formal, calling him Mr Eliot all the time.

The second Mrs Eliot is sixty-seven but looked much younger.

She told me how *Cats* had come to be turned into a musical. I said, 'Wouldn't he have been surprised?' She said, 'He would have been utterly amazed.' She must be very rich, that lady now.

Then along came Margaret Anne Du Cane.[12] She moaned that we hadn't seen her for a long time, we hadn't been in communication. I said, 'We must rectify that. You're looking as young as ever.' She said, 'Yes, that's a face lift. It does you no end of good.'

Debo Devonshire was not there.[13] She hardly every comes to London and she certainly wouldn't go to Pratt's. She is now writing an immensely tripish column in the *Telegraph*.

Also came to sit in our little circle the Librarian at The London

12. Margaret Anne, née Du Cane, interior designer, m (1979) 2nd Viscount Stuart of Findhorn.
13. Née Mitford, writer, m (1941) Andrew Cavendish, now Duke of Devonshire.*

Library.[14] When Andrew wasn't there, he explained how generous Andrew had been to The London Library, making possible all kinds of additions and continuation.

The crowd at Pratt's wasn't as philistine as it usually is.

When I went, there was Andrew standing in the rain seeing some-body off with his exquisite politeness. Now that he doesn't drink he is altogether different and back to himself, as I used to know him. When I got back I said to Verushka, 'Maybe Debo was right when she asked us to leave Chatsworth on that occasion because he was so drunk and we stood by him.'[15]

Wednesday 18 May
Sarah Hogg comes to lunch. She is carelessly dressed, frumpish, dark with a round face. I can see bits of her father and mother in her but she is better looking than either of them.

A young woman (she is forty-eight) who is sure of herself, almost, though there are faint wisps of uncertainty in the background.

I gave her some of the Tursan wine, possibly the best white wine in the world, and we had Château Léoville-Las-Cases 1937.

We talked of how to help John Major. She is his closest adviser. I said he should read the *Sun* editorial which clearly had been dictated by Rupert after the local elections. She read it seriously, even the bit where it said Sarah Hogg should be [got] rid of. She said she is accustomed to that.

It's pointless to change advisers. The error, if any, is in the person who appoints them. Throughout history advisers have been blamed for the failures of kings and prime ministers and attempts are made to dislodge favourites. Whether it is the king or the prime minister who chooses them and then removes them, you get the same again.

After she had gone I decided to ring Rupert. I traced him to his motorcar in Los Angeles.

'What have I done now?' That was Rupert's plaintive cry like a naughty schoolboy's, on hearing my voice on his car telephone. I laughed. 'You've done nothing. I'm very grateful to you for altering the tone of the *Sun*.' I told him that what was worrying me was his

---

14. Alan Bell, Librarian, The London Library, since 1993; the Duke of Devonshire is a vice-president of The London Library, a private lending library in St James's Square, founded in the nineteenth century and much used by writers.

15. See Vol. 1, pp. 467–9, for this episode.

own position. I had said on May 5th in the Lords, when there was a brief question and answer on cross media ownership, that Sky News was the most impartial of them all and I got general agreement for that. 'But now I am told that Kelvin MacKenzie is trying to slant the news against John Major.'

Rupert was alarmed. He said, 'I'll deal with this at once.'

There was a dinner for Charles Wintour at the Soho Soho restaurant.

It was Charles's 77th birthday.

We sat at the top table with Charles, as did Max Hastings.

I sat next to Vivien Duffield whom I like. She understands the Jewish religion and believes there is no afterlife but that one ought to try to behave well and do good because it is the right thing to do. She certainly has done much good with charities and all these gifts to the Tate Gallery and so forth. She has not been a flibberty-gibbet with her vast millions, though she is quite entitled to spend it on herself, taking people on liners in the Mediterranean and all that kind of lark.

Jocelyn Stevens and I discussed the Marx Memorial Library. There was laughter at the table – Jocelyn and I were supporting the Communist Party, which is true, through English Heritage which Jocelyn is responsible for.

Max Hastings was quite funny reading out memos he had years and years ago from Charles. For example, that he was the fifth reporter who wanted to be sent to Vietnam and he was the least qualified of the five.[16]

Charles was a very good editor, severe with his staff but often with a twinkle in his eye and a kind of Mr Chips, though tougher.

Thursday 19 May

Spoke to John Major at two minutes past eight. I told him about my conversation with Rupert who will deal with the Sky News situation.

John Heaton had a long meeting with BT today about the nature of the contract which they are very anxious to settle. Now he gets the impression that we are one of three they are doing this with, which is rather worrying.

We have been told the announcement of the winner will be made on May 25th and there will be no previous notification. I looked, as I always do, in the Patrick Walker astrology pieces in the *Evening Stan-*

---

16. Max Hastings told this story again at Charles Wintour's memorial service in 1999.

dard tonight and the forecast for both John and myself was about as bad as it could be. Is the bid for the Lottery doomed?

Saturday 21 May
In the evening I left a message for John Major to ring me up. He was at a meeting when I rang. He never rang back. I thought maybe it was because he didn't want to get involved in any question about the Lottery. So I think perhaps we haven't got it.

Tuesday 24 May
When I rang Arnold to tell him we were all going to come to sit at GEC tomorrow, he didn't say anything. He was whistling a tune. I said, 'What on earth are you doing? What's that?' 'The funeral march,' he said. 'That's for your bid tomorrow.'

The whole thing is wildly agitating.

Wednesday 25 May
It was difficult to concentrate on much. I hadn't slept a great deal but I was able to get quite a few things done as ten o'clock approached. At five to ten we were told by fax that we hadn't got the Lottery. I was utterly surprised and shocked. It had been given to GTech, the lottery firm from America.[17] All that stuff about absolute integrity and getting everybody to sign sworn statements about bogies in their pasts was clearly a joke.

In the letter he wrote to us he had to admit that ours had been a very good bid and he was attracted by our profit-sharing scheme but he had taken the overall higher percentage offered by GTech, even though it could have been exceeded by our profit-sharing system.

I was distressed. It was the one last big thing I hoped to do before I die, to secure the National Lottery to help racing as the betting shops and the levy for racing decline against the Lottery and the government eventually decides on the end to the levy in any case. Now I fear I shall be blamed by racing as being too old and too inefficient and having kept too low a profile over our Lottery bid. But it wouldn't have made any difference, whatever we had done. Obviously GTech have moled their way through.

Knowing how distressed I was, Arnold Weinstock very sweetly persuaded me to have lunch at GEC and drink champagne.

---

17. GTech was in the winning Camelot consortium.

Arnold foolishly said, 'I didn't think your friendship with Major would help.' Jim Prior[18] said, 'Good heavens, was he backing you for it?' I said, 'Good gracious me, no, of course he wasn't.' He said, 'I'm glad the government isn't as corrupt as all that, with the Prime Minister giving you a present in return for your help to him.'

I moped about fairly wretched. I was particularly sad for John Heaton who had worked his heart out, but at least I shall now have the benefit of him, I hope, still at the Tote.

Verushka went to Hungary. Petronella and I had dinner with Irwin and Cita Stelzer. Previously I went to see him with the tape from the Business News on the BBC on October 23rd last, when they had the piece about the GTech lobbyist bribing the Senator and the Senator admitting it. And the Senator had been sent to jail. That was in order to establish and get the lottery in California.

I also enclosed blank questionnaires about probity which were very lengthy and some correspondence on the subject with and from Peter Davis.

I said, 'You are not to tell Andrew Neil where it comes from because he might be put off and also give me, his enemy, away.'

The *Sunday Times* has already exposed some of GTech's antics.

I had brought pre-Castro cigars for Irwin and myself.

I asked Cita if she would like to taste the cigar. She said she wouldn't. I said, 'Put it in your mouth. It is wonderfully sensual. It must be just like kissing you.'

I said, 'I wish I could go off with you for the day looking at architecture, plus the sensuality of being with you, while Irwin's working.' He looked slightly glum. I said, 'I don't think Irwin would like that very much.' He said, 'No, I certainly wouldn't.' He takes a joke like that over seriously.

I thought about how shattered I was and all the failures in my life. I found it one utter disaster. Irwin said, 'How can you possibly say that? Only recently you were so great that you had the most powerful media man in the world and the most powerful man in Britain to a secret dinner with you at Cavendish Avenue.' I said, 'Heavens, how on earth do you know that? It was supposed to be a

---

18. James (Jim) Prior, chairman, GEC, 1984–98; Conservative politician; Lord President of the Council and Leader of the House of Commons, 1972–4, in the Heath government; then Secretary of State for Employment, 1979–81, for Northern Ireland, 1981–4, under Mrs Thatcher; life peer 1987.

dead secret,' to which he replied 'Rupert can't keep a secret. Didn't you know that?'

Thursday 26 May
Arnold very sweetly rang in the afternoon to ask me how I was. I said, 'I am making a sharp recovery now. We have decided to buy Coral.' He said, 'What a good idea.'

Friday 27 May
My article was not as good as I would have liked. I am too confused and tired, not sleeping and waking in the middle of the night with my brain rattling about over the Lottery.

Wednesday 1 June
The Derby.

I went into John Derby's box to see how he was.[1] The usual people were there, Drue Heinz and the lot. I talked to him briefly. I nearly said, 'You are looking much better than I thought you would,' because he is apparently dying of cancer

I remembered with sad nostalgia how he used to walk down the course to the paddock at the far end, and then Isabel and I would watch the horses coming in and make jokes and guesses about them. She distanced herself entirely from the party of the Queen which John Derby always accompanies. She never liked the Hanoverians and she particularly disliked Princess Margaret. Dear, wonderful Isabel with her quick, sharp wit and her flashing eyes, her elegance and beauty.

The snaky Stoker Hartington spoke to me. He said how sorry he was about the Lottery and how much he supported me. The more he says he supports me, the more I think he is really meaning to make an attack on me to try to get me out again.

Thursday 2 June
There was a party for Bernard Levin's two hundred thousandth article at 74 St James's Street, given by Peter Stothard, the editor of the *Times*. He welcomed me quite effusively. He said he was now very pro-Major and thought he was an extremely good man and should stay. I wonder how long that will last – probably only until Rupert decides to go back, if he does, on his promises to support Major.

Bernard is still not quite right, poor fellow. But he does seem to be able to give lectures and talks about his book. It is about Utopia and the various views upon it, and his views. It reads very well.[2]

---

1. 18th Earl of Derby (1918–94); m (1948) Isabel, née Milles-Lade (1920–90).
2. *A World Elsewhere.*

Monday 6 June

A dinner at Cavendish Avenue designed to please Peter George [of Ladbroke's]. I am trying to get him to come in with his fifteen hundred shops to join us in Tote Direct.

Tony Quinton and his wife came.

He has been not only President of Trinity, Oxford, but head of the British Library. He is quite young[3] and he has completely retired. I said, 'I think that's very bad of you. You have no right not to use your gifts as long as you are able to, for the benefit of others.' He took this quite well and Marcelle was delighted. But I don't think it will have the slightest effect on him.

As Micky Suffolk was coming, I got out some excellent Chassagne-Monrachet 1983, a lovely bottle of old champagne undated, and then I gave them 1968 Château Latour which was rated unexpectedly high in a blind tasting some years ago at Château Latour.

I hope my propaganda to Peter about how we are going to save racing together will have some effect. He said he didn't want to save racing – he didn't think it needed it. It has plenty of money. But he did want to save his business which has not been doing well in the betting shop area.

Wednesday 8 June

I went to the meeting of the television and radio All Party Committee because the BSkyB man, Ray Gallagher, was there. I did it to help defend BSkyB and Rupert against all these people who say he shouldn't be allowed to own newspapers and satellite television at the same time. Gallagher did very well. By the time he had finished everybody realized Rupert hasn't got a monopoly at all and anybody could set up satellite stations. He had paved the way for them.

In any case, Pearson are half owners of BSkyB and they own the *Financial Times* and a lot of provincial newspapers, too.

Continuing this endless round of dinner parties, we went to the Metcalfes.

Their idea of a dinner party is to collect a number of rich people with no particular brains and nothing to commend them except that they are rich. There was Kerry Packer, a sort of media man, a kind of rival of Rupert from Australia, who promoted one-day cricket and made everybody dress up in horrible clothes.

---

3. He was born in 1925.

The dreadful Carla Powell was there, whom I had to embrace and pretend to be pleased to see, which of course I was not. Charles, her husband, asked did I think Major would last if the Euro election result was bad. I said, 'Yes, certainly. Margaret's supporting him against a challenge.' He said, 'She's saying that now but only because she's frightened of Heseltine taking over. She's told me let's wait until next year.'

I was very hurt at this idea that she lies to me, which obviously she does. She is not entirely straight, Margaret, and clearly she wants to wait a year or so and then bring forward Portillo who would be a disaster.

Friday 10 June

I felt I had to ring John Major as I had not spoken to him for some time and he might think I was annoyed or upset about not getting the Lottery.

He said, 'If we do very badly [in the European elections], I may not be able to hold the position for myself. I think that although the economy is coming right, I am perceived very badly by the general public. For one thing they say I lied to them about tax increases; and two, because we opted out of the ERM and I had said we wouldn't leave it.'

I said, 'That's quite wrong. You're going to win the next election and I am going to fight like mad to see you do.'

This conversation lasted nearly half an hour.

Meanwhile, Ladbroke want an answer by June 24th as to whether we are prepared to give them shares, have them on the Tote Direct Board and give them the terms they want to buy the terminals and put them in their shops.

I got hold of Charles Darby before his Bass Board meeting (where he is the Director of Leisure) and again afterwards. Unfortunately, he is retiring. I wish he wasn't.

Finally he said, 'We had better not get Ladbroke on the Board yet, until we have cleared up all these shenanigans at Wigan and over the running of the computers at Tote Direct.'[4] I said, 'I agree with that.'

---

4. There had been a series of incidents when the computers had become overloaded and broken down.

Sunday 12 June
It was a sunny day and warm. But instead of being able to sit in the garden and sunbathe, work on this manuscript and things I like doing and need to do, we had to go on this dreary trip to Headley in Hampshire to Trottsford Farm for Eric Arnott. Verushka kept saying to me, 'If you don't go, you won't be at the head of his queue when you want your eyes examined.' I said, 'But is it worth it? He's a nice enough fellow, but gosh what a waste of a day.'

And indeed it proved so.

Lunch didn't start until half past two. It wasn't bad, though it was full of cream. They have no idea, medical people, of the terrible things they do to their hearts with all the fatty stuff they eat.

Petronella was a great success, as she usually is, men being drawn to her like bees, or maybe it's wasps, round the honey-pot.

Like an idiot I sat up until half past two waiting for the results of the famous Euro elections. The BBC anti-Major people were gloating with glee. They said, 'Great disasters for the Tories. They won't get more than one or two seats,' and so forth. Then they began to look fed up as Major seemed on course to get at least fifteen, which, compared with the prognostications of all the opinion polls, would be a great victory.[5]

Monday 13 June
Spoke to Major at five to nine and we talked for ten minutes.

Like every other human being, when he'd escaped from danger, he'd forgotten his terrors as the danger approached, namely of being more or less wiped out at the Euro elections.

I said, 'You're now absolutely safe. Even the *Sun* hasn't mentioned you unfavourably this morning in the leading article.' He said, 'Yes, but did you see that photograph on the front?'

Once again they were pulling out that photograph at the Chamber of Commerce when his head was slumped over the table because he was roaring with laughter at a joke which had been made. It was put on to the front page of the *Sun* again to show how dejected he was as a result of the Euro election. It's monstrous.

He is going to do a reshuffle before the end of July.

---

5. The Conservatives won 18 seats (32 in 1989), Labour 62 (45), Liberal Democrats 2 (0), SDP 2 (1).

Later in the day I rang Gus Fischer and told him about the picture in the *Sun*.

Then it was along to the Norman Lamont party. Norman is increasingly shifty when he sees me. He wasn't very amused when I said, 'Is Michael Heseltine here?'

Present was Arabella von Hofmannstahl.[6] She introduced her husband to me and we had a very jolly talk. I said, 'How's Piers (her first husband)? Do you see him at all?' She said, 'Yes. I've got two husbands now. They're both going off on a trip together at the end of this week on business in the Philippines or somewhere.' He is very good-looking, and her present husband isn't bad-looking.

To my astonishment I discovered Arabella's now fifty.

Her nose is very Jewish, disfiguring her otherwise pretty face. Of course her father was Jewish. His father, the great lyricist and poet, pretended not to be.[7]

Her mother, Liz, was perhaps the most beautiful woman of all. Pandora Clifford was lovely, but like a china doll with her blue eyes and fair hair. Her mother had classic features with strength behind them and she moved better.

Michael Howard I thought was unpleasant. We were talking about drugs. He said he didn't mind my disagreeing with him over something about which I was so patently and obviously wrong: 'It would be terrible to decriminalize them.' I said, 'Why? What's the point. You've got nowhere criminalizing them.' I don't think I like him very much.

Tuesday 14 June
Ascot.

We went to tea with the Queen after the fourth race.

As usual, I sat next to Queen Elizabeth the Queen Mother. I told her I had just put on a large bet, for me, at £500, that John Major would have the largest number of seats in the next Commons.

She seemed rather doubtful about Major, 'He seems so weak.' 'He's not at all. You wait and see.'

She is more frail now and she finds it difficult to walk, much more than she did before.

---

6. See 10 October 1992, p. 113, note 8, for her marriages.
7. Hugo von Hofmannstahl, Richard Strauss's librettist.

Then we talked about the various creeps in the Tory Party, members of parliament. Somebody said, 'What are you talking about?' She said, 'We've been saying unkind things about some people we know.' I said, 'Not so much unkind, Ma'am, as accurate.'

She wanted to go home because she hates the flat racing. She prefers the jumping over the fences and so forth. 'Not yet,' the Queen said to her.

When the Queen came back from seeing some horse of hers which was running in the last race, she came over and rather curtly said, 'Good-bye. It's very nice to see you.' I think she was wanting to finish and take her mother home.

Wednesday 15 June

Peter Jones had lunch [at Ascot] with his wife. He's the one who wants to get rid of me because he wants the BHB to take control of the Tote and thinks I am the main obstacle.

I explained to him that we nearly got the Lottery, how we were fighting back and were in the middle of very delicate negotiations with Ladbroke. I gave him some idea of how it was going and that pleased him, being taken into my confidence. But I can no longer trust him a yard.

Peter Lloyd, in charge of racing at the Home Office, came down with me to the control room and was duly impressed.

I said, 'We're fighting back against the Lottery as we didn't win it.'

Suddenly Prince and Princess Michael of Kent came dashing in.

Prince Michael kept saying how sorry he was to be no longer on the Tote Board and it was very funny that when he went out to the West Indies to stay in the Bahamas with the Governor of the place, it was Waddington, who had been Home Secretary. He said, 'I greatly embarrassed him by saying, "You were the person who fired me from the Tote. You sacked me." '

I thought to myself, it would have been doubly embarrassing if he, Prince Michael, had realized it was I who told Waddington we couldn't hang on to Prince Michael any longer because he had served his purpose and wasn't doing what I asked him to do properly.

Then she rushed off and locked herself into the betting area.

But she hadn't got an account number.

I said, 'Her Royal Highness can bet on anything she likes, not beyond £10,000.' Poor old Prince Michael shuddered and said, 'Let her have the credit she wants.' I don't know if she lost or won in the end, but I hope there won't be any default. It would be extremely embarrassing.

I said, 'Are you up in the Royal Box?' She said, 'Yes. It's terribly boring. It's much more fun down here. They never gamble and I get so bored.'

Thursday 16 June

To Ascot again, perhaps for the last time if I am not reappointed.

When we got back we had to go to dinner with Michael Howard. I was not looking forward to this. I would much prefer to have gone to The Other Club.

On my left was Mary Archer. We talked about what she had done for the distressed names at Lloyd's.[8]

She has fought immensely hard for these people because she says there is nothing worse than being in debt and saddled with it. I said, 'I know. I've been in debt once or twice.' She said, 'I know a great deal about it,' meaning [through] Jeffrey.

Afterwards I had a talk with Michael Howard about people who feel they have to take the law into their own hands and how appalling it all is.[9]

I thought I liked him rather better than before.

Saturday 18 June

Off to the Test at Lord's.

Bob is not looking or feeling all that well. However, he had staggered up the steps each day of the match.

We had long talks about his father and my father.

I told him how I discovered that my father, who was supposed to be very clever, had only got his pass degree at Oxford after four years. He was the idlest man alive.

'Not as idle as my father,' said Bob. He described how he died almost a pauper. Bob was due to have gone to Christ's Hospital but they couldn't even afford the fees there so he was sent to a local Birmingham school as a day boy. I said, 'If you had gone to a decent school, you'd have been on that 1928 tour of Australia, and you would also have been Captain of England much earlier and you would have

---

8. She was a member of the Council of Lloyd's, 1989–92.
9. WW wrote in the *News of the World* of 26 June about victims of crime being taken to court for using too much force defending themselves and their property.

made far more Test centuries.' He said that was quite true. Plum Warner[10] and the others were so snobbish that they thought anybody who hadn't been at a public school, a real one like Harrow or Marlborough or Eton or Winchester, wasn't really quite the right class.

Monday 20 June

In our Ascot room on Thursday Arnold had a very good conversation with the German Ambassador about something it seems they [GEC] are trying to get through with Siemens and our government doesn't really help. I said, 'The German Ambassador, I am sure, will help Siemens if he can.' He politely agreed though he said he couldn't interfere in these matters. But he could put the case to his government. Neither government is doing enough to help the joint German–British venture which could get a huge export order and is now likely to go to the Americans or some other country.

Tuesday 21 June

At the great dinner at the Ritz given by Carla Powell, the Keswicks and Barbara Black for Jimmy Goldsmith's birthday, I found myself seated rather grandly next to Tessa and Olga Polizzi, now Olga Shawcross.

When Tessa told me that Petronella was sitting next to Jimmy Goldsmith I said, 'I hope he doesn't marry her too.'

When Tessa went up to make a little speech about him for his birthday and the birthday cake was being cut, she suddenly said, to my horror, in front of everybody, 'Woodrow said of you, Jimmy, when he heard you were sitting next to Petronella, "I hope he doesn't marry her too." ' There were great roars of laughter.

Chips Keswick started counting out £10 notes for Verushka to bet on Saturday night at Wimbledon for the dogs. She said, 'Chips, you can't do that in front of everybody. It looks as though you are paying me for something.' 'Well, I am. But I don't care what they think.' He said again how we had introduced him to the world of politics and high social life fifteen years ago.

I think he is a very good friend. He said to Verushka, 'Any time you or Woodrow need any help I will always be there.' I don't quite

10. (1873–1963); Sir Pelham (Plum) Warner; educated Rugby School and Oxford University; Middlesex and England cricket captain; chairman of England selectors, 1926, 1931, 1932, 1935–8; President MCC; cricket writer.

know what that meant. If I asked him for £100,000, I should think he would vanish pretty quick.

There are high jinks going on at the *Telegraph*, all sections. Simon Heffer is apparently about to be made deputy editor. He and Max Hastings hate each other. Max Hastings is too frightened to do anything about it because he thinks he may be on his way out. The circulation is falling but it is not his fault. It is partly because Black doesn't understand anything about newspapers, any more than Stevens does. They are about to cut the price, on Thursday morning, to 30p. This is in the hope of getting back some of the circulation which they have lost to the *Times*. The *Sunday Telegraph* is doing remarkably well but not really making any money.

Dominic Lawson is probably going to be asked to be deputy editor or editor of the *Sunday Telegraph* because Frank Johnson may be editor of the *Spectator*. They are all going around like frightened rabbits.

Wednesday 22 June
Rupert has responded [to the *Telegraph* price cut] by cutting the *Times* to 20p. Conrad is in hot water. He sold large chunks of *Daily Telegraph* shares on May 19th. He is now accused of doing this with the insider knowledge that they were going to bring the *Daily Telegraph* price down on June 22nd.[11]

I think he is in the clear though.

It is quite obvious that on May 19th he was still thinking he could get away with not cutting the price of the *Telegraph*. In fact he would have been wiser never to have cut it.

Friday 24 June
When I said I would be attacking the rail signalmen's strike, Mrs Tamborero was very wise. She said, 'No, you ought to look into it more thoroughly. I think there is something to be said for the strikers.'

I have talked now to Railtrack and the Ministry of Transport, and with the RMT (National Union of Rail, Maritime and Transport workers). It is clear that there has been the most awful mess made with Railtrack and the authorities, including the Transport Ministry,

---

11. These were newspaper rumours; a stock exchange investigation was launched immediately and he was cleared.

and the strike is completely justified. I have written accordingly for the *News of the World* today.

Meanwhile, John Major is in Corfu. He is about to have a great battle over his refusal to accept the Franco-German nominee for the next President of the Commission to follow Delors. The fellow they promote, Prime Minister of Belgium [Jean-Luc Dehaene], is an out-and-out anti-British federalist and wants everything controlled from Brussels and centralized.

Saturday 25 June
To the Wimbledon Stadium to see the Greyhound Derby. Verushka took her £80 with which she had been armed by Chips. I took about £50. I lost the lot. Verushka begun by winning but finished slightly down. It is very difficult to follow if you have got no one there who knows the inside form.

Sunday 26 June
The Pejacsevichs to dinner. I was told at the last minute that not only was Petronella coming but Robert Hardman from the *Telegraph*, a friend she stays with sometimes in the South of France. So I got another bottle out.

I was urging Petronella to marry this nice young man. I said, 'He's taller than you. He's more intelligent than you. You could get on very well. Also, he's quite well off.'

He thought it all great fun. 'But she won't have me.' 'She's impossibly difficult,' I remarked. He then said, 'But she stands up for you and tells everyone how marvellous you are when you're not there.' I said, 'That's really sweet of her and I do the same for her.' I really do adore that little Petronella, maddening though she is.

At six I had rung John Major to congratulate him on his marvellous stand at the Corfu conference.

I asked him how he got on with Berlusconi,[12] whom Rupert had wanted him to talk to. 'First class. To use a phrase once used by Margaret (of Gorbachev), "He's a man I can do business with." It's not his fault that parts of the Italian government alliance contain neo-Fascist types: no one ever minded any government depending on an alliance including Communists in the past.'

I told John about Simon Heffer becoming Deputy Editor of the

---

12. Silvio Berlusconi, newspaper magnate, at this time Prime Minister of Italy.

Telegraph. I said, 'Barbara Black seems pretty innocent and didn't realize how strongly Heffer was against you, nor did Conrad.' 'Oh yes he does. He knows perfectly well.' 'In that case he is either being very duplicitous or he is hopelessly weak, which I think is the case. He can't rule his editors because he doesn't know enough about newspapers.'

I then rang Rupert and told him some of what John Major had said because I knew he would be pleased at his meeting Berlusconi.

Friday 1 July

We were at Oare before anybody, except for Henry. Tessa hadn't arrived yet, nor had the two guests, John Goodfreund and his wife, Susan. He is a very rum fellow, boasting about all the people he knows like Princess Margaret and Prince Charles ('Had we met him?').

He worked for Salomon Brothers and built it up very largely in New York.

Saturday 2 July

Went to dinner at Simon and Laura Weinstock's. Very odd.

When we eventually got our food it was what John Goodfreund called 'plated'. That means you were just served with whatever the course was with vegetables around it and you were not allowed to help yourself and get the amount you actually wanted.

There was Lynch-Bages, which was quite a good fourth growth but ruined by not being looked after properly and not decanted properly, obviously swirled around. It was already poured into the glasses when we sat down for dinner.

Simon I like, but the poor boy has never got over being in the shadow of his father without his charm. He also has a façade of great superiority, I think mostly to hide his shyness and nervousness. He is actually very clever.

Sunday 3 July

Henry and I watched a lot of sport which annoyed Tessa.

Yesterday Martina Navratilova, the lesbian, was beaten by the Spanish girl, Conchita Martinez. I sat there putting a spell on Navratilova making her serve double faults.

I had wanted to watch the whole of the men's final but Verushka began saying she had to get back to London to get her hair done and arrange for my birthday party the next day.

I said, 'Henry and I are forming a Harassed and Battered Husbands

League and we are co-chairmen.' Verushka didn't think that was very
funny, nor did Tessa.

Monday 4 July
My birthday.

Being short of a man, Frank Johnson was asked. He has become
Deputy Editor of the *Sunday Telegraph*. Netta and Arnold were there.
Netta had kindly brought me a weird thing like a huge gun or cannon
which was a cigar lighter. She had it brought over specially from
Switzerland. The next morning I couldn't even make it work, and still
can't.

Chips Keswick, sweet fellow, brought twelve bottles of 1982 Dom
Ruinart champagne.

Sweet Beryl Bainbridge brought me a book about cricket and
inscribed it to me. There was a pressed red rose in it.

She sat next to Bernard Levin. Curiously they didn't have much in
common and to my surprise, unlike some of the others present, he had
never read anything she had written, though he tried to pretend he
had.

Friday 8 July
Most of the newspapers were about Jeffrey Archer. It is alleged that
from insider share-dealing he made at least £50,000 profit over buying
Anglia shares – his wife is a non-executive director of Anglia – knowing
in advance that Anglia was about to be taken over by MAI, Lord
Hollick's company. I find this very odd. The Board of Trade, run by
Michael Heseltine and with his authority, issued a statement saying a
number of people were being investigated including Lord Archer.[1]

At half past eight I rang John Major, mainly to wish him luck on
his trip to Naples for the great G7 summit.

He raised the question of Jeffrey Archer, which I had not mentioned
to him. I said, 'There's no problem to you. You're not involved in it.
It can't possibly rub off on you.' He said, 'No, but I feel very sorry for
him. He's an old friend.'

John said, 'How could it be true? He's got £25 million. What would
he want to mess about at such a risk trying to make £50,000?'

John is pretty annoyed with Michael Heseltine who personally
authorized the naming of Jeffrey Archer.

---

1. Michael Heseltine announced three weeks later that no action would be taken.

I wrote, after I had spoken to John, to Jeffrey Archer.

In my letter I said he obviously has some enemy at work and I don't believe the story. I enclosed a copy of *To the Point* and thanked him for his new book of short stories, *Twelve Red Herrings*, he had just sent me.

Sunday 10 July

Ten past nine p.m. An enchanting evening. It reminds me of when I was a child and got very excited because I could read a book without the light on so late on a summer evening.

Today we went to Wormsley, to Paul Getty's cricket match between his selected team and Oxford University.

Wormsley cricket field is astonishingly beautiful, carved out of the hills all round at enormous expense by Paul Getty.

After lunch we went to the library. It is in a building beautifully constructed from scratch in a Gothic style of a semi-castle with a tower.

There are thirteen thousand books there.

A number were laid out, the beautifully illustrated and illuminated ones.

In particular, I found touching the psalter of Anne Boleyn which had been given her by Henry VIII just before their marriage. Their illustrated armorial bearings were merged together.

When we got home, Nicholas [Banszky] turned up.[2]

I asked him why he had not done any more [business] with Skadden Arps: were they too expensive? He said they weren't any more expensive than anybody else and they were very good. I said, 'Will you then kindly arrange to do more business with them because I get £25,000 a year from them and it may be on the line if I can't get them some business? In that case your grandmother will be deposited in a plain van in your garden as a present and you will have to look after her. I have done it for twenty-seven years and she costs me more than £25,000 a year to keep, so you had better stir your stumps.'

Wednesday 13 July

The Tote girls came to try on new uniforms and examine them with Verushka.

Verushka was relentless, correctly, that they should be classical-style dresses which look indefinitely as though they have been bought at

---

2. WW's stepson was a director of Smith New Court at this time.

Chanel. She allowed but a few modifications. They wanted to do incredibly silly things with pleated skirts which would have made the ones with big bottoms look appalling.

In the evening we went to have dinner with Andrew Roberts.

Andrew Roberts' girlfriend was there.[3] She is a very attractive lady and clever. She is a brilliant lawyer. She told me about some of the cases in the Family Division.

I talked to Simon Heffer at great length and said, 'You've got to stop rubbishing Major. You don't want a Labour government, do you?' He said he didn't necessarily mind.

We talked about the current scandal of MPs from the Tory side who have been taking money, £1,000 a time, to put down questions. They were entrapped by *Sunday Times* investigative journalists into doing this.[4]

At this point Simon said, 'I think Jeffrey Archer ought to be made the Party Chairman.' I said, 'You must be crazy. It's the exact opposite of what you have just been saying. You know what he's like. You know that the Royal Family, for example, won't have anything to do with him.'

He said, 'But does it matter if he were Chairman?' I said, 'You mean on the grounds that he is just like the Card in Arnold Bennett – the most valuable thing anybody can do is cheering everybody up.'

I was amused by the hatred which exists between Max Hastings and Simon Heffer.

Simon said, 'The best thing about it is that if the price-cut Max urged doesn't work, he is going to resign, and as it isn't going to work, he will have to.'

Thursday 14 July

Drue Heinz's annual bash at her very attractive house in Hay's Mews.

It was said before the War, when Piccadilly was a very much smarter place than it is now, that if you stood in front of Swan and Edgars long enough you would meet everybody you knew. I felt this was exactly what was happening to me at Drue's.

---

3. Camilla Henderson who married Andrew Roberts on 22 July 1995.
4. Graham Riddick and David Tredinnick were alleged to have taken £1,000 to put down bogus questions about non-existent firms; both MPs appeared before the Committee of Privileges, apologized to the House of Commons and were fined, in April 1995.

I found myself sitting next to a Mrs Cleese.[5] Her husband is the Fawlty Towers man, a Liberal Democrat.

She is a psychiatrist. We had a long talk about the subconscious.

I said, 'I believe in extra-sensory perception to some extent,' and told her about Arthur Koestler, how I had written his entry in the *Dictionary of National Biography* and how he founded the Chair for this at Edinburgh University.[6]

Opposite me was Annabel Goldsmith. She said, 'I hear that Jimmy took Petronella to a night club and they stayed there until three in the morning. I was very worried as to what might happen because I know what Jimmy is like.' I said, 'It was OK. Petronella knows how to look after herself.'

I gave Ian Gilmour a lift back to the Lords.

He can see no longer any point in our sovereignty, which is strange considering that he is a cousin of almost every duke in the land and might be thought to have some feeling for his country and its independence. However, he is extraordinarily wet, wracked by guilt at his privileges of birth and wealth. He is not prepared to share them with others but thinks he ought to act as though he shouldn't have them.

I felt a little stronger, having taken an extra dose of ginseng, by the time I got to The Other Club.

Jacob was, unexpectedly to me, in the chair.

He was full of warmth and friendliness – the granite melted for a while. I told him I had been talking to Serena at lunch time. He hadn't been able to go because he had been trying, with Isaiah Berlin,[7] to get money for a Jewish charity out of Leonard Wolfson. I said, 'It must be easier now he is married to that charming girl, and happier.' He said he thought it was and he gave them a million or so. Isaiah Berlin said, 'But why did we have to have the lunch, too? Couldn't we have just collected the million?'

He agreed that Serena's extravagance was a fair return for him doing whatever he liked, more or less, which means, as I said to him, pursuing Princess Diana as well. He said, 'I wish I could have some luck there.' I said, 'Well you try hard enough but she doesn't like sex.'

5. Alyce Faye McBride, psychotherapist, m 1 (1966) Davis Eichelberger, m 2 (1992) John Cleese, writer and actor.
6. (1905–83), Hungarian-born writer and polymath.
7. Sir Isaiah Berlin OM (1909–97), Oxford philosopher.

Of Jacob's wealth I said, 'I don't envy any friend of mine or anybody their riches and their good luck. I like to see somebody enjoying themselves with what they have got, not sitting miserably and worrying about it like Ian Gilmour does.'

As he was in the chair, he presented magnums of Lafite of 1982 – a very good year. He also provided cigars which as a rule are not on supply there.

Robert Armstrong[8] felt there was no need for the White Paper on civil service modernization presented by William Waldegrave. I said, 'Do you think he is in danger of being removed?' He said, 'Quite possibly. He once said something extremely cutting to John Major and he never forgets such affronts.'

Sunday 17 July
Spoke at some length to John Major.

I told him about my talk with Simon Heffer.

I said I would work on Norman during the holidays in Italy when he would be staying with me. John said, 'I'd like to have him back in the government. He's got a very good brain. But he's having difficulty in finding a seat now since his present constituency broke up.'

On the William Waldegrave situation I said, 'I hope you are not going to remove him. I know he said something very offensive to you once.' John said, 'That's true, but I've forgotten about it.' (Curiously, John doesn't seem to bear malice like many in his position.) 'Anyway, you can take it from me he is not going to lose his job or be out of the Cabinet. Don't say anything to him about it.' 'Good heavens no. Have you ever had any indication that anything is leaked from me?' He said, 'No. You're safe as the Bank of England.'

We talked about Tony Blair making one mistake after another, rubbishing away about abolishing the House of Lords, for instance.[9] John said, 'Why on earth would one want to waste parliamentary time on a thing like that?'

I asked if he was going to Jeffrey Archer's today. I said, 'I was wondering whether it would be wise.' 'I must go because he's an old friend, as you know. If I didn't go, it would draw attention and have the reverse effect.' I said, 'I still think it's dirty work at the crossroads

---

8. Secretary of the Cabinet, 1979–87, Head of the Home Civil Service, 1983–7; life peer 1988.

9. Blair was elected Labour Leader on 21 July 1994.

by Michael Heseltine,' to which John replied, 'I have to keep distant from this.'

At the Archers' party I had a talk with Carol Thatcher. She is writing a book about her father. Eve Pollard said, 'What is there to write about him?' I said, 'Everything in the world. He was the rock on which she rested.'

When we were about to go, John Major waved across to us and came over. I deliberately hadn't gone up to him. I had been talking to him in the morning anyway and it is not good for business for me to be seen to be too thick with him.

Robert Rhodes James was there. I asked him about the Chips Channon diaries he edited. He said, 'I wish Paul would let me do some more.' 'Perhaps he can't while so many people are still alive.' 'Some of it could be released now.' I vaguely thought of him as an editor for this manuscript but he is too drunk most of the time. He'll probably be dead before me in any case.[10]

My mind keeps coming back to the proposition that Andrew Roberts might do it. His book *Eminent Churchillians* is being serialized in the *Sunday Times*. I am worried (a) about whether he can keep a secret and (b) whether he would work hard enough with all his Kentucky Chicken money.

At home Petronella had asked to dinner Andrew Roberts and his girlfriend, the barrister girl who was at his dinner the other night, and Frank Johnson and his current German girlfriend. She was quite pretty and very intelligent.

I asked Andrew Roberts if he would like to see some Churchilliana. I showed him the *Banbury Guardian* special issue of February 1965 covering Churchill's funeral and on sale by the evening. It was in full colour. The quotations were chosen by Bernard Levin and myself, mostly by Bernard Levin, and the captions were done by me. It was wonderful web offset colour, the first time ever done in England. Oh dear, I wish I hadn't had to lose the *Banbury Guardian*.

He found my copy of his book *The Holy Fox* (Halifax).

While I wasn't looking he wrote an inscription in it, 'To Woodrow, 17 July 94, in fealty and devotion (and fondest regards) Andrew.' But he hadn't given me the book at all.

---

10. He died after WW, in 1999; historian, writer, Conservative politician (MP, 1976–92, having been a House of Commons clerk, 1955–64); knight 1991. See Vol. 2, pp. 455–6 and 554–6, for WW's spat with him about Petronella.

He laughed when I said he had only written some sensational things about Churchill to draw attention to himself. He said, 'That's something you never did, isn't it, Woodrow?' Of course, I often used to do it when I was his age: a good point.

Monday 18 July
Under great pressure from Petronella I went to the *Evening Standard* Londoners' Diary party.

I immediately went to sit next to Michael Foot with Petronella sitting on the other side. He said, 'You've got the most marvellous daughter.'

He was drooling away over her.

Then he thanked me for what I had written in the review of the book about him. He said my review was very kind but ill-informed.

He is somewhat puzzled by Tony Blair and his approach. I said, 'I would like to be able to say one day that it is safe to vote Labour again, but I don't think it will be so by the coming election. It might be before I die.' 'What does that mean?' 'If they really distance themselves from the unions and welcome the union reforms and don't try to go back on them, and if they recognize this really is a capitalist society, and also if they become thoroughly Eurosceptic as they used to be until they turned turtle.' He didn't altogether dissent.

My goodness he is friendly and kind and sweet, Michael. He has always been very fond of me and I of him though most of the time he never agreed with me, except in the 'Keep Left' days. Poor dear, his face is blotched with dreadful skin and his asthma hurts. He needs a stick. When he left, he hitched his belongings and bag untidily around him and with difficulty climbed the iron stairs. He was off to use his pensioner's pass on public transport back to his beloved Hampstead where he still walks with his dog. When talking about the Lords, I told him he'd find the atmosphere amusing and congenial. 'Why don't you go into it?' To my astonishment he answered, 'No one's ever asked me to.' I hope that was a hint he'd be willing.

I talked to Bill Cash.[11] I did my best to persuade him that Mr Santer was just the bloke, very pro British even though he might make

---

11. Conservative MP since 1984 and a leading Eurosceptic.

contrary noises, and about Major's great achievement in rejecting the choice of Germany and France.[12]

Tuesday 19 July
Rang John Major. Tried to get him several times because I wanted to tell him about Bill Cash.

I said, 'I think I persuaded him [Cash] not to make any trouble.' 'Woodrow, you're a star.'

Sent a fax to Irwin Stelzer. Later he rang and we had a very agreeable chat. I said to Irwin on the telephone, 'Major is very pleased about the change round in the attitude of News International newspapers and that so far as the Brussels determination to make Sky (and British TV) show a quota of incomprehensible, tedious Euro films with sub-titles, Major acts on the principle that one good turn deserves another. Rupert has nothing to worry about in this score or on the banning of cross media ownership which Labour is mad keen about.'

Wednesday 20 July
Later in the day came some of Major's changes. He did make Jeremy Hanley Party Chairman.

Also, as promised, Major has kept William Waldegrave in, but shifted him to the Ministry of Agriculture where I think he will do extremely well, arguing with the French and the Germans in particular.

I was delighted to hear that MacGregor's out.[13] I am sure John had been taking on board what I told him about the hash up he and Horton[14] had been making of the signalmen's strike.

Thursday 21 July
I spoke to John and congratulated him on the clever way he had put people in the right slots in his Cabinet.

When I complimented him on Robert Cranborne he said, 'I don't know if you noticed but when I gave him his accelerated elevation to a Viscountcy and put him in the Lords, that was always my intention,

---

12. Britain had agreed to Jacques Santer, Prime Minister of Luxembourg, as the next President of the EU Commission.
13. Brian Mawhinney replaced John MacGregor at Transport; Lord Cranborne replaced Lord Wakeham as Leader of the Lords; Portillo moved from Chief Secretary at the Treasury to Secretary of State for Employment.
14. Robert Horton, Chairman, Railtrack, 1993–9; knight 1997.

to give him this job.' 'You've certainly fixed young Mr Portillo. Now
he'll have to show what he can do in a real life Department. He won't
be able to rock the boat.'

There was a strange party for the launching of Andrew Roberts'
book at the Wellington Barracks. He'd had an enormous chunk cut
out of a newspaper and blown up which said how he had recently
given a dinner party and the guests were Lord and Lady Wyatt and
their daughter, Petronella.

That was to show how with it he is in the social and political world.
I suppose it was a compliment.

I only stayed a few minutes because I had to get on to the Stafford
Hotel for the dinner party to say goodbye to Stoker Hartington and
welcome to Tommy Pilkington who succeeds him as Senior Steward at
the Jockey Club, while Stoker goes on as Chairman of BHB.

I sat next to Peter Jones who I was told had been rotting me and
trying to get me out of my job. I spent a great deal of time buttering
him up.

Saturday 23 to Sunday 24 July
It was off to the King George VI and Queen Elizabeth Diamond Stakes.
Lunch with the Oppenheimers.[15]

I sat next to darling Jean Trumpington from the Lords.[16]

She is pleased about Robert Cranborne being Leader of the Lords
but said, 'He can be a bit overbearing.'

Robert said it was fascinating sitting with Major and seeing how
he matched people's temperaments with each other in their departments
sensibly and wisely.

I told him how I have a very close relationship, which I don't want
anybody to know about, with John Major.

At dinner [at Badminton] David [Duke of Beaufort] produced some
marvellous Château Lafite 1975.

He's still almost as handsome as when I first met him in 1959 or a
bit earlier, tall and lean-looking with a wonderful figure, marvellously
athletic, with a narrow, aristocratic face.

Caroline said she would come to Italy next year if we asked her. I
said, 'If I still have enough money to go there.'

---

15. Philip Oppenheimer (1911–95), Chairman, The Diamond Trading Co., Jockey
     Club member; knight 1970; m (1935) Pamela, née Stirling.
16. A government Whip in the House of Lords, 1992–7; life peer 1980.

On Sunday we left in time for me to go to Lord's to see the funeral rites of the English being buried alive by the South Africans.

When I got to the box, I found John Major had not long gone. He had signed my bats for Jill Radnor as soon as he heard they were for me.

Andrew Devonshire was there. He said he had spoken to Major, he thinks he is very good and he has rejoined the Tories again now.

I told Paul Getty how Andrew Devonshire got frightfully angry with Margaret when she was first Prime Minister. He had written to her saying would she come to do the annual Conservative fête at Chatsworth, because it had always been the practice of Tory prime ministers. She wrote back she was very sorry she couldn't but he would be pleased to hear she was going to the annual Blenheim Conservative fête. Andrew blew up. 'I'm not going to support that woman any more,' and he joined the Liberal Democrats.

Monday 25 July
I rang John and thanked him for signing my bat.

He's pretty cheerful now.

I remember how down he was a couple of months or so ago, saying he thought he'd give up and there was no point in it.

When I told John that the bat he signed was for the dyslexia charity he said, 'A very good charity.' I said, 'Yes. None of the proceeds are intended for Michael Heseltine.' He laughed a lot. He's a dyslexic, Heseltine.

Stoker Hartington came to see me. I don't know what to make of him. We drank champagne in the garden.

Stoker asked me my intentions about the Tote. I said, 'I need to carry on for at least two years. I don't think it makes any difference what age I am. Adenauer ran Germany when he was eighty-nine. It's not all that much more difficult to run the Tote.'

I explained to him about all the detailed negotiations now going on with Ladbroke and the football pools,[17] and how I have to see it through because there were difficulties and breakdowns. I told him confidentially that I want John Heaton to succeed Brian.

Referring to how the Jockey Club [membership] had been widening, he said of Charlie Wilson, who used to edit the *Times* and now runs the News International newspapers, 'I was very glad he was willing

---

17. There were plans to enable betting on football pools through Tote Direct.

to join the Jockey Club.' I laughed. 'How do you mean "willing to"? They'd all give their eye teeth to.'

The question of how to deal with my future term at the Tote has been exercising me severely. At one moment I thought I would speak to John about it, then to Michael Howard. My appointment ends on April 30th, 1995. I want to get it absolutely securely settled long before that, if I am going to go on. I need to, of course, for the money.

But my overriding need is to make sure that all I am building, under considerable difficulties, is solid and will last and will be really good for racing.

I don't want to get John Major involved in it unless it's a crisis.

Thursday 28 July
After dinner I wandered around the garden. I love this house and its garden. Sometimes I feel I want to get away from the inhabitants. But tonight it was calm and quiet.

I then thought I must ring Margaret. This was around a quarter to ten.

She thought John was doing pretty well though she had some doubts about whether he would stick to his plan to resist further encroachments from Brussels.

I hope she was being truthful and doesn't still nourish a hope that Portillo could suddenly take over. I referred to him as too inexperienced yet.

She switched then to the unions and Communism. 'I am writing a second book, now. I am getting to the part where I must deal with what the unions were like and what we had to cope with. You've written a bit about that, haven't you?'

So I have to arrange for *Confessions of an Optimist* and *The Peril in our Midst* to be delivered in the morning.

It was very much like old times.

Monday 1 August *Porto Ercole*
There is a staff of God knows how many here. I wasn't warned about this and I have hundreds of pounds to pay out, which I had not expected, in wages to people who seem to me to be largely superfluous.

The house is like a Scott Fitzgerald multi-millionaire's palace on Long Island in the twenties. (The King of Greece, Constantine, lived here after his exile.) The swimming pool is absolutely glorious, with wonderful lighting and movements in the water, every trick you can think of.

Wednesday 3 August
When I got up and went to see Verushka she was in tears. She had fallen straight into a hole when she was trying to turn the lights out [in the garden last night].

She landed on her heel and was writhing in agony.

Verushka was taken to Orbetello local emergency unit, equivalent of the NHS. They put on her a huge plaster cast which went from her toe to her thigh, weighing about a ton.

We arranged to go the next morning to Pisa to see the best orthopaedic surgeon in the teaching hospital nearby.

So here we are, plunged into calamity and our holiday is ruined. But she is taking it much better than I expected.

I rang John Major to tell him about my conversation with Margaret and said she would like to see him.

John said would I please arrange the meeting for early in September before the party conference. He wants to work on her for the party conference and genuinely wants her advice.

The news had come through that Kelvin MacKenzie had left Sky Television. I said, 'I think I was indirectly responsible for that. I had been telling Rupert that this was the jewel in his crown, the impartiality and the high prestige of Sky News, although they said they didn't get much of an audience for it.'

It was then off to Pisa, in an ambulance arranged by Amy Corsini

who is head of the Red Cross in Italy. Five hundred thousand lire to
go there and back. I was in agony because there was no rest for my
back and I had to sit upright against some tins. But Verushka was
quite comfortable on a bed.

There were three in the team, including a full-breasted young girl
with plenty of make-up and very nice legs.

When I took the hand of the rather attractive girl [to say good bye]
and kissed it she said, 'Oo, wow, wow', shouting in the air and clen-
ching her fist as though she had won a great football victory.

I had the distinct impression I could have kissed a lot more of her
if the opportunity had been available.

But doubtless that was just an old man's optimism.

Friday 5 August
Arnold has been ringing daily wanting to know the registration number
of each car he will pick up on Saturday at Grosetto.

He is bringing God knows how many crates of luggage. That is
because he hired Paul Getty's yacht, which is supposed to be very
secret, Paul not wanting anybody to know he has hired it out to
Arnold. It will take him off, with an eighteen-man crew, when he leaves
here.

It has never been so hot, it seems, for years and years. It makes it
very tiring and hard to work or write, as well as deal with the constant
Tote battles I had hoped I would be released from during August.

Sunday 14 August
It was jolly having Arnold to stay. They went off on Monday morning
which was when we had to go back to Pisa again. We've been having
all these blasted international telephone calls about Verushka's Achilles
heel, which has caused more commotion throughout the world than
the original Achilles heel at Troy.

Having been alarmed by a statement which Rupert appears to have
made to the effect that he might support Blair at the next election (and
Peter Stothard, the silly chap, had followed it up in the *Times* saying
the *Times* might support Blair in the next election, too) I thought I
must ring Rupert before he went away on holiday.

He was just off to Alaska within about ten minutes of my speaking
to him.

He said, 'We're going to be following whales and fishing and
catching wonderful salmon. I am only taking Anna and my sister

and her husband. Lachlan may join us for a few days but he is now in Australia working and Jamie is at his last year at Harvard. Elisabeth is seven months pregnant and she is working too hard.' I said, 'I want to meet that young man [her husband]. He's been fighting very well against these corrupt dictators in Ghana.' He said, 'He hasn't got a hope though he's very optimistic.'

'What did you mean when you said you might back Tony Blair at the next election?' He said, 'Nothing at all. It was a throw-away remark. I had a long interview with *Der Spiegel* and they talked about my attitudes in my newspapers. I replied I am completely independent. I've supported Labour candidates in Australia and I might even support Blair.'

I said, 'Well it caused me a lot of alarm.' He said, 'Don't worry.'

He said, 'Major ought to get rid of Hurd.' I said, 'That's exactly what I think. Hurd is a completely Foreign Office man and the Foreign Office have always been against Britain. They're at it again now. They're wanting to knuckle under Brussels.'

Rupert said, 'He should get rid of Heseltine, too. He behaves in a most disloyal manner.' (I shall tell John Major about that.)

Rupert said, 'There have been so many attacks on Jeffrey Archer that I think people are beginning to feel sorry for him.'

Friday 2 September

On return I found a few replies to postcards I sent to newly promoted ministers and commiserations to the forcibly retired ones. One I particularly liked was from Jonathan Aitken, at last in the Cabinet as Chief Secretary to the Treasury. I was greatly touched by his remembering and treasuring what I had written about him in one of my columns years ago.[1]

A retake on some of the holiday: I thought Fiona Allsopp looked very pretty but less so the more she got sunburned.

She was always very pleasant but I think she tends to be bossy. When Carmelo said about his boat that he could never have children on it because it was the law and you can't take them, she didn't believe it. She said, 'In that case we won't go. We'll stay behind.'

On the day they did not go on the boat, Charlie painted some water colours rather prettily.

One of the jolliest days we had was when Norman and Andrew Roberts were there. A group of us, including Sophie, the Lamonts' very sweet daughter, went off to see the beautiful abbey, Sant' Antimo, near Montalcino.

With unerring instinct for the most expensive, Petronella chose a restaurant called Poggio Antico, four kilometres from Montalcino.

When we sat down the menu was vast and over £60 a head. I said, 'For heaven's sake don't choose anything other than *à la carte*,' which we did, and we tasted a bit of each other's.

When we came to the third course, a cold zabaglione, I asked if we could have five spoons, the number of our party. The woman was

---

1. Aitken, then a journalist and a Conservative candidate, had in 1971 been tried at the Old Bailey under the Official Secrets Act, after leaking to the *Sunday Telegraph* a classified document on the Nigerian civil war, shown him by his constituency chairman. He was acquitted but lost his candidature. Aitken recalled that WW had written 'There is no reason why he should not make an excellent Tory MP and Minister one day.'

beginning to laugh. She solemnly brought us five spoons so we could all dip into the zabaglione Sophie had ordered.

I needn't have worried because Norman said he would pay for it on his credit card but, it having said in the Michelin Guide they did take credit cards, they wouldn't take his.

I must write to the Michelin Guide about that.

At last we have got everything signed, sealed and delivered for the proper use of the Cornish Spring Water of which I am the Chairman.

It is sold at Covent Garden, Harry's Bar, Mark's Club and the superior Sainsbury shops as a high-class item.

Spoke to John Major about Sunday evening's dinner [with Margaret Thatcher].

I suggested a quarter to eight because Margaret tends to leave fairly early, about ten. 'I think it is because of the tiredness of all those strenuous years in office has caught up with her,' John remarked.

I don't think it's that at all, really. I think she likes to get back to get up at the crack of dawn as usual.

Sunday 4 September

The French chef, hired for £70 with a large bill for provisions he required for the dinner, was asked to sign a confidentiality statement.

Five detectives arrived to eat in shifts the two large chickens prepared for them.

John arrived first.

'Is it true that Norman is trying to get a divorce?' I told him this was in his mind but I had urged him not to be such an idiot.

Elizabeth came in and said, 'I think the other guest is arriving.'

She was striding jauntily along the garden path, having come in not through the front gate as requested but by the side where the wide garage gates were still open. She returned to me my book *The Peril in our Midst*.

She was clearly in a good mood.

To begin with, both in the drawing-room and in the dining-room, she banged on a lot about not attacking the other side so much as preaching 'the vision'.

John mentioned Simon Heffer. I said, 'Can you use your influence with him not to be so foolish in the way he attacks John? After all it [the *Daily Telegraph*] is supposed to be a Tory newspaper and it does a great deal of harm. Could you, too, use your influence if you speak to Rupert on the side.' She said, 'He doesn't always know what's in his newspapers.'

I thought to myself, 'I've often told you that but perhaps not quite truthfully.' Aloud I said, 'That is so, but he has to be kept up to the mark and he'll listen to you.

'When I spoke to Rupert during August, he was sticking to his promise to support John. He said John should sack Heseltine.' They both laughed. He is a busted flush but John didn't think it would be wise to have him roaming on the back benches, making even more trouble.

There was some discussion about the sleazy appearance of the Tory Party and whether it involved Jeffrey Archer. Margaret said, 'I think he was quite innocent and didn't realize what he was doing would be wrong.' I said, 'That is not the impression of the country. He has behaved well beyond the limit and the Tory Party must not in any way seem to be condoning him.' That was generally agreed on.

The conversation zig-zagged as we were considering various people in the government and who could replace them. Margaret said that Virginia Bottomley is absolutely useless. John made no reply.

About Hurd, Margaret said, 'He has been loyal.' This was dittoed to by John.

Jonathan Aitken was mentioned and despite his bad behaviour with Margaret's daughter, Carol, whom he dropped rather cruelly, Margaret was very pro him.[2]

John said, 'I don't think he's got the *gravitas* required for it.'

John made a splendid defence of Maastricht.

He was not going to allow Kohl and Mitterrand to get away with some kind of special inner core from which we were excluded.

Margaret said, 'Kohl is dishonest and a bully. He thinks he's a kind of Bismark. He's not done as much harm but he's nearly in the same class.'

We diverted to talk about the Scott Inquiry.

John said, 'Mackay (Lord Chancellor) said we must have an inquiry and he recommended Scott.'

Margaret expressed her contempt for Kenneth Clarke. 'He's really a socialist. He's attacking our people the whole time.'

She praised John Redwood who is now Secretary of State for Wales. Quickly John Major broke in to say, 'He is very disloyal.' He has been

---

2. See Vol. 1, p. 340, for Aitken and Carol Thatcher.

engaged in all kinds of cabals to get rid of John behind his back. This surprised Margaret. I hope she will say something to him.

In talking about sexual peccadilloes of Ministers, Margaret wondered how they allowed themselves to get involved in such states so easily made public. I said, 'Because they are carrying an excess of libido, being in the main ambitious and energetic. We're talking about human nature. It cannot be changed.'

At the beginning of dinner Margaret kept calling John 'Prime Minister.' After two or three times John said, 'Please don't do that, Margaret. I always see you as my Prime Minister. Why are we so formal?' So I laughed. She laughed, too, and went back to calling him John.

She greatly enjoyed the dinner. She had two helpings of the French chef's excellent soufflé, which was made with mozzarella cheese and was spiced up in an enticing manner. She also ate heartily of the roast beef and well prepared vegetables and she had a large helping of the crêpe Suzette at the end. As well as the champagne, she drank a fair amount of the white wine, Baron de Bachen, arguably the best white wine in the world. She also appreciated the Haut Brion 1976 which was excellent. John refrained from drinking as much as usual, saying, 'I don't want to get drunk. I've got to keep a clear head talking to Margaret.'

On the subject of Yeltsin Margaret said, 'His trouble is he is not a hard worker. He will never go into any detail and spends most of his time drinking or on other pursuits.' John said, 'Nevertheless, he's the best bet we've got.' She said, 'Yes. Gorbachev was extremely good in his way but he could never stop being a Communist. When I tried to explain to him what private enterprise was all about he couldn't comprehend it.'

While we were on the subject of Hong Kong, I said, 'Do please give Henry Keswick that knighthood. His younger brother's got one, and he's been absolutely firm, rock solid for Christopher Patten.' John said, 'Yes, you're right. I must do that.'

The subject of the Royal Family came up.

John said he was worried at the moment about the activities of the Prince of Wales with Jonathan Dimbleby. He said, 'He is letting him write an authorized biography.' He has had access to all the letters, ministerial [ones]. John can stop those under the Official Secrets Act, but he can't stop the sort of things he has been saying and has said and written and that have been allowed to go forward, such as attacks on his parents.

Margaret said Prince Charles ought not to have made his confession of adultery in his broadcast. I said, 'I think that was OK. It brought him a great wave of sympathy and assured his position as the heir to the throne. In any case, we would never have had a king half the time if a rule about not being an adulterer was in force.'

John said the stories about the telephone calls Princess Diana has been making are absolutely true. He knows that from his intelligence services.

They were doubtful about Prince Charles being king.

John said Princess Anne might be the best of the bunch to succeed.

John said it is pathetic when he talks to Prince Andrew how much he is still in love with that dreadful Fergie. He wants a reconciliation after all she's done to him. He would clearly be no good as king.

Margaret said, 'The greatest loss will be when Queen Elizabeth the Queen Mother dies. The whole nation will feel it and wonder if that's the end of the monarchy.'

I said I knew Jonathan Dimbleby very well. 'I wonder if I could do something with him on this book.' John said, 'Please don't. That might make matters worse.'

Doubtless I shall remember more details of the conversation and put them in. It was very long. Margaret had arrived at a quarter to eight and didn't go till ten to twelve.

When she had gone John said, 'Well that was the most remarkable conversation. It would make a sensation if it ever got into the newspapers.' Then he smiled at me and said, 'That's one for the memoirs, Woodrow.' I thought to myself, 'Oh God, does he think I'm writing a diary because I am,' but I said, 'I'm too old now to write memoirs.' I wonder whether he guessed, because he is very intuitive, that I must be taking some form of notes of these conversations. Of course, in their way they are of historical interest.

Tuesday 6 September

My *Times* article this morning has caused a mild sensation in Italy. Some newspapers asked if they could reprint it. A lady from the television (Italian) wanted to interview me. It seems there was great surprise at what I said about Berlusconi and that he must be allowed to carry on. Also that he is a great ally of John Major's.

Wednesday 7 September
At just gone a quarter to eight I was eating a small piece of haddock with a poached egg on top when the telephone rang with the Prime Minister at the other end. It was to thank me for the great evening with Margaret.

I then rang Margaret.

I told her what he said about calling her and she said, 'Yes of course I will talk to him. I've got a secure number.'

I asked her how her book was going. She said, 'I'm not a writer like you, Woodrow. I find it very difficult to keep it going and find the right words.'

She said, 'I'm making liberal use of Roget's *Thesaurus*,' (and she pronounced it in such a funny way – tesaurus – that I didn't know what she meant but just guessed it).

Lunch with Peter Mead, the live wire at Abbott Mead advertising agency.

For years he tried to give himself a posh accent, thinking cockney, which he was born with, was not acceptable in the circles he aspired to, and it wasn't when he first started looking for work.

Now it would be regarded as highly fashionable.

He is one of those acute, intuitive, perceptive people who knows exactly what you mean when you start explaining something and finishes your thoughts off for you.

He is rather large and has a plump, round, fast moving face. He will soon become Chairman of Millwall (Football Club).

Thursday 8 September
There was a thank-you letter from Diana Wilton.[3] Mysteriously, it referred to her stay at Badminton and Caroline being so brave. On enquiry we found that Caroline Somerset has got some tumour or disease on her pancreas, a cancerous one, and there is no way they can cure it. She has been writing her will, expecting to die in a few weeks.

The news set me crying for a longish time. I remember so many delicious times with her and attractive things about her: that marvellous head, tossed sideways, when she is making a point.

It seems the old rip David is completely shattered.

I rang, but she had already gone to visit Tony Lambton, who is an

---

3. The Wiltons had been among the Wyatts' guests in Italy.

old friend, at Durham, where Bindy[4] is with him. I couldn't pursue the matter much further for the time being because I have to go up north to Doncaster to make the main speech at the renewed St Leger dinner. It had been dropped some six years ago but now restarted in the new banqueting hall on the racecourse. I am to stay the night with Dickon Lumley (Scarbrough).

Friday 9 September
After the dinner was over I came back and sat for two hours talking to Dickon and to his wife Liz, sister of Sarah Keswick.

Sandbeck Park is very handsome. It was built by an architect called Paine[5] who did a lot of excellent work in the North, but it was pretty chilly. Verushka would have hated it.

We had a very jokey run around about all our friends, such as Julian Amery who is drinking too much.

Saturday 10 September
The St Leger.

Princess Michael was also there.

As usual in the box she was making a bloody nuisance of herself.

She made out an awful lot of bets in hundreds of pounds which she duly lost. Her credit card was in order. She has paid what she owed.

Sunday 11 September
At last I got hold of Caroline. She was sounding extremely cheerful, having come back from Tony. I said, 'I expect he was very kind.' 'Yes, he was, wanting me to do all kinds of impossible cures.' I said, 'He's an extraordinary man that. A mixture of kindness and generosity and extreme mischief-making.' 'Yes,' and she imitated his drawl. I said, 'You are not to die. I will not hear of it. You cannot die while I'm still alive.'

Monday 12 September
To Rupert's party. We took Verushka and her leg. We got her up in the service lift and along through the kitchen and we came back the same way. She found a sofa and a seat at a table. She was very pleased. She was a centre of attention as many came to speak to her.

---

4. Belinda, née Blew-Jones, m (1942) Viscount Lambton.

5. James Paine, 1725–89.

The first person I saw was Anna. I gave her a hug and a kiss and said, 'My beautiful queen, you're looking lovely.' That went down well. Rupert thought I was looking too thin. I said, 'I try to keep thin.'

Margaret Thatcher was there. I gave her a great kiss.

She was ticking off various grumbling people around who said the increase in interest rates was a great mistake and it hurt 'our people.' She said, 'It's much better for them because they'll have a lasting, smooth recovery without inflation coming back again which it was tending to do.'

(Of course, the next morning in the *Sun* came an attack on the increase but that is par for the course. The *Sun* said it is all about people who have mortgages and so forth, but Rupert himself still has very heavy borrowings and that is the real reason why he doesn't want any increase in interest rates sparked off round the world.)

Tony Blair was there. I told him that he was a very good columnist and when he was finished with politics he could write my column. I asked him did he do it all himself. He said he did and that he took a great deal of trouble with it.

I said to him and his wife, 'You won't win the next election. You've got too many difficulties ahead of you. You're still too much lumbered with the past and the trade union element. But you might do it the next time round if you complete your modernization.' I actually said to her 'good luck' when she went.

She is fairly attractive with dark hair and a small, finely formed face. Strangely, I never met either Neil Kinnock or his wife.

Tuesday 13 September
Spoke to John Major.

'Are you having some difficulties with Albert Reynolds?'[6] He said, 'Wait a moment, let me close the door.' I thought he must be at Balmoral because they said, when I originally rang, that he was in the country and they would get him to ring me. But he wasn't. He'd been with Charles Moore and Frank Johnson the night before at Number 10. So where was he? At Chequers or somewhere else?

Charles Moore is quite bright but totally bereft of political judgement, as is Frank Johnson, though he can be brought round for a while by flattery which I suppose John was up to.

He said, 'Yes. Albert Reynolds is trying to push me into saying the

---

6. Prime Minister of Ireland, 1992–4.

IRA assurances are good enough and we ought to be satisfied with them.'

He said he had been thinking of letting Gerry Adams be broadcast live, particularly as he is now going to America. I said, 'Maybe, but it would look like a concession.' 'Yes but an advantage is he could then be questioned.'

He then told me he had made arrangements, after talking to me, for Arnold Weinstock to be invited to Chequers for the great concert when Yeltsin will be there.

Nadje is playing up again. She was hammering away at her machine to get everybody up and downstairs from the kitchen for no particular purpose. She said to me, 'I want to go back to the hospital and for nobody to visit me there.' I said, 'Don't be foolish. You'll only want to come back here again immediately, as you did last time.'

While I was out I got a great pot of white chrysanthemums in a container for her. She was so delighted, 'You're the nicest person I have ever known.' 'Not at all. I'm extremely unpleasant.' She said, 'Can I stay here until I die? Do you want me to go to the hospital?' 'No, certainly not. You'll stay here until you die and that will be in a very long time.' Poor old thing, all she really wants is attention.

Wednesday 14 September
Had to get up at six o'clock to leave for Wigan for the Tote Board meeting there.

I enjoyed wandering around after lunch, talking to the girls (there are only one or two men) on the telephones and in the various departments. Some of the girls are extraordinarily pretty and look at you in quite a sexy manner. Oh well . . . They have lovely voices with their Lancashire accents. Credit customers adore them. They are also very successful at doing the mailshots and the telephoning out to people for firms like Mercury, banks and so on, which we make quite a bit on.[7]

Thursday 15 September
Spoke to Rupert at about twenty past eight in the morning.

I said, 'I think Major's doing very well.' Rupert wasn't quite so sure.

Anyway, he's not going to withdraw his backing.

---

7. Tote INTRAC was responsible for telesales.

He agrees that the great distinguishing mark is that Major is much more against the EU than Blair.

I said to Rupert I had never heard of anybody winning an election while actually promising to put up taxes.

A meeting of Cornwall Light and Power Board.

It emerged that BT are interested in Cornwall Light and Power on the Goonhilly Downs, next to their Telstar, not only supplying that with electricity when our contracts with SWEB (South West Electricity Board) run out but also because they want to make us a main supplier.

There seems to be a possibility that they would like to offer to buy the whole of the equity, or part of it. The chap from the Nat West said it wouldn't be worth less than £2 million even now and it would probably be worth a great deal more in 1998. I thought to myself, 'That's good – with twenty-five per cent of that lot I'd get £500,000.'

Dinner with the Radnors at the Berkeley.

On my right sat a hefty but handsome and well-proportioned blonde called Emma, just forty, daughter of the Marquess of Aberdeen and the niece of the previous Marquess of Aberdeen (Archie Gordon) whom I knew well.[8] He used to conduct programmes about the week in Parliament on the BBC agreeably and effectively.

Her husband [Dr Rodney Foale] was very anxious to talk to me about raising money for medical research.

As we were going (we left rather late because we had drunk so much) I went over to the amazing woman, Raine Spencer, step-mother of Princess Diana, now married to a Frenchman and having a blissfully happy time.[9]

She says she is madly in love with him and has the best sex ever. She has been, though she looks very cool, a very hot piece indeed, and still is.

I thought her husband a fairly miserable looking fellow.

As we moved into the foyer, there was darling old Ted Heath. We

---

8. Lady Emma Gordon, daughter of the 6th Marquis of Aberdeen, m (1980) Dr Rodney Foale (consultant cardiologist, St Mary's Hospital, 1985–98); her uncle, the 5th Marquis (1913–84), was a writer and broadcaster under the name Archie Gordon.

9. She m 3 (1993–6) Comte Jean-François Pineton de Chambrun.

physically embraced each other, kissed each other on both cheeks. Everybody was amazed. Men in staid England don't do that.

I said, 'You have a very good time, stirring things a great deal.' He roared with laughter. I said, 'Why not enjoy yourself? We're not alive very long.' We started making our Oxford kind of jokes again which nobody could understand watching this strange encounter.

Saturday 17 September
On our way to Badminton I had to stop at Newbury to present the Tote Autumn Cup, and also to be entertained by Joe Scanlon, the manager of Tote Bookmakers.

Mrs Scanlon was there. I hadn't really focused properly on her before. She is a charming, attractive girl, quiet, extremely pleasant, with a good sense of humour; tall, brown hair, a soft round face full of maternal love which she pours on to her children and no doubt on to the would-be raffish Joe Scanlon who in many ways is a fairly good egg.

It was a great joy to see Caroline.

She said it was all nonsense, she was never going to die in a week, or whatever. She is going up for tests and things may be improving. She is immensely active, running around, looking after her garden, and full of gossip. She is going on, naturally, with her scrap books. She has recorded all the terrible things which happen to her friends, disasters like my losing Banbury, as well as the good things. She pops in all the divorces and the children's activities.

Sunday 18 September
I rang John Major. I just caught him before he started on his travels to South Africa.

I told him that as a result of my article about Italy and Berlusconi in the *Times* I had been invited to dinner with the Deputy Foreign Minister tonight. He said, 'You can give him a message from me. I'm very grateful for their support and we can do a great deal together. They're very much on our side in their approach to Germany and France.'

Daphne [Fielding] came to lunch.

We talked of Beaverbrook and how much he had helped Henry [Bath] and her when they were very young and hadn't got much money.

Caroline said, 'You must go on ringing me. It always cheers me up.' I do love that girl.

Tuesday 20 September
Petronella and I went to *Arcadia* by Tom Stoppard. It is far too long and pretentious.

Wednesday 21 September
Lunch at NERA where the new Permanent Under Secretary at the Home Office, Richard Wilson,[10] was the chief guest. I pressed upon him the use of identity cards and said the Tote could produce them with its on-line system.

I said we should have won the Lottery. 'I thought you were going to come on to that.' He seemed pretty bright.

Thursday 22 September
A Levy Board meeting. It was commendably brief because John Sparrow was all of a twitter. Michael Howard, Home Secretary, was due to arrive at a quarter to one. He said we must be all out of the room by twelve o'clock so there'd be time to clear away my cigar smoke and lay the table.

He arrived late, as he always does. He told us not to expect any more help from the government in the forthcoming Budget. He was aware of the dangers to racing of the Lottery and they will be monitoring its effect on the levy and on bookmakers generally.

There was general discussion in which he said the government had given racing the opportunity to help itself, which is quite true, and it was up to them to follow it through.

Saturday 24 September
Verushka, quite reasonably, didn't want to go to Ascot. She gets very tired and can't sleep very well. The appalling leg hurts her a lot. She wanted to reserve herself for Chequers.

I asked Richard Evans of the *Times*, who is now a friend, to join us in the paddock to judge the best turned-out horse. He told me he thought I would get another year at the Tote and thereafter retire. I made absolutely no comment. I have to get more than that. I need at least two years, and I sometimes feel why should I ever retire. I feel pretty fit.

---

10. Permanent Under Secretary of State, Home Office, 1994–8; Secretary of the Cabinet and Head of the Home Civil Service since 1998; knight 1997.

Part of the treat for sponsors – the Tote was one for the Festival
Handicap Stakes – is to go to the Royal Box.

Princess Margaret was in one of her tiresome moods. On the surface
she was very friendly, but when I said to her would she mind if I
smoked my cigar sitting beside her, she said she hated the smell of
cigars, so I put it away. She goes on puffing cigarettes the whole damn
time.

When I was talking to Princess Margaret I turned to Piers Bengough,
Her Majesty's representative at Ascot: 'Is the audience up or down?'
He said, 'I keep telling you, Woodrow, it's either an attendance or a
crowd. You shouldn't call it an audience.' I said, 'We're in the entertainment business and it is an audience.'

Petronella had rung up saying they had it in Mandrake in the
Sunday Telegraph that I had given a private dinner with only Margaret,
John Major and myself present. They allegedly covered what we had
discussed. A tiny part was right, about it being the first meeting they'd
had for years and so forth. Fortunately, they didn't know what we
discussed afterwards, which was dynamite. Though it was true there
was a great reconciliation.

When I got to Chequers I took John aside briefly to say, 'I am
terribly sorry but Margaret has leaked about our private dinner. She
wanted to show all three of us are friends and she's backing you.
She told Charles Moore and he's putting it in the *Sunday Telegraph*
tomorrow. Petronella rang to say so and she is furious.'

John was totally relaxed. 'Oh I don't mind a bit. It doesn't matter.
It's a very good thing.' In fact I discovered that both sides had leaked,
Major and Margaret. I thought, 'Oh my goodness. It was supposed to
be a dead secret, and now they both go out and leak it. If you can't
even rely on prime ministers not to leak things which are dead secret,
where are we?'

Yeltsin told Viscountess Rothermere it would be all right if they
called on him in Russia, saying 'If I am still President,' rather doubtfully
but jokingly.

I congratulated Heseltine on his letter in the *Times* this morning.
At first it looked as though he didn't want to talk to me. But I ploughed
on, and said, 'It's funny how they don't want to admit that Blair was
in the CND.' He agreed. I said, 'It was very good fighting stuff.' He
actually smiled.

Arnold, back in the great hall later, asked for a cigar. He didn't have one of his own. He can't afford them, I told those standing around to their amusement.

When we were sitting in the great hall afterwards, the lovely Viscountess Rothermere came up to me and sat down.

She kept putting her hand on me. I thought, 'Oh my goodness, she'll set fire to me.' She easily could with that glorious, round face, strong black eyes, deep, and that wonderful black hair. But I don't think there is much prospect of it.

Sunday 25 September

The news of the great private dinner in Mandrake in the *Sunday Telegraph* caused a sensation. The press and TV kept ringing to ask what was said at the dinner. Verushka kept saying 'No, it was a private dinner.'

Major told me at Chequers about his now regular conversations with Margaret.

The two-way traffic has been set up brilliantly, thanks to me.

I spoke to Caroline. The result of the second opinion is that an operation could be done to remove the tumour from the pancreas, but there would be a ten per cent chance of living. She said she might take that.

They are quite confident nothing is going to happen instantly.

She said, 'If I have to go into hospital for this operation, you must come to see me often.' Poor child. It is really terrifying.

Nicholas [Banszky] came with all his tribulations on Sunday evening briefly, for Verushka's birthday. He is setting out his divorce plans now.

I decided that Nadje should take part in the birthday celebration and insisted on everybody going to her room. I gave her a glass of champagne and Mark and Eva [Pejacsevich] took theirs in.

Nadje got almost drunk. At any rate, it sent her to sleep in a more cheerful mood than usual.

Poor Beryl Bainbridge rang up before dinner.

Her great friend had died, Colin Haycraft, the publisher.[11]

Now she is in a terrible state.

---

11. (1929–94); publisher and classicist; chairman, Gerald Duckworth & Co., from 1971; President, Classical Association, 1993–4.

Monday 26 September

Got up at twenty past six in order to catch the aeroplane to Glasgow.

I saw six betting shops plus a new one being built and a Ladbroke shop.

After the racing at Hamilton there was the glorious drive down to Hexham.

It was a merry dinner party on Monday. Charles Enderby [Chairman, Hexham Racecourse] turned out much more intelligent than I thought. He produced the head of the northern area of the Tory Party and also Hexham Tory MP, Peter Atkinson, plus one or two other local notables.

I think they are very poor. There was only a cru bourgeois for dinner and no champagne so I had to have gin and Dubonnet which I had not drunk for years. The food was not at all bad, cooked by Mrs Enderby who is charming and still pretty, hence their daughter Amelia's good looks.

Atkinson, the MP, said that Major was making a mistake with his classlessness. Heads of the northern areas and other areas of the Tory Party used to get knighthoods and their wives looked forward to that. Now they only get CBEs or something less.

They say nothing about it but it means they don't work as hard for the party as they would have done.

A pleasant fellow, but too keen on Kenneth Clarke.

Tuesday 27 September

I came down to breakfast which was cooked by Mrs Enderby. There were no servants in sight. I ate it in the kitchen which at least was warmed by the cooking apparatus. I rather took to her. She is sprightly.

Then it was off to see the Roman Wall.

The workers at Vindolanda are all voluntary. There were only six of them and they do all the excavations, unpaid. They have got about two hundred years' work left. Early that morning they had found a gold coin of the Roman Emperor, Trajan, in beautiful condition as mint.

I told them to write to me about what their requirements were and the finances they needed to do the job a bit quicker than in two hundred years.

I might try to get Paul Getty interested.

Thursday 29 September

A disagreeable meeting with Michael Howard.

I said I wanted another two years. He said, 'You can't have that because it would come in the middle of an election, in two years.'

There is a mole in the Home Office. Richard Evans told me at Ascot on Saturday that he had heard I was going to get a one-year extension.

It is exactly what Howard offered me.

I said, 'No. I would just be a lame duck. I have always had two years.' I also said that I wanted to have a proper increase in salary because of my pension and all the work I had been doing to develop so many other things including the Lottery. I said, 'At the moment my Chief Executive is paid more than I am. I want £120,000 a year.' He said, 'You can't have it. You know what the public sector pay policy is.' 'But we're not anything to do with the public sector. We've never had a ha'penny from the government, we've just given money to you.' 'But I appoint you. That makes it public sector.'

I said, 'I want to go on for at least another two years because I have so much to do. For example, I am hoping to buy Coral.' 'You can't do that.' 'Why not?' 'Because that would be merging the public sector with private industry and that's against government policy.' I said, 'That's not so. We nearly bought Coral before and the Home Office knew all about it and thought it a jolly good idea.' 'Oh, well I don't,' he said. 'You ought to privatize yourselves.'

I started getting crosser and crosser and it was very difficult for me to keep my temper. I can see now why he is so hopeless at man management. He is aggressive, unfriendly when he thinks he has a little power. I have been supporting him colossally and he rings me up every now and again to thank me effusively.[12] I am beginning to wonder whether he is any good as Home Secretary because he rubs so many people up the wrong way.

When I came back Verushka said, 'You must take the one year and not argue about it.' I said, 'Nonsense. I am going to argue about it. I'm going to think carefully what I am going to do first and one of the things I am going to do is to ring John Major and tell him that I want the two years.'

I also said to Howard that we are already merging with private industry by having an arrangement with Bass over Tote Direct and

---

12. In the *News of the World* of 18 September 1994 WW had defended Howard against attacks concerning recent prison security breaches.

Coral which they own. 'My whole intention is to merge with private industry.' The trouble is that man has got a blind spot in his head and he hasn't really thought about it at all. I have been asking him for months, ever since he has been Home Secretary, to come to talk to him about the Tote but he has never let me until now.

I shall be up a gum tree soon if I lose the Tote, and maybe I'll lose the *News of the World* and the *Times*.

Friday 30 September
I had a dream about Attlee. He said, 'Don't get over-excited. Keep calm. Did you really think I was a great Prime Minister?' 'Yes of course I did. I wouldn't have said so otherwise.' He seemed pleased, not at all alarming as he could be in real life with his curt ways.

Saturday 1 October

Sometimes I wonder whether I shouldn't really concentrate on the manuscript and start publishing it now. But it would end up with me never being able to talk to people again because they would know I was writing it all down. Also, I might not like to look in the eye of the people I would seriously offend.

I went through great chunks of the pieces I intend to show to the Macmillan lot. Some of it was very good but some of it was very badly corrected, mostly by my failure to notice errors. I thought, 'My goodness, if I die and it's all in a state, the editor won't be able to understand where I've said "she" when I should have said "he", or where I am referring to myself speaking when I ought to have been referring to the other person. But it's a pretty big order trying to read a million and a half to a million and three quarter words.'[1]

Sunday 2 October

The alarm by the side of the bed, set for 6.15, rang like a fire engine. I leapt out of bed and rang up Petronella, telling her to be ready to start at a quarter past seven. We had to go to Gatwick to pick up the chartered aeroplane.[2]

For the first time in my life I had lobster for breakfast.

I took a glass of champagne into the lavatory and scored another first, drinking champagne while peeing.

I was pleased to find myself sitting next to Fiona Allsopp. 'How did you get those wonderful blue eyes below your marvellous black hair?' 'Because I'm Irish.'

Charlie was very chuffed when I told him I had framed his water colour of the view from the house [in Italy] across the marina and on to the fort and the sea.

---

1. WW never managed the onerous task. In the end the manuscript totalled over three million words.
2. The Fortes were taking a party to the Arc de Triomphe race at Longchamp, Paris.

I talked to Vere for an hour or more. He liked Major and enjoyed it very much at Chequers.

He said that Major couldn't understand the people and couldn't lead them properly or inspire them. 'Only aristocrats understand the people, like Macmillan, Home and myself.' I said, 'Macmillan was not an aristocrat. The people you name are defeatist in any case. They believed in the decline of Britain and accelerated it.'[3]

Vere said his ancestors were Cromwellians and Republicans and didn't believe in the monarchy. I said, 'That's why you've been telling so many lies about it and exaggerating the Queen's wealth.' Oh no, he didn't want to get rid of the monarchy. He wanted to get rid of foreign proprietors of newspapers like Rupert and Conrad Black.[4]

I didn't point out to him that he himself is a tax exile.

There was also a man called Taki[5] there whom I had never met before. He had been trying to get Petronella to go out with him. He goes around London saying he spoke to Petronella's mother and he imitates her accent. 'She will never go with you,' and she was quite right.

I talked quite a bit to Jeremy Paxman who was standing around with not quite such a smirking smile on his face as usual. I told him, 'The best thing about you is your yellow waistcoat.' We talked about smoking and I said it's all a racket and, 'You must do a thorough programme about it one day.' He was helpful and interested. I congratulated him on various things he had done. That is one way of repairing a breach.

Jacob Rothschild and Serena were there. I was very amused by them joining the common queues. Jacob said he had never walked so far in his life.

Petronella and I thoroughly enjoyed the day. She had been telling me two days before about Anna Pasternak, the great-niece of the great Boris Pasternak.

She had been writing the book for this fearful guardsman [James

---

3. Harold Macmillan's forebears were Scottish crofters; his grandfather had left the Isle of Arran to make his fortune in England and founded the publishing house Macmillan; his wife, Lady Dorothy, was the daughter of the 9th Duke of Devonshire; Sir Alec Home was the 14th Earl of Home before he renounced his title; Vere Rothermere was the 3rd Viscount Rothermere.
4. Conrad Black is now a British citizen.
5. Taki Theodoracopulos, gossip columnist.

Hewitt] on the five-year affair he had with Princess Diana, and the silly letters she wrote to him.

He is clearly not a gentleman.

Now he hopes to make three million pounds out of betraying Diana. Anna Pasternak was at St Paul's with Petronella. I have met her several times and thought her a serious, nice girl. She has now done this despicable thing with Major Hewitt.[6]

Monday 3 October

I rang John Major before starting my *Times* article. I told him of my conversation with Vere Rothermere.

I said, 'I want to come to speak to you, if I may, partly about personal things. I am having a ridiculous dialogue with Michael Howard. I find him extremely tiresome about the Tote.' He said, 'Tact isn't his middle name.' I said, 'But I will leave it until after the conference when you've got more time.'

Friday 7 October

I have had a triumph with Gus Fischer, in charge of News International. Instead of referring my request to have £150,000 a year instead of £140,000 to Rupert, he took it on his own bat and arranged it himself. 'I'm not going to bother Rupert with it. I have the authority to do it.' I thought 'My goodness, why didn't I ask for a bit more?'

Saturday 8 October

We got to Oare in good time for lunch. Henry, as usual, was very welcoming. Tessa is somewhat subdued. All over the newspapers is the complete collapse of the Lovat estates which they have had for six hundred and forty years.

By dinner time Conrad Black and Barbara had arrived. During the course of the evening I attacked Conrad severely.

At one time he said I was being insulting.

Sunday 9 October

I took the trouble to butter Conrad Black up, having played the hard man the night before.

There was a good deal of discussion about the *Sunday Times* raising

---

6. The book was *Princess in Love*; see Vol. 2, pp. 648–9, for WW meeting Anna Pasternak.

again, years after the event, the question of did Mark Thatcher get money from the great deal with the Saudi Arabians to sell them Tornados, which produced fifteen thousand jobs and £20 billion in orders still on-going into the next century.

It was to coincide with the start of the Tory Conference, to illustrate how sleazy the Tories are.

Henry is very proud of his horses which run mainly in Tessa's name. He has been breeding them and having success at it, more he says than Serena [Rothschild] has with hers.

He is amazing, that fellow. Anything he touches turns into money – he has the proverbial Midas touch. I told him, 'You're the best businessman of them all.' 'Oh no. I'm very cautious.' 'Nonsense. You may be cautious but you know exactly what you're doing.'

When we got back to London in the evening I had a long talk with John Major.

On Black I said, 'I have got him swearing that he is going to back you. We've still got the problem of Simon Heffer but I will try to work on him a bit more. At one time I thought you might offer him [Black] a peerage,' to which Major replied, 'But he's got to deliver first.'

I said to Major he should accentuate the positive in his own speech which he said he is going to do.

'I'm feeling very chipper.' 'That's very good. Convey that feeling to the conference, to the lot of them.'

Monday 10 October
Spoke to Margaret. She is in great distress over the attacks on her in the *Sunday Times*, and on Mark.

The National Audit Office had examined the thing for three years and didn't want their report published because various people in Saudi Arabia were concerned and publishing their names could lose us this huge order. 'I shall get on to Rupert and say that after all she has done for you it is absolutely appalling that this has now happened.' 'How glad I am to hear a kind voice.'

I couldn't track down where Rupert was immediately. Eventually I got a number to ring his flat in Sydney, Australia, though no one was supposed to know where he was.

When I told him and asked if he would do something about it he said, 'Yes, of course I will.' He had been asleep at the time and I had woken him up. Then I told Margaret.

I had lunch with Robert Cranborne at Wiltons.

I wouldn't have the whitebait because it was cooked in vegetable oil. 'That means palm oil which is a killer.'

There was a general sending things back and saying they were wrong which caused the waitress great disturbance. Robert said, 'I think she believes we're mad.' I said, 'Never mind. We're not, are we?'

As the night wore on and nothing had happened, I rang Rupert again.

I made him come out of a meeting, which annoyed him a good deal. 'What are you doing about it?' 'Nothing. It's all Mark Thatcher's fault and I'm not going to do anything about it.' I said, 'What? After all she's done for you? It's a disgrace. You must stand by the poor girl. In a few hours time she'll be on that platform at Brighton. Everybody will be looking at her saying "You've poured sleaze upon the Tory party and you've heightened the whole atmosphere of sleaze." '

He started shouting at me and I at him. He said I was bullying him and he wouldn't put up with it. I said, 'You need bullying. For God's sake do something.' 'Get off the telephone then, now. I'll pay some attention to it. I can't let you go on shouting at me. I'll ring you back.' It was very acrimonious. We were both furious.

I slept by the telephone on the floor in my library, but the brute never rang.

Tuesday 11 October

The *Times* ran the story this morning, giving more of the real facts and quoting from an official who had been involved throughout who had never seen or heard of Mark Thatcher having any connection with the famous arms deal. It was quite a good piece and it put the record very much more straight. So Rupert had acted.

I wondered whether I should send a fax to Rupert saying thank you, but I simply never got round to it so this matter is still in the troubled air between him and me.

Lunch with Beryl Bainbridge at The Ivy. She is still in an appalling state about this wretched publisher of hers from Duckworth.

Wednesday 12 October

I was very sad not to be able to send Margaret her roses for her birthday which I've always done in the past. I did not know where she was, nor did her office. So I sent her the following birthday greeting telegram for her sixty-ninth: 'Many happy returns and there will be many. There is sunshine behind the clouds. Love Woodrow.'

Then it was off to stay with the Zetlands, prior to the great race [at Redcar] the next day, with the first prize of £100,000 being put up by us, though in various ways it doesn't cost us anything like £100,000.

Mark started by being friendly and Sue, his wife, certainly so.

As the conversation wore on, Mark began to attack me. 'You ought to go at once. You ought to have new ideas at the Tote and you haven't got any.' I said, 'On the contrary, I invented the Placepot and now the Quadpot. The Placepot is the sole reason why Ladbroke and William Hill are interested [in entering the Tote pools] because it is very popular with their punters.' He said, 'You didn't invent the Placepot. Your organization did.' 'I'm sorry but that's totally untrue.'

I then began to realize he actually hates me. Perhaps he wanted to be Chairman of the Tote himself – very likely.

When the guests disappeared I went to bed, considerably disturbed.

Thursday 13 October

This morning at breakfast Mark told me he had a terrible beating up from his wife for being so unpleasant. He pointed at me, 'You didn't mind, did you?' 'No. I didn't mind at all.' I wasn't going to show anything, though it had been extremely unpleasant, having invited me to stay in the house and then being thoroughly abused and grossly insulted in front of his guests.

During the day I telephone Caroline at least once and sometimes twice. It's not going too well for her. All the tests were pretty bad. She has now got jaundice back again. There seems to be only a slim chance they'll cure her.

She is extraordinarily brave.

Saturday 15 October

The day of the Cesarewitch. We had a very good breakfast [at the Howard de Waldens] with field mushrooms. Angela [Oswald], who is lady-in-waiting to Queen Elizabeth the Queen Mother, said that she dates the deterioration in the health of Queen Elizabeth, who is now a bit doddery, from the publication of the ghastly Morton book about Diana.

I was wrong in believing that Lady Fermoy, grandmother of Diana, had urged them not to let the match proceed. On the contrary, she had told them it would be a great success. When the whole affair collapsed in misery there was a strain between Queen Elizabeth the

Queen Mother and Lady Fermoy who had been her main lady-in-waiting for many years.

Now the forthcoming publication in the *Sunday Times* of the serialization of this new book, written by Jonathan Dimbleby with full approval of the Prince of Wales, is a dreadful blow. He had been advised by Nicholas Soames and William Astor not to do such a silly thing.

We all agreed he is a total chump to publish this self-pitying stuff and attacks on his parents, just as he was winning the battle against Diana. He has become a 'kiss-and-tell' wretch, elaborating all the detail about Camilla. It is demeaning and hurtful of him to say he never loved Diana at all and was ordered to marry her by his father. Actually, I think he was in love with her at the beginning but it suits his selfish arrogance to pretend otherwise.

The Howard de Waldens are extremely nice. I told them about Caroline.

Angela knows much about homeopathy because Queen Elizabeth and the Queen are very much into it. The great advantage is that it can do no harm and may well do you good.

Angela said Caroline must take a type of homeopathic pill.

Before we left Gillie cut me an apricot rose to wear in my tweed suit. Apricot rose are their racing colours.

It looked as though Grand Lodge [their horse] was going to win [the Champion Stakes] when a horse I had looked at with Lord Donoughue (Bernard) in the paddock, called Dernier Empereur, suddenly caught it at the line.

Once economics adviser to Callaghan, Bernard Donoughue has made a great deal of money out of Robert Maxwell and in other ways in the City. He is very keen on racing. He is divorced.

He said [to Verushka], 'Tell Woodrow – if you have an affair with anybody these days, they go straight to the newspapers and sell the story.' He said he had been very careful himself.

Bernard Donoughue is very tall with a round, chubby face and black hair, curly, not bad-looking and with plentiful Irish blarney.

Sunday 16 October
Had a long conversation with John Major.

He said he read Petronella's [column] and he hadn't liked that very much. I said, 'I told Petronella beforehand that you wouldn't like the rubbish she wrote about your being frightened of Sarah Hogg.' He was particularly annoyed about it. I said, 'Of course she feels she has to say some uncomplimentary things from time to time, or some criticism, as indeed I do. Or it looks like a put-up job.'

It's one thing to criticize somebody and quite another to say he is being domineered by a woman or adviser when he's not.

I told John the saga of the Rupert story.

Unfortunately, Zetland is a friend of Michael Howard.

Tuesday 18 October
Peter Stothard wanted to know whether it was true that Queen Elizabeth the Queen Mother objected to Charles having a divorce and that this was a bar to it.

I rang Robin Janvrin, the assistant private secretary at the Palace.

He said it was absolute nonsense.

I also rang Angela Oswald. She said, 'Of course it's not true. Total rubbish. She would never stand in the way of his divorce if he wants one.' The *Times* is now trying to act responsibly.

Dinner with John Robb, who runs Wellcome, and Sir John Sparrow who is Chairman of the Levy Board. John Robb is one of the government members on the Levy Board. We drank a fair amount of champagne, a very decent claret and talked our heads off.

They are both against the BHB and the Jockey Club trying to take over the Tote or the Levy Board. I said, 'If three top people get together in any small area, they can always get what they want. We must act in concert.'

I then told them about Zetland. They were horrified.

I shall need them to support me, both, with the Home Secretary and with John Major if necessary.

Friday 21 October
Things have not been going so well for darling Caroline. They did something wrong in London and they want to do it all over again. She is absolutely fed up with it. Now they are frightened in London because they made a mistake that she is going to sue them. I said, 'I wouldn't bother with that.' 'No, certainly not. There's no point in it.'

Saturday 22 October
I woke up early for Badminton to have time to look at betting shops in Gloucester and Cheltenham as well. I felt absolutely ghastly. I could hardly get out of bed.

When I got there I said to Caroline, 'I'm in a terrible state. I'm afraid I'm the invalid,' which indeed I was.

I couldn't eat anything at lunch and could only drink clear fizzy white water. Caroline was very concerned and so was David. She took me up to a bedroom and I went to bed there.

When I got up we had tea together which she made for me.

Sunday 23 October
I rang John this morning. I told him I thought he had done magnificently over Ireland.

He said, 'I'm really beginning to feel, now, that I have done it. I haven't felt so before but now I think we're very nearly there.'[7]

I said, 'I think you really must tell that fellow Hamilton[8] that he's got to resign, as least while he's going on with this legal action.' He said, 'Well, it was a matter which was cleared up some years ago, in about 1987, when he stayed at the Ritz Hotel at the invitation of Al Fayed.' 'I don't think it was cleared up then. He'd been there several times and also he'd been asking questions for Al Fayed to get at Tiny Rowland.[9] Anybody who has such little judgement as to have something to do with Al Fayed isn't a person who should be a Minister in any case.' 'But it is difficult. He's not been proved guilty yet.' I broke in, 'But being a case of this kind, more mud will be thrown by the ghastly Al Fayed and it'll be even worse.' 'You'll have to leave it to me. I follow what you're saying.'

I also referred to this man Ian Greer.[10] 'He's very bad news. He's

---

7. The Loyalists had announced a cease-fire on 14 October, following the IRA announcement of a cease-fire on 31 August.
8. The *Guardian* of 20 October had accused Neil Hamilton, Conservative MP for Tatton, and another Conservative MP, Tim Smith, of taking cash to ask questions in Parliament. Smith apologized and resigned immediately from his office as Parliamentary Under-Secretary for Northern Ireland; he did not contest the 1997 general election. Hamilton began a libel case against the *Guardian*, later abandoned; he reluctantly resigned on 25 October from his office as Under Secretary of State for Trade and Industry; he was defeated in the 1997 general election by Martin Bell standing as an Independent; his now famous libel case against Mohamed Al Fayed followed later.
9. Mohamed Al Fayed and Tiny Rowland (1917–98; chairman, Lonrho Group, 1981–93) had fought bitterly over the Fayeds' acquisition of the Fraser group including Harrods.
10. Parliamentary lobbyist (Ian Greer Associates).

admitted he's responsible for getting MPs paid to put down questions and raise matters in Parliament. If they are matters which should be raised, then anybody would be willing to deal with them. If they don't think that, they shouldn't be raised in any case. I think these dreadful lobbying people are responsible for a lot of the trouble.'

John said, 'I agree that they do tempt Members of Parliament.' 'Also, I would stand very clear of Greer yourself, if I may say so.' (I said that because he had been attending parties at this ghastly man's headquarters where they have a turnover of £3.5 million a year.)

I told him I had been talking to Tebbit several times and that each time I speak to him he says he is in the middle, at the heart of the party as far as Europe is concerned.

John was very pleased. He said, 'I have been cultivating him lately. I think his talent has been greatly wasted. He could do a lot of good for the Party. He did far more for the Thatcherite revolution than he is generally given credit for. I am going to try to find him something really important to do in connection with winning the next election.'

We discussed Blair. He said it was very interesting for him last Tuesday when he first had him across the table at Questions. He hadn't been able to place him in his mind. He said, 'I like to feel I've got the character right of the person I am dealing with. Then it is much easier. After the last Question time, when he was making all those pious remarks and vague assertions about his policies, I got him right. He's a cross between Hugh Gaitskell and Roy Jenkins.'

Andrew Roberts came to dinner. His girlfriend, the barrister with whom he lives, was ill with flu so he came by himself.

We teased him about his pending marriage.

'Remember Punch's advice to those about to marry, "Don't",' I said.

David frequently asks Caroline what I talk to her about. I said, 'You should tell him that we merely read love poems to each other and some that I have composed for you. That should put him off.'

Monday 24 October
Dashed off to the Waldorf Hotel to meet Diana Rawstron, Mrs Tamborero and Mrs Sarah Curtis, the potential editor. She seems pleasant in appearance, fifty-eight years old, with remnants of a type of prettiness which does not appeal to me. At first I thought, as she spoke about her approach to the job, that she might be suitable. She is Liberal in politics. She also admired Mrs Thatcher.

The more she talked I wondered whether her prejudices wouldn't guide her editing selections. The manuscript is mine, not hers, and I don't want it to be altered in its flavour and approach by someone antipathetic to my political views or maybe to other aspects of my life. We let her see a chunk, as we had done with the Macmillan people – the episode dealing with the assassination of Mrs Thatcher. She seemed to warm to these and said how interesting and almost exciting they were. But I began to wonder, also, about her sense of humour. I asked her whether she liked P. G. Wodehouse. She hesitated, then said she thought he could be funny but her husband and son liked him more – a bad sign.

Cita's birthday party at the Connaught.

Cita was very pleased with the Lees-Milne book[11] I gave her which are his most recent edition of his highly snobbish diaries, beginning with the proposition, agreed to by both Somerset Maugham and himself at dinner, that Kipling 'was not a gent'. I remarked that Kipling was a man infinitely greater than either of them could ever be.

Tuesday 25 October
Irwin Stelzer and John Witherow, the editor of the *Sunday Times*,[12] came to lunch in the Barry Room at the Lords. I attacked Witherow for publishing the ancient story about Mrs Thatcher and Mark to match the opening of the Tory Party Conference.

He replied that they ought to expose corruption wherever it is. 'But you can't get any jobs outside England without some form of corruption, back-handers or commissions. If you want to expose all that, we won't get any orders at all. How do you think Hong Kong was built?' He said, 'That's nothing to do with us. We're a newspaper.' 'It is something to do with you because if you lose everybody's jobs in England, you won't have a newspaper either because nobody would be able to afford to buy the damn thing.' This last point scored the most with him.

He swore he is not anti-Tory though he has reservations about Major.

I am expecting him to be more restrained about the government in future and start backing it.

---

11. *A Mingled Pleasure*; James Lees-Milne (1908–97), cultural and architectural historian, on the staff of the National Trust, 1936–66.
12. Acting editor, *Sunday Times*, 1994; editor since 1995.

Thursday 27 October
I had a fascinating lunch with Professor John Ashford from Exeter University.

And also Judith Hatton, the lady from FOREST [researcher].[13]

Judith Hatton is a bit wacky but she has some interesting notions. Professor Ashford repeated that all these statistics are meaningless, and from uncontrolled experiments. He said you could do them with mice and rats but they weren't quite suitable. You couldn't get them inhaling and not inhaling.

'Why couldn't we do the experiment with chimpanzees?'

'You would get all the animal rights people protesting.'

He also said there were lots of people in the medical profession who knew the campaign against smoking was total rubbish but dare not say so because of the 'political correctness' involved.

I had rather a sweet letter from Mrs Curtis which makes me feel a heel.

Maybe Mrs Tamborero and I may withdraw our reservations.[14]

Saturday 29 October
Talked at some length to John Major.

I told him the Nolan Committee was a brilliant idea.[15] He said he doesn't care what it discovers or discloses. It's got to be done. They have to clear this ghastly sleaze up wherever it may fall.

I told him what I was saying in the *News of the World*, that the Fayeds should be deported for the tricks they are up to. John laughed. 'I can't say that, but thank goodness you can.'

Later on during the day I talked to Caroline. She had been to see the Prince of Wales. They had a very pleasant talk about his garden and they walked all round it. It is very beautifully done. I said, 'And

---

13. Freedom Organisation for the Right to Enjoy Smoking Tobacco.
14. The letter which pleased WW thanked him for lunch, said I enjoyed meeting him and that I had suggested to Diana Rawstron some points which should be clarified at the outset, about the scale of the task and the likely requirements of the publishers. At this period I was working full-time at the RSA (Royal Society of Arts); I met WW only twice again (in April and November 1995) and did not sign the contract with Macmillan to edit his journals until September 1997, shortly before he died.
15. The Nolan Commission on Standards in Public Life which published its first report on 11 May 1995.

what about the conversation?' She said, 'Nothing of interest to me, like my health or his wife.'

Sunday 30 October
The *Sunday Telegraph* has produced the astonishing revelation that the *Guardian* forged a request to the Ritz in Paris on House of Commons writing paper, signed as though it were Jonathan Aitken's secretary, giving the fax number to reply to which was really the *Guardian*'s.[16]

I spoke to Richard Ryder. He said the *Guardian* situation would be brought to the Committee of Privileges and it would be raised in the House. I said, 'I think it would be very foolish to have any part of the Committee of Privileges investigation of the £1,000-a-question people in public. Blair and co. would no doubt summon Mohamed Fayed who would lie his head off, as per the article I wrote in the *News of the World* this morning.[17] A hell of a lot of people are in the pockets of these Fayeds who are causing incredible damage.'

The papers are full of hysteria, like a McCarthyite witchhunt. A few of the things McCarthy shouted out and labelled people with were true but the rest was innuendoes and smears from which people never recovered their characters.[18]

I spoke to John Major.

I said, 'It wants reading very carefully, that section of conclusions in the [1987] DTI report [about the acquisition of the House of Fraser]. Many journalists were criticized for accepting the facts dished out to them by the Al Fayeds. I am sure they were given all kinds of freebies at the Ritz and elsewhere.'

I said, 'You've got to deport the bloody buggers. There's no reason to delay any more. Just throw them out of the country.'[19] John replied, 'There may be some legal problems.'

---

16. The fake fax was to obtain a copy of Aitken's Ritz bill paid by his friend Said Ayas; these revelations were the start of the events that led to Aitken's resignation, libel case, perjury and subsequent imprisonment.
17. In his *News of the World* article of 30 October WW quoted the 1987 DTI report which said that the Fayeds had lied about the sources of their wealth which enabled them to buy the House of Fraser including Harrods.
18. Senator Joseph McCarthy's notorious 1950–4 campaign against alleged communists and fellow-travellers.
19. Mohamed al Fayed's brother Ali was granted a British passport in 1999.

I said to John Major, 'C. P. Scott, the man who laid down the dictum "facts are sacred but comment is free", must be spinning in his grave at what the present editor of the *Guardian* is doing.' 'So must a lot of other people,' said John Major.

I said to John, 'You've been absolutely brilliant over this. You're going to win.' He said it didn't feel like it at the moment.

I also asked him whether he thought the Nolan Committee inquiry could be widened to include the fourth estate, as journalism and the press are colloquially called. He said he would think about that to see whether there were some way of doing it.

Monday 31 October
Strenuous arguments with the *Times*. The lawyer came on. The copy was altered. All kinds of fearful things. It was a follow-up to my yesterday's article in the *News of the World*, expanding it very much. It continued the attack on the Fayeds and the *Guardian* reporting.

At the party at the Ritz, London, for Selina Hastings' book about Evelyn Waugh I met Moorea. We agreed to meet again to talk about judges arranging for conciliation between people when their marriages break up so that they don't spend lots of money on lawyers' fees sorting out their affairs.[20] I thought to myself it would have been much better if Moorea and I had had a similar arrangement when we divorced instead of masses of fees for lawyers and accountants.

---

20. Lady Moorea Black, half-sister of Lady Selina Hastings, was at this time a magistrate on the Inner London and City Family Proceedings Panel.

Tuesday 1 November

A visit to Mr Martin, the dentist.

I had to take my plate at nine o'clock and leave it with him. So I went to lunch with Vere Rothermere (for the Hungarian Ambassador) minus teeth. I hope they didn't notice.

We were in the magnificent boardroom which used to be in their old establishment.[1]

In the library section is a picture of Lord Northcliffe before he had gone round the bend, looking strong, young and handsome.[2]

I talked at great length to Vere. I hoped he was getting on with backing Major. He said, 'I'm trying to but it's very difficult with all the sleaze and the troubles he's in. How is he going to win?' I said, 'He'll win,' and gave him my standard answer.

Vere told me the story of the Perrier water. It was a great uncle of his who called it Perrier – and had discovered that particular well – after a doctor he had, named Perrier, and who gave the shape to the bottle like an Indian club. He had had some trouble with his arms and used clubs for exercise and thought what a good shape that would be for a bottle.

Vere said that his great uncle was otherwise not very bright.

Later on I went back to Peter Martin who pulled out my tooth and put in the plate which he had adjusted in the morning.

Wednesday 2 November

Annoying at the Tote Board to find we are obliged to keep the blasted Zetland race for three years.

Dinner at Cavendish Avenue. The Hungarian Ambassador and his wife were the guests of honour. Unfortunately, Verushka had asked seventeen people without realizing it.

---

1. The *Mail* moved in 1989 from Fleet Street to Kensington.
2. (1865–1922); founded the *Daily Mail*, 1896; became chief proprietor, the *Times*, 1908; cr. Viscount 1917.

Virginia Fraser was there. I made a tactless ass of myself. I said I was sorry about the great estates being lost and surely if they could be held together for a while, they could produce a lot of money again. She looked very gloomy and said, 'I'd rather not discuss it. It's so awful.'

Frank Johnson was not drunk but very tired and washed out.

It was one of our most successful dinner parties in its extraordinary jumbly way. And quite useful in keeping Frank Johnson in line, though he is worried about the privatization of the Post Office possibly not proceeding.

Thursday 3 November
Ken Baker's sixtieth birthday party.

Ken Baker has got rather a pleasant little house in Pimlico on the other side of the railway tracks. Lots of cartoons of the eighteenth century and early nineteenth century lined the staircase.

There was dear old Lew Grade[3] who offered me immediately a Montecristo No. 2 which he said was his favourite cigar and I said was mine, too.

His wife is a very sweet little woman. They have been married for thirty-one years. She said they have never had a cross word. She is not a doormat by any means. He left at once when she said she had to go though he wanted to stay.

Margaret came up to me straight away. 'You wrote an absolutely brilliant, marvellous article about the Fayeds in the *Times*. Wasn't it wonderful?' she said to those seated round her. 'Of course they should be deported, the dreadful people.'[4]

Friday 4 November
I was so horrified by the government's failure to carry through the privatization of the Post Office that I wrote about it in the *News of the World*. Before I started I wanted to speak to John Major but he wasn't available.

He rang me at six in the evening. I had an argument with him. He said, 'But you don't realize that there is such a small majority.' I said, 'I do realize that but I think it's a very fatal thing to do. It looks as though you have no power.' He said, 'Well we haven't, really, without

3. (1906–98); impresario; m (1942) Kathleen, née Moody; life peer 1976.
4. See note on 30 October 1994.

a majority.' 'But you can always make them vote for you. You can threaten them with a general election.' 'I can't keep doing that. I did that on Maastricht.'

Sunday 6 November
I rang John in the evening. They said he was having a bath. I said, 'If he feels like talking to me, I shall be here the whole evening.' Two or three hours later he rang.

I said, 'I think they may well cut down their attempts on smear stories now because of the backfiring involved. There has been a lot of sleaze on the Labour side. They wouldn't tell me how much money Maxwell had given to their party funds from the stolen pension fund. I know one case where he gave at least £38,000 to do with a boundary commission deal.'[5]

Monday 7 November
The main feature of the day was dinner at Norman Lamont's.

It was a lame evening on drink. We only got cru bourgeois Château Cissac 1983. It was fairly good but not the sort of wine for a dinner party.

Norman was very pleased I had come out in the way I did on the Post Office in the *News of the World* and we had agreed for once. At one point they were talking about the coronation of Portillo 'which might now have to be delayed'. I think they were referring to an unlikely challenge against John at the last moment but the time will come, whether it is before the election or after it.

Norman confidently expects the Tories to lose the election.

Tuesday 8 November
A very tiresome meeting of the Tote Direct Board at Cavendish Avenue. Unfortunately, the machines had gone for six again on Saturday and on Monday.

You get no credit if it works well but you get a hell of a lot of blame and loss of confidence if it doesn't.

I am so worried about dear Caroline.

She has got to go to the damn hospital again for ten days.

---

5. WW gives no further details of this allegation.

Wednesday 9 November

The great dinner party at the Allsopps. They have given or are giving at least three of these gigantic affairs. I assume that they are funded by Christie's as an intelligent way of mixing up some extremely rich people with people who are also amusing and socially elevated and unlikely customers at Christie's, being minus cash or unwilling sellers.

Fiona has a great talent for buying houses and transforming them. This must be the sixth house within the last six or seven years.

They are beautifully equipped with pictures. (I don't know whose they are, perhaps borrowed from Christie's or perhaps vaguely family pictures.)

Charlie Morrison and his tall wife were there before us.[6] She is blonde and well built.

He is no longer an MP. He has nothing to do except look after the farm and property they have.

He is certainly a great deal more contented than he ever was with Sara.

Charlie always hated Mrs Thatcher, perhaps prompted by Sara, for long his wife, who is a fan of Ted Heath's.

He more or less supports Major, but it doesn't matter who he supports now he has vanished from the political scene.

The next arrivals were Paul Channon and his wife. I like Paul Channon. He has a cheerful, round and friendly face and considerable intelligence.

We talked about Jerry Hall, that tall, slinky model. Paul said that she was very distressed when she found that after all his promises her husband, Mick Jagger, was secretly having an affair with somebody who was actually in the house when she arrived to see him. Paul said she is a self-educated girl. I said I found her very intelligent on the few occasions I had spoken to her, and very agreeable. Also, of course, she is extraordinarily sexy with those amazing six foot, snake-like legs.

Alan Clark's diaries are much praised by Paul. I said I thought they were very shallow and that he didn't understand as much about politics as Paul's father did. Paul said, 'Well, he's much more into them than my father who was completely wrong about Chamberlain and Churchill.' I

---

6. The Hon. Sir Charles Morrison, Conservative MP, 1964–92, knight 1988; m 1 (1954–84) the Hon. Sara Long, vice-chairman, Conservative Party Organization, 1971–5, when Heath was Prime Minister; m 2 (1984, separated 1998) Rosalind, née Lygon, who m 1 Gerald Ward.

said, 'But he did see a great many people and on a wider basis than Alan Clark did. Alan Clark's judgements are also hopeless.'

Henry [Keswick] tells me business is very bad now for Jardine Matheson in Hong Kong. It is not merely because they have moved their headquarters out of Hong Kong – others like the Hong Kong and Shanghai Bank haven't suffered from doing that – but there has been enormous hostility because of his support for Chris Patten.

The food was extraordinarily good.

The wine, however, was no great shakes, there being no red wine as there was fish as a second course, which I do not like.

Thursday 10 November
A highly successful meeting with Sir Bryan Carsberg, head of the Office of Fair Trading.[7] Despite the lawyers, Rowe & Maw, who charged us an enormous amount of money to write a very long and absurd essay saying why we would not get away with putting up our Tote Authority rate, I decided to plunge on and tackle the Office of Fair Trading ourselves.

Bryan was charm itself. They had all studied it and they saw no reason why we shouldn't go ahead with the planned increases, as I had wanted from the start.

I do not think that I could have managed Bryan Carsberg if I hadn't known him for years and got on with him very well. We had an easy ride.

Friday 11 November
Caroline is very pleased with herself. The day after she got a charming letter from Prince Charles and flowers, she got one from Princess Diana. She said, 'It's such a sweet letter, full of kindness.' She has quite changed her view about her and thinks there must be more to the story than Charles's version. I said, 'What a muggins you are. Don't you realize somebody must have told her that you had been to see him at Highgrove and he sent you flowers, and she thought, "Gosh, I must get in on this and make it evens to stop the rot of his getting a significant somebody on his side." '

---

7. Arthur Andersen Professor of Accounting, LSE, 1981–7; Director General of Telecommunications, 1984–92; Director General of Fair Trading, 1992–5; knight 1989. See Vol. 2, pp. 63 and 66, for WW's good opinion of Carsberg.

Saturday 12 November
Rang John.

He is very exercised about this ghastly crew of malcontents who threaten to prevent the contribution we have to make to the EU going through.

John said, 'Did you see in the *Times* this week they said the whole question of leadership is coming up again? Well, who do you suppose had lunch with the editor the day before?' 'Norman Lamont?' 'No. It was Bill Cash.'

He said, 'I sometimes think I can't go through with it all and I don't know what to do.'

I said, 'I know what you've got to do. You've got to stick at it, and I shall keep telling you that. You'll win.' He laughed.

Before she went off to the hospital tonight I had another talk with Caroline. She was very thrilled that the whole of nearly one page in the *Times* was about her. 'I do love publicity,' she said, 'don't you?' I said, 'No. I'm always trying to avoid it.'

She said she isn't reading now. I said, 'You must read to keep your brain active. The most attractive thing about life is it's so interesting. You should never be bored.' 'I'm never bored.'

She said she would retain a belief in the after-life, being a strong believer in the Church of England.

When I finished talking to her, I read this remarkable article in the *Times*. It is so like her, down to the picture of her captioned 'the young Duchess soon after her marriage'. (But she wasn't a Duchess for ages.) She was beautiful. I loved her since I first saw her thirty-five years ago looking in to a shop window to see what was on sale.[8]

The mutterings about a leadership challenge to John Major seem to have died away. They couldn't get enough signatories to produce the challenge. Norman Lamont would have been the stalking horse. Ludicrous!

Monday 14 November
In the evening we went to the ballet.

Tonight it was 'Frederick Ashton Remembered'. Though a queer, or perhaps because he was a queer, he was a damn good choreographer.

While we were eating our supper during the interval, Andrew Knight came up.

---

8. In Venice; see *Confessions of an Optimist*, pp. 266–7.

He was going on about my saying there should be a privacy law and all the sleaze stuff being overdone. 'But how would you get down to the truth of the financial scandals if they didn't follow the sleaze?' I said, 'The two things are quite distinct.'

He has made about £23 million, that fellow, first of all through dealings with Conrad Black.

Also, by sucking up to Rupert Murdoch and Anna and wheedling his way in to managing everything in England. But he has not the character to be effective. So he's only a non-executive director now. But, from being editor of the *Economist*, he has certainly made a great fortune. I must hand him that.

They are no longer serving Cornish Spring Water at Covent Garden. I must enquire from the Sirdar what is going on.

Tuesday 15 November
Rang John early in the morning to congratulate him on his Mansion House speech. We talked about Northern Ireland and about his Nolan Committee. 'By coincidence,' I said, 'this morning in the *Times* I have written on the subject of the Nolan Committee and my views parallel what you were saying last night.' 'So I must be right, then.' 'No. It means that I must be right.' We both laughed.

Had an amusing meeting at the Jockey Club with the trainers and their representatives. I was in my role as unpaid trade union representative – a trustee with members of the committee from the Stable Lads Association.

In private at one moment our side were willing to accept only a £27 premium, from which a lot else flows, for Sunday racing payments. I said, 'No. It's got to be £29.'

We got away with it.

Thursday 17 November
The Other Club. I was in the chair. I brought along some cigars to give to members of which four were smoked. I told them to leave the rest for the December meeting and whatever is left after that I will take away.

A fierce discussion broke out. Both Norman [Tebbit] and Armstrong (former Cabinet Secretary) agreed that John Major was weak. I said, 'I think he's very tough and strong.' 'No,' said Norman. 'He has the mulishness of a weak man with stupidity.'

I said, 'What would it take for you to back John properly?' 'Have

an entirely new department, the sole job of which would be to deal
with the Brussels machinery in every aspect. I agree that we don't want
to leave the EU, but we've got to manipulate it and block every single
advance we don't like. No, no, no must be his weapon. Veto everything
he disapproves of or that we disapprove of.'

Some of what Norman Tebbit said makes sense. Some of it was
rubbish, such as that Heseltine could form a government.

Arnold (Weinstock) was sitting opposite. He talked a great deal of
nonsense about how the government didn't help business and frustrated
him and it was all very bad. He indicated that he would rather like to
have a Blair government.

I had a discussion with Max Hastings, who was sitting nearly
opposite to me, about A. L. Rowse.

I said, 'I tried to get Margaret again and again to give him an
honour. She said she couldn't, after making enquiries, because he had
written such rude things about people. I said to her that would rule
out about every single literary person from ever getting an honour.'

I said, 'If he doesn't get this honour, will you make a great row
about it in the *Telegraph*?' He said, 'Yes, I certainly will.'

At the dinner was poor old Fitzroy MacLean.[9] He's bent double.
He can hardly hobble along with his stick. I thought to myself, oh my
God, he's going to ask me to take him home and I won't be able to
refuse. That is exactly what he did.

He agreed completely with what I said about not interfering and
getting muddled up in the affairs of the former Yugoslavia.

Fitzroy asked if I thought he had done the right thing in persuading
Churchill to back Tito. I said, 'Yes, you were right. But Tito was greatly
helped by the Russian menace.'

I said Tito was quite mad though to leave this revolving presidency
behind him in his legacy. Fitzroy said Tito discussed it with him at
length. Fitzroy had said to him, 'I can't see that it will work.' Tito
said, 'Nor do I but it's the best thing I can think of now they are no
longer frightened of the Russians.'

Sunday 20 November
Had an amazing, disturbing conversation with John Major.

He started off, poor chap, by saying I had caught him in a very bad

---

9. (1911–96); Conservative MP, 1941–74; commanded British mission to Yugoslav
   partisans, 1943–5; writer and journalist; 1st baronet, created 1957.

mood. He had been reading all the newspapers and they do nothing but attack him.

John said, 'I cannot see why Vere Rothermere in the *Mail*, and the *Daily Telegraph* which is supposed to be our paper, keep doing this drip, drip, drip thing saying I'm no good and the party's no good. They can't suddenly turn round at the end and say "nevertheless, you've got to vote for them." '

Caroline Beaufort has been getting tired and I am getting worried. 'Are you eating enough?' 'I am getting thinner.' 'I'm sure that's not a good idea, to get too thin.' 'The doctor says it's OK.'

The Trees were there, the Wiltons were there, and the nice Ferdie, the Archduke of the Austro-Hungarian Empire with his very nice wife.

Monday 21 November

Rummaging around in my head and feeling, 'Gosh, can I go on with all this myself?', rather like old John Major, with so many problems, money pouring out of my boots and nobody gives a damn.

At the great lunch today [at 19 Cavendish Avenue] each person signed a *Carte des Vins* so they had a copy to take home with them, which they thought an entertaining idea. Particularly young Andrew Roberts, who lapped everything up eagerly. At one point he said he was my 'Boswell'. I referred to him as the boy, which pleased him.

Kingsley [Amis] sat on my right, Bron Waugh[10] on my left. Petronella sat on Kingsley's right, with Andrew Roberts on her right. Next to Bron sat Frank Johnson and at the other end on the left sat Richard Hough.[11] He had a real understanding of wine. He knew what it was all about, with particular appreciation for the old champagne.

Richard Hough said he knew I had been entirely responsible for getting the Mountbattens the money released from Edwina's trust (from her grandfather, Sir Ernest Cassel, Edward VII's financial pal). I said I was quite seduced by her, I don't mean physically though I would have rather liked that. 'She sat up on that sofa with her beautiful legs tucked underneath her and smiled provocatively, just as she carried on in India. It was very difficult for someone of my age, which was twenty-six or twenty-seven, not to feel it.' I got some help for breaking this

---

10. Novelist, journalist, editor and wine connoisseur; son of Evelyn Waugh.
11. (1922–99); biographer, novelist and publisher; his *Mountbatten: Hero of Our Time* was published in 1980, *Edwina, Countess Mountbatten of Burma* in 1983.

trust through the Commons (where a lot of them were Tories, anti-Mountbatten) because I was a socialist MP.

Before we started on the chicken course, we carefully decanted, Elizabeth and I, the fantastic bottle of 1869 Château Montrose.[12] I said, 'You've all got to stop talking. It's a sacred moment. Nowhere else in the world is a bottle of this age being opened, also one which has been so well preserved. Look at the colour.' I gradually pulled the cork out and I passed the cork round. I said, 'Look at that. It's still firm, the cork.'

I nearly broke it in the bottle but I just managed not to. That was passed around as though it were an ancient Roman Catholic relic. I passed the capsule around to show the capsule was still the same on the Montrose 1869 as it was on the Montrose 1970, the top thereof.

It was felt to be a great experience and it drank extremely well, amazing.

Bron then became a bit bossy. He said, 'Let's start on the 1970 Montrose now to compare the two.' I said, 'It's not the right order on the list of the wines.' 'Never mind,' and he started pouring the 1970 out to compare them side by side.

The bottle of Château Latour 1940 was greeted with great interest. The bottle glass wasn't green but white. It was a bad year for France but a good year for Château Latour.

Kingsley was greatly pleased when I said his book *You Can't Do Both* was a sign of his continuing and maturing development and was as good as *Lucky Jim* in its way. He doesn't now care for *Lucky Jim*.

By the end Kingsley was getting really drunk. His sobriety had not been improved by his having a large whisky with a tiny drop of water in it which he had begun to drink before lunch. He confused the Graves Royal 1947 with the Tokay and he couldn't tell the difference.

Tuesday 22 November
Dinner at the German Embassy, 22 Belgrave Square.

I bumped into Norman Tebbit. He looked around the marble hall and magnificent staircase and said, 'Is this the same embassy that Ribbentrop had?' I said, 'Yes, certainly. There have always been Huns

---

12. Michael Broadbent of Christie's told WW that the 1869 Montrose came from the cellars of Sir George Meyrick, 7th baronet, and was sold at Christie's in June 1970. Meyrick had nearly 100 bottles, never moved, originally binned in May 1888.

1994

here, ever since Bismark united Germany.' 'Oh,' he said, looking as though he wished to blow the whole place up.

Later I talked to him about John Major.

'Aren't you going to back him?' 'I don't know. He told me himself that half his Cabinet are madly pro-Brussels and he has great difficulties with them. I said to him he should sack the lot.'

I replied that would be a rather tricky exercise at the moment.

Originally I was talking to Clarissa Avon.[13] She said, 'You're looking over his shoulder,' meaning the other man she was talking to at the same time. I said, 'I couldn't possibly look over his shoulder. He's about twice my height.' She said, 'You're looking for someone better to talk to.' I said, 'Absolute nonsense.' We had a very long conversation about George Weidenfeld who she said always looked over her shoulder for someone better to talk to, and how he got away with his social life in England.

Wednesday 23 November

Had a long chat with Caroline. I missed her yesterday. By some mysterious way I learned someone else had been talking to her. I said, 'Who is my rival?' It was Tony Lambton.

Caroline said he shouldn't have disclaimed his peerage but gone to the Lords. I said, 'He didn't because he was convinced he would've got higher promotion than junior Minister if he stayed in the Commons. In the end the scandal forced him to resign his Commons seat but if he'd gone to the Lords, he could still have been playing a part in politics.'

Alan Meale (Labour MP, PPS to John Prescott, the Deputy Leader of the Labour Party) and Peter Jones (of the BHB, racehorse owner and member of the Levy Board) came to lunch with me in the House of Lords. We had a bottle of champagne. Poor Alan Meale couldn't eat anything because he is starving for Oxfam. I said, 'I often advise my readers not to send them anything because it's too highly politicized.' However, Peter Jones gave him £20.

I took a bet at even money, £50, with Alan Meale that Labour wouldn't win the next election.

---

13. Widow of the 1st Earl of Avon (Sir Anthony Eden, Prime Minister, 1955–7) and niece of Sir Winston Churchill.

Thursday 24 November

I found myself sitting next to Jeffrey Archer in the Lords' Gallery, looking down on the Commons during Question Time for the Prime Minister.

I said to Jeffrey Archer, 'He did extraordinarily well, didn't he?' Archer said, 'Yes. He's in command.' He's a brazen bloke flaunting himself after so publicly injuring John (who now has nothing to do with him) and his party with his shady share dealings.[14]

Went to Alastair Goodlad's reception at the Great Locarno Room in the Foreign Office. Poor Sarah Hogg embraced me warmly, I having rung her up the day before to tell her how sorry I was she was leaving. She said it was nothing to do with the attacks on her. She thought she had been there long enough. She wanted to get out into the world again and give John a chance to find somebody to settle in, ready to accompany him at the general election.

The place was thronged with dull people. Kenneth Rose[15] said, 'They look like a lot of yesterday's men.' I replied 'There's one just behind you.' He turned round. It was Douglas Hurd. He laughed.

Douglas looks very earnest and flaps around attempting to look like a great statesman which he is very far from being. He must be one of the worst Foreign Secretaries we have had. He still makes silly speeches saying we must all get into Europe properly and love it. But recently he has popped up one interesting thought, shared no doubt with Norman Tebbit, that maybe there could be a referendum before the question of the single currency comes up in about 1999.

Having talked to Irwin Stelzer, now in London, about the appalling way in which the *Times* and the *Sun* were treating Major, he said, 'Why don't you ring Rupert up?' I did. I had forgotten it was Thanksgiving Day. I tracked him down to his ranch.

I said, 'I know you've been flirting with Blair. But there's nothing there. He won't support you against the EU.'

Rupert said, 'I am not looking for favours.' 'Are you not going to back Major any more?' 'I will if I can but he's hopeless, he's so weak.

---

14. WW was referring to the allegations of insider dealing concerning Archer's transactions in Anglia Television shares in January 1994; his wife was a director of Anglia; an enquiry concluded there was no evidence on which a prosecution could be founded.

15. Historian and journalist; *Sunday Telegraph* diarist 'Albany', 1961–97.

How silly of him to threaten all the Tory MPs with a general election if they don't vote the way he wants on Monday.'

Finally he said he would look at his papers and see whether he thought I was right and whether he could soften them a bit.

Rupert does take me seriously on these things.

Friday 25 November
I duly reported to John Major what Rupert had said. I told him I thought we might get a slight improvement but at the moment he is in one of his megalomaniac moods and thinks he can choose the Prime Minister.

John said he was in a far more robust mood than when he last spoke to me. He had taken the view that they could do what they damn well liked because he is going to carry on with what he thinks is right.

I told him I traced Norman Lamont to where he was holding a meeting in Yorkshire for the local Conservative Association. He denied that he had any intentions of standing against Major, but he did it in such a peculiar way that I wasn't certain I was quite convinced. Lamont had said there are various plots going on but they will come to nothing.

Sunday 27 November
Michael Howard gave an interview to the BBC David Frost TV programme saying that he didn't think there would be a leadership challenge and that Norman would make himself utterly ridiculous if he were to act as a stalking horse.

When questioned about this later on Sunday, Norman said he had made his position clear that he had no intention of standing in a leadership contest, as he didn't think there would be one. This apparently clear statement, when tested by the interviewer, seemed not to rule out (though Norman didn't say so) acting differently if the situation had altered on Wednesday morning.

I have told him he will ruin his political career if he does such a thing. There is also the question of Evelyn de Rothschild who for certain will ask him to depart from Rothschild's where he is earning £100,000 a year.

I had a long talk with Jonathan Aitken.

Jonathan is rather hoping that five or six of the rebels will vote against or abstain on Monday night [on Europe]. This means they will automatically have the whip withdrawn from them, preventing them taking part in any leadership election.

[When I was] talking to Margaret on Sunday night, she thought that John was quite wrong to make all these threats.

I asked her if she had been talking to John lately. She said, 'I haven't because we'd only disagree. But I am still convinced he's got to be supported, even though he has made mistakes in the way he has handled this situation. There's nobody else who could hold the party together.' I said, 'He'll win the election, you know.' 'Not if he carries on like this.'

When I told John that Rupert was still going on about the sleaze and saying Jeffrey Archer was still the Prime Minister's best friend, or one of them, always with him, John said, 'I haven't seen him for about three months.' 'I know. I think you must keep it that way. He's too dangerous.'

Monday 28 November

I had a row with Peter Stothard. I had written an article which I thought was pretty good, saying why I thought Major was a good egg.

Unfortunately, I had slightly misquoted the *Times'* leading article.

We had an up-and-downer.

I said, 'I will write an article for you on Wednesday when we have seen what happens with the leadership challenge and we have the Budget behind us. But I don't want to write a second one and have it spiked.' Peter said, 'We would not do such a thing to so loveable a person as you and one of such great distinction. I will let you know immediately if we don't want it.'

A most extraordinary dinner at the Hyde Park Hotel. It was given by the Blacks for George Weidenfeld's book.[16] It was the most elaborately arranged affair, with extracts of the book printed large on tablecloths and on display stands all round.

I talked to Edna O'Brien [novelist] whom I hadn't seen for a long time and gave her a good kiss. She was talking to David Owen.

I said to David, 'I always told you never to go to that blasted place, Yugoslavia. You would never get anything done.' He said 'At one moment I thought I might. But you are, of course, quite right. I shouldn't have had anything to do with it. It was hopeless from the word go. They all lie the whole time.'

---

16. His autobiography *Remembering My Good Friends*.

Old Frank Longford said to me, 'I see the *News of the World* has turned against Major.' 'Maybe they have, but it doesn't affect me.' He said 'No. You've always been very loyal.'

I am fond of Elizabeth Longford.

She said, 'I admire you though I don't often agree with what you say. But I think you are basically a good person.' I said, 'Thank you. That is very kind of you. I know you are and I know that Frank is.'

There must have been a hundred and fifty people. Olga Polizzi was there, deep in shame because the Hyde Park is a Trusthouse Forte hotel and the dinner had been absolutely ghastly.

Tuesday 29 November

Norman rang. I told him his speech hadn't been too bad, in fact in some ways nearly statesmanlike. He wanted to know how I had got hold of where he was in Yorkshire [on Friday] and why I had done it.

I said, 'You don't know how far flung my intelligence system is.' 'But why did you do it? I regard you as a friend.' 'Yes, exactly. That is why I was ringing you. I didn't want you suddenly to plunge into a leadership challenge which I thought you would do no good in, and particularly because I thought that Evelyn de Rothschild would be very upset.' 'Yes, but I would never do such a thing without consulting or telling Evelyn first. I have told him all along I wasn't going to stand as a challenger to John.' I said, 'Why didn't you tell me?' 'Well, I was teasing everybody. I did tell you, actually, when you got hold of me on Friday.' 'But you did it in such a funny way I didn't quite know what you meant.'

I congratulated Richard Ryder, the Chief Whip, on the government's victory last night.[17] He thinks it unlikely there will be a leadership contest.

I have started something. In my St Leger speech at Doncaster I attacked the length of stewards' inquiries which lose around a million pounds a year in levy for racing.[18] Christopher Foster, now secretary to the Jockey Club, and Sir Thomas Pilkington, on the disciplinary

---

17. In the confidence vote on the European Communities (Finance) Bill.
18. WW's argument was that punters will not put new bets on until they know the result of the race they have just betted on. Thus, if stewards' inquiries are lengthy, postponing the results, fewer bets are laid and there is less revenue for the Levy Board and racing.

side of the Jockey Club concerned with stewards' inquiries, came to see me. They are very keen to take up my offer for the Tote to help them finance speeding it all up.

Friday 2 December
I wrote for the *News of the World* an article about the approaching change of mood towards Major.

Young Piers Morgan said, 'Why doesn't he ask me to see him? He might be able to persuade me. Why don't you give us lunch or dinner and we could talk about it and I could give him some advice?' I thought that was a bit of a tall order for a twenty-nine-year-old editor of the *News of the World*. He hasn't the slightest glimmering of how politics work. He is a trifle too pleased with himself though I still seem to get on OK with him.

Sunday 4 December
Absolutely livid with Petronella. She has written the most nasty gossip stuff about John Major. She said she was compelled to do it by Charles Moore. He couldn't possibly have compelled her to put in, for example, that Major chucked her under the chin and held on to it, in a piece poking fun at him over being tactile.

Monday 5 December
I talked to Kenneth Baker. He made a vehement attack on Major, saying he was crazy ever to have taken the whip away from these people[1] and it was ridiculous, like an authoritarian Labour Party effort. I remembered how, when the whip was taken away from Nye Bevan and one or two others in the Labour Party,[2] I actually fought against it, so I am not being particularly consistent. But it is a different issue when you only have a tiny majority. Labour was in opposition at the time.

---

1. The eight Tory MPs who had abstained from voting on the European Communities (Finance) Bill on 28 November.
2. In 1955 over defence policy.

Tuesday 6 December
I had a sweet letter from Honor Wyatt. She enclosed a photograph of
my father with his strange old-fashioned collar and peaky face.
Somehow this was extraordinarily moving and the letter showed a fair
amount of insight. She is quite wrong, however, about my father being
very clever academically.

Thursday 8 December
I went to the lunch at the Cavalry Club in Piccadilly for the Rawlinsons'
fortieth wedding anniversary.[3] Elaine doesn't look anything like as old
as that.

Peter Rawlinson's brother-in-law, an American like Elaine, made a
charming, rather moving speech. When twelve he used to follow the
courting couple around, peeping at them behind bushes and catching
them making love. He once saw them naked on a sofa. He spoke so
agreeably that no one could in any way have been shocked.

He was followed by Peter himself.

It was a tremendously lovey-dovey oration. All the ladies in the
room were crying at the story of eternal and undying love and his
wonderful phraseology (he is an extraordinarily good speaker, looks
very handsome still, tall and slim with greying hair and fine patrician
face, with brains you could almost feel coming across to you with
immense quality).

One who listened to him avidly was Elizabeth Harris. She has long
blonde hair and is still amazingly attractive. She was married to the
great actors Richard Harris and Rex Harrison and then to Timothy
Aitken, a close relation of Max Beaverbrook. She was born Elizabeth
Rees-Williams, only daughter of the first Baron Ogmore, a bloke who
was made a peer by Attlee when he lost his seat and then left the
Labour Party, much to Attlee's disgust.

When he sat down the ladies on either side of me asked, 'Why
didn't the men cry? What's the matter with them?' 'Maybe they were
keeping a stiff upper lip.' Actually I was thinking they probably knew
too much about Peter to be fooled by all the sentiment, even though
it was genuine because there is a deep love between them.

At the end of lunch the Lord Chief Justice came up to me. He is a

---

3. Peter Rawlinson, lawyer and Conservative politician; Solicitor General, 1962–4;
   Attorney General, 1970–4; m 2 (1954) Elaine, née Dominguez, of Newport, Rhode
   Island; life peer 1978.

man called Taylor. He said, 'I read your astonishing, disgraceful attack
on the judges. You don't understand anything about the law.' He was
referring to my saying that the terrible judge, the son of Georgette
Heyer the historical novelist, was so out of touch with the world he
might be living on the moon.[4]

The angrier the Lord Justice Taylor got, the more livid he got, until
he was almost shouting at me. I was highly amused. It meant it had
obviously gone home.

Sunday 11 December
Talked to John Major in the morning.

'You're so marvellous to talk to, Woodrow, so wonderfully encouraging. I'll tell you something I haven't said to anybody before. The
real difficulty about a referendum,[5] which I am now in favour of, is
that Heseltine and Clarke don't want one because they are afraid of
the answer. Also now Portillo appears to be saying much the same.'

He said, 'I've got to overcome the dissentients in the Cabinet first.'

I said, 'You're not going allow this business of cringing to the
whipless rebels to get them back?' 'Good heavens no. They've got to
show that they consistently support the party, voting for it, before they
can get back.' 'If they don't, they'll be deselected, won't they?' He said,
'Yes. I'm prepared to get whole parties abolished and replaced by new
ones in constituencies if they don't deselect them.'

I said, 'The *News of the World* is being very foolish lately. The
editor asked if perhaps you would be willing for me to ask him to
lunch here with you.' To my surprise John said, 'Yes, let's do it in
January.'

I apologized for Petronella's nasty remarks in the *Sunday Telegraph*
gossip column last week. 'I long for her to end this gossip stuff. Now
I think she's achieved that and is going to write a straight political
column.' He said, 'Never mind. She was very kind about Norma. She
was delighted and so was I.'

I then raised the question of my period at the Tote.

John said, 'When did you see him [Howard] last?' 'About a couple
of months ago.' 'Things have moved on again since then. There's been

---

4. The Hon. Sir Richard Rougier had awarded damages against an 82-year-old man
   for using excessive force against an intruder on his allotment.
5. On Britain entering the single currency.

a change and you'll get your two years.' I had explained to him I'd be a busted flush if I didn't because I have a great deal more to do.

This is a great relief. It will give me a chance to make a bit more money before I disappear.

John said he was feeling on the top of the world. He is totally confident. His feeling of despair has completely gone.

Monday 12 December
We had a mildly acrimonious meeting of the Tote Direct Board. Beforehand Ian Napier of Bass had come to see me. He was [complaining] about my behaviour in raising the Authority fee, saying it wasn't done very tactfully. I said, 'I know of no way of telling people that an increased fare on a train is actually a lower one and being convincing in so doing.'

Another binge chez George Weidenfeld. This time given and paid for by him, or probably his publishing firm. It was in honour of Alun Chalfont's seventy-fifth birthday. Numerous notables were there, including, alas, the increasingly noisy, boisterous and ill-mannered Robin Day.

We sat at the same round table. Within three minutes he became totally bored by one of his neighbours, the frowzy in appearance Lady Carver. She is the wife of the mad Field Marshal Lord Carver, former Chief of the General Staff, who on retiring announced that we ought to get rid of all our nuclear weapons unilaterally though he had been in charge of ensuring we kept them and that they were in full use.

He talked either straight across her, ignoring her, or to the lady on his left who was Marcelle Quinton.

He cross-questions people and shouts at them as though he were Perry Mason in a B film and rarely says anything remotely funny. But I feel sorry for him. He was excellent when he did the *Question Time* programme for the BBC and was a fool when he abandoned it because he could have hung on. He has got sturdy points.

Marcelle Quinton, as usual, chatted away at high speed, but entertainingly. I like that girl. She lived in America for quite a long time,[6] on and off – her family had some wealth and she has a flat in New York. But she is stoutly English.

She looks down on the Americans as uncivilized, tedious conversationalists, ignorant and too eager. 'I find that one of their attractions,

---

6. She is American by birth.

particularly in the young at universities. They are so admiringly anxious to learn and charming, particularly the girls. They thoroughly appreciate one.' Marcelle sniffed, at least metaphorically.

Tuesday 13 December
I took Mrs Tamborero to the Venice exhibition at the Royal Academy. We both enjoyed it greatly, I particularly because she is so kind and helpful and dashes off to read the inscriptions under the pictures and bring back the information as we go round.

Caroline's voice worries me. It is rasping and she finds it difficult to speak.

I am beginning to get an edge of fear for her which I didn't have before.

Wednesday 14 December
During the night I am always woken by Nicholas [Banszky] tramping down past my bedroom, either to go for a run, or by that damn telephone with Ratna [his girlfriend in India] ringing it. I am not getting enough sleep – this adversely affects my character, making me unkind when deep down I'm longing to be considerate.

In the morning I had a fascinating conversation with Straker, the Chairman of Ayr Racecourse.

We took away our sponsorship from Ayr. They had whored after Ladbroke and gave them a betting shop.

They could make a fortune from a housing development for which there would be planning permission but Brussels won't allow any more houses to be built there until human excreta stops being pumped raw into the sea.

They claim that Ayr is the most unhealthy beach in Europe, so they clearly never visited Italy. However, it will be cleared up when they can get a new sewage works.

Meanwhile, I have promised them that under certain conditions we might be willing to renew our sponsorship at a reasonably high level.

Dinner party at 19 Cavendish Avenue. Michael Dobbs, Deputy Chairman of the Tory Party and author of *To Play the King*, the book and highly rated television series with the same name, was the first to arrive.

In came Vere Rothermere with the enchantingly beautiful Maiko, his Korean wife. Her dress was gorgeous, her jewellery was magnificent. Her legs are delightful, her figure neat and precisely the right shape in the right places.

Vere adores Verushka because her great-uncle wanted to make his father the King of Hungary after the First World War, when the *Mail* alone supported Hungary against the cruel break up of the country into three bits by the Versailles Treaty.[7]

Maiko told me of her fifteen years in a tiny apartment [in Paris] with Vere when he was still married to Bubbles. They had a bedroom smaller than our dining-room, a kitchen which was tiny and a sitting-room about half the size of our dining-room. I said, 'Good gracious. You must be very tidy.' She said no she wasn't, she was very untidy. But it was great fun and they enjoyed it enormously.

Eventually the ladies left the dining-room, Petronella in violent protest because she wanted to hear the political conversation.

Maiko accepted it as completely normal.

Michael Dobbs is extremely intelligent.

He helped a great deal in the onslaught on Vere to start backing Major before it was too late. I urged Vere to anticipate events, not just follow them. He said, 'It's a newspaper's job to follow events.' I said, 'That is taking a very unusual view for an original person like yourself. Great newspapers initiate events, as Northcliffe did when he got rid of Asquith in the First World War.'

Vere attacked Rupert, his great rival.

'You owe a great deal to Rupert. Without him breaking the unions you would never have been able to start the *Mail on Sunday* and make so much money.'

'Why did Rupert allow Andrew Neil to make all those attacks on Mrs Thatcher?' 'Because he was making money. Anyway, the nature of his ownership of the *Sunday Times* was that he was not supposed to interfere with editorial freedom.'

Then Verushka put her head round the door. 'When are you all coming back into the drawing-room?'

Thursday 15 December
The Other Club.

William Rees-Mogg is a complete ass but very sympathetic to talk to.

---

7. Verushka's great-uncle Emile was Hungarian Minister of Justice in the Horthy government.

He asked me, for confidential guidance, what did I think about the Andrew Parker Bowles' possibility of divorcing.

I said, 'They don't want a divorce. They believe in keeping the family together. They live their separate lives. They've always been having affairs and it's never meant the end of their long-term marriage. They think of their children in this respect as well.'[8]

William is bewitched by Diana. The chump thinks her badly wronged. She confides in him and William regards himself as her wise, experienced counsellor. Crikey!

Saturday 17 December
In the Royal Box [at Ascot] I talked to Queen Elizabeth the Queen Mother. A great children's party had been going on with a Father Christmas.

She was looking remarkably well despite a swollen right leg. A thorn got into it. It's been there for the last two months and the effects are likely to stay for another two. But she gets about with a stick quite nippily.

I said how beautiful she had looked on the Christmas card she sent out. 'The horse did but I thought I looked silly standing by it.'

We held our usual review of the world. I told her I thought Blair wouldn't win the election, mainly because he's still looking like an undergraduate larking about at a university debating society.

She said she had never been worried about the future of the monarchy.

I said that the Prince of Wales did extremely well with his good works and caring for the young with his business enterprises, even to the extent of involving young offenders.

But I thought it a great mistake to have talked so freely to Dimbleby in the book.

She raised her hands in disdain, 'That Jonathan Dimbleby!'

I told her how brilliantly I thought John Major was doing in Ireland. She said, 'Do you think Southern Ireland will ever come back into the Commonwealth?' 'It's not inconceivable.'

She laughed away, raising her arms in almost childlike excitement. She is utterly charming.

Badminton – again masses of children.

Worryingly, Caroline was looking extremely beautiful. She reminded

8. The Parker Bowles divorced in 1995; Andrew Parker Bowles remarried in 1996.

me of dear darling Liz Paget (Arabella's mother) when she was dying of cancer. The omens do not appear good at the moment.

They appear to have given up hope – those nice intelligent doctors at the hospital at Gloucester. It seems the Evening Primrose Oil homeopathic treatment has not worked.

Caroline kept thanking me for coming down. I said, 'Don't be absurd. I love to see you. I want to see you. I want to talk to you. It's for me to thank you for asking me.'

I'm terrified she may be going. I tell her to say to herself every night, and when she wakes in the morning, 'Every day in every way I'm getting better and better.' This could have some effect, surprisingly so.

Sunday 18 December

For lunch came Daphne, Caroline's ninety-three-year-old hale and hearty mother. I always sit next to her and have merry chats with her. Her head has improved. She no longer appears to think everybody is pinching her money and all those things which old people get frightened and worked up about.

Last night when Caroline got up to go to bed I stood up and she put her arms round me. 'I want a big hug.' So I hugged her in front of everybody for about two minutes and held her. She squeezed me tight. Then she went. Piers von Westenholz said, 'That was the most touching thing I ever saw.'

I couldn't answer him because my eyes were pricking with tears and with great difficulty I didn't burst out crying. But some of the tears forced their way through down my cheek.

It was a strange but often entertaining weekend with shocking, tragic undertones. To her face I had never shown any anxiety or worry, but smiled and laughed and told jokes to her.

I had promised to ring John Major again at about half past six.

We discussed the pros and cons of a referendum being before or after the 1996 conference. He is inclined to have it after the international conference.

Previously I had spoken to Norman Lamont. He thought it was necessary [to put up interest rates] because a boom was coming and it had to be stopped. I said, 'I don't think governments can stop booms or control inflation. It's caught up in world situations.' Norman disagreed. Norman now really wants the Tories to lose because he thinks it his best chance of becoming leader of the Tory Party. He's such a foolish fellow.

Monday 19 December
I got to the Italian Institute just in time [for Jo Janni's memorial service].[9]

I was put to sit next to Frederic Raphael[10] who was to speak just before me.

He spoke very amusingly but far too long, for twenty-five minutes. I followed him and did pretty well, explaining about the brilliant book *A Kind of Loving* which Jo hadn't wanted to do to begin with. I said to him, 'You'll be able to show a girl naked for the first time in a respectable cinema.' That was in the days when there was still censorship. She was rather a pretty girl and the scene was touching and not offensive.

I explained how I had made money by advising him on ideas, reading books for films. I also talked about how I gave him the idea of doing *Far From the Madding Crowd*. I recounted my quarrel with the great John Schlesinger [film director]. I had said the film was too long.

John Schlesinger was in the audience and he took that pretty well. Jo discovered Julie Christie. She, too, was there. She still looks amazingly pretty.

She was a silly girl, keen on CND, but my goodness, she was a dream of beauty when I used to see her on location when they were shooting *Far From the Madding Crowd* and Jo was staying with me at Conock, not far from Hardy country.

Unfortunately, I couldn't stay to the end of John Schlesinger because I had to have lunch with Patrick Sheehy, who runs British American Tobacco.

He is a solid, red-faced, fat fellow, but vigorous.

I said, 'Have you ever thought of printing on your cigarette packets, "We're sorry we have to print these lies about smoking but we're compelled to do so by the government."?'

---

9. (1916–94); film producer; see Vol. 1, pp. 288–9, for anecdotes about him.
10. Novelist, biographer, translator, and screen-play writer.

Tuesday 20 December

A hilarious lunch at the *Oldie*. We were thinking of people for various awards.

John Mortimer wanted to name Michael Howard as the shit of the year. Others agreed. I said, 'That's because you're all anti-semitic – a feeling which lurks not far below the surface in a great many English people and also with Jews themselves.'

I wanted Cilla Black made as the woman of the year for her bogus and miraculous *Blind Date*. I couldn't get that through.

Sat next to Anna Ford. I said, 'I am terribly sorry, I ought to know your name but I'm afraid I can't remember it.' 'My name is Anna Ford. I know your daughter through Frank Johnson.' 'Oh yes, of course. And you do the news sometimes now.'

I said, 'Are you going to get married again?'[11] 'No, certainly not. Though I might when I am very old and feel I must have a man about the house. But now I enjoy very much being without men, that is as living-in mates.' We became very friendly.

It was agreed that we should ask [to the to the awards lunch] Nicholas Soames as the person who most wants to be an Oldie.

It was agreed that Larry Adler [mouth organist] could be one of the award winners.

I told them how I had got him sent to Korea to play to our troops when the Americans wouldn't have him, and that had rehabilitated him in America. He had been one of the Hollywood Ten accused of being Communist, which he wasn't.

I had forgotten that Terry Wogan would be one of the judges.

In the *News of the World* I had often been extremely rude about him, pointing out that he earns about £400,000 a year from television and radio which he cannot possibly deserve, and as BBC employees earn such enormous sums, why do they keep jeering at captains of industry getting £200,000–£300,000 a year?

As we continued to talk, I began to like him and felt I had been unjust to him.

In the evening we went to the first anniversary wedding reception for Vere and Maiko.

She wore a greyish dress and looked quite lovely. Verushka said she nearly bought one exactly the same. It came from Dior. A little later I

---

11. Anna Ford, journalist and news presenter, m (1982) Mark Boxer (1931–88), cartoonist and editorial director, Condé Nast Publications.

said, 'I see your dress comes from Dior.' 'How did you know that?' 'I know about these things.'

Thursday 22 December
Verushka goes to Hungary.

She was soon ringing me after she had got to Hungary, in the afternoon, to know who I was having dinner with tonight. I said, 'A girlfriend.' She said, 'Don't be silly.' I said, 'Why shouldn't I? Actually I'm having dinner, maybe at Pratt's, with Arnold.'

In the end we went to Mark's Club. I was very cross to find that Sonny Marlborough has got round Mark Birley to remove our Cornish Spring Water and to supply instead Blenheim Water.

Friday 23 December
A ghastly journey to Hungary.

We went to Gundels for dinner. Petronella sang to an enchanted audience of diners who clapped mightily.

I had to give dinner to the new Hungarian Ambassador from Budapest to London, who takes over in January from Antalpeter who is leaving.[12] His wife is fairly pleasant, speaks English well.

Saturday 24 December
We went to the British Embassy. The new Ambassador to Britain, according to John Birch, the British Ambassador [to Hungary], was the group party secretary of all the hard-line Communists in the Foreign Office.

I told Birch that Kovacs was very upset at his appalling treatment and I was worried.[13] I'd been advising people like Chips Keswick of Hambros, and other bankers and people interested in putting money in Hungary, that it was safe to do so. Now they seem to be going back to Communism. He didn't think that was quite true.

He's a miserable little fellow, Birch. He doesn't want to get involved in any trouble. He's retiring, at the age of sixty, in June.

In the morning I had rung John Major to tell him he had done

---

12. HE Tádé Alfödy, m (1968) Orsyda Baraczka.
13. Kovacs had advanced money from his bank for a privatization scheme in exchange for some of the equity. He was then arrested and tried, WW thought, on a 'trumped up' charge, but see below.

magnificently well during the year and was bound to come through on the right track.

He said, 'Sometimes I feel like giving it all up. If they don't want me, I'll go.' 'You mustn't talk like that. You must keep on. It's your duty and you should be cheerful today because it's beginning to move your way, and it has to do so – everybody knows there's nothing to Blair.'

Sunday 25 December
To old Kovacs in his strange house.

It has a wonderful position overlooking Budapest and cost him a fortune. It's full of Herend and valuable Japanese and Chinese stuff, all exceedingly badly put together.

He himself cooked the dinner because he loves cooking.

I said, 'I've rung all the alarm bells with the new Ambassador to Britain and now with the British Ambassador.'

I feel sorry for the fellow. He had shrunk and visibly aged. He's only sixty-eight but years have gone from his life.

He was put in a tiny cell and wasn't allowed to speak to a lawyer – everything which was done to him violated all human rights, and even the Hungarian law.

Tuesday 27 December
I was thinking of writing something about Kovacs.

I decided to ring Birch. He said that he did speak to Kovacs in the end.

He will use as much pressure as he can but he is not very pleased with Kovacs. When he went to see him he had not told him that there were other charges against him connected with currency.

I decided it would be wiser to abandon it until things calm down and we know where we are.

The news is not all that cheerful about darling Caroline. Her voice is getting worse. She's getting more tired.

David obviously fears the end cannot be far away.

I am still hoping for a miracle.

Friday 30 December
This morning I talked to John Major at some length. I said I wanted to write about all these constitutional matters which Blair has been bashing away at and all the silly mistakes they've been making over

taxing school fees with VAT and slaughtering the independent schools.[14]

He was extremely helpful.

I was, however, a bit cross with him because he hadn't given Henry [Keswick] his knighthood.

I raised the question of Rowse with him as well. He said he would take that up, too. I don't know whether it's a case of, 'Put not your trust in princes.' I hope not, particularly as I am myself depending on his promise that I will get my two years reappointment and he will deal with Howard himself on it.

---

14. Labour's dilemma about whether to charge VAT on independent school fees was topical because it had become known on 2 December that the Blairs were sending their son to a grant-aided school.

1995

Tuesday 3 January

It is fair to record that most of the *Times* article I wrote for publication today was basically John Major's idea. I don't know why people think he is a fool. He's far from it.

I mentioned to John the possibility of Rifkind succeeding Douglas Hurd.[1] But this was at a time when he said, 'We're not on a secure telephone.'

The weekend at Oare had amusing moments.

Tessa invites an eclectic lot of people.

For the Saturday night into the New Year evening she asked Elinor Goodman and her appalling husband. Elinor Goodman is the commentator and reporter on Channel 4 which is a hotbed of socialists. They always attack Major. She brought her husband who is the economic adviser to Blair. He is a lunatic. God knows what would happen if Blair becomes PM and this fellow is advising Blair.[2]

One of the visitors was Drue Heinz. She's a friendly old soul, but almost totally wrong about everything.

After she left Oare she went straight on to Badminton.

She told Caroline that Verushka was so beautiful – and she couldn't be less than fifty. Caroline refrained from saying she had known Verushka for a very long time and she has a son of forty-two.

On Sunday I did an extraordinary broadcast sitting on the bed in Verushka's room at Oare. It was by telephone.

It arose out of a woman leaving £2 million to help pay off the National Debt. She had no close relations and that was what she wanted to do because she was proud to be British. The question was, 'Are you proud to be British?'

I argued with some crazy fellow who runs something associated with the homeless. He said, 'How can anyone be proud to be British

---

1. He did succeed Hurd but not until the reshuffle of 5 July 1995.
2. Elinor Goodman m (1985) Derek Scott (since 1997 on the staff of the Number 10 Policy Unit).

when there is so much homelessness?' I said, 'There have never been higher levels of social security payments and if anybody wants to be homeless, it's their fault.'

I asked John Major why he had given Rocco Forte a knighthood. He is far less distinguished than Henry. 'Because he's done so much for exports and tourism.'

Henry now thinks Chris Patten got it all wrong, unnecessarily provoking the Chinese which has harmed British business generally, not only Jardine Matheson.

In the midst of all this, Caroline told me the mischievous Princess Michael is in the same hospital as she was. She had a very bad fall, while out hunting. She didn't want people to know about it.

Verushka has just rung Prince Michael, as I told her to.

Prince Michael was delighted she rang. She had a virus in her middle ear. She was not able to stay on her horse because she was giddy and unbalanced. She is now better though she was in the hospital (where they said she wasn't) and she is coming home tomorrow.

Poor Princess Michael. She is a very jolly girl with all her faults.

Meanwhile poor Bob has had another stroke.

Wednesday 4 January

Major was delighted with my article in the *Times* yesterday.

We talked about Yeltsin and my feeling that he may have actually been doing the right thing in Chechnya but I don't see what we can do to help him. He said, 'I think that's correct.'

I asked him if he could do something about my appointment at the Tote.

He said, 'Would you like me to ring Howard again now? Or perhaps it would be better if I did it next week. I will ensure that he does it.'

We had a heavenly afternoon with Verushka's granddaughters, Genevra and Antonella.

We went to a Chinese restaurant to begin with. I had given them false cigarettes which looked very real and which they were smoking all round the place.

Oliver Twist, as performed in Lionel Bart's version, is brilliantly done.

When I said to Genevra *Oliver Twist* was written by Charles Dickens, she said, 'Oh no, that's not true. Look at the programme. It says it's by Lionel Bart.'

I don't think little Genevra was fully convinced until we got home and I showed her a nineteenth-century copy of *Oliver Twist* by Charles Dickens.

Being rather mean, I was totting up my wounds with all the expense going on. I worked it out that by the time we left the theatre, having bought lots of Oliver cups and various other items on sale at the theatre and chocolates to eat there, what with the price of the seats at £30 a head, I had spent about £220. But I was in such a pleased mood by the end of the evening that I didn't grudge it a bit.

It took me a long time to get on to Caroline tonight.

'I have had an X-ray of my chest this morning. They say it is absolutely clear. There's nothing wrong with it, even though I have got this slightly hoarse voice.' I was delighted. She went on, 'They say downstairs (meaning David and her family) that I only have this hoarse voice because it sounds so sexy.'

I had a lovely talk with her. She was sounding so much better and stronger.

Before I spoke to Caroline I had spoken to David. 'How is she really?' 'Not too good but a bit better today.' 'I am not giving up hope.'

Sunday 8 January
Talked to Major.

On the press he said, 'I'm taking your advice, Woodrow. I'm seeking them out one by one and talking to them.'

I said, 'I hope you don't mind my bothering you but perhaps you could ring Howard this week.' He said, 'It's already in hand.'

As usual we talked a bit about the cricket.

Tuesday 10 January
Alexander Bath went to lunch with his sister, Caroline. He brought a wifelet with him. Caroline said she was quite pretty in a barmaidish sort of way, immensely common and she enjoyed talking to her. Alexander is in many ways vile, though Caroline has a sisterly affection for him. He hated their father and did the most terrible things to him, as has been recorded here before.

Alexander on one occasion refused to speak to his own mother, Daphne, for two years. That was because she had got very cross with Alexander for attacking Christopher, another of her sons, in the most vile, appalling language, and excluding him from Longleat. Alexander's retaliation was, 'I'll not speak to you for two years.'

He wrote it in his diary. When the date came he rang his mother and said, 'I am prepared to speak to you again now.'

David, of course, was not present. He cannot bear Alexander.

Wednesday 11 January
Had quite a jolly Tote Board meeting at Putney. No one mentions that nothing has been heard of my reappointment, or not. They are too polite. I can see they are wondering.

The Tote at the moment is running at about forty-one per cent higher profits than last year. That is excluding the one-off benefit of the huge dividend from SIS. I had to fight the Board, this time with the rare support of David Swaythling, to take up the shares I got [for the Tote] in it and to invest some more.

Martin Charteris is in a pickle. He gave an interview to a woman[3] from the *Spectator*, the undergraduate journal always cutting people up. He thought it was background material for a profile they were going to do of him. 'Very conceited of me, I know,' he said to me. They printed what she had taped, containing a lot of adverse comments on the Royal Family. Prince Charles he considered would make a good king in the end, but a pity he whined so much.

He said the girl told him she would send him the manuscript of the tape to check. She never did.

She did not tell him that her husband is a fellow called Greenslade, once editor of the *Daily Mirror* and a leading light of an organization called Republic which is out to destroy the monarchy.

I said, 'Was she attractive?' He blushed and looked shy. He looked down at the ground (we were standing in the Division Lobby at the Lords). 'Yes, I'm afraid she was rather.' I laughed. 'Did you really say, "Now let's go and get pissed"?' 'No I didn't. I said, "Now let's go and have a drink,"' which sounds a great deal tamer than the words attributed to him in the interview.

Thursday 12 January
I had tea with Patricia Hollis, a Labour member of the Lords. She is rather pretty with her gingery red hair, and very attractive. She was

---

3. Noreen Taylor, née McElhone, m (1984) Roy Greenslade, journalist and author, editor *Daily Mirror*, 1990–1, a member of 'Republic: People Before Privilege'.

enquiring, for a book she is writing on Jennie Lee, about Nye Bevan, his life with Jennie Lee and the effect she had on Nye.[4]

A most mysterious thing is that she left a great deal more money than could ever be accounted for in the account books.

I told her that Nye was a natural aristocrat, a theme which fascinated her; how he never went to his constituency, and how he told me that all local government was corrupt, particularly so in Wales.

She is an academic, as is her husband.[5] I told her I liked her but her excellent speeches tended to be repetitive and too long. 'They could have more effect – people can only remember about three points.' I thought she might be irritated but in fact she was very grateful.

The postcard I had from her read: 'Thank you *so* much for tea, talk and books. All of them a treat and much enjoyed. I am most grateful.' On the other side of the postcard is a picture of the youthful Jennie Lee, very beautiful, addressing a miners' meeting before the war in a La Pasionaria manner.[6]

Saturday 14 January
I went to a betting shop first in Cheltenham, then to the racecourse where I presented prizes to two lady jockeys. The picture (helpful to Tote publicity) only got into the *Racing Post* and *Sporting Life* because I gave them each a kiss as I presented them their prize. I am trying to help these lady jockeys who have been discriminated against by male chauvinists in the Jockey Club for years.

Then it was to Badminton. David Metcalfe arrived before dinner. Caroline quite liked him when she was very young. He used to take her out and make passes at her which she rejected. I said, 'He is pretty brainless.' (This was before he arrived.)

The ghastly Wheatcroft, Geoffrey, came.[7] Caroline said she also quite likes him. I told her the story of how he brought the ghastly Germaine Greer to Newmarket for a luncheon where everybody had

---

4. Her book, *Jennie Lee, a Life*, was published in 1997.
5. Martin Hollis, Professor of Philosophy, University of East Anglia, from 1982, d 1988.
6. Dolores Ibarruri, called La Pasionaria, was a famed Communist leader during the Spanish Civil War, returning from exile after the fall of Franco and becoming a Communist member of the Cortès.
7. Author and journalist.

place names and was seated when they arrived nearly an hour late. Germaine Greer hadn't even been invited.[8]

We talked a little bit about lady jockeys and so on and I was friendly, as I promised Caroline I would be.

Also came Emma Soames.[9] She is now editing the magazine section of the *Sunday Telegraph*.

She has very attractive legs and quite a pretty, podgy little face.

At the end of dinner, David asked me to sit down with him.

We talked for half an hour or so. David said, 'I have been a very bad husband.' I said, 'I wouldn't worry about that. Caroline isn't disturbed about it any more.'

'I have been very promiscuous, as you have, too, Woodrow.' I said, 'Most men are. But the sins of the flesh are not as bad as the sins of unfaithfulness of the mind. They are not to be compared.'

He is now in a terrible state because he feels so guilty. I said, 'You don't have to. It's a waste of time your doing that. You're like many couples who have had terrific ups and downs but at the end they are still together. You mean an awful lot to her as a husband. She would particularly like you to do one thing – take your seat in the House of Lords. You would have interesting and important things to say. You're a duke and you should be there. What's the point of it if you don't sign on? You're just as bad as Henry Anglesey who won't sign on either.'

Of course David has his current mistress living on the estate. I talked about that to Caroline but she is well past caring about that sort of thing. She said, 'He is just like his predecessor,' whom he inherited the title from, called The Master because he was the Master of the Queen's Horse. He had his mistress living on the estate.

If David does take his seat, he'll have all those peeresses from all sides of the house gazing at him in adoring admiration. He's still about the most handsome man I have ever known, the great and dashing Master of the Beaufort Hunt, rider at international contests in showjumping, etc. for England, a fantastic horseman.

I said to David, 'I've always admired you enormously. You hadn't a ha'penny to you when I first knew you.' (His father, Bobby, had zero.) 'But you got cracking and you made a lot, with those two funny chaps you started the Marlborough Fine Art Gallery with.'

---

8. See Vol. 1, p. 3, for this incident which seems to have set WW against Wheatcroft.
9. Daughter of Lady Soames (Mary).*

Wednesday 18 January
The *Daily Express* Ross Benson column is very nasty. It said if I do continue at the Tote, it is only because I write two columns, one in the *News of the World* and the other in the *Times*, which are very important to John Major and so Wakeham (who they say wants the job) was beaten by 'a distance of two columns'.

Thursday 19 January
The *Spectator* has written an unpleasant profile of me. Likewise, Andrew Neil in a new column he is writing for the *Daily Mail* has made a very disagreeable attack on me.

I am saying to myself I mustn't take it seriously, it's only their envy and it won't make any difference. But I am beginning to fear it may, particularly as the question of quangos is coming up so vividly in the Nolan Committee inquiring into the behaviour of the government and MPs. Maybe they will now suddenly get cold feet and think I oughtn't to be given the job at all, even for a year, on the grounds of nepotism. This would be ridiculous.

The Other Club. I was touched. Before dinner Robin Day came up and said he was sorry about what they had written about me in the *Spectator* and he had written me a personal letter. I am beginning to wonder whether I shall ever get any more letters – there has been a strike all week at the Post Office.

Bernard Levin was very friendly. We can't talk politics these days because he has gone bananas against Major. But I and others congratulated him on his beautiful articles in the *Times* about New Zealand. He made it sound a perfect paradise – a time-stopped England.

Friday 20 January
Dinner with Margaret Anne (Lady Stuart of Findhorn).

We had two bottles of excellent 1975 Pichon-Longueville. They had been given to her in a box of twelve by Andrew Devonshire the Christmas before. She was nettled that she hadn't been given another box, or any wine at all, this Christmas.

Thursday 26 January
Pericles came with his Japanese girlfriend just after lunch. I gave them champagne. She is a funny little creature. She has a daughter who is married and having a child or already has one.

However, she has her head screwed on. The more I talked to her the better I liked her.

I think she will have a good effect on the way Pericles runs his businesses.

Of course whenever Pericles does come here, or to Hungary, he always dashes about with various friends and he always brings somebody with him, so I don't see very much of him.

He has got his beard back on again and he's got extremely fat. But it was very nice to see the dear boy. I am extremely fond of him.

I have been speaking every day to Caroline in Barbados. Her voice doesn't sound too good though she says she is feeling well. She swims and enjoys the sunshine. She wishes she could stay longer which I am very pleased to hear.

In the afternoon I saw Professor Pounder. I am disturbed, even if I do have some sleep, by feeling very slack in the mornings and tired. I almost fall asleep, sometimes in a meeting. I forget things and I do not do my articles as well as I should. I am worried about that.

There is a lot of pressure on me from the *News of the World*. They have now an idiot called Michael Winner,[10] a boasting figure in show business, always showing off new girlfriends at restaurants, having arranged for paparazzi to be present.

They give him more space than I have which seems intolerable.

Saturday 28 January
Yesterday Professor Pounder rang up and said, apart from one test which hadn't been completed, there was nothing wrong with me at all. He is now giving a report to Professor Thomas to see whether I am still getting the right pills to avert Parkinson's and what effect there might be if they were changed.

Professor Pounder is a jolly chap. I don't go through a local doctor – I go straight to him. He was very amused when I told him that when Nye Bevan was living at Cliveden Place and had just started the National Health Service, I asked him who his National Health Service doctor was and his answer was Sir Dan Davies (the physician to the King). Bevan thought in his aristocratic manner that the health service would be all right for ordinary people but he wanted something better for himself. I understand that and follow his lead.

I had a nice letter from Irwin Stelzer with a copy of a rebuke he

---

10. Film producer and director, journalist and broadcaster.

sent to Andrew Neil. It wasn't totally wholehearted, suggesting I may
have an element of self-interest in supporting Major. But I would never
support anybody if I didn't agree with them, as he ought to know if
he read my book and all the columns I have written.

I was very touched by the *Spectator* carrying a letter by Bruce
Anderson defending me against the monstrous profile they wrote the
week before.

Sunday 29 January
Talked at length to Margaret. She was full of complaints.

She said John Major was previously madly pro Europe when he
was in her Cabinet. Now he is reversing himself. He doesn't believe in
anything.

When I said I was convinced he would win she said, 'I hope he
does.' That she said in a sincere tone.

I asked her does she ever speak to him on the telephone to which
she replied in a testy voice, 'I won't speak to him on the telephone
because there are always leaks if I do. And I would only have a row
with him in any case.'

After about half an hour or so we stopped talking. She did say her
old, 'God bless you for ringing, God bless.' She retains affection for
me, that is clear, as I do for her and always will. Indeed, it's more than
affection, it's a love I have for her.

Tuesday 31 January
Saw the Home Secretary. What a despicable little man he is, twisting
and turning.[11]

I had sent him in advance a list of the points which I had agreed.
He said he didn't agree with a number of them. He wouldn't agree to
any increase in [my] salary.

He said, 'I'll give you twenty-four hours to make up your mind. I
have to consult my colleagues,' which he said in a snide way, 'and they
may not even agree to your two-year reappointment.' I said, 'But the
PM and you are already agreed.' 'Ah yes but we have got to have this
consultation document accepted by colleagues with a view to legislation

---

11. WW vented in his journals his frustrations about Michael Howard and the Tote
    but he often defended him in print on other aspects of his work as Home Secretary;
    Howard continued to be a welcome guest at WW's dinner table.

which will alter the whole future of the Tote because it'll be under the BHB.'

I spoke to the Home Secretary again in the afternoon and had a row with him.

After a long argument I said, 'I want not a nominee but a representative from BHB [on the Tote Board] and I want Peter Jones whom I have always had in mind as my eventual successor. I have spoken to him and I have spoken to Stoker Hartington. He is trying to arrange [for] Jones to be the BHB representative, not nominee.'

Thinking about that ghastly swine, Michael Howard, I wouldn't put it past him to cancel it all in the end on the grounds that I am not keen enough in readying the Tote for the BHB. I am quite prepared to do it, if it really is going to take place, and make sure all the ground rules are correct so that the Tote can't be mucked about with and my wonderful staff, who are so devoted and worried about their future when they read all the vicious attacks on me in the newspapers, are allowed to continue as before, providing, as I told him, the best computer service, the best experts in the whole ruddy country.

I had lunch with Robin Day in the Garrick. He was very friendly. I told him in strict confidence that I had been given the two-year reappointment.

I saw Isaiah Berlin across the room talking to Nicko Henderson. I said to Robin, 'Perhaps they're plotting how they can stop poor old A. L. Rowse ever getting any form of decoration.'

Thursday 2 February

I rang John Major.

I congratulated him on his meeting with the Independents [peers in the House of Lords] which he held on Tuesday.

John said he was very tired and he had made a muck of it. I said, 'Not a bit of it. You had a great effect on the lot of them.'

I did not mention to him Margaret's conversation, which I may do later, because I thought it would upset him; nor did I mention the irritating troubles I have with that ghastly fellow Howard.

In the evening we had a very large dinner party of sixteen.

I sat next to John Redwood's wife.[1] She told me how awful Major is, no bloody good and he should go. 'Who would you have instead? Your husband?' 'No. He just would like to be Chancellor of the Exchequer.' She thought Portillo, possibly, but not Clarke, about which I agreed.

So I saw how the wind was blowing in that direction.

After the women left the dining-room we talked more seriously about politics. I put some rather difficult questions to him. 'How do you think you're going to win when you've offended all your middle-class supporters with negative equity on their homes? Nobody believes the economy is coming right although it is.' He gave pretty good answers.[2] At the end I said, 'I don't agree with my questions but I agree with your answers.' The fellow has no sense of humour. He hardly smiled.

He had told Verushka he didn't think any person who ever cheated on or betrayed or was unfaithful to his wife should be in the Cabinet.

---

1. John Redwood, Conservative MP since 1987, at this time Secretary of State for Wales; Fellow of All Souls College, Oxford, 1972–87, and former banker; m (1974) Gail, née Chippington.
2. In his thank-you letter to the Wyatts, John Bowes Lyon, another guest, said he felt a little sorry for the wretched Redwood but if all ministers had to go through such a baptism of fire they would perform better at Question Time in the House.

'If a man cheats on his wife, he will cheat on his country.' An odd declaration in view of all the magnificent prime ministers and statesmen we've had, almost to a man or woman.

I liked Redwood's wife. She told me of her career and how it had been interrupted by having children but she had gone back to it. She is company secretary at British Airways.

Punctiliously and prissily he had come in his own car. They were driving back to wherever they live, somewhere in Berkshire, so he drank little of my magnificent 1960 Gazin.

He certainly didn't make any criticisms of John Major but he might well have done if it had been in private. I am sure she reflects his views.

Sunday 5 February
To dinner at Mark Lennox-Boyd's.

The chief guests were Michael Portillo and his wife.[3] I sat next to her. She had a very good job owning a head-hunting agency and makes a fair bit of money.

Michael Portillo, when the ladies had gone, rattled off all kinds of arguments about the European Union. He is not in favour of actually leaving it but of getting the best out of it, as we all are.

My opinion of Michael was much better that evening. He had lost his boastfulness, or at least it has calmed down. Obviously he would like to be Prime Minister but he has now acquired a little sense and is not rocking the boat. The main attention of the Eurosceptics is directed towards Kenneth Clarke who makes very silly speeches and Michael Heseltine who writes tosh, and of course, Douglas Hurd who sits there looking like an elder statesman which he is far from being. He is just an apparatchik of the Foreign Office. But Major can't sack him or have any further disturbance in his Cabinet without risking a series of backbench revolts which could overturn him.

Monday 6 February
A disagreeable letter from Bruce Buck of Skadden Arps. They no longer want to pay me a quarterly fee but to use me whenever they think it necessary and make a payment then. He has always been against me, that fellow. I don't know why. I have done everything I can to help him. He has failed to follow up my avenues numerous times.

---

3. Portillo, at this time Chief Secretary to the Treasury, m (1982) Carolyn, née Eadie.

It is somewhat of a blow losing that £25,000 a year. It means that I don't think we can afford any more holidays in Italy.

Tuesday 7 February
I took Nordlinger of Skadden Arps and Tom Armitt,[4] a customer, to lunch at the House of Lords.

I told them to write to me about the business rate problems they are having with regard to the unit Armitt is erecting in Cornwall to boost power supply. I think I can probably help them with advice and how to set about it. That would be one in the eye for the awful Bruce Buck.

Thursday 9 February
In the afternoon we had a Board Meeting of Cornish Spring Water of which I am Chairman. Robbie [Lyle] was there being very agreeable and making rather good suggestions. In the morning Tessa had rung to say she had seen me on Westcountry TV. It had been absolutely wonderful and the district had been thrilled.[5]

Unfortunately, there is something wrong with the way I speak. I think it is not to do with my neurological situation but because the plate of my false teeth doesn't fit properly. I must get this fixed pretty sharpish, before the Tote Annual lunch.

In the meanwhile, I have agreed with Sonny Marlborough to make the great Churchill oration at Blenheim on March 4th. It is slightly crazy of me. My Tote annual speech has to be prepared and ready for March 7th. However, he said I had once hinted that I wouldn't mind doing the Churchill speech, and Lord Jay[6] was suddenly ill and couldn't come.

I said, 'I don't think I hinted that but I am prepared to do it for you if you will do me a great favour in return.' 'What is that?' 'You

---

4. Tom Armitt worked for Destek Energy Incorp., the US company which set up the Indian Queens power plant now in operation near Newquay in Cornwall.

5. WW was interviewed on 8 February after asking a question in the Lords on 7 February about enforcing fishing quotas on Spanish vessels operating in Cornish waters: 'Will the Minister advise the Government to turn a Nelsonian blind eye to the Devon and Cornish fishermen as they seek to sink the larger Spanish ships?'

6. (1907–96); Labour politician and writer; MP, 1946–83, and Treasury Minister; President, Board of Trade, 1964–7; life peer 1987.

have used your rank as a duke to get Mark Birley to take away my Cornish Spring Water, which is absolutely delicious.

'What I want you to do is to withdraw this unfair competition because I am not a duke, and let them supply it again.'

He promised he would. We shall see.

Poor John Major had to accept the resignation of a junior minister [Allan Stewart], a curious bloke who apparently attacked with a pickaxe protesters over [the M77 motorway].[7]

He is a jolly looking fellow. I think he was quite right, but because of the state of the government he had to go.

Saturday 11 February
A dreadful, pouring wet, windy day. The Tote Gold Trophy at Newbury looked as though it might be threatened by abandonment. We plodded down there. Verushka wore a lovely hat, pink and black. It looked like a bird. It was really attractive and appeared to be waterproof. She looked extremely pretty.

The hat, I fear, came from Chanel. Goodness knows how I am going to keep that sort of thing up when all my money dries up or a large quantity does.

It was a great delight to see Caroline. She is not looking too bad but rather beautiful. She held my hand a lot before dinner. After dinner she went to bed early because she was very tired.

The highlight of the weekend was Hugh Barr, the surgeon in charge at the Gloucester hospital, coming to lunch with his pretty little wife, dark and petite. He was shortish and baldish with a highly intelligent face and keen eyes.

I told him I admired his wonderfully open-minded approach to medicine. 'You don't say, "It's not in the medical books." You'll try anything.'

I feel she is in the best possible hands. He strikes me as a bit of a genius.

I didn't dare tell him I told her to say every night as she goes to sleep 'Every day in every way I'm getting better and better,' and to do the same as she wakes.[8] I thought he might think I was a bit of a crank, though I am not sure. He might even agree.

---

7. The motorway was being built through his constituency, Eastwood, near Glasgow.
8. The Coué system – see 15 May 1994.

Sunday 12 February
I rang Major at around ten to seven on Sunday. Poor fellow, he is fairly upset and discouraged by all this blowing up of Cabinet rows.

He said, 'I don't want to go on with it. I don't care what they all do.' 'You are not to talk like that. You've got to do it. You're going to win the next election and you've got to stick it through.'

I told him that Redwood had been to dinner. I said, 'He's not exactly a barrel of fun.' He laughed.

I also told him about Portillo at the dinner at Mark Lennox-Boyd's.

I told John I had asked Margaret whether she speaks to him on the telephone at all now and [what] she said.

He was a little bit gloomy about that.

He finished off by saying, 'God bless,' which made me laugh because it is exactly what Margaret said to me, as I had just told him.

Monday 13 February
It makes no difference whether I send in the *Times* article early or late. That awful man, McCue [sub-editor], doesn't even begin to look at it till about half past five. It is then a scramble to get the necessary cuts in and to stop him committing all kinds of solecisms and perversions of what I have said. He loves using different dull words for the more entertaining ones I have chosen. When I say, 'interest has sharpened,' he changes it to, 'interest has increased,' just to make it as boring as possible.

Wednesday 15 February
A very jolly lunch with David Swaythling at his Rothman headquarters.

Before it began David said, 'I hear you've done it again, Woodrow. You're a miracle.' 'What do you mean?' 'You got your two years.' I said, 'I've heard nothing.' 'Well everybody knows about it. It was leaked from the Home Office.'

He is very two-faced, David, although he pretends great friendship. But I can't help liking him. I think my real trouble is I seem to like everybody, almost – I can't manage [liking] Heseltine.

Thursday 16 February
Caroline told me she sent a postcard to Princess Diana while she was away in the West Indies. She told her how sorry she was about the adverse and unfair press comment. Mysteriously (or was it mysteriously?) it got from Kensington Palace, where it was addressed

to Princess Diana, to the Prince of Wales who is based in St James's Palace. He wrote Caroline a four-page letter saying how grateful he was to have this postcard from her. It meant a great deal to him that she felt that way about the unfairness in which the press were treating him.

Caroline asked me, 'Should I tell him it was all a mistake?' 'No, for God's sake don't. If he hears about it and speaks to you, say it was meant for him and somehow you put her name on it, or dodge it in some way. Otherwise he'll think you're playing a double game being nice to him and to Princess Diana.' 'In a way, I was.' I bet that vixen, Diana, had it sent on to Prince Charles to show she had a friend in Caroline and that Caroline wasn't his friend at all.

I am now helping Jane Reed [of News International] to see if there [can be] an All Party Media Committee meeting addressed by people from News International

The Other Club dinner was entertaining. Tom King[9] is on the Nolan Committee.

He said that when he was a very junior minister, [Harold] Wilson wanted to come to see his department and discuss an offer made by [Robert] Maxwell to save a firm of bookbinders in his constituency employing about two hundred people. The Secretary to the Cabinet, who was Robert Armstrong at the time – he was sitting next to Tom King as he spoke – advised he should not see him unless there was a civil servant present. If it had just been Maxwell himself, they would have refused to see him, but they had to see him because an ex Prime Minister was coming too.

Maxwell was trying to get back on the approved list of candidates for the Labour Party. He wanted to fight the subsequent election, his Buckingham seat having gone for six.[10] The deal with Wilson apparently was that if he propped up this company, which he did do for two weeks or so and paid their wages while they looked for a buyer, Wilson would get him on to the approved list. What they also wanted was a grant from the government which could have been issued to help in an area of high unemployment.

Tom King asked me should Nolan see Mohamed Fayed. I said no. 'It will get you all lost in a maze of contradictory statements, about

---

9. Conservative MP since 1970; Minister for Industrial Development, 1972–4; Secretary of State for Defence, 1989–92.
10. Maxwell was Labour MP for North Buckinghamshire, 1964–70.

his great innocence and various hints about the ill doings of God knows who.'

Sunday 19 February
Talked at some length to Richard Ryder, the Chief Whip. I said, 'That fellow Nicholas Fairbairn[11] always was a very tiresome fellow.' 'He just died.' 'Exactly what I mean. He's gone and died deliberately at an awkward moment. He's got a seat with a majority of only two thousand in Scotland and you're going to lose it in the by-election.'

When I rang to speak to John on Sunday night they said he was too tired to speak. Very unusual. I wondered whether I had offended him – perhaps with the article I wrote in the *Times* last Tuesday, February 14th.[12]

Tuesday 21 February
Lunch with Bruce Buck. I had done him an injustice. There is simply a new rule that they don't have any consultants now on their payroll but they get paid for anything they may do.

He was very friendly and I felt a little ashamed of doubting him.

In the evening David Swaythling gave a great party for John Freeman's eightieth birthday.[13]

I gave John Freeman Alan Bennett's book, *Writing Home*. In case he had one already I didn't inscribe it until I was pretty drunk. I then wrote in it, 'For John Freeman who could have been Prime Minister but disdained it as a sordid toy of vanity.'

---

11. Flamboyant Conservative MP, elected 1974; Solicitor General for Scotland, 1979–82; he survived cries for his resignation after a rejected lover was alleged to have staged a suicide attempt outside his house but resigned from office in 1982 over his remarks about a rape case to the *Glasgow Daily Record* the day before he was due to make a Commons statement; knight 1988; the seat was lost to the SNP in the by-election on 25 May 1995.
12. The article put arguments against entering the single currency but said the Europhiles in the Cabinet had started a useful debate.
13. Former Labour politician (MP, 1945–55), journalist (editor, *New Statesman*, 1961–5), diplomat (British High Commissioner in India, 1965–8, Ambassador to the US, 1969–71); chairman, London Weekend Television, 1971–84; Visiting Professor of International Relations, University of California at Davis, 1985–90.

Saturday 25 February

Up at seven o'clock and off to swim my furlong at the RAC.

After various repairs to my *News of the World* article I set out at twelve for Kempton.

Left after the 2.30 race for Salisbury to see the betting shop.

I then had to go on to Bowden with two large orchids which needed to be renourished for the next season.

[At Badminton] David had brought his own chef from London, wishing dinner to be better than usual as there were a number of grand people there. It wasn't better than usual. It was tarragon chicken which is nothing in particular, and I can't remember the soup. However, the wine was very good – Château Pichon-Lalande. It was 1983, a splendid year of a super second growth neighbour to Château Latour.

When we went back into the library, Caroline was slightly peeved. 'You always stay so late at dinner when you're here,' meaning David doesn't usually do that. So I apologized.

Sunday 26 February

It was off to the great surprise eighty-fifth birthday party for Cousin Honor.

We found the Meadow Cottages, two of them joined, in which Prue, the daughter of Honor by her first marriage to Gordon Glover, lives. Julian Glover, whom I like a lot and is now a leading actor of the Royal Shakespeare Theatre Company, had arranged it all with his sister.

I talked for long to Honor who was absolutely thrilled and surprised that I had come. The poor little soul was wispy and couldn't stand steadily. She had shrunk, could barely see, was deaf and can't hold a pen to write properly. Yet she seemed suddenly to hear and see me well, perhaps through excitement.

She showed me a picture of herself cradling me as a beautiful baby. When she told her father, Horace, how beautiful I was, he said, 'Don't be proud, I looked like that when I was a baby and now look at me.'

When I asked Petronella if she would sing, she did without demur. I was very grateful. She sang 'As Time Goes By'[14] in that beautiful voice which startled them all, including Julian.

Then I made a little speech, recounting how she had taught me to write, and she cried out, 'I wish I hadn't,' and everybody laughed.

---

14. From the film *Casablanca*.

We've had some acrimonious passages in the public newspapers in which she always contradicted what I wrote about my father.[15]

Bob spoke [on the telephone] to Honor. He was quite lucid. It was a great treat for her. She told me she had been in love with him – he was marvellous and so good-looking at the time. He had been a great hero of hers. I said, 'Just as he was of mine.'

I was wrong to think I was out of favour with John Major. He had genuinely been tired the last time I had wanted to speak to him. But he let fly at me in a furious rage about the way my friend, Murdoch, had criticized and persecuted his son, James, working at Marks & Spencer.[16] Also the unfortunate lady who is managing a store and now has lost promotion chances. He said, 'If I had a majority of a hundred and fifty, I would crush Rupert Murdoch and make sure he had no newspapers at all.

'It's the reason why no decent people want to go into public life these days. If they can't get something on him, they get it on his family. He's a perfectly normal, healthy boy and they persecute him. It's disgraceful. How would Rupert like that done to his sons or daughter?' I said, 'He wouldn't. He takes great pains to see that it doesn't happen.'

John quaintly thinks the boy did not go to bed with the lady whose husband is now citing John Major's son in his divorce.

If John believes that, he'll believe anything. Norma, poor girl, believes it too. Nevertheless, it is a vile and unnecessary persecution and he is right about Rupert being indifferent to making harmless, unimportant people miserable.

After he calmed down a little I told him he was doing fantastically well over Ireland.

He apologized, 'I know it's not your fault, Woodrow. I just felt I wanted to get it off my chest. You were the unlucky recipient.'

Monday 27 February

A message came from the Home Secretary. Could I be available to take a statement about my reappointment and say whether I agreed with it or not? Latish in the afternoon the statement arrived. I was surprised how reasonable and fairly put it was. To the relief of Mr Newcome,

---

15. See Vol. 1, pp. 197–8 and 264, for her 1986 article in the *Observer*.
16. The press had splashed James Major's alleged affair with an older, married woman.

the private secretary who was dealing with it, I rang and said I thought it was a very civilized draft announcement.

The Duff Cooper prize presented at the Mayfair Hotel.

It was a party for the rather élite. The prize went to the David Gilmour boy[17] for his life of Lord Curzon.

John Saumarez-Smith from Heywood Hill [bookshop] was there. I said to him, 'Do you think that if a horny-handed Glaswegian had a book written for the Duff Cooper prize they would award it to him?'[18]

Tuesday 28 February
The usual mole in the Home Office had leaked the announcement to the press. Vile attacks once more were made upon me by all kinds of people, even elements from the Labour Party (including the jackass Jack Straw, Shadow Home Secretary), though Alan Meale expressed admiration for me and said I had out-tricked everybody.

The *Guardian*, the *Financial Times* and the *Independent* have kept on asking me to do interviews with them. I refuse. They're always distorted, they always send one up. I am going to have nothing to do with being interviewed by anybody ever again.

---

17. The Hon. David Gilmour, writer, son of Lord Gilmour (Ian).
18. The prize is awarded for the book published during the previous year which the judges think Duff Cooper would have liked most.

Wednesday 1 March

All was anticipation for the great Euro debate. I had told John he would win.

He did. He got a majority of five on the most important matter. It would have been seven if Norman hadn't gone into exhibitionist mood and decided to vote against the government. He has become totally idiotic, as I will write for the *News of the World* on Sunday.

A jolly dinner at Mark's Club with Tessa and Henry Keswick. Henry was telling us his views about Nick Leeson and what happened over all the betting he was doing on behalf of Barings.[1]

They're still serving that Blenheim rubbish.

Saturday 4 March

I duly delivered my speech in the huge long library [at Blenheim]. Three hundred and fifty people were there.

Mary Soames gave me a great hug at the end and said, 'That was the nicest thing I've ever heard about my father, so original, personal and so new.'

When the guests of the Duke go in, everybody stands up as they go by to take their seats. I find it slightly comical, slightly embarrassing. But Sonny carries it off very well. He, as it were, looks every inch a duke.

Sunday 5 March

I was amused when we arrived at Cavendish Avenue to find Sonny had put in the back of the car a box full of Blenheim water, I having brought him what I called some decent water, i.e. Cornish Spring Water. I propose to have his analysed by the public analyst.[2]

Talked to John Major. I told him I had spoken to Gus Fischer (Chief

---

1. Leeson had lost £700m in the futures market and brought down Barings, the merchant bank.
2. WW does not record doing so.

Executive at News International) and told him would they please lay off about James.

I told him that I'd advised Evelyn de Rothschild to get shot of Norman. He'd had enough warnings. John said, 'I don't want to advise or have anything to do with that.' I said, 'Nobody is asking you to. I was just telling you what I said. Evelyn's intention now is to not renew his directorship in April.'

If I had tipped all the staff at Blenheim £5, I would be bankrupt. So I gave £40 to the butler and £15 to the little valet who was so pleased to see me. He is as queer as a coot but nice and has been there a long time. He is immaculate, laying out one's clothes and packing everything up at the end.

I was disturbed by the *Sunday Telegraph* Mandrake column this morning. The first piece was a replica of my end of the conversation with Evelyn de Rothschild when he was asking my advice about what to do about Norman and I had given it to him. Evelyn will be certain it came from me.

Probably Major will assume that Petronella is the source.

Oh dear, but I love her just the same.

Monday 6 March

Finishing touches, I hoped, to the Tote Annual Luncheon speech. I altered it later in the evening because of an extraordinary article in the *Evening Standard*.

It was by some fellow Rory Knight Bruce.

I counted at least thirty-three mistakes before I gave it up. I then included one or two of the most extraordinary ones in my speech.[3]

I had a lot of very nice letters, particularly one from Julian Wilson, the BBC racing commentator, on my reappointment. A number of the messages seemed absolutely genuine.[4]

---

3. In the first paragraph the article said the chairmanship of the Tote was a sinecure.
4. For example, William Whitelaw wrote that he was delighted to think that he was told in 1983, when Home Secretary, that WW should not be reappointed 'but you were! There you are, and look what you have done for racing – a very great achievement'.

Tuesday 7 March
Peter Jones made a bit of an ass of himself by giving out his great
plans for bringing the Tote into the ownership of the BHB, when he
hadn't even yet been appointed as a member.

In the evening we went to dinner with Aly Aziz at the Boltons.

I found myself sitting next to the Russian Ambassadress, who was
a trifle heavy going but very hot on music.

She was full of nonsense that nobody knew Pushkin in England. I
said, 'Of course I do. For example, he wrote a very long poem about
a man who was friendly with a girl who was very much in love with
him but he didn't want her. When he did want her she was already fed
up with him and it ended in some sadness.'[5]

'But the ordinary people don't know that or anything else about
Russian literature.' I said, 'That simply isn't true. You can fill any
theatre in London with plays like *A Month in the Country* or *The
Cherry Orchard*, if they're well acted.'

The Ambassadress talked quite freely about Yeltsin, saying he was
no good.

I said, 'You're supposed to represent your government.' 'Yes, but
I'm talking privately to you. I wouldn't say that in public.'

Wednesday 8 March
Beryl [Bainbridge] has a half million pound contract with Hamish
Hamilton to write three books. She told me in great confidence that
the first one was going to be about the *Titanic*, the next would be
about the Crimean War and workers connected therewith. The third
would be about Doctor Johnson.[6]

She was amazed when I said I may be his most senior living connection. I told her about his mother's sister having married into the Wyatt
family and I am directly descended from her.

Beryl was also paid £18,000 years ago for the rights to a film of a
book she wrote.[7] The première is to be on April 5th with Hugh Grant.
He has to act a homosexual. I said, 'That won't do any good for his
image.' 'No, but he wants to be a serious actor and show he can act

---

5. A basic plot summary of *Eugene Onegin*.
6. *Every Man for Himself* (the *Titanic*) was published in 1996, *Master Georgie* (the
   Crimean War) in 1998, and *According to Queenie*, about Dr Johnson's relationship
   with Mrs Thrale, as seen through the eyes of a servant girl, Queenie, in 2000.
7. *An Awfully Big Adventure* from her 1989 book.

anything.' Hugh Grant is the famous fellow now from *Four Weddings and a Funeral*.

Caroline felt quite well today and very pleased with the doctors saying she was getting on much better than expected. She had a rehearsal for her doctorate presentation by Bristol University. They had all come out and she had put the robes on. She was disappointed she wasn't going to wear a mortar board but a little Elizabethan crown cap.

I fear that when I got back I was extremely irritable and cross. I was so tired. It was not at all fair on poor Mrs Tamborero who works so hard.

Friday 10 March

In the evening Pericles rang saying two journalists, one a photographer, employed by the *Mail on Sunday*, had come out to see him. Apparently they had hoped to find a drop-out with tattoos on his back and front, washing and scrubbing the floor in his bar, as they called it. Actually, it is rather an agreeable restaurant.

He rang me to ask what he should do. I said, 'The first thing you must get into your head is they have not come out for the good of your health. They've come out to do anything they can to discredit us, you and me.'

I spoke to Vere in Paris and explained what had happened.

Saturday 11 March

I went [to Oxford] to have a general chat with Dick Smethurst in Worcester College. During the day I had made some notes of what to say to the Mercury Society organized by Edmund Glynn, Dermot Glynn's son.[8]

I talked to them about the inaccuracy of modern journalists and how they didn't take the trouble to find out any facts.

If I leave Worcester my papers, I fear they won't have room for them. Should I leave them £5,000 or so? They never made me an Honorary Fellow despite my giving quite a lot previously and paying for putting the original James Wyatt decorations in the Hall back. It was natural for Worcester to make Rupert an Honorary Fellow. He's

---

8. See Vol. 2, pp. 604–5, for WW's talk in November 1991 to the political society at the City of London School with young Edmund Glynn, son of the chief executive of NERA, as chairman.

given them a fortune. But I'm more distinguished than most other Honorary Fellows of my time. Now it's so late I wouldn't enjoy it if they did offer me one and I wouldn't take it.[9]

Tuesday 14 March
Up at a quarter to seven. Had to get to Cheltenham to be photographed with all the [Tote] ladies and a few men in their new uniforms. They don't look good. They've been made shoddily. The buttons are falling off and there is an ominous split in the crutch of the skirt pointing to the Mound of Venus. No notice was taken of Verushka's inputs.

On the way back I stopped to have an early dinner with Caroline.

During dinner Caroline said to me that when Petronella had been there by herself for the weekend she had told her that everybody in the house was making tape recordings of their diaries, or words to that effect, and they were getting muddled up so they hear each other's. All that could mean is that Petronella listens outside the door as I am dictating this manuscript.

Thursday 16 March
I'd a wretched night [at the Suffolks]. As Linda wasn't there, none of the normal things were available, like tissues or soap in the right place. There were no blankets, just one huge duvet. You either had to sweat under that or throw it off and get frozen.

At breakfast I said could I have some of the honey I'd had last time I was there. Micky said, 'I've got some new honey,' and he produced a jar of honey which comes from an old English type bee, black, small and very aggressive. The honey was absolutely delicious.

He's allowed people to take some swarms away so that they may be bred all over the country.

Charlton Park is very ancient with its trees, and these rare English bees have been there for centuries.

[At Cheltenham] Princess Anne, I think, had wanted to present the prize [the Gold Cup], but I always said that if it's not Queen Elizabeth the Queen Mother then it has to be Verushka. She was bustling in and out a lot at one point, then she disappeared for an hour and a half with Andrew Parker Bowles.

I thought how much better it would have been if he'd had an early divorce from his wife and married Princess Anne. Then she wouldn't

---

9. WW left Worcester College £65,000 in his will.

have married the ghastly Mark Phillips and the new one, whose name I can't even remember.

Next to me sat Mrs Vincent O'Brien.[10] She is the wife of the great trainer. The last and seventh race of the day is in his honour and named for him.

She is doing books about Irish architecture, or architecture in Ireland, which is really all or mostly by the English.

Of course she is doing the James Wyatt houses of which there are two or three in Ireland.[11]

I have rarely enjoyed talking to the lady next to me as much as I did on that occasion. She is bright, small, cheerful, obviously had been very pretty; lively, quick, interested in everything.

Friday 17 March
Trouble in paradise. Gus Fischer has been moved by Rupert from being in charge of News International here. His secretary rang saying he wouldn't be coming to dinner on March 28th. I immediately got on to him. 'Why not?' 'I didn't think you'd want me to come.' 'Of course. I want to see you. We like you very much, both of you.' So he was pleased because he thought he'd be dropped immediately he was of no importance.

He then told me he had been there six years.

He brought all their business up to date and scratch. But now Rupert really wants to be an old-fashioned newspaper proprietor and have everybody running about doing exactly what he tells them, right or wrong. He said the new man is also an Australian and, 'He'll ask permission before he goes to the bathroom.'

Rupert was here for a few days but he doesn't ring me any more.

I was much touched to get a letter from John Major, in his handwriting and the envelope likewise. What an amazingly kind thing to do just as he was leaving for his visit to Israel.[12]

Allan Davis, I am glad to say, thinks my play is rather good and

---

10. Jacqueline, née Wittenoom, m (1951) Vincent O'Brien (trainer of three consecutive Grand National winners, six Derby winners, six Irish Derby winners, etc.; retired 1994).
11. Castle Coole, Fermanagh, is one.
12. In the letter he says he had read WW's Blenheim and Tote speeches with huge enjoyment and ends, 'keep writing your wonderful columns'.

suggests for a name, *For God's Sake*. He's sent it on to a director who he says is very good.

I am beginning to think I'll be quite pleased to leave the Tote at the end of two years, April 30th, 1997. It will give me a chance to write in a reflective way, think about things more and perhaps write a decent play or a children's story.[13] I just want to be there for two years in order to make sure I win this battle with the bookmakers over Tote Direct, and that whichever way the Tote is set out in future, it will not harm that glorious staff.

I took Peter Jones to the Control Room [at Cheltenham].

If he's any good, I will see that he does get the job but he has to prove himself first.

Sunday 19 March
The article about Pericles is in the *Mail on Sunday* but not, obviously, as originally intended. It is not such a disagreeable article entirely, though it makes the usual sneers at me, saying there was a sense of shock that I continued at this geriatric age to be the Chairman of the Tote instead of retiring gracefully. It describes me as a Tory, which I am not, and there are all the usual petty mistakes. But it is spread over two pages about Pericles with a very nice photograph of him and a picture of his steak house.

I rang Pericles up in the middle of the night and read the entire piece to him and Kyoko.

We all thought he should pin it up, splash it all over the place in Wyatt's Steak House and the Cross Roads Café.

He said, 'I did say you are proud of me now.' 'I was never anything else but proud of you. I just hoped that everything would be sorted out OK.'

Talked to Irwin Stelzer. He says that Gus Fischer did do well and that I am right to insist on him coming to dinner.

When I attack his newspapers in my column, Rupert gets rather fretful. He refers to me as 'that old bastard' when speaking to Irwin. Irwin says to him, 'Why don't you ring Woodrow?' 'I dunno. I don't want to have a row with him.' I said, 'Is he going to sack me?' Irwin said, 'No. He wouldn't dare. For some reason he won't ever sack you.' I said, 'It's because, I'm sure, he knows I really love him. And it's a

---

13. WW had written two books for children, *The Exploits of Mr Saucy Squirrel* (1976) and *The Further Exploits of Mr Saucy Squirrel* (1977).

very good thing to give some credibility to his papers through my
articles in his newspapers and my opinions, and not trying to prevent
my writing what I do.'

But you can really never tell with Rupert.

Spoke to John at about half past nine.

I asked him how it had gone with Clinton.

He said, 'He won't do that again,' meaning muck about with the
peace process in Northern Ireland.[14]

When I told him about Rupert calling me 'that old bastard', John
said, 'I do that often about my people. It can be a term of affection,
you know.'

Each time I was trying to sign off he wanted to go on talking, which
somewhat amazed me as it was coming on half an hour since I had
been talking to him.

Monday 20 March

Caroline was amusing about Lavinia Norfolk[15] and 'Master', as they
called the previous Duke of Beaufort, Master of the Queen's Horse.
He had a passionate love affair with her. Constantly he invited her to
stay at Badminton where she was immensely bossy. She kept
rearranging the menus, going into the kitchen and telling them what
she wanted to eat and what the guests should have. Mary (Cambridge),
wife of Master, was furious. When she found out about the affair she
forbade her to come to the house. This greatly upset Master who had
to carry on his illicit amours elsewhere.

We had to be at half past six at the Royal Academy for a gala
evening connected with the Poussin exhibition. Vere Rothermere had
a table for about ten people. I thanked him for the much kinder article
in the *Mail on Sunday* about Pericles.

The concert, connected with the gala evening, was performed by
the school set up by Yehudi Menuhin. I was amazed that I enjoyed it.

---

14. It had been announced on 9 March that President Clinton had invited Gerry
    Adams to his St Patrick's Day Reception and that the US ban on fund-raising for
    the Provisionals was being lifted. Major says in his memoirs that Clinton sub-
    sequently telephoned and wrote, swearing he would hold Adams and Sinn Fein
    to address the hard questions of decommissioning arms.
15. (1916–95); she was Lord Lieutenant, West Sussex, 1975–90; m (1937) 16th Duke
    of Norfolk (d 1975); 'Master' m (1923) Lady Mary Cambridge.

One of the boys was Korean. He came to sit next to Vere Rothermere's wife. She was looking gorgeous.

She gave me several great hugs, slightly to the surprise of the onlookers. She is very happy with Vere, but she remains flirtatious.

Wednesday 22 March
An early start to Exeter.

Before the off of the first race the Jackpot had gone to over £2 million, as I had thought it would. The Tote hastily prepared a lovely placard with the figures on and I held it up for the photographers.

Alas, the Jackpot was won, as was to be expected in the end. But it had infuriated the big bookmakers. William Hill immediately tried to rubbish it by pretending that two of their customers had had an SP accumulator which paid more.

Thursday 23 March
At The Other Club they were having the Haut-Bage-Libéral 1984 which I had given in honour of Roy's Order of Merit. He was there too. It drank extremely well and Roy said how nice it was and how kind it had been of me to give it for that occasion.

Conversation was lively and then it became quite nasty. Roy turned on me and said, 'Why did you change your principles? You've gone back on everything you once believed in.' I said, 'But Roy, I haven't. I've simply developed along different channels to you. I didn't want nationalization of steel, nor did you. But you stayed in the Labour party then. I opposed all the trade union swindles and found myself extremely unpopular with the old union members for washing their dirty linen in public. I think Mrs Thatcher did a damn good job.'

Roy began to shout abuse at me, 'Rubbish, rubbish. How can you talk such terrible rubbish? It's all nonsense,' to which I replied in a fairly soft voice, 'Roy, I don't think it's appropriate for the Chancellor of Oxford University to shout in that childish, abusive way without any reasoned argument whatever.' He nearly blew up with apoplexy.

I said, 'You've changed too. You started a party of your own. I would never have been in any other party, except for the Labour Party. I don't see how you can levy changeability and turncoatism and all the rest of it against me, when you've been an arch practitioner of it.'

Roy said, 'We should observe the rules of the club. Party rancour is not to interfere with agreeable intercourse.'

Saturday 25 March
During the week there was a great attack by Jonathan Aitken on the *Today* programme in particular.

This caused commotion. Unfortunately, not long after Jonathan Aitken's onslaught, the *Independent* ran a story about his being a non-executive director of a firm in 1980 which later went bust. It exported arms, and he ought to have known that one of the shipments legally directed to Singapore would eventually finish up in Iran. The *Independent* story was not wholly convincing, but Jonathan has always been a bit hot so there may have been something in it. It was a long time ago. I wasn't surprised Jonathan couldn't remember all the details, but it has an unpleasant odour.

Tuesday 28 March
I bet Chips Keswick 500 to 1 that the Tories would have the most seats in the next parliament. I sent him a note about it. He returned it signed in agreement, hoping I would win.[16]

Friday 31 March
Julian Lewis came to see me.[17] There was the old distress story about the powers that be in the Tory Party being determined that he should never get a seat in Parliament. They say he has a personality problem. Actually, I know precisely what they mean. He is so didactic and utterly charmless. But he is a stout-hearted fellow, idealistic and determined. He has done marvellous work for the Tories, for the cause of curbing the trade unions, bias on the BBC and so forth.

He warned me about David Hart[18] being very close to Rifkind.

He likes Robert Cranborne very much. I said, 'He ought to be Chairman of the Party when poor old Jeremy Hanley has to go.'[19]

---

16. The bet was that if the Tories got the most seats in the next Parliament, Chips Keswick would pay WW £500; if they did not, WW would pay Chips Keswick £10.
17. Research director and director, Coalition for Peace Through Security, 1981–5; director, Policy Research Associates from 1985; deputy director, Conservative Research Department, 1990–6; Conservative MP for New Forest since 1997; see Vol. 2, *passim*, for his role in the campaign for impartiality in broadcasting.
18. Property developer and newspaper columnist; see Vol. 1, pp. 404, 406, 436 and Vol. 2, p. 629.
19. It was rumoured that Hanley would be moved after he had made a number of gaffes.

Robert has put Julian on various secret committees to do with defence. He has to write the papers saying what the effects on us in the world are following the break-up of Russia and the adventures the successor states may undertake westwards.

Saturday 1 April

Went to Badminton for lunch with Caroline. The poor girl is not looking very well, not as well as she has been.

We watched the Boat Race together. She is very knowledgeable on it.

'How do you know so much about this?' 'The Master had a great deal to do with the Boat Race.' They used to follow together in a launch immediately behind the boats.

'Next year,' she said, 'let's go on the river behind the crews. I should so love it. It'd be marvellous, wouldn't it? We'd have a lovely day out.'

It was all I could do not to burst into tears. But I hope and pray it comes true. I still believe a miracle will happen.

It was then on to a strange restaurant in the Hyde Park Hotel with three Michelin Guide stars. You have to be there on the dot or they give your table away.

The bill came to over £700. It's true we had a bottle of Haut-Batailley 1978.

I agree with Arnold [the Wyatts' host] that I never want to go again to a restaurant which regards it as a favour to let you go in. The name of the restaurant is Marco Pierre White.

Monday 3 April

The young man, Rory Knight Bruce, who wrote the article in the *Evening Standard* with thirty-one counted, verifiable mistakes came to see me.[1] He was very nervous. He was also highly apologetic. I liked him.

I told him that if you are going to be a good journalist and make your attacks effective, it is far better to have your facts right.

I think he will be not against me in the future.

---

1. On 6 March WW said there were at least 33 mistakes.

Tuesday 4 April

An interesting meeting at the Office of Fair Trading. They still haven't sent their letter to the complainants, BOLA [Betting Officers Licensees Association] and Ladbroke and William Hill.[2] William Hill are trying to get a judicial review against us. The Office of Fair Trading will turn up on our side but they wanted to know a lot more facts and make sure they don't get themselves subject to a judicial review.

At lunch-time I had Diana Rawstron and the lady who is projected as the editor of this manuscript, Sarah Curtis. The conversation went quite well. I agreed to see Ian Chapman Jr. to get some notion of their concept of how the memoirs are to be published.

As we were sitting there, suddenly Olga Polizzi came in with a team of people from Forte. They were making some kind of film or having photographs for a brochure. She was striding around the elegant Edwardian dance floor and on to the platform level with us. I am not sure whether she saw me or not. I said to the others, 'For heaven's sake, don't make yourselves visible or get caught by the camera with me. Our secrets may be blown.' Maybe she did see me. I shall be interested to see whether something comes back to Verushka that I was sitting with two ladies in the Waldorf Hotel, one of them a pretty blonde and the other not unattractive.[3]

Wednesday 5 April

To the première of Beryl Bainbridge's film. I took some champagne around to her house where we had little bits, quite agreeable, to eat. There was to be no further dinner for me as I was not invited to the jamboree after the film, reserved for her family. I was not in the least bit put out because I would never get to bed otherwise.

It was not a very dramatic première. Hugh Grant was the main star. His girlfriend [Elizabeth Hurley], who is famous for being famous, did not come – she was in America.

The film itself was remarkably good, driven with Beryl's brand of bare, unadorned life combined with humour and will to get somewhere.

---

2. The bookmakers were opposing the Tote's increase in the Authority fee which allows bookmakers to offer bets at Tote odds.
3. This was the second of the three times I met WW. The scene at the Waldorf, where we had lunch, was exactly as he describes it, with WW telling us to dodge behind the pillars so as not to be seen.

What a remarkable girl Beryl is. That brain turns out weird fantasies shot through with truth.

Saturday 8 April

I have been telling Caroline about my feeding the birds and looking at them to see which ones they are, and about the flowers in the garden. She said, 'I didn't know you were like that. I didn't realize you watched birds and fed them.' I said, 'Oh yes. I'm a dreamy sort of person. I'm not at all the entirely matter-of-fact, administrative businessman.'

On the subject of my play, I have been rather shattered by a letter from Allan Davies who had heard from the lay reader who might have been director of it. He says that I haven't made enough differentiation between one character and another.

He is right, I am afraid. This means a lot more work.

Monday 10 April

I began by ringing John Major at a quarter to eight. I told him I was going to write a comparison between his government and Blair's shadow cabinet which would be his first government.

When I told Martin Ivens my proposed article, he said, 'But you can't do that. You must write about Richard Spring and his resignation after the three-in-the-bed scandal, as covered in full detail by the *News of the World*.' I tried to avoid this but I was told I must do it, after he had spoken to the editor of the *Times*, Peter Stothard.[4]

The editor, Peter Stothard, took out the bit I had written saying the *Times*, a sister paper of the *News of the World*, had been happy to live on its immoral proceeds to keep itself going when it was making losses. I was annoyed.

Tuesday 11 April

During the day I heard from Irwin Stelzer.

I had sent him faxes of my original article and the deletions made by the editor. Irwin doesn't agree with my law of privacy.

Irwin had shown what I sent to him to Rupert. Rupert was jumping

---

4. Spring had resigned from his post as Parliamentary Private Secretary to the Secretary of State for Northern Ireland; WW used the episode – Spring's comments on the Majors were allegedly tape-recorded at a dinner party after which he had enjoyed sex with his guests, Odette Nightingale and a friend – to argue for a privacy law.

up and down with annoyance and fury for a bit. Then he suddenly said, 'But it is a brilliant article, isn't it?'

Later in the day I had the following fax from Rupert: 'I am quite prepared to concede both that the *News of the World* was over the top on Sunday and that you are entitled to your opinions. However, your column in today's *Times* makes life difficult for all of us! With best wishes, Rupert.'

I was very pleased to have this. It contrasted sharply with the one I had in the morning from Piers Morgan: 'Your article in this morning's *Times* was a disgrace.' I replied to him: 'I am sure you know there is a Rupert Murdoch rule that writers and papers within the News International Group are free to criticize each other without censorship, whether the criticism affects the paper they are writing in or other News International papers they are writing about. This rule has often been taken advantage of by the *Sunday Times* and the *Sun* in attacks on me. Cheer up. You become ever more famous, which can't be bad for business. And you are a brilliant editor. Yours, with great affection, Woodrow.' My *Times* article has caused something of a sensation.

Meanwhile, after a long and dreary examination of my accounts the conclusion is that I have to pay £24,000 in tax. I paid £12,000 at once and said will they take four months at £3,000 a month [for the rest].

The question is how do I get this damn money. I have had to sell a number of shares I would rather have kept. I don't want to have another overdraft. I am feeling badly hemmed in.

It was then off to lunch with James Hanson who runs the conglomerate of the same name.

I was glad to see Chris Collins who used to have a perfume business.[5]

He is a terrifically good egg who was on the Levy Board as representative of the Jockey Club.

What did I think of the BHB and what the Jockey Club has been doing, and the idea of taking over the Tote? I said, 'It's all going to plan. I've got the man I wanted, Peter Jones, on the Board. I wouldn't have agreed to another two years otherwise. Now I've got lots to do

5. Managing director, Goya, 1968–75; amateur steeplechase jockey, 1965–75; director, corporate development, Hanson, 1991–5, vice-chairman, 1995–8, chairman since 1998; member of Levy Board, 1982–4; member of the Jockey Club.

to bring the bookmakers to heel. I don't think you will find the BHB taking over the Tote in the way it is talked about. It has got to be a hands-off operation, entirely independent.'

Hanson said that Blair had come to see him and had lunch where we were sitting. Hanson was not at all impressed.

Thursday 13 April
Bob is in a terrible state. It looks as though he may pop off any moment. He got out of bed at the hospital and fell and cracked his hip in God knows how many places. Nevertheless, he has been talking in a rational manner. I speak to poor Molly several times a day, as well as trying to talk to Caroline.

In the evening the Hungarian Ambassador and his wife came to dinner. The other guests were Mark and Eva Pejacsevich and Charles Powell.

There was talk about Jonathan Aitken and his determination to sue the *Guardian*, with his great statements on the television.

I said to Charles, 'I have always been nervous of Jonathan. He's the sort of fellow who if he went sailing, would always want his sail to be almost touching the water. He is very close to the edge, it seems to me, with some of these things. But I like him.'

Charles said, 'Yes. Mrs Thatcher was nervous of him, too. We never knew what skeletons were going to come out of the cupboard.' He thought Jonathan's plan was to continue the libel action which will take years to come on, and then hope it would become *sub judice* until after the election so nothing more could be said about it – by which time he, Charles, supposed the Tories would be out in any case.

Saturday 15 April
I rang David to say would he mind my coming. He said, 'I'm afraid you won't find her talking.'

I arrived at about a quarter past twelve and went straight up to her bedroom and held her hand. She wasn't conscious. She was making awful bubbling noises.

I had brought my Easter egg for her which I had got in the Burlington Arcade. It was a beautiful hand-painted affair made in Dorset, with 'I love you' on the top. I had also bought one for Verushka and one for Petronella without 'I love you' on the top.

Anne [Somerset] arrived.

She said how good I was to come and how sweet I was with her mother. I said, 'I'm getting more comfort from holding her hand than she is from me,' which was absolutely true.

After three hours I left. I had no lunch, though Steve (the butler) had brought me up a glass of champagne which I drank, but only half of it. Then the nurse made me a cup of tea, which was all I had until I got back to London and demolished a crumpet with Patum Peperium on it.

Alan Hare died earlier this week.

Alan always referred to me thus: 'I'm Woodrow's oldest friend.' I am not quite sure if this was true but he was maybe just about, my having met him so early on at Oxford. He was very brave, got the MC and belonged to that glorious gang: Billy McLean,[6] now dead, Julian Amery, now on the verge of finishing himself off with drink; Randolph Churchill; Fitzroy Maclean. I shall be the only one left of the group from Oxford.

When I fall over, as I did just now while writing this, I think I'll be gone soon.

To dinner came Andrew Sinclair and Sonia. I like him quite a lot now.

I asked him what he thought of Hobsbawm.[7] I had been reading his latest book which I thought was written pretty objectively though I thought he was a Communist.

Andrew said, 'Yes. Did you get as far as the end where he says that after all, communism turned out to be better than capitalism?' 'No, I haven't reached that absurdity yet.'

Sunday 16 April

The best news of the day was when Molly rang up.

The surgeon had decided to take the great risk of operating on Bob.

He had come through enormously well, he was talking rationally. They had given him a local anaesthetic and a light general anaesthetic and they had entirely repaired the hip he had smashed. Amazing.

I talked to John Major. I apologized for neglecting him lately because I had various things which had interfered. I told him about

---

6. (1918–86); Lieutenant Colonel Desmond McLean, Conservative MP, 1954–64; see Vol. 1, p. 226.
7. Professor Eric Hobsbawm, Emeritus Professor of Economics and Social History, University of London, since 1982; his *Age of Extremes: the Short Twentieth Century* was published in 1994.

Caroline without giving her name – 'a dear friend in Gloucestershire'. I also told him about Bob.

I said, 'I know it's very impertinent of me, but do you think you could give him some kind of decoration? He's never had anything other than being a life president of the MCC.' He said, 'I think it would be too late for June to decorate him now. I didn't know he'd never had any recognition.'

I thought how different that is from when I rang Ted Heath and said Les Cannon was dying, the man who was a Communist and then came over to the other side and helped me expose all the Communist ETU vote rigging.

It was about December 21st when I rang Ted. Les was informed immediately he'd have a knighthood in the New Year's Honours and survived a few days into January.

I told John that there should be a privacy law. He said his lawyers were very much against it. I said, 'They must be crazy. Do you ever talk to Blair?' He said he did occasionally. I said, 'I think you would find that they would support one. If they supported it, it would be unanimous and you would have no trouble with it.' He thought that was a good idea. I said, 'Blair and co. need it. They've got all kinds of sex scandals in their outfit.'

We had a jolly dinner on Sunday night with the Stelzers at the Connaught Hotel.

Irwin asked me why I was so busy persecuting the Fayeds. I said, 'Because they're crooks and they oughtn't to have British citizenship.' He said they had done a lot of good for the country. 'Absolute nonsense. They've done no good at all. They're trying to destabilize the government and obviously the Fayeds are behind the attack on Jonathan Aitken.'

'Why do you defend him so strongly?' 'Read carefully what I wrote about the man on the flying trapeze in the *News of the World* and my saying he was taking a daring risk by attacking the *Guardian* in the law courts.'

Monday 17 April

I got to Badminton just after four. I went in to see Caroline. She recognized me straight away.

I held her hand and she gripped it very hard. I said to her, 'I adore you. I always will. I always have.' She said, 'I adore you, too. I shall always be with you.' I said, 'You look beautiful and you're the most wonderful girl in the world.'

The nurses told me not to overexcite her. David didn't say that because he didn't think it mattered at all.

I was so happy I went.

Thursday 20 April

An enormous lunch at 19 Cavendish Avenue was arranged by Graham Turner for the *Sunday Telegraph*. We were going to do a repeat, but this time about Major, of the type of lunch we had in June 1992 about Margaret.

I produced all the wines. Miraculously I had a wine for each year which was significant in his life. There was a champagne Bollinger Grande Année 1979, the year he first went into Parliament. Followed by a Premier Cru Chablis, Mont de Milieu 1992, the year he won the general election. Then came Sancerre, Croix du Roi 1990, the year in which he was for a time Foreign Secretary and then became Chancellor of the Exchequer when Geoffrey Howe resigned.

Then we had Château Gazin (Pomerol) 1989. That was the first time John was in the Cabinet. The Château Cantemerle 1985 was for when he was first in the government as a junior Minister. That was followed by Château Mouton Rothschild 1970, when he and Norma were married. Finally Tokay Szamorodni 1943, the year of his birth.

Paul Johnson made his usual attacks on Major. We pinned him down to admitting he'd written he wanted Blair to win.

Peregrine Worsthorne thought Major was no good, too, and had to go. Trevor-Roper thought he wasn't much good but he was more neutral. Kingsley Amis, on the other hand, was pretty well on my side.

I had scarcely recovered when it was off to the Saintsbury Club. I had to take Mark Pejacsevich because Harry Hambleden, who was longing to come, had rung up in the morning to say he was in a terrible state, ill in bed and couldn't move, with some awful bug.

Hugh Johnson, of the wine book fame, was sitting next to me.

I congratulated him on making a fortune out of the Japanese.

When I got home, to my horror I learned that Bob had died. After all the trouble he had recovering from the operation when his hip was put together again, suddenly something got to his kidneys and it was all over.

Saturday 22 April
Arrived at Oare. There was a message waiting for me to ring David. Caroline died at eleven this morning. She never spoke since the time I saw her last. She died very peacefully with her family surrounding her.

I was stricken by gloom. It was an extraordinary coincidence that Bob and Caroline died within forty-eight hours of each other.

By myself I kept bursting alternately into tears and into bouts of cheerfulness because both Bob and Caroline had no more pain to suffer. They had given me much joy. Instead of moping about I must be grateful to them both.

There was an aura of sadness at Oare. Poor Tessa had not only seen the death of two brothers in quick succession, but then her father as well.

Weird Barbara Black was staying.

She is a good soul at heart and despite the turmoil in her head she writes frequently very balanced articles. She says Conrad won't let her write any more in the *Sunday Times* because Rupert is openly trying to destroy the *Telegraph*. I told her she ought to write a book, setting out her general philosophy of life as there's a great deal of merit in her views. However, I could not persuade her that identity cards were essential. She, in her old-fashioned libertarian way, regards them as an intrusion into privacy.

Amabel Lindsay came to dinner.

She is very jolly and likes to tease me, sometimes aggressively. She said my socks were too short – I shouldn't show flesh between the top of my socks and the bottom of my trousers. She said the cuff links I was wearing were false fashion jewellery. I said, 'They're gold and lapis lazuli.'

She took one of my cuff links off and said, 'There's no gold hallmark on them,' which oddly made me feel I wouldn't wear them again.

However, she complimented me warmly on my waistcoat from the Victoria & Albert Museum with its extravagantly flowered pattern, and also on my tie, saying 'You're a very smart dresser. That's why you shouldn't wear such short socks.'

Charles Powell was there. He was very pleased about a dreadful man, Howard Davies, he said was a friend of his, becoming the Deputy

Governor of the Bank of England to succeed the unfortunate Pennant-Rea.[8]

Charles Powell has little judgement of people.

Tuesday 25 April
Lunch with Ian Chapman, the son of ex-Collins managing director, at the Waldorf. Macmillan have been bought out by a German firm.

However, it makes no difference to his dealings with me.

'My main motive, as I told you, in doing this diary, is to leave a record of the times I live in, in their widest sense, personal, political and all the people I had contacts with and my thoughts about life itself. I would like that to be there after I have gone. I believe it has some value. The other prompting motive is to leave money for Verushka who will never be able to live on a pension from the Tote. I have not accumulated as much as I had hoped because it has always been sucked away from me, the capital I have.

'They are a long-living lot, the women in her family. I would hate to think of her being strapped for money. Possibly the wind farm will come to produce real money but I am not counting on that.'

Ian Chapman intends at least three books in chronological order, which is correct. They would each have about 220,000 words in them, maybe more. I think we must have done about a million and a half words already.[9] I would like to have a hand, if I can, in the editing of the first one and show how it should be done. I rely a great deal on Mrs Tamborero. She must not let her emotions rob the diary of how I think and feel by erasing the unpleasant side of my nature which is amply present.[10] Like most, I am part good and part bad.

---

8. Rupert Pennant-Rea had resigned after admitting being *in flagrante delicto* in the Bank of England boardroom; Howard Davies, director-general, CBI, 1992–5, succeeded Pennant-Rea, moving to be chairman, Financial Services Authority, in 1997.
9. An underestimate: the manuscript thus far totalled over two and a half million words.
10. See 29 August 1995 when Mrs Tamborero tells WW he should not write in a way that makes him sound spiteful and petty; but the loyal Mrs Tamborero never 'erased' anything – WW checked the manuscript, which is a transcript of his tape-recordings, until almost the end.

Thursday 27 April
Badminton for Caroline's funeral.

There was poor Daphne, Caroline's aged mother, sitting in a confused and tearful state.

Johnson (my godson) thanked me 'for being so kind to Mum these last few months. She loved you being with her.' Johnson's wife is sweet and quite pretty. It was she who gave me the photograph of Caroline in her Doctor of Law togs with the Tudor Rose hat on her head.

Henry Bath's widow, Virginia, his second wife,[11] a tall and lovely woman, still has a face made for temptation.

Sometimes during the service I couldn't stop the tears falling and I gripped my arm fiercely to control myself, thinking Caroline would be ashamed of me if I were to cry.

We went out to the grave where the new bright yellow coffin lay bare and uncovered yet by earth.

To my surprise I was accosted by Charlie Shelburne (heir to the Marquess of Lansdowne).

He wanted to have a bet with me that Major wouldn't win the next election, or the Tories wouldn't.

He was the official representative of the Prince of Wales. Prince and Princess Michael were there, too, but I couldn't be bothered to talk to them. I thought it was nice of them to come. I was screaming inside, wanting to get away from all these people.

I went back to the grave to say a last farewell. The earth was beginning to fall on the yellow coffin. Ferdl, the Hapsburg Archduke, was coming away from the grave alone. He returned with me to the grave. 'It's a pretty day for her.'

Saturday 29 April
Went to Sandown racecourse.

I was one of the last to go into where we were having lunch. Andrew Parker Bowles came rushing out to me.[12] 'Hurry up, Woodrow. Queen Elizabeth is waiting to have her lunch.' Nobody had told me she had asked for me to sit next to her. She was looking exquisite with a light

---

11. The 6th Marquess of Bath (Henry, 1905–92) m 1 (1927–53) The Hon. Daphne, daughter of the 4th Baron Vivian; Alexander, 7th Marquess, and Lord Christopher Thynn are the sons of this marriage, Caroline was the daughter; Henry Bath m 2 (1953) Virginia Tennant, née Parsons.
12. Chairman, Sandown Racecourse, at this time.

blue outfit matching her blue eyes and a lovely bracelet. All about her was attractive. Old people can look really pretty. Her leg is still painful but not so bad as it was.

On her other side was Sir Michael Angus, the new Chairman of Whitbread, sponsors of the Whitbread Gold Cup.

Queen Elizabeth said later to me, 'What a pleasant surprise he was. He had some good jokes. I thought he was going to be another of those boring businessmen. He looked like one, but he wasn't.'

He was fat and bulky, had no braces and his tummy stuck out so his shirt was fully exposed.

Queen Elizabeth thought Blair would win.

She said, 'We always found it difficult to get on with Mr Wilson. He was a bit touchy and he was an uncomfortable man to talk to.' 'I find that very surprising. Of course, I used to like Mary very much. She was quite a good poet.' Queen Elizabeth said, 'I didn't think she was, really. It was over-sentimental, not very well done.'

We then talked about Martin Charteris.[13]

I said, 'He had said before about the Duchess of York, that she is vulgar, vulgar, vulgar.'

I said, 'Was everybody at the Palace cross with him?' 'Oh no. He's got such a lot of wisdom, don't you think?'

Sunday 30 April
John Major rang. He wanted to know Molly's address. He was writing her a letter.

He said, 'I did do what you asked me.' 'What do you mean?' 'About the honour for Bob. I took action immediately. What a pity he didn't last until June.' I forbore to say it would have been more imaginative, as he was so critically ill, to give him a knighthood or whatever while he was still alive.

---

13. His *Spectator* interview.

Tuesday 2 May

We went for lunch to Sotheby's.

My neighbour was Julian Barnes [novelist].

He told me that he used to sub my reviews for the *Sunday Times* when he was the deputy literary editor and Claire Tomalin was the literary editor.

I asked him which he preferred, Martin or Kingsley Amis. He said, 'Actually I prefer Kingsley.' 'So do I. I can't get on with Martin Amis at all. I haven't even managed to finish one of his books, but I admire his great skill in getting £5m, or whatever it is, from the publishers for a novel he hasn't yet written.'

He asked how many bottles of wine I had. 'About fifteen hundred. Rather a lot. I keep it in my house in London.' He said, 'Oh. I've got five thousand.' I collapsed. 'Where are they?' I wailed. 'In various warehouses, stored for me.' 'It must cost you a lot to keep them there.' 'A bit.' 'But when you collect them or have them sent to you, you have to keep them for at least nine months before you can drink them.' He agreed. So I felt slightly back on course.

Julian Barnes must be pretty rich.

Wednesday 3 May

Birthday party for Ian Curteis who is sixty. Joanna Trollope is fifty-one. I arrived early to get her to sign *The Choir*, a first edition I had bought.

She wasn't very pleased with the serialization on BBC television. They had mucked about with her husband's script. He is a very good scriptwriter.

The BBC who for long spurned him for being too right-wing have now repented.[1]

Robin Day was there and then Nicko Henderson came in. Robin Day had said, 'I was horrified to read in the *Evening Standard* all

---

1. His *Yalta* was produced on BBC television in 1995.

about the row at The Other Club you had with Roy Jenkins and Nicko Henderson.' I suspected Robin, possibly unjustly, of being the leak. Nicko was very upset. 'It'll put a stop to Blair and Brown and the other leading figures coming now they see the rule of total confidentiality has been breached.'

At 11 Downing Street there was a political party for saying goodbye to Tessa Keswick who had been six years and a quarter working as special adviser to Kenneth Clarke, often disagreeing with him, which was good for him.

Thursday 4 May
I had been having a bout of nervousness about making the speech for Jill Radnor in the Covent Garden restaurant owned by Christopher Gilmour.[2]

I sat next to Jill, the birthday girl.

I talked about their [the Radnors'] fairy-tale romance beginning in the Argentine when they were both at the age of Romeo and Juliet, though Jake was a bit older.

I put in a Shakespeare quotation after saying that events and oceans had intervened in their great romance (in fact they both got married to other people): 'But love is not love, Which alters when it alteration finds.'

The best bit was when I was talking about her enthusiasm for her dyslexic charities.

I told them how, although she knew nothing whatever about cricket, she knew that cricket bats autographed by famous cricketers could be auctioned. She had made me obey her commands.

At the table where Petronella was sitting one guest said, 'Is he plastered?' Petronella said, 'No, he always speaks like that.'

Friday 5 May
An enchanting telemessage from Queen Elizabeth. 'Grateful thanks for [sending me] the fascinating Churchill tribute, no wonder Mary Soames was pleased. Elizabeth R.' How she finds the time to do all this when getting ready for the VE day celebrations, in which she will be the star, I cannot think.

---

2. Son of Lord Gilmour (Ian); the restaurant is called Christopher's.

Tuesday 9 May

The All Party Meeting on media for News International and Bill O'Neill[3] to explain policies and why it isn't a monopoly and so forth.

The Labour members in particular were making a great deal of attacks on Rupert Murdoch for his papers' disregard of the code on privacy. O'Neill and Jane Reed admitted there had been a disregard of it. Some members asked what happened. 'The guilty person was punished.' I was wondering what they meant by punishing Piers Morgan because I never heard of it.

As Lord Donoughue was leading the attack about monopolies, backed by Clive Soley[4] from the Commons, I think there is a serious situation for Rupert if Blair wins.

John Patten had a party given for him by Jonathan Aitken in his Lord North Street house.

Hart and Rifkind were lurking about the place.

I wonder if Rifkind is up to something mischievous. Perhaps he thinks he can be Leader of the Tory Party.

He is in favour of devolution.

It is true he put in a number of caveats this week, saying that all kinds of things would have to be sorted out and it would be no doubt difficult. Being intelligent, as he is, he must have realized the undermining effect it would have.

A number of Tory MPs were mooning in defeatist mood. They are quite certain they are going to lose, though, to his credit, Jonathan Aitken is very bullish.

Petronella was very much in evidence at the party. Surrounded by admirers, she kept a longish way from me but we came home together for dinner.

Wednesday 10 May

Greg Barker came. He is doing a documentary about Rupert Murdoch. He thinks it is too boring to go on attacking him as a monster and wants to develop the other less publicized side. It will go out through the public broadcasting system in Boston, will be taken by the BBC and go round the world, particularly to Australia.

I said, 'Are you going to pay me?' 'Oh yes.' 'How much?' 'We might manage £100.' 'Don't bother.' 'We might run to £200.' I said,

---

3. Successor to Gus Fischer.
4. Labour MP since 1979.

'Don't bother. By the time I've paid tax on it, it's not worth my having it. I'll do it for nothing.'

Saturday 13 May
Off to Lingfield to the races.

Charlie Benson was there. He said I looked 'very smutter.' 'What on earth does that mean?' It was a word quite unknown to me. It's a modern word for saying someone is smartly dressed.

When I went to the Parade Ring to see the horses for the Derby trial, there Charlie was with his ex wife, chatting away like billy-o.

I said, 'Can I get this straight? Are you two married or not? Half the time you seem to be together.' He said, 'I'd like to be married again.' She said, 'Well you haven't asked me.'

Charlie is a round, tall, grossly overweight bloke, with wit, pleasant smile and a generally ingratiating manner interspersed by occasional insults to show his independence, a sort of court jester.

He always plunges on hot tips on horses which are not as good as he thought they were going to be.

Sunday 14 May
While I was gardening Norman Lamont rang.

He said he had been reading the piece in the *Sunday Telegraph*[5] and he was ringing up as 'my lightweight friend' which I had referred to him as. I said it was 'a slightly flippant remark, but you do behave in a rather rum way. I usually agree with just about everything you say on the European Union. But you have a wonderful tendency to say it at the wrong moment. I hope you are not gunning for Major any more.' He said no, in a sense he was trying to support him.

I asked him how he was getting on with finding a new constituency.

'I am still the MP at Kingston. The boundary revision hasn't gone through Parliament yet.' 'It'd be a jolly good thing if it didn't.'

Monday 15 May
Talked to John Major in the morning. He is hard pressed but buoyant. I told him I thought Virginia Bottomley ought not to be removed. She has been very brave and done very well and was let down by the dissident chumps on her own side in the vote last week on London hospital [closures]. John said that she had wanted to move last year

---

5. The article described the John Major lunch.

but he had told her to stick it out. He made no further comment. It sounds as though he is perhaps thinking she can now be relieved of this ghastly job. I also had added that Julia Cumberlege is very good in the Lords on health service matters. I was glad that he agreed.

Once again I promoted Robert Cranborne as the potential Chairman of the Party. He agreed he had done magnificently over the VE Day functions, but he is a person who is not in touch with the ordinary people. 'Maybe that's a good thing. It will give him a more objective view.' He didn't seem impressed by that proposition.

Tuesday 16 May
Some excitement. A huge bunch of flowers, variegated, arrive with a card inscribed, 'Thank you for your support. God bless, Reg Kray.' It came from the Commercial Road, the Kray brothers' stamping and murdering ground. I couldn't recall having supported Reg Kray or his brother.

Petronella, by coincidence, had dinner with a man who is the Deputy Police Chief of New York. She told him about this curious incident. He said it was a very familiar present in gangland. He asked whether there were roses included. There were, twelve. He said, 'That's a way of letting the recipient know he's going to be bumped off.' However, he didn't suppose that necessarily it followed that Reg Kray was intending to bump me off, or Michael Winner, the ghastly columnist and show-off who writes another column in the *News of the World*, who also received a Reg Kray bunch of flowers.

Dinner at the Metcalfes.

Before dinner I was talking to Mark Birley. I was telling him about Sonny Marlborough and his getting his dreadful Blenheim water sold in Mark's Club, instead of our Cornish Spring Water. He said he didn't know anything about it, but that I do not believe.

He has cold eyes, rather sinister.

Thursday 18 May
In the evening I went to the great Middle Temple, Masters of the Bench, dinner presided over by Sir Ronald Waterhouse who is now a judge.

I piled into my full evening dress, wore my six medals and my Knight's badge.

I was terrified of meeting the Lord Chief Justice, Lord Taylor. He

was the man who nearly hit me at the Peter Rawlinson marriage party.[6]
I had written in the *News of the World* that we have the worst judges
this century. But I did bump into him in the lavatory. I said, 'I think
the judges are getting better now. Are you still angry with me?' He
laughed. 'No.' 'I have now written that it is utterly absurd that judges
should retire at the age of sixty-five or seventy when they've got so
much wisdom and experience.' He said he'd seen that and was grateful.

Rupert is in a furious rage because of that idiot Dorrell[7] at National
Heritage, supposed to be in charge of the media. He has issued mad
proposals to curb Rupert. It's as bad as the stuff that Donoughue
spouted at the All Party Media meeting. When I challenged Donoughue later, he said it wasn't to be taken all that seriously but he likes
to keep them on their toes, Rupert and co. As they are trying to get
Rupert to support them, Labour is more friendly to Rupert than the
government are – Major has not forgiven Rupert for the persecution
of his son.

Saturday 20 May

It was off early to Bangor-on-Dee, a racecourse I had never seen before.
Charming. A lovely view. Everybody was very affable and friendly. I
decided to give a £30 prize to the best turned-out horse which had not
been allowed for in our sponsorship.

The drive to Plâs-Newydd was beautiful.

There was Henry [Anglesey] sitting in the sun outside the house.
He got up and hugged me, embraced me, and we put our cheeks
together. I had brought him half a dozen bottles of champagne, likewise
Belgian chocolates for Shirley. There was no one to dinner that night.
We talked volubly about Pericles, about their children, about everything
that's going on.

The room I was sleeping in was very handsome, overlooking the
Menai Straits both ways and on to the fine property once owned by a
man called Michael Duff who married Caroline, Henry's sister.[8]

---

6. See 8 December 1994.
7. Stephen Dorrell, Conservative MP since 1979, at this time Secretary of State for
   National Heritage. The Broadcasting Act 1996 prevented newspaper companies
   with over 20 per cent of the market expanding into television.
8. Lady Caroline Paget, d 1976, eldest daughter of the 6th Marquess of Anglesey, m
   (1949) Sir Michael Duff (1907–80), 3rd baronet.

However, Caroline had always had a close relationship to Rex Whistler,[9] a homosexual.

She was in love with him and he seemingly was in love with her – maybe it was romantic dreaming unsullied by sex. In the wonderful mural downstairs, which I knew so well from when we used to breakfast in front of it when Henry still had servants, she appears endlessly with him in gondolas and sailing boats. His dog is there, so is Liz Paget's dog. It made my eyes water a little thinking of Liz.

Before we went to bed I was shown how to make my own breakfast, which Shirley thought I might not be capable of. There was a kettle and a toaster and some bread and marmalade. I thought a number of times how much Verushka would have hated the whole trip, the racecourse, the betting shop, the book fair,[10] and making her own breakfast.

Sunday 21 May
I had a superb tour of the gardens with Henry.

Among the rhododendrons and the azaleas were fabulously beautiful combinations of colours. There were hybrids sowing themselves but some of them had a slight air of the chocolate box cover. Henry goes towards such groups and shouts 'Vulgar! Vulgar! Vulgar!', meaning they are too vulgar and nature has slipped.

Martin Charteris is Henry's first cousin, which I had not known.[11] He is a good sculptor. He has done a sculpture of a black tiger which has on it the Anglesey crest and arms with a beautiful collar round its neck carrying Henry's family motto, which roughly translated is 'I will do as I like.'[12]

Monday 22 May
The *Sunday Times* yesterday carried a huge front-page story about Margaret attacking Major.

---

9. (1905–44); artist; he painted the Plâs-Newydd mural in 1937 for the 6th Marquess of Anglesey.
10. WW had on the way visited a betting shop in Oswestry and spent £47 on buying 30 books at a church book fair.
11. Their mothers were sisters, daughters of the 8th Duke of Rutland; Diana Duff Cooper (Viscountess Norwich) was the third sister, making John Julius Norwich another first cousin.
12. There is a bust by Martin Charteris of Percy Herbert, Bishop of Norwich, in Norwich Cathedral.

I rang Margaret. Relations with her are not the same as they used to be. We are conspicuously not asked to any reunions or to Denis's birthday party. Only the mad-hats like Simon Heffer and her flatterers who tell her everything she says, does and did is marvellous.

My reception on the telephone was friendly but not warm. I asked her what these attacks on John's lack of inspiration were intended to mean.

She cut in briskly. 'In the *Sunday Times* yesterday they distorted what I wrote. They had the right to print what they like from my book but not to distort it. They have bought the serialization rights.'

When she was referring to policies 'to be carried out by others', she meant not by a replacement for John but the whole of the Western world, the Council of Europe and all the rest.

I then rang John. 'Margaret sounded a bit contrite about the commotion over the passage from her book.'

'I'm bloody angry and I'm going to give her a hell of an attack and go for her.' I said, 'Please don't. Do it rather like Gower playing elegant leg cuts to the boundary and not like Botham trying to smash everything for six.' He laughed. He liked the analogy.

Later on in the morning came a statement from Margaret's office that she had been misinterpreted.

I thought to myself, 'Ho, I've had some effect on her, calming her down, thank goodness.'

I then wrote my article for the *Times* on the basis of what I had heard from both of them, without of course quoting them, but weaving in my own opinions.

When I got the proof, I was still anxious that Major would blow off in a rage and make things worse and damage himself. I sent him through his political office (rather painfully but with the help of Verushka who understands how to work the damn machines) a fax of it, marking it 'Urgent' for him to see.

Anxiously, I watched the news later on in the evening but Major had restrained himself.

When I had been talking to Margaret she said, 'It would be terrible to have Brian Mawhinney (whom she dislikes for some reason) as Chairman of the Tory Party. He's got an Irish accent and it wouldn't go down at all well.' I said, 'What about Cranborne? He's of the old school with plenty of guts and ability.' She froze. 'Don't you remember? He left the job I gave him in about two weeks. He couldn't stay the course. He wouldn't stay the course. He doesn't understand ordinary people.' I thought, there goes an irritated woman. Still nourishing her wounds from being made to feel small by Robert in her little kitchen in the flat at the top of Downing Street, as I have related previously.[13]

I am exhausted. I don't know whether it is all the travelling, or whether it is *anno domini*, or whether it is because I have not got the right pills.

Thursday 25 May
A nasty situation has developed.

Rupert is naturally doing his nut.

He is beginning to drop hints, and almost saying it in his papers, that Blair will be better than Major and that Major is all washed out.

Friday 26 May
I am still trying to reach Rupert to tell him not to go too far.

I decided to make no reference to the subject [cross media ownership] in my article. It is too difficult to explain at such short length. Anyway, everybody would say, 'He would say that.'

It is pretty crazy for a government which claims to be a de-regulating government to put in all this regulation.

Sunday 28 May
Suddenly the day became sunny and warm, up to 73 degrees. I popped off to Lord's to watch a fascinating one-day Test.

After my lunch I decided to see whether Paul Getty was in his box. He had just arrived. Also there was John Major. The moments he can get to a cricket match 'are complete bliss to me. I forget all my trials and troubles.'

I told him how Rupert felt it was very unfair – he had innovated all these great things in the media with newspapers. He had made it possible for anybody to publish and print a newspaper which they couldn't before he broke the print unions and now you didn't need much money to do it. He's paved the way and risked everything on his satellites which he made a great success and now everybody is able to copy them.

John said, 'It would have been much worse if the others had had their way in the Cabinet. They want to close some of his newspapers immediately.'

---

13. See Vol. 2, p. 497.

He thanked me for my advice not to mix it publicly with Margaret.

Margaret had said that Blair's a conviction politician like herself. (This, by the way, does not particularly please the Blair camp who don't want praise from Margaret although Blair had previously said what a remarkable leader of a revolution she was.)

John put his arm round me very affectionately and shook hands with me when he had to go back to his Cabinet meeting.[14] By this time the cricket had become really exciting. England beat the West Indies after they looked like winning.

---

14. A Sunday Cabinet meeting had been called over British soldiers, members of the UN peacekeeping force in Bosnia, being taken hostage by Serbs.

Thursday 1 June

Alas! It rained in the evening for Paul Getty and Victoria's great party.

I was in my customary predicament of not remembering the faces of many. A grey-haired old lady came up to me. 'Don't you remember me, Woodrow?' I racked my brain. She said, 'I'm Janetta.'

Janetta was married to Robert Kee[1] when I first knew her. She then married Derek Jackson.[2] Derek had one third of the *News of the World* and the Carr newspaper empire. He had wonderful paintings in his house in Paris. He showed the French by accident how to make a nuclear bomb from calculations they asked him to do in the laboratory they gave him. He was a great physicist as well as a very fine horseman, having been third or fourth in the Grand National riding his own horse. Janetta was famed for her beauty and skill at entrancing men who adored her silken web.

Derek left Janetta for her sister. He got married again after that.

Janetta became a great girlfriend, if she hadn't been already, of Andrew Devonshire.

Teasingly she said to me, 'What about me?' I laughed. It's what I often used to say to her when we were together with Robert Kee.

I found myself in front of a poor twitching boy with ginger hair in a wheel chair. He is Paul's son who had his ear cut off by kidnappers. It was sent to his family but his grandfather was reluctant to pay the ransom demanded.

---

1. Writer and broadcaster; m 1 (1948–50) Janetta, née Woolley.
2. (1906–82); Professor of Spectroscopy, University of Oxford, 1947–57; m 1 Poppet, daughter of Augustus John, the painter; m 2 (1936–51) Pamela, née Mitford, daughter of 2nd Baron Redesdale; m 3 (1951–6) Janetta Kee; he eloped with Janetta's half-sister, Angela Culme-Seymour, in 1953, lived with her for three years but they did not marry; m 4 (1957–59) Consuelo, née Eyre, widow of Prince Ernst Ratibor zu Hohenlohe Schillingsfurst; m 5 (1966–7) Barbara Skelton, former wife of Cyril Connolly and George Weidenfeld; m 6 (1968) Marie-Christine, daughter of Baron Georges Reille.

Old Paul Getty was pretty mean but I think his reluctance may well have stemmed from the feeling that if he gave in to that blackmail, future blackmail would be never-ending.

I felt desperately sorry for Paul. What is the point of having all this fantastic money if one can't even give happiness to one's son? Paul himself is in very good health these days. Victoria saved him. But he still has difficulties resulting from his earlier drug addiction.

The champagne was excellent, Veuve Cliquot. Naturally it was not a vintage champagne. It would be pretty good madness to serve anything really good to such an enormous number of people, most of whom don't know plonk from good.

The fireworks looked well enough over the lake, but unless you have music like Handel's Firework Music it's not the same thing at all. That is what they had at Hampton Court when Rupert gave a great party.

Similarly at Chatsworth, at the ball for Andrew's grandson, the fireworks display was infinitely better.[3]

I feel that Victoria and Paul don't have any idea of how to organize a great occasion like this. They leave it to some kind of party planners.

Monday 5 June

At the Ivy Restaurant, Eve Pollard, previously editor of the *Sunday Express* and wife of Nick Lloyd, editor of the *Daily Express*, gave a reception to launch a book written by three ladies, herself included, called *Splash!*.[4]

As copies were going for £10, special offer, instead of £14.95, and I thought it as well to be obliging, I bought one. It is the most appalling jejeune sex with nothing spared: a ridiculous story by three sex-mad passé ladies. But I like Eve Pollard, fat and jolly with vast bosoms attempting to roll out of her dress, and nearly succeeding. She has blonde hair, whether real or not I have no idea.

The next day I was amused to read that John Major had gone to the party.

He went because he wants to keep on-side with the editor of the *Daily Express*.

---

3. See Vol. 2, p. 325.
4. Eve Pollard's co-authors were Val Corbett and Joyce Hopkirk.

Wednesday 7 June
To Thatched Lodge House where Princess Alexandra and Angus Ogilvy
live. Not a very large house, but sufficient for them.

The garden is huge and goes down at one point to a swimming
pool, then on towards the river.

Vere Rothermere was there. He told me he had just had lunch with
Blair. 'He is a fine liberal politician. He'll make a very good Prime
Minister.' 'Are you going to back him publicly?' 'I may do. I'm very
nearly there. We can't go on with Major and this gang of Tories, full
of sleaze.' 'But he'll do immense damage to the country.' 'Not to me
he won't. I won't be affected one way or the other.' 'Well, you could
be.' 'How?' 'All this cross media stuff, cutting down on what he regards
as monopolies in newspapers.' 'That won't bother me.' 'The extra tax
might.' He laughed.

Of course Vere has arranged his tax affairs so he pays none in
England.

It was his newspapers which began all the lies about the Queen's
wealth. But I can't help liking the fellow. I am amused by his icono-
clasm.

Thursday 8 June
William Waldegrave rang up as planned. He gave me a lot of useful
background on which to defend him.[5] The whole story begins with the
Matrix affair, when some exporters working for the government,
getting intelligence from Iraq, were arrested. They were nearly sent to
prison because Alan Clark lied to the customs people when he was
asked was it true that they had been helping the government and he
said no. It had to be retracted. But for Clark there wouldn't have been
this ridiculous inquiry.

Saturday 10 June
An early start to Epsom for the first Saturday Derby except for Coronation year, 1953.

It was poor weather, cold with bouts of rain. That doubtless kept
many away. Also the competing excitements on television – the World

---

5. *Newsnight* had leaked a draft of the Scott Report which blamed Waldegrave for
   writing to MPs that guidelines on arms to Iraq had not been changed; WW
   defended him in his *News of the World* article of 11 June; the Scott Report was
   not published until February 1996.

Rugby Cup in South Africa, the Test Match, the international soccer games and the Paris tennis championships.

I had lunch with the ghastly BHB organization.

I felt that the people's Derby had been taken over by a lot of second-class toffs who are now allowed into Jockey Club areas by Egalité Stoker Hartington.

I went on to Badminton.

It was deeply sad without Caroline. I went to look at her grave in the little graveyard by Badminton House Church. The grass mound seemed to have shrunk so it wouldn't have covered her whole length in the coffin. But I suppose that is quite natural. Some loving person had spelt out in little flowers the letters L O V E and left a bunch of her favourite flowers beside it.

I think it is better for the living if the dead are not cremated.

Bindy Lambton was also staying. I have grown fond of her. She talks a good deal of nonsense but is also shrewd. She is not drinking as much and is easier to talk to accordingly.

David is acutely lonely. Diana Wilton thinks he'll marry the Miranda Morley girl. I don't think so. David says because one has had a long affair [that] is not a reason for marriage.[6]

Monday 12 June
I had chipped a piece off a front tooth on a lobster shell while having dinner with the Stelzers last Tuesday. I went to the dentist at nine o'clock to have another piece put on. Surprisingly he did it within about five minutes.

I had to go to Windsor Racecourse for the opening of the new stand by Queen Elizabeth the Queen Mother.

I told her I had to go back for Petronella's 'official' birthday, her other one having been on May 6th. She laughed. 'Do send her my love and good wishes. She's such an attractive girl.'

The Portuguese mafia, headed by José, cooked and served at the dinner party which was a joint birthday for Petronella and Miriam Gross at St Petersburgh Place, W2. A tall house, a pretty house, though the rooms are small.

After dinner came dancing on the top floor. Miriam made me dance with her. She politely said I did it very well, which of course I didn't.

6. They married in June 2000.

Tuesday 13 June
Tony Blair addressed the crossbench peers. Most of them were fairly
wet and fell for him. I had sent in a question to the effect that he had
referred to altering some of the trade union reforms and which ones
did he have in mind.

When I put my question Tony Blair said, 'Woodrow, knowing you
were going to ask this question I thought I would bring this along.'
He pulled out a package with the joke Christmas present from Piers
Morgan. On the top it read 'Woodrow Wyatt says' then there was a
very recent picture of myself and underneath, 'Labour is good for
Britain and good for you.' That was below my photograph. There was
a great deal of laughter. I joined in.

He dodged and weaved around. He said he wouldn't remove the
ballots before strikes and that sort of thing. But he would see that
employees have more rights to join trade unions and other rights at
work. I had been wrong to say this meant a closed shop.

He made it very clear that I get thoroughly under his skin.

There was a *frisson* of withdrawal when he said he was determined
to abolish hereditary peerages and to prevent any who remained in the
Lords, because they were needed as spokesmen, from voting. Blair
said, 'This could not be done overnight,' for which there was a muffled
'Hear, hear.'

He had a good deal to say about everything being referred to the
Court of Human Rights when there was a case to do so, and he would
not seek to overturn their judgments or prevent them. He also said,
'With this audience it is possible to go beyond the normal soundbite.'
I didn't think he went particularly far but at least he had a try.

My next entertainment was to go to the reception for Margaret's
latest book, followed by her speech. I went because last Saturday I had
received by post a copy of *The Path to Power*, which she had inscribed,
'To Woodrow, with warm regards and many thanks for all your help,
Margaret Thatcher.'

This was a belated recognition of all that I had done for her, but
with very little detail. She did at least, however, on page 306, describe
me as a close friend from whom she had a lot of help. She also said
that I had written her first Conference speech after she became leader
of the Tories. She had rung me up and told me something about it. I
said that would never do and she came round for supper.

But there is nothing in it about the tremendous work I did introducing her to trade union leaders and getting the trade union reforms

through. She pretends she did it deliberately, step by step, when we did nothing of the kind. I had to fight Jim Prior with the aid of Frank Chapple to get on with it faster. We should have done the whole lot in one go. Her memory is extremely variable and always favourable to herself in its inaccuracies.

I talked at some length to Peter Stothard's eleven-year-old daughter. This girl is brilliant. She had already read all the Brontë sisters' works and quoted extracts from them to me freely.[7]

The signing of books was marvellously arranged like a religious ceremony.

I adored the bit [in the instructions] about going up with your copy to be signed, as it were to the communion rail.

At times I was quite moved by her because I remain very much in platonic love with the girl.

It seems that one day when I couldn't see when I got up, I actually had a mild stroke behind the eyes.

If word gets out, I shall be done for at the Tote. The Home Office will say I am not well enough to carry on. That is, by the way, in my contract.

Wednesday 14 June
Jonathan Aitken's into a great scrape again. It isn't his fault. It's that dreadful man, Heseltine, who has suddenly decided to have an inquiry into an arms firm he was a non-executive director of. It exported arms to Singapore and they apparently got passed on to Iran, not that it matters one little bit. It was over two years before Jonathan joined the company.[8]

I was amused to see that I might be called to court as a character witness [for him].[9]

I tried to get hold of John Major this morning on the telephone but was told that he was already in a meeting and he would ring back.

---

7. Anna Stothard completed her first novel in 1999, aged 15.

8. WW says that Aitken was a director of BMARC from September 1988 until March 1990 and the alleged events took place in 1986.

9. In a letter to WW dated 7 June, Aitken thanked him for his *News of the World* column of 16 April, 'Daring Aitken's a trade winner'; he was flattered to be compared with George Leybourne's young man on the trapeze; he thought his QC was planning to use WW's column as the basis of one part for his cross-examination.

But he never did. I don't know if he thinks my going to Margaret's great book show was in some way unfriendly to him. If he does, he's a real chump.

Thursday 15 June
It was off to see Doctor Charkin, on to whose National Health Service books I have got myself registered. That's because, as I am over seventy, I am entitled to free prescriptions.

My prescriptions come to about £700–£800 a year. I don't see why I shouldn't, having paid many thousands in taxes, get a little bit back.

Eventually the nurse came out who had to interview me and talk to me about my health, my allergies and all that rot before I could be signed on to the doctor's register. He is the one who attends to my mother-in-law who, as I said to the nurse, has smoked like a chimney since she was fourteen and is still doing so at the age of ninety-five.

She was a very nice girl, the nurse. She took my blood pressure. I told her it would be well below normal. 'I've got to take it just the same.' She did and said, 'You're right. How much do you weigh?' 'Eleven stone two.' 'How tall are you?' 'Five foot seven and three quarter inches.' They do it all in Euro-speak now. She persisted in weighing me again. With my clothes and shoes I weighed 77 kilos which seems fearful to me.

She asked me to give her some urine. I duly went and peed in a spotless lavatory with a wonderful spotless little tube to pee into. I wiped it very carefully so she wouldn't have to handle it with my pee on it, and came back in triumph with this tube. She tested it. 'Oh it's fine. There's no sugar in your blood even though your brother had diabetes.'

I was greatly impressed by the elegance and the cleanliness of the whole establishment. Also the efficiency, as I told her.

Friday 16 June
Richard Ryder tells me he is giving up being the Chief Whip as soon as he can which is when the House rises in July.

Factions within the Tory party appear to have become uncontrollable: not grown men, they are a lot of frightened children. I put it all down to the ludicrous change in their constitution invented by

Humphry Berkeley[10] by which a leader can be challenged once a year even though he is Prime Minister.

Sunday 18 June

It was Mick Jagger who put Paul [Getty] on to cricket. He would go to see him in the dark years, which were long, when he was a recluse and spent most of his time in the London Clinic or other such places trying to get rid of his drug addiction.

Mick Jagger said, when cricket once went on the screen, 'Why don't you watch this?' 'I don't understand the game.' Mick Jagger began to explain the finer points to him. He was absolutely fascinated.

Paul helped Bob enormously in his last years. [Without Paul] Bob would not have had the halcyon period of sitting in a box at Lord's, once more talking about cricket with all the famous cricketers he had known and ones who were new since he gave up playing, and being treated quite correctly as the country's great sage on cricket.

Monday 19 June

Spoke to John at about half past eight in the morning. He apologized for playing cox and box, having to go to the G7 Conference so he was unable to speak to me.

I said, 'You're not seriously thinking of standing down, are you? You mustn't. You've got to go on.' He said, 'This is something we really shouldn't be talking about on the telephone.'

Tuesday 20 June

Ascot.

As usual, I was sitting next to Queen Elizabeth the Queen Mother.

Kissinger, who was sitting opposite, suddenly got up and said, 'Oh, you're Woodrow Wyatt.' He shook my hand warmly. 'We met with Arnold Weinstock.' He was doing that over her face, almost, but she didn't mind.

We discussed Brussels and the European Union. Queen Elizabeth hates it with all her might and main. I said, 'I would like to join

---

10. (1926–94); Conservative MP, 1959–66; joined Labour Party 1970; joined SDP 1981; rejoined Labour, December 1988; social reformer and writer; the rules he devised allowed a leadership contest if one was requested by 10 per cent of the parliamentary party.

NAFTA, the North Atlantic Free Trade Area. But we're not allowed to do that unless the European Union joins as a whole.'

We discussed the association between Britain and America. I said, 'You need us badly. In the event of a war, when something has to be done, like Kuwait, we make you respectable.' Queen Elizabeth laughed. Kissinger didn't care for my observation at all.

She said, 'But you are exaggerating some of the things you are saying to Mr Kissinger.' I said, 'Yes, but only to stimulate him.' She laughed but Kissinger didn't.

She was proposing to have a hip operation. I said, 'My goodness. Do be careful. They can be very difficult. My old cousin, the famous cricketer (she knew about him at once) had one when he was ninety-five and it didn't do him any good.' She said, 'Well, I'm going to take the risk. I can't bear this pain.' I thought 'Oh my goodness, oh dear.' I said, 'How awful for you.' I do love that woman.

Earlier Queen Elizabeth had said how wonderfully Petronella writes. I said, 'Yes. But she's been very naughty in the last article she wrote. She said that I could only get people to go to bed with me if I married them. She hadn't even read *Confessions of an Optimist* which explained about the large number of affairs I have had. When I complained to her, she said, "It makes a better story." '

Wednesday 21 June
We had a jolly lunch party in our entertainment room at Ascot.

Rosita sat next to me. She is thrilled. She has had two pictures accepted by the Royal Academy. She has got a big order for a picture in America. She is making real money with her painting. 'Enough, perhaps, to make good some of your Lloyd's losses?' She laughed. 'Well, it helps.'

In the evening we went to the dinner organized largely by Charles Churchill but given by Prince Khalid Abdullah, the brother-in-law of the King of Saudi Arabia. It was in a private room at the Café Royal. There may have been twenty there.

On my left sat Sally Metcalfe. When I was saying to Khalid how wise I thought he was and how much I valued his judgement, she suddenly burst out saying, 'He says that to everyone.' So I put my hand over her mouth and said, 'Stop being silly. You may be pretty but you're foolish.' Khalid thought that very funny, being no doubt the way Arabs treat their women. But it did shut her up.

Thursday 22 June

Thursday is still Ladies' Day at Ascot. The Gold Cup is the feature race. We have in the corner always a Tote lady taking bets, either cash or credit. She is much used and the guests like it greatly. The Duchess of Marlborough came back again, with Sonny Marlborough, not merely to talk to our other guests but for the betting. It's about the smartest place on the racecourse, if you rule out the Royal Box where you can't bet anyway.

During the afternoon Major made his announcement that he is going to have a leadership election immediately to put an end to all the mischief-makers' plots for once and for all. Nominations have to be in by next Thursday and the voting and the result will be the following Tuesday. Though the announcement did not break up the interest in the racing or the Test Match entirely, politics have now become the supreme spectator sport.

Ken Baker thought Major had made a mistake and he might not support him, but it would depend on the main contender, if there is one.

Verushka is now sad that we have only got one more Ascot, though she has to work very hard preparing everything. The lunches on both days were perfect due to her drilling and bullying the caterers. She also arranges the seating excellently. Verushka looked exceedingly attractive on both days, though for the first time I can remember she twice wore the same white hat, with lots of flowers on it. But the dress was different.

I got to The Other Club in reasonable time.

When Duke Hussey came in, I said, 'Here comes the Chairman of the Blair Broadcasting Company.' Everybody roared with laughter.

Friday 23 June

Norman is still being enigmatic, having himself photographed everywhere, coming out of his house, buying newspapers, grinning away and not revealing his hand. Evelyn de Rothschild is fuming. I think he will chuck him out or certainly not renew his contract.

Meanwhile, Rosemary is about to bring divorce proceedings against Norman.[11]

Redwood, having said he would consider whether to support John Major or not, vaguely said he would but he would make an

---

11. The Lamonts did not divorce until 1999.

announcement on Monday. I think it would be a good thing if Redwood does stand because he would be a real challenger and Major should trounce him completely. The party could then return to calm.

Sunday 25 June
I had a call from the Prime Minister, returning my calls.

John said he had spoken to Redwood and he had said he wasn't going to stand against him. But now it seems that maybe he is changing his mind.

I said, 'Even the press has got to admit that you have the weight of the country on your side, according to the opinion polls.'

Monday 26 June
John Redwood, having plotted with Norman Lamont over the weekend, announced in dramatic form his standing against the Prime Minister.

The crew with him are a dastardly lot: Marlow, Leigh and the scandalous mischief-makers on the back benches.[12] Norman was sitting there grinning away. Originally he said he was going to run his campaign but that was soon scotched. Norman said he was merely going to give advice on the campaign and would campaign for him.

Redwood is a sort of Puritan. How he came to be a Tory I don't know – he doesn't approve of anybody having any money.

Margaret Thatcher is now being ambivalent. She said in America, where she is, that both are very sound Conservatives. 'Are you endorsing Mr Redwood?' 'No. They are both very good people.' Her latest is that she is backing Major in the first round – a rather sinister form of backing, suggesting there should be a second round and hoping that Redwood would win. I fear she has not come out of this very well.

She says now it was a great mistake of Major's to have announced a contest. As she made a total mess of the leadership challenge to herself, I don't think she has much right to criticize him.

I had a row with both Verushka and Petronella. 'You both listen outside my door. You rumple through my papers.' Petronella said, 'I know you're keeping a secret diary.'

---

12. Antony Marlow, Conservative MP, 1979–97, a Eurosceptic; Edward Leigh, Conservative MP since 1983; in his *News of the World* article of 2 July WW said Leigh was 'still angry that Major sacked him from a junior post'.

I said, 'I don't think either of you realize the dangers and risks you are playing with. What I am doing could be accurately described as collecting material for memoirs, which won't be published until after I am dead, as a sequel to *Confessions of an Optimist*. I am trying to make a small fortune for your mother after I am dead and the pair of you are trying to destroy it. You had no business to listen outside the door when I was talking to the Prime Minister.'

Petronella said, 'It was because I just came up to tell you dinner was ready.' (It was on Sunday night.) 'Don't you trust me?'

'I love you very much. I adore you, as you know. But you really mustn't let me down because you don't know what damage you might be doing. If anybody thinks I am keeping a secret diary, no one will talk to me, even though it has nothing to do with the Official Secrets Act.'

Tuesday 27 June
Portillo has now said that if there is a second round, he will be standing. To this extent he has broken rank. Heseltine is still stoutly saying he doesn't believe there will be a second round and he is fully supporting John Major. I don't believe that either.

Wednesday 28 June
Talked to Jonathan Aitken. He's afraid that if there are more than eighty or so abstainers and Redwood voters put together, John might be in an impossible position.

I said, 'I have always been afraid in talking to John that he may decide to chuck it all, write his memoirs and get a job in a bank.'

Thursday 29 June
At home we are all very amused by Redwood saying he wouldn't put anybody in his government who had cheated on his wife – nor who had personal debts or scandals in the background, financial or of any other kind.

In the afternoon Major was dazzlingly brilliant at Question Time. He floored Blair and all his critics and came out hitting sixes all over the pavilion. As I left the Commons chamber I bumped into Norman Tebbit.

'Why on earth are you coming out telling people to vote for Redwood? You know perfectly well he could never be a vote-winner at elections. He's too grim and ghastly and too much of a Puritan.'

'I have to be careful. I can't afford to offend our proprietor – our employer.'[13]

This was the most astonishing revelation.

Andrew Roberts is behaving in a disgraceful manner. He leans out of the window in the Redwood campaign HQ.

I rang up and left him a fake message, with my voice, saying, 'I hear that Robert Cranborne is extremely worried about your political judgement and is now considering not letting you do the biography of Salisbury because if you can get it all so wrong about Major, you could get it wrong about Salisbury too.'[14]

What a chump the fellow is. He is enormously ambitious and fantastically vain. He thinks he is the cat's whiskers, which he is not.

Friday 30 June
Charles Moore is writing an attack on Major saying Redwood is the man to back.

The truth is that Charles Moore and people like Peter Stothard consider themselves to be intellectuals. As Major isn't one, they feel more at home backing an intellectual. They're all completely distant from how ordinary people react and feel.

---

13. Tebbit was a columnist in the *Sun*, 1995–7.
14. Andrew Roberts' biography of Salisbury was published in 1999.

Saturday 1 July

Norman Tebbit has now come out publicly, saying we must have Redwood. All these fools think they can somehow arrange a situation in which their favourite candidate comes through in later rounds, though it is quite impossible. Even Tory MPs, however dim and stupid, must realize they cannot go on with another of these contests.

The *Sun* offered £150,000 to the prostitute Divine, the black girl with whom Hugh Grant had sex in a car and was then arrested. What the *Sun* didn't know was that their rival paper, the *News of the World*, had already found her and had paid her more. When I rang Piers Morgan I said, 'What are you up to, young man, apart from getting hold of the black hooker?' He immediately said to me, 'Rupert thought I shouldn't have done it because it is lowering the standards of the paper.' 'That's absolutely ridiculous. It's perfectly legitimate. Hugh Grant got himself arrested. It will do no harm to his career because no one will think anything of it. In fact it will probably enhance his career when it's seen in perspective.'

I can't help liking this fellow, Piers Morgan, but he is really all over the shop. He raised absolute Cain when somebody referred to him having a girlfriend in the *Evening Standard*. He said he would have them followed everywhere about their private lives if they didn't drop it. Clearly what is sauce for the goose is not sauce for the gander in his philosophy.

Major asked me about Tebbit. I said Tebbit doesn't matter a hoot. Everybody thinks he is round the bend among the MPs, except for the nutters.

With all this political confusion the FT index has been sliding. I have got myself now an account with City Index. I have bought the proposition that it will rise from its present level between now and 10 September making me £10 a point.

I hope to win at least £1,000. Mrs Tamborero thinks this is sheer folly.

Sunday 2 July

The consensus of opinion is that Major will either lose on the first
ballot and then probably would not dare go to a second round, or,
even if he wins, it will be by so little that he will be severely wounded
and will probably have to give up. That's the verdict of the BBC, the
SKY programmes and the Sunday newspapers, but not mine. I am
certain that John will win comfortably.

Richard Ryder, who is departing as Chief Whip, thinks it may be
too close to call but on the whole believes Major will win. 'But there
are so many liars out there that it is very difficult to tell.'

I have a bet with Piers Morgan for £100 that Major will win on
the first round and there will be no second round.

Tuesday 4 July

My birthday. The day of the vote by Tory MPs on the leadership. Prince
Michael's birthday and the party at Kensington Palace. Petronella gave
me two hand-made cushions in beautiful needlework with flourishes
on the front. One says 'Welcome.' The other says 'Go away.' I can
hang either according to my mood on my door in the improbable hope
of not being disturbed if I hang the latter.

Finally the results came through. It was a convincing win by Major,
two hundred and eighteen to eighty-nine for Redwood and twenty
abstentions only, though there were, I think, one or two spoilt papers.

I rang Piers Morgan. 'What about that then? I've won £100 off
you. I told you not to be taken in by your own propaganda.' 'Ah, but
it is not final yet. We've got to wait three days.' 'What, to clear your
cheque? Haven't you got any money in your account? If you haven't,
please don't pay me if you can't afford it.' 'No it's not that. I don't
think it was convincing enough. He might be forced to resign.' 'You
must be mad.'

At Kensington Palace I found myself going upstairs side by side
with Conrad Black.

'I congratulate you on your perspicacity,' I said to Conrad, his
papers having confidently asserted that Major would be out and that
there would be a new Prime Minister, probably Portillo.

He admitted that Major had shown great courage and flair in
making this challenge and he had won it fair and square and he would
get his papers to support him. I said, 'Are you sure? Do you promise?
You'll get Blair if you don't.' He said he would, though he thought it
probably too late to beat Blair.

We had to listen to a strange version of *Tosca* – the entire opera. There were no musical instruments, only a piano.

The heat was intense. Some people almost fainted. I actually rather enjoyed the music though the opera is scarcely a laugh a minute.

We sat next to Anouska and Mark Weinberg. He, poor fellow, was in terrible agony. He had done something awful to his back.

He said he needed to swim but he didn't know of any pool near his office. I said, 'There's the RAC,' and explained it to him. 'I'll try to get you to be a member and Prince Michael will either propose or second you. He is the President.'

I told him of the wonderful Karnak-like swimming pool and the magnificent Grade I building, built in 1895 by the same people who built the Ritz.

Mark Weinberg is a very interesting, self-effacing man.

He is gentle. I can hardly see him being tough in business. He is a great friend of Jacob Rothschild and of the Marlboroughs where he is a trustee of the Blenheim estates. He is arranging for the unfortunate Blandford not to be able to take possession but to receive some form of allowance when Sonny Marlborough dies.

The place was thronged with immensely rich people. One of them, who wasn't named, had paid for the whole of the opera as a birthday present to Princess Michael in February, but she thought she would delay it until tonight for her husband's birthday.

We drank his health for his birthday and he asked everybody to drink mine and that of Mrs Lemos (wife of the great Greek ship owner), who also had a birthday on the same day. A special birthday cake was provided for my table.

During the day I had sent messages to John Major.

I quoted Churchill: 'In defeat defiance, in victory magnanimity,' and suggested that he put back John Redwood into the Cabinet. This fell on stony ground.[1]

---

1. WW's memo to Major dated 4 July commented on the aptitudes of twelve ministers or potential ministers. He said of Aitken, 'A possible Foreign Secretary but I am worried about the mist and hot potatoes around his head despite my belief in his innocence'; of Portillo, 'Too arrogant and conceited. I suggest he should be left to stew and prove he can do a good job at Employment'; of Howard, 'Comes over badly. It would be dangerous to make him Foreign Secretary though his views are sound'; of Mawhinney, 'Could be a good Party Chairman'.

On hearing of Jonathan's resignation I understood why he was subdued when I talked to him.[2]

Wednesday 5 July
During the day details of John's Cabinet came out.[3]

Heseltine, who has abandoned all hope of ever being Prime Minister, has been given the same derogatory title as Geoffrey Howe had – Deputy Prime Minister, which doesn't exist in the constitution.

He now seems clearly on side with John Major and will be a kind of cheer-leader, which is a role he is well fitted to.

Portillo has been put in Defence. This is regarded by many idiotic commentators as being a demotion. But it is not. In Defence one has a great role preventing such lunacies as common foreign policies and the joint use of European troops in circumstances which we would rather not have. I think his ambitions are not stifled but are certainly stilled.

Others might overtake him. For example, Ian Lang, who has been put in charge of Trade and Industry.

Pru Murdoch[4] had rung to say that because her baby was coming in September and there might be complications, she couldn't come to dinner with us. I would guess she was told not to by Rupert, who is in and out of London without ever calling me. It is rather sad because I am very fond of Pru and I have been promising to ask her to dinner for ages.

Chips told me he had won £500 because, when he had rung me on Monday asking was Major going to win, I didn't hum and ha. I said, 'Yes,' immediately. He took that as a very good sign and had lots of bets with his friends. So he brought me a box of cigars.

Monday 10 July
I went to Heywood Hill to find books for Queen Elizabeth's birthday on August 4th. There was a first edition of Edith Wharton's best book,

---

2. He resigned to fight his libel action.
3. In addition to the changes WW mentions, Rifkind replaced Hurd at the Foreign Office, Alastair Goodlad became Chief Whip, Virginia Bottomley went to National Heritage, Stephen Dorrell took Health, Mawhinney replaced Hanley as Party Chairman and William Hague joined the Cabinet in Redwood's former job, Secretary of State for Wales.
4. Rupert Murdoch's daughter by his first marriage (1956–66) to Patricia Booker.*

The Custom of the Country. I bought it, wishing I had bought it for myself because I don't suppose she really minds whether it is a first edition or not. Anyway, it is without a wrapper, so less valuable.

I also bought her a first edition of Maurice Baring's *Lost Lectures*. The Edith Wharton book was published in 1913 and the Maurice Baring, which is fine stuff, in 1932.

Wednesday 12 July

The Drue Heinz lunch party.

Douglas Hurd came up and said how grateful Major was to me for my support 'which you do in your robust and vigorous way'. We discussed Bosnia. I said, 'You're crazy ever to have gone in. I said that to Carrington. I said it to David Owen and I said it to you.'

He was somewhat reluctant to agree, naturally, but he was very friendly.

He's had many offers, some of them, he thought, from dubious sources. I said, 'I'm sure you'll do very well and you can write a book.'[5]

George Weidenfeld told me he had just been to see Kohl. He is very friendly with Kohl. George is the standard forgiving Jew who receives great respect in Germany. About Major, Kohl had said to him, 'He's the most remarkable man. Never underestimate him.'

Saturday 15 July

There is now commotion from Prince Michael's office about Mark Weinberg. The Prince says that he has already sponsored several people lately for the RAC with accelerated memberships and he doesn't think he can do any more.

Then it was off to the Radnors.

There were more than forty people staying in the house in the end. I hate sharing a lavatory and I hate sharing a bathroom.

I sat next to one of the Barney Miller daughters. (He is the bloke from Argentine where he arranges cricket teams and matches.) Her brother is drummer in the band of Sting who, it seems, is a world famous character.

Eventually came the great Sting himself and sat briefly beside the drummer, his sister and me.

---

5. Hurd became a director of National Westminster Bank and deputy chairman of Nat West Markets in 1995; his *The Search for Peace* was published in 1997 and *Shape of Ice* (novel) in 1998.

He looks so scruffy, more awfully clothed than I suppose even the most grizzly of tramps sleeping on the Embankment.

I asked him if he knew Mick Jagger. 'Oh yes, a fabulous musician.' 'I know him a bit, too. He taught Paul Getty the finer points of cricket,' preening myself. Sting treated me respectfully thereafter.

Sunday 16 July

I had practically no sleep during the night with these awful people making a noise outside and going to the lavatory and making a commotion.

I got Mrs Tamborero to ring to say that we must go at once. My mother-in-law was so ill and the doctor was coming, very worried, and so on. I then rang Jeffrey Archer and said, 'We are coming to your party after all.'

Mrs Tamborero played her part magnificently, as she always does on these occasions. A portable telephone was brought up by Martin, the butler, to Verushka. It had some sort of memory on it. I hope to God they can't play it back and find out how our departure was all fixed.

Oddly, when we eventually got back from the Archer party, Nadje really was very ill. She hadn't been eating and it was true, the doctor had been called. She had a temperature of 103°. She now looks as though she may seriously be about to die, but I will believe it when I see it.

[At the Archers] I was told we had to sit at the table with Margaret Thatcher and Denis, with a couple of judges, Wakeham and so forth. I didn't speak much to Margaret but Denis was absolutely foul about Major.

By chance a man at the same table was a lawyer, Michael Beloff.[6] He is conducting our [the Tote's] defence against William Hill. I said, 'They told me you were very left-wing but I said, "That doesn't make any difference. He can be a Communist if he likes, provided he's a good counsel."'

He said, 'I don't like to tell clients that they will win, but I think it looks as though you must win on it. A pity I can't talk direct to you about it.' 'Well you are now.' He laughed.

Mrs Beloff (Judith) is a great admirer of Mrs Blair. I said, 'Yes, she's

6. The Hon. Michael Beloff QC, President of Trinity College, Oxford, since 1996, m (1969) Judith Arkinstall; Cherie Blair was a member of his chambers.

got lots of guts and I thought it very brave of her when she carried out the instructions she had to against people for not paying their community charges. I defended her.' She said, 'She's got many more brains than Tony Blair.'

Judith is an ardent cigar smoker. She smokes them to relieve stress and varies in the number she smokes a day according to mood and state of mind. I gave her a huge Hoyo de Monterrey. She was delighted and gave me a kiss, which I returned.

Margaret had been staying the night with the Archers.

Mary Archer said, when I rang her up to thank her for the party, that Margaret has become totally Messianic.

It was very noticeable how few politicians there were there. They think Jeffrey's behaviour, particularly on that strange insider-dealing business, too much for them. But I still find him a likeable rogue.

Monday 17 July
I rang Margaret.

She launched into a part tirade. Portillo should have stood against John in the leadership election but he chickened out.

I said, 'I thought you were very nice with your congratulations to John Major. Are you going to support him now?' 'I will because the alternative is even worse.' I said, 'I am sure he is going to win the next election.'

'I hope he does but if he doesn't, the Tories will be out for twenty years. Blair will get the backing of Ashdown and give him proportional representation in return. There'll never be another Tory government, perhaps.'

When I told her what George Weidenfeld had said about Kohl's views on Major she said, 'I never trusted Kohl. That's no recommendation at all. He lies all the time. In any case, he's got Major in his pocket.'

Tuesday 18 July
John Major rang at a quarter past eight.

I told John he is a bit of a genius: the way he had constructed his Cabinet was masterly.

I said, 'Another thing you did very cleverly was to let Jonathan Aitken disappear with all the troubles around his head, without anybody apparently noticing. It all got mixed up with everything else. So he's not a liability for you any more.'

I told him how unpleasant Denis Thatcher had been about him.

I told him that Max Hastings never wanted to write that beastly leading article about him during the leadership election but Conrad made him. 'I think it is worthwhile having him for lunch or asking him to come round to see you because I think Max Hastings can be a brand plucked from the burning. I also believe that Conrad will keep his word to me that he is going to support you but it will take a little bit of time for them to back-pedal, having said you are useless to saying you're extremely good and the only chap who can win the election.' He laughed.

I said, 'But Rupert is a different matter. It will take me quite a struggle to get him off the Blair track.

'I think he's really waiting to see which way the cat jumps. All this stuff about him seeing Blair is to do with your cross-media plans which he hates.' John said he understood that, but there it was.

'I am very sorry you have dropped the idea of having a law of privacy.' To my astonishment he said, 'So am I, but it was the lawyers.'

I think, obviously, Major took some notice of that memo I sent him on the morning of his great victory when I assumed he was going to win. Mawhinney is the Chairman of the Party, Lang has been given a very good job. He didn't make Howard Foreign Secretary though he has risked Rifkind who doesn't come over quite as badly on television as Howard does.

Thursday 20 July
The Other Club.

Quintin Hogg [Lord Hailsham] was in one of his gloomy moods. He said he was thinking of the future after he died.

I told him the story of my saying to Bertrand Russell,[7] 'What would you do after all your atheism if you were summoned before God?' and how he had replied to me in his high, reedy voice, 'I am very sorry, God, but your propaganda was so bad.' Quintin laughed. 'But that won't save him from eternal damnation.'

Roy won't even speak to me now. He looks very unkindly towards me.

On my right was that jolly fellow, Dr Dickson Mabon, ex-MP and

---

7. (1872–1970); 3rd Earl Russell OM, philosopher, social reformer and campaigner for peace.

Labour minister, who joined the Social Democrats and now has gone back to Labour. He is giving advice, if you please, to Blair.

I wonder if Roy is so testy and unpleasant because he's ill. His face is very red.

Dear old fellow. I am extremely fond of him.

Saturday 22 July
In the evening we went to the great Andrew Roberts and Camilla wedding dinner at the Inner Temple.

There was a pavilion erected in the gardens of the Inner Temple. There was a negro band playing all the time. It was lovely music while out of doors. When we got in for the dinner and it played there, the noise at some times was totally deafening.

I had some interesting conversations with Christopher Monckton who is the heir to the second Viscount and therefore grandson of Walter Monckton whom I knew very well. His wife said there were lots of his father's papers at home. She would have loved to have looked at them, but he bundled them all up and sent them straight off to Buckingham Palace. Walter was the absconding Prince of Wales' lawyer.[8]

Somebody asked, 'Why do people use prostitutes?'

I said, 'I couldn't bear to have sexual relations with anybody whom I wasn't deeply fond of or in love with. It is utterly mechanical otherwise and you might as well masturbate. But I hate masturbation and won't do it.'

Saturday 29 July *Italy*
Gingo [Sanminiatelli] hadn't realized that the aeroplane was late. He had driven out in his own car to pick us up. He is immensely kind. He doesn't look all that well and he couldn't stand for very long.

Monday 31 July
Went over to the great castle where the Gambas, Baba and her husband, live. We drank from fantastic, hundred-and-fifty-year-old crystal glasses bought by his ancestors in Paris a hundred years ago.

We ate off ancient early willow-pattern Wedgwood plates.

They may have some glorious fun in Castle Desolation, as I sometimes call it. Everything is to be turned into a luxury modern hotel.

---

8. Most of Walter Monckton's papers were made public in March 2000.

There is to be a golf course attached to the hotel. It will be one of the finest in Italy. Peter Parker's[9] firm Arcadian International has at last got all the permissions.

---

9. Chairman, British Rail Board, 1976–83; a director, Arcadian International, since 1990; knight 1978.

Petronella interviewing the Prime Minister, John Major,
for the *Daily Telegraph*, in July 1996.

The Wyatts with Peter Jones at the 1996 Tote lunch. Peter Jones succeeded
Wyatt as Chairman of the Tote in August 1997.

Top: Pat Chapman when Editor of the *News of the World*.

Left: Piers Morgan when Editor of the *News of the World*.

The Duchess of Beaufort (Caroline) in her robes for her honorary doctorate from the University of Bristol, March 1995.

Lord Weinstock (Arnold).

Clockwise from bottom left:

Miriam Gross (Lady Owen)

Viscount and Viscountess Rothermere (Vere and Maiko) in 1997.

Beryl Bainbridge after nomination for the 1996 Booker Prize.

R. E. S. Wyatt (Bob), Woodrow Wyatt's cricketer cousin.

John Heaton, Secretary of the Tote from 1983, appointed Chief Executive in 1996.

Mr and Mrs John Prescott at the races.

Baroness Thatcher applauds Prime Minister John Major during the 1997 general election campaign.

Michael Howard, Home Secretary, and his wife, Sandra, at the 1996 Conservative Party Conference.

The Queen Mother presents Woodrow Wyatt with a special
gold cup at Cheltenham on 13 March 1997 (centre: Lord Vestey).

Martina Hingis in the 1997 Wimbledon women's singles tennis championship which she won.

Tuesday 1 August

Verushka drove beautifully [to Porto Ercole].

We arrived in time to go to the discount stores (as they are quaintly called – there is no discount) to buy some wine.

To dinner were coming Amy and Gino Corsini and Daisy Corsini, their daughter, and Vere Rothermere and that incredibly beautiful girl, part Korean and part Japanese, Maiko.

She was looking extraordinarily lovely with her fabulous jewellery – real – diamonds and rubies. Verushka was wearing imitation jewellery which Maiko thought was real but it had come last year from a shop by the sea below.

Vere is very jealous. I said to Maiko, 'I want to show you a wonderful view where Charlie Allsopp (now Hindlip) painted a pretty picture for us.' I took her down to the end of the swimming pool and on to the raised platform beyond on the right. We stood there looking at that view for hardly more than a minute when Vere rushed up saying, 'I've brought your champagne,' looking at me very suspiciously.

She is naturally flirtatious, part of her appeal to men, but I would be amazed if she were disloyal to Vere. Unlike Bubbles, whom Vere, in the early days of their marriage, saw kissing me enthusiastically, standing by a car at night.

The place where poor Verushka broke her heel, and incurred agony for months as a result of falling into it, has now been blocked up.

I suppose we could have sued the charming owner, Count Maro, not that I ever would, but he clearly feels guilty about it and was anxious to ensure that Verushka couldn't have another accident.

I had an argument with Vere on John Major as a good Prime Minister. I said, 'You're as bad as Rupert,' which rather put him out.

He asked what I think of Rupert nowadays. 'It's a case of power corrupts and absolute power corrupts absolutely. You may have a danger of that yourself, Vere.' He laughed. I said, 'I disagree with Rupert frequently.'

Wednesday 2 August

Darling Maiko had her two little dogs, one white, a Pekinese, and one brown, a little Yorkshire terrier. She carries them in the same bag. She shampoos them every other day. They sleep in the bed with her and Vere. Vere complains sometimes that he has to carry the bag with the dogs walking behind her.

The reason why Vere and Maiko were staying at the Pellicano [hotel] is that she came to be a godmother to Alexander Corsini's triplets.

Huge bunches of flowers, orchids, lilies and so forth preceded the churchgoers to the place where we all had to gather, in the arboretum belonging to Gino Corsini.

I went to find darling little Maiko. She was sitting alone with one of the baby godchildren and her dogs on her lap, wearing a wonderful white outfit and a fantastic brooch on which I complimented her.

Tuesday 29 August

The holiday has been a hotch-potch. Sometimes very agreeable and at others quite horrible.

The worst moment was when I was told suddenly by Petronella that the ghastly, low-level gossip columnist, Peter Mackay was arriving in two days' time plus his wife and two children, wrongly described as being twelve and fourteen. They turned out to be eight and ten.

His wife had once been a gossip columnist on Nigel Dempster's column.

Anyone who can work for Nigel Dempster's column has to be pretty ghastly.

She had a beautiful figure, wonderful breasts, very nice legs, very flat tummy, all the things which would make a woman desirable. When she was looking at all relaxed her face also became reasonably pretty.

The staff couldn't cope with these four demanding horrors to feed and wait upon. To cap it all, Petronella took no notice of them. I took more notice of the children than she did, and even of the ghastly parents.

I extracted from him a promise that nothing he heard while he was with us would be repeated and that not even the names of guests who were there, nor people who came before or afterwards. But I expect it will be all over London.

Peter Lilley went white when Petronella told him that Mackay was very indiscreet. He had been palling up with him when going to the beach and talking to his family. (He rather liked the children. He has none of his own.) It seems that he had been making anti-Major statements to Mackay of a silly kind and is now terrified they will get back to him either in print or from verbal sources.

I liked Peter Lilley a lot.

He has a fascinating ministry, being in charge of social security. He is very bright, with most ingenious ideas and ways of stopping fraud, cutting down unjustified benefits and making the money go round more.

He is not very keen on identity cards.

He was also against a law of privacy.

He did grudgingly agree to the tenor of my article in the *Times* published on the first Tuesday in August, written before I left. I had a very nice letter from Calcutt agreeing with what I had written.[1]

Gail Lilley is a variable character.

She is not a particularly pretty woman, though once was. She is a year or two older than him. He's fifty-three. She really supports the family while he's a Cabinet Minister, which is inadequate for any serious purpose in salary terms. She designs clothes and has made a lot of money that way. She even makes money out of painting her pictures, which I have never seen, having dodged going to her exhibition.

Earlier Mary Soames when staying with us had joined in the singsongs. She and Petronella together did the 'Chattanooga-Choo-Choo Express' song beautifully, Mary raising her hands at the right moments and dancing about and wiggling away. Together they made an almost professional act.

She told a fascinating story about being invited to dinner by Max Beaverbrook[2] during the war when she was nineteen or so and in uniform. When she got to his apartment, Arlington House, she was puzzled why there were no other guests and why her parents hadn't been invited. Then Max, after he had been immensely complimentary to her, shouted to his weird butler-valet, 'Bring in those trays you got

1. Calcutt said that the generosity of WW's article compelled him to write a brief note of thanks. The sadness was that the Government *could* have done something earlier, but did nothing.
2. (1879–1964); 1st Baron (cr. 1917), proprietor of Express newspapers from 1916; Conservative politician; Minister of Information, 1918, and Minister of Aircraft Production during the Battle of Britain.

from the jewellers.' There were laid on the table, masses of marvellous, fabulously expensive jewellery. 'Take any one you like. You choose,' Max said. Eventually she chose the earrings she was wearing as she spoke to me – large round, gold with emeralds and diamonds, very beautiful. 'Ah, you want those, do you? Don't you want something better?' 'No, that will do be beautifully, Max. It's very kind of you.' They cost then about £1,800 so I suppose they must be worth at least £30,000 now.

Her mother hated Max Beaverbrook and couldn't understand why Winston liked him.

There was, of course, the fact that he'd helped him out financially pretty often with his system by which he would invest money on behalf of Winston. If it went up, it was Winston's. If it went down, it was Beaverbrook's. Dear Winston would never have survived in the modern House of Commons with its ludicrous register of interests.

On her father and what the ghastly Moran (his doctor, made Lord Moran) said in his book which Churchill never read, fortunately, she said it was obvious that he would see him only when he was feeling low.[3] He always had a mercurial temperament, down in the depths at one moment and up in the sky at the next. She admits there's a little bit of truth, though a lot of it is inaccurate, in the psychiatrist Anthony Storr's account.[4]

She said even in the days just before he died her father could have flashes of his old self.

Mary said how upsetting it was at the end when he kept saying he'd worked so hard all his life and nothing had come of it.

It is extraordinary how many great men feel they have accomplished nothing. Their sights are set so high that the achievement they think themselves capable of is beyond any human being. Beaverbrook always used to say to me he had done nothing, his life was no good, he was useless.

John Wilton told a funny story about their visit to the Onassis yacht in the Monte Carlo harbour.

---

3. *Winston Churchill, The Struggle for Survival* was published in 1966, the year after Churchill's death; Lord Moran (1882–1977) suggested that Churchill's health deteriorated more than the public knew during his last years as Prime Minister, 1951–5, when he resigned at 81.
4. Storr's *Churchill's Black Dog and Other Phenomena of the Human Mind* was published in 1989.

Maria Callas, still amorously involved with Onassis, was there. John was about to see an opera and he asked her what she thought the performance would be like. Maria Callas said, 'It'll be quite good even though I won't be singing.'

Both the Wiltons and the Pejacsevichs contribute pretty generously, (a) by bringing me cigars and (b) by buying lots of drinks for the house, though it is mostly the drinks which Mark and Diana like, such as vodka which I never drink nor does Verushka.

Addition (Mrs Tamborero says I shouldn't write in this way: it makes me sound spiteful and petty. But I am often both though I try to be good and do good, even if I fail intermittently.)

Simon Sebag-Montefiore came.

He was painfully writing an article for the *Sunday Times* which he has a contract with. It was not a good article when he'd done it, but we had to listen to it and have it faxed backwards and forwards, and there were telephone calls backwards and forwards.

I grew fond of Simon Sebag-Montefiore, suddenly called by Petronella 'Sandbag.' He answered very cheerfully to that. I drew him up very sharply, and also the ghastly Mackays, for calling her 'Petsy', saying, 'She would have been christened Petsy, if that were her name, but she was christened Petronella, after the heroine of a remarkable short story, "Till September Petronella" by Jean Rhys.[5] Petronella is actually the name of a Scottish dance. Petsy is not a nickname but a vulgar corruption of a very pretty Christian name.'

Delightful guests were Miriam Gross and her husband, Sir Geoffrey Owen, a former editor of the *Financial Times*, good on economics and a consultant to various businesses now. What I didn't know was that he had played at Wimbledon, when it was still amateur, seven times after the war. Twice he got into the second round. On one occasion he took several games off Rosewall, the great Australian player.

He was invited to play tennis with the Grimaldi people, Antoinetta and her son (who fancies himself a fine tennis player) and her husband.

He is sixty-one. To the horror of the son and the amusement of the father, he played with Antoinetta and they won all three sets.

It is my habit on these holidays to play little jokes at breakfast time, not very funny but they amuse me and usually the guests. One of my jokes is, if I have my boiled egg long before anybody comes down, I scoop out the inside completely and turn it upside down again in the

---

5. First published 1960, in *The London Magazine*.

egg cup. Then I offer it to somebody. They always get taken in first time.

Sonia and Andrew were a good inclusion. Andrew has mellowed a lot since he was very left-wing.

He has just written a vast tome on the history of the Arts Council. He was accused by Gowrie in a review of having taken the side of the Arts Council because he had been paid £50,000 to write the history.

He was deeply hurt about these criticisms. I said, 'Just ignore it. People idly say hurtful things. You should see some of the things that have been written about me.'

When Verushka went off to Austria for the great bean feast in honour of Vere Rothermere's seventieth birthday, sweet Sonia was stuck with most of the running of the house, insofar as it was needed.

Another good value guest was the strange Professor Norman Stone.

I keep telling him that John Major will win, which he doesn't believe. He has taken against him because Margaret has and he's one of her ghost writers.

Norman was learning Turkish while with us. He will teach at a Turkish university at Ankara next summer and take a villa by the sea, or so he says. I wouldn't mind having him back next summer.

He is good at bridge, particularly when drunk when he makes the most astonishing opening bids like five spades, and then pulls them off. I usually played with him.

As usual, Petronella leaves her room in the most filthy condition imaginable, with clothes all over the floor.[6]

She comes out looking like a beautiful model, elegant like her mother with the same sort of style, and her brilliant conversation. They can entrance all males and quite a lot of women, so long as they don't fear their husbands are too interested.

Thursday 31 August
I had my last swim at half past seven, with nothing on as usual.

I suppose we will somehow come back to this place next year though it's hard to see how I am going to find the money.

I have done quite a lot to my play.

I showed it to Norman Stone. He read it very quickly. I don't believe

---

6. See Vol. 2, p. 23, for WW's admission that he himself always leaves his clothes on the floor for somebody to pick up.

he could have read all my writing. But he thought it very good and entertaining.

I swore him to total secrecy on the subject. I hope he observes it. Unlike Peter Mackay, who has written in the *Evening Standard* since he left us, having promised not to repeat anything he saw or heard when staying with us.[7]

If we come again to Italy, there will have to be a different arrangement, as I have told Petronella and Verushka. I have got to be able to vet any proposed guests before they are asked, and also to have one or two of my own.

---

7. The item did not mention the holiday but said WW was intrigued to hear Nigel Lawson had secured a handsome advance for a book about his dieting and wondered if he could also 'crack this market' with a health book. It added that he lit his first Havana cigar of the day after breakfast, preferred to use lavatory paper rather than conventional toothpaste 'to polish his fangs' when necessary and enjoyed swimming in the nude.

Saturday 2 September
Up to Lord's to see the final of the Benson and Hedges match between Warwickshire and Northants.

John Major came in. When we had the opportunity we had a talk without the others in the box hearing. He said, 'Don't say it to anyone but I postponed the start of the Irish summit at Chequers on Wednesday until after lunch so that I can come to Bob's memorial service in the morning and hear your great oration.' I thought, 'Oh my God, "great oration".'

I mentioned that Prescott had written my column the week before.[1] 'A terrible man, absolutely awful and a hypocrite,' said John. 'I'm not so sure about that. I'm quite fond of him. But he's certainly very old fashioned and he is supposed to be Deputy Leader of the party.' John almost snorted. 'Supposed to be, but nobody takes any notice of him.'

Victoria was in a very jolly mood. She said she wanted to get to know Verushka much better because she felt she was her type of person. I told Verushka, 'I'm not at all keen on the idea. All she'll do will be encourage you to spend even more money on clothes you don't need with money we can't afford or I haven't got.'

Tuesday 5 September
Number 10 rang while I was shaving and naked. I had to run fast into the top sitting-room to deal with the call. John Major is giving some parties, for eminent husbands with wives, about twenty in total. Would Rupert Murdoch like to come to one of them – for luncheon at Chequers. I said, 'Give me twenty-four hours to think about it.'

Meanwhile, the editor of the *News of the World* [Piers Morgan] has disappeared to the *Mirror*. When I went to have my hair cut on

---

1. The *News of the World* usually asked a leading politician to write a column in WW's place during August when he was on holiday. See Vol. 2, p. 554, for Virginia Bottomley asking WW for advice on the task.

Saturday, I was asked by Eddie O'Brien[2] what did I think about having a new editor at the *News of the World*. I said, 'I have nothing to say.' I was almost ashamed to admit that nobody had told me.

I have just spoken to Rupert. None of the hint of dodging me or undercurrent of slight hostility of the summer when we disagreed profoundly. He said, 'Thank him very much for the honour of being invited.' 'I don't suppose you would want to go to a gathering of twenty people. You wouldn't be able to talk to him properly anyway.' He said, 'I will be in London on Monday, Tuesday and Wednesday. Maybe he could fit in half an hour for a drink and I would go to see him.'

We discussed the disappearance of Piers Morgan. He said, 'These journalists have got no loyalty at all.'

'I suppose he was attracted by the idea of getting an enormous amount of money to try to save the circulation. You've been very patient with him.' Rupert said, 'Yes. He'll not be welcome back.' We both agreed he would make an extremely good editor of the *Mirror*.

Wednesday 6 September
Robert Runcie[3] played a prominent part in the service [for Bob], though it was led off by the Vicar of St John's Wood, the Lord's church.

With Runcie I think I rate as half a Christian.

Jonathan, Bob's and Molly's son, I like a great deal. He's good-looking, something like Bob. He is now forty-two.

He was at Marlborough. Unfortunately, he had asthma very badly which prevented him from reaching any high level at cricket, though he was not bad.

John Major thought my address was magnificent, marvellous. He said, 'I'd like to book you for my memorial address.' I said, 'I don't think I'll be around at that time.'

As he walked with us from the church all the way across the road to the front entrance of Lord's, where we were all to go into the restaurant, I said to John, 'Have you got no bodyguards?' He said, 'I have actually, everywhere. But it would be a good thing for the Tory party if I were assassinated. It'd certainly send them up in the polls and they might win.'

Petronella looked very pretty and was beautifully dressed, as was

---

2. WW always had his hair cut by Eddie O'Brien at the Waldorf Hotel barber's shop.
3. (1921–2000) Archbishop of Canterbury, 1980–91.

her mother. They are both a credit to the family in their appearance. Denis Compton[4] was very much struck by Petronella's beauty.

He is quite a one for the girls, old Denis, always has been.

Lord Justice Popplewell[5] was amused at my putting in a reference to the beautiful stand with Father Time on the top. He said, 'I knew you were teasing us.' He said they are going through the correct procedures and would I like to see a model they have got of what they propose to do.

Thursday 7 September
After hectic packing we were off to catch the Eurostar train to Paris.

Arrived at the hotel Diane Lever recommended, where she used to stay with Harold, a small hotel but absolutely delightful, charming. It used to be a private mansion. It is now owned by people who are dealers in antiques and art.[6]

However, at once Verushka said the bedroom was too small and, while I was unpacking and sorting my papers out, she went out and came back. 'I've got another room and we're moving to it straight away. It's only 70 francs more,' (which is £10).

We were the first to arrive [at the Rothermeres].

The apartment is exquisitely decorated. The ancient oblong wooden beams of the ceilings were painted in lovely colours as were the spaces between them. There were excellent *trompe l'oeil* paintings. Everything was executed in perfect taste by Maiko.

The dining-room was delightful where the picture of Vere's mother – she was very beautiful – was the sole picture on one wall.

The food was fabulous. When we were still talking before dinner the most delightful little prawns in Far East crispy light containers came round too often. I had about ten of them. The first course was a fascinating kind of jellied soup with masses of caviar put in it on the top. Then one course followed another, about six.

At the end I thought I had now had everything but then came some superb ice cream and special chocolate cake which I didn't really want to eat. Maiko, on whose right I was, said, 'You must have a piece,' so what could I do but have one?

---

4. (1918–97); Middlesex and England player; made 123 centuries in first class cricket.
5. The Hon. Sir Oliver Popplewell, High Court Judge, President of the MCC, 1994–6; knight 1983; a new stand was being planned at Lord's, to WW's dismay.
6. Hôtel Duc de Saint-Simon.

Vere was agitated about the wine.

Unfortunately, he had told the servants by mistake to put the red wine in the refrigerator so we had it pretty cold. It was almost disgusting.

He told me how his grandfather had met Hitler at Berchtesgaden when his grandfather was saying, like Beaverbrook, that there was going to be no war. Hitler was an appalling little man, very common, terrified at being at the top of the mountain in the 'Eagle's Nest.' He built it to look down on Austria where he was born but he could easily have got trapped in the tunnel by which you got to the house so he always came downstairs at the end of a meeting, such as the one with Chamberlain, and stayed in the house at the bottom, heavily guarded.[7]

Vere was very keen on telling me again that he is a republican.

He tries to show rather unconvincingly that he is not conventional.

He told Verushka how jealous he was of Bubbles and that's why he had lots of mistresses himself. Now he has no worries at all about Maiko and if anybody tried to make love to her, he would shoot him. That's why he keeps a gun in the house.

Bubbles when young was extraordinarily pretty but deteriorated into most vulgar behaviour and dreadful fatness as the years went by. She was profoundly unhappy.

I feel Vere basically is thoroughly decent. He likes to tease and be mischievous and he has an odd sort of boyish naïveté, not fully grasping the political scene. I am pretty certain now that he will stick by his promise to back Major.

Sunday 10 September
I spent some time on fixing the meeting, between Rupert and Major for twelve o'clock on Wednesday.

Tuesday 12 September
Rupert rang. I told him to have a bang at John about the cross-media restrictions, to tell him that communications were moving so fast that they made no sense. Also that Major's the great deregulator. That's how we got the Lottery.

---

7. The 'Eagle's Nest' was a tea-house, Kehlestein House, built on a crag above Hitler's house, the Berghof, at Berchtesgaden; the tea-house was reached by a lift which was a security problem; Chamberlain saw Hitler at Berchtesgaden in September 1938 to discuss Sudetenland and Czechoslovakia.

Rupert immediately chipped in, 'That's a disgraceful thing. It's just raising taxes. The Lottery should never have been allowed.'

He said, 'The distribution's all wrong, too; they give it to the wrong causes,' and so on.

Rupert was extremely friendly.

Meanwhile, I had sent the enclosed material to John Major.[8] I said it was very important that he should read it – at least the references to Rupert – before he saw him. Knowing that he has a great policy meeting with all his Ministers at Chequers on Thursday, I also gave Major my various thoughts on the weaknesses of his case and the counter arguments or remedy as well.

Wednesday 13 September

As promised, Rupert did ring after he had seen Major. He had raised the whole question of the cross media and the ownership of channels.

Major listened with some attention. 'I can see what you're talking about. You should have your man come to talk to my people.' He said he would also be present.

I said to Rupert, 'That's some advance, isn't it?' He admitted grudgingly it was.

Rupert didn't exactly promise to back Major but as good as on the whole.

Very satisfactory meeting of the Tote Board this morning. I was quite chuffed at our winning with the Office of Fair Trading and their refusal to invalidate our increases in the Authority fee. Also, to my surprise, they favoured my idea for a different kind of jackpot, taking races from different courses, [thus] making the jackpot more difficult to win and at the same time giving greater participation in the jackpot to more courses. It needs a lot of preparation but I am sure it could be done.

Thursday 14 September

Southwark Cathedral for Alan Hare's memorial service.

The Pearson family were very much in evidence, as his brother had married a Pearson and his son, the present Lord Blakenham, had

---

8. A list of seven 'Obstacles' facing the Tories, including sleaze; then 'A Way Round', his suggested answers to the obstacles; he emphasized that Rupert's 'basic gripe is cross-media regulation' and included a copy of his address at Bob Wyatt's memorial service.

married Marcia, Alan's daughter. That is how Alan became in charge of the *Financial Times* and Château Latour.

I always liked him and thought him amusing and intelligent. I was sad as the service went on, thinking of his great bravery in the War, for which he got the MC. Also the undercover operations we did to push back the threat of Communism in India and the Far East after the War.

He was a member of the Saintsbury Club[9] and a regular attender.

He was tall, slim and very good-looking, but he had been suffering with debilitating cancer which finally did for him. When at the end 'Let's Face the Music and Dance' was played and sung, Verushka remembered how he would whirl her around in a dance. She began to cry. I held her hand and we both felt sad together.

When I said to Jill, his wife, after the service, the effect it had on us making us very weepy, she said, 'Oh, why? It was all meant to be a very jolly, happy occasion.'

But I don't think you can just wipe out sorrow with resolutions to be cheerful.

Julian Amery was there.

He looks absolutely ghastly, as though it were he being taken out to be put in his coffin. Oh dear, another old friend going.

Adam Macmillan[10] said he is constantly being an usher at memorial services. 'They are cocktail parties for geriatrics. They enjoy them enormously.'

Friday 15 September
I told Irwin I hadn't met the new man in charge of News International. Irwin said, 'He's quite good.' 'I want to speak to him on a delicate subject. I want more money.'

I am on £150,000 at the moment and something in the order of ten per cent or so would be appropriate – I understood that the fearful show-off Michael Winner gets £200,000 for his article in the *News of the World* and others get paid far more than I do for writing articles. Not only am I the only political columnist in the *News of the World*, but I have a fortnightly article in the *Times* and write book reviews

---

9. Founded in 1931 in honour of George Saintsbury, literary historian and wine connoisseur, its members consist of 'men of letters' and 'men of wine'.
10. Son of Viscount Macmillan (Maurice), 1921–84, and Katherine Viscountess Macmillan (Katie).

for which they don't have to pay extra. Plus helping Rupert in all kinds
of ways with the government and so forth.

Saturday 16 September
To Newbury for the Tote Autumn Cup.

Arnold was there in a very unhappy mood. He is being attacked by
the *Telegraph* and various newspapers, particularly by the *Telegraph*,
about his position as Managing Director. I said, 'You're not intending
to go yet, are you?' 'Oh no, not for years, but there is an agreement,
secretly, as to who my successor will be.' I didn't ask him then for fear
of somebody overhearing him.

Also under attack is Needham.[11] Having left the government and
not standing for Parliament again, he is being taken on as Deputy
Chairman of GEC to Jim Prior. This is felt to be an unfair use of his
knowledge of Whitehall and exports. In a sane world it would be held
as an excellent arrangement for somebody who does know about trade
and has also been on trade delegations not only with GEC but with
numerous other firms as well.

To make matters worse, both his horses failed.

Back at Cavendish Avenue I was tired. I was content with sweetcorn
on the cob, fruit, a little pink champagne and half a glass of white
wine for my supper.

The first part of the last night of the Proms consisted of pleasant
and soothing music. I begin to feel that I am starting to fall for
music and will have to drop quoting Chesterton, 'I understand so little
about music that it doesn't even annoy me.'

For the second half there had been a concerted move by the authorities to tone down the noisy exuberance bursting with youthful
patriotism of the audience as they got to 'Rule Britannia' and 'Britons
never, never shall be slaves.'

The real villain appears to be John Drummond,[12] whom I have met
and thought to be sensible. He is sixty-one and is unmarried, probably
not likely to be now. It is extraordinary that these effete musicians
want to take the robustness and the fervent belief in the future of their

---

11. Minister for Trade at the DTI, 1992–5; executive director, GEC, 1996–7; he had
    been personal assistant to Jim Prior, 1974–9, when Prior was Opposition
    spokesman on employment.
12. Director, Edinburgh International Festival, 1978–83; Controller, BBC Radio 3,
    1987–91; Director, BBC Proms, 1985–95; knight 1995.

country away from them [the promenaders], even though it is displayed merely at the end of one out of seventy-one promenade performances.

Major was in a box with that strange bird John Birt, the Director General of the BBC. He, Major, understands that our bounds are being made 'mightier yet' because of the resilience of the British and their skill in making a new empire across the seas – this time in financial services and investment.

Sunday 17 September
Rang John Major. I asked him how he got on with Rupert. He thought fairly well and did I have any reaction from Rupert?

I said, 'I gather there is to be a further meeting with representatives from both sides.' He said, 'Yes, there is.'

When I mentioned Trimble becoming the leader of the Ulster Unionists, he agreed with me completely. There was nothing to worry about because he's a clear thinker but it shows the IRA and Sinn Fein that he's a tough customer.

He said, 'He's a lawyer and a very good one and, being on the very right wing of the Ulster Unionists, he'll be able to make them agree to things which his predecessor couldn't.'

Saturday 23 September
At Princess Michael's insistence, I had to have lunch in Piers Bengough's room and sit next to her at Ascot. She was in a very merry state. She exudes sex all the time. I asked her which she would prefer, to have a handsome young lover of excellent physique or go to bed with Goethe who was still chasing girls when he was nearly ninety. She said she would choose the young man and have dinner with Goethe.

Sunday 24 September
We entertained a lot of guests in the Tote room at luncheon. On my right sat Lady Berry, the widow of a Tory MP who was killed in the Brighton bomb attack by the IRA during the Tory Party Conference when they tried to murder Margaret.[13]

I said, 'Are you going to marry Bernard Donoughue?'

She seemed surprised by my question. I said, 'No questions are indiscreet. Only the answers can be, sometimes.' She told me that despite his being the Labour spokesman for a variety of matters

---

13. Sarah, née Clifford-Turner m (1966) Sir Anthony Berry (1925–84).

including racing in the Lords, she was going to vote Conservative as she always did. She thinks nothing whatever of Blair and indicated that Bernard didn't have a very high opinion of him either.

Alan Meale and his wife were there. She is quite a pretty girl.

He said why don't we get the Tote privatized.

I said I would send him my paper for the consultation document on the future of the Tote.[14] Opinion is moving to the proposition that this consultation document won't be issued until after the next election – that will be after I have finished my last term at the Tote.

Ladbroke's and Hill's are working up a great campaign which they aim to take to the European Court to prevent us having an exclusive licence to run pools. Ladbroke want to run them as well. The old days when the bookmakers thought we were uncommercial and could be safely ignored have gone. They are terrified of us.

Monday 25 September
John Major had an enormous success at the Majorca conference over the weekend. The newspapers simply will not publish the details because they like to go on pretending he's no good.

I wrote about this in the *Times*.[15] I had a lot of help from John's personal and private secretary who was at the conference. I wrote a number of things, by agreement with him, which had not been known before.

In the evening we went to a concert of the Royal Philharmonic Orchestra, of which Vere Rothermere's wife, Maiko, is the patron.

At the end of the performance we all moved off to a restaurant in Elizabeth Street (a new one). Maiko had taken the whole of the upstairs. It was extraordinary. Champagne, Dom Pérignon, was being poured out by the bucketful.

---

14. WW's paper began by saying it was unwise to consider the future of the Tote in isolation from the rest of the racing industry, including the Levy Board. It set out four possibilities for the future of the Tote: a) for it to remain as it was; b) for its assets to go to another body (privatization by legislation); difficulties are outlined with the bookmakers, if the BHB were to be given the Tote; c) for it to be sold as a whole with conditions, the principal proceeds of its revenues to go to racing; d) for the Home Secretary informally to delegate his powers to a suitable body.

15. On 26 September; WW said the meeting of European leaders took place on Major's initiative and that one of Major's basic points had been that Europe must keep its ties with the US; WW quoted Clinton's telegram to Major congratulating him on setting up the Rapid Reaction Force for Bosnia.

I would have enjoyed the evening much more if it had been shorter.

Tuesday 26 September
I succeeded in buying at the Christie's sale yesterday twelve bottles of 1977 Graham's port which Harvey, who organizes the cellar and the Saintsbury Club, had asked for from some generous member. It has cost me about £250. I do not know quite why I did it. I love port but can't drink it any more because it upsets my whole body. But I felt I'd had a lot of pleasure from that club. I thought of it as like a subscription. The one we pay is very small.

I am alarmed by the ending of the net book agreement. Not only will it damage a lot of small bookshops but I fear the position of the authors may be injured.

Saturday 30 September
To Uttoxeter where I had to open Woodrow's, named after me as a compliment, the new restaurant bar complex, very elaborate, very fine, very well designed.

On the way back I called in at Weeford Church to see the inscription on the main Wyatt grave tombstone, done beautifully by that marvellous stonemason attached to Lichfield Cathedral. It looks exactly the same as the old script.

I said to the vicar, Mr Martin, 'I now want to have a plaque for my cousin [Bob] in the Church.'

I told him I would leave some money as a charitable gift in my will so they can keep up the Wyatt graves, including mine, and also provide money for other purposes.

I selected the plot for my grave. 'I want to look out over all these acres of fields that we used to farm.' 'We'll have to cut the trees down for you to do that.' 'I don't think that's necessary. I'd just like to feel that something of me will be preserved in that same air we breathed over the centuries.'

The vicar is a very pleasant man with a round, perky face, keen, intelligent and interested. I wondered why he wasted his time in so small a place. He is of course vicar, or rector, of a number of churches.

Sunday 1 October

Up at 6.30 again. This time to catch the Forte aeroplane for Paris and the Arc de Triomphe. There was a breakfast beforehand, but not the lobster Petronella and I had got the year before.

We had quite a Tote display here. For the first time the French PMU allowed us to have an external building clearly marked Tote Credit just near the paddock.

We took more money than ever before but we only get two and a half per cent.

At least a third of the crowd was British.

We got a lot of applications for new Credit Club members so the whole trip more than paid for itself, including the parties we took over to stay the night in a hotel.

The table we sat at included John Howard de Walden and Gillian, his wife, plus Nigel Dempster, the *Daily Mail* gossip columnist, whom I have always avoided before. He turned out to be very funny.

Poor Arnold is very much concerned about the monstrous attacks being made on him in the *Sunday Telegraph* Business News.

In the aeroplane on the way over was John Jay, now in charge of the *Sunday Times* financial pages, who used to be in charge of the financial pages of the *Sunday Telegraph*. He was very angry about the rubbish they are writing.

I went over to see Arnold where he was sitting in the President of the Republic's box.

'You should talk to John Jay but don't let anybody know, not even your secretary, in case something gets out inadvertently. He must ring you up and come to see you privately in Grosvenor Square. Don't let Tim Bell, your publicity man, know anything about it either. Then there can be no leak and it will just be John Jay giving his personal objective account.' Arnold thought this a very good idea but pessimistically assumed it wouldn't do any good.

Caroline Moore (Charles Moore's wife) said she heard two Englishmen in the crowd saying, 'Look at Woodrow Wyatt there with that cigar. They're not like that now. He has a different bird every day. He's got a lovely one now (this was Petronella!). That's what I call a real gent.'

Monday 2 October

Over to Lord's to meet the man in charge of the project to create a new stand instead of the Baker Stand.

When I looked at the model for the new stand it looked infinitely better than the pictures I had seen in the newspapers. I congratulated them on the tracery at the top and was assured that the old Father Time weather vane would have precisely the same prominence as before. Accordingly I wrote to Jocelyn Stevens[1] saying I withdraw all my objections.

I was then obliged to go to a party at Andrew and Sonia Sinclair's. It is a long way and I was very tired.

However, Allan Davis was there, bouncing up and down. He said he couldn't do any more plays now because he is too old and it isn't worth it unless it is something absolutely fantastic which he really believed in. That indicated he didn't quite believe in my new play.

Tuesday 3 October

Cita Stelzer came with me on the promised outing. We began by going to the Matthew Boulton house in Soho, Birmingham, not far from my old constituency of Aston.

I pointed out to Cita some of the streets which were actually in my constituency in 1945. I explained to her that we began to think we'd win, despite the large Tory majority, when my photograph began to go up in the windows of the kippers and curtains area. They were better off than in the slums and back-to-back houses in Aston generally because they could afford kippers for their high tea and lace curtains to prevent people looking in on them.

The redone Matthew Boulton house, developed for him by James and Samuel Wyatt, looked divinely pretty, white, elegant and character-istically Wyatt.

Matthew Boulton's family came from Lichfield, only a few miles from Weeford. The families were very close to each other. James helped

---

1. Chairman, English Heritage, 1992–9; the new Grand Stand was designed by Nicholas Grimshaw.

enormously in designing the coins manufactured by Matthew Boulton for which he was famous.

The table at which the Lunar Society sat is a James Wyatt one.[2]

I like to think of James Wyatt walking about in those rooms, instructing the workmen and his clerk of works. There he was amongst those extraordinary men, philosophers, as they called themselves, and scientists of the Lunar Society who in that very house were the foundation of the Industrial Revolution, the revolution which made England rich and powerful throughout the world.

At the great house Ragley Hall, belonging to the Hertfords, the Wyatt rooms were done by James for visits by the Prince Regent. The then Marchioness of Hertford was one of his mistresses.

The first of the three rooms we went through by James Wyatt was a drawing-room. The ceiling was beautifully done in James Wyatt's very best style. In the corners were depicted various sporting activities. One was of a cricketer with three stumps behind him. That was just after they put in the third stump, which our guide foolishly thought was in order to prevent the ball going through. I said, 'No, it was not to do that. It was in order to show the man was out without any doubt if the ball hit the stumps. Before when you only had two stumps there was uncertainty whether it had gone in between the two stumps or outside them.'

I wished dearly I had seen it before Bob had died and could have told him about it.

The present Marquess arrived in a white and yellowish coloured jeep which looked as though it was about to collapse. He got out and bumbled towards us. He had an enormous hole in his jersey. He looked utterly dishevelled. He had a friendly grin. He was the replica of Lord Emsworth at Blandings,[3] to be mistaken for a gardener or a farmhand. It was a deliberate ploy.

He announced he was not afraid of Blair. 'They're very rich that pair, Blair and his wife. They won't put heavy taxes on me.'

---

2. Matthew Boulton (1728–1809) was a co-founder of the Lunar Society in 1766; its members included Dr Erasmus Darwin, Josiah Wedgwood, James Watt, Joseph Priestley and Samuel Galton.
3. The P. G. Wodehouse character.

Thursday 5 October

We went to dinner with Cita and Irwin Stelzer to meet Les and Mary Hinton. He is now Rupert's representative here, the second successor to Gus Fischer who was an urbane and civilized man. Les Hinton was pretty brash, an ardent worshipper of Rupert. He was puzzled by anybody, including myself, who ever disagreed with him.

He started life in Liverpool. Somehow he emigrated to Australia, then he and his wife went to America. His wife also came from Liverpool. She has charm and is far more sophisticated than her husband. She is nice, round and plumply attractive.

I had to say to Cita and Irwin that I liked him very much, though I didn't.

I told him, as we were leaving, I wanted a ten per cent increase.

Perhaps I am jaundiced but I don't feel the evening was a mad success so far as getting a reasonable salary out of Rupert. Hinton told me that Michael Winner attracts a much bigger post-bag than I do and arouses more interest.

Saturday 7 October

Not a good day.

Petronella is in the *Evening Standard* again now because she didn't pay her Council tax.

It all comes back to me to pay in the end.

Sunday 8 October

I have told Verushka that I cannot go to Hungary this Christmas. We can't afford it, staying at the Hilton, paying for parties at restaurants and at Gundels. She said it's all right, she doesn't want to go.

'We'll manage somehow. I haven't many Christmases left. This is my country and I would like to be in England for Christmas for a change.' 'But it is not my country.' 'It is. You're Lady Wyatt of Weeford.' She laughed: 'That doesn't mean anything.'

Monday 9 October

When Martin Ivens (features editor of the *Times*) rang I was not one hundred per cent. I told him I wanted to write about the forthcoming Tory conference and various aspects of Blair.

'I would much rather you wrote about what it is like to leave your party.' 'Mine is not an exact parallel with that extraordinary man,

Alan Howarth.⁴ I didn't leave my party or see it drift away from me beyond recall until about the mid seventies, when I wrote *What's Left of the Labour Party*.' Martin Ivens was very insistent. I agreed to do it.

Tuesday 10 October
I asked Arnold if he had been pleased with what they wrote in the *Sunday Times* Business Section. This was the result of the meeting I set up between John Jay and Arnold to be held secretly at his flat. 'Yes, except they sent a list of questions which I answered and then, instead of setting it out as questions and answers, they wove them into an article.'

My article in the *Times* received numerous compliments, so maybe I was on the ball.

Friday 13 October
I got my *News of the World* article off in relatively good time so that I could get to John Howard de Walden's house for dinner.

I dressed in a white silk shirt and had my tie ready to put on before I left. Angela Oswald was staying there with her husband, Michael.⁵ She said she didn't like my tie so I went to put another one on, a large pink one which she preferred. She's a very bossy lady, one of the women in my life who bully me. Gillie Howard de Walden is another, and Jill Radnor is another.

Poor Queen Elizabeth (Angela is her chief lady-in-waiting) is in terrible pain. It's that damn hip thing, just like Bob had.

Michael said it is quite true she will have the operation before the end of December. She wants to go to the King Edward VII hospital. I said, 'That's absolutely no good at all. She must go either to the London Clinic or lay on emergency equipment of every kind, which might be needed within five seconds if something goes wrong. It's a nice old place, the King Edward VII hospital and I belong to it, too, but I would never go there for a serious operation.'⁶

---

4. Elected a Conservative MP in 1983, Howarth joined the Labour Party in 1995 and has been a Labour MP since 1997, for a different constituency.

5. Lady Angela, née Cecil, daughter of the 6th Marquess of Exeter, m (1958) Michael Oswald (Manager, The Royal Studs, 1970–97, Racing Manager to the Queen Mother since 1999, knight 1998); Woman of the Bedchamber to the Queen Mother since 1983.

6. The Queen Mother's operation there was successful.

Sunday 15 October
Following upon Max Hastings' departure to the *Evening Standard*,
where he will be paid an enormous amount by Vere Rothermere,
numerous names had been canvassed for the editorship of the *Daily*
and *Sunday Telegraph*. Conrad Black has not yet given his decision. I
rang him up and spoke to him at great length, pushing the virtues of
Frank Johnson, and saying I believed that one of the front runners,
Dominic Lawson, would be a disaster.

Conrad said he had made a great success of the *Spectator*, turning
it into a half million a year profit. I said, 'No doubt, but the *Sunday
Telegraph* is a different animal.'

I spoke to Frank Johnson. 'You've got to ring him and say you
want to see him.' He did and reported back that Conrad remarked,
'One of your admirers has already been on to me about you, singing
your praises.' When Frank asked who he said, 'I can't tell you but he's
got a beautiful daughter.'

Monday 16 October
The great Thatcher birthday dinner at Claridge's.[7]

Margaret was immensely friendly. She thanked me for sending her
the twenty-four red birthday roses.

The Queen was there and Prince Philip. Bill Deedes (the father of
Jeremy Deedes on my Board) made a wonderful speech. He has always
been a buddy of Denis Thatcher and the John Wells column in *Private
Eye* about Bill Deedes' conversations with Denis Thatcher always rang
true.

At one moment I swung around with my cigar in my hand and
found I had bumped right into the Queen who was standing apart at
that moment. 'Oh, my goodness, ma'am, I'm terribly sorry.' I started
trying to bow my head to her. She said, 'Don't worry. You can't do
anything with that glass of champagne in your hand.' She was laughing
away. 'You look very pretty, Ma'am. I love your dress. You're looking
absolutely gorgeous.' 'Oh how kind of you. Do you really think so?'

That went down very well. But I thought, my goodness what a
scandal if I had actually knocked her down.

Norman Lamont and Rosemary were there.

The divorce proceedings have not yet materialized and seem to have
been put on the back burner while Norman hunts for a safe seat.

---

7. She was 70.

I was one of the few people named in the press at this party and there had been at least two hundred people.

So I must be really back in Margaret's favour who is now being much more helpful to Major.

Thursday 19 October
For Petronella the worst has occurred. Charles Moore has gone to be the editor of the *Daily Telegraph*. Frank Johnson's to edit the *Spectator*. Dominic Lawson is to edit the *Sunday Telegraph*. She is convinced she will lose her column, there are tears all round.

Dominic Lawson wants to put in [as political columnist] a man called Boris Johnson[8] who writes quite well on politics but is very anti-Major. It's going to be a great blow to poor old Major, too. Petronella's columns were very supportive of him.

They're saying she's too young to write a political column. She hasn't enough experience. That I believe to be a by-product from that ghastly Peter Mackay. He suddenly wrote in his ghastly column that Petronella is a *femme fatale* (which she had been writing jokingly about in her column) and could boast as admirers Jimmy Goldsmith, Conrad Black and a number of others.

She spends all her time in tears.

I said to Frank Johnson, 'Why don't you make her assistant editor of the *Spectator*?'

The guests [at our dinner party] were the Louise MacBain girl – we met her and her husband, who have *Exchange and Mart* type journals, at Vere Rothermere's in Paris – Charles Churchill, Vyvyan[9] and Mrs Harmsworth, Mark and Lady Lennox-Boyd, Annabel Astor, the Euro MP John Stevens, Philip Hapsburg, (Lady) Romilly McAlpine from Venice, Rodney and Lady Emma Foale, the Argentine Ambassador[10] and his wife, Charles Jencks, brother-in-law of Tessa Keswick.

Jencks is an architectural historian of great distinction and a designer of furniture.

He appears to be very rich. He was thrilled with the 1967 Château Branaire-Ducru (St Julien Fourth Growth, opposite Château Beychevelle).

---

8. Not related to Frank Johnson whom he succeeded as editor of the *Spectator* in 1999.
9. The Hon. Vyvyan Harmsworth, first cousin of Vere.
10. HE Rogelio Pfirter m (1980) Isabel, née Braun.

The sweet little Argentine Ambassadress, Isabel, wife of Rogelio, is exquisitely pretty with a round, jolly little face with dimples in the right place, very dainty hands and fingers. She and her husband are about five foot two inches high, I suppose, or a little bit taller.

She has a delicious smile. It makes you want to eat her or put her in your pocket.

I'm always nervous of Charles Churchill sitting on these little chairs – he is such an enormous weight. He is huge, like a vast teddy bear, but kind and generous and nice.

I had been cross with Verushka for asking all these people, forcing us to have two tables. But I had to hand it to her, she had assembled the most varied and entertaining group.

Sunday 22 October
Frank Johnson said he was doing everything he could for Petronella.

I told him surely she could still get her lobby correspondent's pass.

Meanwhile, the great birthday party of Sarah Keswick has taken place at the Ritz. Diana Wilton was invited though she only met Chips Keswick through us. We have been totally ignored. Diana said it was full of the young. Camilla [Parker Bowles] came to be with Prince Charles there. This provoked adverse comment. She is now acknowledged publicly as his mistress.

Maybe we might have been asked but Prince Charles knows that I think he has behaved like a lunatic and was made a fool of by Jonathan Dimbleby. Maybe he thought I was contemptuous of him, but at least Chips might have rung up to explain that.

I was amused in the Lords.

I saw Eirene White (Baroness) glaring at me.[11] I had said in my article dealing with the Howarth defection (*Times*, October 10th) that she always looked at me as though I were something the cat had brought in. It's funny how you can feel a malevolent gaze on you.

Friday 27 October
I went to see Nadje in her room. She sat up in bed, wagged her finger and pointed it at me in a most dramatic manner. 'Take care. There are thieves in the house. They're stealing my cigarettes. Livia says the same. They did it when she was here.'

Poor Nadje, she is having more and more of her shouting spells

---

11. (1909–99); Labour MP, 1950–70; life peer 1970.

these days. They are very disconcerting to me, just above my head when I am trying to write an article.

During the week the worst of all things happened to my darling Petronella.

Every time I thought about it during the week I literally wept for the poor child. She is so very vulnerable but it wouldn't be pleasant for anyone, however tough they might be.

Then all began to get better. Frank hadn't let her down. She will be assistant editor of the *Spectator* and Charles Moore has promised, and I think he will keep his promise, that she will be able to write a weekly article, presumably political, for the *Daily Telegraph*.

Petronella is now much more cheerful. She says she will get paid much more than she does now.

Saturday 28 October
Verushka was very eager that we should go to the party given by Louise MacBain in Paris, at Versailles.

All this going to Paris and similar activities, Verushka dressing as she does, and Petronella too, always trying to keep up with the ultra rich, is madness. We haven't got the money. I also worry that I may have made a horrible mess of my bet about the French franc weakening against the pound. Since I made it, and it's a very expensive one, it has moved the other way. I could lose £6,000 on it. I have to try to ring on Monday to take another bet with the franc going stronger against the pound, as it is at the moment, not weaker.

Petronella is now afraid that a lady called Applebaum from America who works for the *Spectator* will be taken by Frank Johnson to a dinner for journalists at Chequers.[12] John Major has already written to congratulate him, telling him to bring a colleague along. I said I would speak to Major which I did and she'll be OK to go.

Verushka is quite extraordinary the way she rings people up. She had a tremendous telephone call with Charles Moore who is terrified of her, as indeed is Frank Johnson. He said, 'I hear nothing but Petronella all day long. Everybody is coming to me about Petronella and saying something's got to be done about her.'

Verushka has this admirable quality of fighting like a tigress, or a leech, whichever is the more appropriate, for her family.

---

12. Anne Applebaum, at this time deputy editor of the *Spectator*.

Tuesday 31 October
At the Lords at four o'clock I met the three prize-winners from Eastbourne.

One of the girls was entrancingly pretty with blonde hair, very nice legs and mischievous.

We had an enormous tea, even I ate muffins and toasted tea cakes, which was mildly insane of me. When I took them downstairs to see how the fire had started in Parliament, I bought them each a box of House of Commons chocolates – £2.50 each. I really enjoyed the day with those lively young creatures.

Norman and Rosemary Lamont came to dinner. I felt all my old warmth and friendship towards Norman bubbling again. He is very clever, but can be such an ass, unfortunately. He is much exercised about getting another seat.

'Why do you want to be in the House? Why aren't you just content to make money? You don't still think you're going to be Prime Minister, surely?' No, he didn't think that any more. He thought he might be in the government again and anyway he thought he had a useful contribution to make. He is not sanguine about the Tories winning the election and thought it would be agreeable to be in opposition.

Eventually I asked them if they would like to come to Italy again next summer. I felt so pleased at being back in friendship.

Wednesday 1 November
A Tote Board meeting. I had spoken to Peter Jones in New York a couple of days before. 'I hope you're not going to be stuck in America all the time because there are a great many things I need to talk to you about.'

I am not quite having reservations about him.

Thursday 2 November
Down to the Lords to meet Les Hinton and Philip Hall, the editor of the *News of the World*. I said to Les Hinton in the morning, 'I assume we're not going to talk about my request for a ten per cent rise because I wouldn't wish to discuss it in front of Philip Hall. I have my contract with Rupert.' He said, 'There's no question of that. We want to talk about the *News of the World* generally.' I felt that to be slightly sinister but couldn't explain to myself why.

I gave them a tour which they much enjoyed. I was affable, they were affable. I ordered a bottle of champagne. The lunch began. With it arrived the bomb. Philip Hall, who is tall, dark, not particularly clever, with an exceptionally smug face, was brought to the point of revelation by Les Hinton. They don't want me to write every week, only fortnightly, in the *News of the World*. 'We are coming up to an election and it is only right and fair that there should be other voices on that great political pair of pages.'

I said, 'I have a lot of following from those articles. All surveys that have ever been carried out show I come pretty near the top of the items the *News of the World* readers read.' (I believe the editor has been suppressing the letters I get because I haven't had as many lately, even though I have written provocatively about things like immigration.)

My dislike for Philip Hall increased as the lunch went on. Also for Les Hinton.

This Liverpudlian-Australian-American has a jerky face. There's something wrong with his eyes. They don't look in the same direction as his face is going. Very strange.

'Have you told Rupert about this?' 'He knows Philip Hall wants to rearrange these pages,' they said rather shiftily. I said, 'It's unacceptable to me. My contract is to write once a week in the *News of the World*. Continuity is important and it will not be the same at all if I only write once a fortnight.'

After a lot of pointless argument from the sneery young editor, who is obviously pro Blair and is sucking up to him, having been, doubtless, sucked up to by Blair (who is astute at stepping in when there is a change in a newspaper and nobbling the new editor), the lunch came to an end.

I was so annoyed I forgot to pay the bill. I shall have to go back there next week to do it but I daresay they are not unduly worried at the House of Lords refreshment department.

I felt shattered and shocked. Since 1964 I have been writing a weekly article either for the *Daily Mirror* or the *Sunday Mirror* or the *News of the World*. Prior to that I was a weekly columnist in *Reynolds News*, until it packed up. I have lost my platform.

At home I talked to Verushka. I said, 'I shall sue Rupert. I shall take him to an Industrial Tribunal. He's been an absolute swine after all I've done for him. He's always promised I could write for as long as I liked. Bill Deedes is writing steadily on and he's over eighty-three, and Hannen Swaffer[1] wrote his last article at the age of eighty-three in the week he died.'

To Irwin I said, 'Surely he must have some gratitude for what I did for him?' 'He's very selective about that. Why don't you ring him?'

I did. He sounded guiltily evasive. 'Well it was these new people and I didn't want to override them, but you can go on writing once a fortnight.' 'But you always promised me I could write every week unless I became gaga.' 'Who's going to say when you've become gaga?' 'It'll be pretty obvious to the editor if I send in rubbish, won't it?' 'Nothing lasts for ever.'

We argued a long time. He said he would ring the *News of the World* and ring me back. Of course he didn't. He's a real coward when it comes to sacking people, particularly old friends. He gets somebody else to do it, which was what the meeting with Philip Hall and Les Hinton was all about.

---

1. (1879–1962); journalist and dramatic critic.

We then had to go to dinner with Charles and Irene Forte. I was in a shattered state – almost as bad as Petronella, but she has plenty of years to go and will find many places to write in. It is hard for me to find a new billet at the age of seventy-seven.

I hardly knew what I was doing or saying at the dinner party.

On the other side of Irene Forte sat David Stevens, Chairman of United Newspapers. He is trying to sell them. They have got worse and worse and the circulation of the *Sunday* and *Daily Express* is sliding non-stop.[2]

His wife still seems furious with me. He said, 'If you just go up to her and say you're sorry, I'm sure it will be all right.' I said, 'I wouldn't dare. I might get a black eye.'

After dinner I did try once or twice but I didn't get a chance or a moment.

It is absurd that every time I meet this terrifyingly awful and silly woman anywhere, she pointedly turns her back on me and I have to resist the temptation to tell her what a stupid, ignorant and uneducated woman she is, not being able to understand English.

It wasn't me saying he was a nonentity. I just reported it.

Friday 3 November

I tossed and turned during the night. I woke up partly in panic. My salary from the Tote comes to an end on 30 April 1997. If I have no income from Rupert, I shall have nothing to live on other than my savings and a miserable £60,000 a year pension from the Tote from which will be deducted my other little annuities, bringing it down to £40,000 or less a year.

It was tough to get moving on my *News of the World* article, having had little sleep.

Before I had actually finished dear Irwin rang. He had spoken to Rupert at length himself. He said Rupert had three messages for me. One, an expression of undying affection and love which hasn't changed. Two, he couldn't muck about with these new people.

The next point was would I use the alternate Fridays to write him a personal letter about what's going on – political, factual and gossipy – because he badly needs to be kept accurately in touch. (This is true, not because of what he may or may not think about Major, but what Major or others may do to him. A great deal of the money he makes,

---

2. United News (owner of the *Express* papers) merged with MAI in February 1996.

in fact the core of it, comes out of BSkyB, the *Times* and the *News of the World* in England to finance all his other operations.)

I said, 'What about my pay?' Irwin said, 'That's fine. There's no question of reducing your pay even though you're only writing a column once a fortnight.' 'What about an increase?' 'You can raise that with him when he comes.'

I'm now adjusting to what is to me a tremendous blow. I don't know if I am humiliated, exactly, but people will think it strange, and it is a demotion, not having the great Woodrow Wyatt column once a week in the *News of the World*. But I still seem to have some resilience.

Verushka is greatly relieved. She had already been trying to weaken me by saying, 'Do anything he asks.' I said, 'That's always your position, give in, give in.' Well, I hadn't given in and I had got somewhere with Rupert.

I was much comforted by Irwin.

Saturday 4 November
I dropped Verushka off at Oare and went on to Chepstow where we had an important Tote race and prize.

Old Harry Llewellyn[3] was there with others in the Directors' Box. He is seven years older than me (eighty-four) but looks rather younger which is a little irritating. He is a splendid guy with enormous courage as a rider.

On reaching Oare I could find nobody about. It was a glorious late afternoon with a fabulous sunset, red and pink. I walked all the way round the garden to the swimming pool and further on by the fields where the horses usually are. It began to get dark and I began to stumble. It is increasingly difficult for me to see in the dark but I had taken a stick.

It was lucky that my article would still be in the *News of the World* tomorrow so I did not have to mention the alternating fortnightly article I have now been driven into.

Sunday 5 November
Petronella went out riding with Tessa.

Verushka got into a terrible state.

---

3. Sir Henry Llewellyn (1911–99), 3rd baronet; captain, riding Foxhunter, of the British show jumping team which won the Olympic gold medal at Helsinki in 1952.

'Let her do what she wants. She won't fall off,' I said and nor did she.

I heard on the news that Arthur Bottomley had died.[4]

I first met him on a parliamentary delegation spying out the land for the possibility of achieving a smooth handover to India. It was at the very beginning of 1946.

He was round-faced, humorous, calm, dependable, jolly, very persuasive. He'd been a NUPE trade union leader, mayor of Walthamstow and so forth, very young. I liked him enormously. He was always very kind to me. He was eleven years older, not brilliant but a damn good Commonwealth Relations Secretary with his honest charm and ability to persuade and coax. He made friends for himself and Britain wherever he went. He was a first-class 'old' Labour man.

He and Bessie would have celebrated their diamond wedding this year. They had no children. Mischievously I sometimes wondered whether in their unworldly innocence they knew how to create them.

It was Mrs Thatcher who made Arthur a peer (because official Labour wouldn't), largely at my prompting.

Tuesday 7 November

I rang Philip Hall, editor of the *News of the World*, to say I assumed they would not be running my *News of the World* article this week.

He got in a great tizzy. 'No, no, that was only a distant thing we were thinking about. It's not going to happen like that at all. We're talking about much nearer the election. Would you please go on writing.'

Obviously there has been more backtracking than I had supposed.

I wrote a letter to Bessie in large letters to help her read it with her diminishing sight.

Wednesday 8 November

To the party given by Rupert and Anna in their apartment in St James's. We got there fairly early because I was intending to talk to Rupert about increasing my salary, but then felt it wouldn't be a suitable place. He was very warm and friendly.

I was talking to a man quite senior in BSkyB.

While I was speaking I chewed on some nougat in the canapés

---

4. (1907–95); m (1936) Bessie, née Wiles; Secretary of State for Commonwealth Affairs, 1964–6, Minister of Overseas Development, 1966–7; life peer 1984.

which stuck to the roof of my mouth and my teeth fell out. I said, 'I am so sorry, my teeth have fallen out and I have to put them back in again.' He was immensely embarrassed and kept looking the other way.

If he tells Rupert, he'll probably think I really am going gaga.

I had quite a long talk with John Redwood, to whom I said, 'I think you have many splendid ideas. But you are optimistic in thinking that other people are prepared to be as puritanical as you are.'

He was pretty certain the Tories were going to lose.

Rupert and Arnold kept saying Major hadn't got a chance.

Yet Rupert is slightly worried always that I could be right, as I so often have been.

Thursday 9 November

To Hahn's in Albemarle Street for Rosita Marlborough's exhibition and sale. I forgot, in my hurry, to put on a tie.

'You're not wearing a tie,' said Sonny, having suddenly noticed it. 'It didn't say on the invitation that you had to wear one.' Sonny looked a trifle blank.

Rosita was looking her most striking and beautiful best.

Eventually we looked at a couple of pictures which hadn't yet been sold. There was a small one called 'Marcel' for £1,000.

I fought my way through the crowd and got near to Sonny. 'I want to buy a picture but nobody will sell it me.' Instantly a lady appeared at my side.

Later, after having seen Jacob [Rothschild], I told Rosita, 'I've done a very good deal with National Heritage or whatever it is that Jacob runs. I'm selling "Marcel" on at fifty per cent profit.' Rosita was startled. 'Oh, good,' she said hesitantly. I said, 'I'm only pulling your leg. You rise so easily.'

Prince Michael turned up at Rosita's exhibition. He thought the paintings very good. He is not, maybe, quite a good judge.

Also at this strange gathering was Billy Dudley and Maureen, his wife.[5] They are not divorced and sometimes they appear to be living together again.

He said about Maureen, 'She's always looking to see what I'm doing.' I said, 'You mean to see if you're flirting.'

---

5. 4th Earl of Dudley m 2 (1961) Maureen, née Swanson, actress.

Friday 10 November

Went to Bessie's and Arthur's house first, before the funeral. I remembered well the little dining-room in which Bessie and relations were
sitting. She said, 'I had two Prime Ministers to dinner here, which I
cooked myself. When Attlee came I thought I had better get a new
dinner service and I've had it ever since.'

That very nice man, Ted Graham, Labour's Chief Whip in the House
[of Lords], was there smiling to see me. Bessie had asked me, 'Is it the
duty of the Chief Whip to do all the things he's done for me? He
helped arrange the funeral, he's done everything to help me and look
after me ever since Arthur died and went every day to see Arthur in
hospital.' I said, 'No, it is not the duty of the Chief Whip to do that.
He's done it because he's one of the nicest people you could ever
meet. He's a genuine, warm-hearted man, and I have great affection
for him even though he has never forgiven me for leaving the Labour
Party. He has a noble soul.'

I rang Pericles.

He was delighted to hear Anna (Murdoch) had remembered him.
'She's going to come to your steak house.' 'She could have come to the
one at Monterey. It was only five minutes away. This one's about forty
minutes away.'

Sunday 12 November

We have a register of members' interests in the Lords now. I was
looking forward to doing an Enoch Powell and ostentatiously refusing
to have anything to do with it. But on reading the terms of it [I found]
you only have to mention in it any earnings arising from your being a
member of the House of Lords. As the sources of income I get have
no connection whatever with the Lords, including my Chairmanship
of the Tote, which I had long before I joined the Lords in 1987, I am
in the position of signing a nil return. They've shot my fox.

Monday 13 November

Sir Patrick Sheehy was given the great room at 11 Downing Street by
Ken Clarke for his farewell party. He retires from running BAT in
December.

Is this a sign of the times? There were a number of Labour people
there.

To my surprise, Peter Mandelson, now in the Shadow Cabinet, a
great propagandist and leader of the Labour election campaign, said

he also had read *Confessions of an Optimist* and thought it very good indeed. I spoke to him about his grandfather, Herbert Morrison,[6] and how he said to me that he would have got the leadership of the Labour Party if it hadn't been for the freemasons who ganged up against him and he had hated them ever since.

Mandelson said, 'I didn't know that. Why do you write such nasty things about Blair? You ought to be on his side. He's just the sort of person we thought you supported.' I said, 'I'm not sure he's fully in charge of his party yet, or that he really means what he says.'

Ken Baker said, 'I wouldn't say it to anyone else, Woodrow, but I know we're going to lose.'

Thursday 16 November
The memo I sent to Rupert, confidential, explains just about everything for the time being.[7]

Rupert has stopped production of the *Today* newspaper. I am a little disturbed.

But rightly, Rupert has refused to sell *Today* to the ghastly Fayed.

At the Levy Board meeting this morning I produced a letter I had just had from the Paymaster General at the Treasury, David Heathcoat-Amory.[8] It was an answer to my plea for a reduction in betting duty, accompanied by charts and demonstrations that the tax was too high, irrespective of the present sad position of the betting shops.

I demonstrated that two per cent off betting tax would actually bring in more revenue and increase business in the betting shops. His reply clearly indicated that the Budget will do something about it. He underlined 'very carefully' in the letter.[9]

---

6. (1888–1965); Labour politician; Leader of the London County Council, 1934–40, war-time Home Secretary, Deputy Prime Minister and Leader of the House of Commons, 1945–51, Deputy Leader of the Opposition, 1951–5; life peer 1959.

7. WW's first private and confidential memo to Murdoch, one side of an A4 sheet, covered the Sheehy party, Blair's speech to the CBI about taxes, WW's expectations of the Budget, Tory private polls, Margaret on Major, and Tebbit's view that the Tories did not have a ghost of a chance of winning.

8. Conservative MP since 1963; Paymaster General, 1994 until his resignation in 1996; half-brother of Michael Heathcoat-Amory.

9. The letter said he had read WW's comments with interest and 'can assure you that they will be considered very carefully.'

Sir Paul Fox,[10] who is rather a disagreeable fellow, pooh-poohed it. 'Did you do the underlining yourself?' (I had handed out copies.) 'I have not yet added forgery as one of my attributes,' [I said] somewhat icily.

Saturday 18 November

Very sad. Went to the last meeting of the International Nutrition Foundation for the winding up of the management council and to sign papers to transfer the assets to Reading University, where they will provide a Chair called the Hugh Sinclair Chair. And there will be an annual year's free course for a student selected to do [an MSc thesis] on human nutrition.

All the time I was thinking of dear Hugh and his sometimes puzzled face, sometimes eager, thrusting.

I would sit with him occasionally in the evenings in his large drawing-room, bitterly cold in the winter with a one-bar electric fire. He would be wearing an overcoat and I would take the precaution to bring the heaviest overcoat I could find and a thermal vest.

He was tall, lanky, Scottish, nephew of the Sir Archibald Sinclair who received a peerage in the end – Secretary for Air during the War and a great friend of Churchill's though he was a Liberal.

He had never married. He was surprised when I said to him once, 'You nearly married Dorothy Crowfoot, didn't you?' She was the great scientist, with all kinds of vast prizes.[11]

He flushed deeply. 'Yes, I was rather keen on her.'

I believe he really knew the truth about diet and how it didn't matter how much you smoked if you ate the right diet – that was a sideline to all his other inquiries, though an important one.

I live entirely by his diet, including putting oil instead of butter or margarine on my bread, and I stick as best I can to nothing but fish or game and venison and the healthy foods. I avoid almost entirely

---

10. Television journalist; chairman, ITN, 1986–8, managing director, BBC Network Television, 1988–91; at this time chairman of the Racecourse Association, member of the BHB and the Levy Board; knight 1991.

11. Professor Dorothy Hodgkin OM, née Crowfoot, 1910–94; Fellow, Somerville College, Oxford, 1936–77; Nobel Prize for Chemistry, 1964.

dairy products which are a killer. For those who may be interested I enclose a note of what the diet consists of.[12]

It was then on to Ascot.

Eventually I had a little tea upstairs, having had no lunch, in Piers Bengough's room.

His very nice wife, Bridget, was a great skater, an Olympic skater. I said, 'Are you still going on with the skiing?' She paused and looked severely at me. 'It's skating, Woodrow.' She's not going on with it because she's too old and can't do it as well as she used to. She doesn't care to merely do it for the love of it in an amateurish way.

I said, 'Sir Samuel Hoare, Foreign Secretary before the war, was a very good skater, wasn't he?' 'No. He was absolutely awful. He couldn't skate at all. He wandered around with his hands behind his back just to impress people how sporty he was.'

I said, 'He was certainly a rotten Foreign Secretary.'

In an endeavour to hold out that olive branch to that stupid wife of David Stevens, I did describe him, in my *News of the World* piece connected with Rupert closing down the *Today* newspaper, as a notable businessman who made a fine success of United News and Media, as it's now called. I said even he couldn't refrain from hinting that the Express Newspapers could be for sale because of falling circulations and advertising revenue and increasing costs.

The next Monday I was tackled by dear old Geoffrey Ampthill (the Russell who was born as a result of sperm floating from his father into his mother's vagina. This was established by law and is perfectly true. He looks exactly like a Russell though the heritage was hotly disputed by the father, but overruled.[13]) He came up to me and said after I had written this olive branch, 'You've got it all wrong. You should get your facts right. It has never been for sale and I'm the Deputy Chairman.

---

12. In addition to suggestions about meats, dairy products and other fats, the note explains why 'caviar and lemon is a perfect diet'. WW adds that all Tote employees are entitled to a free issue of powdered ascorbic acid to take daily to meet vitamin C requirements.

13. 4th Baron Ampthill; see Vol. 1, p. 543, note, for the Ampthill Peerage Case ([1976] 2 All ER). In *Russell* v. *Russell* [1924] AC 687 at 721 his mother had said, and his father had admitted, 'that he had been in use to lie between her legs with the male organ in more or less proximity to the orifice of the vagina, and to proceed to emission'; hence Ampthill's conception *ab extra*.

We've had offers. People have approached us. We told them all to go away.'

So now do I have to publish a correction? I'm not sure I will because I don't actually believe he's right. 'I only published it to try to end a rift between his wife and myself.'

He said, 'You may have made matters worse.' Dear, oh dear.

I have been trying to get hold of John Major over the weekend. No luck. I wonder if he doesn't want to speak to me any more. Perhaps I have done something to upset him. I have no idea.

When I arrived at the International Nutrition Foundation smoking a large cigar, Brian Lloyd[14] ostentatiously fetched me a small copy of a funeral urn. 'That's to put your ashes in.'

Monday 20 November
The Diana programme. It was absolutely ghastly. Clearly she had been rehearsed (I expect that will come out later). She did it like an actress with great skill.

It was savage revenge for God knows what. She had instigated the Andrew Morton book. She admitted she got her friends to supply the dirt.

This psychopath, schizophrenic creature is as mad as a hatter, but she has that curious gift of schizophrenics, insight, knowing points which hurt, and needling, knowing exactly where to apply the dagger.

Then we had a ludicrous Barbara Cartland-style passage, that she wanted to be the Queen of the people's hearts.

Tuesday 21 November
It seems that what sparked off her revenge broadcast was reading and seeing pictures of Camilla Parker Bowles openly being with Prince Charles at the party at the Ritz given by Sarah Keswick for her fiftieth birthday.

Wednesday 22 November
At the *Spectator* party I sat next to Brian Mawhinney, Chairman of the Tory Party. He says their private polls are a bit better than the general run of published polls but not as much as he would like.

---

14. Dr Brian Lloyd, biochemist and physiologist; fellow, Magdalen College, Oxford, from 1948; director, Oxford Polytechnic, 1970–80, International Nutrition Foundation, 1990–5.

Paul Johnson said he'll vote for Tom King in his own constituency because he is a jolly good constituency MP.

But he still wants Blair to win the nation.

I said, 'I think many of your articles are silly and not balanced. But when you come to write a book you are absolutely spot on, objective, factual and brilliant. I don't know how on earth you do all this work.'

'I get up at six every morning and I write on for ten hours or more in the day.' He has to fit his articles in as well. There never has been such diligence in a writer. He says he can write six thousand words a day. 'Maybe that's not quite as good as Trollope who wrote a thousand words an hour,' to which Paul reasonably replied, 'Yes but that was fiction and it was easier to do.'

Petronella sat next to jolly John Prescott. He got very drunk. He said he hated Blair and the people around him. 'They insist on coaching me to talk grammatically and "posh" and I don't want to speak grammatically.' When I went over to talk to him he was still going on about it. I said, 'You do it like Ernie Bevin did. It's all perfectly coherent.' But the poor chap has lost confidence. They've taken it away from him and he loathes the Mandelson group.

Thursday 23 November
Peter Jones came at five o'clock.

He said he would do the job full-time and give up his American interests, disposing of them in one form or another. I said, 'You don't have to give everything up. As far as I'm concerned, the Tote is forty hours a week and I'm dealing with it at weekends as well. Maybe sometimes it's more than forty hours a week.'

I am reasonably confident he'll do it all right despite the warnings from Peter Mead that he is not really tough in a fight.

Went to the Redfern Gallery at 20 Cork Street.

I wanted to see the musical boxes Andrew Sinclair has been making. The cheapest was £400. Really I don't think they're worth it because they collapse so easily.

But they are very ingenious with lots of flashing lights and music and very well designed.

Petronella came too. They made the three of us group together in a photograph put into the *Hello!* magazine. I was feeling in a good mood about Petronella – she is the star of the family.

It was then to The Other Club at the Savoy.

Lord Aldington (Toby Low) was in the Chair.[15]

It was one of the jolliest evenings I can remember. Ken Clarke was sitting on the right of Toby Low and on his right was Robert Carr (Lord), a former very wet Home Secretary who was bombed by the Red Brigade at home. (I was next on the list. They had a map of Devonshire Street where I was living at the time and the trial jury were asked whether they had any pro or anti feelings about me.)

Before dinner there had been a discussion about Diana. Some actually supported her.

Talking quietly, Martin Charteris said he thought she was very dangerous.

I said I thought she needs a bit of kindness until the sensation is over. He replied, 'That is exactly what is happening.'

I said, 'Of course she is sick mentally and really unbalanced.' 'That's been the trouble all along.' 'But she had a shrewd point about her marriage being a bit crowded with three in it.'

'Do you think there should be a divorce?' 'I think it's inescapable, even though she doesn't want one.'

All were shocked about the Hewitt affair. It's not on the same level as the Camilla one. At least Prince Charles hadn't fallen for a woman with no mentality just because she had a beautiful body.

On the other side of Bernard Levin was Max Hastings. He, thank God, has seen through Blair, but still doesn't think much of Major.

Ken Clarke said, 'My views are well known about Europe.' I said, 'Yes. I hope one day you'll modify them. You appear to be not so hot on it as you were.' 'Well, I'm keen on standing up for British interests.'

Ken Clarke is one of those who thinks the Tories won't win the next election.

Friday 24 November

After pressure from both Verushka and Mrs Tamborero I very much modified my attacks on Diana, having begun by saying she was a schizophrenic. I decided to couch it in a gentler tone, thinking particularly of what Martin Charteris had said to me.

---

15. (1914–2000); Conservative MP, 1945–62; chairman, GEC, 1964–8, deputy chairman, 1968–84; life peer 1962.

Saturday 25 November

I had a nice letter from A. L. Rowse apropos of what I wrote about Gladwyn.[16]

John Saumarez Smith from Heywood Hill's told me that as a result of my enthusiastic review they had sold a hundred copies of the Gladwyn diaries by Gladwyn's wife.

A hundred copies of that expensive type of book (£25) being sold already is pretty good for a little bookshop like that.

I am still worried as to why I can't get through to John Major.

Sunday 26 November

At ten past one John Major rang up. He apologized profusely for not being able to get back to me.

I told him how the new incumbents, Les Hinton, in charge of News International here, and Philip Hall, the new *News of the World* editor, had said I was to write my column only once a fortnight. 'Oh my goodness,' he said.

I said, 'I had a tremendous row with Rupert about it. Finally I made him agree.'

John was much relieved that I have still got my weekly column.[17]

I told him about Petronella losing her *Sunday Telegraph* column and how Dominic Lawson had replaced [her] the first week by Alastair Campbell, Blair's public relations officer.

I said, 'I may be seeing Vere Rothermere in Paris. I'll have another go at him. He's been fairly OK.'

When we finished talking I thought how silly I am. I'm as neurotic as Petronella and Diana. Just because he was so busy he couldn't answer my calls or speak to me I thought something had gone wrong.

Cita and Irwin enjoyed themselves very much at All Souls.

At the little dinner party at All Souls had been Portillo.

Portillo brought with him David Hart, that terrible adventurer whom I have mentioned often in the diary.[18] He was boasting that he

---

16. WW reviewed in the *Times* of 14 November 1995 *The Diaries of Cynthia Gladwyn* edited by Miles Jebb; Cynthia, née Noble, d 1990, m (1929) Gladwyn Jebb (1900–96; former Ambassador, Deputy Leader, Liberal Party, House of Lords, 1965–88; life peer 1960). Rowse thought Gladwyn was second-rate intellectually not to see that General de Gaulle was a great historic figure.

17. WW seems not to have realized that the stay of the axe was only temporary.

18. David Hart was Portillo's special adviser at this time.

settled the miners' strike. Silly ass. I told Irwin the truth, how the working miners had asked me to get him off their backs because he was making a mess of it all.

When Portillo told Irwin that the Tories would lose the next election, and that Major would have to go, he said that Mrs Shephard[19] would be Leader because she was the only one capable of beating Labour. I said, 'I told you he has no political judgement. The man's a clown. They would never ever make her Leader. If they did, they'd be out for ten years.'

Monday 27 November

There had been turmoil as to whether the Eurostar train would go because of strikes in all trains and public services in Paris. Louise MacBain kindly sent a car to meet us at the Gare du Nord.

We went back to the charming hotel which once belonged to Duc de Saint-Simon. (Duc de Saint-Simon, 1675–1775, at one time a very rich courtier of Louis XIV, he died bankrupt and is best known for his memoirs, particularly his descriptions of Court life.)

We had to leave very early for Versailles.

The crush was enormous, perhaps fifteen hundred people. There was nothing to drink to begin with.

Eventually, over an hour late, the grand party arrived. Mme Chirac was there but the French President was evidently unable to come. I couldn't see why she, at least, couldn't have been on time, but in France the heads of government, as in the days of the old kings, have never heard of the maxim 'punctuality is the politeness of princes'.

We should have been in the Opéra Royale by 8.30 but of course we were not there until 9.30. However, we did get champagne *en route*.

In the concourse was Alexander of Yugoslavia. I said, 'Things don't look too good for a return by you now.'

He thought he could have become King of Serbia at least but he wanted to be king of the whole place.

I rather like Louise MacBain, our hostess. She and her husband took us back together in their car to our hotel – both very pleasant. She is the real brain though he is not without one himself. They are a very good team and created this vast empire, International Exchange and Mart.

---

19. Gillian Shephard, Conservative MP since 1987, at this time Secretary of State for Education and Employment.

She seems brassy on top but has a very soft centre, like many enormously capable businesswomen.

Wednesday 29 November
We assembled for the great gathering of peers and MPs in the Royal Gallery to hear Clinton.

As Clinton proceeded it was clear why Churchill's daughter and two grandsons were in the front row. He gave tremendous praise for what we had done in the War.

Clinton's speech, I felt, was strongly helpful to Major in trying to get peace in Northern Ireland, for which he praised John as the architect.

I was far more impressed than I thought I would be.

In the evening, as a dutiful new colonial, I went to hear Republican Jack Kemp, also in town, at the annual ARCO dinner.[20]

There were Margaret T, Ted Heath, Arnold Weinstock, several Cabinet Ministers, and some from the Royal Household. I thought Jack Kemp spoke rather well about free trade markets, free enterprise and the colossal developments in communications.

Margaret asked me what I thought of Clinton's speech in the morning. I said, 'Pretty good on the whole and effective in backing John in the peace process.' She wagged her finger at me, very cross. 'Woodrow, you're too old to be taken in by that man. There he was, saying how marvellous we'd been in the War and they were naming an ultra-modern, missile-carrying destroyer SS *Winston Churchill*. And all the time I was thinking, you're nothing but a draft dodger and a coward.' 'Perhaps he's undergone a conversion.' 'He's only trying to get the Irish-American vote and doesn't mean anything he says.' I thought that somewhat over the top, and said so.

---

20. US based chemical and petrochemical company; Jack Kemp was a Republican contender in the 1988 presidential election.

Friday 1 December

At about seven o'clock the ghastly Philip Hall rang, saying that the system of writing only once a fortnight was going to come into operation on January 5th. I said, 'What on earth do you mean?' He said, 'Rupert said you've agreed it.' 'I've done nothing of the sort.'

He said, 'We haven't enough room. We might get some in July.'

Rupert does play an extraordinarily dirty game. I don't know what he thinks he's up to. He's such a coward. He'll never tell you anything unpleasant to your face.

Hall kept telling me how good my column is. I said, 'Then why do you want to drop it?' 'I want to do this. I'm the editor and that's what I feel I wish to do.' But he couldn't if Rupert didn't agree.

Irwin and Cita again came to dinner.

I said to Irwin, 'He doesn't seem to value what I did for him. I had all the rules bent for him over the *Sunday Times* and the *Times* when he bought them. Because of the strikes the *Sunday Times* was at that time losing a bomb, and so was the *Times*. Through Margaret I got it arranged that the deal didn't go to the Monopolies Commission which almost certainly would have blocked it.'

We discussed Rupert's almost coming out for Blair, and practically telling him he's going to because he thinks he's going to win the election anyway, even if he doesn't come out for him; he's got Blair not to mention the way he makes his money all over the world and pays a different tax rate (which is not tax evasion but tax avoidance), and not to mention the possible reference of the BSkyB to the Monopolies Commission. You won't be able to get any of Rupert's programmes in England through an aerial unless you pay money to Rupert up front. This is about a little black box.[1] That is a clear monopoly. Blair has ordered his shadow trade and industry secretary not to mention it and not to refer to it, although he wanted to at first.

---

1. At this time it was proposed to sell the 'black box' equipment necessary to view digital programmes.

I said, 'I've never heard of such a thing in my life. It is in order to get Rupert to be favourable to him and for his papers at least not to attack Blair so much. That is the basic reason why they don't want me to write my article every week.'

Dear Irwin said he would speak to Rupert about my position again.

I am really worried though in case Irwin puts himself into a difficult position. I said, 'I'm afraid it is a case of power corrupts and absolute power corrupts absolutely. He's surrounded by nothing by yes-men. I never will be one and never have been.'

Cita and Irwin both said Rupert would give me a tremendous pay-off if I ever went.

'I don't want a pay-off. I want the platform.'

Sunday 3 December
Petronella was the only woman at the lunch for people from the *Telegraph* and the *Spectator* at Chequers.

When they went, they all stood in a line as Petronella went by. She kissed everybody there. John Major said, 'You're kissing all my Cabinet. When am I going to get mine?' so she gave him one too. She had a great success. She loved every minute of it. She's a highly political girl, that.

Thursday 14 December
Roy Jenkins, who was in the chair at The Other Club, is very affable to me now.

Before dinner began I had a jolly conversation with John Mortimer. He asked me whether I saw Jane [McKerron] much. I said, 'Not often. I speak to her on the telephone. I thought Ben was very good as Martin Chuzzlewit.'[2]

Brian Walden lives in the Channel Islands now and hardly ever comes to London. He's made a lot of money on the stock exchange. 'But what I like about him is that he's completely honest. When he was a Labour MP he openly said he was getting £5,000 a year from the bookmakers, which was a lot of money in those days.'

John is not enamoured of Blair. He thinks he's dodgy and gone too far away from socialist principles, not a bit like Kinnock whom John had a great friendship with. He also thinks his wife is terrible.

---

2. Ben Walden, actor, son of Jane McKerron by her former marriage to Brian Walden.

Sunday 17 December
Had a long talk with John [Major].

I told him what had happened between Rupert and myself – the reverse of what Rupert said to me when he was in London.

Monday 18 December
For the Prince Michael dinner (December 13th), wandering in the dark, I went to the wrong door. A Philippine servant greeted me.

He huffed and puffed and went off to go upstairs and then showed me to a lavatory, or what he called the rest room. It had a marvellous door on it, with a lavatory and chain and animals and so on in *trompe l'oeil*. Very realistic. I came out puzzled. I hadn't remembered seeing all this in Michael's household, nor the objects in the hall. The servant then came back and said, 'She'll come down in a moment but she's not having a dinner party.' I had got into Princess Margaret's house by mistake. 'Oh, please tell her I am very sorry to have disturbed her. I mistook the house,' and dashed off.

I sat next to Evelyn de Rothschild. He said did I remember talking to him about Norman Lamont.

'He seems to be well tied up with some other people so it's a convenient moment not to renew his contract.' I don't think it's going to damage Norman too much.

Wednesday 20 December
We have just won the case John Brown [William Hill] brought against us for a judicial review of our raising the Tote Authority [fee].

The judge found on all four issues raised that we were completely right, as I knew he would. Not only that, he refused leave to appeal and has awarded us the costs, so William Hill have to pay £250,000, or thereabouts, and they have no money at all.

We had a dinner party. Cita and Irwin Stelzer, Alex de Gelsey and his wife who is charming, John Stevens the Euro MP, and Margaret Ann Du Cane (Viscountess Stuart of Findhorn) came at the last moment because Diane Lever suddenly couldn't because she was unwell; Alastair Goodlad (the Chief Whip), Petronella, Maurice Saatchi and his wife, Andrew Roberts and his wife.

I like Maurice Saatchi very much. He seems a very gentle, intelligent, sophisticated soul. Later I asked Nicholas should I buy some of his shares.

Nicholas said no.

Goodlad is fairly cagey but he does remain confident of winning.

Thursday 21 December
Pericles has sent me a lovely tie which he thoughtfully picked out.

If the Wyatt Steak House continues on present form, it could do reasonably well. He is such a nice boy. He is the only one who never asks for money. He is pleased I sent him $150 'so you can have a decent meal in another restaurant', which amused him.

I enjoyed the family Christmas dinner on Friday. The two children are adorable.

They loved all my little toys, the exploding fireworks and the bombs that went off from the middle of the table, showering gifts, and the stink bombs to infuriate their mother with and so forth.

Caroline looks very drawn and tense. She is much thinner and looking almost haggard. She says it's because she has to work so hard in the City and it's not a fair deal for women there. She has to be twice as good as any man around, and at the same time she has to come home and do all the housework and put the children to bed. 'Why don't you have a nanny?' 'I've got one but I don't want my children to be brought up by nannies. I read to them before they go to bed.'

Petronella is very good with the children who adore her and think she is the most wonderful aunt in the world.

Friday 22 December
Rupert fell off his boat, or nearly did. He cut the top off his finger which had to be sewn on again. He was in the yacht practising for a race in Australia. Irwin can't quite find out what's happened to him, except that he is going back on to the yacht for the race. 'My God, he may be drowned.' 'You mean like Maxwell?' 'I don't put Rupert in the same class as Maxwell,' I said.

Saturday 23 December
By hand was delivered from Buckingham Palace a letter from Queen Elizabeth the Queen Mother. What an extraordinary woman, so active in her mind and apparently not at all disturbed by after-effects of her dangerous and painful operation from which she is fast recovering. She said she would like me to come for a quiet lunch in the New Year. Obviously she would like to talk to me about the monarchy and the Queen's decision to write to Princess Diana and Prince Charles, saying they have to divorce now, and what flows from it.

Sunday 24 December
I was thumbing my way through Denton Welch's journals,[3] sent to me
by its editor as one of those who had published him (in *English Story*).

As I wandered on through the book, I found that shortly before he
died, Denton Welch had been listening to me talking on the BBC about
books. I had said I thought he was one of the two or three currently
most interesting writers. This had delighted him.

I was very moved, thinking of that dear, tragic young man.

Monday 25 December
There has been much frost, particularly overnight, even a little in our
sheltered garden.

It is extremely unlikely that there will be any racing on Boxing Day,
December 26th. This is tragic. It is one of our biggest and best days.

Tuesday 26 December
Irwin and Cita came to dinner. Cita had watched the Midnight Mass
on Christmas Eve at Lichfield Cathedral. I told her that all the great
ornamental work and rearrangements were by James Wyatt.

Irwin is a wonderfully intelligent thinker. But he doesn't want to
come with Cita and myself to look at the Soho Museum or to go
to Lichfield Cathedral and the little church at Weeford. He says it takes
his mind off more important things. Cita and I said, 'But you will
enjoy it.' 'Maybe, but it would serve no purpose.' I said, 'It would. It
would make you think wider and put even more inventiveness into
your work.'

Wednesday 27 December
A lady came from the BBC to record a sound broadcast about why I
left my party. She was called Trixie. She was tall and rather pretty with
fair hair, nice hands, nice narrow face – immensely friendly. To her
first question – 'What was the straw that broke my back with regards
to the Labour Party?' – I replied, 'It was a haystack, not a straw.'

---

3. (1915–48); writer, severely injured in a bicycle accident at the age of twenty; WW
   may be referring to a reprint of his 1943 autobiography *Maiden Voyage* or of his
   posthumous *A Voice Through A Cloud*.

Friday 29 December

Gloomily I wrote my last but one weekly article for my page in the *News of the World* which I've had for thirteen years.

My writing of weekly columns began in national newspapers in *Reynolds News* in 1949. That came to an end in 1961 when *Reynolds News* collapsed. I was interrupted from writing it during 1951 when I was Under Secretary at the War Office. It was Hugh Cudlipp in 1965 who asked me what I was going to do now I was not in the Labour government. I said, 'Write a book.' Hugh said, 'That's a waste of time. Write a column in the *Mirror.* You'll have far more influence.' So I wrote in the *Daily Mirror* from 1965 to 1973, and in the *Sunday Mirror* from 1973 to 1983, when I began writing my weekly articles in the *News of the World* and also my fortnightly column in the *Times.* I fell out with the *Mirror* because I was heartily opposed to Labour by 1974 and they couldn't stomach my continually attacking Labour.

I try not to be bitter at Rupert who promised me I could go on writing so long as I wanted to and was writing OK.

In the evening Sonia and Andrew Sinclair came to dinner and to play a little bridge. Andrew has turned right against Blair and is now, to my amazement, in favour of John Major. That is surprising considering his long flirtation with Labour and of voting Labour in the past. Sonia remains very much a part of my life after forty years or more.

I must have met her in about 1947, when she married Julian.

I often think of my dear friend Julian Melchett, tragically struck down by a heart attack in Majorca in 1973. He was subject to heart trouble all his life through a hereditary gene, but at least he got British Steel into profit for the only time during its period of nationalization.

Saturday 30 December

I took down an orchid to Bowden. Arnold heard about it, 'Why was that brought?' Netta replied that she always kept Verushka's orchids here. They were treated and sent back to London when they were in good order. Arnold said quite seriously, 'What rent does she pay?'

1996

Monday 1 January
We, including Petronella, went down to Sussex to have a New Year's Day lunch with Maurice Saatchi and his Irish wife.

The Keswicks had come all the way from Oare that morning. Tessa asked what I thought about the new divorce bill.

She said, 'It makes it easier to divorce and destroys family values.' I said, 'It always was easy to divorce. I was first divorced during the war when I was twenty-three or twenty-four.' 'But you had plenty of money and you could get a divorce with that.' 'I did not.'

She said, 'It's no good talking to you. We always disagree.' I thought, my God, I suppose that's true.

Still, I like her and she's pretty.

I didn't like to mention to Henry that Major hadn't fulfilled his promise to give him a knighthood. I wonder whether it was Chris Patten who had turned against him.

Another thing which may have been against Henry was the mess they have all made of Trafalgar House, losing money like billy-o – and also their moving their headquarters off shore.

Maurice Saatchi will evidently have a big part in devising Tory policy again.

He has a fabulous house, that fellow.

He has the thickest padded carpet (white) on the floor, corridors and stairs I have ever walked on.

He was very interested in Irwin Stelzer. I told how he was Rupert's great adviser on economics generally and on his business but he's no yes-man.

He has got a soul, quite a good one in its way, Maurice Saatchi, though he went cockeyed at one time with megalomania, trying to buy banks and over-spending on goodness knows what. I was amused by the title of his new advertising vehicle, Megalomedia. Maurice has a sense of humour.

Tuesday 2 January
In the morning I talked to John Major.

On Rupert I said, 'What upsets him about the Broadcasting Bill is that it turns him into a foreigner, plus the cross-media stuff. He's not a foreigner as far as Britain is concerned. All these gadgets and the instant communication he is inventing are developed here and they go out throughout the world. He thinks it's not sane to stop him doing them from here because we'd lose a great deal of exports as a result and he would lose his business. I think you could look at that again.' He wasn't very friendly about it but I said, 'It's worth doing because that's what his real beef is.'

He said he didn't know the man from the *Sunday Times*, John Witherow.[1] I said, 'I will make arrangements for you to meet him.'

John said he thought Norman had written a very good article in the *News of the World*. 'I have no malice about him. But whenever I see him in the lobby or in the House he always turns away and walks in the other direction. I wish he wouldn't.' I think if Norman were sensible, he could make it up with John. John has already told me that in no way are they trying to block him getting a seat. John thinks he ought to be in the House.

When I told John that Arnold had bet me £100 to £250 that he would win, John said, 'I must win your bet for you, Woodrow.' I should have said Arnold wanted to lose the bet.

Wednesday 3 January
My article was put in the *Times* today, not yesterday. In the evening Peter Stothard, the editor, rang. He wanted to tell me how moved he had been by it and he knew lots of people would be made very happy by it.[2]

Friday 5 January
Had a row with Philip Hall, the editor of the *News of the World*. I had written as an intro, 'This is the last time the weekly Voice of Reason appears on this page. That is not by my choice. I have been told my column will in future be fortnightly and on a different page. Mr Blair is delighted. My column is the one he most fears.'

---

1. Editor, *Sunday Times*, since 1995.
2. WW wrote a lyrical article in praise of Britain for its beauty, its language and the civilizing properties of its games.

He got into a complete rage. 'I never wanted you to do the column again when we came to have lunch with you. I said I didn't want you to write any more.' I said, 'You never said anything of the sort. You said it was going to go fortnightly. I am afraid you are not very accurate with the things you report.' 'You went straight away from that lunch and rang up Rupert Murdoch.' 'Yes. I'm entitled to.' He said, 'That's why you've still got it fortnightly.' 'Maybe.' 'The *News of the World* has done you very well.' I said, 'I've done them very well, too.' He asked me to take out the intro. 'I'll ring you back,' I told Hall.

I decided I didn't want another row.

I learned that the appalling Alan Clark is now to take over my column. It will be full of inaccuracies. Although he was in the government, he never understood anything about politics. Of course, his 'morals' are better suited for the *News of the World*.

I am still wondering whether to call Vere Rothermere, or Piers Morgan even at the *Mirror*, to find out whether I can do a column on the weeks I am not doing one for the *News of the World*.

Geoffrey Owen and Miriam came to dinner. To my surprise he was dead against the Lottery, taking a very narrow, puritanical view that it has been bad for people.

I said, 'Did you know the Westminster Bridge was built by a lottery?' He didn't know that. 'That was a one-off. If you have a lottery this size it is really indecent.'

However, Geoffrey is a very agreeable chap and we had an entertaining dinner.

Saturday 6 January

I am pretty low. I hope I shall have sufficient resilience to shake off the loss of my weekly column. Verushka said, 'Why don't you say you are only doing it fortnightly because you are writing a book?' I said, 'I am not very good at lying in that way and I don't want to start being a liar now.'

I went to Sandown.

Wakeham was there with his pleasant wife and nice little son.

In an interview in the *Sporting Life* yesterday, he said it was not the time for the BHB to try to take the Tote over.

That is a great relief to everybody in our staff, and to me because I can't bear to think of chumps from outside thinking they know how to run the Tote and then ruining it. Wakeham was good enough to say that the Tote is a very well-run business and helps racing a lot. It was the first time I'd had such a nice compliment from anybody in the BHB, of which he is now the Chairman.

Tristram Ricketts[3] was surprisingly agreeable. Conciliation seems to be the order of the day.

We had dinner with Irwin and Cita at an excellent new restaurant called The Avenue in St James's Street, tucked away between Locks, the hatters, and Berry Bros.

I have to get my weight down. I have now gone up to 11 stone 5 pounds, which is really terrifying. I also have something strange in my throat or gullet or windpipe. It's been hurting for a couple of days. I can't seem to get rid of it.[4]

Irwin said Rupert couldn't understand why the government and Major were being so beastly to him. 'Can't you? He's been absolutely foul to Major, telling everyone he's rubbish in his newspapers.'

I said, 'They wouldn't allow anybody in America to buy up all the press and media.' 'Oh yes they would.' 'That is not the case, as you know very well. Rupert had to become an American in order to have television at the same time as owning newspapers.'

He's a brilliant man, Irwin. I love him dearly. But he goes over the top a bit in his violence against anybody who threatens Rupert's interest, although he himself concedes that Rupert has too much power.

Sunday 7 January
I couldn't even bear even to open the *News of the World*.

But I am working on making myself less down-hearted and back to my usual optimism.

Tuesday 9 January
The Lords discusses the BBC Charter. The government announces that Duke Hussey is to take early retirement. He is replaced by Sir Christopher Bland who made a mint of money in independent television.[5] He has been a regulator for the ITC (Independent Television Commission). He is a solidly right-wing Tory. The government has pulled a fast one on the Opposition. However, Donoughue, speaking

---

3. Chief Executive, BHB, since 1993.
4. This is WW's only mention in 1996 of trouble with his throat, though he often reports digestive problems.
5. Chairman, Life Sciences International, since 1995, London Weekend Television, 1984–94; Conservative member of the GLC, 1967–70; knight 1993.

for the Opposition in the Lords said he welcomed the appointment provided he remembers though he is a Tory he has to keep the balance properly.

A dinner party at 86 Eaton Square given by Patricia Rawlings in advance of the Astor ball at the Savoy. I arrived a little late from waiting to hear the end of the one-day cricket match in South Africa.

Patricia Rawlings and her paramour, Paul Zuckerman,[6] live in a beautifully decorated flat on the ground floor. Plenty of rooms for each and an office. Patricia, though now fifty-seven, whom I have known for the last thirty years or so, still looks attractive. She takes the trouble to shave off much of the superfluous hair which dimmed her attractions.

She is intelligent and supports Major. I rather like her and always did.

I said to Paul Zuckerman that I thought his father's infidelities hadn't upset his mother. He said, 'You are quite wrong. She was consumed with jealousy and hated all his affairs, those that were secret and the ones which were more or less public. It was not a happy marriage.' I said, 'She is very happy now with her painting, is she not?' 'Yes, she is. She had a fearful lot to put up with from my father.' He was very fond of his father. I told him how fond I was of him, too.

The noise at the Astor ball at the Savoy was the ultimate in decibels.

Thursday 11 January
Off to Warburg's to hear Margaret's Keith Joseph Memorial Lecture. It was brilliant, though as usual with her a trifle selective in memory. She did not attack Major, as all the newspapers said she would. She urged the strongest support for him, stressing the alternative of Blair and the horror of permanent damage to the country.

She saw me on the way out. To the astonishment of those around, she came over to give me a smacking great kiss. I whispered in her ear, 'It was brilliant and it was true.' She was very pleased. I gave her another kiss.

Saturday 13 January
I have been striving hard for News International, sending out masses of letters to peers and others, trying to persuade them to come to our

---

6. Son of WW's friend Lord Zuckerman (Solly).

great reception and to discuss the absurdities which penalize Rupert in the Broadcasting Bill.

Sunday 14 January

Irwin has been helping me prepare for the article which I have to write on Monday for the *Times*. He has given me lots of figures and he has been showing me where to find more, to destroy the idiotic claim of Tony Blair that Britain has sunk from thirteenth to eighteenth place in the world prosperity league.

Tuesday 16 January

Irwin thought my article in the *Times* was terrific. He complained that he was supposed to be the economist, not me.

In the evening there was a curious dinner party given by the Quintons at the Garrick Club. It was a cramped room. Quite pretty with nice pictures of actors and so forth. The principal guests were Princess Alexandra plus Angus Ogilvy. I sat with Viscountess Norwich on my left. Her Christian name is Mollie. She used to be married to Hugo Philipps. He succeeded his father, Wogan, as the third Baron Milford. An old family – baronets in 1621.

Wogan was a Communist, the first Communist peer to sit in the Lords.[7] He was at one point my previous wife Moorea's stepfather. Wogan had married Cristina (after her divorce from Jack Huntingdon), the Communist daughter of the Marchese Casati, from whom Pericles is descended. For his third marriage Wogan married a Russian, Tamara, widow of William Rust who edited the *Daily Worker*. She was a Russian champion athlete, quite a pleasant woman, small and dark with a lithe figure.

Wogan was one of the biggest bloody fools I ever met. He had been taken up by the very left Bloomsbury set. His first wife was Rosamond Lehmann whom I used to know quite well when she sat on the council of the Society of Authors with me. She was a very handsome woman, despite bad legs, but slightly batty, though I think never a Communist. She wrote excellent novels.

Wogan's son Hugo's first wife was Margaret Heathcote, daughter of a man who played cricket for Hampshire.

She used to be very beautiful. She had a long affair with Alan Ross who was a pretty good writer and poet. This ensured a general muddle

---

7. (1902–93); he stood for Parliament as a Communist in 1950.

all round. I remember dancing with her years ago when I had not long been married to Moorea. She was extremely pretty and flirtatious.

About Diana, Princess Alexandra said that she was not only mad but evil wickedness incarnate. That, coming from the gentle soul which the Princess Alexandra is, must be pretty convincing.

Thursday 18 January
A visit to Peter Davis, the Director General of OFLOT. We broached the idea of an alternative lottery. I said, 'We would not be trying to crowd out Camelot but would want to work with them. We would have a lottery with much smaller prizes and also a numbers game. The prizes from time to time would be of the million mark but they wouldn't be gigantic prizes which have been greatly criticized by all the do-gooders.' He was not unhelpful but said we would have to use the Camelot facilities. He said he would ring them.

Wednesday 24 January
I had written to about a hundred and fifty peers a letter in which I carefully explained my position [vis-à-vis News International]. Quite a few came [to the meeting]. Irwin was masterly.

Jane Reed[8] read her presentation extremely well.

One of the issues is sport. Another is digital broadcasting.

I remarked at one point, 'Maybe Rupert could go to the European Court of Human Rights.' Everybody laughed, knowing how much I hate Brussels.

Friday 26 January
Caught the 2.23 train from Waterloo to Paris.

Hôtel Trémoille is a Forte hotel.

Verushka thought it nowhere near so good as the Duc de Saint-Simon where we had been staying lately in Paris. But it was cheaper and had been arranged by Charles Churchill before the take-over of Forte by Granada.

We were fetched by Luc de la Barre de Nanteuil. He was a great friend when he was Ambassador in London.

Hedwige now seems fully recovered from the cancer which nearly killed her. With that art readily available to women, she looks almost

---

8. Director of Corporate Affairs, News International, since 1989.

as young as when they were in London. She is charming and full of fun.

We went to a restaurant called Récamier, my having insisted they were to be our guests.

The food was first class. It has a star in the Michelin Guide.

Luc said the government were in a terrible mess.

Chirac is a great disappointment, not seeming to know what to do or where he is going or where France is going or should go.[9]

Sunday 28 January

Verushka very sweetly did all my packing for me before we left the hotel to go to the Prix d'Amerique.

At the race meeting, suffice it to say that the operation is so inefficient compared with the Tote that they didn't pay out on the winners of the big race until the next race was over. There would have been a riot if we had done that in England.

Tuesday 30 January

Jane Reed asked me to lead a little group with Cecil Parkinson and perhaps one other to see John Major to see if we can't get this business of turning Rupert into a foreigner and so forth ended. She had asked John Wakeham if he would be willing to join the delegation but he said no.

I am trying to get Harris of High Cross who might carry some weight.

Wednesday 31 January

Went to a meeting of the Lords Broadcasting Group. Not all of them are friendly to Rupert.

William Astor is very insistent that 'he shouldn't have all these newspapers.' I said, 'Your family tried once to get as big a circulation as they could for the *Observer*, didn't they?' 'Yes.' 'Well, you're saying now we've all got to come down to the circulation levels of the *Observer* by writing as boringly as we can so that Rupert's papers won't exceed the new cut-off point of twenty per cent of national newspaper circulation disqualifying him from owning terrestrial TV.'

---

9. WW wrote his *Times* article of 30 January about the situation in France.

Friday 2 February
Petronella is having a great triumph today. She has done an enormous article opposite the editorial page in the *Daily Telegraph* – her interview with Douglas Hurd. The photograph taken by *Telegraph* photographers showed her laughing and so was old Douglas who always had a yen for Petronella. The interview itself was extremely amusing and penetrating. She writes better and better, that girl, while thinking she can't write at all.

Saturday 3 February
The three of us went down to Sandown in the bitter cold.

Petronella sat next to Andrew Parker Bowles whom she likes very much. They flirted away.

Throughout the whole of his marriage to Camilla he was habitually chasing women and having affairs, whereas she evidently had only one, and that was with Prince Charles. He was no cuckold, save to the public.

My Quadpot is a triumphant success as everybody now admits.

We're going to ride through this terrible year for betting organizations far higher than all the others.[1] They're dropping their profits enormously whereas we are not.

Since taking the special pill at night from Professor Pounder at the Royal Free, I have lost what I regarded as the hole in my chest or lungs, and don't have anything like so much heartburn. I do it, too, with the aid of the wonderful charcoal tablets produced according to an old English recipe by J. L. Braggs. Professor Pounder said I wasn't to take them because he doesn't approve of homeopathic remedies, but I do and it helps.

---

1. WW said in his Tote speech of 5 March 1996 that the winter had been the worst for racing since 1986, with 86 meetings abandoned between 1 April 1995 and the end of February 1996.

Monday 5 February
Had a longish talk with John Major.[2]

When I said, 'It's all going our way and you are going to win, I'm certain,' he said, 'I feel that, too. We'll have a great celebration when it happens and you must come to it.' 'Do you mean for all those people who never doubted you were going to pull it off?' 'No. That would mean only you and I would be present,' and he laughed.

Tuesday 6 February
In the House I was the only person to make a defence of Rupert's position, apart from a brief reference from dear old Willie Whitelaw.[3]

There was uproar as I spoke. It was a case of Daniel among the lions. But I enjoyed it and gave as good as I got, using more or less impromptu notes.

In the Moses Room I was asked to speak second at the memorial meeting for Arthur Bottomley. As I loved him, it was fairly easy in a sense but I had to write up my notes and compress them while the first speaker was on.

At the back I saw Tony Benn standing.

He didn't look furiously at me as he usually does.

Wednesday 7 February
Before the Tote Board meeting I sent a message to John Major via his Political Secretary suggesting a compromise over the sports issue could be for the BBC to be allowed and encouraged to get sponsors who would pay a competitive price for events which the BBC wanted. They do have sponsored concerts; I can't see why they shouldn't have sponsored sporting events.

On the way to Camelot with John Heaton I had a message from Mrs Tamborero that Les Hinton, in charge of News International, wanted to speak to me.

To my astonishment Les Hinton answered the telephone saying, 'This is the man from Liverpool.' We both laughed. He has some sort of a sense of humour.

---

2. WW told Murdoch in his bulletin of 6 February that he had set the scene for Murdoch's meeting with the Prime Minister on 12 January: 'You should get roughly what you want.'

3. Lord Howell had moved an amendment to the Broadcasting Bill to prevent pay-per-view channels acquiring exclusive rights to televise live sporting events.

'I wanted to tell you how much we all appreciated, and Rupert particularly, your defence of him and Sky in the Lords, and what a wonderful speech you made. It needed saying. I read all the Hansard and what they said about Rupert was abominable.'

I took John Heaton up to the Peers' ante-room where Willie Whitelaw buttonholed me.

Willie was outrageously indiscreet about Margaret, Portillo, the Tory wets, disloyal mutineers against Major like crazy Redwood, too pushy and pleased with himself. I warned the astonished John not to repeat anything Willie had said.

I said to Tim Holley, Chief Executive of Camelot, the Lottery operators, and his sidekick that we were not trying to displace them as Lottery owners but perhaps deflect some of the criticism from them, by making it look as though they were willing to have competition. I also said we would be interested in having a share in Camelot or any new consortium they were concerned with when the next bidding comes along in five years' time.

They took that on board so maybe, after I have gone, the Tote can join a consortium even though it has to be with GTech, and make some money which would go to racing to offset its sufferings from the National Lottery.

After the meeting with Camelot I went to see Dermot Glynn [NERA]. They have been asked by the Centre for Policy Studies (the affair which Tessa Keswick is running) to do an analysis of how successful privatization has been. But they had only been able to raise some £15,000 or so. He said what is needed to do a really good job is at least £30,000. I said I would think of approaching Margaret because she has got this great fund which is supposed to be promoting her privatization ideals throughout the whole world.

Saturday 10 February
When I came back [from Newbury] I found to my horror that Petronella had been working in Mrs Tamborero's office. On the table beside her was a file of all my most utter secret memos to Rupert which she had forgotten to put away. Oh dear, security!

I cannot believe that Petronella, who is the nosiest person out, didn't read all those memos.

If she did read that stuff and leaks it anywhere, it will do me great damage and, incidentally, harm her mother who will be the chief beneficiary of the proceeds from the diaries (or memoirs as I call them as a cover story).

The winner of the Tote Gold Trophy is a Yorkshireman, called Robert Ogden. He is Chairman of the Harrogate Conservative Party who chose Norman.

I said, 'How did it go at the selection committee with Norman? I gather it was not unanimous.' He said, 'No, it wasn't, but he pulled it off by being very humble, admitting he had made mistakes.'

Monday 12 February

Had a long conversation just before dinner with Rupert. He said he was going to have a row with Major when he saw him. I said, 'Don't be so foolish. Use your boyish charms and win him over. I'm sure you can win on the sports front and I still believe you'll get much of what else you want. I hope you've noticed that Blair's men in the Lords have been attacking you hip and thigh.'

'Why were they so against me?' 'Surely you must realize that they smart and want revenge, particularly the Tories (and that's why they are combining with Labour), for all your exposures of their three-in-a-bed and somebody taking £1,000 to ask questions – and for calling them the sleaze party. Also your vilification of Major. Major especially didn't like your hounding his son.' Rupert replied, 'My son, Lachlan, is pursued everywhere.' 'Yes but not because he's having an affair with a woman older than himself who is senior to him in Marks & Spencer.' 'Oh, I don't think he'd do a thing like that.' 'Are you sure?' 'If he is doing that, he hasn't told me.' 'I don't suppose he would,' I said.

Wednesday 14 February

Rupert seemed surprised that Major had mastered all the details and intricacies of the Broadcasting Bill, with all the problems he has with Northern Ireland, Scott and so forth. I said, 'I've always told you he's a much under-rated man. He's extremely clever.'

He said on terrestrial TV the government were sticking rather to their guns on it, even though it's nonsensical.

Rupert said he thought Michael Heseltine doesn't seem quite so enthusiastic as Major to stick to the bargaining agreements they made.

I said, 'I've a wheeze that somebody, it could be me if you liked, who is absolutely British, could have a golden share which ostensibly controls News International's shareholding in Sky.' He said, 'There would be no need to do that because my boys have got British passports, and Pru is a British citizen, and lives here.'

He sounded very exuberant, on top of the world, which I was pleased to hear.

I think he was impressed by Major in a way he hadn't been before.

Thursday 15 February
The Other Club. I told Roy Jenkins I was annoyed with the BBC's methods in the programme about him. I had spent a lot of time looking things up, on the understanding that I would appear in the programme. They then told me they didn't want me.

Roy looked embarrassed (they had actually told me it was Jennifer [Jenkins] – who mysteriously hates me – who didn't want me to appear in it) and said, 'They told me you had been very kind about me.'

Friday 16 February
I've had another letter from 'the man from Liverpool' congratulating and thanking me for what I did for News International in the Committee stage of the Broadcasting Bill. The thanks I'd really like is getting my column back to weekly again. They put my fortnightly one on the gardening page.

Saturday 17 February
John Bowes Lyon was staying at the Wiltons.

He is always full of gossip and talked non-stop with John Wilton, their voices never ceasing as they discussed their friends and the various escapades they had been involved in.

John said that when Camilla Parker Bowles was due to get married to Andrew and they were hesitating, her parents were very keen that Andrew should marry her and suddenly they put a notice in the *Times* announcing their engagement. So Andrew thought that as it had been publicly announced he could not go back on it. Camilla was very much in love with him. But soon she found his roving eye rendered him repeatedly unfaithful to her and she began to resent the marriage and eventually, as is well known, wished to get out of it. Hence the affair with the Prince of Wales, but she never thought she would marry the Prince of Wales or, early on during it, that she would be divorced from Andrew.

Monday 19 February
Dinner party.

Both John Bowes Lyon and Jane Churchill were a great success. Jane was thought to be very pretty and much appreciated by the men like Vere Rothermere and the German Ambassador.[4] The German Ambassador was overwhelmed by the excitement of John Bowes Lyon being a close connection and favoured relation of Queen Elizabeth the Queen Mother whom John sees constantly.

Kenneth Baker was in a jolly mood, very cheerful. He is now convinced that Major will win the election.

Kenneth thinks Mawhinney is not right as Chairman of the Tory Party going into an election. He dislikes his voice, thinks he makes too many bloomers and doesn't attack on the right issues.

Mrs Baker sat on my right.[5] She is a teetotaller and a slight bore. She is clever and a very successful businesswoman. I find her slightly intimidating though she makes agreeable conversation.

On my left was Gail Lilley, very pleased at being asked to come to Porto Ercole again in the summer. She can be charming. I find it a puzzle that she so often treats Peter disdainfully in public. I can't make up my mind whether I think her pretty or not. She has a good figure but her face varies, maybe according to the make-up and hair arrangement she chooses. I like her.

After the women had gone into the drawing-room – Petronella with great annoyance as she regards herself as such a serious politician that she ought to be allowed to stay – I put the German Ambassador rather through the hoop. I asked him why Kohl had made this extraordinary remark about having to have a federal state and a single currency in order to prevent a war breaking out internally in the European Union.

The German Ambassador, Dr Jurgen Oesterhelt, is a very good arguer – I liked his staunch defence of his country. He kept saying, 'You can't do without us. You have to be in this great union to protect yourselves from the forces roaming the world economically and militarily.'

I said, 'I want to be in an ordinary free trade area – and to join

---

4. Dr Jurgen Oesterhelt had succeeded Dr Peter Hartmann as German Ambassador in April 1995.
5. Mary, née Gray-Muir, m (1963) Kenneth Baker; non-executive director, Barclays Bank since 1989, Thames TV, 1975–90, Camelot Group, 1994–8.

NAFTA (the North American Free Trade Area: USA, Canada, Mexico).'

Afterwards Ken Baker said to me, 'All that dinner-table conversation will be going first thing in the morning off to Chancellor Kohl, lamenting that the British will never play a whole-hearted part in the European Union and will never accept economic domination by Germany through Brussels.'

One useful fact had emerged – Vere Rothermere's assurance that he will back Major.

Wednesday 21 February
A good Levy Board meeting.

I then proceeded to see *The Shakespeare Revue* with my lawyer. It was fabulously good, wonderfully amusing, beautifully performed, a laugh every half minute. I took her back to the Lords. The first person I saw there was Alun Chalfont. I had told him I couldn't attend the meeting on the Broadcasting Bill on the point about impartiality and so forth because I had a meeting with my lawyer. When I introduced her as my lawyer, he was totally startled and unbelieving because she looked very handsome and attractive. 'Your lawyer?' he inquired. 'Yes,' said Diana Rawstron.

It was then back to Cavendish Avenue to put on my dinner jacket.

We were the first to arrive at the Carlton Club and I saw Margaret, the guest of honour, following up the stairs behind us.

Dear old Willie Whitelaw, when the loyal toast had been given and a toast to her, waffled away.

I fear he was a little bit over the top.

After Margaret had made a few friendly remarks, he turned to me and asked had I got any comments to make.

When I was commending Major, Denis Thatcher, who was exceedingly drunk, kept shouting out, 'He's awful, he's weak, he's hopeless, he should be got rid of.'

I said, 'Well there's nobody else who could do it any better than him at the moment. We certainly can't change prime ministers now,' at which point Margaret said quite sharply, 'You must be quiet, Denis. Don't go on about what you think of John, whatever you may think privately. This is not the place to say it.'

No woman can be a member of that club, not even Margaret, which is utterly absurd, though there was a portrait of her.

I was happy that she did say yes, she would support Major as best she could but it might be counter-productive if she did it at the wrong moment. I knew exactly what she meant.

Monday 26 February
To dinner came early Cita and Irwin Stelzer, Larry and Susan Kessler,[6] Richard Ryder and Tony and Marcelle Quinton. This was the night of the motion on the adjournment on the Scott Report which Labour was so confident of winning. Richard said he would dash off fast to the Commons and return immediately to finish his dinner and tell us all about it.

I bet Irwin £10 that Major would win the vote tonight.

We heard on the news that the government had won by one. Irwin said we should have kept Richard Ryder here and stopped him voting, then the government wouldn't have won. I said, 'On the contrary, the rule is that the Speaker must give a casting vote in the event of a tie, to maintain the status quo which was the position of the government.'

Irwin paid up his debt of £10 to me with poor grace.

Tuesday 27 February
To lunch at Clarence House. Lashings of servants everywhere, as usual, and standing behind one's chair at luncheon. But she's worth every bit of the cost of cosseting her. I was on her right.

I told her I thought there was a whiff of republicanism in the air. She said she couldn't believe it after all the patriotic fervour and love for the monarchy there was during the VE and VJ celebrations.

She said she hoped now to come to Cheltenham to present the Tote Gold Cup, 'if Verushka doesn't mind'. I said, 'She'll be thrilled, as everybody else will be. It's only when you can't come that she steps in.' She said, 'How remarkably young she looks. It's extraordinary. I think she's got a Hungarian secret of how to make oneself look young.' 'Perhaps you've got the same secret, Ma'am.'

After lunch was over, and it didn't end until about a quarter to three, she was utterly charming. She showed pictures connected with her family and her husband's family, pointing out all the details.

There was a lovely Augustus John portrait of Bernard Shaw.

That morning I had rung Major.

I told him how Rothermere and the German Ambassador had been here to dinner.

---

6. Larry Kessler compiles the Zagat guide to London restaurants.

Thursday 29 February
I certainly got under Labour's skin with my article in the *Times* on
Tuesday about the virtues of privately run pension schemes. There was
a not very effective reply on Wednesday by Chris Smith.[7]

---

7. At this time chief Opposition spokesman on social security.

Tuesday 5 March

The Tote lunch at the Hyde Park Hotel was beautifully cooked and prepared and delivered at great speed by the waiters who had been bullied by Verushka, as the chefs had been.

John Prescott had been forbidden to come on the grounds that he had to face Heseltine at Prime Minister's Questions because the Prime Minister was away in the Far East. It is thought below Blair's dignity to question a mere Deputy Prime Minister, so Prescott was told he had to do it.

Prescott had told me he wanted to tell lots of jokes about his father who was very keen on betting and for whom he used to make rounds to the bookmaker.

I had a tiff with Michael Howard. He said we would have to carry out the Nolan recommendations requiring interviews by a panel with a Nolan nominee for candidates for the Board or Chairman, and no one, not even the Chairman, should serve for more than two years. I said, 'This is absolute nonsense. It doesn't have the force of law. It would ruin our business. No one could run a commercial enterprise like that.'

The weakness of Michael Howard is that he rushes at official papers, not giving himself time to understand them fully.

After a bit he said, 'I think I can see a way through. We must talk about it.'

I was pleased with Robin Cook, Prescott's replacement. He not only spoke brilliantly but gave me a great deal of help in saying the big bookmakers must join Tote Direct if they are going to get any sympathy from a Labour government.

Wednesday 6 March

Tote Board meeting.

Peter Jones was a little troublesome about his ideas for bets, wanting to have a straight forecast and to have a Tote bonanza bet with points allotted on Saturday mornings on Channel 4. I began to wonder whether he would be any good as Chairman.

Went down to the Lords. I asked a supplementary question about the dreadful Fayed brothers, ought they not to be chucked out of the country for their dishonesty and lying and cheating to get Harrods. This received murmurs of approval from some and of disapproval from others, including Lord Spens.[1]

He asked the original question saying why shouldn't the Fayeds now be given British citizenship.

Thursday 7 March

In the evening Netta and Arnold came to dinner. I gave them some delicious Sancerre, 1990. Even Arnold thought it was good.

When the ladies went into the drawing-room, poor Arnold told me, which nobody knows, that Simon [his son] three or four weeks ago had a fearful stroke and was paralysed in his right arm and left arm. He somehow managed to ring his father and said, 'I can't move. I can't think.' His head had gone and so had his body. He was whisked off to hospital where they said it had been a colossal brain haemorrhage.

Arnold said wistfully, 'His absence from the office is a great handicap. He is needed, because he knows a lot about various issues, by me and others. Yet they say it's only because he's my son that I want him to be managing director. He would have been a very good one.' I am not sure that Arnold is right about that, but certainly Simon is very able.

Arnold retires as managing director in a year, though he will be honorary president with a mild consultation role. He said, 'It's awful when one's been used to doing a job and being engrossed in it, and then to have it taken away from you. Don't you feel that?' I said, 'Yes, in a way. It occupies a great deal of my time, running the Tote and directing it. I am very keen on it, fascinated by it. It exercises my brain. But in some ways I don't mind turning my attention to writing more and trying to earn some money that way.'

I sent off my belated memo to Rupert. I'll have to keep this up or he might say he'll cut my salary.[2]

---

1. 3rd Baron Spens, chartered accountant.
2. As usual, WW summarized the events and conversations recorded in these memoirs.

Saturday 9 March
If Aston Villa win both cups and get to be third in the League, I shall collect several thousand from the bookmakers. This would be highly satisfactory as I am nervous about my running bet on the French franc with the City Index.

Monday 11 March
Church House for a debate organized on behalf of the Centre for Policy Studies by Tessa Keswick. She was looking very pretty, as I told her. She organized it all beautifully.

Easily the best speech was made by Rodney Leach, that Europe needed us far more than the other way round.

At Boritshka Karolyi's we were fascinated by the Rumanian Ambassador, Sergiu Celac.

Celac told us every interpreter that Ceausescu had was always shot at the end of two years. I asked, 'Good heavens, why did anybody ever take on the job?' 'They always hoped there might be a change in policy.'

Tuesday 12 March
Decided to go to Cheltenham for the first day.

Unfortunately, the Jackpot had been won the day before – there was nothing to go forward. But there was a big pool of £47,000 and my Quadpot did very well, the bet hated by all, including Peter Jones who is supposed to be my successor.

He is rattling me.

I am beginning to wonder if I have made the right choice.

Maybe the funny idea about having two candidates to choose from on the Nolan plan I might accept in his case. I might ask John Sanderson[3] if he would like to have a go. He is much better, I realize more and more, than Peter Jones.

Wednesday 13 March
During the day we were £400 ahead on my bet on the French franc. Alas, I should have told Mrs Tamborero to close it at once. Owing to

---

3. At this time Chief Executive, International Racing Management, responsible for Doncaster, Catterick and Redcar; chairman of Wetherby; a director of Thirsk, of the BHB, Racecourse Association and Televised Racing; member of Tote Board since 1983.

the general terror raised by the Chinese threatening Taiwan with missiles and military attacks, the Hong Kong market collapsed and my French francs rose against the pound. That was on the closing day [of the bet]. I finished owing £200 instead of collecting £1,100 which I could have had earlier. Mrs Tamborero is now under strict instructions never to let me bet with the City Index again. I shouldn't really bet with anybody again. I lost all my money betting at Cheltenham.

Thursday 14 March

I have a deep affection for the Tote staff we have now, and have had for the last seventeen years or so since I started weeding out the villains and the villainesses in 1976 when I became Chairman.

The staff, women and men, remain cheerful and patiently courteous to the customers, however cold [it is] and however stupidly or rudely or drunkenly the customer may behave – though most, perhaps ninety-eight per cent, are well mannered and appreciate the trouble the Tote staff take with them.

This is an aspect of the Tote I shall miss very much in a year's time, though I can't rush as eagerly and quickly and over the mud and rough places and up and down steps as I could five years ago or even three years ago. Weirdly, I feel like a father to them all. I am immensely grateful for their unfailing response.

Queen Elizabeth was wearing a lovely pink outfit with a beautiful brooch and a pretty hat, on all of which I complimented her. She is always delighted like a young girl: 'How observant and kind you are.'

She was walking in sprightly manner – not with two sticks but one walking stick. Amazing.

At lunch I told her I felt somewhat woozy, having stayed at Micky Suffolk's for the night, but was recovering fast on seeing her.

She was telling me 'what a good fellow' Prince Charles is. 'It is so wicked that they tell all these lies about him in the newspapers. Hardly anything they write about him is true, and he can't reply. It's so terribly unfair.' She is bitterly angry with Diana, even more so than with the other 'silly girl', the Duchess of York.

Robin Cook was having lunch in the huge Tote entertainment room we have as sponsors of the race. I told him to come up and see Queen Elizabeth, which he did.

They got on very well. His knowledge of horses impressed her.

She was amused at my description of him (in the *News of the World*) as 'Labour's Ginger Lenin'.

At The Other Club it was not one of the most entertaining evenings. Max Hastings was in the chair. I do not like him. I think he was beastly to Petronella. He is so absorbed by the impression he is making.

I gave Arnold a lift afterwards. He is desperately worried about Simon, poor man.

Wednesday 20 March
Verushka and Petronella went off to Naples, Florida, for a week in the sun.

A boring set of meetings at the Levy Board. We considered our strategy, long-term, a complete waste of time. No one can foretell what will happen with regard to the twice-a-week Lottery and the decline of the betting shops.

A memorial service for Stephen Spender. It was thronged with the literary *haut monde*.

Stephen's poems were read by various people, including the poet laureate Ted Hughes, Harold Pinter, James Fenton (Professor of Poetry at Oxford), and Stephen's son-in-law, Barry Humphries, otherwise known as Dame Edna Everage from Australia.

I had not realized Stephen was as religious as the service made him out to be. In fact I don't think he was religious at all. He was a mixed character. He adored publicity, he was very vain.

He was part of the furniture of my life. I met him first in 1944 when he was in the Fire Service and I was on leave – in the days when I mixed with Cyril Connolly and the *literati*, when I wrote for *Horizon*.

He was one of the editors of *Encounter*. He pretended not to know the money financing it came from the American CIA. *Encounter* was floated, a great magazine, to counter the communism which had caught hold of so many intellectuals in Britain.

Dinner at the Cranbornes in Swan Walk. Strange. There were all Robert's whips in the Lords (he is Leader of the House and in the Cabinet) and their wives as well as the wife of Alastair Goodlad, Chief Whip in the Commons.

Because Verushka wasn't there, Flora Fraser[4] came in her place. Her book is having excellent reviews. When I went I gave her a hug: 'Your father would be very proud of you.' Indeed he would have been, and now that I've had a chance to read some of *The Unruly Queen* I find

---

4. Writer; daughter of WW's Oxford friend Sir Hugh Fraser (1918–84, Conservative politician) and Lady Antonia Fraser, née Pakenham, who m 2 (1980) Harold Pinter.

it a much better history than ever her mother Antonia wrote. She has taken since 1988 to produce this life of Queen Caroline of Brunswick whom she describes with reasonable objectivity. She was not, as the newspaper reviews make out, just like Princess Diana, though in her way she was as much of a bloody nuisance. But in those days nobody thought of getting rid of the monarchy because of their extraordinary behaviour.

It is quite a pleasant house, though exceptionally untidy.

I left about a quarter to twelve. I had promised to ring Verushka. When I tried to get her I was told the alarming news that she had gone out shopping for dresses.

Thursday 21 March
Board Meeting of Cornish Spring Water. Naturally Tessa and Robbie didn't turn up.

I rather like Aly Aziz, though I think he is a rum character. It is possible we may get Cornish Spring Water off the ground. He has some very good ideas, including a contract with people in America. He has permission to increase the take of the water considerably. It is really an underground well and has no connection whatever with the water supply in the area which mainly comes, as elsewhere in England, from rivers.

To dinner at the Wolfsons, wearing a black tie. I am very fond of Estelle, and Leonard. They are still like a honeymoon couple, chirping away. Her dinner party had far better food, better organized, than Hannah's [Hannah Cranborne].

Ted Heath was there wearing his white tuxedo. I said to him before we went in to dinner, 'Now Ted, you must behave yourself tonight. Very often you don't talk to either of the ladies on your sides, your head sinks on your chest and you fall asleep.' He laughed with his face and shoulders.

He did very well to start with. Marcelle Quinton was on his right. She never draws breath. He couldn't help but listen to her, and even to reply, as she can be very amusing and was being so.

Naturally, Estelle was on Ted's left and he kept going with her, obeying my instructions. Then suddenly towards the end of dinner I looked up and I saw his head sunk on his chest and he had gone to sleep.

I think his difficulty is digesting the vast quantities of food he eats, extending his huge stomach ever outwards.

Also present were the Stevens. We are now reunited. I gave her a kiss and she said she was very pleased to see me.

As we were going I said to David Stevens, 'Would you like me to write some articles for your papers?' He said yes he would but would they be free. I said, 'No, they'd be very expensive.' Something may come of this. But there is no doubt that my reputation has sunk violently as a result of my column in the *News of the World* appearing only once a fortnight and on the wrong page anyway.

Sunday 24 March
I am busy searching for material for the article I want to write which is related to, but not particularly about, Mad Cow Disease hysteria. My theme is the absurdity of expecting governments to provide risk-free lives. I have been reading again the copy of the Richard Dimbleby lecture Victor Rothschild sent me in 1978 called 'Risk'.[5]

In the evening, while I was having my supper of smoked salmon and scrambled egg, Pericles rang. He had just returned from watching Aston Villa beat Leeds on television. There's a restaurant about an hour away which charged $15 each to watch the game.

The steak house, thank God, is doing well. He said he would bring over some steak for us to eat from America. I said, 'There's nothing wrong with the steak here.'

Tuesday 26 March
Off early to see betting shops in the East End and the newly done-up one at Chelmsford.

I had arranged to meet Jane Walden [McKerron] at a quarter to one at a Trusthouse Forte Little Chef near Debenham.

I was delighted by the house she has now moved into. Extremely pretty with a little Georgian front.

We had a lovely lunch. I brought up caviar and smoked salmon and a bottle of the good Sancerre and a couple of bottles of champagne. I also had a large sardine sandwich for Woody, the now eleven-year-old whippet looking like a greyhound, still very active. I hadn't seen him for years. He wagged his tail excitedly the moment I got into Jane's car. I was touched by his enthusiasm at seeing me. Perhaps he remembered the sardine sandwiches.

5. Victor Rothschild (3rd Baron, 1910–90, father of Jacob) was a distinguished scientist as well as a banker.*

Wednesday 27 March

Eventually I did speak to Verushka. She said she felt terrible from what she had been eating and oh dear, why does something always go wrong with her when she goes away?

I was relieved there was no attack on the lines of, 'Where have you been? What have you been doing?' as there often is, a kind of inquisition and long distance spying. She apparently felt too shaken for that. I think by Thursday morning she'll be OK after a good night's sleep and I hope she will enjoy the rest of her holiday.

Peter Sherlock, who used to be on the main board of Bass and who got Tote Direct going from the Bass side with me, came to see me about his idea of buying William Hill.

I told him it was quite impossible. The moment we entered this territory we would be fringing close to an examination by the Monopolies Commission because of our exclusive licence for pool betting, as well as an investigation by the Department of Trade and Industry. I didn't want to have any more investigation.

Monday 1 April

Forgot to play an April Fool before twelve o'clock. I thought with a touch of melancholy maybe I wouldn't be here to do it next year, but on reflection I am pretty sure I will be.

My article in the *Times* has attracted attention intellectually. Stefan Tietz[1] sent me a copy of a similar paper by Solly Zuckerman, 'The Risks of a No Risk Society'. Stefan Tietz was the man who, with John Burkett, designed the Park Village East building I organized and arranged when I had shares in the property company I had to give up as part of the divorce settlement with Moorea.

Another letter, from John Harris,[2] was amusing about Victor. Of course Victor was a ghastly man to work for, very petty.

But I only knew him as a delightful friend and a good judge of wine, as I wrote to Harris. He did love mystery. He was very anxious to get me to persuade Margaret to clear him publicly from ever being a risk, security-wise, despite his membership of the Apostles in Cambridge.[3] Margaret wouldn't do it quite like that. She simply stated that there was no evidence to show he had been implicated.

Tuesday 2 April

Petronella is very chuffed. John Major has agreed to give her an interview for the *Daily Telegraph*, with photographs, in the manner, no doubt, of the successful interview she had with Douglas Hurd.

She will use similar feminine appeal when interviewing John Major, of whom she is a great fan, thank goodness.

---

1. Consulting engineer.
2. Former staff manager of Shell Refining; he said in his letter that Rothschild was brilliant but 'a bugger to work with'.
3. See Vol. 1, pp. 229 ff. The Apostles was founded in 1820 as the Cambridge Conversazione Society; members read and discuss each others' papers; it was targeted by Soviet intelligence in the 1930s.

Wednesday 3 April

I am getting worried about Peter Jones.

I asked John Sanderson whether, if the Nolan recommendations were to prevail and we had to have a choice of two, he would be willing to be one of the two. He said yes, he would be, which surprised me. I thought he had too many business interests. He said his business wouldn't conflict with doing the job of Tote Chairman.

I am beginning to think he would do it much better than Peter Jones who is too keen on himself.

Saturday 6 April

In his Diary page in the *Spectator* this week, Alan Clark writes, 'Mrs Thatcher had [as intimate advisers] John Hoskyns,'[4] (he was in her think-tank at one time; he was not at all close to her so Clark was quite wrong); 'Alan Walters,' (until after she was deposed); 'David Young,' (that was true) 'Woodrow Wyatt and Charles Powell.'

I was amazed Clark included me. In his published diaries in book form he wrote that I was gaga.[5]

I think we should discard the editress-in-waiting and I should set about preparing the diaries myself.

I will explain to Macmillan it would be better if I did the editing and then they can get the volumes before I die but they are not to be published until I do.[6]

I am thinking of talking to 'the man from Liverpool' and asking him whether they will provide me with a secretary when I leave the Tote at the end of April 1997.

I am also worried about locomotion. I don't really like driving about in London during the daytime though I could just manage it. [But] I can't do it in that huge Tote car which normally they would let me keep on retirement. I am thinking of taking a bow at a venture and seeing whether News International will provide me with a motor car.

---

4. Head of the Prime Minister's Policy Unit, 1979–82; Director-General, Institute of Directors, 1984–9; knight 1982.

5. Clark in fact said something different and more perceptive: 'With the exception of Macmillan (and *he* does it on purpose) Woodrow is the only person I know who seems to be more gaga than he is.' (*Diaries*, p. 142.)

6. This plan, not communicated to the 'editress-in-waiting', was subsequently dropped.

However, this is unlikely. They are more likely to provide me with the sack from my fortnightly column.

Thursday 11 April
To a concert in the Purcell Room in the hideous South Bank Centre.

I sat directly behind Princess Diana. Her hair had been beautifully done and her skin from the back view was totally free of blemish and very sexy. I resisted the temptation to touch it.

I was embarrassed at coming, wondering whether I shouldn't have warned pretty Louise Patten that Princess Diana must hate me. I have written so many rude things about her, called her a schizophrenic and dangerously mad.

Unwisely, I thought, Verushka's hairdresser had asked her to tell Diana that Verushka is the lady in St John's Wood who shares her hairdresser. Verushka did so. She said Diana seemed very pleased and interested.

As I was about to go out, the German Ambassador pounced on me. 'I suppose you're going to write another attack on Germany?'

He said, 'Of course they're all cheating over the BSE affair, not reporting the cases, of which there are many in Germany and in France and all over the Continent.' I reported that to John the next morning.

I found the concert – the music – very attractive. It was George Weidenfeld's wife who taught me to appreciate music. She lived with Rubinstein, the celebrated pianist, very much older than herself. He died aged ninety-four. He left her large sums and she is now married to George.

I had told George I had a book called *Lantern Slides: the diaries and letters of Violet Bonham-Carter 1904–14*, to review for the *Times*.[7] 'So far I find them overblown and on the whole tedious. Would you, as the publisher, mind my saying that?' 'Not a bit.'

I remember having lunch once at the Ritz with that formidable lady, Violet Bonham-Carter. She had been very much in love with Winston Churchill but I found no mention of this in the book. She spoke much more entertainingly than the letters in the book but I must read it more thoroughly. Maybe it is better than my first impression.

---

7. In his review on May 30th of the book, which was edited by Lady Violet's son Mark Bonham-Carter and Mark Pottle, WW praised 'the charm and freshness dotted around' but thought it should have been pruned by half; Lady Violet was the daughter of the Liberal Prime Minister, Asquith, and herself a Liberal politician.

Friday 12 April

In a long talk with dear John I found him gloomy.[8]

He was actually willing to go on talking but I said I had my article to write.

Saturday 13 April

I left Verushka and Petronella at Oare and then dashed off to Salisbury to look at our betting shop there.

I love that town. I popped into Beech's bookshop and picked up the odd book, including a copy of *Precious Bane* by Mary Webb, a book once fulsomely praised by Stanley Baldwin when he was Prime Minister, which put up its sales.[9]

Henry and I somewhat annoyed the ladies for insisting on watching the golf. Faldo is six points behind Greg Norman in the US Masters.

Sunday 14 April

At Oare we had an hour's walk, charging through the grass, looking at Oare Sparrow who won six races and is now in foal, and at the stables. Henry rather sweetly kept trying to help me. 'It's all right. I'm not going to fall over.'

Frank Johnson came to lunch. I congratulated him on the rising standards of writing in the *Spectator*, including his own.

Arnold and Netta came to lunch, too. I told Arnold that Major had heard about Simon's illness and was very sorry.

There is a new drug being developed in New York at one of the great hospitals there by first-rate medical scientists. It could cure his sort of cancer. It hasn't been tested properly yet.

Arnold says he thinks about it all the time, saying to himself, 'I don't believe it. It can't be true.' When he has to do his work, he forgets for a while but it's always sitting on his head.

I had to agree to take Tessa up to London.

The drive was not so awful as I had expected though I had hoped to do some browsing work. Suddenly she began to talk sense. She said how appalling it is that Ministers don't even know what legislation

---

8. Labour had won the Staffordshire South East by-election from the Conservatives with a 22 per cent swing.

9. Mary Webb, née Meredith, (1881–1927), novelist; her success was mainly post-humous, due to Baldwin who praised her at a Royal Literary Fund dinner after her death; he wrote an introduction to a reprint of *Precious Bane* in 1928.

they're responsible for, nor do they know what their officials are doing when they issue new laws arising from what they conceive to be the delegated authority given to the Minister.

They put out directives from Europe, leaving out the parts which say that this piece or that piece is left to the government of the country (subsidiarity) to be resolved with regard to local conditions.

Wednesday 17 April

John Robb, Chairman of Wellcome 1994–5 and Chief Executive 1990–5, came to NERA for lunch at my request for Dermot Glynn and NERA to learn more about pharmaceutical firms for whom they might do jobs. John Robb sits next to me at the Levy Board of which he is a government-appointed member. I have always liked him. He is tall, impressive looking, a down-to-earth Scotsman with an excellent brain.

He was extremely helpful, not only over pharmaceuticals but in the nuclear area. He is now Chairman of the nuclear fuels company which was originally a government affair and is in charge of all the nuclear reactors.

I was pleased I had been able to help NERA so thoroughly, as it ensures, I hope, my continued employment by them – £15,000 a year.

John Major has taken up my theme about 'the message' – the subject of my article in the *Times* on April 9th. There is nothing wrong with the message but they are simply not getting it across. I advocated an enormous poster and a newspaper advertising campaign. When I spoke to Maurice Saatchi he said they haven't got the money. He said if somebody would give them £10 million, which used to happen in the old days when Alistair McAlpine was Chairman of the Party, he could get cracking. They have an overdraft of £2 million.

It seems that big businessmen won't help because they think Blair's going to win, nearly all of them. They don't want to be on the wrong side of Blair.

As we talked, he said could I think of anybody who has some money. Suddenly I had a brainwave. It could be Paul Getty.

I said, 'I've never approached him for money because too many do. But there may be some advantage in his adoring Major because of his love of cricket.'

Thursday 18 April

Arranged to see Paul Getty on Tuesday, April 30th by myself. When I told Maurice Saatchi, he was wild with delight. 'You are a miracle man. I'll polish your shoes.' 'I've got servants here who do that. It's odds on against Paul agreeing.'

Friday 19 April

Lunch with Les Hinton, 'the man from Liverpool'. He was very modest in his ordering in the Lords' dining-room, unusually open on a Friday.

He didn't know the extent of my association with Rupert. He hadn't realized that, but for me, he would never have been able to buy the *Sunday Times*. Nor that he wouldn't have been able to get it printed after that strike.

'What got the plant going was my secret meetings, with Eric Hammond and with Rupert, which took place at my house. Eric got the electricians' union, which was always at odds anyway with the TUC General Council, to blackleg by setting up the printing operation which easily could be done by members of the electricians' union. This was all done secretly. Rupert wouldn't have been able to defeat the strikers otherwise. I can tell you that now. Eric Hammond wrote about it in his autobiography.[10] I was rather annoyed. I like these things to be kept secret so that people don't know what I'm doing behind the scenes.'

The more important Hinton thinks I am in Rupert's life, the more help I am going to get from him when I want to ask for a secretary when I leave the Tote and maybe a car driven by a chauffeur.

I said, 'Are you happy with the column as it is?' 'Yes, very. Are you?' 'I'd like it to be once a week again.' He laughed. Maybe I'll get back to it again.

I hadn't wasted my time with that lunch. I had an instinct it would be a good idea and we're now firm friends.

Monday 22 April

In the evening we had to go to a concert by 'Great Orchestras of the World – Budapest Festival Orchestra' at the Barbican Centre.

The invitation was from Vere Rothermere but neither he nor his wife turned up. Vyvyan Harmsworth, acting as the host, was highly apologetic.

---

10. *Maverick: the Life of a Union Rebel*, published 1992.

Sandbag (Simon Sebag-Montefiore) is a terrible fellow. He's attracted by every girl who is at all pretty.

There was quite a pretty girl with blonde hair, who looked a little common, sitting at a table checking off the guests as they arrived. We, as usual, were far too early: Verushka gets so nervous we're going to be late. Simon at once started chatting her up. When we first sat down a little way away from her, he said, 'I wonder what her legs are like.' 'You can see them now. There's a slit in her skirt. They're not at all bad.'

He went over to her, started asking her about herself, her name, what her telephone number was. When we came back through the same room for the dinner after almost everyone had gone in, I saw him kissing her. She was blushing away and looking rather pleased about it. I asked Simon, 'Has she got a boyfriend?' 'She soon won't have.' What an extraordinary man.

Tuesday 23 April
John and Diana Wilton came to dinner.

Diana, the new convert to Roman Catholicism, is going to Lourdes but John is not going with her, rather sensibly. He seems recovered from what looked like at one time being a very serious illness which could have killed him. Poor Diana has had such a lot of trouble in her life, with her own dangerous cancer which has nearly knocked her off completely once or twice.

She now worries that if she dies before John he won't know what to do with himself – he can't look after himself. She has a very generous heart and genuine feeling for others and remains looking extraordinarily elegant.

Thursday 25 April
Once more into a dinner jacket, with which I wear a silk shirt for comfort.

Arnold Weinstock came with me to the Vintners' Hall as my guest at the Saintsbury Club. Seeing this great man, numerous [people] oiled up to him.

To my amazement, on the list of wines was Château Calon-Ségur 1971, presented by Lord Wyatt of Weeford. I got hold of John Harvey and said, 'This surely is under false pretences. I thought I had given you some special 1977 port.' 'Oh yes, you gave us that too. But you gave us this years ago.' I had forgotten.

When the dinner ended (the food was surprisingly good, as Arnold said and he is the most critical of all people) Hugh Johnson got up and made a savage attack on the wines. He said he had never seen so many full glasses left undrunk. But he did say the Château Calon-Ségur was 'acceptable'.

We talked in the car going home (I dropped Arnold off at Grosvenor Square) about his successor. He said he, Arnold, would have an office there and although he had only got some eight per cent of the shares, it represented a lot of money and he was jolly well going to see that they did the job properly. I said, 'Won't that cause conflict?' 'I don't think so. I won't be telling him what to do. But I expect him to ask my advice.' I thought, poor fellow.

Goodness how I like that man, Arnold. Inside he has a gentle soul but on the outside he can be a terror. He's bloody good at getting his own way, which I admire because his way in business happens to be the right one.

Saturday 27 April
Andrew Parker Bowles was a bit peeved with me. It was only the day before that I had said could I come to have lunch at Sandown because I wanted to look at various things there. When I arrived he said, 'You should give me more than a day's notice. Anyway, Queen Elizabeth will be here soon and she wants to talk to you before lunch.'

I told her Blair wouldn't win.

She was delighted. 'How can you feel that?' she asked. 'Because Major's got the instincts of the British right and Blair, with his willingness to do anything Brussels says, has not.' The Queen Mother hates Brussels and all its works.

When the Whitbread Gold Cup was finished – I had backed the winner at 14 to 1 and got £89 – its connections came up to the Royal Box. There were a lot of young among them, including some girls. They crowded round Queen Elizabeth and said would she please ring their father as he wasn't there to receive the Cup because he was ill in bed. They handed her a mobile telephone. With great spirit and gusto, she started to try to make the call. 'How do I work this? I don't understand it.' They got the number and they got the father. There she was surrounded by all these laughing young people, as gay as anything herself, congratulating the owner on his great win. She handled the situation with a combination of dignity, charm and gaiety.

Sandown is the only racecourse on which we don't have a separate and large, comfortable room [for credit customers] with security people at the door to prevent non-members coming in.

I told Andrew about the problem. 'You're losing business. We give you money on every Tote bet that's taken.'

He's very quick, Andrew, and very domineering. When I mentioned a member of his committee who said he supported the idea, he said sharply, 'It's nothing to do with him. I give the orders here.' I laughed. 'At least you have his support.' 'Right, something will be done about it.'

Those fools, Aston Villa, lost 1–0 to Manchester City.

Monday 29 April
Set off with Cita at half past nine. First stop was the church at Weeford. Mr Martin, the vicar, fresh from a funeral, was there.

Selected a place for the plaque for Bob which Molly is keen on.

A window I had never noticed before shone beautifully in the sun. It was taken from the chapel of the Dukes of Orléans by revolutionaries. When it was discovered, it was brought to Weeford Church by James Wyatt and rebuilt by him. The vicar had thought that the church was rebuilt in 1804. I had always maintained the new church was built by James Wyatt in 1802. The lettering on the window at the bottom said quite clearly that it had been put in Weeford Church in 1802, which seems to settle the matter.

Cita was very interested in all she saw, particularly in the site of my grave.

Then to Lichfield where we went round the cathedral.

We had lunch at Mrs Thrale's, a very suitable restaurant. She was a lady with whom Dr Johnson was long in love and who refused to marry him when her husband died.[11]

We quickly looked at the statue of Dr Johnson in the market square near where he stood in the rain and wept and rebuked himself publicly for not having gone to Uttoxeter on a rainy day to help his father sell his books in the market place. The poor man was always tormented by the sins he had committed, rather like Quintin Hogg (as I explained

---

11. Hester Lynch (1741–1821) m 1 Henry Thrale, a wealthy brewer; m 2, after Thrale's death, Gabriel Piozzi, an Italian musician, a marriage to which Johnson was much opposed. Her *Anecdotes* and *Thraliana* are, after Boswell, a primary source for Johnson's talk.

to Cita) who still believes he is going to burn in hell fire for the many evil things he's done.[12]

Tuesday 30 April
Went to see Paul Getty.

I plunged straight into what I came about – the backing for Major.

He thought him simply marvellous, as I knew he did. Then he said, 'I don't know if they told you – Major knows. Did he speak to you? I've already given them half a million pounds a couple of weeks ago. I also gave them a million and a half at the last election.'

'Would you be prepared to guarantee an overdraft of £10 million to the Conservative Party? They would have to pay you back.' He said, 'That is an interesting idea. Would you please give me a fortnight or so to think about it? I felt that was a good sign.

Paul has a very attractive sitting-room with memorabilia of cricket. There was a wonderful screen with a picture of the Lord's pavilion on which he has superimposed rather skilfully pictures of some of the great players.

Arnold and Netta came to dinner by themselves.

Arnold was in an angry state. He almost shouted at me. He said Major wouldn't win, didn't deserve to, was no good.

When Netta and Verushka went for a natter in the drawing-room, I turned to Arnold and said, 'You're very distressed tonight. Is it to do with Simon?' He said, 'Yes.' He had just come from seeing him. The drug is taking a long time to work.

Poor Arnold. He went on, 'What's it all for? All that effort and there he is. There's nothing to hope for. What is life? Nothing. What is there in life? It's meaningless. A lot of despair and unhappiness.' Poor old Arnold. I felt deeply sorry for him.

---

12. See Vol. 2, p. 552, for Lord Hailsham's beliefs on the Day of Judgement.

Thursday 2 May

The *Spectator* for lunch at which Petronella was the hostess.

The lunch was for only some nine people, partly political, partly racing.

Stoker Hartington was slightly put out when I said, 'The BHB is not mature enough yet even to contemplate having any control of the Tote, even if it were desirable, which it is not. The Tote must remain a free-standing organization.' He said, 'How long do you think it will take for the BHB to mature?' 'About thirty years.' He didn't like that very much.

Next to me sat Gillie Howard de Walden. She had been asked for her knowledge of racing. The crass Bruce Anderson said, 'What do you know about racing?'

Dear little Gillie was looking rather drawn. Poor John has been so ill, strokes, speech loss and God knows what else, nearly at death's door and couldn't speak at all for a while.

The lunch was really for Robin Oakley, the famous BBC commentator, reporter and political man in charge.[1] He also writes a column on racing, which he adores, in the *Spectator*.

The question of the sleaze factor came up fairly often. I'm afraid that is a difficult one to beat. Robin Oakley, however, thinks that Major will win, contrary to the belief of the others present.

Maria, from here, cooked the lunch. A weird kind of butler was hired. He was short and confused.

The way they were going to do it before would have cost them £800. This cost them £50 for Maria plus £100 for the food and about another £50 or so for the champagne which Petronella took there in the morning.

---

1. Political editor, BBC, 1992–2000.

Monday 6 May
Petronella's birthday party. I was instructed to give her £100 for a new hat.

The guests, chosen by her, were Geoffrey and Miriam Owen, Simon Sebag-Montefiore, Frank Johnson, Andrew and Camilla Roberts and Robert Hardman. We had a 1947 bottle of Perrier-Jouët, Pavillion Blanc and Lafite Rothschild 1963, followed by Château Capbern 1937 (a magnificent year) Tokay, port, etc.

Camilla Roberts sat next to me. I began to like her. She was in a Cambridge tasting team in competitions. She knows a lot about wine, to my surprise.

Tuesday 7 May
We gave a demonstration of the Tote's increase in profits and help to racing to the All Party Racing Committee. Unfortunately, they had mucked up the dates and we were given the wrong room in which to assemble; only about ten people were present.

Tom Phillips's lantern slides[2] conveyed a great deal plus my commentary and John Heaton did well also. The Chief Executive came along for the ride.

Thursday 9 May
Dramatically Verushka announced that Netta [Weinstock] had said only a miracle can save poor Simon now. He's given up eating, he doesn't speak. For Laura, his wife, it is terrible. Her mother died when she was very young and so did her father, and now she's lost her husband at a very young age and will be bringing up the children without him. She has been very good, Laura.

Arnold is still going to The Other Club tonight. I obviously can't cheer him up but at least I can talk to him.

Nigel Kent-Lemon came to see me at the Lords. Primarily it was about his activities with other members of the Racecourse Association to improve the image of bookmakers.

He told me that Peter Jones has been telling people he is going to be the next Chairman of the Tote. This is causing some dismay. Kent-Lemon said he wouldn't do the job properly, quite apart from wanting to push the owners' interests in the Tote.

I then thought of Wakeham. He said he thought that would be a

2. Phillips was presumably using an overhead projector.

possibility. 'The drawback is he's going to be the Chairman of BHB in June.'

I now have to have a serious talk with (a) Wakeham and (b) later on May 23rd with Howard. Also possibly with Stoker Hartington.

The Other Club.

I asked Ken Clarke what he thought Blair would do, if he won. Kenneth thought almost the worst thing would be that his ministers are so utterly inexperienced that they would be entirely in the hands of civil servants.

He assumed that they would join the social chapter and have a minimum wage, with all the consequences we know which would ruin our employment situation. He said, 'Whatever they may say about not putting up spending, they couldn't do any of the things they say they're going to do without raising taxes. And they have to do some of them.'

There is a great dislike of Margaret among those liberally minded men. Kenneth Clarke said he had admired her enormously and he had actually voted for her in the leadership election when she was deposed. But he thought some of her ideas were rather crude and she was getting too dictatorial. He had been staggered when Howe got up to make his resignation speech. He thought it was just going to be a friendly speech saying how honoured he'd been to serve with her and wish her luck, and he was disappointed he couldn't stay because he had one or two disagreements.

It was that one single speech which dislodged her.

However, there was a general agreement in that little group that she had done something quite remarkable and will be remembered as such in history – as having revitalized the country.

Nicko had been doing some work on Chamberlain, going through all the papers in the Foreign Office and in the Cabinet Office.

I said I felt there was some excuse for him in his appeasement and his bit of paper after seeing Hitler. He knew we hadn't got any arms.

Nicko said, 'You're quite wrong. I have read all the papers and the Cabinet minutes and what Chamberlain noted himself. He really believed that he had persuaded Hitler to drop his warlike approach and aggression and he trusted him.' 'After all we knew about what he'd been doing to the Jews?' 'People didn't realize that here. They turned a blind eye to it. They didn't want to know. The previous war was so close, they lost their nerve and couldn't bear to bring about another one.'

In the car [going home] poor Arnold said, 'It's very bad. I can't see any chance whatever. They can't operate on the tumour in his brain, a cancerous one.'

I held Arnold's hand to console him in the car. I think he found it a little comfort to talk to me.

Saturday 11 May
Went with Petronella to some very pretty shopping precincts near Covent Garden opera house. It was to visit a cheese shop she wanted me to see.

It sells only English cheeses and some of them are really remarkable, even better than their foreign counterparts.[3]

We spent £49, which included a large slice of Stilton which I hoped to get into my Wedgwood honeybee cover for such cheeses. When we got it home it was a very tight fit, so I fear either the valuable Wedgwood article will be damaged or the cheese will be.

Petronella said it would make Frank Johnson's world if I could get him into The Other Club. He would then think he really belonged. He is so conscious of his origins, though no sensible person would take any notice of that.[4] I did canvass it with the ghastly Montague Browne.

He thinks there shouldn't be any journalists in the Club at all. I was surprised that he didn't think Frank Johnson would necessarily be a failure.

Sunday 12 May
Netta says she has never known Arnold not go to work before. Several times he hasn't been to the office all day. I spoke to him. 'Arnold, you've got to carry on. You've got to do things normally. You have so many dependent on you in your firm and in your family. Is there really no hope?' 'No. It's only a matter of days now.'

Wednesday 15 May
The appalling Chirac in the Royal Gallery. After a quantity of humbug flattery and thanks for saving France with the Normandy invasion, he started trying to persuade us to join a single currency.

I don't think Chirac liked being reminded by Betty Boothroyd of the celebrated paintings on the wall of the Royal Gallery with

---

3. Neal's Yard Wholefoods.
4. His father was a pastry-cook and confectioner, as he himself notes in his *Who's Who* entry.

prominence to Blücher and Wellington at the Battle of Waterloo and Nelson at the Battle of Trafalgar.

Later in the afternoon I saw Margaret in the Lords library. She beckoned me to sit beside her. She said, 'That man is glib and treacherous despite his charm.'

Saturday 18 May

Netta and Arnold Weinstock had not gone to the country for fear that Simon might die while they were away. They came to dinner with us. When Netta and Verushka had left the room, Arnold and I went into a long discussion about Simon.

We found ourselves speaking of him in the past tense.

Suddenly a call came through from Susan,[5] whom Laura had told that Arnold and Netta were having dinner with us. Verushka handed the mobile telephone to Arnold and left the room. I said, 'Would you like me to leave?' 'No, I'd rather you stayed.' Then Susan said, 'He's dead. Simon is dead.' Poor Arnold. His face crumpled. He slumped and staggered from the shock. I held his hand and put my arm round his back.

Sunday 19 May

Dear Arnold. Still very shattered, obviously. He's talking of selling all his racehorses. Apart from working every day with Simon, that was the great recreation they had together. He thought him very intelligent in selecting horses to buy and breed and when they were to run. The day he died they had a winner called Election Day – the horse was actually born on election day in 1992, April 9th.

Arnold wants no one to come to the funeral, not even me. He wants it very private.

The funeral is on Monday, tomorrow. Jews always have to be buried within forty-eight hours.

Tuesday 21 May

Saw John Wakeham at the Lords in a room once used as the Consort's Robing Room.

I showed him a copy of my letter to the Permanent Under Secretary at the Home Office. That was in reply to the absurd Nolan desires to make us advertise for the post of Chairman [of the Tote] and not have

---

5. The Weinstocks' daughter, married to Charles Lacroix.

Board Members for more than three years at a time, or certainly not more than two terms.

I then switched to the question of my successor.

I was pleased and surprised at his interest. 'I would like to think about it for a week or so.'

I said, 'What is important about it is that the person who is Chairman of the Tote should have "a presence". He must be able to get people to go to our Tote lunch and the right sort of people to be entertained on the racecourses.' John interrupted me: 'And argue with Prime Ministers, as you do.' We both laughed.

The good part is I don't have to say anything to Peter Jones about his not coming up to scratch. It is done for me by the BHB not nominating him.

Noël Annan these days mildly excites my curiosity. I get copies of the catalogues from a firm called Any Amount of Books. Featured in the last issues were books given to Noël by authors such as Graham Greene, Maurice Bowra, James Pope-Hennessy, Victor Rothschild, and signed with messages by them. He is now selling them off. He must be either very hard up or have very little room in his new living quarters.

Wednesday 22 May
Dinner with David Metcalfe.

On my left sat Virginia Fraser, the widow of the last Lord Lovat. We discussed how we are all different according to the person we are speaking to. 'I'm not talking to you in the same way as I have been talking to the girl on my right. When different people are involved, the composition of thought and emotion is different.'

I said how much I like Frank Johnson. She said he is still very unsure of himself because his father was a pastry cook. 'I know. It's perfectly ridiculous. But he's wonderfully well educated and he did it for himself. He's very clever. I think he's becoming less self-conscious now.' She said she wasn't sure how much he enjoyed being editor of the *Spectator*. 'He likes the excitement of a daily newspaper.' 'But he's doing it very well. The *Spectator* is much better than it was when that terrible fellow, Dominic Lawson, was running it.'[6]

She has a part-time job for the German Ambassador as his social secretary. She vets the people who come and suggests people who might be worth having there. 'Do we owe the honour of being invited to

---

6. Virginia Fraser and Frank Johnson married in 1999.

dinner there to you?' 'No. He wanted you anyway because he likes talking to you and having arguments with you.' Virginia was looking prettier than she sometimes does. She is not at all a bad-looking girl.

Thursday 23 May
Went to see Michael Howard, at last. I was asked by his Private Secretary if I would like to talk to him alone or have officials present. I said I would like to talk to him alone.

We talked about the political situation, briefly.

The way he talks about the political situation made me feel that he sees himself on the cards to be Prime Minister, or at least Leader of the Tory Party if they lose.

On the question of our being required to comply with the Nolan Committee, he was very negative. He had seen my letter to the Permanent Under Secretary to the Home Office, who he said was a very good man.

'You must talk to him about it. I dare not interfere in any way with a Nolan matter – it is all so very dicey and I might be accused of not accepting Nolan's recommendations.'

He is inclined to be helpful on our being allowed to take bets on the Irish Lottery as all the other bookmakers are. I said, 'Please do that quickly because I wrote on April 15th and nothing has happened. We are losing a lot of custom because people come into our betting shops and ask if they can bet on the Irish Lottery numbers. They're told no, so they go straight out and into another betting shop.'

The Howards are coming to dinner with us fairly soon. This is going to be important because I have got to jolly him along about not having Peter Jones as Chairman after me, and wanting, if he agrees, to have John Wakeham.

Friday 24 May
A lovely fax from Irwin about my article in the *Times* on Tuesday.[7]

Arnold is off tomorrow morning to Venice with the children and Laura. I ring him every day.

Thursday 30 May
I had telephoned Number 10 saying I would rather like to speak to John Major.

---

7. About the benefits of privatization.

I told him about a poll which I thought boded well for him. He said, 'Do you mean in the *Observer*?' I said, 'Yes. But there is one in this morning's *Times* which is not so favourable.' 'Can you read it to me?'

When I got it and read him the headline 'Beef Conflict Fails to Bolster Major', he said, 'Isn't that extraordinary reporting? It wasn't intended to bolster me. It was intended to get something done in the national interest.'

When I asked, 'Have you spoken to the editor of the *Sunday Times*?' he said, 'Yes. He's a complete wet. What I am very annoyed about with the *Sunday Times* is that they do nothing but publish stories, which they did again last Sunday, saying that the money we have from donations comes from tainted sources, terrible crooks and all the rest of it. This is very much handicapping our fund raising.'

I said, 'Remember General Booth, the founder of the Salvation Army? When he was attacked for taking money from bookmakers and other disreputable sources, including crooks, his answer was, "I don't mind where the money comes from. I'll make it holy." '

While the good news accumulates, John's definitely not going to hold an election until next year, unless he's forced out.

I told John about my conversation with Michael Howard. 'He wants to be Prime Minister.' He said, 'Lots of people want to do that. It's not an unworthy ambition.'

We talked for quite a long time, as though he had all the time in the world.

We had a huge dinner party in the evening.

We had a premier cru Chablis and then three magnums of 1975 Château Lafite. I suppose they were worth about £1,000 each, perhaps more – David Somerset gave me six magnums after the 1987 election.[8]

I told Frank Johnson I had this day written to Nicko Henderson saying when there is a vacancy at The Other Club I thought he should be considered because he is very amusing and a lively talker.

---

8. See Vol. 1, pp. 372–3.

Sunday 2 June

Took the Kinders, Gordon and his wife, Juju,[1] to Paul Getty's cricket match and to see the library.

The Paul Getty side, cobbled up from various teams which weren't playing this Sunday, was playing Oxford University.

I had to choose a moment to start talking to Paul about our previous conversation – money for the Tory Party. The first time I tried, Kenneth Baker, not knowing what we were talking about, plus his wife, Mary, interrupted. He was brandishing his book on cartoons of British royalty through the centuries.[2] 'Are you giving this to me?' 'No but I'll send you one.' 'I thought you were carrying a stack of them in your car to sell to anybody who'd be willing to buy one.'

Later on Paul said, 'I think to give them any money would be a waste of money because they are obviously going to lose the next election.' I said, 'That's not so. He's going to win it. But it will be much more difficult for him if they [the Tories] can't get their posters and big advertisements in the newspapers out. Did you think any more about my idea of guaranteeing?' 'Yes, but they'd have to pay it back, and maybe they won't be able to raise the money, particularly if they've lost the election.'

Finally, as we went, he said, a little shamefacedly, 'If he's still there in the spring, then I'll look into it again. It could be interesting then.'

I hate this business of trying to get money out of rich people.

Tuesday 4 June

A great farewell dinner at the Berkeley Hotel for Stoker Hartington, now ceasing to be Chairman of the BHB, his place being taken by John Wakeham. John Wakeham had already said to me in the Lords when I bumped into him that he could not now leave the BHB as he had made a commitment to them and it wouldn't be sensible. I said to him

---

1. American friends; Juju was at school with Verushka.
2. *Kings and Queens – an Irreverent History of the British Monarchy.*

what would he think about Cecil Parkinson [for Tote Chairman]? He said, 'It might well be a possibility.'

I was fortunate in my placing between Sandra Howard, who stays very pretty and wore an attractive blue dress with silver piping, and Amanda Hartington, Stoker's wife. She, too, is a pretty woman.

She is very fond of Andrew [Devonshire], her father-in-law, and was wearing a beautiful bracelet he had given her. I said, 'Are those diamonds real?' 'Yes.' Her pearls were real, too. She said you could tell if pearls were real by biting them. They were round her neck. I said, 'I would love to do that but I don't think it would go down very well.'

Wednesday 5 June
Tote Board meeting.

Peter Jones is very keen, obviously, to put his name forward, even if there is advertising, though he hasn't a chance now. He is irritating. When I described my proposition that we should have a dual forecast in four races, he said, 'What about the market research?' I said, 'You can't market research on something which hasn't happened. I don't believe in market research. I believe in intuition and observation. Every time I've raised this with punters in the shops, they've all thought it a good idea, including the managers.' Peter snorted away about how valuable market research is but I moved on to something else.

At the Home Office, Richard Wilson, Permanent Secretary, was extremely friendly. I told him, 'If I can't get you to do anything, I will have to go to see Lord Nolan himself.' He said, 'That might well be therapeutic for you but I don't think you'll get him to do much about it.'[3]

Dinner at Rocco Forte's.

Rocco is determined to try to get back into the hotel business. Olga, who was there, said she won't go anywhere near it now.[4]

---

3. In a letter to Wilson dated 10 June WW noted that Wilson had agreed to arrange the reappointment to the Tote Board for two years of John Sanderson and Jeremy Deedes; he hoped Wilson would 'progress the question of an order being laid for us to take bets on numbers in the Irish Lottery'; and he repeated the dangers of altering the current status of the Tote or the way its Board members were selected.
4. By 2000 Rocco Forte was chairman and chief executive, RF Hotels, of which Olga was a director; she was also managing director of Hotel Tresanton in Cornwall.

Thursday 6 June
Dinner at the Wolfsons with Vere Rothermere and Myoko.

Evelyn de Rothschild had rung me earlier in the week about an appalling double-page extract [in the *Daily Mail*] from a book of scurrilous nature. This was about Tess [Rothschild] having an affair with Blunt, who was a homosexual, and Victor and her being mixed up with spies, suggesting they were probably spies themselves. It was published on the day after her funeral.[5]

I tackled Vere. He said, 'I read it. I thought it very interesting, very amusing. Of course they did get mixed up with all kinds of strange people.' 'Yes, but they were not spies.' 'Who knows?' 'The implication was that they betrayed their country and neither Victor nor Tess would ever have dreamed of doing so.'

'It's a tough, competitive world out there,' said Vere. 'We're fighting for circulation. I can't interfere.'

Vere was also in his anti-Major mood, attacking him very dishonestly. He says he leaves it to his editors whom they back.

At the Fortes last night, Max Hastings, editor of the *Evening Standard*, another Vere newspaper, said he hadn't made up his mind yet whether to say that people should vote for Blair or not, but he thought it quite likely.

Saturday 8 June
Derby Day. I walked for the last time over the Downs.

Is Saturday a success for the Derby? It couldn't really have been because the crowds were much thinner on the stand side, though the Epsom PR lady swore they were bigger than last year, which I simply don't believe. This year the Derby was the second race in order not to clash with the European football cup. So the Saturday Derby didn't have a fair chance. Sunday would be better.

---

5. The *Daily Mail* of 5 June 1996 published a two-page article by Tom Bower, author of a biography of Sir Dick White, former head of MI5 and MI6. At the outbreak of war, Tess Mayor, who married Victor Rothschild in 1946, shared with Anthony Blunt, the art historian, and Guy Burgess, a house in Bentinck Street, Mayfair, owned by Rothschild. Tess, Blunt and Rothschild were members of MI5. The spy Burgess defected to the Soviet Union in 1951 and Blunt confessed his treachery in 1964. The article ended by saying that Tess was 'guilty of overzealous loyalty to her friend [Blunt] rather than treachery'. See Vol.1 for rumours about Rothschild in 1986 at the time of the Australian court case about Peter Wright's book *Spycatcher* and Vol. 2, pp. 104 and 294, for denials of such allegations.

Sunday 9 June
Robbie [chauffeur] took us to Bowden.

Arnold produced some beautiful old champagne for us and a delicious dry white wine made in the champagne style, followed by Haut-Brion 1966.

Petronella brought him a disc of all the recordings that Gigli had made between 1926 and 1937.

I asked riddles from my childhood like, 'What did Farmer Jones first plant in his potato field?' Arnold fell into the trap and said, 'a potato'. 'No, his foot.' 'He might have done it from the side.' 'I don't think so.'

I asked him, 'Can you tell the difference between a pillar box and a nigger's behind?' 'What is it?' 'I shan't ask you to post any letters for me then.' 'You wouldn't get away with calling anybody a nigger now. You'd be reported to the race relations people.'

After we finished lunch, he went off to listen to a race in France. He didn't have a horse in it but he did have considerable interest in it because a granddaughter of Troy won it.[6] He has not entirely lost his fascination for horses. I hope he won't because it will occupy him, however much it distresses him with regard to poor Simon.

He is now working away. It helps him to put despairing sadness out of his mind for a while, though alas he will never fully recover from Simon's death.

Monday 10 June
Natasha Spender came to tea at the Lords.

She is looking for a biographer [for Stephen Spender] of suitable stature. I suggested A. N. Wilson.[7] When it has been done, she wants to give the archives, after a due gap after the appearance of the book, to the British Museum. I said, 'You ought to sell them to the British Museum. You should get a lot of money for them.'

She is still a good-looking woman, though getting on somewhat.

She told me she was the first pianist ever to be televised. That was in a BBC Promenade Concert with Malcolm Sargent who was very cross when he saw she was being made up by a BBC make-up girl. He

---

6. Troy was Weinstock's famous 1979 Derby winner.
7. John Sutherland, Lord Northcliffe Professor of Modern English, University College London, since 1992, was subsequently appointed Spender's official biographer.

said, 'Why can't I be made up?' and brought out a powder puff and applied a lot of pink to his face.

Wednesday 12 June
A meeting of Cornwall Light and Power at 19 Cavendish Avenue. We're a bit behind budget because the wind has not been blowing. We've made a good deal of profit, millions, since we started.

I told Tessa that the Sirdar [Aly Aziz] would like her to take over the supervision of the production of the Cornish Spring Water. Things are going very well but the cost of production is far too high.

'I've told him how brilliantly you run the wind farm.' She was very pleased at that. She said she would like to consider it.

At The Other Club Peter Carrington said he couldn't believe I was serious when I said that the Tories would win.

I told him the story of my punters in the betting shop. 'Whatever they may say to the pollsters, people will in the end vote for the person who'll leave them the most in their pockets.'

He said, 'I hope you're right.' This was rather different from what Paul Getty had told me he said, that not only are the Tories going to lose, but they ought to lose because it was time for a change. He is rather two-faced, old Peter Carrington.

Saturday 15 June
Badminton. At lunch Miranda Morley was not present. John and Diana Wilton were and some members of the family including Daphne, Caroline's mother. She moved fairly briskly around once out of her wheel chair.

At dinner Miranda sat next to me. She is a sweet and sensitive girl. She behaved impeccably, as well as a mistress can living in a house on the estate away from the Duchess's Badminton House.

Anne Somerset was there. Soon her book will come out on the Thomas Overbury murder mystery. Her husband, Matthew Carr, is a moderate painter and earns little money.

I shall always be grateful to him for his solicitude for Caroline in her dying months and his thoughtful kindness to me then. He is agreeable, tall, dark with a thin face, moving eagerly, lightly and quickly. You can see there are potentially good scholarly genes there, inherited from his father, Sir Raymond Carr, the eccentric former Warden of St Antony's College, Oxford, who writes about foxhunting of which he is a devotee.

Sunday 16 June

In the evening I took Irwin Stelzer to dinner at Pratt's.

Bobby Corbett, son of Lord Rowallan, former Chief Scout and a Colonial Governor, was bobbing about. He came and sat by me, kneeling down.

He said did I realize that Aunt Dorothy (who left Jacob the fortune and lots of racehorses which Serena now races) 'never ran her Jewish horses on Saturdays'. I said I thought that was most unlikely. He bet me £5 that this was so. The following day I rang Jacob. He said, 'Aunt Dorothy did run her horses on Saturdays but in the name of her trainer. On the other days of the week they ran in her name.' So Bobby Corbett was wrong.

Irwin was convinced he was deeply anti-semitic because he had referred to 'Jewish horses'.

Among others there was Bruce Anderson.

Alexander Hesketh pushed his claim and got him elected.

Irwin was totally taken by the turtle with the tail which you wag to get servants, 'George' or 'Georgina' who preside highly efficiently.

Tuesday 18 June

First day of the Royal Ascot meeting. For the last time we attended the routine lunch given by Piers Bengough, Her Majesty's representative, in his rooms.

For the last time we were summoned to tea with the Queen, which meant really sitting at Queen Elizabeth the Queen Mother's table.

I told Debo Devonshire, sitting on my left, when somehow the conversation turned to set-aside and the absurd nature of the Common Agricultural Policy, 'Did you know that if you have a charitable event on your set-aside land, you will lose all your set-aside grant?' She nearly had a fit.

When we were standing in line to shake hands with senior members of the Royal Family, Prince Charles came up to me with a great smile. 'How are you, Woodrow? Very nice to see you.' As I have written rather unpleasant things about him in relation to what he said about his parents to Dimbleby, I thought it very handsome of him and naturally I warmed to him. Now I shall be more favourable to him, no doubt.

After tea was over I went back with Queen Elizabeth, to sit with her overlooking the races.

She is a miracle. She didn't need any help at all when we went back to sit in the front of the box. I offered her some and she said, 'Oh no, I can manage.' She didn't even have her stick with her.

Wednesday 19 June
Our first party in the [new] Tote entertainment room so beautifully arranged and decorated by Verushka.

At lunch, just before people started to go betting and to see the first race, Willie Whitelaw got up and banged on the table. He made a little speech thanking me for all I'd done for the Tote and the wonderful hospitality we'd given them.

In the evening we went to a weird exhibition for the anniversary of the founding of the new Saatchi firm. There was a lot of peculiar modern architecture which was supposed to be marvellous.

Maurice was extremely friendly; so was Howell James, the political secretary to Major.

He said he thought my article on Northern Ireland was very good but the difficulty was getting the Irish Government to play.[8]

A woman came up to me and said, 'Are you Mr Saatchi senior?' I said, 'I wish I were. Then I'd be very rich.' When I told Maurice this, he thought it very funny. He is a nice guy, but sometimes I just wonder a little bit about him.

Thursday 20 June
Royal Ascot entertainment room for the last time.

The German Ambassador and his wife were there, so were the Kenneth Bakers and William (Viscount) Astor and his wife. Also Victoria Getty, for whom Verushka managed to get the Royal Enclosure ticket although she had applied too late. She was wearing the famous hat she wanted to show off and a grey, beautifully cut costume. She looked really superb.

Drue Heinz was there bustling about in a friendly manner. The Lamonts came, so did the Joplings.[9] Peter Lilley and his wife were there, the Mexican Ambassador and his wife and the Argentine Ambassador and his wife. Diane Lever was there and Marcelle (Lady)

8. WW had argued in the *Times* of 18 June for a return to internment of IRA members, following the Manchester bomb and other outrages.
9. Michael Jopling m (1958) Gail, née Dickinson; Conservative MP, 1964–97, former Chief Whip and Minister of Agriculture; life peer 1997.

Quinton, the Wolfsons and the Sieffs and Netta Weinstock, the last fully in black. Laura decided not to come after all.

I had told Arnold the night before that it had been very moving when the commentary over the loudspeaker said the favourite, which might well have won, had belonged to Simon Weinstock, how tragic his death was but they knew he was there in spirit. There was great applause. Unfortunately, the horse only came in fifth and I had backed it.

Yesterday Prince Michael of Kent and the Princess came in [to the Tote room]. She insisted on sitting by me. 'I'd like to sit here and flirt with you,' she said rather publicly. Micky Suffolk, sitting on her other side, said, 'Why not with me?' 'You, too, if you like, but I prefer Woodrow.' She's a jolly girl, despite her waywardness.

Just before the last race we thought we would go. Margaret [catering manager] insisted on lining up the six waitresses who always waited on us and presenting them to us before we finally said goodbye. She was in tears. I was almost in tears. Verushka was crying. So were the waitresses. Charming, some of them. I kissed each one and thanked them for all they had done for us.

Then off we went into the sunset so far as Royal Ascot is concerned.

Sunday 23 June
Lunch at the Howard de Waldens in the country. To my mild horror I found Max Hastings there. He seems to pursue me, or I him, perhaps he thinks.

He seemed much more friendly. Maybe I should cultivate him a bit more.

Sue Baring[10] had her new friend, an American lawyer who works with the European Bank for Reconstruction in London.

He is a tremendous federalist. So is silly Sue, who once stood as a Lib Dem candidate.

He said everything in the world was moving towards integration.

There was the usual argument.

Sue was looking quite pretty but rather like an overblown rose.

I had asked Number 10 to tell the PM that if he had a moment I'd like to speak to him. His call came through as Petronella and I were watching *Showboat*, the latest version. Petronella was very cross. 'Can't

---

10. The Hon. Susan, née Renwick, m 1 (1955–84) the Hon. John Baring, m 2 (1997) Andre Newburg; chairman, Inner London Probation Committee, 1996–9.

you tell him to ring back?' 'No I can't tell the PM to ring back. He's a rather busy person. You'll have to keep quiet.' In a fury she turned the TV off and listened to my end of the conversation which put me off and worried me on security grounds.

I congratulated him on his brilliant handling of the beef affair in Florence.

He sounded very chirpy. Fights like the one he'd just had at Florence energize him.

Tuesday 25 June
After lunch Richard Wilson, the agreeable Permanent Secretary to the Home Office, came to the Tote. He's backing us as best he can. I told him about my idea of getting Field Marshal Sir Peter Inge[11] to succeed me. I didn't mention that Arnold had put the idea in my head.

He also told me that an announcement would be coming out shortly concerning no change in the status of the Tote. 'That's what you want, isn't it?' 'Yes, thank goodness. It will help a great deal in dealing with all these business people, Ladbroke and the banks.' That takes a great weight off my mind.

Wednesday 26 June
Richard Wilson rang to say the Home Secretary thought Peter Inge a splendid idea, but as ours is a brilliantly commercial successful operation, the Home Secretary was wondering whether a Field Marshal would be able to cope with all the business people on all these negotiations we have to do financially. I said, 'He's pretty good at beating down the prices, I gather, on arms and tanks and procurements for the army.'

In the meanwhile I've got to ring round the Cabinet to get support from Ken Clarke, Peter Lilley and co. to back our being allowed to take bets on the Irish Lottery numbers. For some extraordinary reason it's become a Cabinet issue. They're scared of breaching the principle and opening a demand to allow betting on numbers in the English Lottery.

Went with Diana Rawstron to see *Salad Days*.

I found the performance almost unbearably nostalgic. 'Never look back' is the starting theme of the Oxford undergraduates getting their degrees at the Sheldonian. But I frequently look back. It was one of

---

11. Chief of Defence Staff, 1994–7; knight 1988, life peer 1997.

the very happiest times of my life at Oxford. I see no reason for not looking back to a period. The music was enchanting and so was the story, insofar as it existed.

Thursday 27 June
Lord Nolan, whom I had not met before.

He is a tall, friendly man with a kind face and intelligent, though not one which indicates a piercing, brilliant intellect as Sir Stafford Cripps's did.

I said, 'If a man is not honourable and doesn't declare his interests, it's very difficult to make him honourable by a set of rules now he's got this register.'

I [also] said, 'The real trouble is that when you go to Roman Catholic countries, corruption is the order of the day. The Roman Catholic Church never seems very disturbed by it.'

He laughed a little. When I looked him up in *Who's Who* later, which I should have done before, I saw he was educated at Ampleforth, the Roman Catholic school, and had been on the Board of the Convent of the Sacred Heart, Woldingham.

He had read the matter I had sent him [about the Tote].

After a little more agreeable conversation he said, 'The person you want to see now is Len Peach, who is the Commissioner in charge of implementing the Nolan Committee's proposals[12] – I am really out of it. But I'll let him know what you have said and our conversation.'

The charming fellow insisted on taking me to the lift in case I lost my way and we parted on the friendliest of terms. I had the clear impression that he thought I was quite right in assuming that 'Nolan' did not cover the Tote, [it] being really, as I had put to him, *sui generis*.

I popped in briefly at the annual summer drinks party at Sotheby's and wished I hadn't. People I couldn't remember bombarded me.

Saturday 29 June
Up at an unearthly hour to catch an aeroplane for Newcastle.

John Wakeham, Chairman of BHB, was also *en route* to Newcastle for Stan Clarke's great semi-opening of the new buildings and arrangements at Newcastle racecourse.

Rodney Brack, Chief Executive of the Levy Board, and his wife

---

12. Personnel and management expert; Chairman, Police Complaints Authority, 1992–5, first commissioner for Public Appointments, 1995–9; knight 1989.

were proudly on their way. He is to make the official opening of the new betting hall because the Levy Board contributed £309,000 or thereabouts. The Tote also contributed £100,000 plus to this part of the enterprise.

The first person I saw at Newcastle was Ginnie Beaumont.[13]

She is very large with a very good nature. She shouted to me that Stan Clarke had given Nicky, her husband, the push.

His brother, Lord Allendale, is patron of Newcastle racecourse and was present. I thought it very rum that Stan Clarke said how marvellous it was to have Lord Allendale as patron, and made various friendly references to Nicky, when he had just booted him out. Nicky sat there smiling when he was thanked for this, that and the other, as though nothing had happened. But Ginnie made faces at me.

In practice Stan Clarke has done a terrific job. He has resurrected a racecourse which was very popular before the war but in decay ever since.

---

13. Jane, née Wallace, m (1953) Captain the Hon. Sir Nicholas Beaumont (Clerk of the Course, Ascot, 1969–94; Director, High Gosforth Park, 1994; knight 1994.)

Thursday 4 July

Seventy-eight today. Though I get tired from time to time, I think I am still in reasonably good shape. I would like to last at least another ten years with my brain in order.

Mrs Tamborero gave me some strawberries picked in Sussex and some Sussex honey, 'to keep me sweet,' she said. I hope it works.

In the evening there was a *Spectator* party in their garden. As usual it was crammed with people, some of whom one doesn't want to meet at all.

There were many tall men and I felt over-shadowed.

We moved on to Christopher's Restaurant, run by one of the Gilmour boys.

Suddenly entered a singer with a musical instrument and a song composed and written in my honour.[1] It contained items such as my falling in the lagoon at Venice.

It had been arranged by Olga Polizzi who had been unable to come to the dinner. She'd hired the musician and I think William Shawcross had written the words. It was very funny and I was very touched by what she had done.

After it, up popped the rather awful Bruce Anderson and began, 'I have been asked by Petronella to say a few words about her father.' Petronella indignantly cried out 'I did NOT.' He carried on, with rambling praise calling me the country's chief elder statesman, describing the glories of my famous cellar. It was no doubt well meant and I thanked him for it.

There was a birthday cake with candles (I can't remember how many, perhaps eight). I had to blow them all out at once, which I achieved.

So I got up and rather feebly thanked everybody.

A little later I rose, banged the table and said, 'You're now going

---

1. The first two lines, repeated at the beginning of most stanzas, were 'Baron Wyatt of Weeford / Woodrow to his friends'.

to have to listen to something whether you like it or not. And you *will* like it. My daughter is going to sing.' Then Petronella did sing, beautifully.

I was not drunk because I hadn't drunk all that much. But I felt rather sick and exhausted. I staggered down the stairs, nearly slipping once or twice but got to the bottom.

They were all immensely kind.

Friday 5 July
I wasted time watching the Test Match against India and bits of Wimbledon. I must remember that I have but a few years left to cram in all I want to do.

Monday 8 July
Robert Cranborne said, 'Your tie is not up to your usual standard. Why are you wearing such a dull one?' It was white with little red spots.

He sits on the Government front bench about four or five yards away and points at me and waggles his tie, as though to say, 'Ho, you've got rather a jolly one on today.'

I congratulated him on his very fine speech in defence of the Lords in a debate on Labour's constitutional reform proposals. 'However, there is one point which is worth considering. That is the choice by representative peers of some of their numbers who are hereditary peers to sit and vote in the Lords but not all of them. That was done in the past with the old Irish representative peers quite successfully.'[2] 'Ah yes, but it wouldn't work today because they don't go to Eton any more. They wouldn't know what their other fellow representative peers were like. How would they know which to select?'

Tuesday 9 July
Yesterday Petronella had an interview with Major.[3] It lasted two hours. His officials and the press secretary were amazed at the *badinage* between them.

Something I liked particularly was that when there is a Test Match going on, a coded message comes in on a bit of paper with the latest

---

2. A solution on these lines was adopted by Labour in 1999 for the interim House of Lords arrangements.
3. Published in the *Daily Telegraph* on 15 July; see illustration.

score to the Prime Minister conducting a meeting. When one arrived that England had reached the five hundred and twenty-one total of an Indian innings, Major passed it to Michael Heseltine who was astonished. He said, 'What does that mean? We've only got to cull five hundred and twenty-one cows after all?'

Tonight came very sad news. Amschel, the son of Tessa and Victor Rothschild, was found dead in his hotel room in Paris, where he had gone with his wife.

He'd had a heart attack.[4] I don't think it could be anything to do with his distress at the horrible vilification by Vere Rothermere's *Daily Mail* of his mother. But perhaps it added to some stress he felt. He was a charming fellow, very good-looking and slim, well built.

Ralph Harris has just written an introduction to a re-publication of Samuel Smiles's *Self Help* which he sent to me ecstatically.

I wondered to myself, have I really lived up to Samuel Smiles? The answer is no. I have wasted my small talents. I have frittered many hours away on pointless pursuits and done very little. If I have ten years left, I must try hard to produce something worthwhile. It is the parable of the talents. It's a crime not to use what talents one has to the full.

Wednesday 10 July

To see Sir Leonard Peach, Commissioner for Public Appointments. To my astonishment he showed me the Home Office entry about the Tote, where it put in that our expenses were £33,050,000 as though they had been paid by the government.

Figures were just taken from our accounts from 1994/5. I said, 'This is absolute nonsense. We've paid those, not the Home Office. They're operational expenses.' Again he pointed to my salary, £97,000. 'That's a very large salary.' 'I daresay it is. But it's probably not as much as it ought to be, considering the salaries of the people I have to deal with.'

He said, 'It's the Home Office who put you in the "box" and they could take you out of it.'

---

4. In his report to Murdoch dated 12 July WW said that Amschel Rothschild had committed suicide by hanging himself; in his report of 17 July he said it appeared he had not intended suicide: 'Remember the case of the Tory MP who did strange things with an orange, strangling himself? It was the same sort of thing.'

Fortunately, he is a cricket lover and enthused greatly about my cousin, R. E. S. Wyatt.

I went to the [Foyles] lunch for Winston Churchill's book.[5] In his press hand-out he has put in how I was a great friend of his father, but I am not in the index. He doesn't mention me at all.

The book is only of interest when his father and grandfather were quarrelling bitterly and writing the most horrible things to each other. This is new stuff and it's the best part.

I proceeded to the Centre for Policy Studies to hear Chris Patten. He's as wet as hell, still, but he has suddenly become wedded to the free market. There's a new dodge from Brussels whereby no one is allowed to work more than a forty-eight hour week. Tessa Keswick, who can be very bright, got up and mentioned this directive: 'How would that go down among the Hong Kongers?' Patten's answer was, 'I think they would very much resent being allowed to make money for only forty-eight hours in a week.'

He was very tricky about Europe, indicating he thought we ought to go into it thoroughly, the single currency and all that. But he was trying to reassure the right wing of the party because he hopes to lead it – he is very vain – by saying his heart is now very much in the free market camp.

Thursday 11 July
Poor Nadje, it seems, died at around six or seven o'clock in the morning.[6] She could be very tiresome but I loved her. Lately, when I brought her flowers, she didn't know what they were and she hardly ever talked sense. Verushka said she did talk sense to her yesterday. Otherwise she has been rambling, shouting out, 'Help me, help me, Jesus Christ.' I made a foolish joke to her. She didn't understand it: 'Jesus Christ is on holiday and can't come at the moment.' I regret that.

She was a highly cultured woman. She could recite Goethe by the yard in German, and Schiller. She knew a great deal about German literature. Looking at photographs of her when young, this morning, one of them showed her as an extremely attractive woman of about

5. *His Father's Son*, a biography of his father Randolph Churchill (1911–68, the only son of the great Sir Winston Churchill).
6. She was nearly ninety-six.

thirty-five. That was when she was having an affair with a man who was the Mayor of Trieste, executed by the Yugoslavs during the war.

Another great affair she had was with a Monsignor of the Roman Catholic Church who drowned himself.

She had long been divorced from her husband. Nevertheless, Verushka and Livia, her sister, think it right that the ashes should be taken to Hungary and buried near their father's grave. They are right.

This morning I had a fearful row with Michael Howard. He was furious with me for lobbying ministers such as Kenneth Clarke and Virginia Bottomley, in charge of the British Lottery, and getting their firm opinions that they had no objection to our Tote bookmakers betting on the Irish Lottery. He said, 'This lobbying is counter-productive. You shouldn't be going to Ministers.' I said, 'I am a Member of Parliament, as well as being Chairman of the Tote, and I have got to fight for the Tote.'

Since betting began on the Irish Lotteries, our turnover has gone down by 9.7 per cent and the bookmakers' turnover has remained the same as last year's, approximately. He said he didn't believe me.

When I mentioned to Howard that Sir Leonard Peach had said, 'The Home Office could take you out of the [Nolan] "box" if they wanted to,' he nearly blew up.

Why did he and I'm afraid his Permanent Under Secretary, Richard Wilson (whom I trusted on the principle that Gandhi always worked on, 'I would rather trust somebody and be deceived than not trust them at all,') never tell me that they were going to make us come under the rules of the Nolan report?[7]

When Howard said, 'I make the appointment of Chairman,' I refrained from saying, 'Yes, but the Prime Minister's approval is the ultimate decision,' which is in fact the case. But I can't worry John Major with this sort of thing unless it becomes absolutely unavoidable.

Among other things I said to the horrible Howard was that the Home Office had always been against us. 'What do you mean?' 'They

---

7. Michael Howard had said in a written Commons answer that the new Tote chairman would be chosen in consultation with the racing industry and according to the post-Nolan code. He announced on 18 July 1996 that the statutory framework governing the Tote would remain unchanged. The government review of the Tote had considered selling off and privatizing its constituent parts, an option vigorously opposed by WW.

wouldn't let us bet in the High Streets for eleven years.'[8] 'We've changed all that now.' 'Yes, eleven years late. Now you're doing the same thing with the Irish Lottery, destroying our profits.'

Grudgingly he said he would look at it again. But I don't know that he will look at it impartially.

He doesn't give a damn about the Tote, or racing.

While I was in the Lords I bumped into Norman Tebbit. I said, 'What way are you going to tell your readers to vote when it comes to the election?' 'I shall do what my proprietor (Rupert Murdoch) and the editor of the *Sun* (for which he writes a weekly column) tell me to do.' 'That's very pusillanimous. I would never do anything the proprietor or the editor of the *News of the World* or the *Times* told me to. I state my own independent line.' He shrugged his shoulders.

He's a very bitter fellow. He's probably never forgiven me for interfering during Margaret's last successful election campaign, making them put her on the television when they were trying to keep her off, thinking she was poison to the public, and it was the exact opposite.[9]

Saturday 13 July

The great dance at Grantchester to celebrate the thirtieth wedding anniversary of Jeffrey and Mary Archer.

Because of what Petronella had written [in the *Spectator*] about Margaret Thatcher being unhelpful to John Major, I was alarmed at meeting her. I plucked up my courage and went over to where she was standing in a small group. I gave her a kiss. She seemed a tiny bit frosty, then promptly introduced me to some foreign notables, saying I was one of the most influential journalists in the country and praising me. (I can't be responsible for what my daughter writes even though I agree with it.)

John Major was there, too, and Norma, looking very lovely, as I told her. Major and Margaret did not speak to each other the whole evening.

Dinner was followed by the Royal Marines Band, beating a Tattoo. This was beautifully done, very moving with its rousing, patriotic

---

8. Off-course betting shops were made legal in 1961; in 1972 the law was amended to allow the Tote also to open high street betting shops and to take bets at starting prices as well as at its own odds.

9. See Vol. 1, p. 351.

songs. As the Tattoo was coming to its closing stages, a splendid fireworks display chimed in with it.

In the dancing tent there were speeches. The principal one was made by a Senator called Bill Bradley.[10]

He was very impressive. Of Archer he said, 'He is not English but an American. He is so modest, as we are. He told me when we met at an inter-university athletics match that he intended to win an Olympic gold medal, to be Prime Minister and to be very rich. He has achieved one of those three.'

Later Mary Archer sang some songs specially composed by herself. Tim Rice did the music. The first one, as on a previous anniversary party, consisted of many digs against Jeffrey Archer, her husband.[11] He took them very well. She looked really lovely, with elfin face framed in deliciously coiffured straight black hair, and wearing a top couture yellow gown which set her off most elegantly. No wonder I've always been half in love with this brilliant, ageless girl.

Sunday 14 July
To lunch with Maurice Saatchi and his wife. It was not so large as the entertainment yesterday where there were three hundred and twenty guests. He had a mere sixty-five, sitting at one huge long table.

Michael Howard had been at both events. I said, 'I've been thinking a lot about you,' meaning about his refusal to let us bet on Irish Lotteries and trying to turn us into something governed by Nolan. 'Is that good news or bad news?' 'We'll have to see.'

I had taken the precaution of reading *Damage* by Josephine Hart, Maurice Saatchi's wife.

It is a real horror story, involving incest and despair and suicides. When I told her I hadn't finished it yet, she said, 'It gets worse.' I said, 'It's a deeply powerful work.' 'Coming from you, Woodrow, that's a terrific compliment.' But I was really being a little ambiguous, although it is an extraordinary story written with some skill, devilish.

---

10. Unsuccessful contender for the Democratic nomination for the 2000 American presidential election, Bradley was a Rhodes scholar at Oxford and an Olympic basket-ball gold medallist.
11. See Vol. 2, pp. 553–6, for the Archers' silver wedding celebrations.

Tuesday 16 July
Rang John Major in the morning.

I asked him how he had liked Petronella's article. He said, 'It was absolutely wonderful. What's more important, Norma thought it wonderful and approved of it completely.'

Thursday 18 July
The eightieth birthday party of Ted Heath, paid for by some friends.

When we arrived we all had to shake Ted Heath's hand. He said, 'What a fantastic selection of wine and malt whisky you sent.' I said, 'The one without a label is Bourbon.' (I'm beginning to think it's rum, so he may be rather surprised.) I gave him a 1970 Graham's port which was meant to commemorate his great election victory.

Saturday 20 July
Swam my usual furlong. Went to Oare. It was an extremely jolly weekend. Tessa was not at all scratchy, as she sometimes is, and I avoided all contentious subjects.

John Stevens, MEP, was there. He is clever, having been at Winchester and Magdalen. He also has an American passport – his father was a distinguished British diplomat in the US when he was born. Tessa Keswick tries to make a match between Petronella and him.

Also there was Rebecca, daughter of my darling friend Hugh Fraser, married to a brilliant young QC, Edward Fitzgerald. One of his clients is Myra Hindley, the Moors murderess. She said she would never do anything thing like that again. She was completely possessed by the evil of Brady who made her do these appalling things.

I said, 'Politically it would be impossible to let her out because there would be such a hubbub.' He understands that but [thinks] she was sentenced for thirty years, she's served them and legally she ought to be allowed out.

He does a tremendous amount of work in the prisons. He is vaguely very left-wing.

Sunday 21 July
For lunch came a remarkable Chinese, Larry Yung, supposedly one of the richest men in the world. He has a conglomerate called Citic in Hong Kong. He was in China when the Cultural Revolution took place. He was imprisoned, locked up in cells by himself and made to do terrifyingly hard labour. The punishments were savage but he

managed to survive something like a fourteen-year period. 'Did that make you tough and able to fulfil your business ambitions?' He said he thought it did but he could have done without this kind of 'training'.

His father is Vice-President of China.

The prettiest person there, clearly once very beautiful, was Tessa Keswick's seventy-eight-year-old mother.

She was the daughter of Delves-Broughton, the wicked baronet of pre-war years in [Kenya].[12]

Her life has been clouded by tragedy.

Monday 22 July
Lunch at NERA with Philip Wroughton, Lord Lieutenant of Berkshire. He had been a Council member of Lloyd's and involved in sorting out all the troubles. He said, 'What people don't realize is that no single person insured ever had his claim, a valid one, not paid in full. So the reputation of Lloyd's externally ought to have been maintained. It was internal troubles.' I said, 'Like fraud and dishonesty?' 'More total incompetence and ineptness.'

Wroughton was head of Bowring owned by Marsh & McLennan who own NERA. He is tall with a large friendly face, astute and amusing.

Tuesday 23 July
Dinner party at 19 Cavendish Avenue, [including] Sandra and Michael Howard; Leonard and Estelle Wolfson; Chips Keswick and Petronella; Charles and Caroline Moore; Arnold and Netta Weinstock. Despite the rows I am having with Michael Howard, he is very friendly. I believe he doesn't actually bear malice, likes a tough fight and doesn't resent my persistent pressure on him.

As he and Sandra were leaving, I took them out to their car.

'Are you getting any progress on the Irish Lottery numbers?' 'I am

---

12. Rosamond, only daughter of Sir 'Jock' Delves Broughton, 11th baronet, m (1938) 17th Lord Lovat (1911–95); the 'Happy Valley' scandals in Kenya, culminating in the murder of the Earl of Erroll in 1941, for which Delves Broughton was acquitted, were recounted by James Fox in *White Mischief* (1982); Delves Broughton did not go to Kenya until 1939; he married 2 (1940) Diana Caldwell who became Erroll's lover; WW put Rhodesia rather than Kenya but this was clearly a slip.

now trying to persuade the Home Office. Some of them are against it. But we may be winning.'

It was a worthwhile dinner party, if for that alone.

Michael Howard doesn't believe we'll ever join a single currency.

The odd man out is Leonard Wolfson. I was glad he was there with all these businessmen. The last time at his house he got quite angry. He said all business wants the single currency. It was demonstrated to him that all businessmen did not want the single currency.

There was talk about David Heathcoat-Amory, the junior Minister (Paymaster General) who resigned.[13] Michael Howard thought it extraordinary that he'd been busy writing his pamphlet with all the old arguments against the single currency, using Treasury staff, while he was at the Treasury. I said, 'What is so stupid is that John has made it abundantly clear that he doesn't believe there'll be a single currency, or want it, but that we must take part in the debate as to the form it's going to take.'

Sandra was very amused when I referred to Diane [Lever] as my little Lebanese peasant friend. Everybody knows how rich she is. Diane always giggles at my saying this. The next morning she rang Verushka and said she had cried most of the night. It was so sad that Harold was unable to be there.

I felt very sorry for her. It's a lonely business being a widow. They did have a very happy marriage and she was utterly devoted to him.

Wednesday 24 July
To the Pepper Pot, Dock Street, Wapping, for a party celebrating Ron Pell's retirement.[14]

They are a splendid bunch, these sub-editors. They're not always exactly brilliant but they have the common touch.

Thursday 25 July
Fearful news from Petronella. She went to a party at Grosvenor House and was sitting talking to Anne McElvoy, deputy editor of the *Spectator*, with her bag on the table. A man rushed by, snatched it and ran off.

In the bag were her passport and her diary containing all the tele-

---

13. On 22 July.
14. Sub-editor at the *News of the World* who dealt with WW's copy; see Vol. 2, p. 174, and *passim*.

phone numbers of the contacts she has in America for when she goes to the various conventions in September. She was in tears.

By the time this news came through to 19 Cavendish Avenue, Les Hinton had arrived. Verushka was busily ringing up the Home Secretary, Michael Howard. She said would he get a new passport for Petronella in the morning, otherwise it might take her days to get it. He said he would and immediately rang his secretary; it is to be collected in the morning.

Les Hinton was astonished. 'Are you actually ringing the Home Secretary, telling him to get a passport for your daughter?' She said, 'Yes, why not? He was here to dinner the other night. He was very friendly. Why shouldn't I?' 'Good Heavens. That's the way to get things done. Go straight to the top.' Verushka said, 'I always do.'

Les Hinton arrived in England with the conviction that Britain is a class-ridden, snobbish state, that it ought to be levelled out and become classless, as John Major has often said he wanted. Now he is changing his tune. He told me with great pride that Robert Cranborne had been to see him at News International at his, Robert's, request, to ask for his advice and help on his understanding of our international communications.

I said, 'Blair won't help you.' 'He may do.' 'His man in the Lords, Donoughue, everlastingly denounces you, saying you've got to be cut down to size.' 'Maybe, but I don't think that necessarily will be Blair's policy.'

He said, 'We've overtaken the *Daily Telegraph* on Mondays when we give the paper away for 10p. It's not doing so well on the other days of the week, but better than it has been.' 'Are you making money with it yet?' 'Good heavens no, not yet.'

I like him increasingly.

Friday 26 July
I was invited to the Albert Hall by Sir Christopher Bland, the new chairman of the BBC and Lady Bland (Jenny).

It was to mark the occasion of the fiftieth anniversary of the BBC Russian service which goes out on BBC World Service. The government, with their usual folly, have been chopping down on the money available to them and telling them they can get the rest from private enterprise, which may or may not work.

After the interval came Symphony No. 5 in D Minor by Shostakovich.

He was the alleged hero who stood up to Stalin and denounced Communism. This was not at all the case. Though he was against Stalin's repression, prison camps and murders, the much hailed piece we heard was actually a condemnation of 'capitalist thieves'. When it gets to a real bang, bang, which I rather enjoyed, it was the slaying and slaughter and crushing of anyone who believed in free enterprise.[15]

---

15. The controversy about Shostakovich's views was revived in 2000 with the publication of a biography, *Shostakovich: a Life* by Laurel Fay.

Friday 2 August – Monday 5 August *Porto Ercole, Italy*
Ken Baker is big, bright and breezy. He began, on arrival on Friday, by concluding there was no hope for the Tories.

By the time he had left an opinion poll had come up showing the gap was only thirty-three from forty-five per cent – it was an IBM poll in the *Guardian*.

Ken decided the Tories would win.

Blair's new proposition is that we would not necessarily go into the social chapter at all – he would consult business first because he believes business is against it.

All this must be making the public feel you never know where you are with him. If he can do somersaults now, what will he do if he got to be Prime Minister? New somersaults back to old positions?

Mary Baker has got lots of well-paid jobs, including one with Camelot. One morning we started a discussion about China. She said we ought not to trade with China because of the way they treated their people. I said, 'This is madness. For centuries we've never bothered about the regimes in the countries we get a lot of money from. Charity begins at home. Only by our example will they gradually behave in a more civilized manner.'

Pericles and Kyoko came on August 5th. She looked older than I remembered her. Pericles is still wearing his beard.

He said would I be prepared to put up £100,000 for a new venture. I said no. 'Did you ask your mother?' He said he had and she'd said the same as me.

Wednesday 7 August – Saturday 10 August
As usual there was great confusion about Petronella's journey, changing tickets.

This is costing some extra money but I am delighted that she is coming.

Richard Ryder and his wife arrived. She is slightly severe but quite pleasant.

I put to them, as experienced in Whitehall, Richard Ryder having been government Chief Whip until recently and she for eleven years having been Margaret Thatcher's personal and senior private secretary, the problems I have with regard to Wilson at the Home Office and Nolan.

Sunday 11 August
The Ryders gave me some excellent advice, which I was inclined to myself already, first of all to ring Richard Wilson on Monday and tell him that if I can't get satisfaction about altering this absurd advertisement they are going to put in [for the new Tote Chairman], I will take the matter further. I should not tell him what I propose to do, which is (a) to see Robin Butler,[1] and (b) to apply to the Prime Minister.

I am also inclined to think I should move a new Act of Parliament giving the Tote the right to bet on any events which the bookmakers are allowed to do, and invoking Clause 3 which would give us the right to open betting shops in any area which we chose, not relying on magistrates considering whether there are already betting shops there, and so forth.

Howard is using Nolan as a way of getting real control over the Tote and buggering it up. It's just as bad as Brussels, and yet Howard is very anti-Europe.

Ken Baker's manners are those of a lout. He is always very aggressive and shouting, grabbing things across the table. He has also been using the telephone at enormous length. On one occasion he said, 'I've got to stop now because this is the most expensive telephone system in the world.' He makes no offer to pay for his calls and as they are rather expensive here, it is very irritating.

However, I like him. He has a certain panache and quite good judgement of politicians. I have sent a message to the *Times* that I would like to review his book of war poetry – Faber and Faber.[2]

Talked to Arnold. He is a bit down in the dumps, poor chap.

Sunday 11 to Tuesday 20 August
Aliai Forte's birthday party. Less boring than usual.

On Tuesday 13th was the usual party at John Vestey's and Judith

---

1. Secretary of the Cabinet and Head of the Home Civil Service.
2. *The Faber Book of War Poetry*.

Bathurst's. Old Queen Juliana was there but I managed to avoid talking to her.

The more I saw Richard Ryder, the more I liked him. He is a truly solid citizen. Of Willie Whitelaw he said he is extremely two-faced; he leaked enormously to the press, showing them how wise he was and how he managed to keep a check on Margaret's excesses. He said it was really all drivel about his great influence on her, although he may have had a little.

The Ryders are going to stay with Denis and Margaret at Archie Hamilton's later on. I said, 'Give her my love and tell her that she created a revolution which can never be reversed and that she was the best Prime Minister in peace-time we had since the Reform Act of 1832.' This is something I sincerely believe. She pulled Britain up by its boot straps, demonstrating that a determined individual can make an enormous difference in a country's attitudes.

We had dinner at the Burrells. Margot wants me to take a share in a horse with her. She has some pretty good ones. I said, 'I am going to have nothing to do with racing after I leave the Tote in April. I don't want to go to the courses where inevitably I would be talking to the Tote staff. People would think I'm trying to interfere with my successor, which I don't propose to do. I shall write it right out of my mind.'

Meanwhile, there's been endless commotion with the Home Office.

I have stopped the advertisement by talking to the secretaries of both Michael Howard and Richard Wilson in their absence. It is a ridiculous advertisement, saying it would be an appointment for five years at £60,000 a year and a three-day week. It is absolutely absurd. The Chairman has to act as a leader. He can't do that on a three-day week. I've always worked forty hours a week at least on Tote matters.

Wednesday 21 August

Had an interesting talk with Norman Lamont and Peter Lilley. Lilley thinks that subsidiarity hasn't worked at all as it was meant to. We've not got back any of the powers which we let the European Union have over us.

I said, 'One reason why we can never be part of this idiotic move towards a Federal Europe is that the others are not democracies. They don't understand parliamentary procedures. They've always had elected dictatorships in a real sense.'

Norman is under the impression Jimmy Goldsmith can beat his old friend David Mellor in Putney.

That's potty. I said he'd lose his deposit.[3]

We discussed what would happen supposing Major wins, as I think he will. I said I believed he would go in about two years.

'But if, supposing he is defeated, you have a leadership election in October, what are your views about who would be his successor? Do you think you've got a chance, Norman?' He said he wouldn't even stand for it. He thinks that Stephen Dorrell would stand but that would be a disaster because no one would support him, though Major seems to like him. They both agreed that he's Major's preferred successor. I think that is true, but why I can't imagine. He put his foot in it over BSE by saying there might be a connection between BSE and CJD, the human disease.

Neither of them think much of Major. I am sorry that Peter Lilley takes that view. I haven't told him that Major thinks very highly of him.

Norman asked plaintively would he be too old to be in the Cabinet again at sixty, or thereabouts? I said, 'No, but why not go in one before, if Major, as I expect, wins this election?' He said he hasn't got a chance, he's too far behind, he couldn't possible catch up, there'll be a landslide against the Tories, and in any case he didn't want to be in the Cabinet with Major.

Norman hates Richard Ryder. He said, 'He was the one who persuaded Major, on the famous night when secret talks were going on next door to him at Number 10, to get rid of me.' He then wrote him a grovelling letter of enthusiasm for all he had done as Chancellor of the Exchequer. I said, 'But it was a difficult period because the country was furious, at least your loyal supporters were, at the VAT on domestic fuel, and also you were accident prone.' He said, 'What do you mean, "accident prone"?'

'You know, with all these credit cards and so forth.'

'That had nothing to do with it.' 'Well, I think it may have done. But I did say to Major at the time that you were his shield, and if once you went, he would be in the front line. That turned out to be true.'

Some observations on the guests.

Andrew Sinclair I like always the more I see of him. He is, however,

---

3. Goldsmith, Leader of the Referendum Party, did lose his deposit in the 1997 election, with only 3.5 per cent of the votes, but Mellor lost the seat to Labour.

somewhat of a boaster. Among other things he claims to have written the speech which Gaitskell made at the party conference in 1962 or 1963, 'I'll fight and fight again to save the party I love.'[4] But he didn't claim to have invented that phrase.

I knew Hugh extremely well and I never heard Andrew Sinclair's help mentioned. He may have sent him a few ideas but the notion that he was once Hugh Gaitskell's speech-writer seems far-fetched to me.

He has been very kind in reading my play and suggesting a new type of beginning which I have put in.

When I said, 'Do you think it's worth bothering about?' he said, 'Oh yes, there's something very good there.' So that was a comfort.

For the first time, this year I haven't been out in a boat. They always want Petronella to go, who's rather prettier than I am.

The Vesteys took the Lamonts and the Lilleys. Peter Lilley adored being on the famous motorbike cruising affair at the back, which he guided with great skill. He likes wind-surfing which he does down on the beach not far from here. She is an avid painter, gets up early in the morning. She says she still feels very sexy and she did the splits on the night before Petronella left to go to America. She looked very sexy. I had half a mind to give her a kiss but I decided against it.

Peter Lilley I like a lot. But he is very serious.

Norman, I thought, was getting on better with Rosemary.

Two nights ago he imitated owls with such enormous effect that he got a great reply from a particular owl which came closer and closer. He has got a most extraordinary gift for mimicking birds and calling to them and understanding them.

I have been in one of my jokey moods.

Several times I have had to sing:

> Craven A, Craven A.
> Never heard of fornication
> Quite content with masturbation.
> Craven A, Craven A.
> His behaviour at the varsity was most grotesque
> He went up and laid his penis on his tutor's desk.
> Craven A, Craven A.

---

4. Gaitskell said at the Party Conference, Scarborough, 1960: 'There are some of us, Mr Chairman, who will fight and fight and fight again to save the party we love.'

That is all to the tune of 'Steamboat Bill'.

On the whole I have enjoyed it greatly, except that I have no energy in the morning. That is despite the fact I go swimming with nothing on and the water is quite chilly at half past seven or a quarter to eight in the morning. It still doesn't bring me to.

Petronella was very sweet, bringing me all kinds of jolly things back from America.

She handed me a cigar with a Republican cigar band on it. She said, 'How do you like it?' I had taken only one puff. 'It's not as bad as I'd feared.' There were shrieks of laughter. 'It's one of your own. We took it out of the box. It's Montecristo No. 2.' I hadn't had much chance to smoke it but everybody thought she scored a great triumph.

Spoke to Pericles, wishing him a happy birthday. He said while he was in Europe President Clinton wanted to have dinner at his Steak House. His entourage came to check it out and they had to be told it was closed because he was in Europe. I said, 'My goodness, that was a great pity.' He said, 'Never mind. People in the neighbourhood got to hear about it and that was quite a good boost.'

Eva and Mark [Pejacsevich] were, as usual, very jolly to be with.

I like John and Diana Wilton very much, too. But Diana also gets very bossy and goes into the kitchen and tells Verushka she's doing this wrong and that wrong – which is totally untrue because Verushka manages it all extraordinarily well, in fact brilliantly.

Unlike last year, all the guests have been a success.

Wednesday 28 August

Last dinner at the Burrells at the top of the ruddy mountain with a terrible road to get there. We lost our way once although we'd been several times. It's badly signposted.

Bischoff was there, very friendly. He said Nicholas Banszky is one of the thirty-five most significant operators in the City of London. This pleased Verushka.

We're all alone in the house now and it's rather fun. Verushka is enjoying not having all the people around. She decided she didn't like to sleep at the other end of the house so she got into my bed yesterday morning. However, this morning she slept very well and didn't turn up until after I had gone swimming.

Wednesday 4 September
At last I got through to a reluctant Richard Wilson who had obviously been dodging me. I gave him absolute hell about the advertisement.

I also said, 'What are you doing about the Irish Lottery numbers? You've completely let us down. We've lost nearly a million already in profit which would have gone to racing.'

He said, 'I shall get on with it immediately now, if only to avoid another conversation like this one.'

Yesterday morning I had been rung from 112 Eaton Square to say that Julian Amery was dead. He had died in his sleep at about three in the morning.

Boritshka [Karolyi] rang. Did I know Julian was dead? 'Yes, I've known for a day and there's a funeral service at St Peter's, Eaton Square, on Thursday at 6 p.m.' She said she wasn't going to that, she couldn't bear it.

Poor Julian. He dwindled drunkenly to death. It could have been the effect of his heart operation, but I don't think so entirely. He grew this terrible beard, quite extraordinary. I haven't been able to get any sense out of him for a longish time.

I remembered how he used to have cheese and wine for breakfast when he stayed with us in Italy and the servants said, 'Is he a peasant?' because only peasants do that in Italy. 'No. He did it in Albania, and now always had wine and cheese for breakfast.'

I feel bereft of one friend after another. They are all disappearing.

Thursday 5 September
Julian's funeral.

In the front row were Robert Cranborne and Jonathan Aitken. Immediately in front of us were Alexander Stockton and his mother, Katie, with whom I have made it up now. She apologized for her appalling behaviour during the last time they were in Italy.[1] I said, 'I use that splendid egg cutter you gave me and I think of you every time I use it.'

Jill Hare, naturally, was there, as her son married Julian's youngest daughter who mixed up the Hares and the Listowels and the Pearsons and the Cargills and the Blakenhams.

She misses Alan terribly though she had been very philosophical and rather gay about it at his memorial service. I reflected for the umpteenth time how short life is and how sad for the survivors – husbands, wives and lovers.

Arnold and Netta came to dinner.

It had been Arnold's last day at GEC.

Arnold is a bit uncertain what to do with himself.

I said, 'Why don't you sell all your shares in GEC?'

'That would look very bad, as though I had no faith in the company.'

He is not certain he has chosen the right man [as successor] in Simpson.[2]

He proposes to sit there prodding him. Poor Mr Simpson.

Friday 6 September

Managed to polish off my *News of the World* article pretty quickly so I was in time to go to the meeting with Michael Beloff and John Heaton to see if we can't mount a judicial review against the government.

I showed him a draft letter I had written to Robin Butler, the Cabinet Secretary.

He suggested a modification, which I adopted, to ask him what legal authority his proposition to muck about with the Tote rested on.

When we had finished we went outside and there was Mr Justice Hoffman[3] who had sat with Victor Rothschild on the Rothschild Committee on Gambling.

'Have you been getting a lot of extremely complicated and difficult

---

1. In August 1987; see Vol. 1, pp. 400 ff., for the rows, and Vol. 2, p. 323, for the egg cutter present.
2. George Simpson, chief executive, Lucas Industries, 1994–6; managing director, GEC, 1996–9, chief executive since 1999; life peer 1997.
3. Leonard Hoffman, a Lord of Appeal since 1995, was a member of the Royal Commission on Gambling, 1976–8.

to understand advice from Michael?' Michael quickly said, 'No. We're
both very clever and we understood each other immediately.'

When I spoke to the *News of the World* acting editor this morning,
she said Rupert Murdoch is coming tomorrow. He never lets me know
when he comes these days or appears to want to speak to me. I don't
know whether he's still ashamed about cutting my column down to
once a fortnight, or what. It's slightly worrying because an enormous
amount of my income after April 30th next year will depend almost
entirely on Rupert, or News International.

Saturday 7 September
I was back in time [from Kempton] to go to the second part of Lanca-
shire v Essex, the Nat West Trophy final at Lords. I sat with Paul
Getty.

A kind of ritual comes at the end of these matches now. I'm given
a lift back in Paul's Rolls Royce and I stand to protect him till it arrives
outside the ground. I said, 'You've got to take care, you know, Victoria.
Somebody might take a pot shot at him because not everybody loves
him.' Paul had been saying it was extraordinary how many hate letters
he gets from people who write to say, 'Will you let me have half a
million or so to buy a house or save myself from bankruptcy, etc.'
When he declines he's assailed with vituperation and hate.

Monday 9 September
Lunch with John Baker of Powergen at NERA.

He was friendly. He obviously remembered how I had helped him
because I thought it right to get through his privatization of electricity.[4]
I said, 'Now you have to blow away this nonsense of £2 billion or so
being collected as a windfall tax.' He said he thought he'd write to all
the shareholders.

Tuesday 10 September
Geraldine Bedell came to interview me for the *Independent on Sunday*
magazine.[5]

Miss Bedell is aged forty, slim, very good figure, good legs, dark,
and a pretty, pert and quizzical face, narrowish but well constructed.

---

4. See Vol. 1, p 527; Baker was then Managing Director of the Central Electricity
   Generating Board (CEGB).
5. Her interview was published on 24 November 1996.

She told me she's written a novel, a detective story of a literary kind which is yet to be published.[6] She was supposed to be here for an hour. In the end she was here for two and a half hours. I enjoyed the conversation. She was jolly and has a good sense of humour – that is to say she laughed at my jokes.

I said some things I said were not to be included because they would be hurtful to various people. I told her that my daughter had suggested I should see her because if I didn't they might write the profile anyway and cut me up, which, my daughter added, they may well do in any case. She laughed. I said, 'Are you going to cut me up?' I got an evasive answer.

She said I was very rich. 'I am not rich at all.' 'What about this splendid house?' 'First of all it's falling to pieces and second it's only leasehold.'

She asked me about my background and about my cousin Honor who had written some nasty things about me at one time. I said, 'She did that because (a) she's getting old and (b) because I had disproved conclusively in my autobiography, *Confessions of an Optimist* and elsewhere, her passionate belief that we were descended from Sir Thomas Wyatt the poet.

I showed her the genealogical table which she showed interest in.

Wednesday 11 September
We had to be at the British Museum by 7.30 p.m. Ted Heath was about to open an exhibition sponsored by the *Times* of early Chinese art.

Les Hinton was there. I whispered to him about how Jeremy Deedes had to leave early from our Board Meeting in the morning for an emergency meeting held by Conrad Black. He'd said, 'Rupert is in town and we have to consider what harm he might be doing to us. He always does some when he's here.'

Friday 13 September
Had a long talk with John Major at half past eight this morning. He has agreed to be the guest of honour at my last annual Tote lunch after twenty-one years, early in March. I offered him March 3rd, which is a Monday, or the 5th, which is a Wednesday, saying that Tuesday he

---

6. *Party Tricks* was published in 1997.

would be at parliamentary questions. He laughed. 'This is far more important than parliamentary questions which I don't like.'

I gave him my wheeze for tax cuts in the Budget – cut the standard rate which will help the middling people but also cut the top rate from forty to thirty-eight per cent. 'That won't make much difference to what you collect but it'll put Blair on the spot. Is he to say of your tax cuts that he'll reverse them if he wins?'

He told me he was at the moment going for a 20p standard rate and doing something about capital gains tax which could well be abolished (I hope).

I told him of my conversations with John Baker of Powergen.

I said, 'It's all very well for the fat cats to be punished, no doubt, by this crazy scheme to raise £2–3 billion for potty-training courses but there are millions of lean cats at the bottom who'd have their food taken away from them.'

We discussed the election date. I said, 'I assume it'll be on May 6th to coincide with the council elections.' He said, 'No, May 1st, that's when the council elections are.'[7]

He said he was feeling great and on top of the world.

As I had no *News of the World* article, I sent my asked-for spiel to Rupert.[8] What a weird chap. I get no reaction from the missives I send him, except once when he said there was too much social gossip which he wasn't interested in. Les Hinton said to me on the evening of the Chinese exhibition in the British Museum that he values them very much.

Tuesday 17 September
Professor Chandra Wickramasinghe from Cardiff University came to lunch.[9] He is the author of *Our Place in the Cosmos*. He has collaborated with Fred Hoyle on similar subjects.

---

7. It was held on 1 May 1997.
8. WW included Jeremy Deedes' quip to Les Hinton at the Chinese exhibition, his own conversation with Major, conversations while on holiday, and his *Times* article of 3 September about northern Italy which had been followed up in the media.
9. Professor of Applied Mathematics and Astronomy, University of Wales, since 1988; author of a series of books on cosmic theory of life, 1978–88, some with Professor Sir Fred Hoyle as co-author; *Our Place in the Cosmos* was published in 1992.

'Are you twin souls, automatically thinking what the other one thinks?' He said, 'No. To begin with Hoyle wouldn't accept my theory that life did not start here on earth but resulted from bacteria from outer space – much coming from the tails of comets. When I'd convinced him, he helped tremendously to develop and find the evidence and we worked without disagreement, or very little.'

Professor Chandra is a most delightful man, slim, with a quick moving face, always searching, following up and asking questions. I gave him the parts of my play which deal with life from space.

Wednesday 18 September
At the Levy Board meeting even the bookmakers thought we should be allowed to bet on the numbers in the Irish Lottery.

After the meeting was over John Sparrow, Chairman of the Levy Board, spoke to me privately. He said, 'This business of advertising for jobs is a terrible nuisance. For example, Mrs McCurley is due to come up soon for reappointment. We have to have a Scottish member. There'd be an absolute riot in Scotland if we don't. But how do we frame an advertisement which says only Scots need apply? We'd be considered racist and discriminatory.'

The British Horseracing Board and the others are all intent to back me. I hope they will approach the Home Office.

Thursday 19 September
Petronella and Verushka went off to Hungary, all at my expense, costing me about £700 for their air fares and a birthday present for Livia of £100.

Saturday 21 September
At Newbury I was a kind of host to the party of Worcester College graduates who came racing. We'd got them all free tickets.

I took some of them to judge the best turned-out horse in our race, including the charming lady who was called the development director and wants to talk to me about my giving the college a lot of money.

They're trying to raise £10 million because they think they're inadequately endowed. I'm not sure why everybody thinks £10 million is always the right sum. It's what Maurice Saatchi tried to persuade me to get out of Paul Getty.

Wednesday 25 September

Verushka's birthday. I sent her the usual collection of flowers and two Hermès pins Mrs Tamborero and I had bought yesterday. She thought them marvellous.

But she was cross that there had been nobody there when she had tried to ring from the airport to find out what cigars I would like. She deliberately didn't buy any. 'I couldn't get Mrs Tamborero either,' she said. 'We were out.' I wrote her a little poem. The curious thing is I do love funny little Verushka, however tiresome she can be.

I went to a memorial service for Fitzroy MacLean.

Mary Soames made a wonderful speech or address about Fitzroy and how he had argued furiously with her father and Winston had apologized for his rudeness. That was when he was at the Foreign Office as expert on Russia and Winston had invited him to lunch to discuss his opinions.

Fitzroy was tall and slim with a long, interesting face and was a good talker in conversation either alone or with others or somewhere like The Other Club. But he was quite hopeless in the Commons. He was Under Secretary for War, or in a similar job, and could make no sense at all against the Opposition.

His books about Russia and Eastern Europe were read for a long time. He was one of that band of fellows who also played 'the great game'. I feel very forlorn sometimes at these memorial services. Down they go like poppies in the wind. Alan Hare, Julian Amery, Fitzroy MacLean, Billy McLean, Jim Meadows (my old friend at Aston who became Lord Mayor of Birmingham long ago, an old and trusted loyal friend even when I'd left the Labour Party).

Thursday 26 September

The enormous difficulties with the Home Office have caused me frequently to ring Howard and his office, Richard Wilson and other Cabinet servants. I've said there will be a public scandal. (I will make one.) During this I was very rude to an unfortunate Home Office secretary who apparently burst into tears. I sent her a letter of apology and a copy of *To the Point*. She rang Mrs Tamborero later on to say how thrilled she was with the letter and the present.

Friday 27 September

I asked Brian McDonnell to come to 19 Cavendish Avenue this morning. I had to drive myself up for the deadly deed.[10] It was agonizing.

He took it very well but said he'd hoped to stay till I retired. I told him I wanted the new Chairman to start with a new slate and to have had time to get to know John Heaton.

I had spoken to all the Board members I could find. They all agreed my action was right. David Sieff said, 'I think you'll find he's very relieved,' which in a curious way he was.

Sunday 29 September

Ascot.

John Sparrow, Chairman of the Levy Board, definitely doesn't want to take on my job. I think it sounds too much like hard work for him.

I told Bernard Donoughue how badly the Tote was being treated over the Irish Lottery and how much money we were losing.

I said, 'I propose to write to the All Party Racing Committee and ask them to help.' He thought that a very good idea. Wakeham thinks so, too. Wakeham is going to put in a word for us. He is quite skilful at that kind of intervention.

Monday 30 September

I have been pretty rude in my *Times* article to Howard and the Home Office.[11] Knowing the spiteful nature of Howard, this may put his back up and make him delay even further our betting on Irish Lotteries. On the other hand, he likes to be popular in racing and they'll be after him like hell for our losing all this money, particularly as Arabs and other foreign owners are moving their horses away from Britain because the prize money is so low here.

---

10. To ask him to take early retirement. John Heaton was to succeed him as Chief Executive of the Tote.
11. The article, published on 1 October, castigated Howard and the Home Office about their tardiness over the Irish Lottery question, the inclusion of the Tote as a body subject to Nolan regulations and the plethora of bureaucratic rules 'emulating Brussels'.

Tuesday 1 October
To dinner came Pru Murdoch and her husband.

Pru said that when her father heard just before she came out that she was having dinner with us, he said, 'Tell Woodrow that I'd like a £100 bet with him that the Tories will lose the general election.' I said, 'They're not going to win it but it's not a very good price. I could get a much better one from the bookmakers.' But actually, for the first time I am beginning to wonder if they really will catch up on the enormous gap. People are not concerned about Europe as they should be.

Friday 4 October
The concert in memory of Simon Weinstock at Covent Garden was a remarkable affair. Riccardo Muti flew over specially to conduct it.[1]

Jim Prior made a very stolid speech about how clever Simon had been. Prior is still Chairman of GEC.

The music, even to a novice in music like myself, was of exquisite beauty and excessively moving. Poor Arnold was weeping. We were sitting in the row behind them as very special friends.

Poor dear Arnold.

Saturday 5 October
I rang Arnold and asked him about his horse, Pilsudski, in the Arc tomorrow.

Arnold obviously thinks it's not likely to win.

I told him about General Rous[2] who had written to me after he read my article in the *Times*. He politely asked whether he would have a chance of succeeding me. I said to Arnold 'It's the most interesting thing. He is a direct descendant of Admiral Rous who arranged all the

---

1. At this time Music Director, La Scala, Milan.
2. Lieutenant General the Hon. Sir William Rous, Quarter Master General, Ministry of Defence, 1994–6; m (1970) Judith, née Persse; knight 1992.

original handicapping system which still happens today. He seems to have the right qualities.'

Sunday 6 October
The Arc de Triomphe. An amazing race. Heliffio led from the front but closely followed by Pilsudski. They led the whole way round the course.

It was the first time anyone can remember the first and second leading from start to finish. I kept thinking of poor Simon. He would have been delighted.

I had £5 each way at 20 to 1 on it.

Monday 7 October
General Rous came. He is very impressive. I told him the nature of the job, that it was about man-management, leadership, PR, attention to detail.

He is not interested in betting except occasionally but loves horses. When he commanded the Coldstreams in Trooping the Colour, he turned sideways to salute the Queen on the march past and he noticed how she saw not only him but the horse. Afterwards, at Buckingham Palace, she remarked, 'That was a very good horse you were riding.' She is possibly the greatest expert on horses in the country.

I told him to look out for the advertisement in the *Sunday Times* on October 13th.

His being a direct descendant of Admiral Rous, and the younger brother of the present Earl of Stradbroke, could be a remarkable coup. Racing would love it. I think, too, he would be listened to with respect in Whitehall, knowing it all through and through from serving on the Army Board.

In deepest confidence I have told John Heaton and Tom Phillips, 'Not a word to anyone. We have got to see that you get this man unless somebody better turns up. I have told him that might be a possibility.'

Meanwhile, my spats with the Home Office continue.

I have won all kinds of victories. The person appointed will be paid around £75,000 and not the ridiculous £60,000; the job is described as being up to four days a week, not three days; the nonsense about doing a review by the end of 1997 has been eliminated. I have won just about everything except the nonsense of going through this farce of advertising. If in the end we do succeed in getting General Rous, it will not have come through the vast waste of money on advertising and all the labours of the Home Office and people who don't understand the business at all, but from my writing that article in the *Times* which prompted him to ask whether there were a possibility of his succeeding me as Chairman.

Wednesday 9 October

Peter Jones insisted on coming to see me before the Tote Board meeting began to ask my advice, and would I help further his application to be Chairman. I said, 'I'm afraid I can give you no promises at all. It's out of my hands. You'll just have to answer the advertisement like everybody else.'

He still doesn't seem to understand that I think him totally unsuitable and the BHB (British Horseracing Board) think so, too. He's blown it by boasting that he's going to be the next Chairman, and also by his staying in America the whole time so I could never talk to him anyway.

He has a very blinkered vision. He thinks we should start a super bet straight away, although we haven't got the shops to do it in; he was against the Quadpot which is now immensely successful.

Friday 11 October

My usual twenty roses were sent to Margaret Thatcher for her birthday. She was going away on Saturday so we delivered them on Friday.[3]

Saturday 12 October

On the Channel 4 *Morning Live*, McCririck said that the removal of Brian McDonnell showed that I was still completely in control and my appointment of John Heaton as Chief Executive shows that I intended to remain in control at the Tote for many years. I certainly will give any advice when I am asked for it or if I think they may be making some gigantic mistake. But I don't propose to go to any racecourses again or to be seen breathing down my successor's neck, particularly if it is General Rous.

---

3. In his note accompanying the roses WW said, 'I was so glad to see you supporting John on the [Conservative conference] platform . . . He's still pushing your frontiers forward and is your pupil. It *may* be safe to elect Blair in five years' time. To do it now would be to put us in chains to Brussels . . .'

I have written individually to every member of the All Party Racing Committee, asking for their support on the Irish Lottery numbers issue and various other matters, including my Bill to make it possible that anything the bookmakers do we can do, too.

Mrs Tamborero has told me in the politest and kindliest terms possible that my play is actually no good.

I fear she is right.

Sunday 13 October
I put through a call to speak to John Major. They didn't quite know where he was but in half an hour he rang back.

John said, 'Have you seen Norma's book on Chequers? It's already third in the best-seller list in the *Sunday Times*.' I said I hadn't noticed that but I must get a copy at once.

I asked him if it was true that Jeffrey Archer had not come to the conference and not given his usual party because he hadn't been put in the government. He said yes. I said, 'It would have been far too risky at this stage to put him in. You were quite right, even if it has annoyed him.'

I told him what Irwin told me about Margaret shouting in a crowded dining-room at Bournemouth. She saw Irwin at a table and called out to him, 'How nice to see you, Irwin. How wonderful. At least there are two Conservatives in the room, thank goodness.' I said, 'She's terrible the way she goes around doing this sort of thing and it's so silly of her. She really goes right over the top now.' Naturally John agreed.

Tuesday 15 October
Had a nice letter from Margaret thanking me for the flowers. She had it typed which is unusual. I can't have much to do with her these days without getting a flea in my ear. She is giving covert backing to the lunatic Jimmy Goldsmith.

Friday 18 October
Quite a day. Had to broadcast on the BBC *World at One* about Dunblane.[4]

---

4. New restrictions on handguns were proposed in the aftermath of the slaughter of sixteen young children and a teacher at Dunblane primary school on 13 March.

I maintained vigorously that the gun laws wouldn't stop anybody from mass murdering or killing wildly.

Sunday 20 October
Had a very jolly chat with Gregory Le Strange. He is an American from Boston, very pro English. I told him a lot about the *English Story* and Edward J. O'Brien who died in 1940 or 1941, early on in the War, who was 'godfather' to me in the production of *English Story*.[5]

He asked if I had met his beautiful wife. They were married abroad when she was fifteen. 'She was usually about his house.' 'How interesting. Maybe I did meet her but I have forgotten her. But I usually notice a beautiful girl.'

He has been studying *English Story* and my introductions, and about the O'Brien prize I gave with each issue. He knows more than I can remember now about *English Story* and all the writers I published. 'Why did Collins do it?' 'First of all, they actually made money with it in the War, though it was very good of them to do it because of the shortage of paper. But they thought they would also get some new writers for Collins, though I can't remember whether they ever did or not.'

He asked why didn't I write more short stories now. I said I thought perhaps they weren't good enough. 'I think they would have been.' 'I was very proud when O'Brien put me in his 1940 collection of the best short stories, English and American, and there I was with all these great names surrounding me.'[6] 'Why don't the English like the short story version more?' I said, 'I don't know. But they like, of course, Somerset Maugham's brilliant short stories, they like O. Henry's, and Robert Louis Stevenson's short stories. In the war people didn't have much time to read, particularly if they were in the trenches or in the blitz, so short stories became extremely popular. They fell back again once the war was over. Then they turned to the trashy airport muck.'

He said he would send me a copy of his thesis. He's been working on it for three years.

---

5. Edward Joseph Harrington O'Brien (1890–1941), born in Boston and educated at Harvard, writer and editor of many volumes of British and American short stories; m 1 (1932) Romer Wilson (d 1930), m 2 (1932) Ruth Gorgel.
6. WW's contribution in *Selected English Short Stories* (1940) was 'Iron on Iron', written when he was twenty.

Monday 21 October
Today and yesterday that ghastly woman, Carla Powell, is plastered all over the newspapers as the hostess with the mostest because she's been giving parties on behalf of Jimmy Goldsmith at Brighton. She now supports this lunatic although she is supposed to be in favour of the Tory Party.

Tuesday 22 October
Paul and Victoria Getty came to dinner, so did Leonard and Estelle Wolfson, David Somerset (Beaufort) and Miranda Morley.

Victoria, talking to me, was very funny.

She said she'd known Paul for aeons but she got angry with him and to annoy him she married three people.

With Estelle on my left we discussed how it wasn't possible to have sex with someone who one didn't in some measure love. I said I did once – the first time I had any sex with a woman. It was somebody who turned out to be a tart but I hadn't known it at the time. I met her in a bar in Munich when I was eighteen. She was very pretty and very sexy, darkish. When I discovered she was a tart I was absolutely horrified and deeply distressed.

Frank Johnson got on like a house on fire with Paul because of his love of music. Paul daren't go to Covent Garden because he's a very secret person.

I would be frightened, too, if he did, that somebody might take a pot shot at him, one of these madmen.

Miranda Morley was, as ever, enchanting. She is very dignified and correct, the longstanding girlfriend of David's. She reminds me of the girl who insisted on dying with Arthur Koestler when he committed suicide after discovering he had Alzheimer's.[7] Her devotion to David is dog-like and she obviously enjoyed the evening enormously.

Frank Johnson is to have lunch with Paul. They will listen to all these wonderful musical recordings. I hope to goodness that Frank won't say that Major hasn't got a chance. (Later Frank was primed to say he would win.)

---

7. Koestler committed suicide in 1983 with his third wife, Cynthia, née Jefferies; WW wrote in Koestler's *DNB* (*Dictionary of National Biography*) entry that Koestler had Parkinson's disease and leukaemia.

Thursday 24 October

Endless chasing around of Marcus Kimball[8] and seeking him here, there and everywhere. He has introduced the first reading of the Bill for the Tote to be able to bet on any event, deleting all these ridiculous provisions in the Act before Irish Lottery numbers or anything else were thought of. It will have all-party support.

We got a date for the second reading on November 6th from the clerks in the Whips' office.

To the Saintsbury Club with General Rous. He loved it all, even the immensely tedious oration given by Roger Morgan, Shirley Anglesey's brother. He used to be Librarian in the House of Lords and was very helpful at that job.

The only decent wine was a Chassagne-Montrachet, Morgeot, 1987, which was quite delicious.

I dropped the General back at the Guards Club where he said he would spend the night. He asked if I'd have a drink with him at Pratt's.

I said, 'Usually I find it pretty boring but sometimes it can be entertaining.' He was very startled and said he always thought it fascinating, talking to the people there. The more I see of him the better I think he will do the job of Tote Chairman, though he must be a bit dim judging from the kind of person he likes.

Friday 25 October

Spent much of the day trying to find John Greenway, Chairman of the All Party Racing Committee.[9]

I have asked him simultaneously to move in the Commons the same Bill being introduced in the Lords.

'But the government may be against it.' I said, 'It doesn't matter if they are. There's overwhelming support for it, I believe, all party. It's not a matter of vital policy and the government could be defeated if they tried to block it.'

I have got a bet of £20 at 3 to 1 with funny old John Brown of William Hill, whom I am rather fond of in an odd way, that the election date will be May 1st. So at least I shall get £60 because it is obvious that is what John is leading up to, unless he is suddenly defeated beforehand, which I think unlikely.

---

8. Conservative MP, 1956–83; life peer 1985.
9. Conservative MP since 1987.

Robin Birley is thrilled with the help he's getting at Vindolanda at Hadrian's Wall from Paul Getty.

It's been organized by Christopher Gibbs who looks after some of Paul's charities. It took me a year and a half of nagging to get it on the slipway.[10]

I spoke to Howell James, political adviser to John Major. 'Perhaps I am a bit *mal vu* at Number 10 because I said in the *News of the World* what nonsense the proposed gun laws are.' 'Oh no, I don't think that's the case.' 'Well, give John my best regards and say the gap is narrowing enormously.' He said that their private research shows it even narrower than the NOP poll last Sunday.

Saturday 26 October

Paul really is a noble fellow. I am glad I have found one of the 1914 books on Lord's. It will cost me £170 but he was fascinated by it and had never seen it before, so I shall happily give it him. He gives so many valuable presents to people that I like to give him unusual ones he couldn't have bought.

Monday 28 October

Lunch early with Stephen Littlechild at NERA.[11]

NERA acts for electricity companies which think that the regulator (Stephen Littlechild) has put unfair and unnecessary burdens upon them to stop them making profits.

I took the opportunity to ask Stephen whether we [Cornish Light and Power] would get 3.5p per kwh after December 1998 when the contract with the South West Electricity Board (SWEB) ends. He said he didn't know that we would. I said, 'If not we're done for, and so are many other little wind farms.'

Later I wrote him a letter. I also wrote to Iain Vallance, Chairman of BT, that we should do a deal with BT in December 1998 to supply Telstar which is only a hundred and fifty yards away from the Goonhilly Downs.

We are so close that the transmission charges would vanish. I think this the only chance we now have of making any serious money out of the wind farm. Fortunately, gales have started taking us up to budget.

---

10. WW first visited Vindolanda on 27 September 1994.
11. Professor Stephen Littlechild, Director General, OFFER, 1989–98.

Having done the article for the *Times*, which I thought wasn't bad, I went to the Lords to find people to support our Bill. Then I went on to Ken Baker's party for the launch of his anthology of war poetry. It was at the Imperial War Museum.

I was very glad I went, otherwise there would hardly have been anybody there.

Tuesday 29 October

Dinner with Arnold at Pratt's. A strange man, Needham, who is really the Earl of Kilmorey, was there. Before Arnold arrived he said, 'Have you seen this? People proposed as members for Pratt's.' He showed me a name. 'That man is one of the ultra loyalists in Northern Ireland. He kills people. He's a terrorist. How can this club have terrorists?'

When he was out of the room, I whispered to Arnold, 'Would that fellow have done for you as Chairman of GEC?' 'No. He was very helpful to us at one point, getting us orders, and he was always very good to deal with when he was a Minister, but he cannot write a proper memo.' I said, 'He seems to be making a lot of money at various jobs.' 'Yes, he's the sort of fellow who will.'

It was heartbreaking when one or two people congratulated Arnold on the success of Pilsudski in the Breeders' Cup race in Canada. His eyes almost filled with tears. He thinks always of Simon, poor fellow.

Wednesday 30 October

Had lunch with Diana Rawstron at the RAC. Macmillan still haven't come forward with a proper contract.

I keep wondering whether I should follow Irwin's suggestion and offer it to HarperCollins, but there is so much about Rupert in it, some not flattering, that it might be difficult.

My big appointment of the day was with Paul Getty, for over an hour. He is prepared to do something. He is quite attracted by the idea of a guarantee of £10 million which they would have to pay back, naturally.

The proposition I left him with was that I would bring Maurice Saatchi to see him with all his plans.

He likes to do these things secretly. Every time I speak to Maurice Saatchi, if he's not alone I nearly have kittens.

The Lamonts' dinner was one of excruciating boredom.

Rosemary will stay with Norman till the election is over. God knows what will happen after that.

Sunday 3 November

Went to Bowden with Verushka and Petronella. Also present was Bernard Donoughue and his very nice girlfriend, the widow of a Tory MP who was murdered in the Brighton bombing by the IRA when Mrs Thatcher was nearly killed.

During lunch the subject of Maxwell came up.

I asked Bernard how it was that he could have had anything to do with Maxwell and been one of his directors when he had a label over his head which said, 'This man is not fit to be a director of a public company' (the label that of the Department of Trade inspectors who had closely examined his crooked dealings). He had nevertheless been passed fit for consumption by the greedy City.

Bernard said everybody told him he was OK and it had all been exaggerated by the Department of Trade inspectors. A previous Lord Chancellor told him that and a former Labour Attorney General, Silkin, had been working for Maxwell. All the people surrounding him seemed very respectable.

Bernard got into trouble because it was said that he got a million pounds in compensation when he left his job with Maxwell. He said it wasn't like that. He had a contract with Maxwell by which he could give notice any time he liked. When he did, Maxwell said to Bernard, 'You're a bloody traitor,' and refused to give him the terminal payment he was entitled to. Then he gave him only half of what he should have done. The figure was much exaggerated in the newspapers but he felt he had done nothing wrong at all.

At this time nothing had come out about Maxwell pinching money from the pension funds. He always had plenty of money at his disposal and nobody realized how crooked he was, except he, Bernard, was a trifle worried about some aspects and demanded that there should be an independent scrutiny by the non-executive members of the Board. Maxwell got very angry and said, 'No, you can't do that,' and accused him of personal treachery. Bernard began to wonder what was going on behind the scenes.

I rather like Bernard Donoughue. He is very bright. He was Callaghan's economic adviser and political adviser when he was Prime Minister. He asked me what was happening about the Chairman of the Tote. I took him on one side and said, 'It's a deadly secret,' and explained to him. He said he sounds a really good chap. He also told me that his side of the Lords had been told by him and by the Party that they have got to support our Tote Bill.

That was the most useful part of the visit to Bowden.

Monday 4 November
Saw Professor Schapira. He is now the top neurologist at the Royal Free Hospital.

I asked Professor Schapira did he think I'd got some awful cancer in my testicles. I did a lot of naked sunbathing in Italy and it was only halfway through the holiday that I thought I had better cover that area up when lying on my back. He laughed. 'You couldn't possibly get a cancer from the sun in so brief a time.'

'What's the trouble?' 'I forget things more than I used to. My computer doesn't record accurately or fast enough names and so on. Mind you, I used to forget names before, but I don't recoup them as quickly as I once did.' He said that was natural.

He made me walk up and down. 'You shouldn't do this juddering. Every time you move off, lift your feet high as though you were crossing some invisible line. That will make a lot of difference.' I tried it and I tried it afterwards. He is quite right. It was worth the visit for that alone.[1]

Tuesday 5 November
In the evening I talked to Baroness Blatch.[2] 'What is going to be your policy to our Bill tomorrow?' She said, 'I think the government are going to support it.' I was amazed. She said, 'But Virginia Bottomley fears there is some loophole which would enable you to bet not merely on the Irish Lottery numbers but on our own National Lottery.' 'This is crazy'. So I had to keep ringing until I got Virginia to reassure her.

---

1. WW by this time suffered from 'Parkinsonism', a minor form of Parkinson's disease.
2. Minister of State, Home Office, 1994–7; life peer 1987.

Wednesday 6 November
When our second reading came on, Kimball introduced our Bill quite neatly. I wished, however, that I had not listened to the clerks who said that I ought not to introduce a Bill in which I had an interest myself.

This added considerably to my work in organizing it.

My own speech followed Kimball's.

Ted Graham, on behalf of the Opposition, having been asked by Donoughue, who couldn't be there, gave the Bill his and Labour's warm support.

There was no opposition to it.

Thursday 7 November
At his request, I went to see Richard Wilson, the Permanent Under Secretary at the Home Office.

He said, 'I'll do anything rather than have another fierce argument with you and an article in the *Times* saying how hopeless we are.' I knew it was the article in the *Times*, saying we had all party support, which scared them. They have been magnificent, the members of the All Party Racing Committee, many of them writing in and telling the Home Secretary to get a move on.

We discussed the effects of the Nolan Committee.

'Nolan said you could take us off that list, if you wanted to. I wish you would do it.' He said, 'It's very difficult for us to do it now we've put you on it. I will think about it and see if we get an opportunity or an opportune time to do it.'

We discussed the Chairman. 'So far by far the best I've seen, and I've taken him out to dinner at the Saintsbury Club and talked to him at my house, is General Rous.'

I said, 'The worst I have heard is from Edwin Bramall (Field Marshal) who told me he is pretty good but rather too full of himself. But that might be said of me.' He laughed.

Wilson confirmed that, of course, my recommendation will have the final influence.

During our conversation he said they would like to have somebody who seemed independent on the little panel who are going to interview the shortlist of candidates when they make it up. Could I recommend somebody? I said, 'What about Stoker Hartington? He's no longer with the BHB. I happen to be seeing him tonight.'

Stoker was the host at the Sotheby's Celebration of Turf sale of sporting trophies and pictures.

He agreed unhesitatingly. I told him I had this chap in mind and I think he might be the best. He said, 'Woodrow, you know I always obey your instructions.'

Strangely, in the sale was a Stuart Devlin[3] circular silver tray. We gave it for a Tote Ebor win. The price suggested was £350–£500. I said to Geoffrey Webster, 'It would cost a great deal more now. Why don't we buy it, erase the name and present it for another Ebor or Cesarewitch or whatever we felt like, and also pick up some other cups quite cheaply which we could use for prizes?'

Saturday 9 November
John Prescott was [at Doncaster races] with his pretty wife wearing a delightful black hat.

They have grown-up children but she looks very young. 'You're a great dancer. I've seen you several times on TV dancing with John and he's very good too.' She is dark with fairly full lips and I would say very sexy.

I'd asked John Prescott and his wife and others to judge the best turned-out horse with me. I said, 'There is one rule that nobody knows about in the competition. A: the tail mustn't have been artificially mucked about with. B: the hair on the mane must be in its natural state.' John said, 'That means Tony Blair would be disqualified.' I don't think even now there is much love lost between them.

Gay Kindersley[4] was very prominent. He organizes the races for the amateur lady jockeys. We had two prizes to give and had sponsored a race for them that afternoon. Gay made a little address in our entertainment room: 'I hasten to reassure everybody that my name being Gay Kindersley came long before the war when gay simply meant happy and didn't have any other associations.' He warmly thanked me for all my initiative in giving amateur lady riders more opportunities – they now have seventy races they can go in for – and for awarding the prizes.

---

3. Goldsmith, silversmith and designer; Royal Designer for Industry.
4. Gentleman rider and trainer; champion amateur jockey, National Hunt season, 1959–60; his mother, Oonagh, d 1995, was one of the 'Golden Guinness Girls' – see Vol. 1, p. 270.

Sunday 10 November

Irwin rang. He'd been in Arizona dealing with some complicated legal matters for Rupert.

'Is Rupert going to back Blair – surely not?' He said, 'No, he won't, mainly because of Europe which he detests. Major's much better on Europe.'

Rupert is very annoyed because Lang[5] has decreed that he must let the others use his black box free by which they connect with all this digital stuff.

He says it is a socialist conception not to be allowed to have any profits from the fruit of his endeavours and initiative.

Tuesday 12 November

To see Paul Getty with Maurice Saatchi who brought no end of mock-up posters and advertisements.

Maurice Saatchi put him off my idea of guaranteeing a loan which he would get back when the election is over. Maurice said he didn't agree with that idea. They didn't want to be in debt again. They're not now. They've got about £3 million in hand to do the campaign with, but that's not enough to run it properly.

I found Maurice strangely negative.

As we were going, I gave Paul two pre-war cigars. I said, 'That's nothing to do with our conversation.'

Later Maurice said he's got another address in Pimlico. I told him that's where Victoria lives. She comes in the morning and may stay all day but she always goes back to her own house because she likes her independence.

Thursday 14 November

Memorial service for Molly Wyatt. She was well known for taking in stray dogs and making them well again. Jonathan [her son] read very well the piece from Kipling about how much dogs mean to people. The service was conducted, as usual, by the former Archbishop, Lord Runcie.

John Major's office had rung up the day before to say would I please represent him at the funeral. He wanted that published. He had to be at a Cabinet meeting and obviously couldn't come.

---

5. Ian Lang, Conservative MP, 1979–97; President, Board of Trade, 1995–7; life peer 1997.

I took the chance to say to Paul Getty at the reception afterwards, for which we didn't stay very long, 'I hope you noticed the very good opinion poll in the papers this morning, showing the gap narrowing.'

In the evening we went to dinner with the Wolfsons.

I had a row with the Israeli Ambassadress.[6]

She attacked Bevin. I said, 'No, he was a great man, admirer of the Jews. There wouldn't have been any Jews in Israel at all but for the Balfour Declaration.[7] It enabled Jews to settle in Israel and own land. I don't know why you curse England. We created Israel.'

Saturday 16 November

Petronella was in a great state of excitement because I had got four numbers right on the Lottery. 'You'll get a lot of money, at least £100,000.' When I rang up the office where you make enquiries they said, 'Four numbers this week only get about £73.'

There had been a breakdown in the machinery during the afternoon. There would have been all hell to pay if anything like that happened at the Tote. I think the whole affair is badly run.

Sunday 17 November

Speaking to John Major in the evening, I said, 'I think you ought to make more of the fact that Blair cheers on this forty-eight hour week legislation which is a purely socialist idea and will wreak havoc.'

He was delighted to hear the *Sun* will give him one hundred per cent backing and the *Sunday Times*, too. But there is this question mark over Peter Stothard at the *Times*.

I said, 'Rupert has a difficult position there, owing to the way in which he was allowed to buy the *Times*. He's not supposed to interfere with the editor. But he may make his views felt. I don't think Stothard would dare actually to say "vote Labour" but he might hum and ha and sit on the fence.'

We finished with him saying, 'You always cheer me up, Woodrow. I'm so glad you rang.' I said, 'I hope you weren't feeling despondent.' He sounded as though he was.

---

6. Hanna, née Kaspi, m (1955) Moshe Raviv, Israeli Ambassador to UK at this time.
7. The promise of a national home for the Jews in Palestine, made in 1917 by the British Conservative politician, Arthur Balfour (Prime Minister, 1902–5) when Foreign Secretary in Lloyd George's coalition government.

Monday 18 November
The General (Rous) and his wife came to dinner. She is an agreeable, not bad-looking, greyish haired, county set lady, well used to entertaining which she had to do frequently in the various high posts he held in the army.

Tuesday 19 November
Black tie as Christopher Sporborg's guest at the £150-a-head dinner at Claridge's ballroom. It was put on by a charitable organization for medical aid to Cuba. They were presenting for the first time a new brand, Cuaba cigars. They smoked tolerably well but were far too young.

There were numerous very pretty Cuban girls dishing out cigars and drinks and so on. At least, we thought they were Cuban but when spoken to their accents were distinctly English – Cockney and some came from Nottingham.

Christopher Sporborg sought to sound me on the Chairmanship. I used my standard answer that it was out of my hands.

Wednesday 20 November
Lunch at the Lords for Maurice Saatchi's introduction as Lord Saatchi. I sat next to Margaret Thatcher and had Black Rod on my other side. One of the supporters for Saatchi was Norman Tebbit, which I thought odd as he does nothing but belabour Major with attacks and derision, and Maurice Saatchi is handling the [advertising] account for the Tory party.

Margaret was in cheerful style. We got back to chatting in our old way about various people and her contempt for them or liking for them. She thought Portillo could make a good Leader when Major goes, but maybe he was too excitable.

She will come out very strongly for Major but she doesn't want to seem as though she is taking the limelight away from him and will only speak in constituencies for her own friends.

At The Other Club there was a fair amount of jollity. I was told by Nicholas Henderson, in charge of the Club, to sit in front of the Chancellor, Ken Clarke. It was surprising that he was there, with his Budget to be presented next Tuesday. Ken said Nigel Lawson started all this absurdity that Chancellors couldn't meet anybody and had to be in purdah for several weeks before their Budget. I said, 'I thought it began with the Dalton leak in Labour's post-war government.'

He said, 'People may ask me questions about the Budget which I simply ignore. It's silly of them to ask.'

I quizzed him also about selling off the national heritage by allowing chunks of Whitehall to be sold for use by property developers.

My question in the Lords on this matter had attracted attention. Strange how much a short question can achieve.

Thursday 21 November
A lunch at the *Spectator*. Tom Stoppard and John Mortimer were there.

I listened with some fascination to Tom Stoppard and John Mortimer discussing the mechanics of putting on a play.

John Mortimer is looking forward to Major being defeated but he doesn't like Blair. Tom Stoppard was much more cagey. He's obviously going to vote for Major but says he hasn't quite made up his mind.

Sunday 24 November
The *Independent on Sunday* magazine featured the interview with me very prominently as its front piece and on the cover.[8]

The woman had promised to let me see the article to check the facts. She gave me a selected list of facts, most of which were wrong, and I altered them. But she left in other 'facts' which were quite untrue and very silly.

I vaguely considered writing to her to complain, but thought, 'Gosh, what a ghastly bitch, anyway.'

This was the result of my collaboration.

On the other hand, presumably they wouldn't have wasted so much space on me if they thought I was a nonentity. And the *Independent on Sunday* has a very small circulation so hardly anybody will have read it.

Monday 25 November
We had a vast dinner party of eighteen.

It was very much a Hungarian evening.

The de Gelseys came.

They are nobly letting us have their flat [in Budapest] which is more or less opposite the Hilton Hotel, where I can receive faxes.

The head of the Karolyi family and his Austrian wife were there. They invited us to a New Year's party in Budapest.

---

8. See 10 September 1996 for the interview.

The Pejacsevichs were there also.

When the ladies had gone to the drawing-room, I set about challenging Vere. 'Are you going to back Major?' He said, 'I don't know yet. David English (his right hand man)[9] favours Blair.'

I am pretty sure I made some impression on Vere and I believe in the end he will be supporting Major. It has to be in his interest, whatever that ass David English thinks.

Tuesday 26 November
The servants did very well in clearing off the dinner party in time for the ten o'clock board meeting of Tote Direct at 19 Cavendish Avenue.

In the afternoon I saw Richard Wilson at the Home Office. He showed me a complete list of the candidates. There are sixty-two. Some were absurd, like bookmakers; some were racing journalists of a very low level. I said, 'We will have to ask Sporborg to come to an interview so that one Tote Board Member is invited. Leave out Peter Jones. He's been a great disappointment.'

For some reason the Home Secretary is very keen on Marcus Kimball. He is the bloke who introduced, on the Tote's behalf, the Bill to allow us to bet on any event.

He would be quite useless as Chairman and will be sixty-nine next October, although he is an agreeable fellow.

I said, 'We should interview William Astor, although he'd be quite useless at it. He was excellent speaking in the Lords for the government but he's too laid back. I couldn't see him trudging around betting shops, going all round the course talking to them as I have always done.'

I said, 'Still the best on the list is the General (Rous).'

I had to leave Richard Wilson after two and a half hours to get back to change into a black tie for dinner at Baby Steinberg's, aunt of Leonard Wolfson, whose flat is identical with Leonard's below except the pictures are smaller.

The guest of honour was the American Ambassador, Admiral Crowe. He got the job as Ambassador because he was the only military man who said he quite understood why, as a matter of conscience, Clinton was a draft dodger. This gave Clinton some more prestige in military circles. He struck me as pretty dumb, though agreeable.

---

9. (1931–98); editor-in-chief, *Daily Mail*, from 1989; knight 1992.

I told him that John Major would win the election, which surprised him.

I was very honoured to sit next to Estelle from the flat below. We had a jolly conversation about sex and how it works with some people and not with others when coupled.

I forget who was on my left, probably some old frump.

Wednesday 27 November

The *Spectator* party at the Savoy.

At the same table was David Trimble.[10]

I said, 'The only way you'll beat these people is to shoot to kill and don't give a damn what the Court of Human Rights says. They say they're an army and they must be prepared to be shot on sight. And internment ought to come back.'

He said he thought it was very much to Major's credit that he'd managed to get some kind of peace going for so long.

'I make a fuss every now and again for the hell of it, but yes, we'll back him. He'll be quite safe until he wants to call an election.'

Also present was Robin Day who showed great glee over the profile in the *Independent on Sunday*.

Thursday 28 November

To dinner at Tite Street with Andrew Roberts and his wife, Camilla.

On his chimney-piece in the drawing-room were all their invitations from here, there and everywhere. I thought that kind of common showing-off went out with Lady Docker who got into trouble for taking out of the country more money than was allowed for travellers abroad in the austerity days of the post-war Labour government. She used to do exactly the same with her invitations, including an aged invitation to a Buckingham Palace Garden Party years after the event. Pathetic.

Andrew's enormously blown up with his own importance and adores every pointless piece of self-generated publicity. For that reason he plays the fool, backing Jimmy Goldsmith's Referendum Party.

I retain much fondness for him despite his posturings, unworthy of a man with so good a brain.

10. Leader of the Ulster Unionist Party since 1995.

Tuesday 3 December
St Margaret's Westminster for the Julian Amery service of thanksgiving for his life. I wish that my memorial service will use the good old-fashioned phrase 'Memorial Service for . . .' etc. There could be a lot of people who wouldn't want to give a thanksgiving for Julian's life and won't want to for mine, but they still might like to come.[1]

The affair was fairly posh with a strong Arab flavour.

Dear old Ted Heath was there. He could have put Julian in the Cabinet, but didn't. He should have done.

Friday 6 December
Verushka has gone off to change the pearl necklace and earrings I gave her for our pearl wedding anniversary which is tomorrow. She found that one of the little diamonds (glass) had fallen out.

Meanwhile, awful things have been happening in politics. The worst is that Ken Clarke told two men from the BBC confidentially, but was overheard [at Chez Nico restaurant] by Frank Dobson, a shadow Labour Party spokesman, how he had warned the Prime Minister not to harden against the single currency or he would resign.

The Tory Party has never looked so much in a mess before as it approaches the election.

I discussed it with Howell James, the PM's political adviser at Number 10. I said, 'My own inclination is that he should sack Clarke and let him go.'

During today there was a tremendous fall in the stock exchange. The ignorant, including the idiotic BBC interviewer on *The World at One* who was talking to Heseltine, put it down to turmoil in the Tory Party. It's nothing whatever to do with it. It's because Greenspan, of the US Federal Reserve, said that interest rates were too low in America and he is contemplating putting them up to avoid inflation.

---

1. A 'Service of Thanksgiving' for WW's life and work was held at St Margaret's, Westminster, on 1 April 1998.

Sunday 8 December

I had left a message for John to ring if he wasn't too busy. He rang not long after 8 p.m. The poor chap began, 'I've had a horrible week. I don't remember anything so awful.'

I said, 'I had been intending to suggest that you fired Clarke, but I thought that would be impracticable at the moment.' He replied 'Yes, it would split the party which would be awful just before an election.'

I said, 'Of course I can write in the *Times*, in a long-term way, that I think we will probably have to get out of Europe and go back to an ordinary trade association, but it's not possible for you to do so.' It's really his view as well that we might have to leave if they don't stop taking on themselves all kinds of things which are purely domestic, in breach of subsidiarity.

Monday 9 December

I shall be quite relieved when April 30th 1997 comes. It is difficult to write the *Times* articles when I have to deal with so many Tote matters during the writing of them. If I can produce enough money without the Tote salary, there will be more time for what I would like to do.

I was made to rush like a maniac to get my black tie on for the Mencap charity affair at the Whitehall Banqueting Hall. As I thought, we arrived far too early. Petronella was in a great tizzy about where to change into her Marlene Dietrich dress lent by Bruce Oldfield [fashion designer].

Geoffrey and Miriam Owen very kindly came to support Petronella.

It was 'an evening with the Lords' who were performing various numbers.

We had paid £75 each for our tickets. Jeffrey Archer rushed around making everybody buy at least £20 of the lucky dip presents – all rubbish. His technique is very good.

The turns were truly terrible. One really large peer sang opera in a gruesome voice. When we thought we had got rid of him, he immediately came on again to do an encore which some ass had shouted for.

During the interval, the good bands led by Lord Colwyn[2] reappeared. Then he announced that Petronella Wyatt was to sing. We were too far away and people kept talking. I couldn't stop them. However, she did sing very well 'It Had to Be You' and Dietrich's 'Underneath the lamplight'. There was a lot of applause.

---

2. 3rd Baron Colwyn; dental surgeon.

Tuesday 10 December
To the gathering of the racing welfare charities at St James's Palace.

Michael Howard, whom I seem to meet everywhere I go, was there with Sandra. I thanked him for helping us along now with our Bill to bet on all events and with the Order to be able to bet on Irish Lottery numbers. He said, 'I'd like you to do a favour for me now. Vote for me in the Lords in support of the gun ban.' I said, 'I think it's a lot of rot.' He said, 'Yes but you'd get something worse if you don't vote against the amendments Labour's going to put down. They aim to widen the number of guns banned.' I said, 'OK, that's a bargain.'

I said to Jeremy Hanley, who was the host (he's the Minister for Overseas Development), 'I wish you were still the Chairman of the Party and not Mawhinney. You put your foot in it but you did it charmingly. He does it all the time with great ill grace and he gets all his facts wrong. He comes over very badly.'

After St James's Palace it was on to Conrad Black's house in Kensington.

The Blacks had a huge party with rather good food which you had to eat on your lap. I sat down with my selections and champagne, which wasn't bad, on the piano stool. Shortly, a terrified young man said, 'I'm terribly sorry but I'm supposed to be playing the piano here. Could you find somewhere else to sit?' I went out of the door and sat at the bottom of the staircase leading to the upper regions.

Everybody went by and stopped to talk as I tried to eat. Serena Rothschild greeted me. I said, 'What is a nice girl like you doing at a party like this?' There were many shady characters present. That rough fellow, Sir Patrick Sheehy came to talk to me.[3] As he left me to go down the flight of stairs to the next landing, he fell into all the drinks arranged on a table. There was an enormous crash and everything was shattered. Shrieks and yells. He's an enormous man. He caused considerable alarm but somewhat comically. I had been telling him that now he was no longer running BAT, he could start to be more daring in his attacks on the lying propaganda cigarette manufacturers are made to put on their cigarette packets.

Robin Birley, Mark's son, was there, the poor boy who was mauled by one of the animals at the Aspinall zoo and his face never recovered. He is standing as a candidate in Jimmy Goldsmith's Referendum Party.

---

3. Chairman, BAT, 1982–95; knight 1991.

I said, 'Are you looking for a political career?' He said, 'No, not really. But I've got to support him.' He is Jimmy Goldsmith's godson.

Algy Cluff[4] talked to me and also to Verushka. He said, 'Frank Johnson is editing the *Spectator* badly. He needs much more for the young in it. Also there's nothing about Europe.'

The Black house is very high with a large number of rooms, some rather small. There is a swimming pool at the bottom.

The furniture is mixed, as are the pictures. They look expensive but not always very good. I was surprised on seeing his so-called library by how few books were in it.

Thursday 12 December

When I met Richard Wilson, the Permanent Under Secretary at the Home Office, at Claridge's, he said everything had been fixed for the General to get the job. I said, 'When do you start the bogus interviewing so you can officially announce it?' 'Not until January.' I am fairly relaxed about that, if it really comes off, because there will be time enough for him to come on to the Board, and be inculcated into the culture of the Tote.

Verushka said I'd be late for the Arco dinner, but I wasn't.

Prince Michael was there. I talked to him at some length. He is more relaxed these days. I also talked to Angus Ogilvy and asked him whether he and his wife, Princess Alexandra, would like to stay with us in Italy. I described the place to him. He thought it a splendid idea. Would I be in touch with him again about it?

I wore the Republican tie which Petronella had got for me at the Republican convention because General Colin Powell, the previous Chief of Staff of the United States, is a Republican.

He made an excellent speech, full of humour and emotion. He described the difficulties of a black man in the army when he first joined. He had risen to the top despite the prejudices. He spoke fondly of his British connections. He was born in Jamaica and had been tracing his genealogy. His brother used to work on the buses in London. He spoke of his enormous affection for England. He became very serious about the need not to be tempted to cut the armed services in these chaotic and changing times.

On my right was William Rees-Mogg.

---

4. Chairman and chief executive, Cluff Mining; chairman, the *Spectator*, since 1985 (proprietor, 1981–5); a director, Centre for Policy Studies.

I asked him if he had read *Our Place in the Cosmos*. He said he hadn't. I said, 'You should.'

I said, 'I can't believe what is postulated by religious leaders.'

William, an ardent Roman Catholic, gravely said, 'But you'll go to Heaven, Woodrow, because you're a good man. I'll meet you.' I said, 'Thank you very much, but what shall we do there?'

Friday 13 December
I had to be at a quarter to one at Paul's.

When we began talking he said, 'I was quite determined I was going to send you away with nothing. The position's hopeless.' 'No it is not,' and I explained to him what the private polls meant.

'Also, did you read the *Spectator* this morning?'

'This was all arranged by Petronella who got Simon Sebag-Montefiore to interview the Spice Girls. She thought it better that a man should do it but she master-minded the questions. Simon actually did the interview very well. They don't trust Blair. They've come out in favour of Major. They sell millions of records all round the world, more than the Beatles ever did. They're madly popular in Britain among the young and I think it will have a very definite impact on the election.'

He said, 'Why am I the only person in the country with any money that the Conservatives can go to?'

I said, 'Would it help if I got a letter guaranteeing that if you let them have £5 million?' – 'I didn't say that.' – 'Well, £2 million or £3 million, that will be the last time they will ask you for money for an election?' He brightened to that.

He said, 'You're a very good persuader.' 'This is a very good lunch,' which it was. I had a glass of beer before lunch, which he did, and drank very little with lunch. The food was excellent – various crab salads.

I said, 'How much money *have* you got? I think it's so much that you don't know how much it is.' He said, 'Maybe, but I haven't got as much as people write in the newspapers.'

We lamented together the poor display of the English team against Rhodesia. Paul said, 'I'm glad you call it Rhodesia. That's what I call it, not Zimbabwe.'

He said finally, 'I'll ring you by Tuesday morning. I'll think about it.'

By the front door with Paul I said, 'I must look at that message of yours again on the cushion: "Money isn't everything but it sure keeps the family coming around." '

Saturday 14 December
At Wigan we discussed my 'Fourtuna' bet which could reach mammoth proportions by having to get the dual forecast right in four consecutive races – extremely difficult. They hadn't been very keen on it. I said, 'I've never been wrong with a new bet. Everybody was against the Quadpot, everybody was against the Placepot, everybody was against my new systems for the dual forecast and also the jackpot, but they all came triumphantly right.'

Louis Skelton said he would examine it at once.

I said, 'I want it done before I go at the end of April.' He's a very nice boy, Louis Skelton, very clever. I will have to ring him on Monday when he's examined it again.

Monday 16 December
Dinner at 19 Cavendish Avenue. As so often, Chips Keswick cancelled at the last minute. He has not been a very loyal friend. I got him his knighthood. I got him on to the Board of the Bank of England. But now he nearly always has some reason for not turning up at dinner. I think he's very mixed up these days with Prince Charles's set, naturally somewhat grander than ours.

Once again John Bowes Lyon, who is a brick, filled the gap at very short notice. Cita, who has Argentine connections (her father having been a correspondent there, she was actually born in Argentina) sat next to the Argentinian Ambassador. She spoke Spanish to him vigorously and eloquently.

I had been apprehensive over Verushka's invitation, without telling me, to Arnold and Netta. Irwin and he previously got on roughly as well as fighting cats in an alley.

I told Irwin that Arnold was coming. He said, 'Oh I can behave myself all right.' And Arnold said he didn't mind Irwin at all. He had forgotten he had a spat with him.

John Bowes Lyon told me that it isn't only Charles who wants to marry Camilla now. She, too, has become determined to marry him and be Queen.

Fortunately, as he agreed, Charles' mother is likely to live for a very long time, maybe ninety plus like her own mother.

Irwin thoroughly enjoyed his dinner and conversation. He had never met John Bowes Lyon before. There's nothing like American snobbery for liking to associate with a cousin of the Queen and the Queen Mother.

That, though Irwin maintains we ought to be a republic.

Peter Lilley had a good joke.

He had been to visit a school and the headmistress pointed out a particularly clever girl. She had told the teacher she had four kittens which were all socialist kittens. When Peter Lilley teased her about the kittens being socialist, to the astonishment of the teacher, she said, 'That was three weeks ago. Now their eyes are open so they've turned Conservative.'

Tuesday 17 December
I had a charming letter from Norma Major. When I sent her *The Wyatts: An Architectural Dynasty*, I wrote in it that her book *Chequers* was beautifully written and showed a great understanding of architecture. I like her comments on that wretched party poor John has to keep together and lead.[5]

Christmas parties to go to, first Claridge's where Vere Rothermere and Maiko were holding court.

A great many people were there whom I knew, many of whom I tried to dodge because I didn't want to talk to them. I did talk to David English who runs everything in England for Vere. 'I hope you're not still proposing to come out in favour of Blair in the *Mail*.'

He replied 'I don't know. We haven't made up our minds yet. But he's very charming. He comes to see us a great deal and he's got some very good ideas, many more than Major has.' I said, 'You really must be going barmy.' However, it was a friendly conversation.

I then dashed off to the Archers.

For sheer publicity reasons, to advertise himself, Jeffrey Archer has produced a Bill saying that the Crown must pass to the eldest child, whether it's a girl or boy. He's very pleased with himself for the spurious attention it got him in the press.

It is quite absurd because, even if Charles doesn't succeed, the two sons which he has means the issue couldn't arise for at least sixty years.

On my left at the Café Royal, where Lili[6] was holding a great party at which John Bowes Lyon was the ostensible host, sat Diana Wilton.

---

5. She said that many of the parliamentary party were completely beyond the pale.
6. Lili Rattan, née Mahtani.

She talked about affairs. Did I have lots of affairs? I said, 'No comment.'

Petronella sang beautifully, a few star turns which she said were new, and also the Marlene Dietrich. I then said would she do my favourite song, 'As Time Goes By', which she did. She received considerable applause. Somebody was talking while she was singing and I shouted loudly, 'Be quiet.'

Lili is exquisitely lovely. She wore a wonderful white gown which revealed her remarkable figure.

She has vast sums of money and she intends to enjoy herself with it. She seems to be very happy, so good luck to her.

It was a strange scene. There was scarcely a poor person in it, except us.

Thursday 19 December
I have been somewhat irritated with John Heaton. He blabbed away to newspapermen after some BHB conference about how the negotiations were going with Ladbroke about joining Tote Direct.

Ladbroke were extremely upset.

However, Tom Phillips said that although they were very angry about it at the time, it does look as though we have got a real chance now of getting Ladbroke into Tote Direct. William Hill would have to follow. This would be an enormous triumph for me. I have been working away at this for years. It would make wonderfully solid the future of the Tote and be a great benefit to racing.

Friday 20 December
On television at 8.30 a.m. for discussion about the Duke of Edinburgh's remark on the impracticability of the gun laws and how silly they were.[7]

Saturday 21 December
Off to the Keswicks.

Tessa banged away about Talitha Pol.[8] She said she was a tart and a prostitute. I said, 'I don't think that's true. I knew her quite well when she was a model and worked in a dress shop and lived with her

---

7. WW also supported Prince Philip's arguments, and his right to state them, in his *Times* article of 24 December.
8. Paul Getty's second wife who died in 1971.

step-mother who was related to Augustus John. She was not by any means a tart when I first met her. She must have been about twenty-one.'

Henry heard some of this at the other end of the table and said, 'I will not have this sort of conversation. If it's going to go on, I'm getting up and I'm having my dinner next door.'

It was an interesting show of force from Henry who can put his foot down at times. Otherwise we belong to the League of Battered Husbands.

Monday 23 December
Wrote my article for the *Times*. They liked it so much that it was put at the top of the features page, opposite the leading article, and not in my thin little column on the right hand side.

Tuesday 24 December
I spoke to John Major. I told him about Rupert's fury over the digital box being referred to the regulator.

I told him about my conversation with David English. He said, 'You know what the trouble with him is, don't you?' 'No.' He said, 'He wants a peerage.' I said, 'Oh my goodness. Well, you can't give him one.' He said, 'Of course not. I'm not going to do that kind of horse-trading.' I said, 'I suppose he's expecting to get one from Blair.'

I told him all the terrific stuff Petronella had done in organizing the Spice Girls and that it would make an incredible difference, in my view, to the election.

I said, 'You must take it seriously. That is the younger generation speaking and they've rumbled Blair all right. It's not true that they have a very juvenile audience. They have one reaching well into the thirties and thirty-fives.'

He thanked me and wished me a happy Christmas.

Wednesday 25 December
The Stelzers came for dinner.

He went on about having a republic and Cita got very cross with him. He said, 'Cita doesn't understand. I put up these sallies to have them knocked about and she doesn't believe in that kind of disputation.' I said, 'I do. I think it's very entertaining.' That's why I like him so much. He stimulates the production of ideas.

Rather foolishly I opened a magnum of 1971 Rauzan-Gassies. Only a quarter of it was drunk. I was rather upset about that but they couldn't drink any more after the Baron de Bachet Tiersan 1985.

Thursday 26 December
Kempton Park was bitterly cold. Nearly all the racing was off at the other courses.

We have been making quite a lot on the Irish Lottery numbers.

Friday 27 December
All my packing got done ready to go to Hungary.

Verushka was not feeling at all well. She really has bronchitis.

Saturday 28 December
Verushka was too ill to go and the doctor said she shouldn't, so naturally I stayed behind with her. Petronella went off, rather fussed, by herself. She asked for £200 before she went. 'Do you never have any money? Am I supposed to be subsidizing Conrad Black indefinitely?'

Monday 30 December
We were still wondering whether Verushka would be able to go if the doctor would say she could. Eventually the doctor said no.

The Stelzers have been incredibly kind. They sent us lots of food from Harrods. Eva Pejacsevich has done the same. They must have thought we were starving. Meanwhile, I eat the little goodies which the German Ambassador sent us.

David Treffry rang me from Cornwall to tell me that A. L. Rowse has at last been made a Companion of Honour. He wanted to have the Order of Merit but David said to him there was difficulty about the Order of Merit because it has to be given by the Queen. He reeled off the numbers of people who had also been given the Companion of Honour who were very distinguished, so he is quite happy now.

It had been nag, nag, nag all the way with Margaret and with Major, but at least it is done in the end. I sent to A. L. a message:

> The asses and the fools depart
> And you shine in Cornwall's heart.

Tuesday 31 December
Richard Wilson is KBE at last. I sent him a little postcard with the man on Wigan Pier, saying now he must come to Wigan.

The General has had the invitation to be interviewed on January 17th. We have arranged for him to come here on January 13th to talk to me and John Heaton. We are sending him the Statute which governs us and which he mustn't agree to depart from.

1997

Friday 3 January

During the day I talked to Irwin. He had sent me a cutting. From it, it seemed that the situation was getting a bit better with regard to what Rupert wants with his digital box and the regulation which might be imposed on the competitive element and so forth.

I told Irwin that when I had spoken to Major about it, he had said it was quasi judicial. I said, 'Yes, but you could get somebody to say something to someone. You have to do it.' I said to Irwin, 'That is what I believe has been done and I think I may have pulled it off for Rupert without too much damage being done to him.'

Irwin said, 'That's what Andrew Neil said in his book, that you were Rupert's great fixer.'[1]

I said, 'What I still find very bitter is my not being allowed to do every week my column in the *News of the World* which he promised me.'

Irwin said, 'He won't go back on that.' I said, 'I don't think the editor of the *News of the World* is any good. The only way he sells the paper is with outrageous, salacious stuff.' 'Yes, but the circulation is going up, or maintaining itself better than its rivals, which is the only thing that counts as far as Rupert is concerned.'

Today I spent a little while over the once-a-year bin-ends sale from Corney & Barrow. I got a dozen and a half, which is all they had left, of Baron de Bachen, at £83 a dozen which is an incredibly cheap price.

Petronella came back from the *Spectator* bubbling with excitement. On Saturday of next week, she goes with Portillo to visit the troops and travel all around Bosnia Herzegovina, going to Zagreb and Sarajevo and so forth.

---

1. Neil's autobiography, *Full Disclosure*, p. 99, explains that at the time of the Wapping dispute WW had brought Murdoch and Eric Hammond, General Secretary of the EETPU, together at a private dinner at his house, thus brokering the co-operation of the electricians to introduce the new printing technology; 'Wyatt loved to be Rupert's fixer in London,' Neil says.

She's a marvellous, wondrous girl. She's got on faster than I did at her age, or perhaps not quite, as I was an MP when I was only just twenty-six and when I was on the Cabinet Mission as Sir Stafford Cripps's personal assistant I was twenty-seven. And I had been writing a lot of articles. How wonderfully ridiculous to measure in rivalry the achievements of my daughter and myself! She will be far more successful than I ever was, and very good luck to her.

Friday 10 January
There was a lovely letter from Queen Elizabeth the Queen Mother thanking me for the books I had sent her.[2]

Saturday 11 January
I went to Wolverhampton where I had to give away a Tote prize for a race on the all-weather track.

Ron Muddle was there with his son. I had some lunch with them. Ron Muddle has been very enterprising, and was entirely responsible for securing the all-weather tracks, to the dismay of the Jockey Club and the BHB who think him no good because he is very common. What asses they are!

Poor Arnold Weinstock is dreadfully ill. At one point he had a heart attack. He was knocked on to a coral reef and hurled on to the beach upside down – he had turned his back on a big wave coming so as not to take it in the front. This was in Barbados.

Christopher Mayhew has died.[3] He was an awkward sort of cuss but he did have quite a lot of pluck.

He was strongly anti-semitic.

Monday 13 January
In the evening I gave a two-hour briefing to the General. I drank nothing. I am leaving off all alcohol except for a little red wine at night which is rather good for you. John Heaton and the General had champagne.

---

2. WW had sent an Edith Wharton novel, Baker's anthology of war poems, John Murray's commonplace book and an Osbert Lancaster collection.
3. (1915–97); former Labour MP and Minister of Defence who joined the Liberal Party in 1974; his daughter Tessa married WW's nephew, Robert Lyle (Robbie), in 1991; life peer 1981.

Tuesday 14 January

This evening Arnold was very pleased, first of all when I went to see him [in hospital], and secondly when Petronella came in bringing a small machine which you just plug into your ears and it plays very high quality discs. The recordings she brought with her were of various operas which he likes. He waved his hands up and down in time with the music.

In the afternoon at the Lords I spoke to Conrad Russell,[4] with Beryl Bainbridge in mind for her new book about the Crimean War. 'Who is the best authority to read on the Crimean War?' He said, 'I've no idea. I don't go any further than the Civil War.' I said, 'You mean nothing's happened since then? You haven't caught up with it yet?' He laughed. 'That's right. I'm locked for ever in the Civil War.'

Meanwhile, Irwin has gone haring after Blair. He has had dinner with him and is having dinner with him again tonight, and I think is thoroughly taken in by his flattery. I left a message on his machine saying, 'You've deserted me for Blair. Dangerous woods and bogs, treacherous ones, are down there. Look out.'

But I bet Cita doesn't like him very much. She is shrewder and more intelligent about character.

Petronella was very taken with the good-looking soldiers [in Bosnia]. They were so kind and polite and very protective. They made her feel safe. They had a kind of gallantry which people of that age whom she knows don't have.

She'd had to jump out of helicopters and aeroplanes before they landed. The ground was so rough they couldn't make a safe landing. She said Anna Ford, who was also with the same party, was very polite to her and very friendly. She was reporting for the *Today* programme.

I am acutely embarrassed. I have been told secretly that on Cheltenham Gold Cup day the Queen Mother, and it is her idea, is going to make a surprise presentation to me in public. Oh my God, and now they want to name a race for me on April 25th at Ascot at the evening meeting.

I told Stoker Hartington in great confidence that Ladbroke are coming in to Tote Direct. He was frightfully thrilled. He said, 'You've pulled it off! That's one of the best things you've done.' He always

---

4. 5th Earl Russell; Professor of History, King's College, London, since 1990; his books include *The Causes of the English Civil War* (1990); Liberal Democrat spokesman on social security, House of Lords.

behaves as though he is a great pal of mine. I hope he is. I said, 'Don't forget my General. He's the best of the bunch.'

I have sent a copy of *Buddenbrooks* [by Thomas Mann] to the boy with the fuzzy hair, of Jamaican origin, Herbert, who is one of the swimming pool attendants at the RAC and who reads deeply Dostoevsky and makes himself even more gloomy. That is when his love affairs are not going very well. He asked me about *Buddenbrooks* and said he couldn't get a copy, so I've got him one. He's a very nice boy. He's so anxious to learn that it must be encouraged.

Beryl Bainbridge said she will ring Henry Anglesey tomorrow at half past ten. I told Henry, 'It is a secret but she is writing a book about the Crimean War and I'm going to give her tomorrow, when I see her, your volume II of *History of the Cavalry*, where you write very well of the ordinary soldiers as well as the officers.' He said, 'I've got some more documents, too.' 'Will you let her have them?' 'I might do, but I'm going to write another book about it.'

He knew all about Beryl Bainbridge. He hadn't read her book about the *Titanic*, which is brilliant, but he will be very pleased to talk to her. I said, 'She's quite left-wing, but that won't matter to you because you live with rather a left-wing lady,' (meaning Shirley, his wife). He thought that very funny.

She said to me, 'What do I call him. He's a Marquess.' 'Call him Lord Anglesey.' 'Is that all right?' 'Yes, of course it is.' Tomorrow I will find out how she got on.

Wednesday 15 January
Lunch with Beryl Bainbridge who was giving it me at the Ivy. I was very glad to see her after so long a time. She has been in America pushing her book everywhere. At last she's got decent people running her publishers.

Beryl would like to see my play.

Friday 17 January
Arnold has now discharged himself and gone off to Bowden. I said, 'Why don't you go in an ambulance?' No, he would rather go in his own car. This is rather foolish because he can't lie down properly in the car and he will be in agony by the time he gets there. He has had these heart attacks twice now.

He hated the food in the hospital and had been getting all his food from us. Verushka sent up various dishes he liked, brown bean soup and vichyssoise.

I was very touched to see that Rupert Murdoch, to whom I had written that Arnold would appreciate it very much if he sent some flowers, had sent some.

Arnold did bump into a bit of coral which is terribly dangerous, but it may not have had anything to do with the situation. I am desperately worried about him, poor, dear Arnold.

Monday 20 January
I have been having a tussle with Cita. After all the arrangements I carefully made for her to sit at the High Table and in the Senior Common Room afterwards at Worcester College, which took a very long time (and we've had no outing the whole time they've been here) – I think they're always haring after Blair and they've been to Rome as well – she said she couldn't come on Sunday. I was absolutely rocked.

She said she had to choose between her two favourite men, namely Irwin and myself. He wants her to be in London because some very important clients of his own business have come over and they all want to watch the Super Bowl at the flat on Sunday evening. 'That's a ghastly perversion of English rugger.' 'Maybe, but that's what they want to do and I have to choose between you.'

Wednesday 22 January
Had a long talk with Bernard Levin at The Other Club.

'You've got to do the Coué system: "Every day in every way I get better and better."[5] That's how I keep going. Have confidence in yourself. You've got a lot of writing left in you.'

I asked if he remembered the days when he used to speak for me on the eve of poll nights and what fun we had, and how well he spoke. He remembered them well. 'You could still speak as well as that if you put your mind to it.'

I asked him how long his parents and grandparents had lived. It was way past ninety. 'So you'll live.'

---

5. See 15 May 1994 for the Coué system.

Friday 24 January

A great treat for me. That ghastly man Alan Clark is trying to get himself selected at Chelsea so I had his space in the *News of the World*.[6]

Dinner with the Stelzers at Scotts in Mount Street.

I sat next to a Mrs Cook, wife of the recently retired Australian Ambassador in Washington. Both he and she were extremely tall.

I could see that once she had been rather pretty, if you like giantesses. She herself is a lawyer and deals with complicated cases.

Sunday 26 January

Still feeling somewhat peeved by Cita's sudden defection, I tootled off to Oxford.

When mention was made of Cita not coming, Dick Smethurst [the provost] said to me, 'Is her husband Irwin Stelzer?' I said yes. He said, 'He writes very interestingly on economics in the *Sunday Times* and about America. He's very good.' The next day in the morning I was happy to pass that on to Cita as an unsolicited testimonial.

Monday 27 January

Caught John before he greeted his Cabinet at Chequers where they were discussing strategy for the manifesto.

I discussed the attitude of John Baker, Chairman of National Power. He wants to send the letter [against the windfall tax] to shareholders and so do the non-executive directors. The executive directors don't. The Cadbury code has somehow wrapped them up in a situation where they can't go against them.

We then talked about the cricket match. He hadn't heard the latest scores in which we did rather better against New Zealand, having got 521 runs.

He always cheers up when one talks to him about cricket.

I rang Cita. 'Who won that Super Bowl?' She said she didn't know.

I had a splendid letter from Beryl Bainbridge about my play. She didn't actually say it was total rubbish but indicated I really hadn't done it in a sensible manner. She makes some wonderful suggestions.

---

6. Alan Clark won the selection at Kensington & Chelsea and the seat at the 1997 general election.

She is such a sweet girl. I really love that lady. Now I must try to see if I can do something with it. But perhaps I am not cut out to be a playwright and should write some children's stories, or even try, under the stimulus of this very nice fellow, Le Strange, to write some short stories.

As a result of his coming, I have found the *Selected English Short Stories 1940*, which is the last volume that Edward O'Brien put together. I noticed, which I had forgotten, that it was dedicated to Woodrow and Susan Wyatt. I was married to Susan at the time. I should never have included her as a joint editor [of *English Story*] because she didn't know anything about it, but I suppose I was in love.

Wednesday 29 January

I had a delicious letter, rather sad in some ways, from dear Beryl Bainbridge. 'Do leave me a message to say you still love me. Perhaps I shouldn't have written such a drastic letter to you.' We sent her some flowers, saying how much I valued her instructions which I would be carrying out as they were most helpful.

She also left a letter for Henry Anglesey. She said he had been fantastic, wonderful, and made her alter her whole view of what happened in the Crimea. She remains terrified of Henry.

I was glad to hear [from Petronella] how well they [the forces in Bosnia] think of Portillo as Minister of Defence who fights for them and their interests very hard.

He is calming down now. He may well mature to be a Prime Minister, whereas poor old Howard, as everybody agrees, will never make it. He comes over so badly on television. What people mean is that he looks too Jewish. They say also he looks too pleased with himself. People don't have the same misgivings about Rifkind who is Jewish.

Thursday 30 January

I am agitated about the General – whether he will be appointed next Chairman. I keep ringing Wilson in vain. Richard Evans of the *Times* told Geoffrey Webster that the General had interviewed very well. That's the only information I've had.

I rang the Home Secretary's office and was put through to him eventually. I said we had got Ladbroke into Tote Direct, a great success for racing, but I don't think he understands this. I asked him about the new Chairman. He was very evasive, perhaps just for fun. He said the recommendations had been made by the panel who've finished interviewing. He would like me to come in one day next week to talk to him about it.

Saturday 1 February

When I leave the Tote at the end of April I get £124,000 which is tax free. They then give me a much lower pension, about £40,000, I think. I can do a lot with the £124,000, if I get my investments right.

Robin Cook has said it is inevitable that we will go into the single currency if it works. He apparently doesn't mind the Chancellor of the Exchequer being unable to present his own Budget or alter the interest rates.

Sunday 2 February

We went to Bowden. Arnold is much better. He came downstairs for lunch.

I wandered round the garden. The column looks fine with the large eagle on top and is well placed. For me, looking at it, bitter-sweet memories are revived. It stood at the left-hand side of the beech hedge in front of lovely, red-brick, Queen Anne, Conock. When we left that house I gave it to Arnold – no room for it at Cavendish Avenue. Also in Arnold's garden are lovely urns from Conock – and two beautiful stone balls from the Knightsbridge Barracks built by Thomas Henry Wyatt. When the barracks were foolishly demolished, the authorities gave me the two balls which had topped one of the entrances. It's always a delight for me to be in Arnold's house built by James Wyatt, who also built an entrancing rustic folly cave in the garden, not far from the column with the eagle.

Tuesday 4 February

The Tory Party has sent out a circular letter about the windfall tax, signed by the Prime Minister. It is quite good but not as good as if I had written it.

I gather the Prime Minister's letter has gone to just about everybody on the share register of the huge privatized utilities in danger from the windfall tax.[1]

At her request, Princess Michael of Kent came to dinner. She was very nicely dressed though she knew we were not having other people. She was also looking prettier than I have seen her for a long time. Perhaps she has got a new boyfriend. She was very friendly, touching my hand. We had a good deal of laughter.

Wednesday 5 February
Ladbroke joining Tote Direct is a great coup, as the whole of the racing world now handsomely recognizes. Even Monty Court had a headline about 'the wonderful Wyatt'. That after he has spent a year attacking us, and me in particular.

It happened without anything to do with Peter Jones, who has been publicizing himself with flattering comments in the *Sporting Life*, *Racing Post* and the *Times*. He can't claim any credit for it. He would if he could. He has all this stuff written up about him to influence the selection panel.

He has very much upset the Tote staff by saying we are no good and need perking up and run more efficiently. It's not very agreeable to me, either.

I spoke to John Wakeham. 'Did you put Peter Jones forward as a BHB candidate?' He said, 'No, I managed to avoid that. There were two from the BHB, Peter Jones and Christopher Sporborg, so we didn't put forward anybody.'

Friday 7 February
The nice young man, Gregory Le Strange, came back during the week.

He's going to send, I think, somebody who's got a grant, a researcher, here to tidy the whole lot [of my papers] up. I would be extremely grateful and maybe he would find the wonderful long handwritten letter I had from Margaret Thatcher the same day, or the day after, she won her 1979 thumping election victory. It was perhaps the

---

1. WW himself received the letter as a shareholder; he wrote a memo to the Prime Minister on 10 February saying there was now a change of feeling at National Power and they might send a letter to their shareholders after a suitable gap. WW also made points about projecting the government's policies on Europe, Mawhinney's failings as a campaigner, the need for Major himself to be at the forefront of the Tory campaign against Blair and how he was keeping Murdoch on-side.

only time she gave me full credit for all I had done to help her with it, which had been a lot.

Saturday 8 February
At Sandown there was a great hurdle race, the Tote Gold Trophy.

Priscilla Hastings,[2] a director of Newbury, was the hostess with Carnarvon. I told her that her son is not the true king of England. When I had to write the entry in the *Dictionary of National Biography* about Jack Huntingdon, I did a lot of research. Because of the Salic law it turned out that the real sovereign of England, if you take it by descent and believe that the Plantagenets were the true sovereigns, is the Countess of Loudon. 'He will be disappointed.' 'I am sorry about that but it will have to be faced.'

He is the Queen's trainer, the present Earl of Huntingdon [her son], who succeeded Jack, a distant cousin.

I was tired. For days I have been feeling somewhat ill in the stomach and intestines. I have had this damn bug for weeks and never got rid of it properly. I don't always have enough sleep. Sometimes I spend too much time looking at erotic movies – but they're not erotic enough.

Monday 10 February
Howard's still driving me mad. I've had a few very short interviews with him. He doesn't take any notice of what I'm saying. He's very evasive. He's not keeping me posted or taking my advice seriously as he promised he would in his letter of July 29th last year.[3]

He's vain and absurd, pretending to know who would be the right person to run the Tote. He's never been to our London HQ at Putney, he's never been to our computer complex in Wigan, he knows nothing about the business whatever. Nor does his side-kick, Sir Richard Wilson, though he at least has been to Putney and has a little bit of understanding and is rather better than the wretched Howard.

---

2. Widow of Captain Peter Hastings Bass, mother of the 16th Earl of Huntingdon; see Vol. 1, pp. 228–9, and elsewhere for WW's former belief that the Huntingdons, including Pericles who was in line of succession through his mother, were the Plantagenet claimants to the throne.
3. Howard's letter had said: 'I will of course be very happy to consider the claims of anyone who has your support.'

Tuesday 11 February
Went to Gail Lilley's exhibition in the Mall Gallery. Her paintings are not at all bad. I bought one which I described to her as a picture of a lady sitting on the loo. Indignantly she said, 'No, it wasn't a loo, it was a box.'

I paid £300 for it, I'm not sure why except that I quite like the woman and she'd been very kind to us and they'll be coming to stay in Porto Ercole in August.

Present at the ghastly exhibition was the fearful woman, Carla Powell.

Petronella tells me she now has living in her house the homosexual Peter Mandelson, the chief adviser to Blair on policy and general election policy in particular.

Wednesday 12 February
Dinner at The Other Club. It was chiefly notable for Nicko Henderson raising the question 'Should the Club continue?' He said the turnout now is never very good, only about thirteen or fourteen, like tonight. The Labour people won't come and it's supposed to be an all-party affair. I said, 'We must not give it up. It'd be a terrible betrayal of all these people like F. E. Smith, Winston Churchill and Lloyd George, of different parties who started it and made such a success of it.'

I've been reading Damon Runyon stories in bed, many I hadn't read before. It was he who invented the phrase 'Hooray Henry'.[4] I thought it came from this side of the Atlantic but I was wrong.

Thursday 13 February
The windfarm debate. It went off pretty well. The government was in full support of windfarms. Those who opposed on the grounds of ugliness in the environment were routed.

I described how awful the Goonhilly Downs were when I was a child, and now we had these marvellous wild flowers growing on them.

I began by saying quite frankly that we didn't build the windfarm for altruistic reasons but in order to try to make some money.

John and Diana Wilton to dinner.

I gave them a jolly good wine, Lascombes 1965, as well as a Premier Cru Chablis. I am very fond of that pair. John is getting better, despite

---

4. In *Collier's* Magazine of 18 April 1936.

all his ghastly treatment which doesn't seem to give him any pain, though it gives him headaches afterwards, which I am not surprised at.[5] He will be all right.

Saturday 15 February
A very exhausting day. Up at 5.30 a.m. to catch an aeroplane to Newcastle.

Stan Clarke is a marvellous bloke and I kept congratulating him, and he kept congratulating me.

Stan has bought an enormous place called Trentham where he proposes to have an amusement park and dining clubs and God knows what. 'How do you know that will work? You may be diversifying too much.' 'I know it'll work because I got the land and the property at such a good price.'

I am quite pleased with Peter Dow[6] who is now coming on fairly well, but he has some rash ideas.

He said he had a great deal coming up with *Punch*. I said, 'Be very careful how you deal with that man [the owner, Al Fayed].' The arrangement is that we send out to all our Credit customers, without giving him the list because it will be kept private, offering free subscriptions.

When I got home and found the copy of *Punch* sent to me, it was the most appalling bloody rubbish from start to finish. That wretched man, Al Fayed, has already changed the editor three times and the thing is an absolute ghastly bloody awful mess.

John Heaton had been driven to the airport, I suppose by his wife, when he left this morning, and he had no car to come back with. Would I drop him at Hammersmith Bridge? 'Why, what are you going to do there?' 'I'm going to walk across it. It's on my way home.'

As soon as he got out at Hammersmith Bridge, I rang his wife. 'Your young man is on his way. It'll take him about twenty minutes to get to you. He's walking. I hope he'll be safe. He's had a lot of walking to do already.' She was very grateful I had rung. He never thinks of that sort of thing with his wife. Curious chap.

---

5. He was having treatment for cancer; he died in 1999, aged 78.
6. The Tote's new marketing director.

Sunday 16 February
The most fearful nonsense appeared in the *Sunday Telegraph* about
Labour wanting to privatize the Tote and raise £400 million for the
Treasury.

Several people rang me up about it and I told them all the same. 'If
we'd have taken the advice of Lloyds Merchant Bank the last time the
question of privatization came up, we'd have had to sell our betting
shops, in which case I would never have got Tote Direct and we would
never have had this revolution which is going to profit racing so much.
And by the way, Lloyds Merchant Bank has disappeared and we're
still going strong.'

On Saturday there was an idiotic thing in the *Times* Diary, saying
that I was courting Beryl Bainbridge vigorously. Utter piffle. Of course
I am very fond of her and we extravagantly exchange notes about love
and all the rest of it but it is utterly platonic.

I am wondering vaguely whether I shouldn't threaten to sue the
Times and get some libel damages. But I don't really want to draw
attention to these absurd things people say.

When Richard Evans rang about the absurd story in the *Sunday
Telegraph* (I told him why it was absurd) he said, 'You're backing the
General, aren't you?' I said, 'I make no comment. I've said nothing to
that effect.'

I like that fellow. He had been my chief enemy at one time but I
think he no longer is. He certainly has somebody who leaks to him the
whole time from the Home Office. When I said that on the telephone to
Howard, he said, 'Impossible, absolute nonsense. Nobody could possibly leak from here.'

When I said that I had heard via Richard Evans that the General
had a brilliant interview he said, 'He couldn't possibly know.'

Saturday 22 February
I had tried to get hold of John Major yesterday to talk to him about
my difficulties with Michael Howard.

While I was talking to John Heaton and Tom Phillips at Cavendish
Avenue, John rang back.

I told him that Howard had delayed enormously over picking the
man he would recommend to John. 'In July last year he wrote to me
saying he wanted to get it done by the end of December so that the
new man could join early in 1997 to learn the ropes from me. It is
now nearly March. He is trying to dodge until after the Tote lunch

because it looks as though he will recommend somebody who I know is no good and will say so. He's been toying with William Astor, who is very agreeable but completely weak and no use whatever. And he will be attacked on "jobs for the boys" and personal friends. (Sandra Howard and Annabel Astor are close friends.) Peter Jones is another possible candidate he wants. I want somebody who will do the job better than I can.' John Major laughed.

I said, 'That has to be General Rous. He's tailor-made for the job. But for some reason which escapes me, Michael Howard thinks his judgement as to who should be the next Chairman of the Tote is better than mine.'

He laughed again. 'I will make enquiries about it straightaway, to see what's going on.'

I had told Howard I would speak to the Prime Minister. I warned him about it, but he will be furious. But that's his own fault. Of course, John may not want to thwart Howard because of the delicate balance within the Cabinet.

Yesterday I made numerous telephone calls to Howard's office, trying to speak to him but failed.

'Beautiful lady here, examining you,' is recorded on my tape machine. I was referring to the girl who asked to see what was in my briefcase as we left Heathrow for [a short holiday in] Marrakech and made me run the machine. She was highly delighted.

The journey to Marrakech was something of a nightmare. We had to change aeroplanes at Casablanca. Petronella would not sit in the middle of the row because she said she would feel ill if she couldn't look out of the window.

I was extremely uncomfortable sitting between Petronella and Verushka, and ached everywhere. By the time we reached the hotel La Mamounia in Marrakech it was about twelve o'clock.

Sunday 23 February
Arnold rang up and said, 'There's a tremendous lot about you in the newspapers again.'

I had a conversation with John Heaton.

'Will you please tell the members of the Board that no one is to say anything whatever about all these proposals to privatize us. I will deal with the whole subject in my speech at the Tote lunch on March 5th.'

I was moving so badly and awkwardly that after I'd had a bath and shampooed my hair I couldn't get out of the bath. I struggled for half an hour.

Eventually, by putting a number of towels on the bottom of the bath, I painfully raised myself. I must recover my old form.

This morning I am feeling a bit better, though I have an ache in my testicles. It is not so warm today. I have been reading *The Three Musketeers* again. How brilliantly that fellow Dumas writes. It's years since I read it and it's as gripping as ever.

Monday 24 February
I have been spending a fair amount of time sunbathing by this fantastic swimming pool. It's huge, about twice or three times the size of the RAC [Club's] Olympic-size pool. I walk past rows of often quite pretty ladies who have their breasts uncovered to get them sunburned. They are quite shameless about it and walk about in this pleasing guise. They lean on their elbows on the chairs with their breasts hanging down in front of them.

There is a games room. I played ping-pong with Petronella. At first my eye focus was so bad, having only the sight from my left eye, that I couldn't get the ball over the net. As I gradually grew acclimatized to it, I started to beat her – so she stopped playing.

The hotel is almost a shrine to Churchill. There is a suite which costs about £3,000 a night and was occupied so we couldn't see it. All along the walls are pictures of Churchill doing this, that and the other, and paintings which he did based in this hotel. He liked it very much and went back there several times when he was in Opposition after 1945.[7]

The Moroccan girls you see in the streets are extremely attractive, with a high degree of pulchritude, as P. G. Wodehouse might have put it.

I was beginning thoroughly to enjoy myself and relax and not worry so much about who would be Chairman of the Tote, when the holiday came to an end.

----

7. WW wrote about Churchill in Marrakech in his *Times* article of 3 March.

Wednesday 5 March
Annual Tote lunch. The affair was a rip-roaring success. The best speech was made by Verushka. She had asked me a few days ago did I mind if she said a few words before I spoke. She got terrific laughter and applause. I was proud of her. She was beautifully dressed and looked very pretty. The PM congratulated her and tried to imitate her Hungarian accent.

The Prime Minister was exceptionally kind to me.[1] Also he declared that no one could ever touch or inquire into changing the structure of the Tote again. It is absolutely safe and secure, which will be a great relief to our staff. Labour agreed.

Thursday 6 March
Tote Board meeting.

Peter Jones was sent for to speak to the Home Office in the middle of the Board meeting. He came back looking nervous and shaken again and is obviously to be interviewed in the final group by the treacherous Howard.

Friday 7 March
I tipped Mr Mulligan in my *News of the World* column for the Cheltenham Tote Gold Cup. I said I had a bet at 33 to 1 on it some time ago with Coral.[2]

Thursday 13 March
In the Royal Box [at Cheltenham] I was due to sit next to Queen Elizabeth the Queen Mother at lunch.

She said, 'Tell me about your early life.' So I did.

---

1. The heading for Richard Evans's report in the *Times* was 'Prime Minister pays tribute to Wyatt legacy'.
2. During the next few days WW gave the same tip to an attendant at the House of Lords and the Earl of Suffolk's butler.

I recounted how I nearly got court-martialled and about the regular soldiers who put the job on to me of getting rid of the cowardly Fearless Fred. I said, 'I was put under open arrest by the General but I knew that justice in the army is extremely good and I knew that I was right so I was never worried.[3] I wrote [when suspended from duty] an article called "Letter from France" for Cyril Connolly which he published in one of the early *Horizon*s and which he later included in his collection in *Golden Horizons*.[4] Do you remember *Horizon*?' 'Oh yes', she said. 'I read it often.'

I told her that I had been staying with Micky Suffolk the night before and we had an enormous amount to drink, so I wasn't drinking very much at lunch. We had thirty-year-old Veuve Clicquot champagne, a brilliant premier cru Montmains Chablis, and terrific Figeac 1961, plus a tremendous Hine brandy twenty-five years in the cask before bottling, and a first-class Croix des Monts dessert wine.

Simon Sebag-Montefiore, invited to lunch in the Royal Box with Petronella, was very anxious to be allowed to speak to Queen Elizabeth. So eventually I presented him to her, saying, 'His cousin was the very left-wing Bishop of Birmingham, but he's not left-wing himself.' She laughed.

She is such a sweetheart, that lady.

I told her the story: 'Do you know what Carruthers did? He took a baboon up to the hills with him. "Male or female?" "Female. There's nothing queer about Carruthers." ' Queen Elizabeth thought that very funny.

After Mr Mulligan had duly won the Gold Cup, at slight surprise from its connections because it had been very off-colour, there was a great presentation.

I was photographed with Verushka with Queen Elizabeth when she presented the great Cup.

Then she made a great announcement saying that she had been asked by the Cheltenham Steeplechase Company to present me with a Gold Cup. I half expected it, then I thought, well I had heard nothing more, so thought it was off the menu or was going to be done privately in the room, or whatever. So I was for once at a loss for words, though I shook her hand and kissed her hand and all the rest of it.

---

3. See 10 February 1993 for the threatened court-martial and the 1944 'Letter from France'.
4. *Golden Horizons* was published in 1953.

Verushka must get that Gold Cup insured rapidly. I am terrified it will be in the house and get stolen. I should think it is worth perhaps £3,000 or thereabouts, but we have to find out – it's always worth less when it's got an inscription on it.

Friday 14 March

Had a longish conversation with Margaret.

She has no recollection of saying that Blair would do no harm to the country, as alleged – maybe she did when a bit tiddly.

On the contrary, she thought he'd do immense harm and she will vigorously campaign for John. She's had numerous invitations to speak and has to choose which ones to select.

The 'leak' in the *Times* was by Peter Stothard, editor, who was host at the private room dinner at the Reform Club.

Sent my usual memo to Rupert.[5]

Monday 17 March

Rupert has behaved like a swine and a pig. He doesn't like backing losers and he thinks Major will lose. Tonight the great announcement has come out that the *Sun* is backing Blair and there'll be huge headlines across the front page tomorrow. How he can do that – he's against the single currency and hates the whole idea of our joining the social chapter – I do not know. But he's so vain that he doesn't want to be on what he thinks is the losing side in the general election.

Irwin says, of course, that he's not the Rupert that he and I used to know. I think, also, that Irwin is not the Irwin I used to know. He's been plotting every time he's been in London, changing the dates to come for dinner here, to suit going out to dinner and giving dinner to Blair and his sidekicks. He's probably been part of the bad advice to Rupert.

I left various messages with Alex Allan at Downing Street (John Major's Principal Private Secretary) saying I hoped he would read my

---

5. The memo covered the Tote lunch, WW's rows with Howard and his talk with Thatcher. WW also says that he heard from Robin Cook that 'the Blair regime is so strict that no one at Labour's top is allowed to be seen in any public place with any woman who is not his wife for fear of the press and photographers unearthing some scandal. Robin thought this ridiculous but Blair has acquired the power of deselecting any MP who disobeys him.'

Times article tomorrow and that I had been afraid Rupert might do something like this.

John will see tomorrow morning from my article in the *Times* that I believe he will win.

Later I have at last been able to reach Irwin Stelzer.

I had done him a grave injustice. It was nothing whatever to do with him; indeed he had advised against it. Apart from not wishing to be on the losing side, which was not the predominant feature by any means, it was because Rupert is so angry with the government for referring the digital box to OFTEL when there was no need to do so. All Rupert was asking for was what I've said before: £75 towards the actual making of each box but nothing for the development costs which ran into millions. He never had any intention, and said so, of barring access to it or making it difficult for anybody to use a digital box. That was the tip-over factor which caused him to turn against Major.

What fools the Tories are, and so is Lang, the Secretary for Industry, as I said to John. I recalled how I'd urged him not to refer it. He is not like Margaret who would have got stuck into that straight away.

Irwin said that Rupert is buying things left right and centre for millions of dollars in America. He hopes his judgement is all right, but some of the things are risky enterprises. I said, 'He's lived on high risk all his life and it usually comes off.'

Irwin still argues with Rupert and is always ready to pack his bags and go if Rupert doesn't like it. But he remains very fond of him, as I do. It was unworthy of me to have thought Irwin could have turned his back on me and Verushka just because he was involved with talking to Blairites. He did that to find out what they were up to and what might or might not be done when they formed a government. That is perfectly sensible.

Tuesday 18 March

Spoke to John Major. He had rung the day before when I was out. I told him why Rupert had turned turtle. He took it fairly philosophically.

He told me about Howard who had said he had met a stumbling block with the Opposition. Because the date of the election has now been announced [1 May], Jack Straw wouldn't agree to the nominee proposed by Howard, who is the wrong General, Watkins, the one from Hong Kong,[6] so there will be no selection of a new Chairman until after the election. Straw had asked to interview the four main candidates and said he might agree to one. Howard refused to let him. I had already fixed with Robin Cook that my General is the right one and they approve of him.

The man from Hong Kong would be totally useless.

They don't have anything like our sophisticated equipment [there]. The service to customers is appalling on the racecourses.

They have no credit business like ours. They don't have to compete with bookmakers. He wouldn't be able to understand the first thing about the importance of Tote Direct and Ladbroke and Coral being in it.

There was a nice dinner party given by NERA.

I had to make a speech because the dour Patrick Jenkin, the evening's chairman, wouldn't seem funny even if someone poured soup on his head.

Wednesday 19 March
At The Other Club Norman Tebbit told me he started by saying in his weekly article in the *Sun* tomorrow that 'The *Sun* may back Blair but I don't'. I said, 'That's excellent.' But when I came to read it the next morning he said it was all Major's fault for not being strong enough about Europe and for not saying we would never join a single currency and so forth. I thought to myself, that's pretty ridiculous. The *Sun* is now backing a man who is hopelessly pro Europe.

Thursday 20 March
Everybody at Doncaster, where I had a very successful day, wondered who would be the next Chairman, obviously. I replied, 'So do I.'

It was the opening of the flat season. We were making an announcement that the charming little Frankie Dettori [jockey] will promote the Tote.

It is regarded generally as a great coup. He won seven races in a row last year which had never been done before.

We have to pay him £50,000 with an option to take him on for another two years. But he is well worth it.

---

6. Major-General Guy Watkins, Chief Executive, The Royal Hong Kong Jockey Club, 1986–96; a director, British Bloodstock Agency and Racecourse Holdings Trust since 1996.

Friday 21 March
Having tried to get hold of either Richard Wilson or Howard for days,
and failing, I suddenly got a call from Howard after Verushka had
gone to Venice this morning.

When he rang me on Thursday, John had asked me not to let
Howard know he told me what had happened with regard to the
Labour Party. When Howard rang he said, 'Would you like me to tell
you what is happening?' 'Yes.' He then proceeded to tell me what I
knew already, that Jack Straw had rejected his selection.

I said, 'This is a very serious position because I had been looking
forward to retiring on April 30th as planned.'

I said, 'I don't think it's wise to leave the Tote rudderless. We've
got two very good young men there and they're fine but I can't let them
make decisions which should properly be made with the Chairman, and
leave them out on a limb if anything goes wrong. Maybe I should go
on for a couple of months and see the new Chairman in, whoever it
may be, even if I disapprove of the choice, and make sure there is a
proper handover.'

He thought it a very good idea and said he would tell Richard
Wilson that was what I had suggested. He actually said he was grateful
to me.

Meanwhile, all evening there was a great commotion going on over
my article for the *News of the World* in which I had said that the *Sun*
had been told by the proprietor to stand on its head. They wanted to
censor it, they wanted to alter it. I said, 'If you do, I will simply publish
the whole thing in the *Spectator*. That won't be very nice for you.'

I told Irwin. He had read it because he and Cita came to lunch. He
thought it OK and that Rupert wouldn't have minded at all. I hadn't
put in the real reason, namely that he was furious with the government
about the digital box, their dislike of him and so forth.

Saturday 22 March
They sent me something in which they had altered the whole bloody
thing. I said, 'You can't do that.' I rang Irwin who said, 'Get on to Les
Hinton,' which I did. I agreed with him a few alterations, not of very
great significance though it did alter the sense a bit.

I never spoke to the editor – he doesn't like to speak to me, or he's
afraid of me. Anyway, he's a treacherous fellow.

But as a result of Hinton's intervention it all got sorted out in the
end and was published.

It was quite an exciting day.

What a curious girl Verushka is. She didn't even tell me before she went [to Venice] that she wasn't coming back until midday on Monday. She is so possessive. She thinks that if I knew she was going to be away as long as that, and not coming back on Sunday as she said, that I would get into mischief by going out with another woman.

Of course I did go out with another woman – dear Mrs Tamborero! We went to the RAC and had a lovely dinner and lovely conversation.

Sunday 23 March
The give-away [in my *News of the World* article] was in the last bit where I wrote about the exchange between Major and Blair in the Commons on Thursday in which John had referred to Blair's trips to Australia where he made newspaper deals – implying that he gave some secret promise to help Rupert's business in exchange for the *Sun* (and probably the *Times*) backing Blair.

Thursday 27 March
The announcement that I was staying on till June 30th went out yesterday.[7]

The press statement was received on the whole well. It was one in the eye for the silly old *Sporting Life* which said I'd completely lost out to Michael Howard and that I'd been humiliated. Complete nonsense. I've won everything so far and I think I will succeed in getting the right General in.

I am getting a bit exhausted going round the courses, travelling long distances, visiting betting shops.

As long as I can hang on to Rupert's £150,000 a year plus the odds and ends from NERA and so on, I will still have an income before tax of pushing £190,000 a year. This could come to an end if I grew doddery. I have noted with great interest that somebody appears to have found a workable cure for Alzheimer's if tackled at the start. I sent particulars of this to Professor Pounder but he hasn't answered.

John Major's having a rough time. The swine [Neil] Hamilton won't resign and will try to fight his seat when everybody knows he's as guilty as hell. The *Guardian* came up with complete details of his hotel

---

7. The Tote press release quoted WW as saying: 'I must have made as many final farewells as Dame Nellie Melba, Maria Callas and Lester Piggott. I hope this will prove to be my last.'

bill which was paid by Mohamed Al Fayed at the Ritz in Paris. It was absolutely enormous, about £4,000–£5,000 for a couple of days. Hamilton has admitted that he didn't disclose this to the Register of Interests. The evidence that he was given money in cash is also overwhelming. It is not good enough for John to keep saying, 'We have to regard the man as innocent until he's proved guilty.' (That is what the *Times* said, too.) Hamilton should be told to stand down now.

A well-orchestrated smear campaign is run by Labour. This morning the newspapers gave full details (in the *Sun* and the *Mirror*) plus a long story by the girl herself, that Tory MP Piers Merchant of Beckenham, a safe Tory seat, had been caught having sex with a seventeen-year-old, not very pretty, night-club hostess.[8]

The fool Merchant paraded the girl round his constituency and was photographed in a public park. The *Sun* paid her £50,000 for her story and to get her making love.

Every time the Tories try to talk about the economy or attack Labour's intention to overturn large parts of the Thatcher trade union reforms, up comes a sleaze story.

Tessa Keswick, on behalf of the Centre for Policy Studies, gave a lunch party for Keith Marsden.[9] He's the man who showed beyond peradventure that the Labour Party have been lying about our economic performance.

Marsden sat on my left and on my right his French wife who was absolutely charming.

We talked about François Mauriac and his books on the Bordeaux country, the strange behaviour of the vineyard owners and those connected with them.

John Redwood turned up towards the end. He is following the party line on the single currency during the election.

It's very amusing. We will, after all, have another Royal Ascot, and

8. Merchant said he met Anna Cox at a Young Conservative meeting and thought she was a secretary in her twenties. She said she left the job in the club after four nights when she found out what type of place it was. They were photographed kissing in a Beckenham park and she was photographed later that night arriving at and leaving his Pimlico flat. His wife stood by him, his constituency party reselected him and he retained the seat in the general election.

9. Economic consultant; his *Miracle or Mirage?* was published by the Centre for Policy Studies.

another 2000 Guineas at Newmarket, and another Derby. Verushka's busy organizing the guests for the two lunches we give, Wednesday and Thursday, at Royal Ascot.

Saturday 29 March
At Oare. Jacob Rothschild came over to dinner with Serena. She is doing very well with her horses.

Tessa is very good at organizing. I told her how well she had organized the publishing of the booklet by Keith Marsden and that I would write an article about it for Tuesday's *Times*, mentioning the Centre for Policy Studies.

Amabel Lindsay, widow of Patrick, was there for the weekend.

Jokingly, I said we were leaving early on Sunday because I was going to see my girlfriend. At the door she carefully brushed my coat collar. 'You must look smarter than that to see your girlfriend.' I said, 'That was just optimism.'

Despite the enormous amount of food, I didn't put on any weight while at Oare. I have to get as light as I can. It is less tiring and less dangerous for what is left of my body.

Monday 31 March
On return to Cavendish Avenue last night I tried to get hold of John Major. I left messages but he wasn't there.

This morning he rang me.

John said, 'Over the weekend I have been doing nothing but deal with shits.' He spelled it out, S-H-I-T-S. We both agreed that Piers Merchant had been set up by the *Sun*.

I said, 'It's all right apart from the fact that it shows the fellow's got so little judgement that he ought not to be an MP, and certainly not a prospect for ministerial rank.'

I said, 'I don't know what you can do about Hamilton.' 'My difficulty is that I don't have the authority that Blair has in his party where they can deselect candidates they disapprove of and have a new one put in his place who is acceptable to the leader. Our constitution is quite different and always has been. The constituency parties are absolutely free to select anyone they like. But one of the first things I'm going to do after the election is to alter that rule, to give the leader of the party the ability to do what Blair is able to do.'

John is remaining very cool and calm. [But] every time they get a lead on them, for example on what they have promised to the trade unions, another sleaze story is manufactured by the demons of darkness, Peter Mandelson and Alastair Campbell.

I think it may be backfiring to some extent because the general public, in its cynical way, thinks all politicians are as bad as each other.

Went to Alan Hall's wedding.[10]

I was sitting about two feet away from where the preacher was blowing off, as Jewish preachers will, with very long passages. Since it was all in Hebrew, I don't think Alan Hall understood much of it, though his bride did.

I was very moved by the whole ceremony, thinking of the enormous strength and vitality of the Jews who survived so many terrible disasters.

A number of extraordinarily pretty Jewish girls were there and a few good-looking men. Mostly, Jewish men aren't so attractive as their daughters.

---

10. Alan Hall, d 1999, was WW's accountant.

Friday 4 April

John Heaton has gone off for the weekend, first to France to do a deal with Pari-Mutuel, if we can, and second to a wedding in Edinburgh. 'You won't be much available during the Grand National tomorrow.' He said he would have his mobile.

Saturday 5 April

A quarter of an hour or so before the Grand National began, up came the notice 'The course must be cleared at once'. There had been coded bomb warnings from the IRA.

I would have carried straight on. Everybody said that would have been a fearful risk. But there is no such thing as a risk-free life.

Does this mean that the IRA are now able to stop every big event – cup finals, Wimbledon, the Derby, anything they have a fancy for stopping?

All our people at the Grand National were prevented from staying at their stations. A lot of the girls there, on orders from David Haslett (Geoff Oke's replacement),[1] stuffed as much money into their handbags as they could. The tills were completely unguarded although the police said they would keep a security check on them. Joe Scanlon refused to leave his office when ordered to do so. Finally, they locked him in there for a bit. Then he was let out again. But he took £60,000 in cash which we had already taken in bets before the Grand National, to make sure it wasn't stolen. They were all very sensible.

And John Heaton wasn't there. I finally got a message through to him but there was nothing he could have done.

Eventually it was announced that the race would be run on Monday.

It's not much good running it on Monday for a crowd.

Meanwhile, the Tories are not really fighting a good campaign. They look as though they know they're defeated and the only one who

---

1. Managing director of the Racecourse Cash Division of the Tote; Joe Scanlon was managing director of Tote Credit; see Racing Appendix.

doesn't think he's defeated is John Major.[2] Petronella's going off on his bus with him one day next week, the only one who doesn't have to pay her fare because she's a special guest. I hope she cheers him up. He's had one hell of a time.

Monday 7 April
At dinner were Mr and Mrs Peter George, Lord and Lady Wakeham, Sir Piers and Lady Bengough, and Mr and Mrs David Sieff.

Lady Wakeham asked the story of my life and marriage, which I told her about. I said Verushka and I have been married for the longest I have ever been married to anybody. I told her about the various wives I've had. When I said that Julian Amery adored my half-Russian wife, the daughter of a Communist, she said, 'But he adored so many women.' I said, 'Maybe, but he liked the songs she sang in Russian as did many others. But then the sex ran out, as it often does. She had an affair with Ken Tynan, which I discovered later from a book written by his second wife. I thought it strange. He had very kinky notions on sex.'[3]

The party was basically arranged so that the others could meet Peter George as he is desirous of moving up in the social world, no bad ambition. If one sees the best, one must try to follow it. It isn't snobbery, it's common sense.

Tuesday 8 April
The Tory propaganda is abysmal. Why John made nice Maurice Saatchi a peer, and the brother of the ghastly Gummer[4] a peer as well, I cannot imagine. They're both working for the Tory propaganda machine.

---

2. In his memo to Murdoch dated 4 April, WW goes through a list of potential successors to Major were he to stand down, ending with William Hague: 'He's thirty-six, the same age as Eden when he became Foreign Secretary; and eight years younger than Blair, which would annoy him. Hague had a comprehensive school background before going to Oxford. Just right, maybe.'

3. WW m 2 (1948–56) Nora (Alix), née Robbins, who later married John Coleman, journalist; Tynan's 'extra-marital fling' in 1953 is described in Kathleen Tynan's 1987 biography of the drama critic, *The Life of Kenneth Tynan*, pp. 105–6; Kathleen Tynan told WW in 1989 that it was Alix who had told her of the affair – see Vol. 2, p. 113.

4. Peter Selwyn Gummer, executive chairman, International Public Relations (formerly Shandwick International) since 1974, life peer (Lord Chadlington) 1996; brother of John Selwyn Gummer, at this time Secretary of State for the Environment.

Perhaps it was in lieu of paying them, as the Tory Party remains strapped for money.

Wednesday 9 April
I spent a long time at the Tote at lunch time, taking my own sardine sandwich and an apple.

Before I was ready to go there came an urgent call from Irwin Steltzer in Washington. I wasn't going to speak to him from the Tote. I was thinking that maybe, when we have dinner with Les Hinton tonight, he would tell me I would never be allowed to write for the *News of the World* at all, nor perhaps even for the *Times*, as a result of my heavy criticism of Rupert for turning the *Sun* into a pro-Blair newspaper.

Back at home Irwin came through. 'I've got Rupert and some smart people (he means brains, not clothes) in Washington coming to dinner. I'm giving them Haut-Brion 1966. How long should I open it before they drink it?'

Mario, the head waiter or the manager [at Harry's Bar], greeted me in very friendly manner. 'We don't see you here very much, M'lord.' I said, 'No, I can't afford to come here unless somebody pays for me.'

I asked Les Hinton was Rupert annoyed about my attacking him in the *News of the World*? 'No, not at all.'

I've become very fond of Les Hinton. I think he will support me quite well with Rupert, except that in the last resort he'll never really stand up against him. Why should he? He has his career and his income to think of. I think he's doing pretty well for money and Rupert now allows share options.

Thursday 10 April
To Coleman Street for a meeting with Aly Aziz of the Board of Cornish Spring Water of which I am the Chairman.

On my way back I thought, gosh, why don't I approach Peter George to ask if someone can come to talk to him about selling Cornish Spring Water to all the Hilton hotels Ladbroke run. I spoke to his secretary who said she would find out who we should speak to about it.

Maybe we'll be able to do a deal, but Ladbroke are always very tough in negotiations.

Friday 11 April
Petronella is writing brilliantly.

She is interviewing David Steel who is not standing again.[5]

David Steel lives in a castle sold him by the Duke of Buccleuch, I gather at a rather cheap price. Buccleuch is a nice chap. I like him very much. I also like David Steel.

It seems that David Steel likes me, despite the fact that I tease him endlessly at The Other Club and elsewhere. David Steel liked and thought highly of Jo Grimond, as did I. He was a fine leader of the Liberals and wasted on them. He should have been in a proper party, like Labour, if he could have brought himself to it. He was a Whig.

David Steel reckons drains to Paddy Ashdown – totally incompetent and a silly ass, always having a different solution for Bosnia every time he comes back from there. He doesn't think he has a chance of getting many votes for his party. All this he was willing for Petronella to print. He said Major is much better than Blair and hopes that Major will win. This will be a help to Major when she publishes the interview in the *Telegraph*.[6]

Sunday 13 April
John Major rang in the afternoon. I was somewhat dopey. I had fallen asleep. I was upstairs and I had been watching television. Rather foolishly I said, 'Have you had any chance to watch some cricket?' He said no and wished he had.

I pulled my thoughts together as well as I could.

'Why can't you keep claiming, in answer to the jeer from the Labour Party that you had twenty-two tax rises, that you had twenty-five tax cuts during the last parliament?' He said, 'I do that sometimes but nobody publishes it.' Later on, when I saw him on the television, he had got going on this.

5. Liberal then Liberal Democrat MP, 1965–97, Leader of the Liberal Party, 1976–88; life peer 1997; elected MSP, 1999.
6. In the interview published on 17 April, Steel is quoted as saying about Ashdown, 'We work together, but we've never pretended to be close friends'; he criticizes Blair for lack of vision and says about Major, ' . . . though I disagree with him, what he says is very thoughtful. He genuinely wants to do what he thinks is right, and he is tenacious.'

Wednesday 16 April
John Major has laid it down now that if he's the Prime Minister, there will be a free vote for backbenchers on the question of the single currency or going any further into Europe.

This is a brilliant move. It exposes the absolute dictatorship of the Labour Party where nobody is allowed to have a dissentient voice. It allows Tory candidates to give their opinion, which they are doing in overwhelming numbers, that they are against the single currency but they agree that the negotiations should go on because, even if we're not in it, we have to make sure that it does us the least harm.

I think this will show very well for him, despite the attempt by Blair and the media to pretend it's weak leadership.

Thursday 17 April
Peter Stothard had a great reception in a huge tent covering most of his garden at Eton Avenue, NW3.

Phil Hall and his secretary were there. He told me that he won't support Blair during the few days until the election. He has told Rupert he is still thinking about it and will take a balanced view. Rupert argued with him but he very bravely stuck it out till Rupert said OK and let it go.

Friday 18 April
Petronella went to Gloucester to buy a papillon bitch, a tiny little thing. It does look like a butterfly, very sweet and very pretty. Petronella was exhausted. Frank [Johnson] had told her she can't bring it to the office because some are allergic to dogs, some at any rate at the *Spectator*.

She said she couldn't sleep last night because the dog wouldn't let her, and she doesn't know what to do about it. She said she would take it back to Gloucester. I said, 'No you won't. It's a sweet little dog. It can sleep with me every evening.'

Tuesday 22 April
Olga Polizzi very sweetly had arranged a dinner party for us at her house in Clarendon Close. The invitations went out that it was a dinner in our honour. Liz Murdoch sat next to me and Olga on the other side.

Liz Murdoch was amazingly friendly. She chattered away about the times we had in Italy. She got very pally with Petronella and wants to have lunches with her. She said, 'But we're very simple and unsophisticated, really. We don't know all these society people,' which sounded as though she would rather like to, if what she means is the sort of people Petronella knows.

Her husband is of the same ethnic tribe as Joe Appiah, who was married to Peggy Cripps, Stafford Cripps' daughter. The young man's father she is married to was imprisoned, not by Nkrumah, as Joe Appiah was, but by Flight Sergeant Rawlinson who took over the dictatorship from the elected government when he overthrew it.

Liz said, 'My father says you're very angry with him for backing Blair.' 'Quite right,' I said. We both laughed.

Thursday 24 April
Finally, a week before the election, I spoke to Paul [Getty] again. He said, 'I had been thinking I'd given enough to the Tories, as you know.' I said, 'What about the idea of the loan?' 'I've been thinking about that, too. I'm prepared to lend them a million pounds repayable in two years at a minimum rate of interest which I have to put in to satisfy my accountants.'

When I told Maurice Saatchi this, he was over the moon.

Friday 25 April
Eventually I heard back from the disappointed Maurice Saatchi. The Chairman, Charles Hambro, and Mawhinney also, had refused to take the loan because they didn't want to get into debt again. They probably have thrown the towel in.

I gave Paul the bad news.

Fortunately, John has taken over the direction of the campaign entirely himself, to remove some of the shambolic box-ups.

Phil Hall has left the deputy editor in charge because he didn't want to be there, I think, when the editorial of the *News of the World* said that the *News of the World* was backing Blair as well. It is a great humiliation for him, poor chap. I thought he had got it straight with Rupert and was able to support Major.

His deputy editor leapt at the opportunity when I said, 'Although it's not my normal week for writing, would you let me do an additional article of about five hundred words?' He said, 'Yes, that's fine. We'll fit it all into a special political page we have that day. Thank you very much.' (I am not asking for extra pay for this.)

I still believe the pollsters can be wrong and there may be an upset when people come to their senses. There are still a few hours left to do it.

I didn't tell the deputy editor of the conversation I have just had with Maurice Saatchi who said there was a moment when the gap narrowed but all their canvassing returns 'are showing that it's gone quite differently again and we're in danger of losing many more seats than we thought we would. It could almost be a landslide.'

All is deep gloom.

We were all going to Ascot for the evening meeting. My own race, the Woodrow Wyatt stakes, was at 6.00 p.m. We left at about 4.30 which should have been ample time, but it was not. We got caught in the most fearful Friday night traffic.

We nearly went crazy. When we arrived at the course it was almost 6.30.

John Heaton had presented the prize for the Woodrow Wyatt stakes race. But Petronella was in time to present the next prize, which she duly did in the rain.

Saturday 26 April
Sandown. I was put to sit at the same table as Queen Elizabeth the Queen Mother. She was very jolly and looked a peach.

I said, 'Have you seen that Blair has now adopted the Imperial Purple, the same colour you are wearing today?' She thought that very funny.

Tristram Ricketts asked if it would be a good idea to ask Wakeham to join the Tote Board. I said, 'I'll think about it.' I talked to John Heaton about it. We both thought it an excellent idea. He'd make the Board more sensible whoever became Chairman.[7]

Monday 28 April
I had rung Peter Martin, the dentist, at his home in Wales. He kindly arranged to see me at 8.00 a.m. this morning to pull this damn tooth out which is hurting and sometimes hurts violently, shooting pain everywhere. In fact, it was so bad that I started to pull the damn thing out myself, which wouldn't have been a very great success. I had to leave my plate there with my teeth on it because he will make me a plastic tooth in place of the lost one. It isn't going to cost as much as I thought it was going to.

---

7. Wakeham became a member of the Board, 1997–8.

Tuesday 29 April

Richard Wilson, Permanent Secretary to the Home Office, came to lunch.

He was charmed by everything he saw, including the pictures.

I gave him 1961 Lynch Bages and also Pavillon Blanc 1985, the white wine of Château Margaux. He had tomato juice, as I did, before lunch. He didn't want any champagne.

We discussed everything very thoroughly. I told him why I had turned against Jones and that nobody wanted him in racing.

Wilson thought it a marvellous move that we were getting Wakeham to come on the Board.

I said, 'I suppose it wouldn't be a total disaster if Watkins were chosen but he wouldn't take anything further forward. Of course my General is very popular in racing.

'Also, I wouldn't mind if Bernard Donoughue became Chairman, but he hasn't applied.'

I told him we'd made a profit of £4.8 million, which is sixty-five per cent higher than last year, and it would have been a million higher if we'd been able to do the Irish Lottery sooner.

Richard Wilson said I was a legend around Whitehall when he was in charge of administration at the Cabinet Office.

He said, 'Margaret never left any instructions as to how the Cabinet minutes were to be framed after she spoke, after she'd decided things at Cabinet.' She left it to him and he had to put the words down properly. I said, 'You know, upstairs is a round table where she used to come and sit and she would say, "Help me, I'm not a wordsmith." '

Wilson is tall and slim. He is not good-looking; he has a clinical look but a charming smile on his long, narrow face. A lucid brain and an expert civil servant. He moves his head quickly and listens with great interest. A flattering approach, always useful.

As he was leaving and I was taking him to his car he said, 'Will you come to have lunch with me?' 'At your club?' 'I don't belong to a club.' I said, 'I thought every civil servant belonged to a club.' 'I don't. We're a new type these days. I go to restaurants. Would you come to have lunch with me?' 'Delighted to.'

I like Wilson, despite reservations that Norman Lamont had about him, that he is a bit two-faced. I decided he wasn't.

Wednesday 30 April
I went to a party given by the publisher for the biographer of Cyril Connolly.[8]

I thought of asking for a discount on the £25 book, but decided it sounded a bit mean. I gave it to the author to sign and he wrote a little message in it about the hair brush – that is the hair brush which Lys [Lubbock] said Cyril Connolly used to beat her with. There are several references to me in the book, including his immense jealousy of me because he thought I was having an affair with her. He might have been right; he was actually.

---

8. Jeremy Lewis; see 10 March 1994 for the information WW gave Lewis; WW indicated then that he did not have an affair with Lys Lubbock.

Thursday 1 May
I had rung 10 Downing Street to try to speak to the Prime Minister but he was on a long call. When I got back [from the dentist's] it was fortunately no later than 8.25 a.m. I was just in time to get a call from him.

We had quite a little chat. He said, 'You've been marvellous because you've supported me in all the bleak times as well as the good.'

I said, 'You are a great man,' and I meant it deeply. History will see him as such.

I hope very much this is not the last time I ring Number 10 and ask for the Prime Minister – however busy he is, like Margaret he has always tried to ring back.

I've been feeling sick inside all day, fearing the worst, not only for dear John but for the country. If they vote Blair in, they will have committed an act of collective lunacy.

At the grisly party [given by the Blacks] at Christopher's, I couldn't hear a single thing as people rushed backwards and forwards.

I said to Paul Johnson, 'I don't think it'll be quite as bad as the first projections show.' I was quite wrong about that.[1]

A. N. Wilson was very polite: 'I got your very touching note and I am so glad to have it.' That was the one in which I said he had written a marvellous article about Major and, 'All is forgiven,' meaning his appalling indiscretions after the dinner he was present at when the Queen Mother was at Cavendish Avenue.[2]

---

1. Labour won with a majority of 179 seats.
2. Wilson's account of the 1987 dinner party was in the *Spectator* in June 1990; see Vol. 1, pp. 308–10, for the dinner party and Vol. 2, pp. 318–9, for WW's reactions to the *Spectator* article.

Friday 2 May
I wrote my article for the *News of the World*. John and I had both
known secretly that it was all up but I didn't say that to him for fear
of discouraging him at the last moment.

Monday 5 May
When I got through to John I said, 'Clinton was very nice about your
contribution to the world and the USA and to him in many difficult
situations.' John laughed: 'They're all very nice about me now I'm
gone. You may detect an air of cynicism.'

'That fellow Clarke even said he hadn't been consulted about the
free vote.' John agreed wearily.

I thought to myself, 'Margaret always used to say "Those dreadful
Hush Puppy shoes Kenneth Clarke wears everywhere. He's really a
socialist at heart." '

I've been having conversations with Peter Lilley who has decided
to go for the leadership.

I said, 'You've got the best intellect in the House. Frank Field started
off by admitting your scheme for pensions in the future is an extremely
good one.

'Now he's gone to the job at Social Security obviously he'll
implement your plan. I can't believe his Number One, Harriet Harman,
is going to last very long.'[3]

Actually Field is an enlightened appointment by Blair.

Tuesday 6 May
Jeffrey Archer rang, returning my call during the Bank Holiday
weekend. All I had wanted to know was John's telephone number
which by then I had discovered by other means.

He was all for Peter Lilley but he said there was a strong movement
blowing up that there ought to be a wider suffrage than just the
hundred and sixty-five Tory MPs left in the House. The constituency
parties and associations should have a vote, too. Basically he's right
but whether they'll succeed in getting it through I don't know.

---

3. Frank Field, Labour MP since 1979 (Director, Child Poverty Action Group,
   1969–79, Low Pay Unit, 1974–80), was Minister of State for Welfare Reform at
   the Department of Social Security, 1997–8; Harriet Harman was Secretary of State
   for Social Security, 1997–8.

Wednesday 7 May

[At The Other Club] I sat next to Nicholas Henderson, the Secretary, and on his other side was poor old Hartwell who looks very ill but at least has got much better from his various heart attacks and was able to come to the meeting.

Nicko at one point said, 'Membership is limited to fifty. Actually we've got seventy-two but so many of them don't come.'

I said, 'What you have to do is to get that fellow Mendelssohn to join.' (Everyone shouted 'Mandelson!'). 'Mendelssohn's the Rasputin.' (Everyone repeated shouts of 'Mandelson'.)

Opposite me was Ludovic Kennedy.[4]

He belongs to the Exit Group. I said, 'I've always thought everybody had the right to take their own life if they didn't want to be alive any more, whether it was because of acute pain or whether it was just because they were fed up with it. But it needs a lot of careful policing.'

A number of us joined in the conversation, including Winston [Churchill]. He said if his mother [Pamela Harriman] had been taken ill in New York and had complete brain damage after she was got out of the swimming pool, she would never have been allowed to die. 'Fortunately, it was in France[5] and although she was taken to the American hospital, where they started making a bit of fuss, I persuaded them because I knew my mother would want it, to switch off the life-support machines as her brain was irreparably damaged.'

I didn't like to say I had read of a case the other day where somebody was presumed dead in his brain but after ten years he began to speak and recovered full speech facility and his memory.

I said, 'You'd have to get a clause changed in everybody's life insurance.' Ludo said, 'Why?' I said, 'Well, if you commit suicide, your relatives, and in my case Verushka, lose a large lump of life insurance because it's not paid in the case of suicide.'

When I asked young Winston had he married his intended yet, he said, 'No. We haven't even got the divorce yet, the decree nisi.' I said, 'But that's automatic, isn't it?' 'I suppose it could be disturbed. Of course the chief obstacle was about money.'

I forbore to mention to him that I thought it an extremely nice gesture of his mother, Pamela, to have left Minnie Churchill quite a

---

4. Writer and civil rights campaigner; television and radio journalist; knight 1994.
5. Pamela Harriman was US Ambassador to France from 1992 until her death in 1997.

lot of money. It was intended as a snub to Winston though he has been left an awful lot of money as well and got a lot from the sale of his grandfather's papers.

She certainly is a very attractive girl, the one he is marrying and deserting poor sweet and pretty Minnie for. She was always loyal to him throughout his sexual and other scrapes.[6]

The odds [for Tory Leader] are shortening on Peter, making Clarke go further out. Everybody at the table, whether they approved of Clarke's approach to Europe or not, and Nicholas Henderson certainly does, thought he would be a disaster as leader. He'd split the Tory Party completely.

Thursday 8 May
Verushka and Petronella set off for Hungary.

When Petronella got to the airport she found she had left her handbag behind in her flat. We had to send Elizabeth in a taxi. It cost £30. Fortunately, she arrived in time.

Before going to Andrew Devonshire's party at Pratt's, I went to take my oath of allegiance at the Lords.

I found myself sitting next to Shirley Williams on a bench with only about five waiting. I told her what Petronella had done over losing her handbag and so forth because I know how scatterbrained dear Shirley Williams is. She was enchanted. 'I admire her all the more. I so often have forgotten my tickets to get on an aeroplane or a train, forgotten my passport and gone to the wrong place for an engagement. I feel for her very much.' I said, 'It just shows that however much brain you have, you can't necessarily organize your own life very well.'

Friday 9 May
I was worried about Mimi [the papillon dog] last night and slept badly. She was getting restless and trying to get to the door of my bedroom at about 2.30 a.m. I took her out. I didn't follow her very far because I only had my socks on. I just went to the front gate to make sure it had been properly shut which it so often isn't. She rooted around among the bushes and I hope did what was necessary.

Later in the night, however, she was coughing badly. Having begun on the floor on a Jacob sheepskin rug, she decided she wanted to come

---

6. Winston Churchill m 1 (1964–97) Minnie, née d'Erlanger, 2 (1997) Luce Engelen.

up on the bed with me. I took her up. She snuffled a great deal and curled up and snuffled again. I put my hand on her to warm her and put a blanket over her and then she went to sleep. Neither of us woke until she started barking, hearing Maria coming up the stairs to wake me.

There is some veiled criticism of John Major for not carrying on longer. But there is no reason whatever why he should, having been let down by so many people in the Tory Party.

I imagine, though he hasn't said so and nor has anybody else at this stage, that as soon as he thinks it's safe to have a by-election at Huntington, where he has a very decent majority, he may go to the House of Lords. I will try to persuade him to take the title of Earl, as is his privilege, but for life only.

While at Pratt's, Andrew [Devonshire] told me he had written a long missive about what the future policy of the Tory Party should be. He's now reverted to type and rejoined the Tory Party some time ago. It arrived this morning but I haven't had time to look at it yet. He has a certain amount of political wisdom inherited from Planty Pal, the real Duke of Devonshire who was fictionalized by Trollope.

Tuesday 13 May
Tote Board meeting. Peter Jones was there. He was forced to praise my efforts at getting Ladbroke into Tote Direct. He looked very nervous and jaded. He's terrified he may not get the Chairmanship which I hope very much he does not.

I almost felt sorry for him, but it is difficult to be so after his blatant lobbying in the sporting press and to anybody he can oil up to in the Labour Party.

Monday 12 May
I referred to Peter Lilley in my *Times* article, saying I thought he was the best choice because he has the best brain on either side of the House.

Wednesday 14 May
State opening of Parliament. I watched it on television. Blair predictably, in his presidential style, upstaged the Queen. He walked through the crowds from Downing Street instead of going by car.

Rodney and Emma Foale came to dinner. He's a splendid man.

He is a great heart specialist and surgeon. He was about to fly out to give a sultan some form of heart operation. He's been paid an enormous amount for that, and good luck to him.

During the evening the great heart surgeon, Rodney, examined Mimi. We had been told by the vet that there might be something wrong with her heart. He listened to it and held it and said there is nothing wrong with her heart at all. She was again taken to the vet the next day and the vet agreed with that, but she has a terrible cough.

It is very cold for her out of doors where she has to go to do her general business of excretion. I am terrified of putting her out there and her getting worse. So I'm afraid she does it sometimes in my bedroom and sometimes in one of the halls or rooms. She is a sweet little soul but she's not helping my sleep.

I received a tremendous shock before the dinner party began. It was a letter sent by special courier from Peter Stothard. I fear it made me rather miserable, losing the regular column which so many people have praised and been encouraged by. My one on Monday, even Lord Jenkin (Patrick) said how delighted he was by it. So did dear little Baroness Cumberlege who used to be at the Department of Health before the election. So did others in the chamber.[7]

Monday 19 May
I spent the weekend rather idly watching sporting events. Also working on my stock exchange investments to see what I should buy and how they are going. I had a great time watching football and cricket but it didn't really cheer me up very much.

I had previously rung Les Hinton who said he feared there was nothing he could do about it but it wouldn't make any difference to

---

7. This paragraph is all WW wrote at this stage about losing his *Times* column. Stothard's letter began by saying he was taking the opportunity of the new govern- ment's arrival to refashion the Op-Ed page to some extent. He thanked WW for his wise and independent-minded articles over almost 15 years but had decided his fortnightly column should be concluded at the end of the month. He hoped WW might be willing to contribute occasional articles and book reviews. WW wrote back on 14 May, a short letter stressing the importance of continuity and regu- larity; he suggested writing once every three weeks or month. WW attached Stothard's letter to his memo to Murdoch dated 27 May, after giving a political round-up, and said, 'I don't think there is anything you can do, as a condition of your buying the *Times* and the *Sunday Times* was that the editor would have complete freedom.'

the money I receive. I hope that is true because I depend very much on that £150,000 with my forthcoming retirement from the Tote.

Thursday 22 May
Dinner party at 19 Cavendish Avenue.

Arnold Weinstock was very grumpy. He was not at all a good guest. However, even he didn't complain about the wine.

Kenneth Baker was easily the best and talked a good deal of sense. He thinks it important to have Kenneth Clarke as Leader of the Opposition. The single currency in any case is going out of the window and he would trim to please the sceptics a bit; he is effective and a populist. I am inclined to think now that he would be better than Peter Lilley who hasn't the fighting quality and language to enthuse the remnant of the Tories.

Friday 23 May
Gregory Le Strange, the charming bloke from Oxford University, where he's doing a PhD on short stories and so forth, came plus the delightful lady, Helen Langley from the Bodleian in Oxford.

I told them very privately that I am also doing a diary which will not come out until after I am dead. We discussed how we could maintain the copyright if the archives are lodged at the Bodleian.[8]

Monday 26 May
I was very sad doing my *Times* article for the last time. I think I did it pretty well but it has been very painful for me to lose that regular column.

The Antelpeters, the previous Ambassador and his wife from Hungary to Britain, came to dinner, as did the present Ambassador and his wife. The present Ambassador had not enjoyed his time as Ambassador. He is a curious fellow, quite agreeable but he was a real tough Communist, high up.

He says he is no longer Communist, but who is?

Antelpeter is making money. He enjoyed very much being the Ambassador here.

They see a lot of Livia and play bridge with her regularly, sometimes at their house, luxurious for Budapest.

---

8. The copyright is held by WW's estate; his papers were bought by the Bodleian and are in the closed collection, not yet catalogued.

Tuesday 27 May
The *Times* laid my column out in a more prominent position than usual, at the top of the page, not the thin column on the right-hand side of the page.[9] The Op-ed staff, including Daniel Johnson, had been sad. They had learned only on Monday morning that my regular column was discontinued. They were surprised and very kind to me.

Wednesday 28 May
Meeting with Jack Straw, the new Home Secretary. Richard Wilson was in attendance. I explained to him why I thought Peter Jones would be wholly unsuitable and said it ought to be the General and gave my reasons.

Jack Straw was charming. I was surprised. He didn't look a bright spark when I watched him at Question Time and in the Commons.

He said there would be no question of privatizing the Tote; he and Robin Cook, who is a close friend, would see that it didn't happen.

He'd been consulting him on the new Chairman, too.

The Home Office had a new air of Puritanism. Everywhere signs said, 'No Smoking'. I was not even allowed to smoke in Jack Straw's office.

Thursday 29 May
I really am desperately worried over who they are going to put in as my successor.

When I said to Jack Straw the reasons I didn't want Peter Jones he said, 'I've got that message. I've got that large and clear in my eyes. I understand that.' So I think he will at least take notice of that.

I asked him to interview the General again, but I don't think he will. I said, 'I gather he interviewed badly because he didn't have all kinds of suggestions for improving the Tote.' 'You mean it's perfect.' 'No, but we've got a policy going forward, making us ever more prosperous. We've never made so much money. We've got record profits and we can go on to make £25 million a year quite easily for racing in a few years. I just want him to carry through the policies of the Board which have been so successful, and improve them, no doubt, if he can.'

---

9. WW wrote a wide-ranging piece about aspects of the new government's 'frantic rushing about to demonstrate a new beginning of energy and purpose, without a coherent plan'.

Tessa Keswick came to dinner. She thought that on no account should Kenneth Clarke be made Leader of the Party.

She was going to support this man Hague. I said, 'That's terrible. He's got this fearful man Duncan whom he stays with.'[10]

I was too ashamed to tell them I had been told I can't write for the *Times* any more. I think it's all to do with Blair as they want to please him.

Friday 30 May

I think I did the *News of the World* article pretty well when I eventually got it going.

I don't know why I am so shattered by losing the *Times* article, but I am.

I asked Conrad Black if he would let me write columns for him. The result was that they got me to write via Dean Godson something for the *Daily Telegraph*.

I thought it was a special feature but what he really was referring to was a tiny piece they have at the bottom of the leading article on a Saturday, 'I believe in . . .' I had to write this directly after I had written my *News of the World* article. If he had explained it properly to me beforehand, I wouldn't have had to re-write it several times. But they will pay me £500 for it.

---

10. Alan Duncan, Conservative MP since 1992; parliamentary political secretary to William Hague, as Leader of the Opposition, 1997–8; Opposition spokesman on health, 1998–9, on trade and industry since 1999; his house in Gayfere Street was used for Major's campaign headquarters in the 1990 Conservative leadership contest; see Vol. 2, p. 412.

Tuesday 3 June

Went to a party in Golden Square given by Maurice Saatchi. John Major was there and I talked to him a bit. 'Are you happy now?' 'I'm free at last and I'm enjoying myself.'

Wednesday 4 June

In the evening there was quite a jolly party at the Weidenfelds. The food was terrible and so was the drink, but otherwise it was amusing. On my right was the daughter of Gladwyn Jebb.[1]

She was annoyed with me because, when I wrote about what her mother said of the snobbishness of Ada Waverley in my review in the *Times* of her mother's diaries, I had said of her mother, 'It takes one to know one.'[2] She said her mother wasn't at all snobbish. She was very angry. I said, 'I don't know what you're complaining about in my review. It was enthusiastic. That was only a tiny observation of no great significance.' She calmed down after a while.

Thursday 5 June

They came in the morning to film me for the BBC with relation to a history of *Panorama*.[3] I was paid a measly £75 on the grounds that that was the same as the tea ladies got and there was to be no distinc-

---

1. Vanessa, née Jebb, m (1962) Hugh Thomas (life peer 1981).
2. See 25 November 1995 for WW's review of *The Diaries of Cynthia Gladwyn*, published on 14 November 1995. Ada, née Bodley, widow of Ralph Wigram, m (1941) Sir John Anderson, OM, 1882–1958, civil servant and politician, Chancellor of the Exchequer, 1943–5, cr. 1st Viscount Waverley, 1952. WW had said in his review that the diaries should be on everyone's bookshelf: 'They are mischievous, often unkind and above all, gloriously snobbish.' He ended the review: 'She describes Ava Waverley as "Becky Sharp personified". How about you, dear Cynthia?'
3. WW's interview was included in the second of three programmes on the history of the BBC, shown on BBC1 on 4 November 1997.

tion between one class and another. Very odd. I knew things the tea
ladies couldn't possibly know.

Saturday 7 June
I woke in agony, all my limbs were in torture, my whole body was
twisted, I felt I was going to die. Verushka, whose [previous] husband
had dropped dead in front of her from a heart attack when he was
sixty-five, is a hypochondriac. Consequently she has masses of medicines. She fed me with what she said were vitamins, but they were
actually a special kind of antibiotic, which if I had known I would
have rejected, as she knew.

   With a temperature of 104°F I was in too bad a way to go to the
Derby or even to put a recommended bet on from Peter O'Sullevan
[racing commentator] who has just been knighted. I can't even write
to congratulate him.

Monday 9 June
I was listed in a gossip column as being one of the people who was
attending Lord Hanson's party to promote the interests of Michael
Howard in the leadership race. I might have popped in just for the fun
of it but I was still lying dangerously ill with this most dangerous
form of pneumonia, as it turned out to be. I would never have supported the ghastly Howard.

Tuesday 10 June
Went to see Professor Pounder, pretty wrapped up. He is the consultant
physician at the Royal Free, a most brilliant man. I gave him an
envelope from Verushka containing details of the medicaments she'd
given me. He said that Verushka had saved my life. He was just a
bystander. I had to have blood tests, X-rays and heaven knows what
else, to see what infection remained.

Wednesday 11 June
Professor Pounder rang up to say there is still infection there in my
lungs. I will have to return to the Royal Free. I had to cancel my eye
test with Mr Arnott. I am frightfully worried about my eyesight now.
It seems to vary a bit. I hope to goodness the glaucoma hasn't spread,
but I am probably imagining it.

Friday 13 June

I wrote rather a good article for the *News of the World*, for which I received congratulations from Irwin Stelzer. He said, 'I can't think how you could do it considering you nearly died and are still recovering.' I said, 'I do it because I must. My reliability as a journalist has to be maintained whatever happens.'

Monday 16 June

Another visit to Professor Pounder for more blood tests and X-rays. I am getting better very fast, quite remarkable. He said I could go to Ascot but he didn't advise it. So I missed all the days of Royal Ascot and watched it on the television.

I couldn't go to Conrad Black's party on June 18th nor to the last party given by the Legco [Legislative Council] of Hong Kong in London. They will be replaced in Hong Kong by a non-elected body promoted by the Chinese on the mainland, which is already passing laws. Nor could I go to the Sotheby's party nor the *Times* party.

Friday 20 June

I spent a lot of time watching the Test Match at Lord's.

In my article in the *News of the World* on June 29th I referred to Bob's record: he was the only captain this century to beat the Australians at Lord's which he did by an innings and thirty-eight runs. Now his record can't be beaten, one of the few of his which hasn't been broken. He never minded his records being beaten but I think he would have been pleased about keeping this particular one.

Tuesday 24 June

Another visit for X-rays at half past eight in the morning to Professor Pounder. He said I am now absolutely normal and can do anything I like with no need to worry.

I got back in time for the Tote Direct Board meeting at Cavendish Avenue. I started smoking cigars again but Verushka said I should try to restrict the number. I said, 'He doesn't mind.' 'It may irritate your lungs.' 'It's OK. There's nothing wrong with anything now.'

Darling Beryl Bainbridge came to lunch.

I asked her how her book was getting on. She said she got stuck. I said, 'Don't forget what Trollope said. "What would you say to your pork butcher and he said he hadn't been in the mood to make his pork sausages today?" '

She's a marvellous girl. I've had a letter back from her since, about how to set about re-writing my play which she feels had some frightfully good ideas about life from outer space and how the bacteria from the tails of comets started off evolution.

She wants 'her upstairs' (Nadje) included. She suggested co-operation with me in writing the play. That would be wonderful. As soon as I can get away from the blasted Tote (which I love dearly, of course) I will be able to get the time and thinking space to do it with her.

Wednesday 25 June
Bruce Anderson is very keen for me to meet William Hague, whom he swears by.[4] I said, 'OK, I'm willing to do that. I don't think much of him so far.' That lunatic Redwood suddenly going over to Hague is barking mad.

Monday 30 June
At the overcrowded party at Christie's, I met on the packed staircases dozens I knew. Nigel Dempster I told that Verushka had saved my life, which he later put into his gossip column. He's not a bad chap.

---

4. Hague was elected Leader of the Conservative Party on 19 June 1997.

Wednesday 2 July

Tote Board meeting in the morning. Peter Jones was not present as he finished on June 10th as a member of the Board. He has now been ousted from the racehorse owners' section of the BHB. It is possible he may finish up with nothing.

I am told that John Wakeham's membership must wait to be agreed with the new Chairman, which is ridiculous – the BHB have nominated Wakeham, the BHB Chairman, to be on our Board and they are entitled to a nomination.

I have been writing an article for the *Times* telling of the confusion and how hopeless it is for people who understand nothing about business to try to choose the Tote Chairman. They got into real trouble when they offered Maurice Lindsay the job.[1]

The Home Office hastily withdrew its offer.

After the Board meeting I spoke to John Sanderson and asked if he would like to apply.

He has already written to the Home Office saying, if they think he could help in any way, he would be willing.

Thursday 3 July

I hadn't slept all that well. It wasn't entirely Mimi who was a bit restless in the night. I was racketing about in my head over the future of the Tote. Also I was thinking of the things I had to do to make sure the lunch for Queen Elizabeth the Queen Mother was set correctly so far as the drink was concerned.

I had rung Alastair Aird, her private secretary and comptroller, to ask how she wanted her dry Martini prepared because I had forgotten. He replied that it wouldn't be a dry Martini on this occasion. She wanted one third gin, two thirds Dubonnet, plenty of ice and a slice of lemon. I carefully mixed this at about a quarter to one. Some of the guests had arrived already. Fortunately, for once in this damp summer

---

1. Bookmaker; chief executive, Rugby League.

it wasn't raining. At one o'clock I waited for her in the road and she arrived, as usual, on the absolutely royal punctual dot.

I said, 'I hope you notice that I have at last been able to afford to raise that bottom step a little higher so it's the same as the others.'[2] She laughed. She looked round the garden and said, 'What a beautiful garden.' Curiously, it did look very nice, particularly on the left-hand side, with the huge bush of hydrangeas in the middle and lots of roses out.

I helped her up the steps, as did her bodyguard, but she didn't need much help. When she entered the house she stopped and said, 'Oh how beautiful. How nice to be back here again.' We went into the drawing-room where they were all lined up and I introduced each of them. Then I gave her drink. 'I hope this is all right, Ma'am. I've stirred it, just like Bond: "stirred not shaken".' She pronounced it to be perfect. I said, 'You used to have Martini, not Dubonnet.' 'That's now in the evenings when I have the Martini.'

Her cousin, John Bowes Lyon (Bowsie), received a kiss before he bowed his head in the appropriate manner.

I sat on her right and Conrad Russell on her left. On his left was Victoria Getty and on my right was Diana Wilton. Paul Getty sat on Verushka's right, next to Petronella. Frank Johnson sat on Verushka's left, I think it was, and then came Lady Russell.

Frank Johnson's got a very good brain, though he is an erratic editor and really wants only academics to read the *Spectator* which would diminish the circulation to zero.

He hated having the famous Spice Girls interview in the paper, which enormously increased the circulation on the street, in the news-agents and by subscription.

What an ass such a clever person can be. Dickens wrote for the masses as well as the mighty.

At lunch itself Queen Elizabeth talked a lot to Conrad Russell. I said, 'He is the acknowledged authority on the Civil War. Who do you think was right, Parliament or the King?' Very tactfully he replied, 'Both were wrong.'

---

2. In her letter thanking WW for the lunch, she referred to his waiting to greet her and 'the ascent of the BIG STEP'. She said it was a great pleasure to meet Frank Johnson, and also WW's enchanting daughter. Having dropped the *Spectator* a few years previously, possibly because it printed something which annoyed her intensely, she had now reordered it.

When the claret came round, I told the servants not to put too much in every glass because we could always have more. Diana raised her glass and said very loudly to Queen Elizabeth, 'Why is he so stingy? There's not enough claret in your glass,' which I thought very rude of her to me.

Queen Elizabeth loved the claret and had plenty more of it. She also adored the Baron de Bachen which is one of the three best white wines in the world.

Perhaps the other two are Pavillon Blanc of Margaux and the Grillet from the Rothschild restaurant at Vienne in France.

She was highly amused by Mimi.

I said, 'She's supposed to be Petronella's dog. She lives in the High Street, not very far away, but she won't get up in time to take her out in the morning. So she sleeps on my bed and tries to give me a good wash all over my face and hands before I go to sleep.'

We talked about [Princess] Diana, very privately between the two of us. I said, 'There always was bad blood there. She's a schizophrenic in my view.' She said, 'I know what you mean.' I said, 'She knew the form but she wanted to get Prince Charles to marry her.' The Queen Mother said, 'She's very clever, getting an enormous amount of publicity for herself.'

Reverting to Hong Kong I said, 'Some people were very silly and said the Queen should have gone [for the hand-over ceremony],' to which she promptly replied, 'She's not giving away possessions.'

She wondered what I thought about Hague. I said, 'Not a lot at the moment. He seems to be like a baby Winston Churchill without any of the content of his brain.'

She said, 'Petronella is very pretty and very clever.' 'She's the great joy of my life. I adore her.' She understood that. She said she read a lot of what she wrote and thought it very well done.

At about ten past three I said, 'What would you like to do now, Ma'am?' That was after she had drunk some Tokay but refused the port which I had got specially for her. She said she couldn't drink port now after all the wonderful lunch she'd had.

I said, 'Would you like to go into the drawing-room now and talk to some of those you haven't spoken to yet?' 'Oh yes, I'll do that. We'll leave you behind for a few moments.' We didn't stay long, though those who wanted them had cigars, including me because she loves the smell of them.

Mimi tried to get on her lap which she didn't mind a bit.

As she was going, she tried to make me not come down the steps with her because she thought I might fall. I may have been looking a bit doddery because I hadn't slept well. I said, 'Oh no, I must come with you, Ma'am.'

As they drove away she kept waving to me and as they turned the corner she turned and waved from the back window which I thought was delicious of her.

Conrad said he'd come by tube to St John's Wood station. I think they're very poor. I said, 'How are you getting back?' 'Perhaps we'll go to find a cab.' I said no and sent the Tote car with them back to Kilburn where they live.

Friday 4 July
My actual birthday, though the dinner party for my birthday isn't until Monday. I had a lovely large jar of caviar, the best Iranian sort, from dear Diane [Lever].

I had a cute cigar carrier which immediately extinguishes a cigar from Mrs Tamborero.

Verushka gave me a beautiful lighter holder which is silver, in which you pop refills.

Went to Elisabeth Murdoch's party at Kingston. We arrived at exactly the same moment as Rupert. He greeted me as a long-lost friend. He embraced me. I walked with him as he talked away.

I said, 'You're looking a bit tired. I think you're over-doing it. I think you're happiest when you're on that wonderful yacht of yours.' 'But that doesn't stop the faxes coming and I can never not read them.' 'But your doctor said you are to have complete rest.' 'I know. I should do but I don't actually.'

He had come that morning from Beijing and was staying in the Stafford Hotel, not in his flat which is undergoing a redecoration and alteration designed by Anna.

As the fireworks display came on, I went out to see it – I adore fireworks. Things were going bang, wallop all over the place. Simultaneously there was a thunderstorm.

We were at a table called Massachusetts. There were no place settings so you could sit anywhere you liked. I sat down next to a very good-looking girl, extremely attractive.[3] It turned out that she has a

---

3. Judith Gordon; Bruce Gordon was President, Paramount International Television, 1972–97.

partner, as they call it these days, and a child by him. She said he is the President of Paramount films. I said, 'Good heavens, that's terribly important.' 'Yes, it is. We're looking for subjects for children.'

So I told her about *The Exploits of Mr Saucy Squirrel* and *The Further Exploits of Mr Saucy Squirrel*.[4] I said, 'They sold better than anything else I ever wrote. Now they are very rare and difficult to get hold of.'

The President of Paramount fetched my food for me because he thought I wouldn't be able to walk through the crowds. But I wasn't shuffling because I put my feet down firmly, as instructed by Professor Pounder.

We were about to go. Verushka had already told me she had danced with Rupert who didn't dance badly at all. He kept embracing her, giving her kisses and saying, 'I love you, you're wonderful.' I don't think Anna would have been very pleased but I doubt if he has ever been unfaithful to her. He's very puritanical in that way.

Then Rupert turned up and sat next to me. He put his arm round my shoulder again and said, 'We've been friends for a very long time.' Verushka had reminded him it was twenty-six years. I had backed him ever since he first came to England.

I said, 'You got over all your difficulties over being able to count yourself British in Europe. But you seem to have been left out of some of this digital broadcasting stuff.' He said, 'Ah, that doesn't matter. Things are moving so fast it'll be out of date before long. Anyway, it's the sports that matter and I've got those tied up.'

By this time Rupert, amazingly for him, was getting drunk, which he hardly ever does. For a time he was a total abstainer. I think it was because he thought the drink would pick him up after his journey. He is also getting deaf. I had to keep shouting my answers to him.

I told him, 'Verushka asked Peter Mandelson would he like to be interviewed by Petronella and he said, "Not for two years." ' I saw him glaring away at me.

Understandably, he doesn't like me because I called him evil.

It was the friendliest conversation I'd had with Rupert for ages.

---

4. They were written for Petronella and published in 1976 and 1977; Mr Saucy Squirrel has entrepreneurial adventures and shares many of the interests of his creator. On the suggestion of Rupert Murdoch, Judith Gordon later contacted WW about the possibility of him writing screenplays based on the stories but he died before the deal was struck.

Eventually Liz said, 'I think my father must go home to bed.'

I went arm in arm with Rupert to where his car was waiting for him.

The editor of the *News of the World*, Phil Hall, was also there. I've grown to like him. From wanting to get rid of my articles, he now likes them very much, he says.

Saturday 5 July

John Sparrow, having first refused to take over the Tote Board when I suggested it would be a good idea, rang me very secretly to say that one applicant in particular for the chairmanship of the Levy Board was so good that he now felt it would be a very good idea if he were to become Chairman of the Tote, though I mustn't say anything to anybody about it as yet. I said, 'Fine. If you would do it, everybody at the Tote would be very happy with you in charge. Anything but that dreadful man Peter Jones.'

Monday 7 July

A message that Mary Archer couldn't come [to WW's birthday dinner] but Jeffrey Archer was coming just the same. Also Norman Lamont was coming, with Rosemary.

I pointed out to Verushka, when I heard another guest was Olga Polizzi, that this was hardly a good mixture. Rosemary no doubt remembers keenly the tremendous furore in the newspapers when Norman was found by the press having a fight with Olga's current friend and he got a black eye in the process. That was something which greatly amused Mrs Thatcher. She didn't think it a case for dismissal from the government, which Norman was in, because she was very broadminded.

As for Jeffrey Archer, Arnold said he thought he would have to leave at once because he couldn't bear to be in the same room. Verushka placated him and got Conrad Black to change his place to be next to Archer, where Arnold was going to be.

He's a strange fellow, as I've noted before, just like 'the Card' in Arnold Bennett's book.

David Somerset [Beaufort] brought a magnum of Lafite 1982, a singularly good year, which was very kind of him. He also brought Miranda, of whom I am very fond.

Jake and Jill Radnor brought a huge and beautiful orchid on two stems with many flowers for me personally. Verushka wanted to leave it down in the drawing-room indefinitely. I said, 'No. It's going up to my library when the party's over.'

Diana Wilton gave me two ties from Hermès. They must have been very expensive but unfortunately they don't tie very well and the colours are not exactly thrilling.

Mark Lennox-Boyd was there. He is trying to get a job. Did I know of one? I said, 'But you've got plenty to do, haven't you, with your making of sun dials and other gadgets which you do so beautifully?' 'Oh yes, but I ought to have a gainful job.' This from a Guinness heir with a marvellous country house where his old constituency was in the North and also a very attractive house in London. However, people have differing views of poverty and the need to have gainful employment. He is not only no longer in the government but lost his seat as well.

Prince and Princess Michael gave me a beautiful box, a round one, brass coloured, with my zodiac sign on the top. I thought that very thoughtful and agreeable. I gave him a bottle of very aged 1963 Graham port. He was delighted with it. His birthday was on July 4th like mine and we had exchanged messages.

Mr and Mrs Andrew Parker Bowles brought a huge magnum of champagne and one very old bottle, 1954, of Ruinart. That was lovely. The Lamonts brought a book about Sheridan which is very good. I think perhaps Norman thinks he is a bit like Sheridan, a man of all parts, politics and other activities, though Sheridan was into gambling. Arnold brought a splendid box of twenty-five Churchill long cigars. And Bowsie Lyon brought a wonderful cigar case which I was very touched by as he has very little money.

The Marlboroughs brought a splendid bottle of Ruinart champagne.

The Metcalfes gave me a most thoughtful and rare present. It was a silver rupee mounted into what I suppose is meant to be an ashtray now, though it seems sacrilege to use it so. It has George V, King-Emperor, on the rupee, one of the last ones, I guess, to be minted. It is [from] 1918, the year of my birth.

I expect, as his grandfather was Viceroy of India, his mother has probably left him a number of these items from the British Raj and all its glory.

Petronella gave me some very pretty Tiffany cuff links with horses' heads each side. The Pejacsevichs brought me some Godiva chocolates

which I have hidden in my library. Kimberly Fortier[5] brought me a
silver spoon which has a hole in the middle so I don't know what on
earth one does with it. Still, it was kind of her as I hardly know her.

Petronella hadn't wanted to sing. She was afraid the Blacks would
think her too frivolous. Eventually I coaxed her into it. 'Silence for the
St John's Wood nightingale who will sing "As Time Goes By".' There
was tumultuous clapping from all, including the Blacks and Arnold,
when she finished.

I didn't hear much politics. Peter Lilley (Shadow Chancellor)
attempted to say that William Hague was a strong leader with a first-
class administrative and political brain. 'You'll be out for ten years,
maybe fifteen, if you don't get rid of him. There's nothing behind that
would-be Churchillian face.'

I sat between Princess Michael and Rosita Marlborough. The former
urged me to look down at her bosom. 'I wore a low cleavage especially
for you.' She's a jolly girl.

Saturday papers said she owed Coutts £3 million, with interest
mounting daily, and they were calling the overdraft in. Poor Michael
was distraught. The leak could have come only from someone at the
bank fully conversant with her affairs.

The borrowings are more than well covered by assets pledged. I
said, 'You should sue the bank and demand compensation, enough
to wipe out the overdraft. They're entirely to blame for the leak in
confidentiality.' 'Do you think I could?' 'Yes, they're bound to settle.'

Wednesday 16 July

John Major came to dinner. The dear wronged and injured man, free
of the strains he was put under, was cheerful. He will give up Huntingdon to let Chris Patten in. 'He's my best friend.'

John said he wanted Patten to be Prime Minister and he would
resign at the appropriate moment, possibly going to the Lords: he
might not even do that.

I said I thought William Hague was pretty ghastly. John said he
would get Chris Patten back in the House to challenge him. This is
allowed under the rules where there can be a leadership change once
a year, unless they alter the rules beforehand which I don't believe
Hague would dare to do. John said he voted for Kenneth Clarke for

---

5. Publisher, the *Spectator*.

the leadership as the best man to rattle Blair on the economy, though he thought Ken a real bastard.

John thought they [Labour] would get two terms. It would be too difficult to disperse such a huge majority after only one parliament. I said, 'It is quite extraordinary how all their ideas are yours and from the Tory Party.'

I suppose it is possible that Patten could be acceptable as a sort of centre candidate. He'd certainly be better than Hague. John said, 'I don't want this dreadful, overdone, right-wing stuff all the time. I want someone to lead from the centre where it's best to be, in the centre or slightly right.'

I remain convinced that Portillo has the best chance now that he has calmed down, but he must be warned to have no connection with David Hart. Rifkind was a fool to have him as his political adviser when he was a senior minister.

I am very fond of John. He was a very capable PM, making the economy the best ever. However, the modern Tory Party is top-heavy with shallow minds and blatant self-seekers. They expect quick results and have little guts or loyalty. They short-change the leader when the going's rough.

It was lucky we didn't have a cowardly crew like that when we stood alone against Hitler. They're nothing like the old Tory MP squires who put first their duty to the country.

Saturday 19 July
Went down to Oare. Poor Henry Keswick is in a bad way. He had a fearful fall, slipping on some wet marble during the Hong Kong hand-over ceremony.

He is, however, thinner.

Tessa, as usual, was deep into politics.

She is very bright and is quite a force in the bedraggled Tory hierarchy.

Sunday 20 July
Over to the Archer party, their annual summer one, at Grantchester. Mary Archer is still astonishingly pretty. She has a new haircut which sets her off extremely well.

Betty Boothroyd, the Speaker, was there.

'You're a very good Speaker. I think you're the best they've had since the War. So long as you annoy both sides you can't be wrong.'

After lunch Archer brought up William Hague and his girlfriend to meet me.[6] She is sparky and intelligent and is Welsh. He didn't make much impression on me.

I cannot see him defeating Blair.

Tuesday 22 July

At last the Home Office have come forward with their choice for my successor.

I had hoped that as a final resort they would choose either John Sanderson or the Chairman of the Levy Board, John Sparrow.

They have now appointed Peter Jones. I issued a public statement to say that I would give him all the help I can. They are much concerned at the Tote whether he will be any good or not. He has promised me to keep on the senior staff.

Saturday 26 July

I went to Ascot for the King George and Queen Elizabeth Diamond Stakes. I had lunch with Netta and Arnold Weinstock.

I went down to the Tote entertainment room where my successor was already holding sway. When I came into the room, to my surprise they all stood up and started to clap and applaud. That I found touching.

Jeremy Deedes talked to me about the *Spectator*. He said, 'Petronella now should become Deputy Editor. She'll get paid more.'[7]

There's a lot of talk in Conrad Black circles about and against Frank Johnson.

Petronella is rung now daily from Canada by Conrad Black.

She said I must speak to Frank.

I said to Frank, 'Beaverbrook couldn't bear it if he rang up shortly after lunch and found an editor wasn't there at one of his newspapers. He would say, "Who's in charge of the clattering train?" ' Frank said, 'Why don't they come to me if they think I'm not doing it properly?'

Wakeham said to me, 'I have now been told that I have got to make an application [to join the Tote Board] under Nolan rules, fill in God knows how many forms and all the rest of it. I'm not going to do it.'

Then Christopher Sporborg told me that he wanted another year

---

6. Ffion Jenkins, his fiancée.
7. In his memo to Rupert Murdoch dated 29 July WW confirmed that Petronella had been made deputy editor of the *Spectator*.

at the Tote. I would like him to have one but he would have to apply with everyone else, just as John Wakeham would have to, and fill in all kinds of ridiculous forms about their politics and all the rest of it. He said, 'I'm not going to do it. It's only for one year anyway.' So already the Home Office is *en route* to wreck the Tote Board.

Monday 28 July

I went up to Wigan to say goodbye to all those splendid people there – the clever boys, Louis Skelton in the computer section and the able ones at Tote Credit where Colin Dingley has done very well.

The heads of departments came to lunch, those who happened to be present that day.

We had a general conversation about the future of the world, the planetary system and life starting from outer space and so forth.

I said I thought the purpose of life was basically to enjoy it. Most people of any worth really enjoy it, if they are doing something useful.

I was presented with a box of twenty-five Montecristo cigars from all the staff. I was very touched by that.

Tuesday 29 July

I sent a last missive before September to Rupert with quite a lot of entertaining stuff in it. I told him, *inter alia*, about Prince Charles not wanting to marry Camilla.[8]

The terrible treachery took place. Darling little Mimi was driven off to the country by Diana Wilton and Verushka. There is an old lady there of eighty-five who loves dogs and she has quite a reasonably sized garden.

All her toys went with her and her basket and lead and the things she likes the most.

Next year we'll get somebody to come and live in the house to look after Mimi at the same time, so she'll know it's still hers and won't be so distressed.

---

8. WW said they both irritated each other when they were together too often. Unusually, Murdoch faxed a reply on 29 July, wishing the Wyatts a wonderful holiday and saying they were going to have two weeks diving with the sharks beside the Great Barrier Reef. In a hand-written postscript he added, 'friendlier than the sharks in Hollywood!'

Wednesday 30 July

I have to get out of my head being annoyed by what Peter Jones says. He's already made an announcement that he'll have over a thousand betting shops or have none.

I told John Heaton, 'For heaven's sake tell him not to make these announcements before he meets the Board. We couldn't run Tote Direct without owning betting shops. The man is an ass.'

But it seems he is now coming around slightly to the idea of the Tote annual luncheon, after my having said I would help him write the speech if necessary.

Thursday 31 July

Off to Italy. It is the last time I shall have a Tote-employed driver to take us to the airport. When we got to Rome, there was Mr Moore, privately paid for by me to bring the car out to Italy, and off we tootled to the house. Verushka, who was very tired, drove extremely well. I was a little nervous towards the end, when she seemed to be not quite as accurate as to which side of the road she should be on as she had at the start from Rome.

We were almost immediately plunged into the local society once more, on the Saturday with dinner at the Vesteys. John Vestey talked a fearful amount of rubbish about politics. I felt sorry for Judith Bathurst. I told her how pretty she was looking, which is true enough for her age, and how nice it was to see her again. My intention was to spread good cheer all around.

Saturday 2 August

There is a young man here called George Osborne, the son of Peter Osborne who is the principal shareholder in Osborne & Little which was floated on the stock exchange by Nicholas [Banszky].

The young man is the chief of staff to William Hague.[1] He is anxious to convince me how marvellous William Hague is and to talk about politics to me.

He said, 'I know Peter Lilley's coming out to stay with you.' 'How do you know that?' 'We keep tabs on all our Shadow Cabinet. We know where they're going.' 'Good heavens, you sound as though you're imitating Blair in the worst possible way, having Mandelson spies following the movements of your senior people.'

I said, 'I think you won't win with William Hague.'

'But he's very bright and very clever.' I said, 'The first thing he'd better do is to get married and have a child.' He laughed. 'I know what you mean.' 'He should marry that nice Welsh girl who's got a lot of spunk and guts.'[2]

I wrote my article for the *Oldie* by hand.[3] Little Kimberly, who is the enterprising manager who runs the business side of the *Spectator* and is technically the publisher, took it back with her to London. She couldn't read all of it, I gather, nor could the *Oldie*. However, we dealt with all that on the telephone.

I am thinking that I must try to write a booklet, or a short book, to explain the nature of the British rule in India and how it was all by consent. Gandhi and Nehru and co. told me repeatedly that it had been the best thing that happened to India. It brought them into

---

1. George Osborne has been political secretary to William Hague since his election as Conservative Leader.

2. He did, on 19 December 1997.

3. A review of *Liberty or Death* by Patrick French, published in the September issue of the *Oldie*; the book was about the transfer of British power in India.

the modern world, eradicated corruption through an incorruptible administrative system.

The *Spectator* article I gather was a great success.[4]

I stated the obvious about India and the inevitability of independence and how we prepared for it for the last seventy years of British rule.

We told Peter Lilley he must be more aggressive and go for the jugular. He is too passive in his role as Shadow Chancellor. He took that very well.

The Lilleys haven't any money. They have this house in Normandy which doesn't need much spent on it. They also have a house in the constituency but Peter says he gets an allowance of about £12,000 a year for having it, so it really doesn't cost him anything. But he has no earning capacity.

Gail says their house in Islington is in a very unpleasant area, full of drug addicts.

I asked Peter if I were to approach one or two people to give him some earning capacity, would he agree. He said provided it didn't conflict with his role as Shadow Chancellor. So we hit upon people in energy about which he knows a lot, and in water, perhaps, and other concerns which don't have any direct relationship to the Treasury.

There would be nothing wrong with declaring all in the Members' registry of interests. Punctiliously honest, he would never do anything one inch out of line, which I respect him for.

Gail made £12,000 from selling her pictures in her exhibition in the Mall Galleries. She says she can't do that very often because it would be the same people again and also she can't get together another collection so quickly. She can be quite pretty when she does herself up.

I told George Osborne that I thought it very stupid to make it a test of anybody being in the shadow cabinet that they had to pronounce against a single currency.

Major had got us into an excellent position by skilful negotiation and we could choose whether to or not.

I am having terrible difficulty swallowing. Verushka has been in touch with Professor Pounder who says if it goes on I should have an X-ray. He thinks it may be connected with the pneumonia I had. I am determined that it should not be. I find it almost impossible to eat thin

---

4. Published 9 August to commemorate the fiftieth anniversary of India's independence.

spaghetti. It is like rope and it won't go down my gullet, whereas ravioli does, and gorgonzola cheese and soft things.

At a dinner we had here when the Burrells came and lots of others, I had to leave the table. I ate chunks of melon which were rather raw and stuck in my throat. It was terrible. Verushka was also ill in bed with a sore throat and a cold and she had the doctor in. She is taking antibiotics. So both host and hostess were absent for a large part of the dinner. However, eventually I recovered. But I really was choking and choking. It seemed like miles of phlegm came up, I suppose an antidote created by the body. It was very unpleasant.

I had been reading the latest book by Frederick Forsyth, called *Icon*.[5] When I began it I thought it very boring and he got all his dates wrong about when Yeltsin disappeared.

However, Frederick Forsyth rang up. He will be staying at the Pellicano on Saturday and he is coming here to dinner.

Tuesday 5 August
Mary Soames arrived with the best gift I have ever had, I think. She brought me a box of fifty Romeo y Julieta 1972. They belonged to her husband, Christopher, of whom I was very fond.

Later I discovered through Arnold Weinstock that they had belonged to Sir Winston. She's a marvellous girl. She talks away like all Churchills do, non-stop, but she is often very entertaining, in fact nearly always so.

She brought all the papers from England, including the *Financial Times*. I couldn't resist looking to see what the racing results had been and whether the Jackpot had been won. I thought, 'I must stop this. I must wipe the Tote out of my mind, apart from what I may have to do to help reduce the clutches of the Home Office.'

On her father, there is a very good addendum to the ghastly book Lord Moran wrote about him. (His thesis was that for a very long time Winston had not been fit to govern. He was in a terrible state of depression and so forth.) She said Martin Gilbert, who finished the biography of her father when Randolph died, found Moran's notes. They were written long after her father died and mostly invented.

I have been reading J. B. Priestley's time plays, as instructed by dear Beryl.

I am beginning to work out the structure of the play I have to do.

5. Published in 1996.

Eva [Pejacsevich] is agreeable and charming but Mark is so bloody bossy and always interfering in the household arrangements. He is obsessive about the swimming-pool and is endlessly cleaning it.

Sunday 17 August
This morning the Sinclairs left. I like Sonia a lot but she is very woolly about politics. Andrew is somewhat didactic on the subject which he knows less about than he thinks. Nevertheless, I like them as guests very much. Andrew is also generous, bringing a dozen of the 'Eye of the Partridge', possibly the best pink champagne.

Geoffrey and Miriam Owen are very agreeable. Geoffrey did his stint at playing tennis with Antoinetta [Grimaldi], her husband and the boys. His side won 8–6, 6–1. I said, 'What went wrong in the first set?' He said, 'We were out of practice. We were OK in the second set. I upheld the honour of the Wyatts.'

Friday 22 August
Norman Lamont and Rosemary should be arriving at 7 p.m.

This afternoon we had another thunderstorm and lightning.

Tomorrow I have no doubt it will be a beautiful day again, as it was after the first thunderstorm. Unfortunately, my mattress (on which I lie on my balcony where I can sunbathe naked) was absolutely soaked and I haven't been able to use it for a few days.

Richard Ingrams said he is very pleased with the review I have done [for the *Oldie*]. It is a pretty solid rebuke of those idiots who think we were forced out [of India].

I always remember meeting Nye Bevan at the Blackpool conference just before the 1945 general election. I was propaganding him, saying, 'We must give independence if we can to India.' He replied, 'Why should we? If all those millions of people have been unable to get rid of a few British troops, they don't deserve to have independence.' I was stunned to hear the great socialist say that.

Despite my ailment, and not being able to go out to dinner because I felt so peculiar with these choking fits, I have been enjoying the holiday. I hope that I am having a rest but I still do get tired, as Professor Pounder said I would.

I rendered to John [Wilton] my version of Shelley's 'I met a traveller from an antique land.'[6] Mine goes: 'I met a traveller from an antique

6. The first line of *Ozymandias*.

land/ I took his hat, I shook his hand./ I said to him "Where have you
been?/ Your face is the dirtiest I've ever seen."

John thought that Shelley's was better than mine. I was deeply hurt.

Saturday 23 August
Frederick Forsyth and his wife came for a drink.

Frederick Forsyth says he is not going to write any more. I said, 'I
can't believe that. You've got to do something.' 'I've got enough money
and I've got a nice farm in Hertfordshire. I've very happy with it.'

I don't believe he will never write any more.[7]

I asked him, 'How do you get your information? You seem to be
very well informed.' 'I sit at the best tables,' meaning that he listens to
other people's conversations or talks directly to the people in the secret
service in which he says he has never been himself. He is a stocky
fellow with a strong head, a trifle grizzled.

His wife is taller than he, about five foot nine and a half inches.
She has very good legs, a strong and beautiful face.

Sunday 24 August
Spoke to Pericles today, a couple of days late for his birthday. I am
worried that he is selling his steakhouse for only about $115,000,
having told me he would get around $150,000.

Norman had asked John Major if he would give him a peerage in
his dissolution honours. He said the top three, Chancellor of the
Exchequer, Foreign Secretary and Home Secretary, have always been
entitled to have one if they want one. He said, 'I got a letter from John
in which he said, "I am sorry I can't give you a peerage. I've had lots
of other applications which take precedence to yours." ' I said, 'I'm
sure William Hague will do something for you.' After saying he
wouldn't give him a peerage, John had said, 'I have a great regard for
you.'[8]

William Hague was Norman's PPS. He thinks very highly of him. I
said, 'I'm in a wait-and-see position. But I am not convinced he has
got the stature or the political skills to beat Blair. Maybe Portillo
could,' to which Norman replied, 'I was at a party given for William
Hague by Portillo and he was swearing undying loyalty to him.'

---

7. *Phantom of Manhatten* was published in 1999.
8. Lamont discusses this episode in his memoirs, *In Office*, pp, 507–9; he was made
   a life peer in 1998.

Norman thinks it was a very good move William Hague made to appoint Cecil Parkinson as Tory Chairman. He has agreed to do it for two years. I said, 'It seems to me like going back into the past.' 'Oh no it's not. He's very good at organization and William Hague is determined to get it right. Conservative Central Office is in a terrible mess,' to which I agreed.

Monday 25 August
Lolli and Giovanni [Ricci], the parents of Aliai Forte, came to dinner.

Giovanni, after hearing about all the medicines I was having, said, 'You're on the right course. You're getting better and you're looking very well.' I told him about my swallowing and that Professor Pounder thought it was something to do with my lobar pneumonia. He said if it won't go away, we would have to do something about it, which is what Pounder says. At the moment it is a bit better.

Thursday 28 August
We went up to the Burrells for a final dinner.

As I didn't know how to make my Polaroid work, I took it up to see if anybody could do it at the Burrells. Mark Burrell had a go. He had a first-class degree in engineering at Cambridge. I said, 'I don't think you'll be able to manage a Polaroid, though,' but blow me down, he actually did. He got it working.

It's amazing that they have this house perched up there. It gets very misty and very damp up there, so near to rain clouds.

His mother was a Pearson, and they are immensely rich, one of the richest families in Britain.

I enjoyed talking to Norman again. Apart from the routine attacks on Major, to which I said, 'Can we stop talking about that, please?' he is full of ideas.

Sunday 31 August
I was having my last swim before leaving this glorious house, garden, swimming-pool, views. Lying on my back I was listening to the news from London, the usual stuff.

Then came the moment when the voice from the BBC Overseas Service said, 'We will now return to the main news. Diana Princess of Wales was killed in a car crash in Paris in the early hours of this morning. She was with a friend, Dodi Fayed, son of the Harrods' owner.'

My first reaction was, it's a good riddance. She was never going to settle down and behave in a normal, sensible way. She was always going to be a terrible thorn in the monarchy. Then I began to reflect on her, thinking she was not all bad. She came from a very unbalanced family. Her father wasn't too bright. Diana never got over her mother packing her bags and leaving the house without saying goodbye when she was very young.

Though she was the vainest and most self-centred girl in the world, she had good in her heart. She genuinely minded about the people helped by the causes she sponsored. She always got the photographers organized before she went on one of her public visits to hospital wards or to shake hands with lepers or people with AIDS, or whatever it might be, which brought some light and happiness into their lives.

She was also capable of doing good by stealth and genuinely so. She wrote a very sweet letter to Caroline [Beaufort] when she was dying, which had no possible publicity value. And I have heard of a number of cases when she went privately to see people in hospital and she didn't want anybody to know she had been there.

I was sad to be leaving the house. We've got it booked for next year at a slightly increased rent. I had some vague presentiment that maybe I wouldn't be there this time next year. It was similar to the feeling I had when I last went into the smoking-room in the House of Commons just before the 1970 election. I looked around and thought perhaps this will be the last time I'll ever be in the smoking-room. I had a sneaking feeling that though I had a good majority and was popular in Boswell, the influx of middle-class housing from Leicester would tip the scale against me. It did and I lost on a recount.

But then I did get back to Parliament in 1987 when Margaret Thatcher sent me to the Lords. So I expect something will send me back again to that glorious house. I spent my last few camera shots – I wish I were a better picture taker. There were photographs of Aurora, the glorious cook who makes pinoli cakes for me.

This damn swallowing has been getting worse, making it more difficult for me to eat anything seriously solid, unless I chew it a hundred times, without having the pain at the end of it and being in danger of choking and spewing up phlegm again. I am going to see Professor Pounder.

Wednesday 3 September

I went to see Professor Pounder. I had a series of X-rays on my throat and the passages down. He was seriously worried on seeing the results, as was another Professor, an expert, whom he called to talk to me. They thought there could be some sort of tumour in my throat. I have to go back again on September 5th and spend the morning in the private patients' quarters.

There was a charming Australian nurse and we discussed cricket and whether or not Australia should go on recognizing the Queen as head.

She said she was going to work in Africa. I said, 'First of all that's very dangerous. Why don't you go to work among the Aborigines who've been treated pretty badly?' She said, 'That's a point.' What a nice girl she was.

Friday 5 September

I had to be there at nine in the morning. I was taken down to an operating theatre. First I was given a sedation and then something was put between my teeth. 'You've got to hold on to that because the camera and the tube which will go down your throat is going through it and it cost £18,000, so we don't want you biting it.' I laughed. I felt very drowsy and I didn't feel a thing while it was going on.

When I woke up, I felt on the whole quite good. But worse was to follow. They looked at the results and said there is definitely some form of cancer at the end of my gullet and it's blocking it more all the time. There's now only a tiny narrow passage to swallow through. I now have to go back again on Tuesday and may have to stay there for a fortnight. They are thinking up alternative ways by which it might be dealt with.

I said to Professor Pounder 'They won't let me smoke in this room.' I had tried and the nurse said, 'I'm terribly sorry but you're not allowed to smoke in this hospital anyway.' I had to put my cigar into the container which Mrs Tamborero had kindly given me for my birthday.

Meanwhile, Professor Pounder had rung Petronella to say, 'Perhaps you are the most sensible member of the family. You must tell your father this is very serious.' The suggestion is that I could die from it very easily and quite quickly, I gather, to which I replied, 'I can't do that. I've got to stay alive for ten years. I've got too much to do before I die and I don't intend to die.'

Actually I don't believe for one moment I'm going to die. Verushka, of course, is in a terrible state about it. Petronella is more realistic.

I had thought originally that the throat situation was part of the lobar pneumonia I'd had which nearly killed me. It is apparently something quite different. I said, 'Are you going to say it has something to do with my smoking cigars?' But Professor Pounder said he thought that had nothing to do with it. It's a factor of old age. He hasn't even told me to stop smoking cigars believing they have a therapeutic value for me. While I'm alive I might as well enjoy them.

Meanwhile, in the last few days there has been mass hysteria about Diana, and why haven't the Royal Family done anything instead of staying on at Balmoral, don't they realize how marvellous she was, etc. Well, was she? She was killed in a car crash with this man Dodi Fayed, a playboy and a drug addict. He had promised to give it up but of course never would. I wrote an article [*News of the World*], fortunately the day before because they wanted it earlier, on the Thursday. It represents my general thoughts on the subject. Of course I didn't say the horrid things I could have said about Diana. It wasn't the moment.

They are now calling her a saint. But her behaviour was hardly saint-like going from one man to another and having scandalous affairs, and her vanity. But people feel she was the most famous woman in the world, photographed more often than anybody, and that she had great star quality. She certainly did have that.

Little Mimi was very cross with me when we came back [from Italy] and very hurt that I had abandoned her. She was thrilled to see us but she won't eat. The vet says it's some kind of punishment for deserting her.

When both Verushka and Mrs Tamborero went to take me off to the hospital together and I was disappearing, she had some feeling I was never coming back – that was unfounded, thank goodness.

Saturday 6 September
There came to lunch Santa Palmer-Tomkinson, the daughter of the
great friends of Prince Charles, Simon Sebag-Montefiore and Frank
Johnson.[1] We watched all the proceedings of Princess Diana's funeral,
when Earl Spencer made his outrageous attacks on the Royal Family.

In the same speech he attacked the paparazzi and those who bought
their photographs and arranged for their sale, the great newspaper
magnates and the editors.

He did not mention that he himself had long been a journalist, had
appeared on television and had made a lot of money out of it, so in
what way was he any better than those he was criticizing?

Nevertheless, I remarked that it needed some grit, some nastiness
in the programme at the Abbey. It was a clear indication as to why
Princess Diana was batty. It's bad blood on her mother's side.

WW made his last correction to the typescript here.

Santa said that at one point (she had been told this by Diana herself)
she had written to Mother Teresa, saying could she please work with
her in all her various missions to aid the poor and so forth. She got a
letter back to the effect that, 'I think it would be better for you to
solve your own problems before you start trying to solve other
people's.' Diana was apparently mortified by this.

From the moment he married her Prince Charles didn't see Camilla
Parker Bowles for five years. He told her he wasn't going to and he
didn't. He only began to see her again when Diana started the Morton
book and the hysteria – falling down staircases and trying to commit
suicide.

The Queen Mother had been specially protective of her at the time
she was getting married.

Of course, she was a danger to the monarchy and now she isn't.
That's why I said in the *News of the World* it would be a nice gesture
to give her back her royal title which she was very hurt at losing, and
make her HRH again.

We all went out to the end of our road when the coffin was due to
go by. It went past the wall of the Lord's cricket ground and we duly
saw it, draped in the royal standard, with flowers being thrown at the

---

1. Santa Palmer-Tomkinson and Simon Sebag-Montefiore married in 1998.

driver of the hearse despite the warning, 'Please don't do it because it's dangerous.'

No doubt when she is buried on the island in the lake at that very pretty place, Althorp, people will conjure up visions of her rising from it, waving a wand like a good fairy for the neglected and the downtrodden; they'll leave out the bits of her having an affair with the villain, the Fayed fellow, and being ready to have the son of the ghastly Fayed of Harrods as step-father to her children. Fayed's aim was not only to get the lustre from being the father-in-law of Princess Diana but also by that means to get his British citizenship.

The service of the son was at Regent's Park mosque. He was then whipped off to be buried at the Woking mosque, founded by my godfather, Lord Headley.[2]

Sunday 7 September

I decided to have haddock with a poached egg on top for breakfast. Like an idiot I started eating too fast. I immediately began to choke again. That gap at the bottom of the gullet must be very narrow and I wasn't chewing it as much as I should have done while listening to the wireless. Poor Verushka got into a terrible state. I said, 'Leave me alone, leave me alone,' and went upstairs to try to get rid of it. I found some fizzy white water in my bedroom and gradually got it down so it didn't hurt any more.

I went to the cricket match final, Essex v. Warwickshire, which unfortunately Essex won easily, having won the toss and choosing to put Warwickshire in to bat.

At the cricket match everybody said how well I looked. Paul [Getty] was concerned saying, 'Have you got over all that pneumonia?'

It was his birthday today, which I hadn't realized. I had brought two pre-Castro Montecristos No. 2, which are very difficult to get hold of. I gave him one. When I heard it was his birthday, I gave him the other which I had been intending to smoke myself.

I did not tell them that I have this apparent cancer, or something like that, a growth or a tumour at the bottom of my windpipe. I don't understand where it is.[3]

---

2. (1855–1935); fifth Baron Headley; a civil engineer, his main work was in Kashmir and Ireland; he was President of the British Muslim Society and made a pilgrimage to Mecca in 1923.

3. It was a carcinoma of the lower end of the oesophagus, where it joins the sternum.

I have to go back into the hospital on Tuesday and perhaps be there for a fortnight. One thing I do wonder is why, with all the X-rays I was given when they were trying to find out what had happened to my lung after the pneumonia, they never spotted anything about my gullet.

Arnold says I ought to go to New York but that's absolutely ridiculous. These two professors must be among the top people in the world. Anyway, I couldn't afford it.

He was most concerned. He was also concerned about GEC. It's being criticized a great deal now.

Pounder and Arnold and co. all seem to think I'm about to die, but I'm not going to. I'm determined not to. Mrs Tamborero said, 'I take the optimistic line too. It's the only thing you can do.' She's the most encouraging of the lot, actually.

I do not want people told about the danger my life is held to be in. They'll think I'm finished completely and not even worth having an article from. John Heaton has been told very confidentially.

Tonight [on television] is the final of the Hingis match.[4] I said to Paul, 'She's a very pretty girl, that. I shall look at her little bottom when her skirt flies up, as a lot of elderly gentlemen will.'

It was quite a merry afternoon. I ate a scone with cream and strawberry jam on it. I ate a few egg sandwiches. I managed to eat it all with[out] choking because I was very careful not to. It would have been terrible if I'd choked there.

WW's recordings for his journal end here. His faxed report to Rupert Murdoch on 22 September said he would be going back to the Royal Free that morning to start chemotherapy and possibly radiotherapy: 'They may have another go at removing the rest of the tumour in my throat by laser but I can now swallow properly. Incidentally, this is nothing whatever to do with smoking and I am allowed to smoke cigars in the hospital as well as at home, for therapeutic reasons!'

He continued writing his column in the News of the World. *On 5 October he covered the Labour Party Conference and Robin Cook's ethical foreign policy; on 19 October the Queen's trip to India and Pakistan, saying her visit to the Golden Temple at Amritsar was an*

---

4. Martina Hingis, who had won the 1997 Wimbledon women's singles championship, beat Venus Williams in the women's singles final of the US Open championship.

error; on 2 November the Louise Woodward trial – 'They treated Louise like a Salem witch' – and his belief that the government should not commit Britain to join the single currency; on 16 November Labour's embarrassment over exempting Formula One motor racing from the ban on tobacco advertising at sporting fixtures; and lastly, on 30 November, he attacked in successive items Tony Blair, Earl Spencer and Cherie Blair. In his final paragraph he said he was hoping to go to Barbados to see England play the West Indies.

WW died in the Royal Free Hospital on 7 December 1997. He would doubtless have been pleased that the immediate cause of his death was not the cancer but a burst aortic aneurysm within his abdomen – a weakness of the wall of the main artery of his body which suddenly gave way. The doctors had known the aneurysm was there but it had been too dangerous to operate because of the cancer. He was buried at Weeford, in accordance with his wishes. His memorial service on 1 April 1998 was as he planned, with the hymns and readings he chose. Roy Jenkins, his friend for over fifty years, gave the address, Petronella and Rupert Murdoch read the lessons, and 'Stand Up and Fight Until You Hear the Bell', from Carmen Jones the Rogers and Hammerstein version of Bizet's Carmen, was sung.

Chronology

1992

9 *April*	General election – Conservative majority twenty-one
10 *April*	Government reshuffle – Kenneth Clarke becomes Home Secretary, Portillo in the Cabinet
13 *April*	Kinnock resigns as Labour Leader
24 *April*	Chris Patten appointed Governor of Hong Kong
2 *June*	Danes reject Maastricht in referendum
18 *July*	John Smith elected Labour Leader
18 *August*	Troops sent to Bosnia
4 *September*	Government borrows £7.2 billion foreign currency to support sterling
16 *September*	'Black Wednesday' – Britain withdraws from the ERM, Parliament recalled
24 *September*	David Mellor resigns
13 *October*	Closure of 31 pits announced
4 *November*	Commons passes Maastricht paving motion, 319–316 Clinton elected US President
9 *November*	Matrix-Churchill arms-to-Iraq trial abandoned
10 *November*	Scott Inquiry set up
19 *November*	Britain sends 2,500 troops to UN relief operation in Bosnia

1993

1 January	Single Market begins
26 January	Interest rate cut to 6 per cent, lowest for fifteen years
12 February	Inflation rate 1.7 per cent, lowest for twenty-five years
4 May	Asil Nadir flees to Northern Cyprus
6 May	Liberal Democrats win Newbury by-election
27 May	Clarke replaces Lamont as Chancellor; Howard becomes Home Secretary
3 June	Opinion poll gives Major lowest popularity rating for any Prime Minister since polling began
21 June	Heseltine suffers heart attack in Venice
24 June	Michael Mates resigns as Minister of State, Northern Ireland
25 June	Jacques Attali resigns as President of the EBRD
22 July	Twenty-three Conservative MPs rebel against Maastricht Bill – Government defeated 324–316
23 July	Major wins Government confidence motion by forty votes
25 July	Leak of Major's alleged 'bastards' comment
29 July	Liberal Democrats win Christchurch by-election
8 October	Major's 'Back to Basics' speech at Conservative Conference
1 November	James Bulger murder trial begins
15 December	Anglo-Irish Downing Street Declaration

1994

5 January	Tim Yeo resigns
9 January	Earl of Caithness resigns

7 February	Stephen Milligan dies
14 February	Deadline for National Lottery bids
6 May	Channel Tunnel opens
7 May	Michael Brown resigns as government Whip
12 May	Death of John Smith
25 May	Camelot, including G-Tech, win bid to run National Lottery
29 June	Prince Charles in television interview admits being unfaithful in his marriage
10 July	Riddick and Tredinnick accused of accepting cash for questions
14 July	New defence cuts announced
15 July	Britain agrees to Santer as President of EU Commission
20 July	Cabinet reshuffle – Aitken in the Cabinet, Hanley replaces Fowler as Conservative Party Chairman
21 July	Blair elected Labour Leader, Prescott Deputy Leader
31 August	IRA declares cease-fire
19 September	Lord Hollick calls for tighter controls on cross-media ownership
13 October	Loyalists declare cease-fire
21 October	Tim Smith resigns over Fayed payments. Office of Fair Trading announces it will take no action on newspaper price war
25 October	Neil Hamilton sacked as minister but does not resign as MP; appointment of Nolan Committee
14 November	National Lottery launched
28 November	Government wins confidence vote on EU Bill; whip withdrawn from eight Conservative rebels

1995

8 February	Allan Stewart resigns as minister
27 April	Purchase of Churchill papers with first Heritage lottery grant
11 May	First Nolan Report
12 May	Rifkind says he agrees with principle of devolution for Scotland
25 May	Scottish National Party win Perth and Kinross by-election
14 June	Commons approves new parliamentary boundaries
22 June	Major resigns as Conservative Leader to seek re-election
4 July	Major defeats Redwood 218–89 with 22 abstentions
5 July	Cabinet reshuffle – Heseltine Deputy Prime Minister, Rifkind replaces Hurd at Foreign Office, Hague in the Cabinet, Aitken resigns to fight libel action
8 September	David Trimble elected Ulster Unionist Leader
9 September	Major rejects devolution proposals
7 October	Howarth leaves Conservatives and joins Labour
28 October	Budget – basic rate tax cut by 1p
20 November	Princess Diana's television interview on *Panorama*
27 November	Goldsmith launches Referendum Party
8 December	Madrid EU summit
20 December	Nato-led forces including 13,000 British to Bosnia to implement Dayton peace accord

1996

9 February	Canary Wharf bomb; end of IRA cease-fire

15 February	Scott Report on arms to Iraq
13 March	Dunblane massacre
20 March	Bans on British beef begin
29 March	Intergovernmental conference on European integration
2 April	Government promises a referendum if a future Conservative government decides to join the single currency
15 June	Manchester IRA bomb
15 July	Prince of Wales and Princess Diana divorce
22 July	Heathcoat-Amory resigns over European policy
30 November	Budget – basic rate tax cut by 1p

1997

18 March	General Election announced
1 May	Labour win election with a majority of a hundred and seventy-nine; Lamont among Conservatives who lose their seats
31 August	Death of Princess Diana and Dodi Fayed

Biographical Notes

Names in bold or italics are of people WW mentions in this volume.

Amery, Julian (1919–96, life peer 1992), Conservative politician; son of Leo Amery (Conservative politician and writer); m (1950) Lady Catherine Macmillan (died 1991), daughter of *Harold Macmillan*, 1st Earl of Stockton, Prime Minister, 1957–63. One son, three daughters (Elizabeth, b 1956, m (1988) Alan, son of *Alan Hare*). Secretary of State for Air, 1960–2; Minister of Aviation, 1962–4; Minister for Housing and Construction, DoE, 1970–2; Minister of State, FCO, 1972–4.

Amis, Kingsley (1922–95, knight 1990) novelist, poet, critic and *bon viveur*; m 1 (1948–65) Hilary (Hilly), née Bardwell (two sons, one being *Martin*, also a novelist, one daughter). Hilly married 2 the 7th Baron Kilmarnock; Amis lodged in their house for his latter years, lunching regularly at the Garrick Club. He married 2 (1965–83) the novelist *Elizabeth Jane Howard*. He won the 1986 Booker Prize.

Archer, Jeffrey (life peer 1992), b 1940, Conservative politician and bestselling author; MP for Louth, 1969–74, and Deputy Chairman of the Conservative Party, 1985–6. He published *Honour Among Thieves* in 1993, *Twelve Red Herrings* in 1994 and *The Fourth Estate* in 1996. He married (1966) *Mary*, née Weeden, scientist; Fellow of Newnham College, Cambridge, and Lecturer in Chemistry, Trinity College, Cambridge, 1976–86; Visiting Professor, Dept of Biochemistry, Imperial College, London, since 1991; member, Council of Lloyd's, 1989–92; a director, Anglia Television, 1987–95; she published *Rupert Brooke and the Old Vicarage, Grantchester* in 1989. The Archers have a flat overlooking the Thames in London and their country house is The Old Vicarage, at Grantchester near Cambridge.

Astor, Major Hon. Sir John Jacob (*Jakie*, 1918–2000), fourth son of 2nd Viscount Astor; Conservative politician, MP 1951–9; member of the Tote Board, 1962–8, of the Horserace Betting Levy Board, 1976–80, and Steward of the Jockey Club 1968–71 and 1983–5.

His older brother, the *Hon. Michael Astor* (1916–80), m 2 (1961–8) as her second husband *Pandora* née Clifford. Pandora had previously married Timothy Jones, son of Sir Roderick Jones of Reuters and the writer Enid Bagnold; *Annabel*, daughter of Pandora and Timothy Jones, m (1976) *William, 4th Viscount Astor*, b 1951, a government Whip, 1990–3, spokesman in the House of Lords for the DOE, 1990–1, on home affairs, 1991–2, on national heritage, 1992–7, and parliamentary under-secretary of state, social security, 1993–4, national heritage, 1994–5. The Astor family seat was Cliveden, now a hotel. Pandora's sister, Anne, was the first wife of 2nd *Viscount Norwich* (*John Julius*).

The *Hon David Astor* (b 1912), older brother of Jacob and Michael, was editor of the *Observer*, 1948–75.

Beaufort, 11th Duke (*David Somerset*), b 1928; chairman, Marlborough Fine Art Ltd since 1977. He succeeded his cousin the 10th Duke ('*Master*') in 1984. Married 1 (1950) Lady Caroline Jane Thynne (*Caroline*, d 1995, Petronella's godmother), daughter of the 6th Marquess of Bath (1905–92, *Henry*) and the *Hon Daphne Fielding* (1904–97, writer, daughter of 4th Baron Vivian; m 2 Major Alexander (Xan) Fielding, travel writer; she was famous for her beauty, affairs and courage in breaking convention; her books include biographies of Rosa Lewis, Emerald and Nancy Cunard, Iris Tree and Gladys Deacon, 9th Duchess of Marlborough). Married 2 (2000) *Miranda Morley*, landscape gardener. Badminton is the Beaufort seat.

The Beauforts' heir is the *Marquess of Worcester* (*Harry*), b 1952, m (1987) *Tracy* (daughter of the Hon Peter Ward, son of the 3rd Earl of Dudley, and Claire Ward, née Baring, Tony Lambton's companion); Tracy Worcester is a trustee of Friends of the Earth). The Beauforts' other children include Lord Edward Somerset (m, 1982, the Hon. Caroline Davidson, daughter of Viscount Davidson) and *Lady Anne Somerset*, writer (m 1988) *Matthew Carr*, younger son of Raymond Carr (historian, Warden St Antony's College, Oxford, 1968–87, knight 1987).

Black, Conrad, b 1944, newspaper proprietor in Canada and the UK; m 1 (1978–92) Shirley (later Joanna) Hishon, two sons, one daughter; 2 (1992) *Barbara Amiel*, Canadian-born journalist. Chairman and chief executive, Hollinger International Inc., since 1985; chairman, the Tele-graph Group, since 1987; director, the *Spectator*, since 1990. Resident in the UK since 1989 and now a British citizen.

Black, Lady Moorea, see Note on Woodrow Wyatt, p.xix.

Brittan, Leon QC (knight 1989, life peer 2000), b 1939, Conservative MP, 1974–88; Chief Secretary to the Treasury, 1981–3, Home Secretary, 1983–5, Secretary of State for Trade and Industry, 1985–6, when he resigned over the Westland affair; appointed UK member of the European Commission 1989 and a vice-president, 1989–92 and 1995–2000; m (1980) *Diana* (m 1 Dr Richard Peterson), member of Equal Opportunities Commission, 1988–96, deputy chairman, 1994–6); younger brother of *Sir Samuel Brittan* (knight 1993), principal economic commentator, *Financial Times*.

Cranborne, Viscount Robert, b 1946, heir to the 6th *Marquess of Salisbury*, m (1970) *Hannah*, née Stirling. Conservative politician; MP, 1979–87, when he left the Commons over opposition to the Anglo-Irish agreement. Entered the House of Lords 1992; Parliamentary Under-Secretary for Defence, 1992–4; Lord Privy Seal and Leader of the House of Lords, 1994–7; shadow Leader of the House of Lords, 1997–8.

Derby, 18th Earl, (1918–94, *John*) m (1948) *Isabel*, née Milles-Lade, d 1990. Their houses were Knowsley in Merseyside and Stanley House at Newmarket, Suffolk. Lord Derby was a member of the Jockey Club.

Devonshire, 11th Duke (*Andrew*) b 1929; he succeeded his father in 1950, his older brother having been killed in the Second World War; m (1941) the Hon. Deborah (*Debo*), writer, née Mitford, daughter of 2nd Baron Redesdale; Conservative Parliamentary Under-Secretary for Commonwealth Relations, 1960–2, and Minister of State CRO, 1962–4; member of the Tote Board, 1977–86, chairman, Thoroughbred Breeders' Association, 1978–81, and chairman, Pratt's Club. Chatsworth is the Devonshire seat.

The Devonshires' eldest son and heir is the *Marquess of Hartington* (*Stoker*) b 1944, senior steward of the Jockey Club, 1989–94, chairman, British Horseracing Board, 1994–7; m (1967) *Amanda*, née Heywood-Lonsdale.

Andrew Devonshire's sister *Lady Anne Cavendish* m (1949) *Michael Tree* (1921–99, painter).

Fielding, Daphne, see under **Beaufort.**

Forte, Charles (life peer 1982), b 1908, was chief executive, chairman and president of Trusthouse Forte and Forte (which he began as a milk bar in Regent St in 1935); retired 1996; m (1943) *Irene*, née Chierico; the Fortes had five daughters and one son. *Rocco Forte* (knight 1995), b 1945, m (1986) *Aliai*, daughter of *Professor Giovanni Ricci* of Rome, one son, two daughters; chairman and chief executive RF Hotels since 1996, of Forte 1983–96.

Their eldest daughter *Olga*, hotelier, formerly director of Forte and managing director of design, a Conservative member of Westminster City Council, 1989–94, m 1 Marchese Alessandro Polizzi di Sorrentino (d 1980), 2 (1993) the Hon. *William Shawcross*, b 1946, writer, son of *Lord (Hartley) Shawcross* (Labour Attorney-General, 1945–51); his books include *Rupert Murdoch* (1992) and *Cambodia's New Deal* (1994).

Hare, the Hon. Alan (1919–95), son of 4th Earl of Listowel, m (1945) *Jill*, née North; their son Alan m (1988) Elizabeth Amery. Oxford friend of WW. Chairman, *Financial Times*, 1978–84, and chief executive, 1975–83; director, Pearson Longman, 1975–83, *Economist*, 1975–89, English National Opera, 1982–8; president, Société Civile du Vignoble de Château Latour (owned by Pearson), 1983–90.

Henderson, John (*Johnnie*), b 1920, m 2 (1976) Catherine Christian; chairman, Henderson Administration, 1983–90; Lord-Lieutenant of Berkshire 1989–95; member of the Jockey Club.

Henderson, Nicholas (*Nicko*) (knight 1972), b 1919, diplomat; Ambassador to Poland, 1969–72, Federal Republic of Germany, 1972–5, France, 1975–9, Washington, 1979–82. Chairman, Channel Tunnel Group, 1985–6; director, Hambros, 1983–9, Eurotunnel 1986–8.

Heseltine, Michael, b 1933, Conservative politician and publisher; m (1962) Anne, née Williams; MP since 1966; Secretary of State for the Environment, 1979–83; Secretary of State for Defence, 1983–6 when he resigned over the Westland affair; candidate in the Conservative Party leadership contest, November 1990; Secretary of State for the Environment, November 1990–2, for Trade and Industry, 1992–5, Deputy Prime Minister, 1995–7; chairman, Haymarket Press, 1966–70, director, Haymarket Group, 1997–9, chairman since 1999.

Hesketh, Alexander, 3rd Baron, b 1950, m (1977) the Hon. Claire, daughter of 3rd Baron Manton. Conservative politician; a government Whip in the House of Lords, 1986–9, Parliamentary Under-Secretary of State DoE, 1989–90, Minister of State DTI, 1990–1, government Chief Whip, House of Lords, 1991–93. President, British Racing Drivers' Club.

Howard de Walden, John, 9th Baron (1912–99, *Johnnie*), m 2 (1978) Gillian (*Gillie*) Viscountess Mountgarret. Member of the Jockey Club

(Senior Steward 1957, 1964, 1976); racehorse owner (including Slip Anchor, 1985 Derby winner).

Hurd, Douglas (life peer 1997), b 1930, Conservative politician; eldest son of Lord Hurd (life peer 1964, d 1966, farmer, Conservative MP 1945–64, and agricultural correspondent of the *Times*), m 1 (1960–82) Tatania, née Benedict Eyre, m 2 (1982) Judy, née Smart (sister-in-law of racehorse trainer Jeremy Hindley). After leaving the diplomatic service in 1966, he joined the Conservative Research Department and in 1968 became Private Secretary to *Edward Heath* when Leader of the Opposition, continuing when Heath became Prime Minister. He entered Parliament in 1974 and although closely associated with Heath became Minister of State at the FCO, 1979–83, in the first Thatcher Government. As Home Secretary (1985–9) he was responsible for legislation about betting and opening hours, and for the Tote. He was Secretary of State for Foreign and Commonwealth Affairs from 1989 until 1995, retiring from Parliament in 1997. A director, National Westminster Bank, 1995–9; deputy chairman, Nat West Markets, 1995–8, Coutts since 1998; chairman, British Invisibles since 1997, Prison Reform Trust since 1997, Booker Prize judges, 1998. He also writes thrillers.

Jenkins, Roy (life peer 1987, OM 1993), b 1920, politician. His father, Arthur Jenkins, was a South Wales miner who became a Labour MP and junior minister. Roy Jenkins entered Parliament as a Labour MP in 1948, having lost the selection for Aston in 1945 to WW. He was a reforming Home Secretary, 1965–7 and 1974–6; Chancellor of the Exchequer, 1967–70; Deputy Leader of the Labour Party, 1970–2. After failing in the Labour leadership contest on Harold Wilson's resignation, he became the first British President of the European Commission, 1977–81, presiding over the creation of the EMS. He left the Labour Party with *David Owen, Shirley Williams* and *Bill Rodgers*, the 'gang of four', in 1981 to form the SDP, becoming its first sole Leader, 1982–83. He won Glasgow Hillhead for the SDP in a by-election in 1982, remaining its MP until his defeat in the 1987 general election. Elected Chancellor of the University of Oxford in 1987, he was Leader of the Liberal Democrats in the House of Lords, 1988–98. M (1945) *Jennifer*, née Morris (DBE, chairman, National Trust, 1986–91), and has written biographies of Balfour, Dilke, Asquith, Baldwin, Truman and Gladstone. His autobiography *A Life at the Centre* was published in 1991.

Keswick, Henry, b 1938, chairman, Matheson & Co., since 1975; Jardine,

Biographical Notes

Matheson Holdings, Hong Kong, and Jardine Strategic Holdings since 1989; proprietor, the *Spectator*, 1975–81; director, *Daily Telegraph*, from 1990; chairman, Hong Kong Association, since 1988. M (1985), the Hon. *Tessa* Lady Reay (née Fraser, daughter of 15th Baron Lovat, m 1, 1964–78, 14th Lord Reay), whose early career was in journalism. She has been director, Cluff Investments and Trading, 1981–95; special adviser (1989–95) to Kenneth Clarke when he was Secretary of State for Health, for Education and Science, Home Secretary and Chancellor of the Exchequer; executive director, Centre for Policy Studies, since 1995.

Chips Keswick (John Chippendale, knight 1993) is Henry Keswick's younger brother, b 1940, chairman and chief executive, Hambros Bank, 1986–95, non-executive chairman, 1995–7, chairman, 1997–8, chief executive, Hambros, 1995–8; director, Bank of England, since 1993; m (1966) Lady *Sarah* Ramsay, daughter of 16th Earl of Dalhousie.

Simon Keswick is the youngest brother, b 1942, m (1971) Emma, née Chetwode; chairman, Jardine Matheson Holdings, 1983–9, Kwik Save Group, 1990–8, Trafalgar House until 1996; director, Hanson, since 1991.

Lambton Viscount, Antony (*Tony*), b 1922, disclaimed his peerages 1970; m (1942) Belinda (*Bindy*), née Blew-Jones; one son, Edward (m (1983) Christabel daughter of Rory McEwen, painter); five daughters including Lucinda, writer, photographer and broadcaster (b 1943, m 1 (1965) Henry Mark Harrod, son of Sir Roy Harrod, m 2 (1986) Sir Edmund Fairfax-Lacy, m 3 (1991) Sir Peregrine Worsthorne (*Perry*, b 1923, knight 1991, m 1 (1950) Claudie Baynham who died 1990), *Anne* and *Rose*, actresses. Conservative MP, 1951–73, Parliamentary Under-Secretary, MoD, from 1970 until 1973 when he resigned after photographs of him with a prostitute were offered to the press. Owner of Villa Cetinale near Siena, Italy, and La Cerbaia which the Wyatts used to rent.

Lamont, Norman (life peer 1998), b 1942, m (1971–99) *Rosemary* née White (son *Hilaire*, b 1977, daughter *Sophie*, b 1980). Conservative politician. Merchant banker at N. M. Rothschild & Sons 1968–79, non-executive director there, 1993–95; currently chairman and director of various investment trusts and adviser, Monsanto Corporation since 1995. MP from 1972 until 1997 when defeated in the general election. Minister of State, DTI, 1981–85; Minister of State for Defence Procurement, 1985–6; Financial Secretary to Treasury, 1986–9; Chief Secretary to Treasury, 1989–90; Chancellor of the Exchequer, 1990–3.

Lawson, Nigel (life peer 1992), b 1932, m 1 (1955–80) Vanessa, née

Salmon, (who married 2 (1983) Sir Freddie Ayer, philosopher, and died 1985), m 2 (1980) Thérèse, née Maclear. Conservative politician and journalist (*Financial Times, Sunday Telegraph* and editor, *Spectator,* 1966–70). MP 1974–92; Chancellor of the Exchequer 1983 until he resigned in October 1989 over differences with Mrs Thatcher about Europe, the EMS and her adviser Alan Walters. Director, Barclays Bank, 1990–8. His memoirs *The View From No 11* were published in 1992, *The Nigel Lawson Diet Book* in 1996.

Dominic, his son by his first marriage, edited the *Spectator*, 1990–5, and has been editor, *Sunday Telegraph*, since 1995; *Nigella*, one of his daughters by his first marriage, is a journalist (the *Times* since 1995) and cookery writer.

Macmillan, Katherine Viscountess DBE (*Katie*), née Ormsby-Gore, widow of Viscount Maurice Macmillan (1921–84, Conservative politician, Oxford friend of WW and son of Harold Macmillan, 1st Earl of Stockton, Prime Minister, 1957–63). Mother of 2nd Earl of Stockton (*Alexander*), b 1943, (succeeded his grandfather in 1986, m 1 (1970–91) Birgitte (*Bitta*) née Hamilton, 2 (1995) Miranda, née Quarry, previously wife of Peter Sellers, actor); *Adam* Macmillan, b 1948; David Macmillan, b 1957; also Joshua died 1965 and Rachel died 1987. The family estate was Birch Grove in East Sussex.

Marlborough, 11th Duke (*Sonny*) b 1926, son of 10th Duke (Bert) by his 1st wife, m 3 (1972) *Rosita* Douglas, painter. His eldest son is the Marquess of Blandford (Jamie). The Marlborough seat is Blenheim Palace, Woodstock, Oxfordshire.

Montagu, see under **Swaythling.**

Murdoch, Rupert, b 1931, newspaper and media proprietor, son of Sir Keith Murdoch, Australian newspaper owner, and Dame Elisabeth Murdoch; educated Geelong GS and Worcester College, Oxford, of which he is an Honorary Fellow; m 1 (1956–66) Patricia Booker, one daughter Prudence (*Pru*, m 1 Crispin Odey, m 2 Alisdair MacLeod, general manager, Times Newspapers); m 2 (1967–99) *Anna*, née Torv, novelist; two sons, Lachlan (head of US print operations, 1999) and James (President, News Corp's Music and New Media, 1999), one daughter Elisabeth, (m, 1993, now divorced, Elkin Pianim, banker; worked with Fox in the US until 1995, at BSkyB since 1996); m 3 (1999) Wendi, née Deng.

Chairman and chief executive, The News Corporation Ltd; chairman and president, News America Publishing Inc.; director, 20th Century Fox (chairman and chief executive officer, 1992–6), News International, UK, since 1969 (formerly chairman), Times Newspapers Holdings since 1981 (formerly chairman), HarperCollins Publishers since 1989, British Sky Broadcasting since 1990. He owns seventy per cent of Australia's newspapers and several TV stations. The UK newspapers he owns include the *Times* and *Sunday Times* (acquired 1981), *News of the World* (1968) and *Sun* (1969). His newspapers supported Harold Wilson (Labour) in the 1970 general election, switched to the Conservatives in 1973 and back again to Labour in 1997. He is a US citizen.

Parkinson, Cecil (life peer 1992), b 1931, m (1957) *Ann*, née Jarvis. Conservative politician; Paymaster General, 1981–3; Chancellor, Duchy of Lancaster, 1982–3; Secretary of State for Trade and Industry from June to October 1983 when he resigned on the revelation that his secretary Sara Keays was pregnant with his child. He returned as Secretary of State for Energy, 1987–9, for Transport 1989–90. He was chairman of the Conservative Party, 1981–3, 1997–8.

Polizzi, Olga, see under **Forte.**

Quinton, Anthony (*Tony*) (life peer 1982), b 1925, m (1952) *Marcelle*, née Wegier of New York, sculptor. Philosopher and broadcaster (*Round Britain Quiz*). Fellow, All Souls College, Oxford, 1949–55; New College, Oxford, 1955–78; President, Trinity College, Oxford, 1978–87; member, Arts Council, 1979–81; chairman of the Board, British Library, 1985–90.

Rothermere 3rd Viscount, (1925–98, *Vere*), m 1 (1957) Mrs Patricia Brooks (*Bubbles*, d 1992), 2 (1993) *Maiko* Joeong-shun Lee. Chairman, Associated Newspaper Holdings from 1970, *Daily Mail* and General Trust from 1978. His father, 2nd Viscount Rothermere, (1898–1978, *Esmond*), m 2 (1945–52) Anne, née Charteris (1913–81, who m 1 (1932) 3rd Baron O'Neill, d 1944, 3 (1952) Ian Fleming, the writer), m 3 (1966) *Mary* Ohrstrom, née Murchison, of Dallas, Texas, d 1993, one son, the Hon. *Esmond*, b 1967.

Rothschild, Victor 3rd Baron (1910–90), succeeded uncle 1937, m 1 (1933–45) Barbara, née Hutchinson, 2 (1946) Teresa (*Tess*) née Mayor. Scientist and banker. Prize-Fellow, Trinity College, Cambridge, 1935–9; military intelligence during the Second World War; chairman, Agricultural Research Council, 1948–58; Assistant Director of Research, Dept of Zoology, Cambridge, 1950–70; chairman, Shell Research, 1963–70; director-general and first permanent under-secretary, Central Policy

Review Staff, Cabinet Office, 1971–4; director, Rothschilds Continuation (chairman 1976–88); N. M. Rothschild & Sons (chairman, 1975–6); chairman, Royal Commission on Gambling, 1976–8.

Succeeded in 1990 by his eldest son by his first marriage, *Jacob Rothschild*, b 1936, m (1961) *Serena* (elder daughter of *Sir Philip Dunn* (d 1976) and sister of Nell Dunn, writer), one son, three daughters. Banker; president, St James's Place Capital (chairman 1971–97, formerly J. Rothschild Holdings); chairman, Trustees National Gallery, 1985–91, National Heritage Memorial Fund, since 1992, National Heritage Lottery Fund since 1994. Waddesdon Manor was bequeathed to the National Trust in 1957.

Evelyn de Rothschild (knight 1989), b 1931, m 2 (1973, separated 1999) Victoria Schott; second cousin of Victor – their grandfathers were brothers – succeeded Victor as chairman of N. M. Rothschild & Sons. Chairman, Economist Newspaper, 1972–89; a director, *Daily Telegraph*, 1990–6 and since 1997, Chairman, United Racecourses Ltd, 1977–94; member of the Jockey Club.

Shawcross, the Hon. William, see under **Forte**.

Sinclair, Sonia, b 1928, née Graham, m 1 (1947) the Hon. *Julian* Mond, later 3rd Baron *Melchett* (grandson of the founder of ICI, chairman British Steel Corporation from 1967, d 1973); one son, *Peter*, 4th Baron Melchett, who sits as a Labour peer, minister of state, Northern Ireland Office, 1976–9, executive director, Greenpeace UK since 1989; 2 (1984) Dr *Andrew Sinclair*, b 1935, writer and former academic, his 3rd marriage.

Her books: *Tell Me, Honestly* (1964), *Someone is Missing* (1987), *Passionate Quests* (1991). She was a board member, Royal Court Theatre, from 1974; Royal National Theatre 1984–94.

Andrew Sinclair's books include *The Breaking of Bumbo* (1958), *The Red and the Blue* (1986), *Spiegel* (1987), *War Like a Wasp* (1989), *Arts and Cultures: the History of the Fifty Years of the Arts Council of Great Britain* (1995); he edited *The War Decade, an anthology of the 1940s* (1989) and has been managing director, Timon Films, since 1967.

Soames, Lady (Mary), DBE, writer; chairman, Royal National Theatre, 1989–95; daughter of Sir Winston Churchill, m (1947) *Christopher Soames* (1920–87, life peer 1978; Conservative politician, MP 1950–66; Ambassador to France, 1968–72, Governor Southern Rhodesia, 1979–80, chairman ICL from 1984).Their son the Hon. *Nicholas Soames*, b 1948, m 1 (1981–90) Catherine, née Weatherall, 2 (1993) Serena, née Smith;

Conservative politician, MP since 1983; PPS to Secretary of State, DoE, 1987–9; Parliamentary Secretary, MAFF, 1992–4; Minister of State for the Armed Forces, 1994–7. Their daughter the Hon. *Emma* was deputy editor, the *Oldie*, 1991–2, editor, *E S Magazine* (*Evening Standard*), 1992–4, editor, *Telegraph Magazine*, since 1994.

Somerset, see under **Beaufort.**

Stelzer, Irwin, b 1932, m (1981) Marian Faris Stuntz (*Cita*); American economist and journalist living partly in London. President, NERA (National Economic Research Associates), 1961–85; Director of Regulatory Studies at The Hudson Institute; columnist *New York Post* and *Sunday Times* (since 1986).

Stockton, see under **Macmillan.**

Swaythling 4th Baron (1928–98, *David* Montagu), succeeded father in 1990; m (1951) *Ninette*, née Dreyfus; son Charles, b 1954, daughter, b 1956 and daughter, b 1952, d 1982. Merchant banker: chairman, Samuel Montagu, 1970–3; chairman and chief executive, Orion Bank, 1974–9; chairman, Ailsa Investment Trust, 1981–8; director (latterly deputy chairman), J. Rothschild Holdings, 1983–9; chairman, Rothmans International, 1988–98. Member of Tote Board for twelve years. Director, *Daily Telegraph*, 1985–96, British Horseracing Board from 1993.

Weidenfeld, George (life peer 1976), b 1919, m 1 (1952) Jane, née Sieff; m 2 (1956–61) *Barbara*, née *Skelton,* former wife of *Cyril Connolly,* writer and critic; m 3 (1966–76) Sandra Payson Meyer; m 4 (1992) *Annabelle*, née Whitestone. Publisher; founded Weidenfeld & Nicolson 1948, chairman since then of it and associated companies. Member, South Bank board since 1986, English National Opera board, 1988–99, trustee National Portrait Gallery, 1988–95.

Weinstock, Arnold (knight 1970, life peer 1980), b 1924, m (1949) *Netta*, daughter of Sir *Michael Sobell* (chairman of Radio and Allied Industries, television sets manufacturers, and racehorse owner, d 1993); son *Simon* (1952–96, m (1976) *Laura*, née Legh), daughter *Susan* (b 1955, m Charles Lacroix). The electrical group GEC bought RAI and its management team, making the Sobell and Weinstock families GEC's largest shareholders. Weinstock become a director of GEC in 1961 and then managing director from 1963 to 1996, building GEC into one of Europe's major electronics companies and a principal defence supplier to the government. Sits as an independent in the House of Lords. Honorary master of the bench, Gray's

Inn, since 1982; trustee, British Museum, 1985–95. Racehorse owner and breeder; member of the Jockey Club. His house, Bowden Park, Wiltshire, was designed by James Wyatt.

Wolfson, Leonard (knight 1977, life peer 1985), b 1927, son of Sir Isaac Wolfson (founder Great Universal Stores, d 1991), m 1 (1949–91) Ruth, née Sterling, 2 (1991) Estelle née Feldman, widow of Michael Jackson. Chairman, Great Universal Stores, 1981–96. Founder trustee and chairman, Wolfson Foundation.

Appendix on Racing

Horserace Totalisator Board (the Tote)

The Tote was set up by Act of Parliament in 1928 to provide an alternative means of betting other than with bookmakers and to give financial support to racing.

The term 'totalisator' originates from the machines used for the aggregation of bets under a 'pool' system of betting, whereby an organization acts as stakeholder to enable people to bet between themselves. The Tote's original name under the 1928 Act was the Racecourse Betting Control Board, changed to its present name by the Betting Levy Act 1961. The Tote was given an exclusive licence to run pools betting on horseracing. For a fee, known as the Authority fee, the Tote can authorize bookmakers to offer bets at Tote odds. In 1972 the Tote was allowed to open high street betting offices with betting also at starting prices, eleven years after high street betting offices were made legal for ordinary bookmakers.

The Tote's 1997 annual report, the last when WW was chairman, stated that on average two-thirds of the Tote's profits went back into British racing, £7.9m in that year. In 1997 the Tote had 209 high street betting shops and was Britain's fifth biggest bookmaker, with more credit customers than any other betting operation, and offered a full betting service to all fifty-nine racecourses in the UK.

The chairman of the Tote Board is appointed by the Home Secretary, who also approves the appointment of Board members. WW joined the Board in 1975 and in May 1976 was appointed chairman by the then Home Secretary, Roy Jenkins. He was reappointed by all subsequent Home Secretaries until his retirement at the end of July 1997 at the age of seventy-nine. The Home Secretaries during the period of this volume were Kenneth Clarke (April 1992–May 1993), Michael Howard until the general election of May 1997 and Jack Straw when Labour formed the government.

WW was succeeded on 1 August 1997 by Peter Jones, a member of the Tote Board since 1995 and of the Levy Board, a director until June 1997 of the British Horseracing Board, and a council member of the Racehorse Owners' Association.

Tote Board members during the years covered by this volume included the Hon. Jeremy Deedes, Peter Jones, John Sanderson, the Hon. David Sieff, Christopher Sporborg and Peter Winfield. On the staff were Brian McDonnell (chief executive, 1981–96), John Heaton (secretary from 1983 until he succeeded McDonnell as chief executive in November 1996), Tom Phillips (finance director from 1991) and Geoffrey Webster (public relations director from 1976 until May 1997).

The Tote's administrative headquarters was in Putney, south-west London.

By this time the Tote divided its activities into three main divisions: the Racecourse Cash Division (based at Sunbury, operating at all 59 racecourses for Tote bets; managing director Geoff Oke, succeeded by David Haslett); Tote Credit (based at Wigan, betting with debit and credit cards, over 50,000 customers, with new racecourse offices opened during this period at Sandown, Uttoxeter and Cheltenham, in addition to telephone and electronic services; managing director Colin Dingley); and Tote Bookmakers (based at Putney, with 67 on-course shops at 39 racecourses in 1997 for starting price bets, in addition to 209 high street betting shops for all bets; managing director, Joe Scanlon).

In addition, there was Tote Direct, formed in 1992 with Bass, owners of Coral bookmakers (based at Putney; managing director, Phil Siers). The Tote technical team had developed a system, using terminals from the Bass subsidiary Barcrest, for betting shops to send bets to Tote pools on any racecourse or to football pools. Roy Hilsey was technical director, based at Putney; Louis Skelton, the computer expert, worked from the high technology base at Wigan where Colin Dingley also ran Intrac, the Tote's telemarketing business.

The government at this period had shelved any plans to privatize the Tote. In the course of the two earlier volumes of these journals the affairs of the Tote were scrutinized first by Lloyds Merchant Bank and then by the House of Commons Home Affairs Select Committee, chaired by Sir John Wheeler. WW had fought to keep the Tote's different operations – on-course betting, credit betting and betting shops – under the single Tote umbrella. On the other hand, he had supported the establishment of the British Horseracing Board, representing all in the racing industry, and the suggestion mooted for a racing trust to take over the Home Office's role vis-à-vis the Tote. In March 2000 the government asked the British Horseracing Board to produce a plan for taking over the Tote and abolishing the levy system of funding racing.

At the beginning of this volume, Coral betting shops were being linked

by the Tote's new technology to the Tote on course. To WW's delight, by
the end of his chairmanship the new management at Ladbroke had
joined the system, greatly increasing revenue. Another boost to Tote profits
came at the end of 1996 when the statute governing the Tote was amended
to allow the Tote, like other bookmakers, to take bets on Irish Lottery
numbers and other non-sporting events. WW reckoned that Tote profits
for the year ended 31 March 1997 would have been around £1 million
higher if the change had been made when he first requested it.

The prize WW fervently wanted, but did not win for the Tote and its
partners in the Enterprise consortium, was the opportunity to run the
National Lottery. The story of their bid is one of the highlights of this last
volume of his journals.

WW was an *ex officio* member of the Horserace Betting Levy Board,
a director of Satellite Information Services (Holdings) and a trustee of the
Stable Lads' Welfare Trust.

Horseracing Betting Levy Board
Established in 1961 by the Betting Levy Act to levy money for the benefit
of racing. It works by taking a percentage of turnover from all bookmakers
(including the Tote) who in turn pass this charge to the punters, along
with betting tax.

The money raised by the levies goes towards prize money, improving
racecourses, technical services at racecourses, training of stable staff, veter-
inary research, improvements to breeding, security, and grants for point
to point races.

Sir John Sparrow was chairman of the Levy Board throughout the
period of this volume. The chief executive was Tristram Ricketts, succeeded in 1993 by Rodney Brack (formerly finance director).

United Racecourses (Epsom, Kempton Park and Sandown Park) was a
subsidiary of the Levy Board but passed to the Racehorse Holdings Trust
in 1994. Sir Evelyn de Rothschild was chairman of United Racecourses,
1977–94.

The Jockey Club
The oldest regulatory body of racing in the world, the Jockey Club 'sets
and maintains standards for racing'. Its rules and the supervision by its
stewards govern the state of the course, starting procedures, discipline on
course, the determination of winners and enquiries.

Jockey Club members are elected for life. Those mentioned in this
volume include Colonel Sir Piers Bengough, the Duke of Devonshire,

Philip Freedman, the Marquess of Hartington (senior steward, 1989–94), Mrs Priscilla Hastings, John Henderson, Lord Howard de Walden, Sir Evelyn de Rothschild, Christopher Spence, Christopher Sporborg, Lord Weinstock, the Marquess of Zetland and (honorary) HH Prince Khalid bin Abdullah.

Christopher Foster has been executive director since 1993; Christopher Haines was chief executive, 1989–93.

The Racecourse Holdings Trust, the Jockey Club's subsidiary established in 1964, by 1997 owned and operated twelve racecourses including Aintree, Cheltenham, Newmarket and the three members of United Racecourses (Epsom, Kempton Park and Sandown Park). Captain Miles Gosling (d 1997) was chairman of RHT, 1990–5, succeeded by Christopher Spence; David Hillyard was managing director. (Tommy Wallis, d 1992, had been managing director, 1975–89.)

The chairman of United Racecourses, when owned by RHT from 1994, was Christopher Sporborg, succeeded in 1996 by Andrew Wates. Brigadier Andrew Parker Bowles was chairman of Sandown, 1994–9.

British Horseracing Board
Formed in 1993 as racing's governing body, the Board includes representatives of the Jockey Club, the Racecourse Association, the Racehorse Owners' Association, the Thoroughbred Breeders' Association and an independent director. The Marquess of Hartington was chairman, 1994–6, Lord Wakeham, 1996–8. Its first chief executive was Tristram Ricketts, formerly chief executive of the Levy Board.

The Big Three bookmakers
At the time of this volume the 'Big Three' were Coral; Ladbroke (Peter George); and William Hill (chairman, Len Cowburn, succeeded by John Brown).

Pari-Mutuel
The first system of betting by means of a totalisator was introduced in France in 1872 and became known as the pari-mutuel. Hence the name of the French equivalent of the Tote. Its head at the time of this volume was André Cormier.

Racecourse Association Ltd
All fifty-nine UK racecourses belong. Its chairman was J. J. Warr, 1989–93, succeeded by Sir Paul Fox.

Satellite Information Services

The Tote had secured a 5 per cent holding in SIS when it was founded in 1986/7. SIS networks television pictures of races to betting shops.

List of Abbreviations

AEU	Amalgamated Engineering Union
ANC	African National Congress
AWACS	Air Warning and Control System
BHB	British Horseracing Board
BSB	British Sky Broadcasting
BSE	Bovine Spongiform Encephalopathy
BUPA	British United Provident Association
CBI	Confederation of British Industry
CEGB	Central Electricity Generating Board
CJD	Creutzfeldt-Jakob Disease
CND	Campaign for Nuclear Disarmament
DTI	Department of Trade and Industry
EBRD	European Bank for Reconstruction and Development
EC	European Community
EETPU	Electrical, Electronic, Telecommunication and Plumbing Union
EMS	European Monetary System
ERM	Exchange Rate Mechanism (of the EMS)
ETU	Electrical Trades Union
EU	European Union
FCO	Foreign and Commonwealth Office
FOREST	Freedom Organisation for the Right to Enjoy Smoking Tobacco
GAM	Global Asset Management
GATT	General Agreement on Tariffs and Trade
GEC	General Electric Company
GLC	Greater London Council
IBA	Independent Broadcasting Authority
ILEA	Inner London Education Authority
IMF	International Monetary Fund
ITC	Independent Television Commission
LSE	London School of Economics
MAAF	Ministry of Agriculture, Fisheries and Food

MCC	Marylebone Cricket Club
MEP	Member of the European Parliament
MSP	Member of Scottish Parliament
NAFTA	North American Free Trade Agreement
NERA	National Economic Research Associates
NGA	National Graphical Association
NUM	National Union of Mineworkers
NUPE	National Union of Public Employees
NUT	National Union of Teachers
OFFER	Office of Electricity Regulation
OFLOT	Office of the National Lottery
OFT	Office of Fair Trading
OFTEL	Office of Telecommunications
OM	Order of Merit
PLO	Palestine Liberation Organisation
PMU	Pari-Mutuel
PPS	Parliamentary Private Secretary
PSBR	Public Sector Borrowing Requirement
RAC	Royal Automobile Club
RHT	Racecourse Holdings Trust
RPI	Retail Price Index
RTS	Racehorse Technical Services
SDI	Strategic Defence Initiative
SDP	Social Democratic Party
SIB	Security and Investments Board
SIS	Satellite Information Services
SP	Starting Price
SWEB	South West Electricity Board
TGW	Transport and General Workers' Union
Tote	Horserace Totalisator Board
TUC	Trades Union Congress
UEFA	Union of European Football Associations
UNICEF	United Nations Children's Fund

Index